Visual Basic 5 Developer's Handbook

Visual Basic® 5 Developer's Handbook™

Evangelos Petroutsos

Kevin Hough

SYBEX®

San Francisco • Paris • Düsseldorf • Soest

Associate Publisher: Gary Masters
Contracts and Licensing Manager: Kristine Plachy
Acquisitions & Developmental Editor: Peter Kuhns
Editor: Pat Coleman
Project Editors: Ben Miller and Kim Crowder
Technical Editors: Scott Player and Rima Regas
Book Designer: Cătălin Dulfu
Graphic Illustrator: Andrew Benzie
Electronic Publishing Specialist: Bill Gibson
Production Coordinator: Amy Eoff
Production Assistants: Beth Moynihan and Duncan Watson
Indexer: Ted Laux
Companion CD: Molly Sharp, John D. Wright, and Kate Kaminski
Cover Designer: Design Site
Cover Illustrator/Photographer: Gregory MacNicol

Library of Congress Card Number: 97-80780
ISBN: 0-7821-1985-9

Manufactured in the United States of America

10 9 8 7 6 5 4 3 2

Screen reproductions produced with Collage Complete.

Collage Complete is a trademark of Inner Media Inc.

SYBEX is a registered trademark of SYBEX Inc.

Developer's Handbook is a trademark of SYBEX Inc.

TRADEMARKS: SYBEX has attempted throughout this book to distinguish proprietary trademarks from descriptive terms by following the capitalization style used by the manufacturer.

The CD Interface music is from GIRA Sound AURIA Music Library ©GIRA Sound 1996.

To the Joy of my Life.
Evangelos

To my wife, Cheryl, who tells me I can do
anything and helps me do everything.
Kevin

ACKNOWLEDGMENTS

One must publish a few books (or spend a few days at a publishing company such as Sybex) to truly appreciate the effort that goes into the process. It's amazing how much teamwork is involved and how many people work to help authors produce a book in which we can all take pride. It makes writing seem so easy.

I would like to thank all the people involved in this project, starting with the Visual Basic team at Microsoft who delivered an awesome programming environment that brought Visual Basic to the corporate world. Who else would have thought of it, and who else could have done it?

At Sybex, I interacted with many people. First, I want to thank Gary Masters, Associate Publisher, for his unique brand of enthusiasm, vision, and encouragement. Working along with Gary, Peter Kuhns, Acquisition and Developmental Editor, turned a bunch of ideas into a real book. In the fast-paced universe of computer book publishing, Peter takes the time to be on the author's side, and I can't thank him enough.

Next, I want to thank our editor Pat Coleman for taking this book personally and improving it in numerous ways. I think of Pat as my closet co-author. Along with Pat, I want to thank Scott Player and Rima Regas for their excellent technical editing and very helpful remarks.

Special thanks go to Ben Ezzell for helping us tap into the power of Visual C++, the interesting examples in Chapter 4, and his valuable input on optimization issues.

To publishers, deadlines are as real as the day that follows night, yet for authors like us, these concepts are hard to master. Kim Crowder and Ben Miller, our Project Editors, who were involved in every phase, were also burdened with keeping track of time for us. I only hope they'll want to work with us again.

I also want to thank Amy Eoff, Production Coordinator; Beth Moynihan and Duncan Watson, Production Assistants; Bill Gibson, Electronic Publishing Specialist; Ted Laux, Indexer; Andrew Benzie, Graphic Illustrator; and Molly Sharp, Dale Wright, and Kate Kaminski, CD Specialists.

And a great thank you goes to the people who manage the intricacies of the Internet. This wonderful structure enabled us to stay connected at all times and trivialized two continents and an ocean. In addition, it antiquated an author's favorite excuse—the chapter's in the mail.

Evangelos Petroutsos, December 1997

They say if your first book-writing experience is a good one, you'll be anxious to do another one, and I agree with that wholeheartedly. So I'd like to say thanks to all the people who helped make my first book-writing experience a great one, and for working so hard to publish a book that we can all be very proud of.

Thanks go to the talented people at Sybex: Associate Publisher Gary Masters; Contracts and Licensing Manager Kristine Plachy, for her helpful and proficient handling of contract negotiations; Acquisitions and Developmental Editor Peter Kuhns, for his guidance, patience, humor, and support in helping me develop ideas and for providing me the opportunity to take part in this book; Project Editors Kim Crowder and Ben Miller, for coordinating all the behind-the-scene tasks from start to finish and for making sure I stayed on schedule; Production Coordinator Amy Eoff; Electronic Publishing Specialist Bill Gibson; Graphic Illustrator Andrew Benzie; CD Specialists Molly Sharp, Dale Wright, and Kate Kaminski; Production Assistants Beth Moynihan and Duncan Watson; Indexer Ted Laux; and all the others for their hard work.

Thanks go to Editor Pat Coleman, for her skillful refining and careful attention in transforming and improving this book in so many positive ways; and to Technical Editors Scott Player and Rima Regas, for their exact and precise scrutinizing of code and helpful suggestions.

Special thanks go to Ben Ezzell, for his contribution in Chapter 4.

And, finally, thanks go to the creative people at Microsoft, who gave us a revolutionary and extraordinarily versatile programming environment to write about.

Thanks, again, to all of you, for making this book possible.

Kevin Hough, December 1997

CONTENTS AT A GLANCE

TABLE OF CONTENTS

INTRODUCTION

Visual Basic is the most popular programming language, but you probably already knew that. What you may not know is that version 5 is the most popular version of the language ever. Visual Basic has been enhanced and improved with every new version and has evolved from a simple environment for developing Windows applications to a full-blown environment for component development, client/server applications, and corporate development. (Visual Basic is also promoted as a Rapid Application Development environment. We prefer to think of it as a very efficient environment; for some reason, rapid isn't the first word that comes to mind when thinking about quality.)

It is no wonder that there are so many books on Visual Basic, yet most books are either introductory or deal with a single aspect of the language, such as ActiveX, database programming, and so on. We believe developers who are familiar with previous editions of Visual Basic need a book that concentrates on the new capabilities of Visual Basic and discusses them from an experienced programmer's point of view. The *Visual Basic 5 Developer's Handbook* fulfills such a need. It's written by two long-time developers and is addressed to developers. Since we couldn't cover every topic of the language in depth, we decided to compile a collection of advanced topics and discuss them in depth. We believe every developer will find something of interest in this book.

In our experience, developers don't read books cover to cover. We took care to make the chapters as independent of one another as possible without repeating ourselves. You will find cross-references in the book, but the chapters are organized to be read independently.

We also believe that you can't master a language through reference material alone. That's why we tried to skip much of the information you can find in the Visual Basic documentation. Where this was not possible or practical, we moved much of the reference material to appendices (which you'll find on the CD that comes with this book). The chapters focus on the concepts and on how you can apply them to day-to-day tasks. To master a language, you have to step through real-world applications, so many of our examples are complete applications. They are not as easy to follow as trivial examples that demonstrate a few functions or methods. We tried to design sample applications that combine many of the techniques involved in building actual applications and that you can use as starting points for other projects.

Who Should Read This Book

Most VB programmers develop database and client/server applications, so more than half the book deals with topics such as client/server programming, SQL, and the Remote and ActiveX Data Objects. We assume you are familiar with database programming, and we focus on client/server architectures and techniques for creating and accessing databases.

But there's more to programming than querying databases. Visual Basic is an excellent environment for developing components (code components and ActiveX controls). We discuss these topics in depth and give you practical examples to demonstrate the more advanced techniques. As you undoubtedly know, the Web is making waves in corporate computing, and it is changing the way corporations look at the Internet and intranets. If you are a VB programmer and would like to apply your knowledge to the Web, you'll find much of the information you need in this book. We don't discuss trivial topics, such as how to build Web pages or how to use HTML. Instead, we focus on the topic that will enable you to apply your knowledge of Visual Basic to the Web: the Active Server Pages.

In short, this is a book for result-oriented people. If you have some programming experience in Visual Basic and want to build on your knowledge, instead of going through trivial material, or if you want to read about practical techniques, instead of general discussions, you will find this book useful.

The Structure of the Book

The book is organized in five parts that each cover a different aspect of the language. In Part I, we discuss a few topics that we feel are prerequisites for advanced VB programming. They are all important, but not all are new to VB5, so we decided to present them early in the book. We start with a discussion of the Windows API. Sure, we know every book on VB includes a chapter on API functions, but how about the API functions that developers really need? Especially the ones for manipulating the Registry? We selected a small fraction of the Windows API functions that we feel are difficult to master and quite useful to VB programmers.

You will probably notice that a few new ActiveX controls have been added to the Toolbox of the IDE in Visual Basic 5. Some of these controls—for example, TreeView and ListView—aren't easy to program. We describe these very flexible and powerful controls in Chapter 3.

In Part I, we also discuss optimization techniques. We show you a few simple and efficient ways to optimize your VB applications. If the optimized application isn't enough, you may want to help Visual Basic with an external DLL. In Chapter 4, you'll see how to develop DLLs with Visual C++. Visual C++ is faster that Visual Basic, and you can speed your applications considerably by implementing a small percentage of the application's code (the calculation intensive code) in Visual C++ and packaging it as a DLL.

Objects are the recurring theme of this book. We didn't plan it this way, but that's how it turned out. No matter what you do with Visual Basic, you have to learn and master a number of object models. Part II is dedicated to using and building objects. It starts with an overview of programming with objects in Visual Basic. In the following chapters, we show you how to build ActiveX components (DLL and EXE servers) and ActiveX controls. In the last chapter, we discuss, in depth, how to extend the Visual Basic IDE with add-ins. ActiveX control design is one of the best-implemented features in Visual Basic 5. Designing ActiveX components isn't any more complicated than building VB applications. Less obvious, but equally important, is that the new features in VB 5 encourage component software development and designing with reusable components.

Part III is dedicated to database programming. We place a lot of emphasis on the client/server model, which is the dominant form of database programming in the corporate environment. The first chapter provides an overview of the client/server arena, data-access methods, and three-tiered architecture. There is a chapter devoted to Microsoft SQL Server 6.5 with information on how to install and set up a server and a discussion of what's new in SQL Server 6.5. Since this book deals with advanced topics, we have included a chapter that demonstrates, through a sample VB application, some advanced SQL programming, including functions and joins. If you use Microsoft Access, be sure to check out Chapter 14, which explores the process of upsizing an Access database to SQL Server. The last chapter in this part of the book pulls this all together as we design and build a complete three-tiered application using Visual Basic and SQL Server.

Visual Basic, being the simplest language for the Windows environment, was chosen as the model upon which a scripting language for the Web was based. VBScript is a subset of Visual Basic, designed to be used for programming Web pages. VBScript is at the heart of Dynamic HTML and is also used on the Web server by the Active Server Pages. In other words, you can use VBScript to program Web pages, create dynamic Web pages by programming the elements of DHTML, and write applications on the server that interact with the clients.

VBScript will present new opportunities for VB programmers, and we devoted two chapters that will help you leverage your knowledge to the Web. In Part IV, you'll find a quick introduction to VBScript and information on how to use VBScript to develop Active Server Pages.

Part V is dedicated to Visual Basic for Applications (VBA). An increasing number of programmers use Visual Basic to control Office applications, and there is good news for them. VBA 5 was made available at the same time as Visual Basic, and you can now apply your VB knowledge to programming Office applications, as well as a host of other applications that support VBA. More and more companies are customizing off-the-shelf applications, rather than developing custom software for their day-to-day operations. Microsoft Office is the most popular suite of applications in the corporate environment, and once you learn the objects exposed by the Office applications, you'll be ready to apply your knowledge to VBA programming as well.

What's on the CD

This book is accompanied by a CD that contains the following:

- The code for all the example projects discussed in the book

- Demo versions of third-party tools for developers

- The book's appendices:

  - Appendix A, Chapter 1 API Functions

  - Appendix B, Chapter 2 API Functions

  - Appendix C, New and Enhanced Features in SQL Server 6.5

  - Appendix D, Visual Basic 5.0 Service Pack 2 Changes and Additions

You'll find the projects in the CH_CODE folder, and each chapter's projects are in their own folder, named after the project. For example, the DEMOALL project in Chapter 8 is stored in the CH_CODE\CH08\DEMOALL folder. All the files necessary to open the project and run it in the Visual Basic IDE are stored in this folder.

We suggest that you use the installation software on the CD to copy all projects to your hard disk, duplicating the structure of the CH_CODE folder on your disk. You can run the projects off the CD, but you can't save them on the CD after editing. To edit a project, you must copy the project's folder to your hard disk and then open the project. Notice also that files copied off the CD have their Read-Only attribute set. To edit any projects you have copied manually to your hard disk from the CD, follow these steps:

1. Select all the files with the mouse, and then right-click the selection.

2. From the shortcut menu, choose Properties to open the Properties dialog box.

3. In the Attributes section, clear Read-Only.

The FRACTAL and REVERSE projects in Chapter 4 require that the files FRACTAL.DLL and REVERSE.DLL be in the current path or in the Windows\System folder. If you attempt to run these projects without building the DLLs yourself (as discussed in the text), be sure that the two DLL files are copied to the Windows\System folder.

We have also chosen to include a few highly useful and relatively new tools for developers. For details, see the list on the "What's on the CD" page at the back of the book.

How to Reach Us

Despite our best efforts, the first edition of a book this size is bound to contain errors. We will spare no effort in correcting any problem you (or we) discover. If you have any problems with the text or the applications in this book, you can contact us directly at:

Evangelos Petroutsos: 76470.724@compuserve.com

Kevin Hough: khough@houghtech.com

Although we can't promise a response to every question, we will endeavor to address any problems in the text and/or examples and will provide updated versions. We would also like to hear any comments you may have about the book regarding topics you liked or disliked and how useful you found the examples. Your comments will help us revise the book in future editions.

PART I

Extending Visual Basic

CHAPTER

ONE

1

Visual Basic and the Windows API

- Understanding API fundamentals

- Using handles in Windows

- Manipulating applications

- Analyzing an application's menu structure

- Programming with the bitmaps and graphics API

- Using the system API functions

The Windows 32-bit application programming interface (Windows API) includes functions, messages, and type structures that enable developers working in many programming languages to build applications that run on Windows 95 and Windows NT operating systems. Because Visual Basic 5 is truly a feature-rich programming environment, you could probably write programs for years and not use the Windows API. But as you develop more complex applications, you will find that using APIs will make your life much easier.

In Visual Basic, text boxes already know how to hold and display text, list boxes and combo boxes already know how to present data, command buttons know how to process a click, and windows know how to open and close. When your application needs capabilities that go beyond the core language and these controls, you can make API calls. By calling API procedures in DLLs, or dynamic-link libraries, you can access the thousands of procedures in the WIN32 API system, as well as routines written in other languages.

As their name suggests, DLLs are libraries of procedures that applications can link to and use at run time rather than link to statically at compile time. DLLs are not compiled into the application's executable; thus, DLLs can be updated independently of the application, and many applications can share a single DLL. Microsoft Windows itself is composed of DLLs, and other applications call the procedures within these libraries to display windows and graphics, manage system resources, manipulate the Windows Registry, and do many other tasks. These procedures are sometimes referred to as the Windows API.

Visual Basic is designed to be extended by having access to the API. VB provides a balance by hiding many of the complexities of Windows programming while still providing access to the Windows environment. More than 1000 API calls are available and can be classified in four areas:

Application manipulation   APIs open and close applications, access menu commands, and move and resize windows.

Graphics   APIs create bitmaps and capture screen images.

System information   APIs determine the current drive, available and total memory, current user, and the computer's operating system.

Registry interaction   APIs interact with the Windows Registry beyond the built-in Visual Basic registry functions of GetSettings and SetSettings to create and query keys and to delete keys, subkeys, and values. (We discuss the Registry API functions in Chapter 2.

The Win32 API allows Visual Basic to exploit the power of the 32-bit Windows family of operating systems. The functions, structures, messages, macros, and interfaces form a consistent and uniform API for Microsoft Windows 95 and Windows NT operating systems. With a simple API call, you can achieve tasks that seem overwhelming or even impossible. This chapter introduces the fundamentals of Windows APIs, shows how to access APIs from Visual Basic, and looks at how to declare and reference function arguments. The example projects in this chapter will show you, the developer, how to unleash and harness the power of the Win32 API functions so that your VB projects are able to do the following:

- Find and control a window

- Manipulate other applications

- Find, access, and execute a menu option in another application

API Fundamentals

To use the Windows API functions, you need to understand the functional categories shown in Table 1.1.

TABLE 1.1: API Functional Categories

Category	Description
Windows Management (User32)	Creates and manages a user interface for applications
Graphics Device Interface (GDI32)	Generates graphical output for Windows devices
System Services (Kernel32)	Provides access to the operating system and computer resources
Multimedia	Accesses audio and video services
Remote Procedure Calls (RPC)	Carries out distributed computing

Windows Management

Windows Management (User32) provides the basic functions required to build and manage the display of your program output and to capture user input. The Windows Management layer determines how your application responds to mouse and keyboard input, retrieves and processes messages sent to your application windows, and supports all the clipboard functions. The Windows Management API functions include:

- ShowWindow, which sets the specified window's visibility.
- IsWindowVisible, which retrieves the visibility state of the specified window.

Graphics Device Interface

The Graphics Device Interface (GDI32) provides the functionality for your application to support all the devices installed on your computer, including the monitor and the printer. The GDI provides the ability to define drawing objects, such as pens, brushes, and fonts and also provides the ability to draw lines, circles, and bitmap functions. The GDI functions include:

- BitBlt, which performs a bit-block transfer of the color data corresponding to a rectangle of pixels from the specified source device context into a destination device context.
- CreateCompatibleBitmap, which creates a bitmap that is compatible with the device that is associated with the specified device context.

System Services

System Services (Kernel32) provide functions to access the resources of the computer provided by the operating system. These include functions for memory, the file system, and resources running on your system. System Services provide information about the hardware, including the mouse and the keyboard. System Service functions include:

- GetDiskFreeSpace, which retrieves information about the specified disk, including the amount of free space on the disk.
- GetVersion, which returns the current version number of Windows and information about the operating system platform.

Multimedia Functions

Multimedia functions allow you to add wave audio, AVI video, joystick support, multimedia timers, and MIDI music to your applications. The MCI Command

String and Command Message Interface provides support for playing various types of media files. The multimedia functions include:

- mciSendCommand, which sends a command message to the specified MCI device.

- MessageBeep, which plays a waveform sound. The waveform sound for each sound type is identified by an entry in the [sounds] section of the Registry.

Remote Procedure Calls

Remote Procedure Calls (RPC) give applications the ability to carry out distributed computing, allowing applications to tap the resources and power of computers on a network. You use RPC to create distributed applications consisting of a client that presents information to the user and a server that stores, retrieves, and manipulates data and performs computing tasks for the client. Remote file servers, remote printer servers, and shared databases are examples of distributed applications. The RPC API functions include:

- RpcServerRegisterAuthInfo, which is a server side API that turns on security for the various server interfaces that are registered. It sets up the server, the principal name, the authentication service to use, and any key retrieval function in the RPC_SERVER object.

- RpcMgmtInqServerPrincName, which is used by the server application to inquire about the server's principal name corresponding to the supplied binding handle and the authentication service.

Accessing the Win32 API from Visual Basic

Using a DLL procedure in Visual Basic consists of two steps: declaring it, and then calling it as many times as it is needed. You must tell Visual Basic the DLL or API function you want to use and then supply the arguments it requires.

Declaring API Functions and DLLs

To declare a DLL procedure, you add a Declare statement to the Declarations section of the Code window. If the procedure returns a value, write the Declare statement as a function:

```
Declare Function publicname Lib "libname" [Alias "alias"] [([[ByVal]
variable [As type] [,[ByVal] variable [As type]]...])] As Type
```

If a procedure does not return a value, write the Declare statement as a subroutine:

```
Declare Sub publicname Lib "libname" [Alias "alias"] [([[ByVal] variable
[As type] [,[ByVal] variable [As type]]...])]
```

Later in this chapter, we will use the function FindWindow. It is declared as follows:

```
Declare Function FindWindow Lib "user32" Alias "FindWindowA" _
    (ByVal lpClassName As String, ByVal lpWindowName _
    As String) As Long
```

NOTE

The underscore character at the end of code lines is used to break long code into multiple lines.

The FindWindow function in this declaration finds the handle of a window. We will also demonstrate how to use this function later in this chapter.

When you declare DLL procedures in standard modules, they are public by default, and you can call them from anywhere in your application. When you declare DLL procedures in any other type of module, they are private to that module, and you must identify them as such by preceding the declaration with the Private keyword.

NOTE

Procedure names are case-sensitive in 32-bit versions of Visual Basic. In previous, 16-bit versions, procedure names were not case-sensitive.

Specifying the Library

The Lib clause in the Declare statement tells Visual Basic where to find the DLL file that contains the procedure. When you reference one of the core Windows libraries

(User32, Kernel32, or GDI32), as we did in the FindWindow example, you don't need to include the file name extension. If you do not specify a path for *libname*, Visual Basic searches for the file in the following order:

1. In the directory containing the calling EXE file
2. In the current directory
3. In the Windows system directory (often, but not necessarily \Windows\System)
4. In the Windows directory (not necessarily \Windows)
5. In the *Path* environment variable

Table 1.2 lists the common operating environment library files.

TABLE 1.2: Common Operating Environment Library Files

Dynamic Link Library	Description
Advapi32.dll	Advanced API services library supporting numerous APIs, including many security and Registry calls
Comdlg32.dll	Common dialog API library
Gdi32.dll	Graphics Device Interface API library
Kernel32.dll	Core Windows 32-bit base API support
Lz32.dll	32-bit compression routines
Mpr.dll	Multiple Provider Router library
Netapi32.dll	32-bit Network API library
Shell32.dll	32-bit Shell API library
User32.dll	Library for user interface routines
Version.dll	Version library
Winmm.dll	Windows multimedia library
Winspool.drv	Print spooler interface that contains the print spooler API calls

Using the API Viewer Application

You can use the API Viewer application (shown in Figure 1.1) to browse through the declarations, constants, and types included in any text file or Microsoft Jet database. When you find the procedure you want, you can copy the code to the clipboard and paste it into your Visual Basic application.

FIGURE 1.1:

The API Viewer application

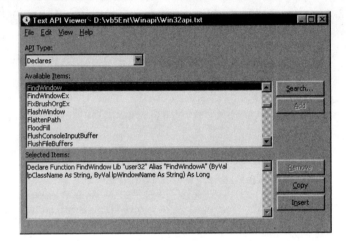

To use the Viewer Application, follow these steps:

1. Choose Add-Ins ➤ API Viewer. If you don't see the API Viewer option, select Add-In Manager and check VB API Viewer to add the API Viewer Application to the list of available Add-Ins.

2. Choose File ➤ Load Text File or File ➤ Load Database File.

> **NOTE**   For your convenience, Microsoft includes a Win32API file with Visual Basic 5. It is in the WinAPI subdirectory where you installed Visual Basic.

3. Select the function you want from the Available Items list box. The selected function(s) are displayed in the Selected Items list box.

4. Click the Copy button to copy the functions to the clipboard.

5. Paste the functions from the clipboard into your application's Code window.

Passing Arguments

Most DLL routines, including those in the Windows API, are documented using notation from the C programming language. This is only natural, as most DLLs are written in C or C++.

To translate the syntax of a typical API routine into a Visual Basic Declare statement, you have to understand something about how both C and Visual Basic pass arguments. The usual way for C to pass numeric arguments is *by value*—a copy of the value of the argument is passed to the routine.

Sometimes C arguments are pointers, and these arguments are said to be passed *by reference*—the called routine modifies the argument and returns it. C strings and arrays are always passed by reference.

Visual Basic usually passes all its arguments by reference (the default if not specified otherwise). To pass arguments to a C routine that expects its arguments to be passed by value, you use the ByVal keyword with the argument in the Declaration statement.

Visual Basic strings do not use the same format as C strings. In Visual Basic, the ByVal keyword is overloaded to mean "pass a C string" when it is used with a string argument in a Declare statement.

Table 1.3 shows the C argument types and their equivalent declarations in Visual Basic.

TABLE 1.3: C and Visual Basic Data Types

C Declaration	Visual Basic Data Type	Argument Type
Char	String	ByVal
Handle	Long	ByVal
Integer	Integer	byVal
Integer Pointer (LPINT)	Integer	ByRef
Long	Long	ByVal
Long Integer Pointer	Long	ByRef
Void Pointer	Any	ByRef

> **NOTE** You will never pass a Visual Basic string or array to a DLL routine unless the DLL was written specifically for use with Visual Basic. Visual Basic strings and arrays are represented in memory by *descriptors* (not pointers), which are useless to DLL routines that were not written with Visual Basic in mind.

Passing Arguments by Value

When arguments are passed by value, only a copy of a variable is passed. If the procedure changes the value, the change affects only the copy and not the variable itself. Use the ByVal keyword to indicate an argument passed by value.

For example, if you create the following subroutine:

```
Public Sub customSub(ByVal addTo As Integer)
    addTo = addTo + 10
    Debug.Print addTo
End Sub
```

and call customSub() with the following code:

```
x = 5
Call customSub (x)
Debug.Print x
```

the Debug.Print command displays 15 in customSub(), but the value reverts to 5 when it returns to the calling subroutine. The value changes only within the customSub() subroutine.

Passing Arguments by Reference

Passing arguments by reference gives the procedure access to the actual variable contents in its memory address location. As a result, the variable's value can be permanently changed by the procedure to which it is passed. Passing by reference is the default in Visual Basic.

For example, if you create the following subroutine:

```
Public Sub customSub(addTo As Integer)
    addTo = addTo + 10
    Debug.Print addTo
End Sub
```

and call customSub() with the following code:

```
x = 5
Call customSub (x)
Debug.Print x
```

the Debug.Print command displays 15 in customSub(), and the value of *x* is 15 when it returns to the calling subroutine. The changes to *x* are global since it was passed by reference.

Handles in Windows

One way or another, Windows API functions can access windows, program instances, bitmaps, files, icons, menus, and all types of objects in Visual Basic. Windows identifies each object with a 32-bit integer known as a *handle*. This handle is generally referred to as the *Windows hwnd*. It is a unique Long Integer data type.

Every window in Windows has a handle, which enables you to find a specific window among all the windows currently running in memory. Once you obtain the handle, it is easy to minimize and maximize a window, move a window, and change a window's size.

As the mouse moves over windows on the Desktop, you can use the API function WindowFromPoint to get the handle to the window currently under the mouse. To take this one step further, you can also store the window's handle and use it later in your program. To do so, you implement the same type of process that Visual Basic DragDrop uses.

Clicking the mouse button on a Visual Basic Form triggers the MouseDown event. This sets the Form as a starting point. Releasing the mouse button triggers the MouseUp event. You can then pass the mouse coordinates to the WindowFromPoint API function and obtain the window's handle. Now that you have the handle, you can use the API function GetWindowRect to determine the size and position of the window. The coordinates of the window are returned from GetWindowRect in WindowRect.Left, WindowRect.Right, WindowRect.Top, and WindowRect.Bottom. Code 1.1 shows how these API functions work.

WARNING When you use API functions in Visual Basic, there is no built-in safety net. If you pass incorrect arguments to a function, unexpected things can happen. You can even cause a General Protection Fault that can crash the system. Therefore, it is good programming practice to use procedure-level error trapping, as we have done in Code 1.1.

Code 1.1: **Sample API Functions**

```
Private Sub Form_MouseUp(Button%, Shift%, x As Single, _
    y As Single)

On Error GoTo ErrorRoutineErr

Dim strCaption$
Dim ptLocation As POINT
Dim i

'Convert the current mouse position to screen coordinates
ptLocation.x = CLng(x)
ptLocation.y = CLng(y)
ClientToScreen Me.hwnd, ptLocation

'Use WindowFromPoint to find out what window we are
'pointing to
hwndCurrentWindow = WindowFromPoint(ptLocation.x, _
    ptLocation.y)

'Create a buffer to hold the caption, and call
'GetWindowText to retrieve it
strCaption = Space(1000)
Caption = Left(strCaption, _
GetWindowText(hwndCurrentWindow, strCaption, _
Len(strCaption)))

'Clear our module-level variable and restore
'the mouse pointer hwndCurrentWindow = False
MousePointer = vbNormal

'Get the rectangle describing the window
GetWindowRect hwndCurrentWindow, WindowRect
```

```
                 'coordinates of the window are returned in
                 '(WindowRect.Left),(WindowRect.Right)
                 '(WindowRect.Top),(WindowRect.Bottom)

         ErrorRoutineResume:
             Exit Sub
         ErrorRoutineErr:
             MsgBox "FindWindow - frmMain, MouseMove" _
                 & Err & " " & Error
             Resume Next
         End Sub
```

NOTE   We'll expand on this code later in this chapter in the FindWindow project.

With WindowFromPoint, you can get the handle for any window and then use GetWindowRect to capture the style, size, and position of the window. The projects and examples that follow will give you plenty of ideas and opportunities for integrating (and controlling!) other applications from your Visual Basic application. If you combine the features from the example projects, you can build an even more robust project.

The FindWindow Project

Armed with the window's handle, manipulating the window is easy for VB. We will use the FindWindow application (shown in Figure 1.2) to find and manipulate a window.

NOTE   You will find the FindWindow project in the Chapter1\FindWindow folder on the CD that comes with this book.

FIGURE 1.2:

The FindWindow
application

The FindWindow program gets the handle from a window and allows you to minimize, maximize, move, resize, and flash the title bar of the selected window with API functions. The project consists of three Forms and six Command Buttons on the main Form. These buttons are as follows:

- The Minimize Window button minimizes the selected window by passing SW_MINIMIZE to the ShowWindow function.

- The Restore Window button restores a minimized window to its original size by passing SW_SHOWNOACTIVATE to the ShowWindow function.

- The Set Position button displays the Set Position Form (shown in Figure 1.3). This Form allows you to pass new coordinate positions to the SetWindowPos function and move the window.

- The Set Size button displays the Set Size Form (shown in Figure 1.4). From this Form, you can set new size values and call the SetWindowPos function to resize the window.

- The Identify button calls the FlashWindow API function and causes the window's title bar to change colors.

- The Exit button terminates the program.

FIGURE 1.3:

The SetPosition
Form

FIGURE 1.4:

The SetSize Form

The FindWindow Project API Functions

The FindWindow project calls the API functions listed in Table 1.4 to find and manipulate a window.

NOTE You'll find a complete description of the API functions in Appendix A, which is on the CD that comes with this book.

TABLE 1.4: The FindWindow API Functions

API Function	Description
ClientToScreen	Converts the client coordinates of a given point or rectangle on the display to screen coordinates.
DrawIcon	Draws an icon in the client area of the window.
FlashWindow	Flashes the specified window once.
GetWindowRect	Retrieves the dimensions of the rectangle of the specified window. The dimensions are given in screen coordinates that are relative to the upper-left corner of the screen.
GetWindowText	Copies the text of the specified window's title bar (if it has one) into a buffer. If the specified window is a control, the text of the control is copied.
IsIconic	Determines whether the specified window is minimized (iconic).
IsWindowEnabled	Determines whether the specified window is enabled.
IsWindowVisible	Retrieves the visibility state of the specified window.

TABLE 1.4 (CONTINUED) : The FindWindow API Functions

API Function	Description
IsZoomed	Determines whether a window is maximized.
LoadCursor	Loads the specified cursor.
SetWindowPos	Changes the size, position, and Zorder of a child, pop-up, or top-level window.
ShowWindow	Sets the specified window's visibility.
WindowFromPoint	Retrieves the handle of the window that contains the specified point.

The FindWindow Code in Action

Now that you've seen the API functions needed to convert the mouse pointer's coordinates to find a window's handle, minimize and restore a window's state, move and resize a window, and flash the title bar of a window, let's take a look at the code needed to put the functions into action.

Code 1.2 contains all the declarations, types, and constants required for the API functions in the FindWindow project.

Code 1.2: **Declarations, Types, and Constants for FindWindow**

```
'API Declarations, Types, and Constants
Public Type RECT
    Left As Long
    Top As Long
    Right As Long
    Bottom As Long
End Type

Public Type POINT
    x As Long
    y As Long
End Type

'SetWindowPos() hwndInsertAfter values
Public Const HWND_TOP = 0
Public Const HWND_BOTTOM = 1
Public Const HWND_TOPMOST = -1
Public Const HWND_NOTOPMOST = -2
```

```
'SetWindowPos Flags
Public Const SWP_NOSIZE = &H1
Public Const SWP_NOMOVE = &H2
Public Const SWP_NOZORDER = &H4
Public Const SWP_NOREDRAW = &H8
Public Const SWP_NOACTIVATE = &H10
Public Const SWP_FRAMECHANGED = &H20
Public Const SWP_SHOWWINDOW = &H40
Public Const SWP_HIDEWINDOW = &H80
Public Const SWP_NOCOPYBITS = &H100
Public Const SWP_NOOWNERZORDER = &H200
Public Const SWP_DRAWFRAME = SWP_FRAMECHANGED
Public Const SWP_NOREPOSITION = SWP_NOOWNERZORDER

'ShowWindow() Commands
Public Const SW_HIDE = 0
Public Const SW_SHOWNORMAL = 1
Public Const SW_NORMAL = 1
Public Const SW_SHOWMINIMIZED = 2
Public Const SW_SHOWMAXIMIZED = 3
Public Const SW_MAXIMIZE = 3
Public Const SW_SHOWNOACTIVATE = 4
Public Const SW_SHOW = 5
Public Const SW_MINIMIZE = 6
Public Const SW_SHOWMINNOACTIVE = 7
Public Const SW_SHOWNA = 8
Public Const SW_RESTORE = 9
Public Const SW_SHOWDEFAULT = 10
Public Const SW_MAX = 10


Declare Sub ClientToScreen Lib "user32" (ByVal hwnd _
    As Long, lpPoint As POINT)
Declare Function GetWindowText& Lib "user32" Alias _
    "GetWindowTextA" (ByVal hwnd&, ByVal lpString$, ByVal cb&)
Declare Function GetWindowRect Lib "user32" (ByVal _
    hwnd As Long, lpRect As RECT) As Boolean
Declare Function WindowFromPoint Lib "user32" (ByVal _
    ptY As Long, ByVal ptX As Long) As Long
Declare Function LoadCursor Lib "user32" Alias "LoadCursorA" _
    (ByVal hInstance&, ByVal lpCursor&) As Long
Declare Function DrawIcon Lib "user32" (ByVal hdc As Long, _
    ByVal x As Long, ByVal y As Long, ByVal hIcon As _
```

```
        Long) As Long
Declare Function ShowWindow Lib "user32" (ByVal hwnd As _
    Long, ByVal nCmdShow As Long) As Long
Declare Function IsWindowVisible Lib "user32" (ByVal hwnd _
    As Long) As Long
Declare Function IsWindowEnabled Lib "user32" (ByVal hwnd _
    As Long) As Long
Declare Function IsZoomed Lib "user32" (ByVal hwnd As _
    Long) As Long
Declare Function IsIconic Lib "user32" (ByVal hwnd _
    As Long) As Long
Declare Function SetWindowPos Lib "user32" (ByVal hwnd _
    As Long, ByVal _
    hWndInsertAfter As Long, ByVal x As Long, ByVal _
    y As Long, _
    ByVal cx As Long, ByVal cy As Long, ByVal wFlags _
    As Long) As Long
Declare Function FlashWindow Lib "user32" (ByVal hwnd _
    As Long, ByVal bInvert As Long) As Long


'Define the icon
Global Const IDC_UPARROW = 32516&


' Holds the handle to the captured window
Public hwndCurrentWindow As Long
```

Drawing the Icon

The Form_Load subroutine sets up the Form and draws a copy of vbUpArrow on the Form using the function DrawIcon. Table 1.5 lists the built-in cursor styles available in Visual Basic. To substitute one of these styles, change the IDC_UPARROW argument in the LoadCursor function.

Code 1.3:   The Form_Load Subroutine

```
Private Sub Form_Load()

    'Size the form and put instructions in the caption
    With frmMain
        .Caption = "Click & drag the arrow!"
    End With
```

```
'Change the ScaleMode to pixels and turn on AutoRedraw
ScaleMode = vbPixels
AutoRedraw = True

'Draw vbUpArrow into the form's persistent bitmap
DrawIcon hdc, 170, 0, LoadCursor(0, IDC_UPARROW)

End Sub
```

TABLE 1.5: Cursor Values

Value	Description
IDC_APPSTARTING	Standard arrow and small hourglass.
IDC_ARROW	Standard arrow.
IDC_CROSS	Crosshair.
IDC_IBEAM	Text I-beam.
IDC_ICON	Obsolete for applications marked version 4 or later.
IDC_NO	Slashed circle.
IDC_SIZE	Obsolete for applications marked version 4 or later. Use IDC_SIZEALL.
IDC_SIZEALL	Four-pointed arrow.
IDC_SIZENESW	Double-pointed arrow pointing northeast and southwest.
IDC_SIZENS	Double-pointed arrow pointing north and south.
IDC_SIZENWSE	Double-pointed arrow pointing northwest and southeast.
IDC_SIZEWE	Double-pointed arrow pointing west and east.
IDC_UPARROW	Vertical arrow.
IDC_WAIT	Hourglass.

Tracking the Mouse Position

The MouseMove subroutine tracks the movement of the mouse pointer and converts the location to screen coordinates with the ClientToScreen function. With the WindowFromPoint function, we retrieve the handle to the window. Finally, we pass the handle to the GetWindowText function to set the caption of the main Form to the caption of the window under the mouse pointer.

Code 1.4:   The MouseMove Subroutine

```
Private Sub Form_MouseMove(Button As Integer, Shift As Integer, _
    x As Single, y As Single)
    Dim strCaption$
    Dim ptLocation As POINT
    Dim i
    Dim hwndTemp As Long

    'Convert the current mouse position to screen coordinates
    ptLocation.x = CLng(x)
    ptLocation.y = CLng(y)
    ClientToScreen Me.hwnd, ptLocation

    'Use WindowFromPoint to find out what window we are
    'pointing to
    hwndTemp = WindowFromPoint(ptLocation.x, ptLocation.y)

    'If a window has been captured, then put its caption
    'in our caption
    If hwndTemp Then

        'Create a buffer to hold the caption,
        'and call GetWindowText to retrieve it
        strCaption = Space(1000)
        Caption = Left(strCaption, _
        GetWindowText(hwndTemp, strCaption, Len(strCaption)))
    End If
End Sub
```

Getting the Handle and Filling the Main Form

The MouseUp subroutine gets the position of the mouse pointer when you release the mouse button and converts the location to screen coordinates with the ClientToScreen function. As in the MouseMove subroutine, we use the WindowFromPoint function to retrieve the handle to the window. Finally, we pass the handle to the GetWindowText function to set the caption of the Main Form to the caption of the window under the mouse pointer, and then we fill in the text boxes with the window's size, position, and state.

Code 1.5:   The MouseUp Subroutine

```
Private Sub Form_MouseUp(Button%, Shift%, x As Single, _
    y As Single)

On Error GoTo ErrorRoutineErr

Dim strCaption$ ' Buffer used to hold the caption
Dim ptLocation As POINT ' The location of the window
Dim i

'Convert the current mouse position to screen coordinates
ptLocation.x = CLng(x)
ptLocation.y = CLng(y)
ClientToScreen Me.hwnd, ptLocation

'Use WindowFromPoint to find out what window we are
'pointing to
hwndCurrentWindow = WindowFromPoint(ptLocation.x, _
    ptLocation.y)

'If a window has been captured, then put its caption
'in our caption
If hwndCurrentWindow Then

    'Create a buffer to hold the caption, and call
    'GetWindowText to retrieve it
    strCaption = Space(1000)
    Caption = Left(strCaption, _
    GetWindowText(hwndCurrentWindow, strCaption, _
    Len(strCaption)))

    'If this window does not a caption,
    'it is not a main window, exit out
    If Len(Caption) = 0 Then
        Exit Sub
    End If

    'Fill the form with the current windows attributes
    Call GetWindowAttributes
```

```
                'If we found a window, enable the action buttons
                For i = 0 To 4
                    cmdWindowAction(i).Enabled = True
                Next

            End If
            'Restore the mouse pointer
            MousePointer = vbNormal
    ErrorRoutineResume:
        Exit Sub
    ErrorRoutineErr:
        MsgBox "frmMain, MouseUp " & Err & " " & Error
        Resume Next
    End Sub
```

Managing the Window

The cmdWindowAction button is a control array that minimizes and restores the window with the ShowWindow function, flashing the window's title bar with the FlashWindow function and displaying the NewSize and NewPosition Forms. Table 1.6 lists the possible values for the ShowWindow function.

Code 1.6:   The cmdWindowAction Button

```
    Private Sub cmdWindowAction_Click(Index As Integer)
        On Error GoTo ErrorRoutineErr
        Dim rc
        Select Case Index
            Case 0  'minimize window
                rc = ShowWindow(hwndCurrentWindow, SW_MINIMIZE)
            Case 1  'show window
                rc = ShowWindow(hwndCurrentWindow, SW_SHOWNOACTIVATE)
            Case 2  'set new size
                frmNewSize.Show 1
            Case 3  'set new position
                frmNewPosition.Show 1
            Case 4  'identify the window, make the title flash
                rc = FlashWindow(hwndCurrentWindow, -1)
            Case 5  'exit
                End
```

```
        End Select
ErrorRoutineResume:
        Exit Sub
ErrorRoutineErr:
        MsgBox "frmMain, cmdWindowAction " & Err & " " & Error
        Resume Next
End Sub
```

TABLE 1.6: The ShowWindow Visibility Values

Value	Description
SW_HIDE	Hides the window and activates another window.
SW_MAXIMIZE	Maximizes the specified window.
SW_MINIMIZE	Minimizes the specified window and activates the next top-level window in the Zorder.
SW_RESTORE	Activates and displays the window. If the window is minimized or maximized, Windows restores it to its original size and position. An application should specify this flag when restoring a minimized window.
SW_SHOW	Activates the window and displays it in its current size and position.
SW_SHOWDEFAULT	Sets the show state based on the SW_ flag specified in the STARTUPINFO structure passed to the CreateProcess function by the program that started the application.
SW_SHOWMAXIMIZED	Activates the window and displays it as a maximized window.
SW_SHOWMINIMIZED	Activates the window and displays it as a minimized window.
SW_SHOWMINNOACTIVE	Displays the window as a minimized window. The active window remains active.
SW_SHOWNA	Displays the window in its current state. The active window remains active.
SW_SHOWNOACTIVATE	Displays a window in its most recent size and position. The active window remains active.
SW_SHOWNORMAL	Activates and displays a window. If the window is minimized or maximized, Windows restores it to its original size and position. An application should specify this flag when displaying the window for the first time.

Moving the Window

To move the window, enter the new Top and Left positions into the text boxes on the NewPosition Form (shown in Figure 1.5 with the Main FindWindow Form) and click the Set button.

FIGURE 1.5:

The NewPosition
and Main
FindWindow Forms

The Set button calls the SetWindowPos function and moves the window to its new location. You must identify the window to precede the positioned window in the Zorder. This parameter must be a window handle or one of the values in Table 1.7.

Code 1.7:   Moving a Window with the SetWindowsPos API

```
Private Sub cmdWindowAction_Click(Index As Integer)
    On Error GoTo ErrorRoutineErr
    Dim rc As Long
    Select Case Index
        Case 0  'OK
            rc = SetWindowPos(hwndCurrentWindow, _
                HWND_TOP, txtLeft, txtTop, _
                frmMain.lblHorizontal, frmMain.lblVertical, _
                SWP_NOSIZE)
        Case 1  'cancel
            'cancel the changes and unload the form
            Unload Me
    End Select
ErrorRoutineResume:
    Exit Sub
```

```
ErrorRoutineErr:
    MsgBox "frmNewPosition, cmdWindowAction " _
        & Err & " " & Error
    Resume Next
End Sub
```

TABLE 1.7: The SetWindowsPos Values

Value	Description
HWND_BOTTOM	Places the window at the bottom of the Zorder. If the hWnd parameter identifies a topmost window, the window loses its topmost status and is placed at the bottom of all other windows.
HWND_NOTOPMOST	Places the window above all nontopmost windows (that is, behind all topmost windows). This flag has no effect if the window is already a nontopmost window.
HWND_TOP	Places the window at the top of the Zorder.
HWND_TOPMOST	Places the window above all nontopmost windows. The window maintains its topmost position even when it is deactivated.

Resizing the Window

To resize the window, enter the new Horizontal and Vertical dimensions in the text boxes on the NewSize Form (shown in Figure 1.6 with the Main FindWindow Form), and click the Set button. The Set button calls the SetWindowPos function and resizes the window.

FIGURE 1.6:

The NewSize and Main FindWindow Forms

Code 1.8: **Setting the Window's Size with the SetWindowsPos API Function**

```
Private Sub cmdWindowAction_Click(Index As Integer)
    On Error GoTo ErrorRoutineErr
    Dim rc As Long
    Select Case Index
        Case 0  'OK
            rc = SetWindowPos(hwndCurrentWindow, HWND_TOP _
                , frmMain.lblLeft, frmMain.lblTop, _
                txtHorizontal, txtVertical, SWP_NOMOVE)
        Case 1  'cancel
            'Cancel the changes and unload the form
            Unload Me
    End Select
ErrorRoutineResume:
    Exit Sub
ErrorRoutineErr:
    MsgBox "frmNewSize, cmdWindowAction " & Err & " " & Error
    Resume Next
End Sub
```

Taking FindWindow for a Test Run

Now that everything is set up, let's test the FindWindow application and move some windows around. Press F5 to start the program and follow these steps:

1. Move the mouse pointer over the Main Form and press and hold the mouse button.

2. With the mouse button still pressed, move the pointer over a window. Notice that the caption of the Main Form changes to display the title of the window.

3. Release the mouse button, and the Form displays the window's statistics (see Figure 1.7).

4. Now, you can experiment with the features of the program.

As you can see from the code samples, finding a window's handle is not difficult. Once you have the handle to a window, it is easy to manipulate it with the API functions. In the next section, we'll explore some of the API functions needed to manipulate an application.

The FindWindow
application at work

Manipulating Applications

Visual Basic is designed to give you, the developer, lots of control over your application as you are designing and running it, but VB does not give you much control over other applications that may be running concurrently. At times, you need to be able to do the following:

- Start another application from within your VB program.
- Terminate the application and know when that application has ended.
- Start another application and deny access to your VB program until the user closes the new application.
- Terminate any application from within your program.

You can take care of all these tasks with the help of Windows API calls. Here are a few API functions that you can call from within VB to launch a new application:

- OpenProcess opens a handle to an existing process. You can use this function after the Visual Basic Shell function, or you can incorporate the Shell function into the call.
- CreateProcess creates a new process.
- PostMessage terminates a running application after you obtain the handle.

The AppShell Project

We will use the AppShell project (shown in Figure 1.8) to demonstrate the application manipulation API functions.

NOTE   You'll find the AppShell project in the `Chapter1\AppShell` folder on the CD that comes with this book.

AppShell loads a ListBox control with the name and Windows handle of all the processes currently running in memory. These processes include Windows level processes and applications such as Notepad and Calculator. The project has four Command Buttons:

Shell and Continue   Clicking this button displays a File Open dialog box in which you can choose an application (EXE) file to launch. Your VB program monitors the new application and notifies you, through a message box, when it is closed. You remain in control of the VB program.

Process and Wait   This button differs from the Shell and Continue button in that you do not maintain control over the VB program while the new process is active. Clicking this button "freezes" the VB program. Your VB program will notify you through a message box and will again gain control when the new application is terminated.

Terminate App   Clicking this button terminates the application you selected from the ListBox.

WARNING   This is a powerful command. You can terminate any process, even Windows itself. Since this example program does not employ a lot of error trapping, use caution and only terminate applications such as Calculator or Notepad.

Refresh List Box   Clicking this button refreshes the ListBox control. You can click this button if you launch an application from the Start menu.

The AppShell
project

Launching a New Application

To launch a new application from within VB, you can use the OpenProcess API function with the Visual Basic Shell function. The OpenProcess function allows you to control how the application is run. It returns the handle to the newly opened process or application and is declared as follows:

```
Declare Function OpenProcess Lib "kernel32" _
    (ByVal dwDesiredAccess As Long, ByVal bInheritHandle _
    As Long, ByVal dwProcessID As Long) As Long
```

When you have the process handle to the new process, you can use the GetExit-CodeProcess function to determine whether the process is still running in memory. Code 1.9 uses the OpenProcess function to start the Notepad application.

Code 1.9:   The OpenProcess API Function

```
Private Sub Command1_Click()
    On Error GoTo ErrorRoutineErr

    Dim hProcess As Long
    Dim RetVal As Long
    Dim slAppToRun As String

    slAppToRun = "c:\Windows\Notepad.exe"
```

```
'The next line launches Notepad,
hProcess = OpenProcess(PROCESS_QUERY_INFORMATION, 1, _
Shell(slAppToRun, vbNormalFocus))

ErrorRoutineResume:
    Exit Sub
ErrorRoutineErr:
    MsgBox "AppShell.Form1.Command1_Click" & Err & Error
    Resume Next
End Sub
```

The GetExitCodeProcess function returns a value of STILL_ACTIVE if the opened process or application is still running. You can code a subroutine to check this value periodically to determine the state of the new process.

Launching a New Application and Waiting

You can use the CreateProcess API function to load and run any application or process you want. Unlike the OpenProcess function, which uses the Shell function to start the application, CreateProcess actually starts the application before it creates a Windows process. When you use this function, you have complete control over how the launched application is run. After you call the CreateProcess function, you can call the WaitForSingleObject function and force the system to wait until a specified process has finished to continue. You declare the CreateProcess function as follows:

```
Declare Function CreateProcessA Lib "kernel32" _
    (ByVal lpApplicationName As Long, ByVal lpCommandLine As _
    String, ByVal lpProcessAttributes As Long, ByVal _
    lpThreadAttributes As Long, ByVal bInheritHandles As _
    Long, ByVal dwCreationFlags As Long, ByVal _
    lpEnvironment As Long, ByVal _
    lpCurrentDirectory As Long, lpStartupInfo As STARTUPINFO, _
    lpProcessInformation As PROCESS_INFORMATION) As Long
```

For the WaitForSingleObject function, you pass the handle of the process you want to wait for and the length of time to pause, in milliseconds. You can set the time-out value to INFINITE and cause the system to wait until the user stops the process.

After the user stops the process, the final step is to close the open handle for the just-launched process. This removes all references to the new process. Code 1.10 uses the CreateProcess function to start the Notepad application.

Code 1.10:   The CreateProcess API Function

```
Private Sub Command1_Click()
    On Error GoTo ErrorRoutineErr

    Dim NameOfProc As PROCESS_INFORMATION
    Dim NameStart As STARTUPINFO
    Dim rc As Long
    Dim slAppToRun As String

    slAppToRun = "c:\Windows\Notepad.exe"

    NameStart.cb = Len(NameStart)
    rc = CreateProcessA(0&, slAppToRun, 0&, 0&, 1&, _
        NORMAL_PRIORITY_CLASS, _
        0&, 0&, NameStart, NameOfProc)

ErrorRoutineResume:
    Exit Sub
ErrorRoutineErr:
    MsgBox "AppShell.Form1.Command1_Click" & Err & Error
    Resume Next
End Sub
```

Terminating an Application

To terminate an application, you use the FindWindow function to retrieve the handle. After you have the handle, it is a good idea to check and be sure that you are not getting ready to close your Visual Basic program. To do this, use the GetWindow function, and compare the handle with your program and with the application you want to terminate. If they are the same, you're getting ready to terminate your Visual Basic program. After this check, use the PostMessage function to actually terminate the application. You declare the PostMessage function as follows:

```
Declare Function PostMessage Lib "user32" Alias _
    "PostMessageA" (ByVal hwnd As Long, ByVal wMsg _
    As Long, ByVal wParam _
    As Long, ByVal lParam As Long) As Long
```

Code 1.11 shows how you can use the PostMessage function to terminate an application whose handle is passed in as TargetHwnd. The FindWindow function ensures that you do not close the current window.

Code 1.11:   The EndTask Subroutine

```
Function EndTask(TargetHwnd As Long) As Long

    Dim rc As Integer
    Dim ReturnVal As Integer
    If TargetHwnd = Form1.hwnd Or GetWindow(TargetHwnd, _
        GW_OWNER) = Form1.hwnd Then
        End
    End If
    If IsWindow(TargetHwnd) = False Then
        GoTo EndTaskFail
    End If
    If (GetWindowLong(TargetHwnd, GWL_STYLE) _
        And WS_DISABLED) Then
        GoTo EndTaskSucceed
    End If

    If IsWindow(TargetHwnd) Then
        If Not (GetWindowLong(TargetHwnd, GWL_STYLE) _
        And WS_DISABLED) Then
        rc = PostMessage(TargetHwnd, WS_CANCELMODE, 0, 0&)
        rc = PostMessage(TargetHwnd, WM_CLOSE, 0, 0&)
         DoEvents
        End If
    End If
    GoTo EndTaskSucceed

EndTaskFail:
    ReturnVal = False
    GoTo EndTaskEndSub
EndTaskSucceed:
    ReturnVal = True
EndTaskEndSub:
    EndTask = ReturnVal
End Function
```

The AppShell Project API Functions

The AppShell project calls the API functions listed in Table 1.8 to give Visual Basic a boost in manipulating applications.

NOTE   You'll find a complete description of these API functions in Appendix A, which is on the CD that comes with this book.

TABLE 1.8: The AppShell API Functions

API Function	Description
CloseHandle	Closes an open object handle.
CreateProcess	Creates a new process and its primary thread. The new process executes the specified executable file.
GetExitCodeProcess	Retrieves the termination status of the specified process.
GetParent	Retrieves the handle of the specified child window's parent window.
GetWindow	Retrieves the handle of a window that has the specified relationship (Zorder order or owner) to the specified window.
GetWindowLong	Retrieves information about the specified window. The function also retrieves the 32-bit (long) value at the specified offset into the extra window memory of a window.
GetWindowText	Copies the text of the specified window's title bar (if it has one) into a buffer. If the specified window is a control, the text of the control is copied.
GetWindowTextLength	Retrieves the length, in characters, of the specified window's title bar text (if the window has a title bar). If the specified window is a control, the function retrieves the length of the text within the control.
IsWindow	Determines whether the specified window handle identifies an existing window.
OpenProcess	Returns a handle of an existing process object.
PostMessage	Posts a message in the message queue associated with the thread that created the specified window and then returns without waiting for the thread to process the message. Messages in a message queue are retrieved by calls to the GetMessage or PeekMessage function.
WaitForSingleObject	Returns when the specified object is in the signaled state or when the time-out interval elapses.

The AppShell Code in Action

The AppShell project uses the API functions in Table 1.8 to help you develop Visual Basic applications that can do the following:

- Launch a new application
- Launch a new application and wait until it is terminated
- Terminate a running application

Code 1.12 highlights the interaction of the VB application and the API functions.

Code 1.12:   Declarations, Types, and Constants in the AppShell Project

```
Public Const GW_HWNDFIRST = 0
Public Const GW_HWNDLAST = 1
Public Const GW_HWNDNEXT = 2
Public Const GW_HWNDPREV = 3

Public Const GW_CHILD = 5
Public Const GW_MAX = 5

Global Const NORMAL_PRIORITY_CLASS = &H20&
Global Const INFINITE = -1&

Public Const STILL_ACTIVE = &H103
Public Const PROCESS_QUERY_INFORMATION = &H400

Public Const GW_OWNER = 4
Public Const GWL_STYLE = -16
Public Const WS_DISABLED = &H8000000
Public Const WS_CANCELMODE = &H1F
Public Const WM_CLOSE = &H10

Public glCurrentHwnd
```

```
Type STARTUPINFO
    cb As Long
    lpReserved As String
    lpDesktop As String
    lpTitle As String
    dwX As Long
    dwY As Long
    dwXSize As Long
    dwYSize As Long
    dwXCountChars As Long
    dwYCountChars As Long
    dwFillAttribute As Long
    dwFlags As Long
    wShowWindow As Integer
    cbReserved2 As Integer
    lpReserved2 As Long
    hStdInput As Long
    hStdOutput As Long
    hStdError As Long
End Type

Type PROCESS_INFORMATION
    hProcess As Long
    hThread As Long
    dwProcessID As Long
    dwThreadID As Long
End Type

Declare Function OpenProcess Lib "kernel32" _
    (ByVal dwDesiredAccess As Long, ByVal bInheritHandle _
    As Long, ByVal dwProcessID As Long) As Long
Declare Function GetExitCodeProcess Lib "kernel32" _
    (ByVal hProcess As Long, lpExitCode As Long) As Long
Declare Sub Sleep Lib "kernel32" (ByVal dwMilliseconds As Long)
Declare Function CloseHandle Lib "kernel32" (hObject As Long) _
    As Boolean
Declare Function WaitForSingleObject Lib "kernel32" (ByVal _
    hHandle As Long, ByVal dwMilliseconds As Long) As Long
Declare Function CreateProcessA Lib "kernel32" _
    (ByVal lpApplicationName As Long, ByVal lpCommandLine As _
    String, ByVal lpProcessAttributes As Long, ByVal _
    lpThreadAttributes As Long, ByVal bInheritHandles As _
    Long, ByVal dwCreationFlags As Long, ByVal _
```

```
        lpEnvironment As Long, ByVal _
        lpCurrentDirectory As Long, lpStartupInfo As STARTUPINFO, _
        lpProcessInformation As PROCESS_INFORMATION) As Long
    Declare Function IsWindow Lib "user32" (ByVal hwnd As Long) _
        As Long
    Declare Function GetWindow Lib "user32" (ByVal hwnd As Long _
        , ByVal wCmd As Long) As Long
    Declare Function PostMessage Lib "user32" Alias _
        "PostMessageA" (ByVal hwnd As Long, ByVal wMsg _
        As Long, ByVal wParam _
        As Long, ByVal lParam As Long) As Long
    Declare Function GetWindowLong Lib "user32" Alias _
        "GetWindowLongA" (ByVal hwnd As Long, _
        ByVal nIndex As Long) As Long

    Declare Function FindWindow Lib "user32" Alias "FindWindowA" _
        (ByVal lpClassName As String, ByVal lpWindowName _
        As String) As Long

    Declare Function GetParent Lib "user32" (ByVal hwnd _
    As Long) As Long
    Declare Function GetWindowTextLength Lib "user32" Alias _
        "GetWindowTextLengthA" (ByVal hwnd As Long) As Long
    Declare Function GetWindowText Lib "user32" Alias _
        "GetWindowTextA" (ByVal hwnd As Long, ByVal lpString _
        As String, ByVal cch As Long) As Long
```

Finding All the Windows and Their Handles

The LoadTaskList subroutine loops through all the windows in memory and uses GetParent, GetWindowTextLength, and GetWindowText to write the Task Name and handle to the list box. This includes all Windows-level processes and applications. Table 1.9 lists the values for the GetWindow function.

Code 1.13:   The LoadTaskList Subroutine

```
Sub LoadTaskList()
    Dim CurrWnd As Long
    Dim Length As Long
    Dim TaskName As String
    Dim Parent As Long

    List1.Clear
    CurrWnd = GetWindow(Form1.hwnd, GW_HWNDFIRST)
```

```
        While CurrWnd <> 0
            Parent = GetParent(CurrWnd)
            Length = GetWindowTextLength(CurrWnd)
            TaskName = Space$(Length + 1)
            Length = GetWindowText(CurrWnd, TaskName, Length + 1)
            TaskName = Left$(TaskName, Len(TaskName) - 1)
            If Length > 0 Then
                If TaskName <> Me.Caption Then
                    List1.AddItem TaskName & Chr(9) & Chr(9) & _
        CurrWnd
                End If
            End If
            CurrWnd = GetWindow(CurrWnd, GW_HWNDNEXT)
            DoEvents
        Wend
    End Sub
```

TABLE 1.9: The Values for the GetWindow Function

Value	Description
GW_CHILD	The retrieved handle identifies the child window at the top of the Zorder.
GW_HWNDFIRST	The retrieved handle identifies the window of the same type that is highest in the Zorder.
GW_HWNDLAST	The retrieved handle identifies the window of the same type that is lowest in the Zorder.
GW_HWNDNEXT	The retrieved handle identifies the window below the specified window in the Zorder.
GW_HWNDPREV	The retrieved handle identifies the window above the specified window in the Zorder.
GW_OWNER	The retrieved handle identifies the specified window's owner window, if any.

Opening an Application and Continuing

The ShellAndContinue subroutine uses the OpenProcess API and the Visual Basic Shell functions to launch the selected application. After it is open, the program monitors the state with GetExitCodeProcess. As soon as the value of GetExitCodeProcess is not equal to STILL_ACTIVE, you are notified through a message box. Table 1.10 lists the access values for the OpenProcess function.

Code 1.14:   The ShellAndContinue Subroutine

```
Sub ShellAndContinue(ByVal AppToRun As String)
    Dim hProcess As Long
    Dim RetVal As Long
    Dim Msg, Style, Title, Response

    'The next line launches AppToRun,
    'captures process ID
    hProcess = OpenProcess(PROCESS_QUERY_INFORMATION, 1, _
    Shell(AppToRun, vbNormalFocus))
    Do
        'Get the status of the process
        GetExitCodeProcess hProcess, RetVal

        DoEvents
    'Loop while the process is active
    Loop While RetVal = STILL_ACTIVE

    'Define message
    Msg = AppToRun & " Terminated by user"
    'Define buttons
    Style = vbOKOnly + vbInformation
    'Define title
    Title = "Termination Notice"
    'Display message
    Response = MsgBox(Msg, Style, Title)

End Sub
```

TABLE 1.10: The OpenProcess Access Values

Access	Description
PROCESS_ALL_ACCESS	Specifies all possible access flags for the process object.
PROCESS_CREATE_PROCESS	Used internally.
PROCESS_CREATE_THREAD	Enables using the process handle in the CreateRemoteThread function to create a thread in the process.
PROCESS_DUP_HANDLE	Enables using the process handle as either the source or target process in the DuplicateHandle function to duplicate a handle.

TABLE 1.10 (CONTINUED): The OpenProcess Access Values

Access	Description
PROCESS_QUERY_INFORMATION	Enables using the process handle in the GetExitCode-Process and GetPriorityClass functions to read information from the process object.
PROCESS_SET_INFORMATION	Enables using the process handle in the SetPriorityClass function to set the priority class of the process.
PROCESS_TERMINATE	Enables using the process handle in the TerminateProcess function to terminate the process.
PROCESS_VM_OPERATION	Enables using the process handle in the VirtualProtectEx and WriteProcessMemory functions to modify the virtual memory of the process.
PROCESS_VM_READ	Enables using the process handle in the ReadProcess-Memory function to read from the virtual memory of the process.
PROCESS_VM_WRITE	Enables using the process handle in the WriteProcess-Memory function to write to the virtual memory of the process.
SYNCHRONIZE	Windows NT only: Enables using the process handle in any of the wait functions to wait for the process to terminate.

Opening an Application and Waiting Until the User Terminates It

The ShellAndWait subroutine uses the API function CreateProcess to launch the application passed in the AppToRun parameter. This process also uses the function WaitForSingleObject to "freeze" the VB program until the new process is terminated; it then uses the CloseHandle function to close the handle to the process and free the VB project.

Code 1.15:   The ShellAndWait Subroutine

```
Public Sub ShellAndWait(AppToRun)
    Dim NameOfProc As PROCESS_INFORMATION
    Dim NameStart As STARTUPINFO
    Dim rc As Long
```

```
        NameStart.cb = Len(NameStart)
        rc = CreateProcessA(0&, AppToRun, 0&, 0&, 1&, _
            NORMAL_PRIORITY_CLASS, _
            0&, 0&, NameStart, NameOfProc)
        rc = WaitForSingleObject(NameOfProc.hProcess, INFINITE)
        rc = CloseHandle(NameOfProc.hProcess)
End Sub
```

Terminating an Application

The EndTask subroutine first checks with the IsWindow function to be sure you do not close the AppShell program. Next, the GetWindowLong function finds the state of the window you want to close. If it is disabled, you don't close it. If the selected window is not the current window and it is not disabled, use the PostMessage API to cancel and close the handle to the window.

Code 1.16:   The EndTask Subroutine

```
Function EndTask(TargetHwnd As Long) As Long
    Dim rc As Integer
    Dim ReturnVal As Integer
    If TargetHwnd = Form1.hwnd Or GetWindow(TargetHwnd, _
        GW_OWNER) = Form1.hwnd Then
        End
    End If
    If IsWindow(TargetHwnd) = False Then
        GoTo EndTaskFail
    End If
    If (GetWindowLong(TargetHwnd, GWL_STYLE) And _
        WS_DISABLED) Then
        GoTo EndTaskSucceed
    End If

    If IsWindow(TargetHwnd) Then
        If Not (GetWindowLong(TargetHwnd, GWL_STYLE) And
        WS_DISABLED) Then
        rc = PostMessage(TargetHwnd, WS_CANCELMODE, 0, 0&)
        rc = PostMessage(TargetHwnd, WM_CLOSE, 0, 0&)
         DoEvents
        End If
    End If
    GoTo EndTaskSucceed
```

```
EndTaskFail:
    ReturnVal = False
    GoTo EndTaskEndSub
EndTaskSucceed:
    ReturnVal = True
EndTaskEndSub:
    EndTask = ReturnVal
End Function
```

As you can see, APIs are handy for helping VB open applications, create processes, find all the currently running processes, and even terminate processes. Now with everything in place, let's take the AppShell program through its paces.

Give AppShell a Try

Press F5 to start the AppShell application (shown in Figure 1.8, earlier in this chapter), and then follow these steps:

1. Click the Shell and Continue button to open a standard Open dialog box in which you can select an application.

2. Select an EXE file to run. You will notice that you still have control of the AppShell program.

3. Now, close the new application. A message box notifies you that the application has terminated.

4. Click the Process and Wait button, and choose an application. Notice that this time you do not retain control of the AppShell program.

5. Close the new application, and control is returned to the AppShell program.

6. Clicking the Terminate App button terminates the application selected in the list box. Be carefull with this one; it terminates any application that you select. Test it on an application such as Notepad.

7. Click the Refresh List Box button to refresh the list box with the name and handle of all open processes (see Figure 1.9).

Being able to control applications from within your Visual Basic program is really a plus. It's important to be able to start, monitor, and terminate applications running concurrently with your applications. Just as important to the VB developer is having a way to spy on an application's menu structure and having the power to activate a menu option automatically. The next section examines the API function and procedures necessary to pull this off.

FIGURE 1.9:

The AppShell
application at work

Analyzing an Application's Menu Structure

Most applications we write and encounter have some sort of menu structure. A menu can be a simple one-level structure that includes File and Exit options, or it can be complex, as is the menu structure for Visual Basic 5. With the aid of API functions, you can analyze an application's menu structure and trigger a menu option in another application.

You can use the FindWindow function to get the handle to an application if you already know its name. Once you have the handle, the function GetMenuItemCount returns the number of top-level menu entries. Top-level items are the menu options visible at the top of an application. In Visual Basic, for example, the top-level menus include File, Edit, View, Project, and Format. After you have the top-level menu items, use the function GetMenuItemInfo to retrieve information about the menu, and then use GetSubMenu to obtain information about the pop-up menus.

After you analyze all the top-level and submenus, it is easy to call the SendMessage function and trigger one of the menu options.

The AnalyzeMenu Project

The AnalyzeMenu project, shown in Figure 1.10, reads the menu structure of Notepad, Calculator, WordPad, and Paint. You can easily adjust it to analyze the menu structure of any application by using the techniques we discuss in this chapter.

As the program reads through the menu structure, it creates a new List Box control for each top-level menu item. Using the List Box's AddItem method, it adds the menu items to the list box. Each menu item and its sub items end up in their own list box. An OptionButton is provided for each of the four sample applications. Two Command Buttons and two Text Box controls are included:

The Analyze button When you click this button, it loops through the application's menu structure and creates and loads a List Box control with the options for each top-level menu. Each top-level menu and its sub and pop-up menus are placed in a separate list box with the caption of the menu option. The handle to the menu is also provided for all top- and sub-level menu options.

The Send button Clicking this button triggers the selected menu option with the SendMessage API function.

The Menu Handle text box Here, you can enter the handle of the menu you want to activate.

The Number text box Here you enter the number of the menu item to be triggered. Menu items start with zero and advance until you encounter another menu option with a handle.

> **NOTE** You'll find the AnalyzeMenu project in the Chapter1\AnalyzeMenu folder on the CD that comes with this book.

FIGURE 1.10:

The AnalyzeMenu project analyzing Notepad

The AnalyzeMenus Project API Functions

The AnalyzeMenus project calls the API functions listed in Table 1.11 to give Visual Basic the power to analyze and access other applications' menus.

NOTE   You'll find a complete description of these API functions in Appendix A, which is on the CD that comes with this book.

TABLE 1.11: The API Functions in the AnalyzeMenus Project

API Function	Description
FindWindow	Retrieves the handle to the top-level window whose class name and window name match the specified strings. This function does not search child windows.
GetMenu	Retrieves the handle of the menu assigned to the given window.
GetMenuItemCount	Determines the number of items in the specified menu.
GetMenuItemID	Retrieves the menu item identifier of a menu item located at the specified position in a menu.
GetMenuState	Retrieves the menu flags associated with the specified menu item. If the menu item opens a submenu, this function also returns the number of items in the submenu.
GetMenuString	Copies the text string of the specified menu item into the specified buffer.
GetSubMenu	Retrieves the handle of the drop-down menu or submenu activated by the specified menu item.
SendMessage	Sends the specified message to a window or windows. The function calls the window procedure for the specified window and does not return until the window procedure has processed the message.

The AnalyzeMenus Code in Action

Using the API functions in Table 1.11, the code in the AnalyzeMenus project demonstrates how Visual Basic, with the help of API calls, can spy on the menu structure of other applications and activate menu options.

Code 1.17: Declarations, Types, and Constants in the AnalyzeMenus Project

```
'Public Constants
Global hwndHold As Long
Global glSpaces As String
Global Const WM_COMMAND = &H111
Global glApplicationName As String    'hold the window to analyze
Public Const MF_BYPOSITION = &H400&
Public Const MF_BYCOMMAND = &H0&


'API Declarations
Declare Function FindWindow Lib "user32" Alias _
    "FindWindowA" (ByVal lpClassName As String, ByVal _
    lpWindowName As String) As Long
Declare Function GetMenu Lib "user32" (ByVal hwnd _
    As Long) As Long
Declare Function GetSubMenu Lib "user32" (ByVal hMenu _
    As Long, ByVal nPos As Long) As Long
Declare Function GetMenuItemCount Lib "user32" (ByVal _
    hMenu As Long) As Long
Declare Function GetMenuItemID Lib "user32" (ByVal _
    hMenu As Long, ByVal nPos As Long) As Long
Declare Function GetMenuString Lib "user32" Alias _
    "GetMenuStringA" (ByVal hMenu As Long, ByVal wIDItem _
    As Long, ByVal lpString As String, ByVal nMaxCount _
    As Long, ByVal wFlag As Long) As Long
Declare Function GetMenuState Lib "user32" (ByVal hMenu _
    As Long, ByVal wID As Long, ByVal wFlags As Long) As Long
Declare Function SendMessage Lib "user32" Alias _
    "SendMessageA" (ByVal hwnd As Long, ByVal wMsg As _
    Long, ByVal wParam As Long, lParam As Any) As Long
```

Analyzing the Top-Level Menu Structure

The AnalyzeTopLevelMenus subroutine loops through the menu structure of the main window and writes the menu text and handle to an array. Figure 1.11 shows the top-level menus for Visual Basic, which include File, Edit, View, and Project. You use the GetMenuItemCount function to get the number of top-level menus for this window. Then, you call the GetSubMenu function to get the handle for the menus. The AnalyzeMenu subroutine uses this handle to determine when to start a new menu. Each time a top-level menu is found, the size of the main Form is increased, and a List Box control is added. This list box holds the menu structure that is found later in the AnalyzeMenu subroutine.

FIGURE 1.11:

Top-level Visual Basic
menus

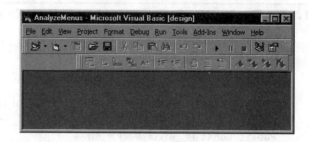

Code 1.18:   The AnalyzeTopLevelMenus Subroutine

```
Public Sub AnalyzeTopLevelMenus(ByVal menuhnd)

    Dim slMenuCounter As Integer
    Dim slNumberOfMenus As Integer

    Dim slMenu As Integer
    Dim slMenuID As Long
    Dim slPopupMenu As Integer

    Dim slMenuInfo As Integer
    Dim slMenuFlags As Integer

    Dim menustring(128) As Byte
    Dim menustring2 As String * 128
    Dim context&

    'This routine can analyze up to 32 popup sub-menus
    Dim trackpopups&(32)

    Dim slXcnt As Integer

    'Find out how many entries are in the menu.
    slNumberOfMenus = GetMenuItemCount(menuhnd)

    'set the number of top level menus
    ReDim aryTopLevel(Str$(slNumberOfMenus))

    'Find out how many entries are in the menu.
    slNumberOfMenus = GetMenuItemCount(menuhnd)
```

```
For slMenu = 0 To slNumberOfMenus - 1
    'Get the ID for this menu
    'It's a command ID, -1 for a popup, 0 for a separator
    slMenuID = GetMenuItemID(menuhnd, slMenu)
    Select Case slMenuID
        Case 0   'It's a separator

        Case -1 'It's a popup menu
            slMenuInfo = GetMenuString(menuhnd, slMenu, _
                menustring2, 127, MF_BYPOSITION)
            slMenuFlags = GetMenuState(menuhnd, slMenu, _
                MF_BYPOSITION)
            Debug.Print glSpaces & Left$ _
            (menustring2, slMenuInfo) _
            & "  Handle  = " & GetSubMenu(menuhnd, slMenu)
            'store the handle to this menu in the array
            aryTopLevel(slMenu) = _
            (GetSubMenu(menuhnd, slMenu))

            'add a list box for each menu and
            'increase the size of the form
            If slMenu > 0 Then
                Load Form1.lstMenu(slMenu)
                Form1.Width = Form1.Width + 3450
                Form1.lstMenu(slMenu).Left = Form1.lstMenu _
                    (slMenu - 1).Left + Form1.lstMenu _
                    (slMenu - 1).Width + 100
                Form1.lstMenu(slMenu).Visible = True
            End If
    End Select
Next slMenu

End Sub
```

Analyzing the Menu Structure

The AnalyzeMenus subroutine uses the GetMenuItemCount function to return the number of menu items. The GetMenuItemID function tells us if the menu is a separator or a pop-up menu. Figure 1.12 shows the top-level menu of Notepad with the File submenu exposed. New, Open, Save, and Save As are pop-up menus, and the gray line below Save As is a separator.

The AnalyzeMenus subroutine loops through the items in a menu and adds each item with the GetMenuString function; it then uses the GetSubMenu function to add the handle to a list box. Each top-level menu is added to a separate List Box control. The items are indented to mimic the look of the menu. This subroutine is a good example of API calls and Visual Basic loops. Figure 1.10, earlier in this chapter, shows the menus of Notepad analyzed.

FIGURE 1.12:

The top-level
Notepad menus

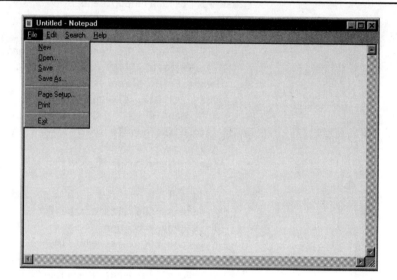

Code 1.19:   The AnalyzeMenus Subroutine

```
Public Sub AnalyzeMenus(ByVal menuhnd)

    Dim slMenuCounter As Integer
    Dim slNumberOfMenus As Integer

    Dim slMenu As Integer
    Dim slMenuID As Long
    Dim slPopupMenu

    Dim slMenuInfo As Integer
    Dim slMenuFlags As Integer

    Dim menustring(128) As Byte
    Dim menustring2 As String * 128
```

```
'This routine can analyze up to 32 popup sub-menus
Dim trackpopups&(32)

Dim slXcnt As Integer

slPopupMenu = 0

'Find out how many entries are in the menu.
slNumberOfMenus = GetMenuItemCount(menuhnd)

For slMenu = 0 To slNumberOfMenus - 1
    'Get the ID for this menu
    'It's a command ID, -1 for a popup, 0 for a separator
    slMenuID = GetMenuItemID(menuhnd, slMenu)
    Select Case slMenuID
        Case 0  'It's a separator
            Form1.lstMenu(lstNum).AddItem glSpaces & _
                "Grey separator"
        Case -1 'It's a popup menu
            'Save it in the list of popups
            trackpopups&(slPopupMenu) = slMenu
            slPopupMenu = slPopupMenu + 1

            slMenuInfo = GetMenuString(menuhnd, slMenu, _
                menustring2, 127, MF_BYPOSITION)

            'Set the listbox according to the top level menu
            For slMenuCounter = 0 To UBound(aryTopLevel)
                If aryTopLevel(slMenuCounter) = (GetSubMenu _
                    (menuhnd, slMenu)) Then
                    lstNum = slMenuCounter
                    'reset the indention
                    glSpaces = ""
                End If
            Next

            slMenuFlags = GetMenuState(menuhnd, slMenu, _
                MF_BYPOSITION)
            Form1.lstMenu(lstNum).AddItem glSpaces _
            & Left$(menustring2, slMenuInfo) _
            & "  Handle  = " & GetSubMenu(menuhnd, slMenu)

            'At least one popup was found
```

```
                     If slPopupMenu > 0 Then
                         For slXcnt = 0 To slPopupMenu - 1
                             slMenuID = trackpopups&(slXcnt)
                             glSpaces = glSpaces & "    "
                             AnalyzeMenus GetSubMenu(menuhnd, _
                             slMenuID)
                         Next slXcnt
                         slPopupMenu = 0
                         glSpaces = "    "
                     End If

                 Case Else 'A regular entry
                     slMenuInfo = GetMenuString(menuhnd, slMenuID, _
                         menustring2, 127, MF_BYCOMMAND)
                     Form1.lstMenu(lstNum).AddItem glSpaces & _
                         Left$(menustring2, slMenuInfo)
                     slMenuFlags = GetMenuState(menuhnd, slMenuID, _
                         MF_BYCOMMAND)
             End Select
         Next slMenu
         glSpaces = ""

     End Sub
```

Activating a Menu Option

The subroutine cmdSend uses the handle and menu number from the main Form and calls the API function SendMessage to activate a menu option.

Code 1.20:   The cmdSend Subroutine

```
Private Sub cmdSend_Click()
    Dim hwnd As Long
    Dim hMainMenu As Integer
    Dim hMenu As Integer
    Dim slMenuID As Long
    Dim rc
    Dim X As Long

    slMenuID = GetMenuItemID(txtHandle, txtNumber)

    rc = SendMessage(hwndHold, WM_COMMAND, slMenuID, 0&)

End Sub
```

The ability to activate a menu option from other applications adds a new dimension to the power and flexibility of Visual Basic. As you can see, you can program VB to do the following:

- Open a help file from another application
- Print a report
- Open a file
- Change properties such as font, color, and format
- Access any menu option

Testing the AnalyzeMenu Program

The AnalyzeMenu program is designed to analyze the menu structure of Notepad, Calculator, WordPad, or Paint. You could easily adapt it to analyze the menu structure of any application. For this test, we will analyze the menus of Notepad. Follow these easy steps:

1. Start and minimize the Notepad application.
2. Press F5 to start the AnalyzeMenu program.
3. Select the Notepad button.
4. Click the Analyze button. The top part of the Form will be filled with five list boxes, similar to what you see in Figure 1.10, earlier in this chapter. Each list box contains a top-level menu option and all the submenus and pop-up menus under it.
5. In the MenuHandle text box, enter the handle number for the &Help menu.
6. Enter the number 0 into the Number text box. This tells the program that you want to trigger the first option, &Help Topics (remember that menu numbers start with zero).
7. Click the Send button to display the Notepad help file.

Menus are an integral part of Windows applications. By employing the API functions and procedures we looked at in this section, you can program Visual Basic to unlock the power of menus in other applications.

The Bitmaps and Graphics API Functions

In visual programming environments such as Visual Basic and Windows, bitmaps and graphics are important. Graphics and bitmaps are used in almost every part of a Visual Basic application—from the menu to the forms that make up the user interface. Visual Basic does not provide a lot of support for graphics; fortunately, API functions can fill the void. The Win32 API includes a vast array of API functions that can be employed in Visual Basic to do the following:

- Create bitmaps
- Copy bitmaps
- Flood a container with color
- Add bitmaps to menus

And the list goes on and on. One common thread is a bitmap.

Understanding Bitmaps

A bitmap is an object in Windows that holds an image. The two types of bitmaps are:

- Device-dependent (DDB)
- Device-independent (DIB)

Device-Dependent Bitmaps

All bitmaps in Windows are device-dependent unless otherwise noted. DDBs are described in a single structure, the BITMAP structure. The BITMAP structure defines the type, width, height, color, format, and bit values of a bitmap. Table 1.12 lists and describes the members of a BITMAP structure.

TABLE 1.12: The Members of a BITMAP Structure

Member	Description
bmType	Specifies the bitmap type. This member must be zero.
BmWidth	Specifies the width, in pixels, of the bitmap. The width must be greater than zero.

TABLE 1.12 (CONTINUED): The Members of a BITMAP Structure

Member	Description
BmHeight	Specifies the height, in pixels, of the bitmap. The height must be greater than zero.
BmWidthBytes	Specifies the number of bytes in each scan line.
BmPlanes	Specifies the count of color planes.
BmBitsPixel	Specifies the number of bits required to indicate the color of a pixel.
BmBits	Points to the location of the bit values for the bitmap.

Copying and displaying a DDB is much faster than copying and displaying a DIB. All Windows needs to do to move a DDB is to copy memory. You can use the function BitBlt to do this. The key to using DDBs is compatibility. The easiest way to determine if a bitmap is compatible with a device is to use the CreateCompatibleBitmap function. On the other hand, you can use device-independent bitmaps to copy or display bitmaps across devices.

Device-Independent Bitmaps

A device-independent bitmap is a color bitmap in a format that eliminates the problems that occur in transferring DDBs to devices that have a different bitmap format. DIBs provide bitmap information that any display or printer driver can translate. The main purpose of DIBs is to allow bitmaps to be moved from one device to another.

Transferring bitmaps from one device to another was not possible in Microsoft Windows prior to version 3. Now, with DIBs, every device can display a bitmap to the extent of its color resolution. An application can store and display a bitmap regardless of the output device.

A bitmap file consists of a BITMAPFILEHEADER structure and the DIB itself. Table 1.13 lists the members of this structure.

TABLE 1.13: The Members of the BITMAPFILEHEADER Structure

Field	Description
bfType	WORD that defines the type of file. It must be BM.
BfSize	A DWORD that specifies the size of the file in bytes.

TABLE 1.13 (CONTINUED): The Members of the BITMAPFILEHEADER Structure

Field	Description
bfReserved1, bfReserved2	WORDs that must be set to zero.
BfOffBits	A DWORD that specifies the offset from the beginning of the BITMAPFILEHEADER structure to the start of the actual bits.

The BITMAPINFOHEADER structure follows immediately after the BITMAPFILEHEADER structure. Table 1.14 lists and describes the members of the BITMAPINFOHEADER structure. The header is made up of two parts: the header and the color table. They are combined in the BITMAPINFO structure, which is what all DIB APIs expect.

TABLE 1.14: The Members of the BITMAPINFOHEADER Structure

Field	Description
BiSize	Should be set to the size of (BITMAPINFOHEADER). This field defines the size of the header (minus the color table).
biWidth, biHeight	Define the width and the height of the bitmap in pixels.
BiPlanes	Should always be 1.
BiBitCount	Defines the color resolution (in bits per pixel) of the DIB. Only four values are valid for this field: 1, 4, 8, and 24.
BiCompression	Specifies the type of compression. Can be one of three values: BI_RGB, BI_RLE4, or BI_RLE8.
BiSizeImage	Should contain the size of the bitmap proper in bytes.
biXPelsPerMeter, biYPelsPerMeter	Define application-specified values for the desirable dimensions of the bitmap.
BiClrUsed	Provides a way for getting smaller color tables. When this field is set to 0, the number of colors on the biBitCount field should be set to one of the following values: 1 indicates 2 colors, 4 indicates 16, 8 indicates 256, and 24 indicates no color table.
BiClrImportant	Specifies that the first x colors of the color table are important to the DIB.

The color table follows the header information. The number of entries in the color table matches the number of colors supported by the DIB except for a 24-bit color bitmap that does not have a color table. Table 1.15 shows the structure of a color table for a 16-color DIB.

TABLE 1.15: Color Structure

Field	Description
bmiHeader	BITMAPINFOHEADER information
BmiColors(15)	Colors

The ScreenCapture Project

The ScreenCapture project (shown in Figure 1.13) demonstrates how to use some of the most popular bitmap API functions.

You can use a bitmap to do the following:

- Capture an image
- Store an image in memory
- Display an image at a different location or on a different device

To store an image temporarily, you can call the CreateCompatibleDC function to create a device context that is compatible with the current window device context. After you create the compatible device context, you can create a bitmap with the appropriate dimensions by calling the CreateCompatibleBitmap function. You can then call SelectObject to select it into the newly created device context.

After the compatible device context is created and the bitmap is selected into it, you can use the BitBlt function to capture an image. The BitBlt function performs a bit block transfer. It copies data from a source bitmap into a destination bitmap of the same size. The BitBlt function receives handles that identify two device contexts and copies the bitmap data from a bitmap selected into the source device context into a bitmap selected into the target device context. The target device context is a compatible device context; so when BitBlt completes the transfer, the image is copied into memory. You use the OleCreatePictureIndirect function to redisplay the image.

The ScreenCapture project has six Command Buttons:

Capture Screen   Clicking this button captures the screen and places an image of it in a picture box.

Capture Form   Clicking this button captures the Form and places an image of it in a picture box.

Create Form Picture   Clicking this button, after you capture an image, sets the Picture property of form2 to the captured image. This is an example of how to copy a bitmap into memory and then use it on a Form.

Save to File   Clicking this button opens a standard File Save dialog box, in which you can set the file name and location and save the picture to a file.

Clear   Clicking this button clears the contents of the PictureBox control.

Print   Clicking this button prints the contents of the picture box on the default printer.

NOTE   You'll find the ScreenCapture project in the Chapter1\ScreenCapture folder on the CD that comes with this book.

The ScreenCapture API Functions

The ScreenCapture project calls on the API functions listed in Table 1.16 to help Visual Basic perform bitmap functions.

TABLE 1.16: The ScreenCapture API Functions

Function	Description
BitBlt	Performs a bit-block transfer of the color data corresponding to a rectangle of pixels from the specified source device context into a destination device context.
CreateCompatibleBitmap	Creates a bitmap compatible with the device that is associated with the specified device context.
CreateCompatibleDC	Creates a memory device context that is compatible with the specified device.
CreatePalette	Creates a logical color palette.
GetDesktopWindow	Returns the handle of the Windows Desktop window. The Desktop window covers the entire screen. The Desktop window is the area on top of which all icons and other windows are painted.
GetDeviceCaps	Retrieves device-specific information about a specified device.
GetForegroundWindow	Returns the handle of the foreground window (the current window). The system assigns a slightly higher priority to the thread that creates the foreground window than it does to other threads.
GetSystemPaletteEntries	Retrieves a range of palette entries from the system palette that is associated with the specified device context.
GetDC	Retrieves a handle of a display device context for the client area of the specified window. The display device context can be used in subsequent GDI functions to draw in the client area of the window.
GetWindowDC	Retrieves the device context for the entire window, including the title bar, menus, and scroll bars. A window device context permits painting anywhere in a window, because the origin of the device context is the upper-left corner of the window instead of the client area. The GetWindowDC function assigns default attributes to the window device context each time it retrieves the device context. Previous attributes are lost.

TABLE 1.16 (CONTINUED): The ScreenCapture API Functions

Function	Description
OleCreatePictureIndirect	Creates a new picture object initialized according to a PICTDESC structure.
RealizePalette	Maps palette entries from the current logical palette to the system palette.
ReleaseDC	Releases a device context, freeing it for use by other applications. It frees only common and window device contexts and has no effect on class or private device contexts.
SelectObject	Selects an object into the specified device context. The new object replaces the previous object of the same type.
SelectPalette	Selects the specified logical palette into a device context.

The ScreenCapture Code in Action

Let's put these functions to work with VB to see how a bitmap can be used to capture a screen and part of a Form and how it can be used as the Picture property of a Form.

Code 1.21: **Declarations, Types, and Constants in the ScreenCapture Project**

```
Global Const INVERSE = 6
Const SOLID = 0
Const DOT = 2

Global HoldX As Single
Global HoldY As Single
Global StartX As Single
Global StartY As Single
Global SavedDrawStyle
Global SavedMode


Option Base 0

Private Type PALETTEENTRY
peRed As Byte
peGreen As Byte
peBlue As Byte
```

```
peFlags As Byte
End Type

Private Type LOGPALETTE
palVersion As Integer
palNumEntries As Integer
palPalEntry(255) As PALETTEENTRY ' Enough for 256 colors
End Type

Private Type GUID
Data1 As Long
Data2 As Integer
Data3 As Integer
Data4(7) As Byte
End Type


Private Const RASTERCAPS As Long = 38
Private Const RC_PALETTE As Long = &H100
Private Const SIZEPALETTE As Long = 104

Private Type RECT
    Left As Long
    Top As Long
    Right As Long
    Bottom As Long
End Type

Private Type PicBmp
    Size As Long
    Type As Long
    hBmp As Long
    hPal As Long
    Reserved As Long
End Type

Private Declare Function BitBlt Lib "GDI32" ( _
    ByVal hDCDest As Long, ByVal XDest As Long, _
    ByVal YDest As Long, ByVal nWidth As Long, _
    ByVal nHeight As Long, ByVal hDCSrc As Long, _
    ByVal XSrc As Long, ByVal YSrc As Long, ByVal dwRop As Long) _
    As Long
Private Declare Function CreateCompatibleBitmap Lib _
    "GDI32" (ByVal hDC As Long, ByVal nWidth As Long, _
```

```
        ByVal nHeight As Long) As Long
Private Declare Function CreateCompatibleDC Lib "GDI32" ( _
    ByVal hDC As Long) As Long
Private Declare Function CreatePalette Lib "GDI32" ( _
    lpLogPalette As LOGPALETTE) As Long
Private Declare Function DeleteDC Lib "GDI32" ( _
    ByVal hDC As Long) As Long
Private Declare Function GetDesktopWindow Lib "USER32" () As Long
Private Declare Function GetDeviceCaps Lib "GDI32" ( _
    ByVal hDC As Long, ByVal iCapabilitiy As Long) As Long
Private Declare Function GetForegroundWindow Lib "USER32" () _
    As Long
Private Declare Function GetSystemPaletteEntries Lib _
    "GDI32" (ByVal hDC As Long, ByVal wStartIndex As Long, _
    ByVal wNumEntries As Long, lpPaletteEntries _
    As PALETTEENTRY) As Long
Private Declare Function GetWindowDC Lib "USER32" ( _
    ByVal hWnd As Long) As Long
Private Declare Function GetDC Lib "USER32" ( _
    ByVal hWnd As Long) As Long
Private Declare Function GetWindowRect Lib "USER32" ( _
    ByVal hWnd As Long, lpRect As RECT) As Long
Private Declare Function OleCreatePictureIndirect _
    Lib "olepro32.dll" (PicDesc As PicBmp, RefIID As GUID, _
    ByVal fPictureOwnsHandle As Long, IPic As IPicture) As Long
Private Declare Function RealizePalette Lib "GDI32" ( _
    ByVal hDC As Long) As Long
Private Declare Function ReleaseDC Lib "USER32" ( _
    ByVal hWnd As Long, ByVal hDC As Long) As Long
Private Declare Function SelectObject Lib "GDI32" ( _
    ByVal hDC As Long, ByVal hObject As Long) As Long
Private Declare Function SelectPalette Lib "GDI32" ( _
    ByVal hDC As Long, ByVal hPalette As Long, _
    ByVal bForceBackground As Long) As Long
```

Capturing the Screen

The CaptureScreen function uses the GetDesktopWindow API function to retrieve a handle to the Desktop. After the handle is retrieved, the VB function CaptureWindow is called to copy the bitmap into memory. The screen resolution is passed as well as the handle.

Code 1.22: The CaptureScreen Function

```
Public Function CaptureScreen() As Picture
    On Error GoTo ErrorRoutineErr

    Dim hWndScreen As Long

    'Get a handle to the desktop window
    hWndScreen = GetDesktopWindow()

    'Call CaptureWindow to capture the entire desktop,
    'give the handle and return the resulting Picture object
    Set CaptureScreen = CaptureWindow(hWndScreen, _
    0, 0, _
    Screen.Width \ Screen.TwipsPerPixelX, _
    Screen.Height \ Screen.TwipsPerPixelY)

ErrorRoutineResume:
    Exit Function
ErrorRoutineErr:
    MsgBox "Project1.Module1.CaptureScreen" & Err & Error
    Resume Next
End Function
```

Capturing the Form

The CaptureForm function is similar to the CaptureScreen function except that it uses the Visual Basic Handle property hWnd to retrieve the handle to Form1. After the handle is retrieved, the VB function CaptureWindow is called to copy the bitmap into memory. The screen resolution is passed as well as the handle.

Code 1.23: The CaptureForm Function

```
Public Function CaptureForm(frmSrc As Form) As Picture
    On Error GoTo ErrorRoutineErr

    'Call CaptureWindow to capture the entire form
    'given it's window
    'handle and then return the resulting Picture object
    Set CaptureForm = CaptureWindow(frmSrc.hWnd, 0, 0, _
    frmSrc.ScaleX(frmSrc.Width, vbTwips, vbPixels), _
    frmSrc.ScaleY(frmSrc.Height, vbTwips, vbPixels))
```

```
ErrorRoutineResume:
    Exit Function
ErrorRoutineErr:
    MsgBox "Project1.Module1.CaptureForm" & Err & Error
    Resume Next
End Function
```

Processing the CaptureWindow Actions

A lot of work is performed in this function. First, the API function GetWindowDC gets the device context for the screen or window. Next, CreateCompatibleDC creates a memory device context for the copy process, and then a bitmap is created with the CreateCompatibleBitmap function and placed into memory with the SelectObject function.

The next task is to get the screen properties. To accomplish this, we use the GetDeviceCaps function to find the raster capabilities and the palette size. If the screen has a palette, we need to copy it and select it into memory. We get the palette with the GetSystemPaletteEntries API function, create a copy of it with CreatePalette, and, finally, select it into memory with SelectPalette.

Now that we are finished with the preliminaries, we can use BitBlt to copy the image into the memory device context. If the screen has a palette, get it back with the SelectPalette function. With the bitmap and palette copied into memory, we can clean up a bit. We use the functions DeleteDC and ReleaseDC to release the device context resources back to the system. The last task is to call the function CreateBitmapPicture and create the picture object with the API function OleCreatePictureIndirect.

Code 1.24:   The CaptureWindow Function

```
Public Function CaptureWindow(ByVal hWndSrc As Long, _
    ByVal LeftSrc As Long, _
    ByVal TopSrc As Long, ByVal WidthSrc As Long, _
    ByVal HeightSrc As Long) As Picture

    On Error GoTo ErrorRoutineErr

    Dim hDCMemory As Long
    Dim hBmp As Long
    Dim hBmpPrev As Long
    Dim rc As Long
    Dim hDCSrc As Long
```

```vb
Dim hPal As Long
Dim hPalPrev As Long
Dim RasterCapsScrn As Long
Dim HasPaletteScrn As Long
Dim PaletteSizeScrn As Long

Dim LogPal As LOGPALETTE

'Get device context for the window
hDCSrc = GetWindowDC(hWndSrc)

'Create a memory device context for the copy process
hDCMemory = CreateCompatibleDC(hDCSrc)
'Create a bitmap and place it in the memory DC
hBmp = CreateCompatibleBitmap(hDCSrc, WidthSrc, HeightSrc)
hBmpPrev = SelectObject(hDCMemory, hBmp)

'Get screen properties
'Raster capabilities
RasterCapsScrn = GetDeviceCaps(hDCSrc, RASTERCAPS)
'Palette support
HasPaletteScrn = RasterCapsScrn And RC_PALETTE
'Size of palette
PaletteSizeScrn = GetDeviceCaps(hDCSrc, SIZEPALETTE)

'If the screen has a palette, make a copy
If HasPaletteScrn And (PaletteSizeScrn = 256) Then
    'Create a copy of the system palette
    LogPal.palVersion = &H300
    LogPal.palNumEntries = 256
    rc = GetSystemPaletteEntries(hDCSrc, 0, 256, _
    LogPal.palPalEntry(0))
    hPal = CreatePalette(LogPal)
    'Select the new palette into the memory
    'DC and realize it
    hPalPrev = SelectPalette(hDCMemory, hPal, 0)
    rc = RealizePalette(hDCMemory)
End If

'Copy the image into the memory DC
rc = BitBlt(hDCMemory, 0, 0, WidthSrc, HeightSrc, _
hDCSrc, LeftSrc, TopSrc, vbSrcCopy)
```

```
'Remove the new copy of the  on-screen image
hBmp = SelectObject(hDCMemory, hBmpPrev)

'If the screen has a palette get back the palette that was
'selected in previously
If HasPaletteScrn And (PaletteSizeScrn = 256) Then
hPal = SelectPalette(hDCMemory, hPalPrev, 0)
End If

'Release the device context resources back to the system
rc = DeleteDC(hDCMemory)
rc = ReleaseDC(hWndSrc, hDCSrc)

'Call CreateBitmapPicture to create a picture
'object from the bitmap and palette handles.
'Then return the resulting picture object.
Set CaptureWindow = CreateBitmapPicture(hBmp, hPal)

ErrorRoutineResume:
    Exit Function
ErrorRoutineErr:
    MsgBox "Project1.Module1.CaptureWindow" & Err & Error
    Resume Next
End Function
```

Constructing a New Picture Object

The CreateBitmapPicture function takes the handles of the bitmap and palettes that were placed into memory in the CaptureWindow function, adds the GUID structure and Pic parts, and, with the OleCreatePictureIndirect API, creates a bitmap picture that can be placed in our PictureBox control on Form1.

Code 1.25:   The CreateBitmapPicture Function

```
Public Function CreateBitmapPicture(ByVal hBmp As Long, _
    ByVal hPal As Long) As Picture

    On Error GoTo ErrorRoutineErr

    Dim r As Long
        Dim Pic As PicBmp
    'IPicture requires a reference to "Standard OLE Types"
```

```
        Dim IPic As IPicture
        Dim IID_IDispatch As GUID

        'Fill in with IDispatch Interface ID
        With IID_IDispatch
            .Data1 = &H20400
            .Data4(0) = &HC0
            .Data4(7) = &H46
        End With

        'Fill Pic with necessary parts
        With Pic
            'Length of structure
            .Size = Len(Pic)
            'Type of Picture (bitmap)
            .Type = vbPicTypeBitmap
            'Handle to bitmap
            .hBmp = hBmp
            'Handle to palette (may be null)
            .hPal = hPal
        End With

        'Create Picture object
        r = OleCreatePictureIndirect(Pic, IID_IDispatch, 1, IPic)

        'Return the new Picture object
        Set CreateBitmapPicture = IPic

ErrorRoutineResume:
    Exit Function
ErrorRoutineErr:
    MsgBox "Project1.Module1.CreateBitmapPicture" & Err & Error
    Resume Next
End Function
```

As you can see, creating a bitmap in memory involves several steps. Without the help of the Win32API, Visual Basic would never be able to pull it off. Now, it's time to take the ScreenCapture project for a test run.

Testing the ScreenCapture Program

You can use the ScreenCapture project to capture a screen or a form with the aid of API calls and then use the bitmap as the Picture property of a Form. You can create a permanent copy of the bitmap by copying it to a file, and you can print the bitmap to the default printer. To test ScreenCapture, follow these steps:

1. Start the ScreenCapture project from within Visual Basic.

2. Click the Capture Screen button to capture the Desktop to the PictureBox control. Figure 1.14 shows the ScreenCapture project with the Desktop captured.

3. Click the Clear button to clear the picture box.

4. Click the Capture Form button to capture the ScreenCapture Form to the picture box.

5. If you want to save the bitmap to a file, click the Save to File button to open a standard Save As dialog box, in which you can select a path and file name and save the file.

6. Click the Print button to print the contents of the picture box on the default printer.

You can create bitmaps from almost any source, and this project demonstrates only the tip of the iceberg. By combining the techniques in the other sections of this chapter, you could really make APIs and bitmaps work for you to create some unique projects.

FIGURE 1.14:

The Desktop
captured

The System API Functions

Visual Basic can tell you a lot about a computer's environment, but as developers we really need even more information. For example, when you get a support call, it's important to know the makeup of the user's system. Many times the problem is simply that the machine running the program does not meet the minimum hardware requirements.

If a computer is running an application that uses a few API functions, developers can have access to information about the following:

- Memory statistics
- Total and free disk space
- Number of colors
- Operating system
- Processor type

You can use the GlobalMemoryStatus API function to investigate the system and report the amount of memory. The GetFreediskSpace API returns, among others, the total disk space and the total free disk space. If your application needs to know the number of colors supported, call the GetDeviceCaps function.

You can use the GetVersionEx function to find out the major version, the minor version, such as NT version 4, the build number, and the service pack level for Windows NT. This last bit of information is especially important for NT users. Most applications written today require at least Service Pack 2 for NT.

Another must in today's programming environment is the type of processor currently running. You can find this information with the GetSystemInfo API function. And if the user is signed on to a network, you can retrieve the user's name with the GetUserName function.

The Statistics Project

We will use the Statistics project (shown in Figure 1.15) to demonstrate some of the API functions you can use to get information about a computer's environment. When the application starts, it makes several API calls to catalog the current environment.

FIGURE 1.15:

The Statistics project

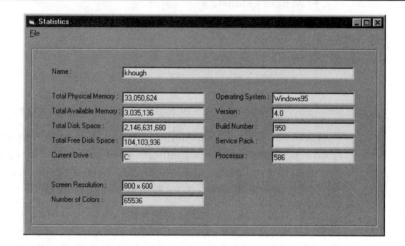

The Statistics Project API Functions

Table 1.17 lists and describes the API functions in the Statistics project.

TABLE 1.17: The Statistics API Functions

Function	Description
GetDeviceCaps	Retrieves device-specific information about a specified device.
GetDiskFreeSpace	Retrieves information about the specified disk, including the amount of free space on the disk.
GlobalMemoryStatus	Retrieves information about current available memory. The function returns information about both physical and virtual memory. This function supersedes the GetFreeSpace function.

TABLE 1.17 (CONTINUED): The Statistics API Functions

Function	Description
GetUserName	Retrieves the user name of the current thread. This is the name of the user currently logged on to the system.
GetVersionEx	Obtains extended information about the version of the operating system that is currently running.
GetSystemInfo	Returns information about the current system.

The Statistics Project Code in Action

The system statistic API functions listed in Table 1.17 can really give you a head start when it comes to troubleshooting application problems. Let's take a look at the functions in some code.

Code 1.26: Declarations, Types, and Constants used in the Statistics Project

```
Global SectorsPerCluster As Long
Global BytesPerSector As Long
Global NumberOfFreeClustors As Long
Global TotalNumberOfClustors As Long
Global BytesFree As Long
Global BytesTotal As Long
Global PercentFree As Long

Public Const VER_Processor_WIN32_NT& = 2
Public Const VER_Processor_WIN32_WINDOWS& = 1

Public Const PROCESSOR_INTEL_386 = 386
Public Const PROCESSOR_INTEL_486 = 486
Public Const PROCESSOR_INTEL_PENTIUM = 586
Public Const PROCESSOR_MIPS_R4000 = 4000
Public Const PROCESSOR_ALPHA_21064 = 21064

Type MEMORYSTATUS
    dwLength As Long
    dwMemoryLoad As Long
    dwTotalPhys As Long
    dwAvailPhys As Long
    dwTotalPageFile As Long
```

```
            dwAvailPageFile As Long
            dwTotalVirtual As Long
            dwAvailVirtual As Long
    End Type

    Public Type SYSTEM_INFO
            dwOemID As Long
            dwPageSize As Long
            lpMinimumApplicationAddress As Long
            lpMaximumApplicationAddress As Long
            dwActiveProcessorMask As Long
            dwNumberOfProcessors As Long
            dwProcessorType As Long
            dwAllocationGranularity As Long
            wProcessorLevel As Integer
            wProcessorRevision As Integer
    End Type

    Public Type OSVersionInfo
            dwOSVersionInfoSize As Long
            dwMajorVersion As Long
            dwMinorVersion As Long
            dwBuildNumber As Long
            dwProcessorId As Long
            szCSDVersion As String * 128
    End Type

    ' Holder for version information. Set on form load
    Global myVer As OSVersionInfo

    Declare Function GetDeviceCaps Lib "gdi32" (ByVal _
        hdc As Long, ByVal nIndex As Long) As Long
    Declare Function GetDiskFreeSpace Lib "kernel32" Alias _
        "GetDiskFreeSpaceA" (ByVal lpRootPathName As String, _
        lpSectorsPerCluster As Long, lpBytesPerSector As Long, _
        lpNumberOfFreeClusters As Long, lpTtoalNumberOfClusters _
        As Long) As Long
    Declare Sub GlobalMemoryStatus Lib "kernel32" _
        (lpBuffer As MEMORYSTATUS)
    Declare Function GetUserName Lib "advapi32.dll" Alias _
        "GetUserNameA" (ByVal lpBuffer _
        As String, nSize As Long) As Long
    Declare Function GetVersionEx Lib "kernel32" Alias _
        "GetVersionExA" (lpVersionInformation As OSVersionInfo) _
```

```
      As Long
Declare Sub GetSystemInfo Lib "kernel32" _
    (lpSystemInfo As SYSTEM_INFO)
```

Getting the User's Name

A call to GetUserName returns the network logon name of the person currently logged on. You can use this name to send mail, verify access levels, mark records for history, and—well you get the idea.

Code 1.27:   The UserName Subroutine

```
Public Sub UserName()
    On Error GoTo ErrorRoutineErr

    Dim st As String
    Dim slCnt As Long
    Dim slDL As Long
    Dim slPos As Single
    Dim slUserName As String

    'Get the users name
    slCnt = 199
    st = String(200, 0)
    slDL = GetUserName(st, slCnt)
    slUserName = Left(st, slCnt) & slCnt
    slPos = InStr(1, slUserName, Chr(0))
    If slPos > 0 Then
        txtUserName = Left(slUserName, slPos - 1)
    End If

ErrorRoutineResume:
    Exit Sub
ErrorRoutineErr:
    MsgBox "Stats.Form1.UserName" & Err & Error
End Sub
```

Getting System Information

The APIs in this section retrieve a lot of valuable system information. The GlobalMemoryStatus function retrieves and reports on the system's memory position—the total available memory and the total memory. After that, a call to GetDeviceCaps gets the number of colors supported. The function GetFreeDiskSpace gets the total disk space and the total free disk space.

Code 1.28:   The SystemInformation Subroutine

```
Public Sub SystemInformation()

    On Error GoTo ErrorRoutineErr

    Dim ms As MEMORYSTATUS
    Dim slDriveType
    Dim slDL As Long
    Dim slDrive
    Dim slPosition As Integer
    Dim slFreeBytes As Long
    Dim slTotalBytes As Long

    ms.dwLength = Len(ms)
    GlobalMemoryStatus ms

    'Get memory
    txtTotalPhysicalMemory = Format(ms.dwTotalPhys, "0,000")
    txtTotalAvailableMemory = Format(ms.dwAvailPhys, "0,00")

    'Screen resolution and colors
    txtScreenResolution = Screen.Width \ Screen.TwipsPerPixelX _
        & " x " & Screen.Height \ Screen.TwipsPerPixelY
    txtColors = DeviceColors((hdc))

    'Current drive
    slDrive = Left(App.Path, 2)
    slPosition = InStr(slDrive, " ")
    If slPosition > 0 Then
        slDrive = Left$(slDrive, slPosition - 1)
    End If
    If Right$(slDrive, 1) <> "\" Then slDrive = slDrive & "\"
    txtCurrentDrive = Left(slDrive, 2)

    'Total free disk space
    slDL = GetDiskFreeSpace(slDrive, SectorsPerCluster, _
        BytesPerSector, NumberOfFreeClustors, _
        TotalNumberOfClustors)
        slTotalBytes = TotalNumberOfClustors * _
        SectorsPerCluster * BytesPerSector
        txtTotalDiskSpace = Format(slTotalBytes, "#,0")
```

```
                slFreeBytes = NumberOfFreeClustors * _
                SectorsPerCluster * BytesPerSector
                txtTotalFreeDiskSpace = Format(slFreeBytes, "#,0")

ErrorRoutineResume:
    Exit Sub
ErrorRoutineErr:
    MsgBox "Stats.Form1.SystemInformation" & Err & Error
End Sub
```

Getting Version Information

The GetVersionEx function finds out the type of operating system and also gets the major version, the minor version such as NT version 4, the build number, and the service pack level for Windows NT. Among other information, GetSystemInfo can tell us the type of processor on which our application is currently running.

Code 1.29:   The VersionInformation Subroutine

```
Public Sub VersionInformation()
    On Error GoTo ErrorRoutineErr
    Dim flagnum&
    Dim dl&, s$

    Dim vernum&, verword%
    Dim mySys As SYSTEM_INFO

    ' Get the windows flags and version numbers
    myVer.dwOSVersionInfoSize = 148
    dl& = GetVersionEx&(myVer)

    'Get the processor
    If myVer.dwProcessorId = VER_Processor_WIN32_WINDOWS Then
        txtOperatingSystem = "Windows95 "
    ElseIf myVer.dwProcessorId = VER_Processor_WIN32_NT Then
        txtOperatingSystem = "Windows NT "
    End If

    'Get the version, build, and service pack
    txtVersion = myVer.dwMajorVersion & "." _
        & myVer.dwMinorVersion
    txtBuildNumber = (myVer.dwBuildNumber And &HFFFF&)
    txtServicePack = LPSTRToVBString(myVer.szCSDVersion)
```

```
GetSystemInfo mySys

Select Case mySys.dwProcessorType
    Case PROCESSOR_INTEL_386
            txtProcessor = "386"
    Case PROCESSOR_INTEL_486
            txtProcessor = "486"
    Case PROCESSOR_INTEL_PENTIUM
            txtProcessor = "586"
    Case Else
        txtProcessor = "586"
End Select
ErrorRoutineResume:
    Exit Sub
ErrorRoutineErr:
    MsgBox "Stats.Form1.VersionInformation" & Err & Error
End Sub
```

Testing the Statistics Program

Testing the Statistics program is simple. Since all the major calls are in the Form Load procedure, all you have to do is start it up. As you can see in Figure 1.16, the Form is filled with information about the current environment.

FIGURE 1.16:

The Statistics project in action

Visual Basic and the Registry

- Understanding the Windows Registry

- Interacting with the Registry from Visual Basic

- Controlling the registration of shareware

The Windows Registry is a unified database that stores system and application configuration data in a hierarchical form. Because the Registry contains all the settings required to configure memory, hardware peripherals, and network components, you may find that it is no longer necessary to configure settings in initialization files. Also, because settings are stored in a central location, you can provide both local and remote support for system configuration.

You can use the Registry to do the following:

- Store the location, size, and configuration of your Visual Basic Forms so that your users see the application the way they want.

- Store the column widths for grids and set them for each user.

- Store the application's color schemes.

- Keep a list of recently used files or reports. Almost all Windows applications do this.

> **NOTE** Notice the list of files at the bottom of the File menu in Visual Basic? This list of recently used files is stored in the Registry.

As your users' needs or requirements change, you may find it necessary to change or even delete Registry keys. You can take care of all these tasks in VB. In this chapter, we'll show you how to create, open, list, and maintain the Registry from your VB programs and how to take advantage of the Registry when creating time-limited shareware applications.

Understanding the Windows Registry

Applications use the Windows Registry to store configuration data. It replaces the large number of INI files that Windows 3.x used, and it is also used heavily by OLE (object linking and embedding). The Registry consists of a hierarchical structure (shown in Figure 2.1) that is divided into six subkeys.

FIGURE 2.1:

The Windows Registry
structure

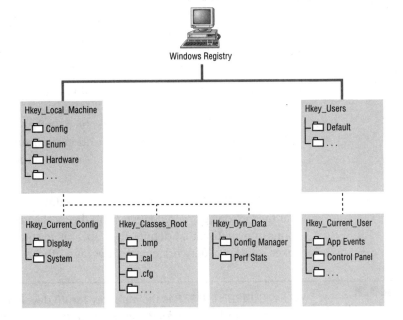

You can access the Registry using the Windows application RegEdit. Here are
the steps:

1. Choose Start ➤ Run.

2. In the Open text box, type **RegEdit** and press Enter to open the Registry
   Editor, as shown in Figure 2.2.

FIGURE 2.2:

The Registry Editor

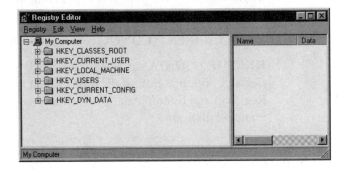

RegEdit is a great tool to use when testing your applications. As you develop a VB program that writes or deletes keys to the Registry, you can use RegEdit to ensure that everything works as you expect.

The six Registry keys are predefined and hold data as follows:

HKEY_CLASSES_ROOT contains the data that associates file types (by file name extension) with the applications that support them. It also contains information about file associations and data associated with COM (communications) objects.

HKEY_CURRENT_USER contains the settings that describe the user profile for the person currently logged on to the local computer. A user profile contains information that defines the appearance and behavior of the individual user's desktop, network connections, and other environment settings.

NOTE

HKEY_CURRENT_USER is the main key for VB developers. By convention, you add your Registry keys, subkeys, and values to HKEY_CURRENT-USER\Software\Vb and VBA Program Settings.

HKEY_LOCAL_MACHINE contains the configuration data for the local computer. The information in this database is used by applications, device drivers, and Windows NT to determine configuration data for the local computer, regardless of which user is logged on and which software is in use.

HKEY_USERS contains profiles for all users who can log on to the machine. If only one person is logged on, this key contains only the Default subkey.

HKEY_CURRENT_CONFIG contains font and printer information.

HKEY_DYN_DATA stores dynamic Registry data. The Windows 95 Registry supports both static data (which is stored on disk in the Registry) and dynamic data (which changes frequently, such as performance statistics).

You can create, delete, open, close, query, and enumerate Registry keys in Visual Basic. A Registry key must be created before it can be used. The RegCreateKeyEx function creates a new key if the key does not exist or simply opens the key if it does exist. Once the key is open, you can use the RegSetValueEx function to set or create its value, if necessary. If you only want to find out whether a value already exists, you use the function RegQueryValueEx. When a key is no longer used, you can delete it with the function RegDeleteKey.

WARNING Changes to the Registry are final once the Registry file is closed. Changing some Registry settings can have drastic and unwanted effects, so exercise caution when working with the Registry. It is a good idea to make a backup of the Registry before you make any changes. To do so, in the Registry Editor, choose Registry ➢ Export Registry File.

The Registry plays an important role in Visual Basic application development by providing a central location for storing and retrieving important information. If you are developing an application with which the user opens and uses files, including a recent file list is a good idea. If your application provides reports for the user, keeping a list of the top five reports that each user requests would be helpful. The Registry is a great place to store each user's preferences for Form sizes and locations, as well as spreadsheets and grids. Users are grateful when an application remembers the way they formatted columns in a spreadsheet or a grid. You can easily store and retrieve all this and more in the Registry.

We'll start our exploration of how Visual Basic and the Registry interact by looking at the Registry project.

The Registry Project

The Registry project (shown in Figure 2.3) demonstrates the API functions necessary to interact with the Registry from within Visual Basic. You can use this project as a stand alone Registry editor or incorporate the code into your application and use it as a starting point for your own Registry functions.

NOTE You'll find the Registry project in the Chapter2\Registry folder on the CD that comes with this book.

FIGURE 2.3:

The Registry project

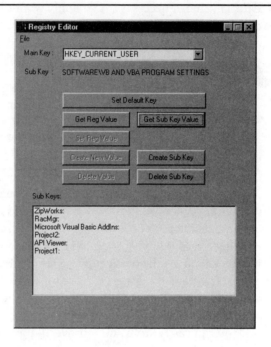

The Registry project does the following:

- Retrieves a list of values associated with a key

- Creates a value

- Changes a value

- Deletes a value

- Lists subkeys within keys

- Creates a new subkey

- Deletes a subkey

The Registry project consists of a module that holds the API-specific information and one Form. The Form has a ComboBox control that lists the six predefined keys and the following eight Command Buttons:

Set Default Key allows you to set the current working key location.

Get Reg Value fills a list box with the values associated with the current key and subkey(s). First, the key is opened with the RegOpenKey function, and then RegEnumValue enumerates the values for the specified open Registry key.

Set Reg Value uses the function RegCreateKeyEx (if the key exists, RegCreateKeyEx opens it) to open the key, and then the RegSetValueEx changes the value.

Create New Value creates a new value for the specified key by calling the function RegSetValueEx.

Delete Value uses the function RegCreateKeyEx to open the key and then uses RegDeleteValue to delete the value from the key.

Get Sub Key Value fills the list box with the subkeys defined for the selected key/subkey combination. It uses the function RegOpenKey to open the key, and then the RegEnumKey function enumerates the values for the specified open Registry key. This button is similar to the Get Reg Value button except that it enumerates the keys instead of the values in the keys.

Create Sub Key creates a new subkey with the function RegCreateKeyEx.

Delete Sub Key opens the key with the RegCreateKeyEx function and then deletes the selected subkey by calling the RegDeleteKey API function.

The Registry Project API Functions

Table 2.1 lists and describes the API functions used in the Registry project.

TIP

You'll find a complete description of these functions in Appendix B, which is on the CD that comes with this book.

TABLE 2.1: The API Functions in the Registry Project

API Function	Description
RegCloseKey	Releases the handle of the specified key.
RegCreateKeyEx	Creates the specified key. If the key already exists in the Registry, the function opens it.
RegDeleteKey	Deletes a key and all its subkeys.

TABLE 2.1 (CONTINUED): The API Functions in the Registry Project

API Function	Description
RegDeleteValue	Removes a named value from the specified Registry key.
RegEnumKeyEx	Enumerates subkeys of the specified open Registry key. The function retrieves information about one subkey each time it is called.
RegEnumValue	Enumerates the values for the specified open Registry key. The function copies one indexed value name and data block for the key each time it is called.
RegOpenKeyEx	Opens the specified key.
RegQueryValueEx	Retrieves the type and data for a specified value name associated with an open Registry key.
RegSetValueEx	Stores data in the value field of an open Registry key. It can also set additional value and type information for the specified key.

The Registry Code in Action

Now let's look at the code in the Registry project. To conserve space, we aren't including the declarations, types, and constants required for the Registry API functions here, but they are in this chapter's folder on the CD.

Opening a Key

Before you can retrieve a key's value, query a key, create or change a value, or delete a Registry key, it must be open. Code 2.1 demonstrates how to make a key and subkey available by opening it. First, an InputBox is displayed so that a new subkey can be entered, and the code attempts to open the subkey with the function RegOpenKeyEx. If the subkey is opened successfully, it becomes the new subkey, and then the function RegCloseKey closes the key.

NOTE   Notice the On Error statements. As mentioned in Chapter 1, when you use API functions in Visual Basic, there is no safety net. It is important for your applications to trap unforeseen errors.

Code 2.1:   The cmdDefaultKey_Click Subroutine

```
Private Sub cmdDefaultKey_Click()
    On Error GoTo ErrorRoutineErr

    Dim NewKey As String
    Dim phkResult As Long

    'Get Registry SubKey from user
    NewKey = InputBox("Enter SubKey Desired:", , SubKey)

    'Exit if user chose Cancel or entered an empty string
    If NewKey = "" Then
        Exit Sub
    End If

    lblSubKey = NewKey

    'See if the new Registry SubKey given exists
    If RegOpenKeyEx(hKey, NewKey, 0, 1, phkResult) <> _
        ERROR_SUCCESS Then
        MsgBox "A Valid SubKey is needed to continue." & _
        Chr(13) & "Changes Cancelled."
        Exit Sub
    End If

    'Close given SubKey
    RegCloseKey phkResult

    'Set the new default SubKey
    SubKey = NewKey

    Exit Sub

ErrorRoutineErr:
    MsgBox "ERROR #" & Str$(Err) & " : " & Error & Chr(13) _
        & "Please exit and try again."
End Sub
```

Creating a New Subkey Value

The SetRegValue subroutine creates a new value under a subkey. First, RegCreateKeyEx opens the key and the subkey. The RegSetValueEx function then sets the value of the subkey. You can think of this value as a heading. For example, if you want to store a list of recent files used in an application, the value could be "Applications Recent File List." The data for the value could be the list of files.

Code 2.2:   The SetRegValue Function

```
Function SetRegValue(hKey As Long, lpszSubKey As String, _
                     ByVal sSetValue As String, _
                     ByVal sValue As String) As Boolean

    On Error GoTo ErrorRoutineErr

    Dim phkResult As Long
    Dim lResult As Long
    Dim SA As SECURITY_ATTRIBUTES

    'Note: This function will create the key or
    'value if it doesn't exist.
    'Open or Create the key
    RegCreateKeyEx hKey, lpszSubKey, 0, "", _
        REG_OPTION_NON_VOLATILE, _
        KEY_ALL_ACCESS, SA, phkResult, Create

    lResult = RegSetValueEx(phkResult, sSetValue, 0, _
        REG_SZ, sValue, _
        CLng(Len(sValue) + 1))

    'Close the key
    RegCloseKey phkResult

    'Return SetRegValue Result
    SetRegValue = (lResult = ERROR_SUCCESS)
    Exit Function

ErrorRoutineErr:
  MsgBox "ERROR #" & Str$(Err) & " : " & Error & Chr(13) _
        & "Please exit and try again."
  SetRegValue = False

End Function
```

Deleting a Subkey's Value

As an application progresses, you may need to delete a subkey's value. Remember, you can think of a value as a heading. If an area of the program is complete and will not be used again, you can delete a subkey's value, freeing the space to be used by another part of the application or by another application. The subroutine cmdDeleteValue uses the function RegCreateKeyEx to open the subkey and then deletes the data value with the RegDeleteValue API function. After the value is deleted, the LoadList1 function is called to refresh the list box.

Code 2.3:   The cmdDeleteValue_Click Subroutine

```
Private Sub cmdDeleteValue_Click()

    Dim Reply As String
    Dim phkResult As Long
    Dim SA As SECURITY_ATTRIBUTES

    If List1.ListIndex = -1 Then
        MsgBox "Please select a Value to delete"
        Exit Sub
    End If
    RegCreateKeyEx Registry.hKey, Registry.SubKey, _
        0, "", REG_OPTION_NON_VOLATILE, _
    KEY_ALL_ACCESS, SA, phkResult, Registry.Create

    'Delete SubKey value specified
    If RegDeleteValue(phkResult, GetValueStr(List1.Text)) _
        = ERROR_SUCCESS Then

        'Refresh the list
        Call LoadList1("Regular")
        lblResult = "Value Deleted"
    Else
        lblResult = "Cannot Delete Value"
    End If

    'Close the current SubKey
    RegCloseKey phkResult
End Sub
```

Creating a New Key

All information in the Registry is stored under a key. Since it is a good idea to keep data separated by application or type of application, you need to create keys to hold subkeys and values. You can think of keys as sections. The function CreateRegKey is called from cmdCreateKey_Click, and the RegCreateKeyEx function creates the new keys. The RegCloseKey function then closes the open key.

Code 2.4:   The CreateRegKey Function

```
Function CreateRegKey(NewSubKey As String) As Boolean

    On Error GoTo ErrorRoutineErr

    Dim phkResult As Long
    Dim lResult As Long
    Dim SA As SECURITY_ATTRIBUTES

    'Create key if it does not exist
    CreateRegKey = (RegCreateKeyEx(hKey, SubKey & NewSubKey, _
    0, "", REG_OPTION_NON_VOLATILE, _
        KEY_ALL_ACCESS, SA, phkResult, Create) = ERROR_SUCCESS)

    'Close the key
    RegCloseKey phkResult
    Exit Function

ErrorRoutineErr:
    MsgBox "ERROR #" & Str$(Err) & " : " & Error & Chr(13) _
        & "Please exit and try again."
    CreateRegKey = False

End Function
```

Querying a Key's Value

A key's value stores the actual data, such as the list of most recently used files, Form dimensions, or the column widths of a spreadsheet. Double-clicking a value in the list box calls the GetRegValue function to return the data value associated with the value of the subkey. The RegOpenKeyEx function opens the key, RegQueryValueEx gets the data value from the value, and RegCloseKey closes the key.

Code 2.5: The GetRegValue Function

```
Function GetRegValue(hKey As Long, lpszSubKey As String, _
    szKey As String, szDefault As String) As Variant

    On Error GoTo ErrorRoutineErr

    Dim phkResult As Long
    Dim lResult As Long
    Dim szBuffer As String
    Dim lBuffSize As Long

    'Create Buffer
    szBuffer = Space(255)
    lBuffSize = Len(szBuffer)

    'Open the key
    RegOpenKeyEx hKey, lpszSubKey, 0, 1, phkResult

    'Query the value
    lResult = RegQueryValueEx(phkResult, szKey, 0, _
        0, szBuffer, lBuffSize)

    'Close the key
    RegCloseKey phkResult

    'Return obtained value
    If lResult = ERROR_SUCCESS Then
        GetRegValue = Left(szBuffer, lBuffSize - 1)
    Else
        GetRegValue = szDefault
    End If
    Exit Function

ErrorRoutineErr:
    MsgBox "ERROR #" & Str$(Err) & " : " & Error & Chr(13) _
        & "Please exit and try again."
    GetRegValue = ""

End Function
```

Deleting a Key

In the course of your Registry programming, some keys will lose their usefulness. You can delete a key when the information it stores is no longer needed. The subroutine cmdDeleteKey_Click uses the RegCreateKeyEx API function to open the selected subkey, and then the RegDeleteKey function deletes it. Remember, a key must be open before you can manipulate it.

Code 2.6:   The cmdDeleteKey_Click Subroutine

```
Private Sub cmdDeleteKey_Click()
    'Open current SubKey

    Dim Reply As String
    Dim phkResult As Long
    Dim SA As SECURITY_ATTRIBUTES

    If List1.ListIndex = -1 Then
        MsgBox "Please select a SubKey to delete"
        Exit Sub
    End If
    RegCreateKeyEx Registry.hKey, Registry.SubKey, 0, _
        "", REG_OPTION_NON_VOLATILE, _
        KEY_ALL_ACCESS, SA, phkResult, Registry.Create

    'Delete SubKey specified
    If RegDeleteKey(phkResult, GetValueStr(List1.Text)) _
        = ERROR_SUCCESS Then
        Call LoadList1("Key")
        lblResult = "SubKey Deleted"

    Else
        'Close the current SubKey
        RegCloseKey phkResult
        lblResult = "Cannot Delete SubKey"
    End If
End Sub
```

In this section, we've looked at API functions that perform some type of action on the Registry—opening a key, deleting a key, and reading a key's value. In the next section, we'll explore the process involved in enumerating, or inspecting, a key's structure. This will include listing the subkeys, the values, and the data in the values.

Enumerating Keys and Loading the List Box

Code 2.7 is a procedure for enumerating a key's structure. You can use this procedure when it becomes necessary to look through a key's structure to find a certain value. Clicking the Get Sub Key Value and the Get Reg Value buttons calls the subroutine LoadList1. In the top part of the code, we use the RegCreateKeyEx function to open the subkey, and then we use the RegEnumKeyEx function inside a While loop to enumerate the subkeys and load them into the list box.

In the bottom part of the code, we load the list box with the values under the selected subkey. The RegOpenKeyEx function opens the key, and then RegEnumValue is used within a While loop to enumerate the values. The RegCloseKey function is called to close the open keys.

Code 2.7: **The LoadList1 Subroutine**

```
Public Sub LoadList1(Action As String)
    On Error GoTo ErrorRoutineErr

    Dim lResult As Long
    Dim Index As Long
    Dim dwReserved As Long
    Dim szBuffer As String
    Dim lBuffSize As Long
    Dim szBuffer2 As String
    Dim lBuffSize2 As Long
    Dim phkResult As Long
    Dim SA As SECURITY_ATTRIBUTES
    Dim lType As Long
    Dim FT As FILETIME

    'Initialize local variables
    Index = 0
    dwReserved = 0
    List1.Clear
    lblResult = ""

    'get keys
    If Action = "Key" Then
        'Add the SubKeys to the list box
        'Open the key
        lResult = RegCreateKeyEx(Registry.hKey, _
            Registry.SubKey, 0, "", REG_OPTION_NON_VOLATILE, _
            KEY_ALL_ACCESS, SA, phkResult, Registry.Create)
```

```
'Loop for each subkey found
While lResult = ERROR_SUCCESS

    'Set buffer space
    szBuffer = Space(255)
    lBuffSize = Len(szBuffer)
    szBuffer2 = Space(255)
    lBuffSize2 = Len(szBuffer2)

    'Get next key
    lResult = RegEnumKeyEx(phkResult, Index, _
        szBuffer, lBuffSize, dwReserved, _
        szBuffer2, lBuffSize2, FT)

    'If found a new key, add it to the list
    If lResult = ERROR_SUCCESS Then
        List1.AddItem Left(szBuffer, lBuffSize) & ": "
    End If
    Index = Index + 1
Wend

Else ' Enumerate Values

    'Open the key
    lResult = RegOpenKeyEx(Registry.hKey, _
        Registry.SubKey, 0, 1, phkResult)

    'Loop for each value found
    While lResult = ERROR_SUCCESS

    'Set buffer space
    szBuffer = Space(255)
    lBuffSize = Len(szBuffer)
    szBuffer2 = Space(255)
    lBuffSize2 = Len(szBuffer2)

    'Get next value
    lResult = RegEnumValue(phkResult, Index, szBuffer, _
        lBuffSize, dwReserved, lType, _
        szBuffer2, lBuffSize2)

    'If a new value is found, add it to the list
    If lResult = ERROR_SUCCESS Then
```

```
            List1.AddItem Left(szBuffer, lBuffSize) & _
            ": " & GetType(lType)


            '_____

            'As an option, you could use the next line of
            'code to return the value and the data in the value
            '_____

            'List1.AddItem Left(szBuffer, lBuffSize) & ":" _
            '     & GetType(lType) _
            '     & ":" & Left(szBuffer2, lBuffSize2 - 1)


        End If
        Index = Index + 1
        Wend

        End If


    'Close the key
    RegCloseKey phkResult

    'Return true if enumerated all values
    LoadValueList = (lResult = ERROR_NO_MORE_ITEMS)
    Exit Sub

ErrorRoutineErr:
    MsgBox "ERROR #" & Str$(Err) & " : " & Error & Chr(13) _
        & "Please exit and try again."
    LoadValueList = False
End Sub
```

The Registry Project in Action

The code listings in the previous sections highlight the main parts of the Registry project. You can use this code as a basis for building a library of routines that access the Registry from your applications. The Registry project shows how you can use the API functions in a Visual Basic program to store and retrieve data.

Now let's take a look at what happens when you run the program. Press F5 to start the application. Your screen should look like Figure 2.3, earlier in this chapter. The default key is HKEY_CURRENT_USER, and the default subkey is SOFTWARE\ VB AND VBA PROGRAM SETTINGS.

WARNING When you set a subkey value, do not add a backslash (\) to the end. If you do, you must remove it to add a new subkey.

The following seven steps demonstrate the major functionality of the Registry project.

1. Click the Get Sub Key Value button. The list box fills with the subkeys that are defined, and the Create Sub Key and Delete Sub Key buttons are enabled.

2. Click the Set Default Key button to set a new subkey. You can enter a value from the list box. For this example, add `\API Viewer\File List` to the end of the default setting of SOFTWARE\VB AND VBA PROGRAM SETTINGS that is currently displayed in the Input Box.

3. Click the Get Reg Value button to fill the list box with the values associated with a subkey.

4. Double-click a value in the list box to see the value data set for that value.

5. Click the Set Reg Value button to set or change a value data.

6. Click the Create New Value button to create a new value and set the data for the value.

WARNING Be careful in the next step when deleting a value. Remember that there is no safety net. When you delete a key, a subkey, or a value, it's deleted!

---

7. Click the Delete Value button to delete a value and its data.

As you can see, combining API functions with Visual Basic makes it easy to add, change, and delete Registry keys, subkeys, and values.

Shareware and the Registry

OK, it's time to put the Registry to work! Put on your shareware author's hat, and let's see how you can use the Registry to control the registration of a shareware application. We can use the Registry to hold information about our application. We can store the application name as a subkey, and we can store the number of times the application is launched along with the registration number.

What Is Shareware?

Shareware is a marketing method; it is not a type of software. Shareware is try-it-before-you-buy-it software—an economical way to see if an application meets your needs. In recent years, it has become acceptable for authors to put time-out code in shareware applications.

Many shareware authors allow their applications to be used for a designated period, such as one month, or for a specified number of times before requiring that the user register it. When this trial period expires, the program stops working.

The RegShareware Project

We'll create a shareware application that allows the user to launch it three times during the trial period. During this period, the user can look at the About screen to check the number of remaining launches or to register the software. When the trial period expires, we'll display a message box that allows the user to register the application by entering a registration number. The registration number can be any string as long as the last character is a 5. You can devise a sophisticated registration algorithm, but for now, let's keep it simple. For testing purposes, we'll include a Remove Registration button that deletes our entire subkey.

> **NOTE**   You'll find the RegShareware project in the Chapter2\RegShare folder on the CD that comes with this book.

The RegShareware project will put the API functions to practical use. In the course of this project we will do the following:

- Create a key and subkey
- Create a value and add data to the value
- Delete a key

Our project has three Forms (shown in Figure 2.4): a Splash screen, a main Form, and an About screen. The Splash screen, which is displayed first, uses the API function RegOpenKeyEx to try to open our shareware registration key. Since we are launching the application for the first time, we will need to create the Registry entries. We will use the existing HKEY_CURRENT_USER key and the subkey SOFTWARE\VB AND VBA PROGRAM SETTINGS. Under these keys, we will create the following subkeys:

DevHand5Shareware holds the name of our application and has one subkey, Settings.

Settings holds the values of the registration number and the number of times the application is used.

Registration Number holds the actual number the user registers with.

Times holds the number of times the application is launched. We subtract one from this value every time the application is launched. When this value reaches zero, the user is denied access to the application unless he or she enters a valid registration number.

FIGURE 2.4:

The three Forms that make up the RegShareware project

Splash Form

Main Form

About Form

Figure 2.5 shows the Windows Registry after the application creates the subkeys and values.

FIGURE 2.5:

RegEdit after registration

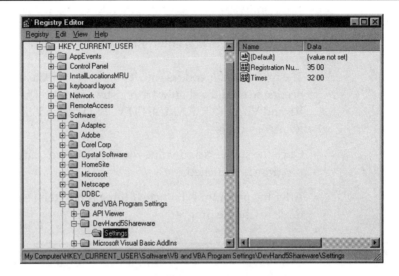

The user can register at any time during the trial period by clicking the Register button on the About screen and entering a valid registration number. Any string that ends in a five (5) is a valid registration number.

Creating the RegShareware Project

To create the RegShareware project, start a new project, and add a Splash Form and a regular Form using the Add Form option. Change the name of form2 to frmAbout. The Splash Form gives the user something to look at while we verify the status of the software, and frmAbout registers the program during the trial period.

NOTE

The RegShareware project uses the API functions in Table 2.1, earlier in this chapter. See Appendix B on the CD for a complete description of these functions. To conserve space, we didn't include the type, constant, and declare statements here, but they are in this chapter's folder on the CD.

Loading the Splash Form The Splash Form, shown in Figure 2.4, earlier in this chapter is the first Form the user sees, and we use it to check the Registry for a valid serial number. If we don't find a valid serial number, this is an unregistered copy of the software, and we must, therefore, check the status of the trial period. The code in the Form_Load subroutine performs the following actions to verify and prepare the shareware environment:

- The first time this code is run, it attempts to create the key, subkeys, and values needed to hold the shareware registration data. The structures SOFTWARE\ VB and VBA PROGRAM SETTINGS\DevHand5Shareware will hold our Registry location.

- Once the subkeys and values are created, we track the number of times the program is launched.

- After the program is launched three times, the user must register to continue to use the program.

NOTE   As you look at Code 2.8, pay particular attention to the comments to see how the trial period is used.

Code 2.8:   The RegShareware Splash Screen

```
Private Sub Form_Load()

    Dim phkResult As Long
    Dim slValue As String
    Dim slData As String
    Dim slTimesRemaining As String
    Dim Msg, Style, Title, Response, MyString
    Dim slRegNumber As String
    Dim rc
    Dim slRegistered

    lblVersion.Caption = "Version " & App.Major & "." _
        & App.Minor & "." & App.Revision
    lblProductName.Caption = App.Title

    'Registry key we want to use
    hKey = HKEY_CURRENT_USER
```

```
'Set Registry SubKey
SubKey = "SOFTWARE\VB AND VBA PROGRAM SETTINGS\" _
   & "DevHand5Shareware\Settings"
slValue = "Times"
slData = 3

If RegOpenKeyEx(hKey, SubKey, 0, 1, phkResult) = _
    ERROR_SUCCESS Then

    'Check to see if there is a registration number
    glRegNumber = _
    GetRegValue(hKey, SubKey, "Registration Number", _
        "Not Found")
    If Len(glRegNumber) > 0 Then

        'It's a registered copy, exit
        lblWarning = "Registered Copy"
        glRegistered = True
        Timer1.Enabled = True
        Exit Sub
    End If

    'The key exists so this is not the first time the
    'program has been run
    'Check to see how many runs are left
    slTimesRemaining = _
    GetRegValue(hKey, SubKey, "Times", "Not Found")
    If Val(slTimesRemaining - 1) = 0 Then

        'No time left
        Msg = "Evaluation period has expired." & Chr(13) & _
        "Would you like to register now?."
        Style = vbYesNo + vbCritical + vbDefaultButton1
        Title = "Register Software"
        Response = MsgBox(Msg, Style, Title)
        If Response = vbYes Then

            'Let the user register
            slRegNumber = InputBox("Enter your " & _
            "Registration Number.")
```

```
                    'Add an algorithm to validate the reg
                    'number, here it only has to end in a 5
                    If Right(slRegNumber, 1) = "5" Then

                        'Put the reg number in the registry
                        If Not SetRegValue(hKey, SubKey, _
                            "Registration Number", slRegNumber) Then
                            MsgBox "Unable to set Value."
                        Else
                            frmAbout.Caption = "Registered Copy"
                            frmAbout.Command1.Visible = False
                            'Set the global registration number
                            glRegNumber = slRegNumber
                        End If
                    Else
                        'Not a validate reg number
                        MsgBox "Registration Number is not valid."
                        End
                    End If
                Else
                    'User does not want to register
                    End
                End If
            Else
                'There is time left so deduct one
                rc = SetRegValue(hKey, SubKey, _
                    slValue, slTimesRemaining - 1)

                lblWarning = "Number of Times remaining = " _
                & slTimesRemaining - 1
                frmAbout.Label1 = "Number of Times" & _
                " remaining = " & slTimesRemaining - 1
            End If
            Timer1.Enabled = True
        Else
            'The key does not exist, this is the first time
            'the program has been run, create the new key
            If CreateRegKey(SubKey) Then

                'If subkey is created, create the value and data
                'For the times counter
                rc = SetRegValue(hKey, SubKey, _
```

```
                slValue, slData)
            rc = ""
            rc = SetRegValue(hKey, SubKey, _
                "Registration Number", "")
            Timer1.Enabled = True
            lblWarning = "Number of Times remaining = " _
            & slData
            frmAbout.Label1 = "Number of Times" & _
            " remaining = " & slData
        Else
            MsgBox "Unable to Create Key."
        End If
        Exit Sub
    End If
End Sub
```

Registering the Software   One part of the process that might get overlooked (because it is the end result of all your hard work) is the About box (shown in Figure 2.4, earlier in this chapter). If the user chooses Help ➤ About, the About box is displayed. This Form shows the registration status of the software.

If the software is registered, the About box displays the registration number, and the title is changed to Registered Copy. If the software is not registered, a Registration button is provided to allow the user to enter a registration number.

Loading the About Form   The subroutine Form_Load loads the Form and sets the caption. If the program is registered, the user has entered a valid registration number, and the caption is set to "Registered Copy"; otherwise the caption shows the title.

Code 2.9:   **The Form_Load Subroutine**

```
Private Sub Form_Load()
    If glRegistered Then
        'It's a registered copy, set up fields
        Me.Caption = "Registered Copy"
        Label1 = "Registration Number: " & glRegNumber
        Command1.Visible = False
    Else
        'Not registered
        Me.Caption = "About " & App.Title

    End If
End Sub
```

Entering a Registration Number   The subroutine Command1_Click is called from the About box to allow the user to register the software. An Input box is displayed for the user to enter a registration number. If the number matches a set value (in our case, the number must end in a 5), the program is registered by adding the registration number to our Registry key with the API function SetRegValue, and the user is notified.

Code 2.10:   Adding the Registration Value

```
Private Sub Command1_Click()
    Dim slRegNumber

    'Let the user register
    slRegNumber = InputBox("Enter your " & _
    "Registration Number.")

    'Add an algorithm to validate the registration
    'Number, here it only has to end in a 5
    If Right(slRegNumber, 1) = "5" Then

        'Put the reg number in the registry
        If Not Module1.SetRegValue(hKey, SubKey, _
            "Registration Number", slRegNumber) Then
            MsgBox "Unable to set Value."
        Else
            glRegistered = True
            glRegNumber = slRegNumber
            Me.Caption = "Registered Copy"
            Command1.Visible = False
            MsgBox "Registration succeeded."
            'Unload Me
        End If
    Else
        'Not a validate reg number
        MsgBox "Registration Number is not valid."
        End
    End If

End Sub
```

Deleting the Test Key

You can click the Remove Registration button on the main Form (shown in Figure 2.4, earlier in this chapter) to delete the Registry key. The Command1_Click subroutine uses the API function RegCreateKeyEx to open the key and then deletes it with RegDeleteKey.

NOTE   This is not part of a normal shareware registration program. We've provided it so that you can delete the key and retest the process.

Code 2.11:   The Command1_Click Subroutine

```
Private Sub Command1_Click()

    Dim Reply As String
    Dim phkResult As Long
    Dim SA As SECURITY_ATTRIBUTES
    Dim slSubKey As String

    'Open current SubKey
    slSubKey = "SOFTWARE\VB AND VBA PROGRAM SETTINGS"
    RegCreateKeyEx hKey, slSubKey, 0, _
        "", REG_OPTION_NON_VOLATILE, _
        KEY_ALL_ACCESS, SA, phkResult, 0

    'Delete SubKey specified
    If RegDeleteKey(phkResult, "DevHand5Shareware") _
        = ERROR_SUCCESS Then
        MsgBox "Registration removed."
        glRegistered = False
        glRegNumber = ""
    Else
        'Close the current SubKey
        RegCloseKey phkResult
        MsgBox "Cannot Delete SubKey"
    End If
End Sub
```

Many shareware authors use the process we just described to control the trial period for their applications. Creating and administrating time-limited shareware can be a daunting task, but with the help of a few API functions, we can cut the task down to size.

Testing the RegShareware Application

Let's take our RegShareware application through its paces:

1. Press F5 to start the program. The Splash screen (shown in Figure 2.4, earlier in this chapter) is displayed. Notice the Number of times remaining = 3 label. This tells the user that the application can be launched three times without being registered. After a couple of seconds, Form1(also shown in Figure 2.4) appears. The Remove Registration button is disabled. After the software is registered, this button is enabled.

2. Choose Help ➤ About Screen to open the About Form (shown in Figure 2.4, earlier in this chapter). Notice that the caption reads "About RegShareware" and that the label reads "Number of times remaining = 3." This reminds the user to register the software.

3. Click the Register button and enter a value that ends in a 5 in the Input box to register the software.

With a little time and effort, you could add a lot of functionality to this program and use it as a starting point for many other applications that require Registry manipulation.

CHAPTER

THREE

3

The Built-In
Visual Basic Developer's
ActiveX Controls

- The ImageList control

- The Toolbar control

- The StatusBar control

- The TabStrip control

- The Slider control

- The ProgressBar control

- The TreeView control

- The ListView control

In this chapter, we will explore the Microsoft Windows Common Controls. This suite of eight ActiveX controls comes with Visual Basic and should be part of every serious developer's arsenal:

The ImageList control contains a collection of ListImage objects, each of which can be referred to by its index or key. The ImageList control is not designed to be used alone, but as a central repository to supply other controls with images.

The Toolbar control contains a collection of Button objects that you use to create a toolbar that is associated with an application.

The StatusBar control provides a window, usually at the bottom of a Parent Form, through which an application can display various kinds of status data. The status bar has become a standard feature of all Microsoft Office programs. It can be divided into a maximum of 16 Panel objects that are contained in a Panels collection.

The TabStrip control is similar to the dividers in a notebook or the labels on a group of file folders. By using a TabStrip control, you can define multiple pages for the same area of a window or a dialog box in your application.

The Slider control is a window that contains a slider and optional tickmarks. You can move the slider by dragging it, by clicking the mouse to either side of it, or by using the keyboard.

The ProgressBar control shows the progress of a lengthy operation by filling a rectangle with chunks from left to right.

The TreeView control displays a hierarchical list of Node objects, each of which consists of a label and an optional bitmap. A TreeView typically displays the headings in a document, the entries in an index, the files and directories on a disk, or any other kind of information that might usefully be displayed as a hierarchy. The left side of Windows Explorer and the Windows Registry are examples of the TreeView control.

The ListView control displays items using one of four views. You can arrange items into columns with or without column headings, as well as display accompanying icons and text. The right side of Windows Explorer and the Windows Registry are examples of the ListView control.

Adding the Windows Common Controls to Your Project

The Windows Common Controls are available as a Visual Basic custom control. You'll find them in the file Comctl32.ocx. To add the controls to your VB project, follow these steps:

1. Choose Project ➢ Components to open the Components dialog box.

2. Check the Microsoft Windows Common Controls 5.0 checkbox, and then click OK.

The controls are now added to your Toolbox.

In the following sections we will look at these controls in detail and create sample projects that will demonstrate how they fit together into an application.

The ImageList Control

An ImageList control contains a collection of images that can be used by other Windows Common Controls—specifically the TabStrip, Toolbar, TreeView, and ListView controls.

You can save valuable development time using the ImageList control as a single image repository instead of writing code that loads bitmaps and icon files at run time. With the ImageList control, you can store and refer to images from one central location with the Key value or Index property.

The control uses bitmap or icon files in a collection of ListImage objects. To use the ImageList control with the Windows Common Controls, you must first associate the ImageList control with the other control and then assign either the Key or the Index property to one of the Windows Common Controls. You can do so at design time or at run time. All the Windows Common Controls, except the ListView control, have an ImageList property that can be set with the name of the ImageList control you are using. The ListView control uses the Icon and SmallIcon properties to associate the ImageList control.

The ImageList control also features the Overlay, ExtractIcon, and Draw methods with which you can create composite images, create icons from bitmaps stored in the control, and draw images on objects with an hDC property.

Adding Images to the ImageList Control at Design Time

To add ListImage objects at design time, you use the ImageList control's Property Pages. Follow these steps:

1. Right-click the ImageList control and click Properties.

2. In the Property Pages, select the Images tab:

3. Click the Insert Picture button to open the Select Picture dialog box.

4. Locate either bitmap or icon files, and click Open. You can select multiple bitmap or icon files to open.

5. Assign a unique key to each image by typing a string in the Key box.

NOTE   Optionally, you can assign a Tag to each image by typing a string in the Tag box. Tags do not have to be unique.

---

6. Repeat steps 3 through 5 until the control is populated with the desired images.

Adding Images to the ImageList Control at Run Time

To add an image to the ImageList control at run time, use the Add method for the ListImages collection with the LoadPicture function. The following code loads an ImageList with a single Open bitmap image:

Code 3.1: **The ListImage Add Method**

```
Private Sub Form_Load()
    ImageList1.ListImages.Add , "open", LoadPicture("d:\chapter3code\
toolbar\open.ico")
End Sub
```

As this code shows, just before the Form is loaded, the open bitmap is added to the ImageList control. Also notice that the Key, open, is used. You can refer to ListImages by their numeric index, or you can use the Key value that you assign.

Using the ImageList Control with Other Controls

The ListImage object's Picture property returns a Picture object, which can be assigned to another control's Picture property. This property can be set to the Picture property for a control that is not part of the Windows Common Controls. The following have a Picture property:

- CommandButton control
- OptionButton control
- Image control
- PictureBox control
- CheckBox control
- Form object
- Panel object (StatusBar control)

NOTE   Populate the ImageList control with images before you associate it with another control. Once you associate an ImageList with a control and assign any image to a property of the control, the ImageList control will not allow you to add any more images.

The ImageList control is demonstrated in the following sections as we explore the other controls that make up the Windows Common Controls.

The Toolbar Control

A Toolbar control (shown in Figure 3.1) contains a collection of Button objects that correspond to items in an application's menu, providing a visual interface for the user. Although the toolbar usually does not include a button for each menu option, it provides access to the most frequently used actions or commands. The Toolbar control can also hold other controls, such as a Label, ComboBox, or TextBox control.

FIGURE 3.1:

The Toolbar control

You use the Toolbar control to easily create toolbars by adding Button objects to a Buttons collection. Each Button object can have text and/or an image, supplied by an ImageList control. You set the image with the Image property, and you set the text with the Caption property, for each Button object in the collection. At design time, you use the Toolbar Property Pages to add and remove buttons. At run time, you use the Add and Remove methods to add or remove buttons from the Button object.

To add other controls to the Toolbar control at design time, simply draw them on the Toolbar. The drawback to this approach is that the controls you draw on the toolbar will not be wrappable; that is, they will not move to the next line with the rest of the Button objects if the Form is resized. If this is a concern, you can create a Button object with a PlaceHolder style and position the desired control over the button in the Resize event. Table 3.1 lists the Button Style properties.

TABLE 3.1: The Properties for the Button Style

Constant	Value	Use
tbrDefault	0	(Default) Button. The button is a regular pushbutton.
tbrCheck	1	Check. The button is a check button, which can be checked or unchecked.
tbrButtonGroup	2	ButtonGroup. The button remains pressed until another button in the group is pressed. Only one button in the group can be pressed at any time.
tbrSeparator	3	Separator. The button functions as a separator with a fixed width of 8 pixels.
tbrPlaceHolder	4	Placeholder. The button is like a separator in appearance and functionality, but has a settable width.

Double-clicking a toolbar at run time opens the Customize Toolbar dialog box (shown in Figure 3.2), with which the user can hide, display, or rearrange toolbar buttons. You can enable or disable the dialog box by setting the AllowCustomize property. You can invoke the dialog box at run time by calling the Customize method.

FIGURE 3.2:

The Customize Toolbar dialog box

NOTE   To preserve the state of a Toolbar control, the SaveToolbar method writes to the Windows Registry. You can restore a Toolbar control to a previous state using the RestoreToolbar method to read the information previously saved in the Registry.

Adding Buttons to the Toolbar Control at Design Time

To add Button objects to the Toolbar control at design time, use the Toolbar control's Property Pages (shown in Figure 3.4). Follow these steps:

1.   Right-click the Toolbar control and click Properties to open the Property Pages.

2.   In the General tab, select ImageList from the ImageList box.

3.   Select the Buttons tab, as shown in Figure 3.3.

4.   Click the Insert Button button to insert a new Button object.

5.   Set the Caption, Key, Style, Tag, ToolTipText, Image, Description, and Value as needed.

6.   Repeat steps 4 and 5 until you have added all the desired Button objects.

FIGURE 3.3:

The Toolbar
Property Pages

FIGURE 3.3:

The Toolbar
Property Pages

Adding Buttons to the Toolbar Control at Run Time

Use the Add method to add Button objects to the Toolbar control at run time. The
following code adds a Separator Style Button object and a Regular Style Button
object.

Code 3.2: **Another Way to Add ListImages**

```
Private Sub Command3_Click()


    On Error Resume Next

    'Remove the separator the second time through
    Toolbar1.Buttons.Remove (10)
    'Add an image to the ImageList control
    ImageList1.ListImages.Add , "Cut", _
        LoadPicture("d:\Chapter3Code\toolbar\Cut.ico")

    'Add a separator button to the Toolbar control
    Toolbar1.Buttons.Add (10)
    Toolbar1.Buttons(10).Style = tbrSeparator

    'Add a button to the Toolbar control
    Toolbar1.Buttons.Add 11, "Cut", , , "Cut"
    Toolbar1.Buttons(11).ToolTipText = "Cut"
End Sub
```

How you use a Toolbar control depends on the type of application you are writing. An application that employs the SDI (Single Document Interface) approach interacts with the Toolbar control differently from an application based on the MDI (Multiple Document Interface).

The SDIToolbar Project

Creating a toolbar for a single Form is easy and can be done entirely at design time. The SDIToolbar project (shown in Figure 3.4) has one Form that contains a Toolbar control and an ImageList control to hold the images used on the toolbar. The Toolbar control has a TextBox and a ComboBox. The six Command Buttons on the Form demonstrate some of the toolbar's functionality, and a TextBox holds some text to manipulate. Here is a list of the Command Buttons and what they do:

Disable, Enable disables and enables the first toolbar icon.

Add Button adds an image to the ImageList control and then adds two buttons to the Toolbar control.

Remove Button removes the buttons added with the Add Button Command Button.

Customize displays the Customize Form (shown in Figure 3.2, earlier in this chapter), which allows the user to customize the look of the toolbar.

Save Toolbar saves the current toolbar configuration to the Registry.

Restore Toolbar restores the saved toolbar configuration to the Registry.

FIGURE 3.4:

The SDIToolBar project

NOTE   You'll find the SDIToolBar project in the Chapter3\SDIToolbar folder on the CD that comes with this book.

Creating the SDIToolBar Project

Toolbar controls, after they are set up, rely on code to do almost all their work. Thus, in this section we're including all the code modules so that we can discuss toolbar functionality in depth. Follow these steps to get this project rolling:

1. Start a new Visual Basic project. Form1 is created by default.

2. To Form1, add a Toolbar control, an ImageList control, a TextBox control, and six Command Buttons.

3. Draw a TextBox control and a ComboBox control on the Toolbar control.

4. Right-click the ImageList control, and click Properties to open the Property Pages.

5. Select the 16 × 16 option button to choose the small image size. Standard Windows 95 and Windows NT toolbar buttons are 16 × 16 pixels.

6. Select the Images tab, and then click the Insert Picture button.

TIP

If you use icons as images and draw them with a transparent background, the Toolbar control automatically adjusts the image to reflect the disabled state of a Button object. You'll find some of the more popular icons already drawn for you if you look in the Chapter3Code/Toolbar folder on the CD that comes with this book.

---

7. From the Chapter3Code/Toolbar folder on the CD that comes with this book, select the New, Open, Save, Print, Bold, Italic, and Underline icons. Your ImageList should look like the one in Figure 3.5.

FIGURE 3.5:

The ImageList Property Pages with images

Now that the ImageList is set, let's add the buttons to the Toolbar control.

8. Right-click the toolbar and select Properties to open the Property Pages.

9. On the General tab, select ImageList1 from the ImageList drop-down list box.

10. Select the Buttons tab. as shown in Figure 3.3, earlier in this chapter. Click the Insert Button button nine times to insert nine empty buttons.

11. Set the Caption, Key, ToolTip, and Image properties as shown in Table 3.2.

TABLE 3.2: The Toolbar Control Properties

Index	Key	Style	ToolTipText	Image
1	New	0-tbrDefault	New	1
2	Open	0-tbrDefault	Open	2
3	Save	0-tbrDefault	Save	3
4		3-tbrSeparator		
5	Print	0-tbrDefault	Print	4
6		3-tbrSeparator		
7	Bold	2-ButtonGroup	Bold	5
8	Italic	2-ButtonGroup	Italic	6
9	Underline	2-ButtonGroup	Underline	7

Changing the Form's BackColor

You must change the backcolor of the Form so that it corresponds to the value in the Combo1 combo box on the toolbar. The combo box has been drawn directly on top of the Toolbar control.

Code 3.3:   Responding to a Change in BackColor Request

```
Private Sub Combo1_Click()
    Select Case Combo1.Text
        Case "Grey"
            Form1.BackColor = &H8000000F
        Case "Yellow"
            Form1.BackColor = vbYellow
```

```
        Case "White"
            Form1.BackColor = vbWhite
        Case "Blue"
            Form1.BackColor = vbBlue
    End Select
End Sub
```

Enable and disable the Open button on the Toolbar control. If the Image associated with the Toolbar button is a transparent icon, the button will be grayed out by default.

NOTE

The ImageEdit program included with Visual Basic is a good tool to use to create icons. You'll find the ImageEdit application in the Tool\ImageEdit folder on the VB5 CD-ROM.

Code 3.4:   Changing the Enabled State of the Open Button

```
Private Sub Command1_Click()
    If Toolbar1.Buttons(1).Enabled = True Then
        Toolbar1.Buttons(1).Enabled = False
        Command1.Caption = "Enable"
    Else
        Toolbar1.Buttons(1).Enabled = True
        Command1.Caption = "Disable"
    End If
End Sub
```

Clicking Command2 displays the Customize Toolbar dialog box, in which the user can customize the look of the toolbar:

NOTE The Toolbar configuration can be saved with the SaveToolbar method, discussed later in this section.

Code 3.5:   **Displaying the Customize Toolbar Dialog Box**

```
Private Sub Command2_Click()
    Toolbar1.Customize
End Sub
```

Adding an Image and Buttons at Run Time

Command3_Click adds an image to the ImageList control and adds two buttons to the Toolbar control. One button is a separator, and the other one is the Cut button with the image added to the ImageList control.

Code 3.6:   **The Command3_Click Subroutine**

```
Private Sub Command3_Click()
    On Error Resume Next

    'Remove the separator the second time through
    Toolbar1.Buttons.Remove (10)
    'Add an image to the imagelist control
    ImageList1.ListImages.Add , "Cut", _
        LoadPicture("d:\Chapter3Code\toolbar\Cut.ico")
'Add a separator button to the toolbar control
    Toolbar1.Buttons.Add (10)
    Toolbar1.Buttons(10).Style = tbrSeparator

    'Add a button to the toolbar control
    Toolbar1.Buttons.Add 11, "Cut", , , "Cut"
    Toolbar1.Buttons(11).ToolTipText = "Cut"

End Sub
```

NOTE Change the drive letter in the LoadPicture code to match that of your CD-ROM drive.

Removing Buttons at Run Time

You can use the Remove method to remove Button objects from the Toolbar control. The following code removes two buttons from the toolbar at run time.

> **NOTE** You can use the Index, in this case 11, or you can use the Key, Cut, to access the Button objects of the Toolbar control.

Code 3.7:   The Remove Method

```
Private Sub Command4_Click()
    On Error Resume Next
    Toolbar1.Buttons.Remove (11)
    Toolbar1.Buttons.Remove (10)
End Sub
```

Saving the Toolbar Configuration to the Registry

After you customize the toolbar to fit your needs, you can save the configuration to the Windows Registry. You save the current toolbar configuration to the Registry with the SaveToolbar method. Here are the parameters:

- The key location in the Registry
- The subkey under the key
- The name of the toolbar

> **NOTE** If the key, subkey, or value you specify doesn't exist in the Registry, it is created.

Code 3.8:   The SaveToolbar Method

```
Private Sub Command5_Click()
    Toolbar1.SaveToolbar "DHBook", "Toolbar", "UserName"
End Sub
```

Restoring the Toolbar Configuration to the Registry

Visual Basic also provides a way for you to retrieve a saved toolbar. You restore the toolbar configuration to the Registry with the RestoreToolbar method. Here are the parameters:

- The key location in the Registry

- The subkey under the key

- The name of the toolbar

Code 3.9:   The RestoreToolbar Method

```
Private Sub Command6_Click()
    On Error Resume Next
    Toolbar1.RestoreToolbar "DHBook", "Toolbar", "UserName"
End Sub

Private Sub mnuExit_Click()
    End
End Sub
```

Responding to the Clicked Button

At the heart of the Toolbar control is its ability to tell you which button the user clicked. In the following code, the Key property is checked to determine which button was clicked, and the code for the action determined by that button is carried out.

Code 3.10:   Responding to a Toolbar Click

```
Private Sub Toolbar1_ButtonClick(ByVal _
    Button As ComctlLib.Button)
    On Error Resume Next
    Select Case Button.Key
        Case "New"
            MsgBox "New code goes here"
        Case "Open"
            MsgBox "Open code goes here"
        Case "Save"
            MsgBox "Save code goes here"
        Case "Print"
            MsgBox "Print code goes here"
```

```
                    Case "Bold"
                        Text1 = "Bold"
                        Text2.SelStart = 0
                        Text2.SelLength = Len(Text2.Text)
                        Text2.FontBold = True
                        Text2.FontItalic = False
                        Text2.FontUnderline = False
                    Case "Italic"
                        Text1 = "Italic"
                        Text2.SelStart = 0
                        Text2.SelLength = Len(Text2.Text)
                        Text2.FontBold = False
                        Text2.FontItalic = True
                        Text2.FontUnderline = False
                    Case "Underline"
                        Text1 = "Underline"
                        Text2.SelStart = 0
                        Text2.SelLength = Len(Text2.Text)
                        Text2.FontBold = False
                        Text2.FontUnderline = True
                        Text2.FontItalic = False
                        Case "Cut"
                                Text1 = "Cut"
                                Text2.SelStart = 0
                                Text2.SelLength = Len(Text2.Text)
                                Text2.Text - ""

            End Select
        End Sub
```

Testing the SDIToolbar Program

To start the SDIToolBar program, press F5. You'll see the screen shown in Figure 3.4, earlier in this chapter. Clicking a toolbar button displays a message box, and clicking a Command Button manipulates the toolbar.

Clicking the Disable button disables the Open toolbar button, and the caption of the Disable button changes to Enable. Notice that the look of the toolbar button changes to reflect the disabled state. Here's what happens when you click the other buttons:

- Clicking the Command button again enables the toolbar button.

- Clicking the Add Button button adds a new button to the toolbar.

- Clicking the Remove Button button removes the newly added button.

- Clicking the Customize button opens the Customize Toolbar dialog box. Select some buttons to remove, and click the Close button. The toolbar changes to reflect the new buttons.

- Clicking the Save Toolbar button saves the changes to the toolbar in the Windows Registry.

- Clicking the Restore Toolbar button restores the saved toolbar.

This is a good example of some of the Toolbar control's functionality. The use of the toolbar control in an MDI (Multiple Document Interface) application takes a little more planning.

Using the Toolbar Control in an MDI Application

Using the Toolbar control in an MDI application is different from using it in an SDI application. In an MDI application, you have an MDI form and usually more than one Child Form. These Forms share the Toolbar control and the code on the MDI Form. If the MDI Form is displayed without any visible Child Forms, you must present the toolbar buttons associated with the MDI Form. When one of the Child Forms is displayed, you need to show that child's toolbar buttons. You can do so by creating the toolbar buttons at run time, depending on the Form displayed, by:

- Calling a routine from the Form_Activate event of the Child Forms to add the proper buttons

- Calling a routine in the Query_Unload event to hide the toolbars

When a button on a Toolbar control is clicked, the code from the toolbar calls the associated menu code in the active Form. This approach keeps track of the active Form and ensures that the proper toolbar buttons are displayed. The MDIToolbar project demonstrates this toolbar approach.

The MDIToolbar Project

The MDIToolbar project (shown in Figure 3.6) has one MDI Form with a Toolbar control, an ImageList control, and two Child Forms. The Child Forms do not have Toolbar controls; they share the Toolbar control on the MDI Form.

FIGURE 3.6:

The MDIToolbar project

NOTE
You'll find the MDIToolbar project in the Chapter3\MDIToolbar folder on the CD that comes with this book.

Creating the MDIToolbar Project

As we did with the SDIToolbar project in the previous section, we are including all the code for the MDIToolbar project in this section so that you can see it working together.

Start a new VB project. Form1 is created by default. Now, follow these steps:

1. Add another Standard Form and an MDI Form.

2. Add a Toolbar control and an ImageList control to the MDI Form.

3. Set the MDIChild property of Forms 1 and 2 to True. This will make them Child Forms of the MDI Form.

4. Add a Module to the project to hold the Toolbar collection definitions.

5. To add images to the ImageList control, set the ImageSize to 16 × 16 pixels, and add the icons shown in Table 3.3.

NOTE   For help on how to add images to the ImageList control, see the section "Adding Images to the ImageList Control at Design Time," earlier in this chapter.

TABLE 3.3: The MDIToolbar ImageList Control Settings

Index	Key	File
1	New	New.ico
2	Open	Open.ico
3	Save	Save.ico
4	Print	Print.ico
5	Bold	Bld.ico
6	Italic	Itl.ico
7	Underline	Undrln.ico

NOTE   You'll find the icons in the Chapter3Code\Toolbar folder on the CD that comes with this book.

Add the menu structure in Table 3.4 to the MDI Form, add the menu structure in Table 3.5 to Form1, and add the menu structure in Table 3.6 to Form2.

TABLE 3.4: The MDIForm Menu Structure

Caption	Name	Menu Position
&File	mnuFile	Menu
&New	mnuNew	Submenu
&Open	mnuOpen	Submenu
-	Space1	Submenu
E&xit	mnuExit	Submenu

127

TABLE 3.5: The Form1 Menu Structure

Caption	Name	Menu Position
&File	mnuFile	Menu
&New	mnuNew	Submenu
&Open	mnuOpen	Submenu
-	space1	Submenu
&Save	mnuSave	Submenu
-	space2	Submenu
&Print	mnuPrint	Submenu
-	space3	Submenu
E&xit	mnuExit	Submenu
&View	mnuView	Menu
Form&2	mnuForm2	Submenu

TABLE 3.6: The Form2 Menu Structure

Caption	Name	Menu Position
&File	mnuFile	Menu
&Save	mnuSave	Submenu
&Print	mnuPrint	Submenu
-	space1	Submenu
E&xit	mnuExit	Submenu
Forma&t	mnuFormat	Menu
&Bold	mnuBold	Submenu
&Italic	mnuItalic	Submenu
&Underline	mnuUnderline	Submenu
&View	mnuView	Menu
Form&1	mnuForm1	Submenu

Defining the Buttons for the Main Toolbar

The subroutine ToolbarSetup loads the Keys for the desired buttons into the colToolbarAction collection and loads the ToolTipText, the text that you see when your mouse moves over the toolbar buttons, into the colToolbarTip collection. After this, it calls the CreateToolbar subroutine where the buttons are loaded onto the Toolbar control.

NOTE The following code is located in the MDIForm1, General Section. Since this code will be called from Form1 and Form2, be sure to change Private Sub to Public Sub.

Code 3.11   **Setting Up the Button Icons and ToolTipText Values**

```
Public Sub ToolbarSetup()
    On Error GoTo ErrorRoutineErr

    colToolbarAction.Add "New"
    colToolbarAction.Add "Separator"
    colToolbarAction.Add "Open"

    colToolbarTip.Add "New"
    colToolbarTip.Add ""
    colToolbarTip.Add "Open"

    Call MDIForm1.CreateToolbar
ErrorRoutineResume:
    Exit Sub
ErrorRoutineErr:
    MsgBox "MDIForm1.ToolbarSetup " & Err & " " & Error
End Sub
```

Creating the Toolbar Buttons at Run Time

The CreateToolbar subroutine is called from FormLoad of the MDI Form and Form_Activate of Form1 and Form2.

First, the CreateToolbar subroutine clears the buttons from the current toolbar, and then it links the Toolbar control and the ImageList control. Next, a Button object is added to the Toolbar control for each item in the colToolbarAction collection, and the ToolTipText is set. At the end of the routine, the Toolbar and ToolTip collections are set to Nothing to release their resources.

Code 3.12:   **The CreateToolbar Subroutine**

```
Public Sub CreateToolbar()
    On Error GoTo ErrorRoutineErr
    Dim slAction As Variant
    Dim slTip As Variant
    Dim slCnt
    Dim btnX As Button

    'Clear the current buttons
    Toolbar1.Buttons.Clear

    'Associate toolbar and imglist
    Toolbar1.ImageList = ImageList1
    'Clear the counter
    slCnt = 0

    'Add button objects to Buttons collection using the
    'add method. After creating each button, set
    'toolTipText properties
    For Each slAction In colToolbarAction
        slCnt = slCnt + 1
        If slAction = "Separator" Then
            Set btnX = Toolbar1.Buttons.Add(, , , tbrSeparator)
        Else
            Set btnX = Toolbar1.Buttons.Add(, slAction, , _
            tbrDefault, slAction)
            btnX.ToolTipText = colToolbarTip(slCnt)
        End If
    Next

ErrorRoutineResume:
    Set colToolbarAction = Nothing
    Set colToolbarTip = Nothing
    Exit Sub
ErrorRoutineErr:
    MsgBox "mdiForm1.CreateToolbar " & Err & " " & Error
End Sub
```

Hiding a Toolbar

The HideToolbar subroutine is called from the Query_Unload event of Form1 and Form2. It checks the Count property of the Forms collection. If the count equals two, the MDI Form will be the only Form visible when the Query_Unload event completes, so you must call ToolbarSetup to add its buttons, for the main MDI Form, to the Toolbar control.

Code 3.13:   **The HideToolbar Subroutine**

```
Public Sub HideToolbar(frm As Form)
    On Error GoTo ErrorRoutineErr

    frm.Visible = False
    'If there are only 2 Forms, show the toolbar for the
    'Main mdi Form, the other Form will be unloaded
    If Forms.Count = 2 Then
        Call ToolbarSetup
    End If

ErrorRoutineResume:
    Exit Sub
ErrorRoutineErr:
    MsgBox "mdiForm1.HideToolbar " & Err & Error
End Sub
```

Loading the Main Form

In the subroutine Form_Load, we call the ToolbarSetup routine to set up the toolbar for the main MDI Form.

Code 3.14:   **The Form_Load Subroutine**

```
Private Sub MDIForm_Load()
    'Setup the MDIToolbar
    Call ToolbarSetup
End Sub
```

Clicking the Toolbar Button

Clicking the Button object on the Toolbar control triggers the Toolbar1_ButtonClick event. All the options are prefixed with ActiveForm so that the code in the proper Form is called, and each Form can have different code for the same button. Clicking the buttons on the MDI Form generates an error because there is not an ActiveForm. The On Error Goto ErrorRoutineErr traps this error and processes code for the MDI buttons.

NOTE For this subroutine to work properly, you must change Private Sub to Public Sub for the menu code in Form1 and Form2. The MDI Form can remain private because it is in the same module as the Toolbar1_Click code.

Code 3.15:   The Toolbar1_ButtonClick Event

```
Private Sub Toolbar1_ButtonClick(ByVal Button As ComctlLib.Button)
    On Error GoTo ErrorRoutineErr

    Select Case Button.Key
        Case "New"
            ActiveForm.mnuNew_Click
        Case "Open"
            ActiveForm.mnuOpen_Click
        Case "Save"
            ActiveForm.mnuSave_Click
        Case "Print"
            ActiveForm.mnuPrint_Click
        Case "Bold"
            ActiveForm.mnuBold_Click
        Case "Italic"
            ActiveForm.mnuItalic_Click
        Case "Underline"
            ActiveForm.mnuUnderline_Click
    End Select

ErrorRoutineResume:
    Exit Sub
ErrorRoutineErr:
    'If the MDI Form is the only Form open,
    'Then there is no active Form
    If Err = 91 Then
        Select Case Button.Key
            Case "New"
                mnuNew_Click
            Case "Open"
                mnuOpen_Click
        End Select
        Err = 0
```

```
        GoTo ErrorRoutineResume
    End If

    MsgBox "MDIForm1.tbToolbar_ButtonClick" & Err & Error

End Sub
```

Defining the Toolbar Properties for Form1

TheToolbarSetup subroutine loads the Keys for the desired buttons into the colToolbarAction collection and loads the ToolTipText into the colToolbarTip collection. It then calls CreateToolbar in the MDIForm where the buttons are loaded onto the Toolbar control. The following codes is located in Form1.

Code 3.16: **The ToolbarSetup Subroutine**

```
Public Sub ToolbarSetup()
    On Error GoTo ErrorRoutineErr

    colToolbarAction.Add "New"
    colToolbarAction.Add "Open"
    colToolbarAction.Add "Save"
    colToolbarAction.Add "Separator"
    colToolbarAction.Add "Print"

    colToolbarTip.Add "New"
    colToolbarTip.Add "Open"
    colToolbarTip.Add "Save"
    colToolbarTip.Add ""
    colToolbarTip.Add "Print"

    Call MDIForm1.CreateToolbar
ErrorRoutineResume:
    Exit Sub
ErrorRoutineErr:
    MsgBox "MDIForm1.ToolbarSetup " & Err & Error
End Sub
```

Activating the Form

In the Form_Activate module, place the code to set up the toolbar for the Form. That way, whenever the Form becomes active, the proper toolbar buttons will be displayed. The following code is located in Form1.

Code 3.17:   The Form_Activate Module

```
Private Sub Form_Activate()
    Call ToolbarSetup
End Sub
```

Unloading Form1

The Form is about to be unloaded; check to see if it is the last Form. If it is, set up the buttons for the MDI Form.

Code 3.18:   The Form_QueryUnload Subroutine

```
Private Sub Form_QueryUnload(Cancel As Integer, _
    UnloadMode As Integer)
    Call MDIForm1.HideToolbar(Me)
End Sub
```

Defining the Toolbar Properties for Form2

The ToolbarSetup subroutine loads the Keys for the desired buttons into the colToolbarAction collection and loads the ToolTipText into the colToolbarTip collection. It then calls CreateToolbar in the MDIForm where the buttons are loaded onto the Toolbar control. The following code is located in Form2.

Code 3.19:   The ToolbarSetup Subroutine

```
Public Sub ToolbarSetup()
    On Error GoTo ErrorRoutineErr

    colToolbarAction.Add "Save"
    colToolbarAction.Add "Print"
    colToolbarAction.Add "Separator"
    colToolbarAction.Add "Bold"
    colToolbarAction.Add "Italic"
    colToolbarAction.Add "Underline"

    colToolbarTip.Add "Save"
    colToolbarTip.Add "Print"
    colToolbarTip.Add ""
    colToolbarTip.Add "Bold"
    colToolbarTip.Add "Italic"
    colToolbarTip.Add "Underline"
```

```
        Call MDIForm1.CreateToolbar
ErrorRoutineResume:
        Exit Sub
ErrorRoutineErr:
        MsgBox "MDIForm1.ToolbarSetup " & Err & Error
End Sub
```

Activating the Form

As we did in Form1, place the code to set up the toolbar for the Form. That way, whenever the Form becomes active, the proper toolbar buttons will be displayed.

Code 3.20: **The Form_Activate Subroutine**

```
Public Sub Form_Activate()
        Call ToolbarSetup
End Sub
```

Unloading Form2

The Form is about to be unloaded; check to see if it is the last Form. If it is, set up the buttons for the MDI Form.

Code 3.21: **The Form_QueryUnload Subroutine**

```
Public Sub Form_QueryUnload(Cancel As Integer, _
    UnloadMode As Integer)
        Call MDIForm1.HideToolbar(Me)
End Sub
```

Testing the MDIToolbar Project

To start the MDIToolbar project, press F5. You'll see the MDI Form displayed with a Toolbar control, as shown in Figure 3.6, earlier in this chapter.

NOTE   You'll find the MDIToolbar project in the Chapter3\MDIToolbar folder on the CD that comes with this book.

To test this project, follow these steps:

1. Choose View ➤ Form1 to open Form1.

Notice that the Toolbar buttons from Form1 are shown on the Toolbar control and that the Menu from Form1 replaces the MDI Forms menu (see Figure 3.7). When Form1 is activated, the code ToolbarSetup in Form1 is run. This passes a collection of buttons to the CreateToolbar subroutine in the MDI Form and tells it to change the Toolbar control's buttons.

FIGURE 3.7:

The MDI Form with Form1

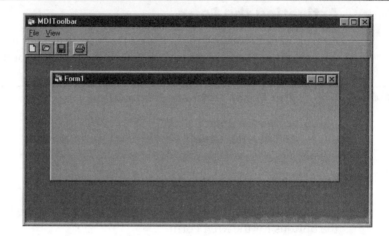

2. Choose View ➤ Form2 to open Form2 with its buttons displayed on the MDI toolbar, as shown in Figure 3.8. The same process is at work here.

FIGURE 3.8:

The MDI Form with Form2

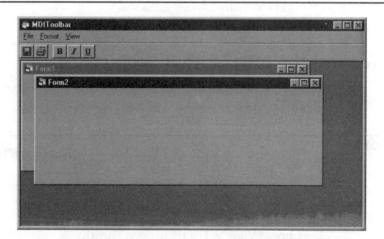

3. With both Form1 and Form2 displayed, activate each Form, and notice the toolbar buttons change. If you close both Forms, the toolbar buttons from the MDI Form are displayed. This all happens in the ToolbarSetup and CreateToolbar subroutines.

As you can see from our test, with a little work, the Toolbar control works as well in an MDI application as it does in a single Form application.

The StatusBar Control

A StatusBar control (shown in Figure 3.9) provides a window, usually at the bottom of a parent Form, through which an application can display various kinds of status data. The status bar has become a standard feature of most Windows programs.

FIGURE 3.9:

The StatusBar project

The StatusBar control is built around the Panels collection. It can be divided into a maximum of 16 Panel objects, or sections, that are contained in a Panels collection. At run time, you can dynamically change the text, images, width, and style of any Panel object. You can also add panels and remove panels from the StatusBar control. At design time, you can create panels and customize their function and style with the StatusBar Property Pages.

A feature of the StatusBar control is its ability to display key states, time, and date by setting the Style property. Table 3.7 lists and describes the values of available styles.

TABLE 3.7: The Values of the StatusBar Control

Style	Value	Description
sbrText	0	Default. Displays text and/or a bitmap image. You set text with the Text property.
sbrCaps	1	Caps Lock key. Displays the letters CAPS in bold when Caps Lock is enabled and dims them when Caps Lock is off.
sbrNumber	2	Number Lock. Displays the letters NUM in bold when Num Lock is enabled and dims them when Num Lock is off.

TABLE 3.7 (CONTINUED): The Values of the StatusBar Control

Style	Value	Description
sbrIns	3	Insert key. Displays the letters INS in bold when the Insert key is enabled and dims them when Insert mode is turned off.
sbrScrl	4	Scroll Lock key. Displays the letters SCRL in bold when Scroll Lock is enabled and dims them when Scroll Lock is off.
sbrTime	5	Time. Displays the current time in the system format.
sbr Date	6	Date. Displays the current date in the system format.
sbrKana	7	Kana. Displays the letters KANA in bold when kana lock is enabled and dims them when kana is turned off. Applies to Japanese systems only.

Use the Bevel, Autosize, and Align properties to control the appearance of the Panel objects.

- Bevel specifies whether the Panel object will have a bevel of inset, raised, or none.

- Autosize determines how a Panel object will be resized when the parent container is resized by the user.

- Align determines where the StatusBar control is placed on the Form.

Adding Panels to the StatusBar Control at Design Time

To add panels to the StatusBar control at design time, you use the StatusBar Property Pages. Follow these steps:

1. Right-click the StatusBar control and click Properties to open the Property Pages:

2. Select the Panels tab, and then click the Insert Panel button to insert a Panel object.

3. Set the Text, ToolTipText, Key, Tag, Alignment, Style, Bevel, and AutoSize properties, and add a picture, if desired.

4. Repeat steps 2 and 3 to add all the panels you need.

Adding Panels to the StatusBar Control at Run Time

To add Panel objects at run time, you use the Set statement with the Add method. Declare a *Panel* object variable and then set the object variable to a panel created with the Add method. The following code adds a panel at run time and adds the application's EXE name and a bitmap image.

Code 3.22:   **Adding Panels to the Status Bar at Run Time**

```
Private Sub Form_Load()
    'The StatusBar control is named "statusbar1."
    Dim pnlX As Panel
    Set pnlX = StatusBar1.Panels.Add()

    pnlX.Text = App.EXEName
    Set pnlX.Picture = LoadPicture _
    ("d:\Chapter3\Codetoolbar\open.ico")
End Sub
```

The StatusBar Project

The StatusBar project, as shown in Figure 3.10, displays a StatusBar control on a Form and creates a Panel object at run time for each of the panel styles, with the exception of KANA.

FIGURE 3.10:

The StatusBar project

NOTE You'll find the StatusBar project in the Chapter3\StatusBar folder on the CD that comes with this book.

The project contains one Form and a StatusBar control. It also contains two Command Buttons:

Add a Panel, which adds a Panel object that has text and a bitmap image.

Remove Panel # 2, which removes the second Panel object.

The option buttons cycle the Panel object 2 Bevel property from Inset, Raised, and None.

The StatusBar Project Code

Let's take a look at some of the more interesting code in the StatusBar project.

Adding a Panel at Run Time

The Command1_Click subroutine adds a Panel object to the StatusBar control with the Add method, and it adds an icon and sets the Panel Text property.

Code 3.23:   The Command1_Click Subroutine

```
Private Sub Command1_Click()
    'The StatusBar control is named "StatusBar1."
    Dim pnlX As Panel
    Set pnlX = StatusBar1.Panels.Add()

    pnlX.Text = App.EXEName
    Set pnlX.Picture = LoadPicture("d:\Chapter3Code\toolbar\open.ico")

    'Change some text
    StatusBar1.Panels(1).Text = "Panel Added"
End Sub
```

Removing a Panel Object at Run Time

The Command2_Click subroutine removes Panel object number2 with the Remove method. After the panel is removed, the AutoSize property is set to resize the panels.

Code 3.24: The Command2_Click Subroutine

```
Private Sub Command2_Click()

    'Remove panel 2
    StatusBar1.Panels.Remove (2)

    'Change some text
    StatusBar1.Panels(1).Text = "Panel 2 removed"

    'Set the style to AutoSize
    StatusBar1.Panels(1).AutoSize = sbrContents
End Sub
```

The AutoSize property determines the width of the Panel. The values are listed in Table 3.8.

TABLE 3.8: The Values of the AutoSize Property

Constant	Value	Description
sbrNoAutoSize	0	None. This is the default. Autosizing does not occur.
sbrSpring	1	Spring. If there is extra space in the panels as a result of resizing the Form, the panels divide up the extra space. The panels never resize smaller than the amount in the MinWidth property.
sbrContents	2	Content. Panels are resized to fit the contents but never below the MinWidth property setting.

Adding Several Panels at Run Time

When the Form is loaded, we add one Panel object and set the Style property to all the styles available, except for KANA.

Code 3.25: The Form_Load Subroutine

```
Private Sub Form_Load()
    Dim pnlX As Panel
    Dim i As Integer
    'Add six Panel objects
    For i = 1 To 6
```

```
            'Create a panel and get a reference to it simultaneously
            Set pnlX = StatusBar1.Panels.Add(, "Panel" & i)
            'Set Style property
            pnlX.Style = i
            'Set AutoSize property
            pnlX.AutoSize = sbrContents
        Next i

        Option1(0).Value = True
        StatusBar1.Panels(1).Text = "Panels created"
    End Sub
```

Changing the Bevel Property

We change the Bevel style of Panel2 based on the Option Button setting.

Code 3.26:   Changing the Bevel Property

```
    Private Sub Option1_Click(Index As Integer)
        Select Case Index
            Case 0
                'Set Panel 2 Bevel = Inset
                StatusBar1.Panels(2).Bevel = sbrInset
                StatusBar1.Panels(1).Text = "Bevel = Inset"
            Case 1
                'Set Panel 2 Bevel = Raised
                StatusBar1.Panels(2).Bevel = sbrRaised
                StatusBar1.Panels(1).Text = "Bevel = Raised"
            Case 2
                'Set Panel 2 Bevel = None
                StatusBar1.Panels(2).Bevel = sbrNoBevel
                StatusBar1.Panels(1).Text = "Bevel = None"
        End Select
    End Sub
```

Testing the StatusBar Project

Start the StatusBar program by pressing F5, and then follow these steps:

1. Click the Add a Panel button to add a panel to the end of the StatusBar control. The text in Panel 1 changes to "Panel added." Most StatusBar controls are used to display changes to their programs or environments.

2. Click the Remove Panel # 2 button to remove Panel number 2. The Remove method is used to delete the Panel object from the StatusBar control.

3. Click one of the Option Buttons to change the BevelStyle Property of Panel 2.

Status bars have become a fixture in most Windows applications, and this project demonstrates some of the flexibility of the control.

The TabStrip Control

A TabStrip control (shown in Figure 3.11) is similar to the dividers in a notebook or the labels on a group of file folders. By using a TabStrip control, you can define multiple pages for the same area of a window or dialog box in your application.

FIGURE 3.11:

A TabStrip control

The TabStrip control consists of one or more Tab objects in a Tabs collection. You can add, remove, and/or change the appearance of tabs at design time and at run time. You can also associate an ImageList control with a TabStrip control.

TabStrip Control Properties

The TabStrip control can take on the appearance of notebook tabs (Tabs) or push-buttons (Buttons). The Style property determines the appearance.

Each page in the TabStrip control consists of a tab and a client area, as shown in Figure 3.12. Visual Basic automatically determines the size and position of the internal area, or ClientArea, of the TabStrip based on the overall size of the control. This area is returned in the Client-coordinate properties of ClientLeft, ClientTop, ClientHeight, and ClientWidth.

FIGURE 3.12:

The TabStrip Control's ClientArea

The TabStrip control is not a container. You must use a Frame, a PictureBox, or some other container control to hold the actual pages. After the container controls are created, a technique is required to position them over the TabStrip control's client area. Code 3.27 uses the Move method with the ClientLeft, ClientTop, ClientHeight, and ClientWidth properties to position the containers.

Code 3.27:   Positioning the Frames

```
Public Sub ResetFrames()
    Dim i

    For i = 0 To Frame1.Count - 1
    With Frame1(i)
        .Move TabStrip1.ClientLeft, _
        TabStrip1.ClientTop, _
        TabStrip1.ClientWidth, _
        TabStrip1.ClientHeight
    End With
    Next i

End Sub
```

A TabStrip control can contain more than one Tab object; however, you must manage the Tab objects and the associated container controls. You can use the following process to do so:

1. At design time, create as many of the Tab objects as you need.

2. Create a control array of container controls, one for each Tab object.

3. On each container control, draw the controls for that page.

4. At run time, use the SelectedItem property to determine the index of the selected Tab object.

5. Use the Zorder and visible properties to bring the container control to the top and make it visible.

NOTE   If you add a Tab object at run time, you must also create a container control to hold the page controls.

Another feature of the TabStrip control is the MultiRow property. If you set this property to True, a large number of Tab objects will appear in multiple rows, as shown in Figure 3.13. If you set this property to False, the same number of tabs appear in a single row with a pair of scroll buttons at the end, as shown in Figure 3.14.

FIGURE 3.13:

A TabStrip control with multiple rows

FIGURE 3.14:

A TabStrip control with a single row

Associating an ImageList Control with the TabStrip Control

To identify a tab, you can assign an image from the ImageList control to the Tab object. First, associate the ImageList control with the TabStrip control. You can do so at design time or at run time.

To associate an ImageList control with a TabStrip control at design time, follow these steps:

1. Populate the ImageList control with images.

2. Right-click the TabStrip control and choose Properties to open the TabStrip Property Pages:

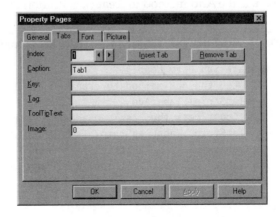

NOTE   You could build the Property Pages with a TabStrip control.

3. Select the General tab, and then select the ImageList control from the ImageList box.

To associate an ImageList control with a TabStrip control at run time, set the ImageList property to the ImageList control.

Code 3.28:   Associating the ImageList with TabStrip at Run Time

```
Private Sub Form_Load()
        TabStrip1.ImageList = ImageList1
End Sub
```

Creating Tabs at Design Time

Follow these steps to create Tab objects at design time:

1. Right-click the TabStrip control, and choose Properties to display the Property Pages.

2. Select the Tabs tab.

3. Click Insert Tab to add a Tab object.

4. Set the Caption, Key, Tag, ToolTipText, and Image properties to customize the Tab object.

Creating Tabs at Run Time

You use the Add method to create a collection of Tab objects at run time.

Code 3.29:   Adding Tab Objects at Run Time with the Add Method

```
Private Sub Form_Load()
    'Use the Add method to create a new Tab object
    TabStrip1.Tabs.Add
    'Count gets the last tab added
    TabStrip1.Tabs(TabStrip1.Tabs.Count).Caption = "Printer"
    TabStrip1.Tabs(TabStrip1.Tabs.Count).Image = "Print"
    TabStrip1.Tabs(TabStrip1.Tabs.Count).Key = "Print"
End Sub
```

The TabStrip Project

The TabStrip project (shown in Figure 3.15) demonstrates a TabStrip control at work. It shows how to add and remove Tab objects at run time, demonstrates the procedures to keep all the containers associated with the correct pages, and demonstrates the MultiRow property.

FIGURE 3.15:

The TabStrip project

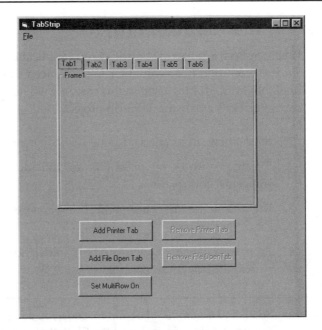

NOTE

You'll find the TabStrip project in the Chapter3\TabStrip folder on the CD that comes with this book.

This project consists of a Form with a TabStrip control. Each TabStrip control has a Frame associated with it to hold the page. Five Command Buttons are included:

- **Add Printer Tab** adds a Tab object at run time. The Caption of the Tab contains text and a bitmap image. The image is retrieved from an ImageList control.

- **Remove Printer Tab** removes the Printer Tab object.

- **Add File Open Tab** adds a Tab object at run time. The caption of the tab contains text and a bitmap image. The image is retrieved from an ImageList control.

- **Remove File Open Tab** removes the File Open Tab object.

- **Set MultiRow On** toggles the MultiRow property on and off.

Creating the TabStrip Project

When you use a TabStrip control in your application, keep in mind that the TabStrip control is not a container. You will need some other container control to hold the control for the user. In this case, we will use the Frame control as our container. Let's create the TabStrip project.

1. Start a new project and add one TabStrip control.

2. Create a control array of six Frames, and add five Command Buttons and an ImageList control.

3. Right-click the ImageList control, and choose Properties to display the Property Pages.

4. From the Chapter3Code\TabStrip folder, add an Open icon and a Printer icon to the ImageList control.

NOTE   You'll find a number of common icons you can use in your projects in the Chapter3\TabStrip folder on the CD that comes with this book.

---

4. Right-click the TabStrip control, and click Properties to display the Property Pages.

5. Select the General tab, and then select ImageList1 from the ImageList box.

6. Select the Tabs tab, and click the Insert Tab button five times to add five Tab objects. Tab 1 is created by default.

7. Set the Caption property of each Tab object to Tab and the index of the tab. Tab1 should have a Caption property set to Tab1; Tab2 caption is Tab2. Do this for each Tab object.

Moving the Frames to the Client Area

The ResetFrames subroutine moves the Frames to the ClientArea of the Tab by looping through the frames and aligning them with the ClientArea of the TabStrip control.

Code 3.30:   The Reset Frames Subroutine

```
Public Sub ResetFrames()
    Dim i

    For i = 0 To Frame1.Count - 1
    With Frame1(i)
        .Move TabStrip1.ClientLeft, _
        TabStrip1.ClientTop, _
        TabStrip1.ClientWidth, _
        TabStrip1.ClientHeight
    End With
    Next i

End Sub
```

Adding a Tab at Run Time

The Command1_Click subroutine adds a new Printer Tab object and then sets properties on the new tab. After the Tab is created, the frames are reset by calling the ResetFrames subroutine.

Code 3.31:   Creating a Printer Tab Object

```
Private Sub Command1_Click()

    'Use the Add method to create a new Tab object
    TabStrip1.Tabs.Add
    TabStrip1.Tabs(TabStrip1.Tabs.Count).Caption = "Printer"
    TabStrip1.Tabs(TabStrip1.Tabs.Count).Image = "Print"
    TabStrip1.Tabs(TabStrip1.Tabs.Count).Key = "Print"

    'Reset the frames
    Call ResetFrames

    Command1.Enabled = False
    Command2.Enabled = True
End Sub
```

Deleting a Tab at Run Time

The Command2_Click subroutine deletes the Print Tab object with the Remove Method and calls ResetFrames. If the TabStrip control has a large number of Tab objects, you will need to realign them.

Code 3.32: **Deleting a Tab Object**

```vb
Private Sub Command2_Click()
    'If you delete the current tab,
    'make Frame1(0) visible
    If TabStrip1.SelectedItem.Index = TabStrip1.Tabs.Count Then
        Frame1(0).Visible = True
    End If

    'Remove the printer tab
    TabStrip1.Tabs.Remove ("Print")

    'Set the command buttons
    Command1.Enabled = True
    Command2.Enabled = False

    'Reset the frames
    Call ResetFrames

End Sub
```

Adding a Tab with the Add Method

The Command3_Click subroutine uses the Add method to create a new File Open Tab object. The Add Method allows you to combine the add and property settings into one command. The Add method has the following parameters:

Object, which is a TabStrip control.

Index, which is optional and is an integer specifying the position where you want to insert the tab.

Key, which is optional and is a unique string that identifies the tab. Use Key to retrieve a specific tab.

Caption, which is optional and is the string that appears on the tab.

Image, which is optional and is the index of an image in an associated ImageList control.

Code 3.33:   **Adding a Tab Object with the Add Method**

```
Private Sub Command3_Click()
    'Use the Add method to create a new Tab object
    'This is the same as in the Command1 Printer add except
    'it is all in one command
    TabStrip1.Tabs.Add TabStrip1.Tabs.Count + 1, _
        "Open", "Open File Tab", "Open"

    'Reset the frames
    Call ResetFrames

    Command3.Enabled = False
    Command4.Enabled = True
End Sub
```

Setting the MultiRow Property

The Command5_Click subroutine toggles the MultiRow property on and off. If you set the MultiRow property to True, a large number of Tab objects will appear in multiple rows, as shown in Figure 3.16 earlier in this chapter. If you set this property to False, the same number of tabs appear in a single row with a pair of scroll buttons at the end, as shown in Figure 3.17 earlier in this chapter.

Code 3.34:   **Setting the MultiRow Options**

```
Private Sub Command5_Click()
    If TabStrip1.MultiRow = True Then
        TabStrip1.MultiRow = False
        Command5.Caption = "Set MultiRow On"
    Else
        TabStrip1.MultiRow = True
        Command5.Caption = "Set MultiRow Off"
    End If
    Call ResetFrames
End Sub
```

Clicking a Tab

The TabStrip1_Click subroutine checks for the current tab and makes the associated frame visible and puts it at the top of the Zorder. Make all other frames invisible.

Code 3.35:   **Maintaining the Correct Frame**

```
Private Sub TabStrip1_Click()
    Dim i

    'Loop through the tabs
    For i = 0 To Frame1.Count - 1
        If TabStrip1.SelectedItem.Index = i + 1 Then
            'Make the current frame visible
            Frame1(i).Visible = True
            Frame1(i).ZOrder 0
        Else
            'All others are invisible
            Frame1(i).Visible = False
        End If
    Next
End Sub
```

The previous code loops through the Frame controls one at a time. When the current frame is located, it is made visible and moved to the top of the stack. All other frames are rendered invisible.

Testing the TabStrip Project

To test the TabStrip project, press F5 to run the project and then follow these steps:

1. Click the six tabs, and notice that the Frame associated with the tab is visible and lined up in the Tab object's ClientArea.

2. Test the other features by clicking the Add and Remove buttons.

3. Try this with the MultiRow property on and again with the MultiRow property turned off. If your project must remain in a limited area, setting MultiRow off can save space.

TabStrip controls have become permanent features in most Windows applications as dialog boxes and list containers. In fact, the use of TabStrip controls for dialog boxes will help your programs maintain the Windows standard.

The Slider Control

The Slider control (shown in Figure 3.16) is a window containing a slider and optional tickmarks. You can move the slider by dragging it, clicking the mouse to either side of the slider, or using the keyboard.

FIGURE 3.16:

The Slider control

A Slider control consists of a scale defined by the Min and Max properties and a "knob" that can be moved by using the mouse or arrow keys. You can set the Min and Max properties of the Slider control at run time to dynamically change the range of the control.

The appearance of the Slider is controlled by the TickStyle and TickFrequency properties. Set the ticks (shown in Figure 3.17) according to Table 3.9.

FIGURE 3.17:

The Slider control tickmarks

TABLE 3.9: The Properties of the Slider Tick Style

Constant	Value	Description
sldBottomRight	0	Bottom/Right. Tickmarks are positioned along the bottom of the slider if the control is oriented horizontally or along the right side if it is oriented vertically.
sldTopLeft	1	Top/Left. Tickmarks are positioned along the top of the slider if the control is oriented horizontally or along the left side if it is oriented vertically.
sldBoth	2	Both. Tickmarks are positioned on both sides or the top and the bottom of the slider.
sldNoTicks	3	None. No tickmarks appear on the slider.

The TickFrequency property returns or sets the frequency of tickmarks on a Slider control in relation to its range. For example, if the range is 100 and the TickFrequency property is set at 2, there will be one tick for every 2 increments in the range and a total of 50 ticks.

Setting the Min and Max Properties at Design Time

The Min and Max properties determine the minimum and maximum limits of the Slider control. To set these properties at design time, right-click the control and choose Properties to open the Property Pages:

Setting the Min and Max Properties at Run Time

To set the Min and Max properties at run time, you can use Code 3.36.

Code 3.36:   Setting Min and Max Properties

```
Private Sub Command2_Click()
    Slider1.Min = 100
    Slider1.Max = 1000
End Sub
```

Changing the Position of the Slider Knob

In addition to adjusting the TickStyle, TickFrequency, Min, and Max properties, you can adjust the SmallChange and LargeChange properties to determine how the slider control increments and decrement. The SmallChange property sets the number of ticks the slider will move when you press the left or right arrow keys, and the LargeChange property sets the number of ticks the slider will move when you press the Page Up or Page Down keys or when you click the mouse to the left or the right of the slider.

Selecting Ranges with the Slider

As you have seen, you can use the Slider control to select a value between the Min and Max properties. You can also use the Slider control to select a range of values by setting the SelStart and SelLength properties. When a range of values is selected, the Slider changes its appearance (as shown in Figure 3.18) to notify the user that it is ready to accept a range. If the user presses the Shift key while clicking the Slider control, the MouseDown event occurs. Code in that event sets the SelectRange and SelStart properties. When the user releases the mouse button, the MouseUp event occurs, and in that code the SelLength property is set, from which a range of values can be extracted.

FIGURE 3.18:

The Slider control in
Selected mode

The Slider Project

The Slider project (shown in Figure 3.19) sets the caption of a Label control according to the value of the Slider control. The Slider project has one Command Button that is used to toggle between selecting a single value and selecting a range of values.

NOTE　　You'll find the TabStrip project in the Chapter3\TabStrip folder on the CD that comes with this book.

FIGURE 3.19:

The Slider project

The Slider Project Code

Let's take a look at some of the code in the Slider project that demonstrates how to set the Minimum and Maximum values and to select a range of values.

Showing the Slider's Value

The Scroll event is triggered whenever the knob of the Slider is moved. As the knob is moved, we put the value in a label.

```
Private Sub Slider1_Scroll()
    lblValue = Slider1.Value
End Sub
```

Getting the SelStart

When the SelRange property of the Slider control is True and the user presses Shift and clicks the control, the MouseDown event is triggered. In the MouseDown subroutine, we capture the starting point, the SelStart property, and put it into the label property of lblMinValue.

Code 3.37:   The MouseDown Subroutine

```
Private Sub Slider1_MouseDown(Button As Integer, Shift _
    As Integer, x As Single, y As Single)

    If Shift = 1 Then
```

```
        Slider1.SelStart = Slider1.Value
        lblMinValue = Slider1.Value
        ' Set previous SelLength (if any) to 0.
        Slider1.SelLength = 0
    End If

End Sub
```

Getting the SelLength

When the user releases the mouse button, the MouseUp event is triggered. In the MouseUp event, the SelLength and SelStart properties are captured and put into labels.

Code 3.38: **The MouseUp Event**

```
Private Sub Slider1_MouseUp(Button As Integer, _
    Shift As Integer, x As Single, y As Single)

    If Shift = 1 Then
    ' If user selects backwards from a point,
    ' an error will occur.
    On Error Resume Next
    ' Else set SelLength using SelStart and
    ' current value.
        Slider1.SelLength = _
        Slider1.Value - Slider1.SelStart
    Else
        'If user lifts SHIFT key, set SelLength
        ' to 0 (to deselect the SelRange) and exit.
        Slider1.SelLength = 0
    End If
    lblLengthValue = Slider1.SelLength
    lblMaxValue = Slider1.Value
End Sub
```

Testing the Slider Program

There is only one button to work with in the Slider application, and it toggles the Range property on and off. To test the Slider project, follow these steps:

1. Press F5 to start the project.

2. Click the slider knob and move it to the right. Notice that the Current Value is increased. Move the slider knob to the left, and the value goes down.

3. Click the Select Range button, and the Slider control expands to notify you that it is in the SelectRange mode.

4. Press and hold the Shift key, click the Slider knob and move it to the right about midway, release the mouse button, and then release the Shift key. Notice that the Min, Max, and Length values are now the labels in the Ranges frame, as shown in Figure 3.20.

FIGURE 3.20:

The Slider project in SelectRange mode

Well, that's about all there is to the Slider control. Not very difficult, but a great tool with which you can set values and limits in your applications.

The ProgressBar Control

The ProgressBar control (shown in Figure 3.21) shows the progress of a lengthy operation by filling a rectangle with chunks from left to right. A ProgressBar control allows your application to graphically represent the progress of an operation, such as:

- Copying or transferring a file
- Sorting a huge database
- Loading a long or complex array or collection with data
- Performing any task that takes more that a few seconds

FIGURE 3.21:

A ProgressBar
control

If users have no indication that an operation is taking place, they may assume that the application has stopped responding. Also, when users get feedback, they feel that the operation is taking less time than it actually is. The ProgressBar is a great tool to use for that reason.

The Value property determines how much of the control has been filled, and the Min and Max properties set the minimum and maximum points.

Setting the Value Property and Min and Max Properties to Show Progress

To show the progress of a lengthy operation, the Value property is continually increased until the value in the Max property is met. The number of blocks displayed in the ProgressBar control is a ratio of the Value property to the Min and Max properties. You can use Code 3.39 to display a ProgressBar and show the progress.

Code 3.39:   The ProgressBar

```
Private Sub Command1_Click()
    On Error Resume Next
    Dim Progress As Integer

    Dim TestArray(2250) As String
    ProgressBar1.Min = LBound(TestArray)
    ProgressBar1.Max = UBound(TestArray)
    ProgressBar1.Visible = True

    'Set the Progress's Value to Min.
    ProgressBar1.Value = ProgressBar1.Min

    'Loop through the array.
    For Progress = LBound(TestArray) To UBound(TestArray)
        'Set initial values for each item in the array.
```

```
            'Workarea(Counter) = "Initial value" & Counter
            ProgressBar1.Value = Progress
        Next Progress
        ProgressBar1.Visible = False
        ProgressBar1.Value = ProgressBar1.Min
    End Sub
```

The ProgressBar Project

We will use the ProgressBar project (shown in Figure 3.22) to demonstrate the use of the ProgressBar control.

FIGURE 3.22:

The ProgressBar project

> **NOTE**
>
> You'll find the ProgressBar project in the Chapter3\ProgressBar folder on the CD that comes with this book.

This project consists of one Form, a Slider control to set the Max value of the ProgressBar, and a ProgressBar control. (See the previous section, "The Slider Project," for a complete discussion of the Slider control.)

There is also a label to show the value of the Slider control. One Command Button is provided to start the ProgressBar. The ProgressBar control notifies you of the progress as a counter advances from zero to the value of the Slider control.

The ProgressBar Code

Let's take a look at the code used to actually start the ProgressBar and give the users some feedback about the status of an operation.

Moving the ProgressBar

The *Counter* variable is set to the Slider's Value property. The Min property is set to zero, and the Max property is set to the value of the Slider control. The counter starts at the Min value and counts by one until it reaches the Max. As the counter advances, the ProgressBar is set to the value of the counter.

Code 3.40: Setting ProgressBar Values

```
Private Sub Command1_Click()
    On Error Resume Next

    Dim Counter As Integer

    ProgressBar1.Min = 0
    ProgressBar1.Max = Slider1.Value
    ProgressBar1.Visible = True

    'Set the Progress's Value to Min.
    ProgressBar1.Value = ProgressBar1.Min

    'Loop until Slider1.Value is met
    For Counter = Slider1.Min To Slider1.Value
        ProgressBar1.Value = Counter
    Next Counter

    ProgressBar1.Visible = False
    ProgressBar1.Value = ProgressBar1.Min
End Sub
```

As you can see, the ProgressBar control is not a difficult control to program, and it helps provide the user with feedback that draws attention away from what might be a lengthier-than-usual operation.

Testing the ProgressBar Project

To test the ProgressBar project, follow these steps:

1. Press F5 to start the project.

2. Move the Slider knob to the right.

3. Click the Process Array button.

The ProgressBar has become a staple in the developer's bag of tools. Almost every application that performs an operation that takes more than a couple of seconds calls on the ProgressBar control to keep users informed of the progress. It does not require a lot of code, and the return is an informed user.

The TreeView and ListView Controls

A TreeView control displays a hierarchical list of Node objects, each of which consists of a label and an optional bitmap. A TreeView typically displays any information that might benefit from a hierarchical arrangement, for example:

- The headings in a document

- The entries in an index

- The files and directories on a disk

The left side of the Windows Explorer (File Manager) and the Windows Registry Editor are examples of the TreeView control.

The ListView control displays items using one of four views:

- In Icon view, which is the default, each ListItem object is represented by a full-sized icon and a text label.

- In SmallIcon view, small icons represent the ListItems, and a text label appears to the right of the icon. Each ListItem appears horizontally.

- In List view, small icons represent the ListItems, and a text label appears to the right of the icon. Each ListItem appears vertically and on its own line with information arranged in columns.

- In Report view, each ListItem is displayed with its small icons and text labels. Additional information can be added in columns with optional column headings.

The right side of the Windows Explorer (File Manager) and the Windows Registry Editor are examples of the ListView control.

The TreeView control is often used with the ListView control. The combination allows the end user to look through several hierarchical layers, with the TreeView displaying the larger structure and the ListView displaying the individual sets of records as each Node object is selected, as shown in Figure 3.23.

FIGURE 3.23:

TreeView and
ListView controls

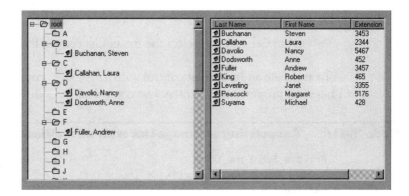

Let's take a look at the individual controls before we examine them together in a project.

The TreeView Control

The TreeView control (shown in Figure 3.24) is designed to display data that is hierarchical in nature, such as lists of names, database records, or a phone list. A tree is composed of cascading branches of "nodes" that can consist of images, set with an ImageList, and text.

FIGURE 3.24:

A TreeView control

Associating an ImageList Control with the TreeView Control

To identify a Node, you can assign an image from the ImageList control to the TreeView control. First, associate the ImageList control with the TreeView control. You can do so at design time or at run time. Follow these steps:

1. Populate the ImageList control with images.

2. Right-click the TreeView control, and choose Properties to open the TabStrip Property Pages.

3. On the General tab, select the ImageList control from the ImageList box.

To associate an ImageList control with a TreeView control at run time, set the ImageList property to the ImageList control, as in Code3.41.

Code 3.41: **Associating an ImageList with a TreeView Control at Run Time**

```
Private Sub Form_Load()
        TreeView1.ImageList = ImageList1
End Sub
```

All about Nodes

As we have already discussed, a tree is composed of cascading branches of "nodes" that can consist of images, set with an ImageList, and text. These nodes belong to the Nodes collection. After you create a TreeView control, you can add, remove, rearrange, expand, collapse, and manipulate nodes in code.

Adding Node Objects to the Nodes Collection

To add a node to the tree, you can use the Add method, whose syntax is:

```
object.Add(relative, relationship, key, text, image, selectedimage)
```

The Add method can take the arguments shown in Table 3.10.

TABLE 3.10: The Arguments of the Add Method (Nodes Collection)

Argument	Description
object	Required. An object expression that evaluates to an object in the Applies To list.
relative	Optional. The index number or key of a preexisting Node object. The relationship between the new node and this preexisting node is found in the relationship argument.
relationship	Optional. Specifies the relative placement of the node object, as described in Settings.
key	Optional. A unique string that can be used to retrieve the Node with the Item method.
text	Required. The string that appears in the node.

TABLE 3.10: The Arguments of the Add Method (Nodes Collection) (continued)

Argument	Description
image	Optional. The index of an image in an associated ImageList control.
selectedimage	Optional. The index of an image in an associated ImageList control that is shown when the node is selected.

Table 3.11 shows the settings for node relationships.

TABLE 3.11: The Node Relationship Settings for the Add Method

Constant	Value	Description
tvwFirst	0	First. The node is placed before all other nodes at the same level of the node named in relative.
tvwLast	1	Last. The node is placed after all other nodes at the same level of the node named in relative. Any node added subsequently may be placed after one added as Last.
tvwNext	2	(Default) Next. The node is placed after the node named in relative.
tvwPrevious	3	Previous. The node is placed before the node named in relative.
tvwChild	4	Child. The node becomes a child node of the node named in relative.

Because the Add method returns a reference to the newly created Node object, it is most convenient to set properties of the new node using this reference. Code 3.42 can be used to add nodes to the Nodes collection at run time.

Code 3.42:   Adding Nodes

```
Private Sub Form_Load()

    'Declare the Node object
    Dim nodX As Node

    'Add Root Node object
    Set nodX = TreeView1.Nodes.Add(, 4, , "root", "closed")
    'Add an A, child node
    Set nodX = TreeView1.Nodes.Add(1, tvwChild, , "A", "closed")
```

```
    'Set the Enabled property
    nodex.Enabled = True
End Sub
```

This code adds a Root node and an "A" child node under the Root and sets the Enabled property of the child node to True.

Another Way to Add Nodes

You can also add nodes using the Set statement with the Add method. The Set statement sets the object variable to the new node as shown in Code 3.43. After the Set statement is used, other properties can be set.

Code 3.43:   Using "Set" and "Add" to Add a Node

```
Private Sub Command5_Click()
    Dim nodex As Node
    Set nodX = TreeView1.Nodes.Add("1 node", tvwChild)
    nodX.Key = "New Node"
    nodX.Tesx = "Added Node"
    nodX.Image = "Closed"
End Sub
```

Node Relationships

Each node can be either a parent or a child, depending on its relationship with other nodes. If a node has child nodes, it can be expanded or collapsed. A tree can have any number of child nodes, but there can be only one Root node. You can use Code 3.44 to expand all the nodes of a TreeView control.

Code 3.44:   Expanding Nodes

```
Private Sub Command4_Click()
    Dim i As Integer

    For i = 1 To TreeView1.Nodes.Count - 1
        TreeView1.Nodes(i).Expanded = True
    Next
End Sub
```

As you can see, we loop through all the nodes and set the Expand property to True. This causes the nodes to expand as shown in Figure 3.25.

FIGURE 3.25:

A TreeView control with collapsed and expanded nodes

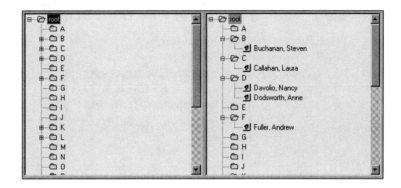

To collapse nodes, you use code that loops through the nodes and sets the Expand property to False:

Code 3.45:   Collapsing All Nodes

```
Private Sub Command2_Click()
    Dim i As Integer

    For i = 1 To TreeView1.Nodes.Count - 1
        TreeView1.Nodes(i).Expanded = False
    Next

End Sub
```

Finding Items in a TreeView Control

The TreeView control does not have a defined Find method, so we're on our own. To find a specific item in a node, you can loop through the nodes and compare the node text to a text string. Code 3.46 shows one way to accomplish this. Here are the steps:

1. Loop through the nodes one by one.

2. When you find the string, use the EnsureVisible method to scroll the tree to the node that has the string you want.

3. Set the Selected property to True to highlight the text.

Code 3.46:   **Finding a String in a TreeView Control**

```
Private Sub Command1_Click()
    Dim i As Integer
    For i = 1 To TreeView1.Nodes.Count - 1
        If TreeView1.Nodes(i).Text = Text1.Text Then
            TreeView1.Nodes(i).EnsureVisible
            TreeView1.Nodes(i).Selected = True
            Exit Sub
        End If
    Next
    MsgBox "No match found"
End Sub
```

You can use this procedure to find text in any node on the tree.

Now that you understand the TreeView control and some basic Node fundamentals, let's take a look at the ListView control. We'll then pull it all together in a sample project.

The ListView Control

The ListView control (shown in Figure 3.26) displays data as ListItem objects. Each ListItem object can have an associated icon. The control is best at displaying items of data, such as database records, lists, and indexes.

FIGURE 3.26:

The ListView control

Views

The ListView control can display data in different views, as listed in Table 3.12. Each view has its advantages and is suited for different data.

TABLE 3.12: Views of the ListView Control

Constant	Value	Description
lvwIcon	0	(Default) Icon. Each ListItem object is represented by a full-sized icon and text.
lvwSmallIcon	1	SmallIcon. Each ListItem is represented by a small icon that appears to the right of the item. The items appear horizontally.
LvwList	2	List. Each ListItem is represented by a small icon and text that appears to the right of the icon. Each ListItem appears vertically and on its own line with information arranged in columns.
lvwReport	3	Report. Each ListItem is displayed with its small icons and text. The icons, text labels, and information appear in columns, with the leftmost column containing the small icon, followed by the text. Additional columns display the text for each of the item's subitems.

Figures 3.27, 3.28, 3.29, and 3.30 show the ListView views.

FIGURE 3.27:

The ListView Icon view

FIGURE 3.28:

The ListView Small
Icon view

FIGURE 3.29:

The ListView
List view

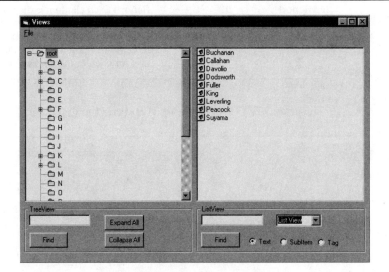

FIGURE 3.30:

The ListView Report
Icon view

Associating an ImageList with the ListView Control

The ListView control, unlike other controls, can use two ImageList controls:

- A ListItem object, which consists of a label and an optional image supplied by an ImageList

- The ImageList control, which is associated to the ListView with the Icons and SmallIcons properties

In the List, SmallIcon, and Report views, you can use a small icon as an image for the ListItem object. You can associate the ImageList control at run time or at design time.

ImageList and the List, SmallIcon, and Report Views   To associate an ImageList control with a ListView control in the List, SmallIcon, or Report view, at design time, follow these steps:

1. Populate the ImageList control with images.

2. Right-click the ListView control and choose Properties to open the ListView Property Pages:

3. In the Image Lists tab, select the ImageList control from the Small ImageList box.

To associate an ImageList control with a ListView control at run time, set the SmallIcons property to the ImageList control.

Code 3.47: Associating an ImageList at Run Time

```
Private Sub Form_Load()
    ListView1.SmallIcons = ImageListSmall
End Sub
```

ImageList and the Icon View   When the ListView control is in the Icon view, it uses a different set of images supplied by a second ImageList control. You can set the ImageList control at design time by following the procedure discussed earlier and choose the images from the Normal Icon Image List list box or at run time with the following code.

Code 3.48: Associating a Second ImageList at Run Time

```
Private Sub Form_Load()
    ListView1.Icons = ImageListIcons
End Sub
```

The Report View Has Column Headers

As an added feature, the Report view has the ability to display column headers, as shown in Figure 3.31.

FIGURE 3.31:

The ListView control column headers

The control contains a ColumnHeader object. There is always one column in the ListView control, which is Column 1. This column contains the ListItem objects. The other columns contain subitems. You can add ColumnHeaders with the Add method.

Code 3.49: Adding ColumnHeaders to a ListView Control

```
Private Sub Command5_Click()
    'Create an object variable for the ColumnHeader object
    Dim clmX As ColumnHeader
    'Add ColumnHeaders. The width of the columns
    'is the width of the control divided by the
    'number of ColumnHeader objects
```

```
        Set clmX = ListView1.ColumnHeaders. _
            Add(, , "Last Name", ListView1.Width / 3)
        Set clmX = ListView1.ColumnHeaders. _
            Add(, , "First Name", ListView1.Width / 3)
        Set clmX = ListView1.ColumnHeaders. _
            Add(, , "Extension", ListView1.Width / 3)
    End Sub
```

Here, we declare a ColumnHeader object and then use the Add method to add three ColumnHeaders.

SubItems

In all the list views, except the Report view, the ListItem object displays only one label. In the Report view, ListItems can have any number of other text items.

The number of ColumnHeader objects determines the number of subitems each ListItem object in the control can have, and the number of subitems is always one less than the number of ColumnHeader objects. When you delete a ColumnHeader object, all subitems associated with the column are also deleted. Each ListItem object's subitem array shifts to update the indices of the ColumnHeader, causing the remaining column headers' SubItemIndex properties to change. Subitems are arrays of strings representing the ListItem object's data that are displayed in Report view. For example, in Figure 3.30, First Name and Extension are subitems.

A ListItem object can have any number of associated item data strings (subitems), but each ListItem object must have the same number of subitems.

Corresponding column headers are defined for each subitem.

You cannot add elements directly to the subitems array. Use the Add method of the ColumnHeaders collection to add subitems.

Code 3.50:   Adding SubItems to a ListView Control

```
Private Sub Command5_Click()
    Dim itmX As ListItem
    'Use the Add method to add a new ListItem
    'and set an object variable to the new _
    'reference
    'Use the reference to set properties
    Set itmX = ListView1.ListItems.Add(, , "Buchanan")
    intCount = intCount + 1
    itmX.Tag = intCount
```

```
'Set SubItem 1 to FirstName
itmX.SubItems(1) = "Steven"

'Set SubItem 2 to Extension
itmX.SubItems(2) = "3453"

End Sub
```

This code declares a ListItem object and then adds a ListItem object and two subitems.

Finding Items in a ListView Control

Another nice feature of the ListView control is the FindItem method. The FindItem method finds and returns a reference to a ListItem object in a ListView control. Once the item is found, you can use the EnsureVisible method to scroll the found item into view. The syntax for the FindItem method is:

```
object.FindItem (string, value, index, match)
```

The FindItem method syntax has the parts shown in Table 3.13, the values shown in Table 3.14, and the match settings shown in Table 3.15.

TABLE 3.13: The Part of the FindItem Method

Part	Description
object	Required. An object expression that evaluates to a ListView control.
string	Required. A string expression indicating the ListItem object to be found.
value	Optional. An integer or a constant specifying whether the string will be matched to the ListItem object's Text, Subitems, or Tag property, as described in Settings.
index	Optional. An integer or a string that uniquely identifies a member of an object collection and specifies the location from which to begin the search. The integer is the value of the Index property; the string is the value of the Key property. If no index is specified, the default is 1.
match	Optional. An integer or a constant specifying that a match will occur if the item's Text property is the same as the string, as described in Table 3.14.

TABLE 3.14: The FindItem Settings

Constant	Value	Description
lvwText	0	(Default) Matches the string with a ListItem object's Text property.
lvwSubitem	1	Matches the string with any string in a ListItem object's SubItems property.
lvwTag	2	Matches the string with any ListItem object's Tag property.

TABLE 3.15: The FindItem Match Settings

Constant	Value	Description
lvwWholeWord	0	(Default) An integer or a constant specifying that a match will occur if the item's Text property begins with the whole word being searched. Ignored if the criterion is not text.
lvwPartial	1	An integer or a constant specifying that a match will occur if the item's Text property begins with the string being searched. Ignored if the criterion is not text.

Code 3.51 demonstrates how you can use the FindItem and the EnsureVisible methods to locate an item. Here are the steps:

1. Create a reference to hold the found item.

2. Use the FindItem method to find the requested item.

3. Use the EnsureVisibility method to scroll the ListView control so that the item is in view.

Code 3.51: **Finding an Item in the ListView Control**

```
Private Sub Command5_Click()

    'FindItem method returns a reference to the found item, so
    'you must create an object variable and set the found item
    'to it

    ' FoundItem variable
    Dim itmFound As ListItem
```

```
                    Set itmFound = ListView1. _
                    FindItem("Steven", lvwText, , lvwPartial)

                    'Scroll ListView to show found ListItem.
                    itmFound.EnsureVisible
                    itmFound.Selected = True
                    'Return focus to the control to see selection.
                    ListView1.SetFocus
                    End If
                End Sub
```

The List Project

As you can see from the sections on the TreeView and ListView controls, you can use these controls to present all sorts of data to users in ways that make it easy to view, select, and find just the right data when it is needed. The List project (shown in Figure 3.32) uses the TreeView and ListView controls to display the Employee's table from the NWIND sample database.

NOTE   You'll find the List project in the Chapter3Code\List folder on the CD that comes with this book. The NWIND sample database comes with Visual Basic and is installed by default in the main Visual Basic directory.

FIGURE 3.32:

The List project

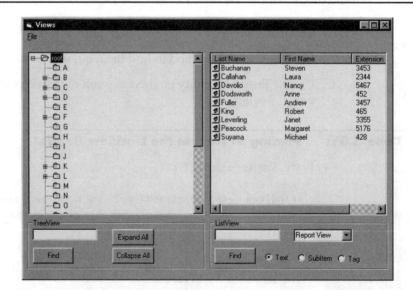

The TreeView Side

The TreeView control is on the left side of the List Form and has a text box in which you can enter a text string. It also has three Command Buttons:

Find searches through the nodes of the TreeView control for a string value. If it is found, it is selected, and the EnsureVisibility method is used to expand the node and scroll it into view.

Expand All expands all nodes in the TreeView control.

Collapse All collapses all nodes in the TreeView control.

The ListView Side

The ListView control is on the right side of the List Form and has the following controls:

TextBox, which you use to enter a text string to find.

ComboBox, which you use to select from one of the four available views:

- Icon
- SmallIcon
- List
- Report

FindButton, which searches the ListView control for a text string, subitem, or tag as selected by one of three option buttons:

Text, which searches for a text string in the ListItem.

SubItem, which searches for a text string in a subitem.

Tag, which searches for a text string in a tag.

Filling the Controls

The FillList subroutine populates the TreeView and ListView controls with data. A Data control is used to create a recordset of the records from the Employee table in the NWIND sample database. After the records are retrieved, the column headings for the Report view of the ListView are set with the ColumnHeaders property. To ensure a clean start, the controls are cleared with the Clear method and the LineStyle property is set to trwRootLines. Table 3.16 shows the settings for the LineStyle property.

TABLE 3.16: The Values for the LineStyle Property

Constant	Value	Description
tvwTreeLines	0	(Default) Tree lines. Displays lines between node siblings and their parent node.
tvwRootLines	1	Root lines. In addition to displaying lines between node siblings and their parent node, also displays lines between the root nodes.

Now that everything is set up, we use a For loop to add the data. A loop is set up to add the letters of the alphabet from A to Z in the TreeView control. The Index and Tag properties are set also.

NOTE We store the index of the current node. This is used later in the program to ensure that the detail names fall under the parent node that is set to the letters A–Z.

Each iteration of the loop checks for any employee records that have the same first letter of the last name as the current node letter. If one is found, it is added to the TreeView node and to the ListView ListItem.

Code 3.52: Filling the List and Tree Views with Records

```
Public Sub FillLists()

    On Error GoTo ErrorRoutineErr
    Dim nodX As Node
    Dim i As Integer
    Dim intIndex
    Dim gRs As Recordset
    'Create an object variable for the ListItem object
    Dim itmX As ListItem
    Dim intCount As Integer
    'Create an object variable for the ColumnHeader object
    Dim clmX As ColumnHeader

    Data1.RecordSource = _
        "Select * from Employees order by lastname;"
    Data1.Refresh
    Set gRs = Data1.Recordset
```

```
'Add ColumnHeaders. The width of the columns
'Is the width of the control divided by the
'Number of ColumnHeader objects
Set clmX = ListView1.ColumnHeaders. _
    Add(, , "Last Name", ListView1.Width / 3)
Set clmX = ListView1.ColumnHeaders. _
    Add(, , "First Name", ListView1.Width / 3)
Set clmX = ListView1.ColumnHeaders. _
    Add(, , "Extension", ListView1.Width / 3)

'Set BorderStyle property
ListView1.BorderStyle = ccFixedSingle

'Clear the views
TreeView1.Nodes.Clear
ListView1.ListItems.Clear

'Set TreeView control properties
TreeView1.LineStyle = tvwRootLines  ' Linestyle 1

'Add Node objects.
Set nodX = TreeView1.Nodes.Add(, 4, , "root", "closed")

'Fill top level A-Z of the treeview
For i = 0 To 25
    Set nodX = TreeView1.Nodes.Add _
        (1, tvwChild, , Chr(65 + i), "closed")
    'Set the tag property of the main nodes
    nodX.Tag = "Name"
    'Set index to current node
    intIndex = nodX.Index
    'Add Names
    Do While Not gRs.EOF
            If UCase(Left(gRs!LastName, 1)) = _
            Chr$(65 + i) Then  '
            Set nodX = TreeView1.Nodes.Add _
                (intIndex, tvwChild, , gRs!LastName + _
                ", " + gRs!FirstName, "word")

                'Use the Add method to add a new ListItem
                'And set an object variable to the new _
                'Reference
                'Use the reference to set properties
```

```
                    Set itmX = ListView1.ListItems.Add _
                        (, , CStr(gRs!LastName))
                    intCount = intCount + 1
                    itmX.Tag = intCount

                    'If the FirstName field is not Null,
                    'Set SubItem 1 to FirstName
                    If Not IsNull(gRs!FirstName) Then
                        itmX.SubItems(1) = CStr(gRs!FirstName)
                    End If
                    itmX.SmallIcon = "word"
                    itmX.Icon = "center"

                    'If the Extension field is not Null,
                    'Set SubItem 2 to Extension
                    If Not IsNull(gRs!Extension) Then
                        itmX.SubItems(2) = gRs!Extension
                    End If

                    'Move to next record
                    gRs.MoveNext
                Else
                    Exit Do
                End If
            Loop
        Next i
        TreeView1.Nodes(1).Expanded = True
        'Set the ListView control to report view
        Combo1.ListIndex = 0
        ListView1.View = lvwReport

ErrorRoutineResume:
    Exit Sub
ErrorRoutineErr:
    If Err = 3021 Then
        Resume Next
    End If
    MsgBox Err & " " & Error
    Resume Next
End Sub
```

Finding a TreeView Record

The Command1_Click subroutine searches through the nodes of the TreeView control, one by one, to find a match with the text entered in theText1 text box. If the text is found, the control is scrolled with the EnsureVisibility method and highlighted with the Selected property. If a match is not found, the user is notified with a message box.

Code 3.53:   **Performing a Tree Search**

```
Private Sub Command1_Click()
    Dim i As Integer
    For i = 1 To TreeView1.Nodes.Count - 1
        If TreeView1.Nodes(i).Text = Text1.Text Then
            TreeView1.Nodes(i).EnsureVisible
            TreeView1.Nodes(i).Selected = True
            Exit Sub
        End If
    Next
    MsgBox "No match found"
End Sub
```

Expanding All the TreeView Nodes

In the Command4_Click subroutine, the Expanded property is set to True as we loop through the nodes of the TreeView control, expanding them as we go.

Code 3.54:   **Expand All the Nodes**

```
Private Sub Command4_Click()
    Dim i As Integer

    For i = 1 To TreeView1.Nodes.Count - 1
        TreeView1.Nodes(i).Expanded = True
    Next

End Sub
```

Collapsing All the TreeView Nodes

In the Command2 subroutine, the Expanded property is set to False as we loop through the nodes of the TreeView control, collapsing them as we go.

Code 3.55: **Collapse All the Nodes**

```
Private Sub Command2_Click()
    Dim i As Integer

    For i = 1 To TreeView1.Nodes.Count - 1
        TreeView1.Nodes(i).Expanded = False
    Next

End Sub
```

Selecting a ListView View

As the Form is loaded, we populate the combo box with the four views of the ListView control. When you select a view from the combo box, the ListView property is set.

Code 3.56 **Setting the Four Views**

```
Private Sub Form_Load()
    Data1.Refresh
    'Load the listview combo box
    With Combo1
        .AddItem "Icon View"         '0
        .AddItem "SmallIcon View"    '1
        .AddItem "List View"         '2
        .AddItem "Report View"       '3
        .ListIndex = 3
    End With
    Option1(0).Value = True

    Call FillLists
End Sub

Private Sub Combo1_Click()
    'LvwIcon = 0
    'LvwSmallIcon = 1
    'LvwList = 2
    'LvwReport = 3
    ListView1.View = Combo1.ListIndex
End Sub
```

Finding an Item in the ListView Control

The ListView control provides a handy FindItem method we can use to find a text string in the ListItem, a subitem, or the Tag.

Code 3.57 gets FindOption—either the ListItem, subitem, or Tag—from the option buttons. It calls the FindItem method with the string from the text box, and it calls FindOption from the option buttons. If the find is successful, the EnsureVisibility method is used to scroll to the item, and the selected property is set to True to highlight the item.

Code 3.57:   Finding a List Item

```
Private Sub Command3_Click()
    Dim slFind As String
    Dim slFindOption As Integer

    If Option1(0).Value = True Then
        slFind = txtListFind
        slFindOption = lvwText
    End If
    If Option1(1).Value = True Then
        slFind = txtListFind
        slFindOption = lvwSubItem
    End If
    If Option1(2).Value = True Then
        slFind = txtListFind
        slFindOption = lvwTag
    End If

    'FindItem method returns a reference to the found item, so
    'you must create an object variable and set the found item
    'to it
    Dim itmFound As ListItem

    Set itmFound = ListView1. _
    FindItem(slFind, slFindOption, , lvwPartial)

    'If no ListItem is found, then inform user and exit. If a
    'ListItem is found,
    'scroll the control using the EnsureVisible
    'method, and select the ListItem
    If itmFound Is Nothing Then
```

```
                MsgBox "No match found"
                Exit Sub
        Else
            'Scroll ListView to show found ListItem
             itmFound.EnsureVisible
            'Select the ListItem
             itmFound.Selected = True
            'Set focus to the control to see selection.
             ListView1.SetFocus
        End If
End Sub
```

The List project demonstrates the major functionality of the TreeView and ListView controls. Now, let's run the project and see it in action.

Testing the List Project

To test the List Project, follow these steps:

1. Start the project by pressing F5.

2. Click the Expand All and Collapse All buttons to see the TreeView nodes expand and collapse.

3. Press the Collapse All button to collapse the nodes.

4. Type **King, Robert** in the text box under the TreeView control, and click the Find button. The TreeView control will scroll, expand, and select the node "King, Robert."

5. Click the different views in the combo box on the ListView side to see the views.

Next, let's test the Find option of the ListView.

1. Select the Report view.

2. Type **Fuller** in the text box, select the Text option button, and click the Find button. The ListView will highlight the "Fuller" record.

Now, let's test the SubItem find.

1. Click the SubItem option button.

2. Enter **Michael** in the text box, and click the Find button. The ListView highlights the last record. The ListItem, column1, is always selected regardless of the type of find performed.

Finally, let's test the Tag find option. The Tag property is set to the record number in the FillList subroutine.

1. Click the Tag option button.

2. Enter **4** in the text box, and click the Find button. The fourth record will be selected.

As you can see, the List controls are flexible and provide lots of options for the developer and the user. If your application needs to show data from a database, a list, an index, or most any kind of tabular data, the TreeView and ListView controls might be just what the user ordered.

Optimizing VB Applications

- Understanding the Visual Basic compiler

- Optimizing Visual Basic code

- Building DLLs with Visual C++

- Understanding dynamic-link libraries

- Calculating fractals

- Calling DLL functions from Visual Basic

- Manipulating strings with Visual C++

Visual Basic is the most popular language for rapid application development, the simplest language to use, and in most respects as powerful as any other language, such as Visual C++. But Visual Basic also has limitations, some of which are inherent in the interpreted nature of the language and others which are simply part of the functionality supplied by VB. This is not to decry the value of Visual Basic, but simply to point out that in certain areas it is valuable to be able to extend or enhance the functionality of the language.

One of these areas is speed. Visual Basic relies on an interpreter, which generates *p-code*. P-code stands for pseudocode, a language designed to be machine independent yet easily mapped to processor commands. P-code is translated into executable statements by the Visual Basic run-time module.

NOTE   You'll find detailed information on p-code in the section "What's P-Code?" later in this chapter.

Visual Basic 5 is the first version of VB to come with a *native code compiler*, which can generate optimized code similar to the code produced by the VC++ compiler. The Visual Basic native code compiler will improve with future versions, but at this point it isn't as efficient as the VC++ compiler.

In this chapter, we are going to discuss the Visual Basic compiler, look at what the native code compiler can do for your application, and give you a few tips on how to optimize math and string operations. Some applications just can't be made fast enough. You can use all the tricks in the book and still not be happy with their performance. To stretch this limit, we'll show you how to implement computationally intensive procedures with Visual C++ and package them as DLLs. Although Visual Basic's native code compiler can improve performance over the interpreted code significantly, Visual C++ is even faster. How much faster, depends on the type of processing. You'll see examples of both math and string operations in the following sections. But first, let's see how to optimize VB code and how to get the most out of the Visual Basic compiler.

The Visual Basic Compiler

One of the most exciting new features of Visual Basic 5 is its ability to compile projects to *native code*. This is a true compiler that produces machine-specific code that the CPU can execute directly. These executable files are the same as those generated by the Visual C++ compiler or the Delphi compiler.

Previous versions of Visual Basic couldn't produce native code, only p-code. Even with Visual Basic 5, you're actually running p-code when you run a project in the IDE. Any project will run faster (marginally or significantly faster, depending on the nature of the calculations it performs) when it's compiled to native code and executed outside the Visual Basic IDE. To understand why native code performs better than p-code, you must first understand the nature of p-code and how Visual Basic uses it.

NOTE   In short, p-code is what makes the environment of Visual Basic so unique and so popular. Without p-code, you wouldn't be able to stop your applications, edit the code, and resume execution.

What's P-Code?

P-code is close to machine language, but it's not quite machine language; in other words, it can't be executed as is. It must be translated into commands for a specific processor. Whether you develop on a Pentium or a PowerPC, the p-code is the same. But before it can be executed on either processor, it must be translated into the target processor's command set. Moreover, this translation must take place while the application is running, which means that p-code will never be as fast as native code.

The text you enter in the Visual Basic editor is translated into p-code as you enter it. Each time you press enter to move to the next line, the IDE translates the line you are leaving into p-code. All the syntax checking and color coding of the statements takes place after the line is translated into p-code—which explains why the current line isn't colored as you type.

To run p-code, Visual Basic uses a so-called execution engine: a DLL that translates p-code into machine-executable code, or native code. This is how your projects are executed in the Visual Basic IDE. To distribute the application, you can create an executable file that contains the p-code plus the execution engine. The EXE files produced by previous versions of Visual Basic were nothing more than p-code and the run-time DLL. That's why running an executable file outside the IDE wasn't any faster than running the application in the IDE.

NOTE

Visual Basic applications were always slower than other compiled applications. All benchmarks showed that languages such as Visual C++ and Delphi were consistently faster than Visual Basic. The reason is that every line of p-code must be translated into machine-specific instructions before it can be executed. This was the price we had to pay in exchange for an unmatched development environment in which we could edit, run, edit, and resume execution of the application.

The VB5 native code compiler, however, is similar to a traditional compiler, such as the one used by Visual C++. It produces processor-specific instructions that can be executed directly, without any additional translation. It's easy to understand why native code executes faster than p-code. You might actually expect a much better improvement over p-code, but Visual Basic's p-code is highly optimized. (It seems that Microsoft couldn't improve it any further, and the introduction of a native code compiler was inevitable.)

Another reason native code outperforms p-code is that it can do global optimizations. P-code is generated on the fly, and it's executed one line at a time. The native code compiler can see the big picture (many lines of source code at once) and produce optimal executable code that takes into consideration the peculiarities and dependencies among multiple lines of code. A native code compiler for Visual Basic was long overdue, and we expect future versions of Visual Basic to produce executables that match the speed of executables generated by Visual C++ or Delphi.

Compiler Options

So, now that we have a native code compiler, which produces faster running executables, you might think that we could just forget all about p-code. But the native code compiler doesn't come without a price. It produces longer files that take longer to load, and, if you are distributing your software on the Internet, they also take longer to download. If these restrictions don't apply to you, you can compile your applications to native code, see what difference the compiler makes, and then decide how to distribute them.

NOTE

We use Visual Basic to implement scientific and graphics algorithms, which benefit the most by the native code compiler, so we're more than glad to exchange some disk space for performance.

Applications compiled to native code don't always run faster. Real-world business applications spend most of their time doing disk I/O, screen updates, and other tasks that you can't speed up from within your VB code. For example, when you call an API function, you're no longer in control. When the API function is executed, there's nothing you can do to improve its speed no matter how much you've optimized the rest of the code. In a way, this is a barrier you can't break, regardless of whether you compile to p-code or to native code.

To create the executable file, start Visual Basic (if necessary), and choose File ➤ Make *File.exe* (*File.exe* is the application's name). Before selecting this command, you must set certain compiler parameters in the Project Properties dialog box (see Figure 4.1). Choose Project ➤ Project Properties to open it.

FIGURE 4.1:

The Project Properties
dialog box

The type of executable that will be created depends on the settings you choose in the Compile tab of this dialog box:

Compile to P-Code compiles a project using p-code. The main benefit of p-code is that it's compact and (in many practical cases) not much slower than purely executable code.

Compile to Native Code compiles a project using native code, which is the machine language the CPU understands and executes.

NOTE

The generated executable created by selecting Compile to Native Code is faster than the equivalent p-code executable by as much as 2000%, according to Microsoft. Only applications designed to exploit the compiler will exhibit such behavior; we have not witnessed improvements more than 100%, and in most cases, less than that.

In the Ch04/Bench folder on the CD, you will find the NATIVE.EXE and PCODE.EXE applications. They generate fractals, such as those shown in Figure 4.2. (We'll use these files throughout this chapter.)

NOTE

For instructions on using these two applications, see the sidebar "Having Fun with Fractals."

Both executables come from the same source code; one was compiled to native code, and the other, to p-code. The application is calculation intensive and was not designed to demonstrate the superiority of one type of code over the other. However, we expected to see a significant difference between p-code and native code for this type of application. If you run both applications, however, you'll see that the native code executable is consistently 20% to 30% faster than the p-code executable, which is typical. Most of our applications run approximately 30% faster when compiled to native code.

FIGURE 4.2:

A fractal generator compiled in both native code and p-code demonstrates the differences in the two executables.

The NATIVE.EXE file is 20Kb, and the PCODE.EXE file is14Kb. Other applications can generate much larger executables, and p-code executables are consistently smaller than native code executables. However, we don't think the size of the executable is an important consideration, especially for an application such as a fractal generator.

Having Fun with Fractals

The Fractal application displays the Mandelbrot set. The application uses palettes, and it may not work well (that is, it may not display the correct colors) on many true color systems. If your video board is set to display true color (16- or 24-bit color), change the color depth to 8 bits (256 colors). To change the palette, click Load Palette and select one of the palettes in the DIBS folder under the Fractals folder on the CD.

After displaying the entire Mandelbrot set by clicking the Draw menu command, you can zoom into any area of the fractal image by drawing a rectangle with the mouse around the desired area. Click the upper-left corner of the desired area, and while holding the button down, drag the mouse to the lower-right corner of the selection and release the button. Then click the Draw command. If you get lost in the filaments of the Mandelbrot set, click Reset Limits to return to the original limits of the Mandelbrot set.

You will notice that the Fractal application can't be stopped and that it doesn't yield control to the operating system. To change this behavior, insert a DoEvents statement in the main loop of the program (we explain this later in the chapter). You can also capture keystrokes and end the drawing of the fractal when the Escape key is pressed. We didn't implement these features, because our primary goal is to compare the performance of the native code and p-code executables.

The Load Palette command lets you select the current palette, by selecting a DIB file with a range of colors. The DIB files are stored in the DIBS folder under the Fractal folder. You can open these DIB files with any application that can manipulate palettes, such as BitEdit or PaintShop Pro, and adjust their contents or create new ones. Notice that the palette files contain smooth gradients (ranges of similar colors).

Options for Optimizing Native Code

The native code compiler must balance various and, usually conflicting requirements. For example, it can't produce the most compact and most efficient code. The Compile to Native Code section of the Project Properties dialog box contains processor-specific optimizations and a number of advanced options that may or may not apply to your project. You specify the options that produce the type of executable that best matches your application and the target systems:

Optimize for Fast Code maximizes the speed of the executable file by instructing the compiler to favor speed over size. To optimize the code, the compiler can reduce many constructs to functionally similar sequences of machine code. This will inevitably increase the size of the executable file.

Optimize for Small Code minimizes the size of the executable file by instructing the compiler to favor size over speed.

No Optimization compiles without specific optimizations. It balances speed and size.

Favor Pentium Pro optimizes the code to favor the Pentium Pro processor. Use this option for programs meant only for the Pentium Pro. Code generated with this option will run on other Intel processors, but it will not perform as well.

Create Symbolic Debug Info generates symbolic debug information in the executable. An executable file created using this option can be debugged using Visual C++ or debuggers that use the CodeView style of debug information. Setting this option generates a PDB file with the symbol information for your executable. This option is most often used by Visual C++ programmers who also use Visual Basic.

Advanced Optimizations displays the Advanced Optimizations dialog box, which is shown in Figure 4.3. You use the options in this dialog box to turn off certain checks that normally take place and ensure that your application works properly. To increase the speed of the executable file, you can turn off some or all these options by checking the appropriate checkbox.

WARNING Enabling the options in the Advanced Optimizations dialog box may prevent the correct execution of your program. You must understand what each option does and be sure that your application doesn't require any of the options you turn off.

FIGURE 4.3:

The Advanced Optimizations dialog box

Assume No Aliasing tells the compiler that your program does not use aliasing. Aliasing is a technique that lets your code refer to the same variable (memory location) by more than one name. We don't use this technique (of dubious value, anyway) in this book, so you can safely turn off this option.

Remove Array Bound Checks checks for array bounds and speeds up applications that use arrays when checked. By default, Visual Basic checks an array's bounds every time your code accesses the array to determine if the index is within the range of the array. If the index is not within array bounds, a run-time error is generated (the out-of-bounds error), which can be trapped from within the code. However, the code that will ensure that the array's bounds are not exceeded may cost more in execution time. If an array bound is exceeded, the results will be unexpected. You can turn on this option if the application doesn't use arrays or if you know that your code will not attempt to access nonexisting array elements. For example, a loop that uses the LBound and UBound functions to scan the elements of an array will not cross the array's boundaries.

Remove Integer Overflow Checks checks for errors and speeds up integer calculations when checked. By default, Visual Basic checks every calculation for integer-style data types—Byte, Integer, and Long—to ensure that the value is within the range of the data type. If the magnitude of the value being put into the data type is incorrect, a run-time error is generated. If data-type capacities are overflowed, you will get incorrect results, but no errors. It's really difficult to make sure that calculations with integers do not result in overflows, and it's even trickier to find out where the overflow occurred.

Remove Floating Point Error Checks checks every calculation of a floating-point data type—Single and Double—to be sure that the value is within range for that data type and that there are no divide by zero or invalid operations. If the magnitude of the value being put into the data type is incorrect, an error occurs. Select this option to turn off the error checking and speed up floating-point calculations. If data-type capacities are overflowed, no error occurs, and you may get incorrect results. Avoid this optimization with scientific applications.

Allow Unrounded Floating Point Operations uses floating-point registers more efficiently, avoids storing and loading large volumes of data to and from memory, and does floating-point comparisons more efficiently (floating-point numbers are slightly truncated when moved from registers to memory).

Remove Safe Pentium FDIV Checks removes safety checking so that the code for floating-point division is faster. Selecting this option may produce slightly incorrect results on Pentium processors with the FDIV bug. (The new Pentiums, 120MHz or faster, are exempt from the floating-point division flaw.)

So, this is how you can automatically speed up your application: by producing a native code executable. Unless the EXE is really large (and you plan to distribute it by means other than a CD), generate EXE files optimized for speed. However, a few bad coding techniques can easily offset any benefit introduced by the native code compiler. If your application calculates squares in a loop that's executed many times and you code it as $x \wedge 2$, no advanced optimization option is going to help your application. As you will see shortly, coding this operation as $x * x$ will make a p-code executable run faster than a native code executable. The trick to writing fast-running applications is to start by optimizing the code itself. In the following sections, we are going to present a few useful optimization techniques. They are quite simple, but efficient. Even if you are an experienced VB programmer, you should take a look at the following pages. You may discover simple optimization tricks you are not familiar with.

Optimizing VB Code

Before we get into how to improve VB code by using DLLs written in other languages, let's look at how to optimize VB code from within. Code optimization depends on the type of application you're writing. In most cases, you'll be optimizing small, tight sections of code that are executed frequently (such as loops or frequently called procedures). Code optimization requires a combination of experience, an eye for detail, and a basic understanding of processors. Seasoned programmers, who have done some assembly-language programming in their days, have an advantage here, but you can pick up a lot along the way.

TIP

Never think your code has been optimized completely, and never underestimate your capabilities. Some expert programmers start with the code produced by the compiler and optimize it. So don't count too much on the machine. Learn its limitations and work around them.

Although there are no hard and fast rules for optimizing code, there are some tricks you can use and some guidelines you can follow. We'll discuss these in the next sections and then look at how these tricks affect the native code and p-code compilers.

There are some simple rules that every BASIC programmer knows. For example, Integer and Long variables are handled faster than Single and Double variables. If your calculations permit it, use Integer instead of Long variables, and use Single instead of Double variables. But, most important, don't use undeclared variables.

Avoid Variants

Variants are convenient when putting together a short program to display the ASCII character set or the ASCII values of the function keys, but avoid variants in your code. They take up much more memory than other data types, and they can't be processed immediately. The compiler must find out their proper type, convert them to this type, and then use them in a calculation. For example, if a variant holds the value 45, the compiler must convert it to a numeric value before using it in a numeric calculation or to a string before using it in a string operation.

Some developers defend variants and explain to you why they are so cool, pointing out that they free the programmer from having to declare variables and use them consistently. They also give you some neat examples—mostly one-liners that could normally be implemented with two or three lines of code. If you're trying to squeeze every drop of performance from your application, avoid variants. Or, if you're the type that learns the hard way, use them and see for yourself.

The VBOPT application, shown in Figure 4.4, performs a number of calculations.

NOTE   You'll find the VBOPT application in the Ch04 folder on the CD that comes with this book.

FIGURE 4.4:

The VBOPT application demonstrates the inefficiency of variants.

The Declared Variables button performs the calculations using variables declared as Doubles. The Variant Variables button does the same calculations using variants. The time to complete the calculations is displayed on a Label next to each button. The actual calculations are shown in the TextBox at the bottom of the Form. A few math operations repeated 1,000,000 times. As you can see, using properly declared variables speeds up the calculations by more than 10% (23.398 versus 20.695 seconds).

The code of the VBOPT application is shown next. The calculations are trivial, but are typical of scientific and engineering applications. You may notice the exceptionally inefficient implementation of some operations; more on this later.

Code 4.1:   The VBOPT Project

```
Private Sub Command1_Click()
    T1 = Timer
    Screen.MousePointer = vbHourglass
    Dim i As Long, j As Double, k As Double
    For i = 1 To 1000000
```

```
        j = Log(i) ^ 2
        k = Cos(Rnd() * 100) ^ 2    Next
    Label1.Caption = Format(Timer - T1, "##.000")
    Screen.MousePointer = vbDefault
End Sub

Private Sub Command2_Click()
    T1 = Timer
    Screen.MousePointer = vbHourglass
    For i = 1 To 1000000
        j = Log(i) ^ 2         k = Cos(Rnd() * 100) ^ 2
    Next
    Label2.Caption = Format(Timer - T1, "##.000")
    Screen.MousePointer = vbDefault
End Sub
```

Let's compile the VBOPT application and see how the equivalent native code does. Follow these steps:

1. In the Project Properties dialog box, check the Compile to Native Code option and the Optimize for Fast Code option.

2. Click the Advanced Optimizations button to open the Advanced Optimizations dialog box.

3. Check all the options to enable all optimizations.

4. Now choose File ➢ Make VBOPT.EXE to generate the executable file.

5. Minimize the Visual Basic window, locate the VBOPT.EXE file, and run it.

The equivalent times on the same system are now 15.82 and 18.953. The native code compiler helped the variants a little, but the calculations with typed variables were executed faster. Notice also that the native code compiler improved execution by 34%.

Now let's experiment with the optimization options. Go back to the Advanced Optimizations dialog box and clear the option Allow Unrounded Floating Point Operations. The compiler will round the results of each operation, as if they were moved to memory, in between calculations. This will add a few cycles, and we are going to lose some accuracy too (one wonders why this is even an option). The calculations with typed variables will take 13.242 seconds, and those with variants will take 15.047 seconds. Rounding intermediate results has a profound effect on execution time.

TIP It is possible to use variants by calling the wrong form of certain functions. The string functions Mid(), Left(), and so on are different from the functions Mid$(), Left$(), and so on. The functions without the dollar sign in their names are more flexible (they work on both strings and numbers), but they return variants. If you are working exclusively with strings, use Left$() instead of Left() and Right$() instead of Right().

Simplify the Math

Now we are going to optimize the code in the loop. There isn't much you can do here, except for the ^ operator, which raises a number to a power, even a non-integer number. Raising a number to a non-integer power is accomplished with an algorithm that is more complicated than multiplying a number by itself (which is what the square of a number is). Many programmers will use the proper operator (x ^ 2) to calculate the square of x, because they don't know better or (in most cases) because they are translating a math formula into Visual Basic statements.

Let's revise the code to avoid the ^ operator. Replace the following line:

```
j = Log(i) ^ 2
```

with the line

```
j = Log(i) * Log(i)
```

And replace the following line:

```
k = Cos(Rnd() * 100) ^ 2
```

with this line:

```
k = Cos(Rnd() * 100)* Cos(Rnd() * 100)
```

Make sure that the advanced optimization options are checked, create a new executable, and run it. The calculations take only 3.680 seconds to complete with typed variables and 9.117 seconds with variants. So, most of the time in the previous runs was spent by the ^ operator. Notice also that, although the calculations with variants improved, they are now much slower than the calculations with typed variables. The reason? With simple math tricks you can improve the performance of your code, but there's nothing you can do about the overhead involved with variants.

You can use the same tricks with cubes and other integer powers. You will still save time if you multiply a number by itself three times, rather than raising it to the cube with the ^ operator.

Another way to optimize code that implements math operations is to save intermediate results. For example, the following statements:

```
Xnew = X * X + X0: Ynew = Y * Y + Y0
{other calculations}
 If X * X + Y * Y > 0 Then ...
```

will execute faster if you save the results of the operation X * X to a temporary variable, as shown next:

```
XSquare = X * X : YSquare = Y * Y
Xnew = Xsquare + X0: Ynew = Ysquare + Y0
{other calculations}
If Xsquare + Ysquare > 0 Then ...
```

The improvement will be more impressive if you store more complicated operations, such as X ^ 2.8 or Y ^ -0.3, to temporary variables and reuse them.

Manipulate Strings Efficiently

The single most important trick in speeding up string operations is to remember that Mid() is not only a function. It's also a statement. In the following line, the Mid() function returns the third through the tenth characters of a string:

```
subString = Mid$(originalStrig,3,10)
```

But in the following line:

```
Mid$(originalString,3,10) = "1234567890"
```

Mid$() is used as a statement to change part of the string.

Let's look at a practical example. Let's say you want to reverse a long string. Many VB programmers would start by building a new string and appending to it the characters of the string to be reversed, starting with the last character and working up to the first, with a loop such as the following:

```
For i = 1 To Len(AString)
    BString = BString & Mid$(AString, Len(AString) - i + 1, 1)
Next
```

In this listing, AString is the string to be reversed, and BString is the new string. If you run this code with a 30Kb string, you'll spend almost a minute looking at the hourglass. It won't be bad with a shorter string, say 5Kb, but as the length of the string increases, Visual Basic needs more and more time to handle it. Reversing a 30Kb string isn't 6 times slower than reversing a 5Kb string 6 times. Not even close.

Let's start with setting up a long string, which is a more fundamental problem. We are going to build a string using random characters. In a practical application they could be read from a file or an incoming stream from a Web server. The basic problem is that a string grows as new characters are attached to it. The following code appends random characters to the end of the string AString:

```
AString = ""
For i = 1 To 30000
    AString = AString & Chr(Rnd() * 26 + 48)
Next
```

It's simple, but very slow. On a Pentium 166 system, it took more than a minute. If the string were only 3000 characters, filling it with random characters would take less than a second. There seems to be something wrong here. The longer the string, the more time it takes Visual Basic to manipulate it. This is a consequence of the way Visual Basic stores strings in memory, but this isn't something you can change.

To speed up the code, we can set up two nested loops, such as the following:

```
AString = ""
For j = 1 To 10
    BString = ""
    For i = 1 To 3000
        BString = BString & Chr(Rnd() * 26 + 48)
    Next
    AString = AString & BString
Next
```

The inner loop creates a 3000-character string (variable BString) at a time and appends it to the AString variable. It must build ten of those strings to fill the long string. This structure took 6.7 seconds on the same Pentium. By limiting the size of the string variable we use to append individual characters, we brought the total execution time of more than 60 seconds down to fewer than 7.

TIP   The conclusion is that you shouldn't manipulate very long strings with Visual Basic. Break long strings into shorter ones, manipulate them individually, and when you're done, concatenate the processed strings. Execution times will be reduced tremendously.

The application VBSTROPT, shown in Figure 4.5, demonstrates the two techniques.

NOTE   You'll find the VBSTROPT project in the Ch04/VBSTROPT folder on the CD that comes with this book.

FIGURE 4.5:

The VBSTROPT application demonstrates efficient string manipulation techniques.

The Create Long String button builds a very long string (30,000 characters) by appending characters to the end of a string variable. The button Create Short Strings builds the same string, using shorter segments, as described here.

Let's process a long string now. The processing is trivial: We'll reverse the order of the characters in the string. Again, here's how many programmers would initially code this operation:

```
For i = 1 To Len(AString)
    BString = BString & Mid(AString, Len(AString) - i + 1, 1)
Next
```

As you might suspect, this is another slow operation. It's implemented with the Reverse Slow button on the VBSTROPT Form. How long does it take on the same Pentium 166? Nearly 80 seconds! A trivial operation like this. What if we wanted to scramble the characters or do a more intensive operation?

We can improve the string reversal operation by using the Mid statement. To enhance the example, we are going to reverse the string in place: We'll reverse its characters without copying it to another string. If you want to keep the original string too, copy AString to BString and then reverse BString in place. Here's the code for reversing the *AString* variable in place:

```
For i = 1 To Len(AString) / 2
    tmpChar = Mid(AString, Len(AString) - i + 1, 1)
    Mid(AString, Len(AString) - i + 1, 1) = Mid(AString, i, 1)
    Mid(AString, i, 1) = tmpChar
Next
```

This operation is implemented with the Reverse In-Place button in the VBSTROPT application. The time? Only 0.6 seconds! This can't be considered an optimization trick; it's more like bad initial coding, right? We bet that many programmers would reverse the string with the first method. They would test their program with a 20-character string and think they had a functional application.

Perhaps we can stop here. Reversing a string in less than a second isn't bad. But maybe we can do even better with character arrays. Let's start by copying the characters of the *AString* variable to an array:

```
For i = 1 To Len(AString)
    A(i) = Mid(AString, i, 1)
Next
```

This operation (which is implemented by the Copy String to Array button) took approximately half a second. If we can speed our string manipulation routines by using the character array we just created, the time to copy the string to an array is well spent. Here's the code for reversing the characters in the array:

```
UB = UBound(A)
For i = 1 To UB
    B(i) = A(UB - i + 1)
Next
```

The string reversal operation in an array took 0.27 seconds. Indeed, the time to copy the string to an array was well spent, especially if you use the array for more complicated types of processing or multiple string operations.

In this section, we measured times while the project was running in the IDE. If you compile the project to native code and run it, you won't see much improvement. The compiler will help all operations a little, but it will primarily help the string reversal operation with the array. So, if you are doing lots of string processing in your code, consider copying the strings onto character arrays and process the array elements instead. When you're done, you can copy the array's characters back to the string.

Access Properties Indirectly

Another simple but effective optimization technique is to avoid referencing the same property many times. Let's say you have an incoming stream of data that you want to display on a TextBox. You already know what to do: Create small string variables, and append them to the control's Text property.

Another common mistake is to reference a property such as Text1.Text in a loop. Let's say you want to reverse the characters of the text displayed in a TextBox. Even if you use the Mid statement in a loop such as the following, the process is going to be very slow.

```
Dim Astring As String
Astring = " "
With Text1
    For i = 1 To Len(.Text)
        tmpChar = Mid(.Text, Len(.Text) - i + 1, 1)
        Mid(AString, i, 1) = tmpChar
        Astring = Astring + " "
    Next
    .Text = Astring
End With
```

Because a lot of overhead is involved every time you access a control's property, avoid too many references to the same property. Copy the Text property's value to the string *AString*, and process this variable. Then, assign the processed variable to the Text property. Reversing 3000 characters on a TextBox control took 8.6 seconds using the Text property, while the same operation using a temporary string variable took less than half a second on the same computer. Clearly, you should avoid referencing control properties directly in your code, especially within loops that are executed many times.

Optimize for Worse-Case Scenarios

Many times we write less than optimal code because we don't test our applications with real-world data or under worse-case scenarios. We write code that works well with short text files, and we assume it will behave similarly with any text file. If an operation takes 90 milliseconds, why optimize it? Because, as we have demonstrated, it may deteriorate by a factor of 100 when the string's length is increased by a factor of 20.

In addition, don't trust anyone's code—not that of the compiler, a code generator, your colleagues or boss, your professors, or book authors. No code (except for truly trivial segments) can be proven optimal; so if you are not happy with its speed, optimize it.

Maximize Apparent Speed

No amount of optimization is going to do you much good unless the users of your application *think it's fast*. Conversely, the sloppiest application need not be optimized if users think it's fast. The most important metric of the speed of an application is its so-called apparent speed. Apparent speed can't be measured in time units (or any units, for that matter). Apparent speed is how fast the application appears to the user. If your Forms load slowly, any amount of optimization in the code that follows the loading of the Form isn't going to help. For example, which image-processing application do you open more often? The one that loads the fastest, right?

Apparent speed can be improved in two ways

- By loading Forms faster
- By displaying flash screens and animation while the program is busy for more than a few seconds

Your best bet is to load Forms at startup and keep them in memory. The Load command loads a Form, but doesn't display it. Once the Form is in memory, you can display it instantly with the Show method. The application may take longer to start, but once it's started, Forms can be displayed and hidden instantly (unless they contain large bitmaps).

Another way to increase the apparent speed is to load new Forms and then ask the user to wait for a lengthy operation to complete. While the user takes a few seconds to study the controls on the Form and think about his or her next move (which parameters to adjust or which button to click), your application calculates the values that will be displayed on the Form or retrieves data from a database.

But how about the initial delay, when the user has to wait for your application's Forms to load? This initial delay is just about the worse thing you can do for the application's apparent speed, but it helps the apparent speed of the rest of the application. When a time-consuming operation takes place, we use the hourglass to indicate that the user should wait. And we've all watched more than our share of hourglasses. Sometimes users go as far as to shake them to see if the sand will move. Well, an hourglass isn't improving the application's apparent speed, and we need something more amusing, something fresher.

An animated cursor or an AVI file with a few small frames isn't going to make the application run faster, but it's not going to slow it down noticeably either. A typical example is the animation that takes place while documents are sent to the

Recycle Bin. Another example is the information displayed on the screen while applications are being installed. The flash screens keep the user from getting utterly bored, and they are more fun to watch than an hourglass. The excitement, however, grows thinner over time, and users want more speed. You may have optimized your VB application as best as you can. Perhaps there are no more milliseconds to be squeezed out, and still you (or your users) are not happy with the application. It may be time to help Visual Basic with an external component.

Building DLLs with Visual C++

A DLL written in Visual C++ is a prime candidate, and we are going to look at the basics of implementing simple, time-consuming operations in Visual C++ and packaging them as DLLs. By time-consuming operations, we mean CPU-intensive calculations, string manipulation, and the like. Accessing a database isn't going to get any faster no matter what language you use. The JET Engine or the SQL Server, for example, doesn't know what language is contacting it. The same is true for API calls. You simply can't make these operations any faster. However, you can make other operations, especially math operations, significantly faster with the help of an external DLL.

Do You Have to Learn Visual C++?

Are we suggesting that you learn Visual C++ to simply make Visual Basic faster? Yes and no. Visual Basic programmers, for whatever reasons, don't like C. But experienced VB programmers shouldn't have any problem picking up the basics of writing C code. We'll show you the mechanics of converting VB code to C and compiling it as a DLL.

Writing code to perform math operations in C isn't any more complicated than writing VB code. Sure, you must end each line with a semicolon and get used to the notation counter++ (which increases the value of the counter variable) and other syntactical differences, but the actual statements aren't that different from the equivalent VB statements.

In this section, we'll show you how to design a DLL with Visual C++, how to call the DLL's functions from within your VB application, and how to pass parameters (including arrays) back and forth. You don't have to master C, just reap some of its benefits, without the hard work. Sometimes you can succeed without trying really hard, but don't make it your banner. To get this far in this book, you've tried hard already.

What Are Dynamic-Link Libraries?

Dynamic-link libraries, or DLLs, are libraries of executable code that another application can call at run time through dynamic linking to provide functions and procedures to perform tasks that are not supplied by the application itself. In your VB application, you must declare the procedure in a DLL and provide the path to the DLL so that your application can connect to it at run time. These DLLs are similar to the ActiveX DLLs discussed in the second part of the book, but they only expose procedures, which are called directly like the API functions. Let's look at this process in more detail.

First, a *library* is a block of code that has been compiled to produce a machine-executable product. A library can consist of a single function or procedure or contain a variety of separate procedures, all of which are externally accessible. These public functions or procedures can be called by other applications to perform specific tasks, to execute calculations and return results, and even to call on the services of other libraries.

A DLL can also contain procedures that are not accessible outside the library but that are used by procedures within the library. These private functions or procedures differ principally in the manner in which they are exposed for external access. We'll discuss both types in detail later in this chapter.

Second, like any Windows application, a DLL can contain resources such as dialogs, bitmaps, and so on that are used by functions within the DLL and that are visible to the user. These resources are not, however, directly accessible to applications using the DLL. (There are exceptions by which resources may be made available externally, but these are not the usual methods for using resources.) The DLLs we'll describe in this chapter don't have a visual interface; we'll leave that task to Visual Basic, and the DLL will take care of CPU-intensive calculations.

Third, unlike a static library that is linked at the time the application is created, a DLL remains independent and separate from the application and is linked only at run time and only if and when specific functions supplied by the DLL are requested. Further, again in contrast to a static library, the machine code supplying the service is not incorporated in the application but remains a part of the dynamic-link library.

You can think of a DLL as a black box that can be asked to perform specific tasks and/or to return specific results, but that does not require the programmer to know anything about what is inside.

Of course, the ignorance permitted for those using a DLL does not apply if you are interested in writing a DLL, which is precisely what this section is about.

Advantages of DLLs

Several advantages are associated with using dynamic-link libraries. Some of them apply to any application written in any language, and others apply principally to using DLLs with Visual Basic.

Common Services

The functions supplied by a DLL can be shared by more than one application at different times or even simultaneously by several applications. When separate applications call a DLL, each individual client application receives a separate instantiation of the requested function—at least in the sense that the data used by the function remains separate for each calling application—even though only one copy of the executable code exists.

The Windows Common Dialog Library, which provides such functions as the Save File and Find File dialog boxes, is an example. In addition to sharing a single functionality across all applications, the shared file also ensures that all applications present a common interface when opening or saving files. Thus, when you are using the Common Dialog control to build an Open dialog box, the users of your application will see the familiar Windows File Open dialog box.

Compact Size

While the current trend toward code bloat seems to almost make a mockery of falling memory prices and increasing CPU speeds, using DLLs is still a valid and useful way to reduce the size of executables. When functions supplied by a static library are used in an application, the code for each function is incorporated into the application's code, becoming a part of the EXE program file.

Some years ago, when an application used a library, the entire library was linked into the compiled application, regardless of how much or how many of the services supplied by the library were actually needed by the application. Later, as smart linkers came into use, only those portions of a library that were actually needed and used were linked to become a part of the executable.

But, regardless of how the application is compiled—or even whether it is compiled or interpreted—the functions supplied by the DLL are never incorporated in the application's EXE file. Instead, all functions supplied by the DLL remain in the dynamic-link library and are called as needed. Further, because there is only one copy of the DLL even when the services are shared among many applications, additional savings in space are realized over duplicating the code.

Ease of Revision

A DLL can be revised at any time to incorporate improvements. In this respect, a DLL is similar to an ActiveX component, except that your application doesn't have to access the exposed functions via an object variable.

Likewise, revised DLLs can include additional public functions that were not provided in the original DLL without affecting applications using the earlier version. Of course, applications that are taking advantage of elements added to a later revision will not be able to function using the earlier version.

TIP To avoid potential version conflicts and crashes, provide a way to test the DLL version in your application.

Speed of Execution

The primary reason for using a DLL with Visual Basic is the need for speed. For example, a graphics application may require a large number of calculations. By implementing a calculation-intensive process as a DLL written in Delphi or C/C++, you can significantly reduce calculation time. In many areas, however, Visual Basic is just as fast as other languages.

NOTE If a DLL written in Visual C++ could run circles around your Visual Basic application, you'd be really disappointed, wouldn't you? Visual Basic is not only an excellent development environment, but a fast language too. It just isn't always as fast as Visual C++.

Third-Party Libraries

With a DLL, you can use third-party libraries to supply functions, features, or utilities instead of developing them yourself. Libraries of functions in DLL format were popular, but are being slowly replaced by classes. However, there is still a significant market for DLLs that contain useful procedures, especially if they are implemented in a fast language such as Visual C++.

Disadvantages of DLLs

Although the advantages of using DLLs far outweigh the disadvantages, short-comings may occur in a few areas.

Loss of Customization and Adaptability

When you are developing every aspect of your application entirely on your own, you are certainly free to adapt every aspect and every element of the application exactly and precisely as you would prefer. By off-loading tasks to DLLs that are not developed in-house, you give up some freedom of design and customization.

Also, DLLs are not as readily adaptable as Visual Basic code, and, when working across languages, trying to debug operations inside a DLL can be a major headache at best and impossible at worst.

Of course, since the ultimate in customization and adaptability would be to design your own operating system, every application consists of some form of compromise. In the case of DLLs, the usual compromise is trading some flexibility for increases in execution speed and savings in development time.

Compatibility Problems

You can encounter compatibility problems between DLLs written in one language and applications written in another. Of course, the same can be said of DLLs and applications that are written in different versions of the same language.

For example, an integer in Visual Basic is not the same as an integer in Visual C/C++. In most cases, such as passing an integer parameter by value, this discrepancy will not be apparent or relevant. In other cases, this difference can be a major problem if you do not take it into consideration. (See the section "When an Int Is Not an Int" later in this chapter.)

The key, of course, is to be sure that you know what the DLL expects and what the calling application can provide. And, obviously, test your application with the DLL to ensure that they are communicating in a compatible fashion. (See the section "Array Dimensions in VB versus VC" for more on this.)

Fractal Calculations

In this section, we'll use the Mandelbrot set in an example, mainly because displaying the set depends on extensive floating-point calculations and is intrinsically slow. Calculating a fractal is a computationally intensive operation, and we chose it to demonstrate how much difference a DLL written in Visual C++ can make.

The Fractal application (written in Visual Basic) calculates an image that is 400 by 400 pixels, a total of 160,000 pixels. Further, since each pixel requires 50 iterations (an approximate average), this gives us a total in the neighborhood of 8 million iterations. However, each iteration requires multiple floating-point operations (FLOPs), bringing us to many million FLOPs to display a single image of the Mandelbrot set.

The Visual Basic version of this operation can easily require two minutes to complete. Therefore, we developed the Fractal.DLL library using Visual C++. It provides one function for performing the calculations (which are the most time-consuming portion of the task) and returning the result (as an altitude) to the Visual Basic program for display. Different altitudes are colored differently.

We'll start by looking at the VB code for calculating and displaying the Mandelbrot set. This application will be the reference point for comparing the speed improvements introduced with the Visual C++ DLL.

You are probably familiar with fractal images, but you may not be familiar with the algorithms used to produce them. Fractal images are generated mathematically. In this chapter, we'll concentrate on the calculations (which aren't complicated, but are repeated millions of times). For more information on what fractals represent, see the fractal.doc file on the Visual Basic 5 companion CD.

Fractals and Fractal Dimensions

The term *fractal* was first coined by the mathematician Benoit B. Mandelbrot in 1975 as shorthand for any object—mathematic or physical—that exhibits the characteristics of a fractional dimension. A detailed discussion of the Mandelbrot set and fractals is beyond the scope of this chapter, but if you are interested in exploring fractals and other mathematically intriguing entities, check out the following:

Fractals Everywhere by Michael Barnsley

Fractals and Fractal Dimensions (continued)

Fractal Programming in C and *Advanced Fractal Programming in C,* both by Roger Stevens

Computer Graphics: Principles and Practice by Foley, van Dam, Feiner, and Hughes

Graphics Programming in Turbo C by Ben Ezzell

The Fractal Application

Don't worry if you are not familiar with the fractal algorithms. They are straight-forward, and you need not understand all the details. Each point of the fractal must be calculated separately. Let's call the Mandelbrot() function, which calculates the color of each point. It accepts as arguments the coordinates of the point and returns the color. The entire image is calculated with two For ... Next loops, which scan the columns of the pixels (the outer loop) and the pixels across each column (the inner loop). Here's the structure of the application that calculates and displays the fractal:

```
nLimit = 100
XStep = (XMax - XOrg) / XSize
YStep = (YMax - YOrg) / YSize
For i = 0 To XSize
    For j = 0 To YSize
        XPos = XOrg + i * XStep
        YPos = YOrg + j * Ystep
        {calculate nSteps}
        Picture1.PSet (i, j), QBColor(nSteps Mod 16)
    Next
    Picture1.Refresh
Next
```

The variables *XOrg*, *XMax*, *YOrg,* and *YMax* represent the limits of the Mandelbrot set. By changing these values, you can zoom into any area of the Mandelbrot set.

The calculations are repeated up to 100 times (variable *nLimit*) for each pixel. The current pixel is painted according to the number of iterations. Points lying in the "fractal sea" exhaust all 100 calculations (or as many as you specify with the *nLimit* variable). To simplify the code, the current point is painted with the QBColor() function.

NOTE   The fractals that are produced with the QBColor() function—which supports only 16 colors—will not look as nice as those colored with palettes, but this isn't the issue at hand. At the end of the chapter, we'll show you how to build smoothly colored fractals.

The actual calculations take place in the section marked as {calculate nSteps} in the previous listing. We didn't implement them as a separate function because this function would be called for each point; we preferred to code the calculations inline. The statements that calculate the color of each point are shown in the next listing.

Code 4.2:   Calculating the Mandelbrot Set

```
XSize = Picture1.ScaleWidth
YSize = Picture1.ScaleHeight
Picture1.BackColor = QBColor(15)
Picture1.Cls
XStep = (XMax - XOrg) / XSize
YStep = (YMax - YOrg) / YSize
For i = 0 To XSize
    XPos = XOrg + i * XStep
    For j = 0 To YSize
        YPos = YOrg + j * YStep
        XIter = 0#: YIter = 0#
        bDone = False
        nSteps = 0
        Do
            XSqr = XIter * XIter
            YSqr = YIter * YIter
            XTemp = XSqr - YSqr + XPos
            YIter = 2 * (XIter * YIter) + YPos
            XIter = XTemp
            nSteps = nSteps + 1
            If (XSqr + YSqr) >= 4# Then bDone = True
            If (nSteps >= nLimit) Then bDone = True
        Loop Until bDone = True
        Picture1.PSet (i, j), QBColor(nSteps Mod 16)
    Next
    Picture1.Refresh
Next
```

Even if you aren't familiar with the math involved, you can easily see that painting each pixel requires a lot of floating-point operations. In the Fractal application, shown in Figure 4.6, choose Draw Direct ➤ Mandelbrot to display the entire Mandelbrot set, or choose Draw Direct ➤ Mandelbrot (Zoom) to display a detail of the Mandelbrot set. These two commands are implemented in Visual Basic.

FIGURE 4.6:

The Fractal project calculates and displays the Mandelbrot set.

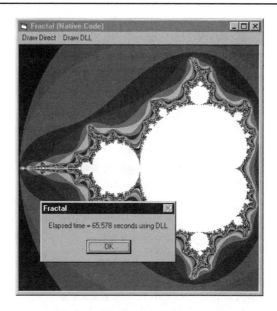

TIP
In our code, we evaluate some squares. As you can see, to calculate the square of a variable, we multiply it by itself. If you didn't know better, you might code these line with the ^ operator (XIter^2 instead of XIter * XIter). Doing so will make your code much slower! The ^ operator invokes a procedure that raises a number to any power. When it comes to integer powers, though, the ^ operator is slow, and you should never, never use it. This trick won't make a difference in a typical application, but avoiding the ^ operator in a loop that repeats millions of times will make a world of difference in your application's speed!

The rule for breaking the calculations is that the square root of the sum of the squares XIter^2 and Yiter^2 be less than 2. This rule is implemented with the line:

```
If (XSqr + YSqr) >= 4# Then bDone = True
```

To avoid calculating a square root for each iteration, for each point, we took the squares of both sides of the inequality. The variables *XSqr* and *YSqr* hold the values of the *XIter* and *Yiter* variables squared.

In the Fractal application, shown in Figure 4.6 earlier in this chapter, choosing Draw DLL ➤ Mandelbrot and choosing Draw DLL ➤ Mandelbrot (Zoom) is identical to using the commands on the Draw Direct menu, but the Draw DLL menu uses the DLL we are going to develop in the next section, FRACTAL.DLL. We still use the same two nested loops to scan the pixels of the image, but instead of using the VB code shown in Code 4.2 to calculate the color of the current point, we call the DLLMandelbrot() function, which is implemented in Visual C++ and is provided to our application by the FRACTAL.DLL.

Before getting down to the details of constructing a DLL in Visual C++, let's look at what the DLL did for the application. Run the Fractal application (in the Ch08/Fractal folder on the CD) from within the Visual Basic IDE. The commands on the Draw Direct menu draw the Mandelbrot set with straight VB code, and the first two commands on the Draw DLL menu draw the same views of the Mandelbrot set using a DLL function to perform the calculations. It takes nearly 36 seconds to draw the Mandelbrot set with straight VB code and just 13.5 seconds to draw the same image with the help of the DLL. The VB/DLL code is nearly three times faster, which is an enormous improvement.

However, this isn't quite fair to VB. The DLL contains native code, optimized by the Visual C++ compiler. If you create a native code executable for the Fractal application and run it, you'll see that the VB compiler will do a great job. Run the FRACTAL.EXE file in the Fractal folder (or create a new executable), and you'll see that the Mandelbrot set is drawn in approximately 13.5 seconds with VB code and in 8.5 seconds with the VB/DLL code. The VB compiler helped the VB implementation of the program a lot, as expected. The DLL can't be helped by the VB compiler (the compiler doesn't do anything to the DLL; it simply calls one or more of its functions). Even so, the VB/DLL approach is almost 40 percent faster than straight VB. Given that calculating a fractal image is an inherently slow process, it makes sense to help VB with a DLL written in Visual C++. Let's look at the implementation of the function that calculates each pixel's color with Visual C++.

NOTE Before calling a function supplied by a DLL, you must declare the function's name, the DLL it belongs to, and its argument, just as you do with API functions (see the section "Calling DLL Functions from Visual Basic," later in this chapter). The commands on the Draw DLL menu will not work if the FRACTAL.DLL file isn't copied to the Windows/System folder.

Alternatively, you can specify the DLL file's full path name in the declaration line, but this approach depends on the system on which the application is run and should be avoided.

Constructing a DLL in Visual C++

Constructing a DLL using Visual C++ is a relatively simple process, but begins with a choice of either using the standard C/C++ format or basing the DLL on the Microsoft Foundation Classes (MFC). In both cases, of course, you can use the Visual C App Wizard to create the project, but which Form you select has definite ramifications.

NOTE   Microsoft Foundation Classes are prepared classes that contain commonly used functions that are not part of the C++ specification (for example, routines to manipulate strings or read from and write to files, similar to the Visual Basic functions and statements).

To create a DLL using Visual C/C++, start Visual C++ and in the IDE choose File ➤ New, and then select the Project tab. For a standard DLL, select the *Win32 Dynamic Link Library* option; for an MFC-based DLL, select the *MFC App Wizard (dll)* option. Then, simply follow the onscreen directions to create the basic files for your project.

To create the Fractal.DLL, select the *Win32 Dynamic Link Library* option.

Standard C++ versus the Microsoft Foundation Classes

The simplest form of DLL begins with a .CPP source file, a .H header file, and an (optional) .DEF definition file. It contains no derived classes and does not depend on the MFC or the MFC DLLs for support. The advantage of such a DLL is that it is lean and mean (figuratively speaking), and you don't have to install other DLLs before you can use it.

On the other hand, if you create an MFC-based DLL using the Visual C App Wizard, you have the advantage of being able to use the MFC classes, including the CString and CFile classes, within the DLL-supported operations, and, of course, you can derive your own custom classes from the MFC library. But, at the same time, in addition to installing your DLL, you will have to ensure that the appropriate supporting libraries are also installed.

Since the expectation here is that you are programming in Visual Basic and are creating a DLL to provide specialized support, there is probably little reason for basing your DLL on the MFC classes. For one thing, Visual Basic already provides support paralleling virtually all the MFC classes—particularly the CString and CFile operations—so there is little point in attempting to duplicate these services. And, for another, creating a straight C/C++ DLL is just simpler, particularly for anyone who is more accustomed to programming in VB than in VC.

Declaring Functions for Export

One of the first tasks in creating a dynamic-link library is to define functions for export. Although you may have any number of functions within the library, it is the exported functions that provide the access for other applications to use the DLL.

TIP   It is possible, of course, to make every function in the DLL an exported function, but, except for relatively simple DLLs, there is usually little point in exporting everything.

The DEF File

The .DEF file, or definitions file, provides a list of exported functions, making them available in the compiled DLL in a format that is accessible to external applications. Although you can compile and link the DLL without including the .DEF file and without producing any error reports, the resulting library will not have identifiable entry points when the VB application calls it.

The Fractal.DEF file is simple, consisting of a list of exported functions by name only, and can also include an ordinal value for each exported function. The sample definition file is:

```
; Fractal.def : Declares the module parameters for the DLL.

LIBRARY      "Fractal"
DESCRIPTION  'Fractal Windows dynamic-link libraries'
```

A standard .DEF file begins with the Library and Description statements. The Library statement simply defines the name of the DLL library. The Description statement is purely optional and simply offers an opportunity to enter a description of the library's purpose.

Next, following the Exports statement, the names of the library's exported functions are listed; optionally, each function name can be followed by an ordinal value.

```
EXPORTS
    ; Explicit exports can go here
    DLLMandelbrot          @1
    DLLMandelbrotArray     @2
    DLLPaintMandelbrot     @3
```

If you do not explicitly define any ordinal values, default ordinal values are assigned (sequentially) when the DLL is compiled and linked.

The Header File

Unlike the optional .DEF file, the .H header file is absolutely essential. If you have experience with C/C++ programming, calling the .H header *essential* may seem redundant since all C/C++ files are expected to be accompanied by .H headers. This format of .CPP and .H files as pairs, however, is more custom and convenience than a hard and fast requirement, and, in many cases, there is really no need for a .H header.

For the Fractal.DLL library, the Fractal.H header serves several purposes:

- The .H header contains the names and specifications for the exportable functions (but may also contain declarations for local functions that are not exported).

- Any other C/C++ applications that want to use the Fractal.DLL library will use the .H header (in an #include statement) to make the exported functions accessible within the application. (Visual Basic does not use the .H header, but does require parallel function definition statements, which we'll discussed presently.)

- The .H header provides a reference for programmers to see which functions are provided by the library and which parameters and arguments are required or returned.

The first item in the Fractal.H header is a #define statement, which identifies the Export macro as:

```
extern "C" __declspec( dllexport )
```

Wherever the term EXPORT appears in the header file or in the .CPP source file at compile time, this macro is expanded to the full term:

```
#define EXPORT extern "C" __declspec( dllexport )
```

Such macros—and many macros are used in C/C++—are simply a convenient shorthand format for expressing complex terms, tests, or other provisions without having to write them out in full each time. The Export macro identifies the exported functions listed both in the header and in the source file.

Following the macro definition, you define three exported functions (as you will see later when the other two procedures are used):

```
EXPORT int CALLBACK DLLMandelbrot( double, double );
EXPORT int CALLBACK DLLMandelbrotArray( int*, int, int,
                                        double, double, double, double );
EXPORT int CALLBACK DLLPaintMandelbrot( HDC*, int, int,
                                        double, double, double, double );
```

Here, the EXPORT term identifies each of these functions as external functions, as using the C calling format for arguments and, for the library, as exported functions. The int for each function is the value returned by the function to the calling application, and the Callback macro, which is already defined in Visual C/C++, expands to FAR PASCAL, identifying the handling required to call the function.

Since the Export and Callback macros are essentially fixed elements, you need not be concerned with them. Note, however, that local functions (functions that will not be exported) will not include the Export macro but will still specify a return value (or void if nothing is returned) and will be identified as CALLBACK.

Following the function name, the calling parameters are identified by their types. Optionally, here in the header, the function definitions can also include variable names. For example, the DLLMandelbrot function definition could also be written as:

```
EXPORT int CALLBACK DLLMandelbrot( double dXPos, double dYPos );
```

However, although you must include the variable names in the function entries in the .CPP file, they are optional in the .H header, and you can include them or omit them. The operational point is that only the types are important; the variable names proper, which are internal to the functions themselves, are not needed outside the source file.

TIP

Visual Basic requires that the complete statement appear on a single line and interprets a CR/LF pair (in the source code) as the end of a statement. In contrast, Visual C (and all versions of C) permits statements to extend over several lines in the source code and, instead of line breaks, requires semicolons as statement terminators.

The DLL Entry Point

Every dynamic-link library requires an entry point that, by custom and practice, is always named `DllMain`, just as the entry point for an executable under Windows is always named `WinMain` and under DOS is always named `Main`. Likewise, the parameters accompanying the call to `DllMain` are also predefined and do not vary.

In short, the entry point function for the DLL, in its simplest form, appears in the .CPP source file as:

```
int WINAPI DllMain( HINSTANCE hInstance, DWORD dwReason, PVOID
pvReserved )
{
    return TRUE;
}
```

Within the `DllMain` procedure, you can make additional provisions if, for example, you have some need or reason to perform some special initialization for the library. In general, however, the `DllMain` procedure does not need to perform any special tasks other than assuring the system that the DLL has been loaded correctly by returning True.

Once you provide the `DllMain` procedure, your source file is ready to compile and link and will produce a valid DLL library.

Of course, it will also be a library that doesn't do anything yet, so the next step is to add some functionality by providing at least one exported procedure.

DLL Procedures

A DLL procedure is not particularly different from any C/C++ procedure except, of course, for the EXPORT specification. The procedure definition from the .H header is repeated in the source file, but this time it does not have the terminating semicolon and does have the variable names as well as the variable type identifiers.

```
EXPORT int CALLBACK DLLMandelbrot( double dXPos, double dYPos )
{
```

Within the procedure, define any local variables that will be used. Unlike Visual Basic, in which variables can be used without being defined, C/C++ always requires that you explicitly define variables before you reference them:

```
double  dXIter, dYIter, dXTemp;
int     nSteps, nLimit = 100;
bool    bDone;
```

Once you define the variables, you assign a few initial values. Again, unlike Visual Basic, which has the grace to zero out variables when they are defined (or dimensioned), Visual C/C++ does not automatically clear the memory allocated for a variable. Instead, any allocated variable must have an explicit value assigned even if it is only a matter of explicitly zeroing the variable:

```
dXIter = 0.0;
dYIter = 0.0;
bDone  = FALSE;
nSteps = 0;
```

Once these local variables are initialized, we're ready to enter a Do...While loop, using the variable *bDone* as our exit condition. We started by assigning a value of False (0) to the *bDone* variable, and the loop is set up to continue until *bDone* has a value of True (1). This means that the loop will not terminate until we explicitly change the value of *bDone* in response to one of two tests.

Before performing any tests, however, we need to carry out an iteration of the Mandelbrot equation for the supplied coordinates:

```
do
{
    dXTemp = dXIter * dXIter - dYIter * dYIter + dXPos;
    dYIter = 2 * ( dXIter * dYIter) + dYPos;
    dXIter = dXTemp;
    nSteps++;
```

The values for *dXTemp*, *dXIter*, and *dYIter* were all initialized as zero, and the *dXTemp* variable is used for temporary storage so that the value in *dXIter* is not updated until the second calculation is complete.

Also, each time these calculations are reiterated, the *nSteps* variable is incremented. The value in *nSteps*, assuming that the calculated distance for this coordinate pair does increase without bounds, will identify the altitude for the point. The following statement:

```
nSteps++;
```

increases the value of the *nSteps* variable by one.

NOTE   This notation was introduced not to make the code more compact, but to help the compiler optimize the native code it produces.

The following line:

```
result = limit * nSteps++;
```

tells the compiler to produce code to multiply the variables *limit* and *nSteps* and store the result in the variable *result*. After the operation is complete and while the *nSteps* variable is in one of the processor's registers, it increases its value. If the variable *nSteps* is increased in a separate statement (`nSteps = nSteps + 1`), the value of the variable would have to be read from memory (an operation that can be avoided).

Last, after the current iteration is complete, one test is performed to determine the distance for the resulting values before a second test checks *nSteps* to decide if *nLimit* has been reached. If either condition is satisfied, the variable *bDone* is set to True, and the DO...WHILE loop is allowed to terminate:

```
        If ( dXIter * dXIter + dYIter * dYIter ) >= 4.0 )
            bDone = TRUE;
        if( nSteps >= nLimit )
            bDone = TRUE;
    }
    while( ! bDone );
```

The ! operator in C/C++ is the equivalent of the logical Not operator. The Not operator in C/C++ inverts every bit of the following variable. Likewise, the logical And operator in C/C++ is &, and the logical Or operator is |.The And, Or, and Not operators are numeric operators that act on each bit of variable(s). The And operator in *value1* And *value2* will And each bit of the variable *value1* with the corresponding bit of the variable *value2* and return the new value. These operators are also known as bitwise operators because they process one bit at a time and don't treat variables as logical ones (True/False values).

Finally, if *nSteps* is less than *nLimit*, the function returns the *nSteps* value modulo 15 (that is, the remainder after dividing by 15) for use as a color index to indicate the altitude of this point. Or, if *nSteps* equals *nLimit* (or is greater), the value of 15 is returned since this is the color index for white in the default palette that Visual Basic uses:

```
    if( nSteps < nLimit )
        return( nSteps % 15 );
    else
        return( 15 );
}
```

And this completes the DLLMandelbrot procedure. We'll discuss the process for calling the DLLMandelbrot function in the section "Calling DLL Functions from Visual Basic," later in this chapter.

Using Arrays As Parameters

Let's see if we can improve the speed of the application by reducing the number of calls to the DLLMandelbrot procedure. The DLLMandelbrot procedure is called once for each point. For an image 400×400 pixels, it must be called 160,000 times. Let's see if we can save any seconds by calling another function in the DLL that calculates the values of all points and returns an array with the pixel color values.

We are going to develop another procedure, the DLLMandelbrotArray, that will set up an array whose dimensions are the same as the dimensions of the PictureBox control, on which the fractal is displayed, in pixels. The DLL procedure will fill in all the values of the array's elements and pass it back to the VB application, which will use the values stored in the array to paint each pixel on the PictureBox.

WARNING This approach increases the apparent speed since the user won't see the fractal being drawn as it's calculated. The calculations must complete before any pixels can be drawn. It's not a very good idea, but we'll explore it anyway.

Besides ruining the apparent speed of the application, this approach does not improve the speed of the application. We'll discuss it because we want to show you how to use arrays to process large sets of data with a Visual C++ DLL. Some interesting issues arise when you pass arrays back and forth to DLLs, and if you are going to use arrays in your Visual C++ DLLs, you will find this information useful.

In the second exported function in the Fractal DLL, an array of integers is expected as a parameter. Or, more accurately, instead of an array of integers, a pointer to the first element in the array is expected, along with two arguments giving the size of the array. (A two-dimensional array is assumed here.)

Since this version will calculate values (altitudes) for all the points in the array, the last four parameters are the dXStart/dYStart and dXEnd/dYEnd arguments, which set the boundaries for the region of the Mandelbrot set that we want to explore:

```
EXPORT int CALLBACK DLLMandelbrotArray( int *pA, int nXSize, int
nYSize, double dXStart, double dYStart, double dXEnd, double dYEnd )
{
    double    dXStep, dYStep;
```

```
        dXStep = ( dXEnd - dXStart ) / nXSize;
        dYStep = ( dYEnd - dYStart ) / nYSize;
        for( int j=0; j<nYSize; j++ )
            for( int i=0; i<nXSize; i++ )
            {
                *pA = DLLMandelbrot( dXStart + i * dXStep, dYStart + j *
dYStep );
                pA++;
            }
        return TRUE;
}
```

Rather than repeating the code for calculating the point values, the same exported DLLMandelbrot function is also called locally. Even though a function is explicitly exported, nothing prevents us from using it locally as well.

Because we have a pointer to the first element in the array, the inner loop simply increments the address of the pointer to the next element in the array after performing the calculations for one point in the array, instead of passing the entire array as a fixed size. The variable pA is a pointer to the array, and it's declared as *pA. When you declare a variable with the asterisk in front of it, like:

```
int *pA
```

you create a variable that points to an integer value in memory. In the code, you use the expression *pA to access the integer you're pointing at. If you assign a value directly to the pA variable, you cause it to point to a different area in memory. The array is a collection of integers stored in sequential memory locations. When you increase the variable that points to the first element of the array, the compiler knows that it should not add 1 to the current value of the variable pA. When you increase a pointer, it should point to the next integer, which is 8 bytes away. The compiler will increase the value of the variable pA by 8 so that *pA will point to the next element in the array.

Notice also that the array we pass from the Visual Basic application is two-dimensional, but in the DLLMandelbrotArray() function, we address it as one-dimensional. No matter how many dimensions an array has, its elements are stored in sequential memory locations, one row at a time. Therefore, when we reach the last element of the first row and attempt to access the next element, this will be the first element of the next row. This trick allows you to access any two-dimensional array declared in VB from within a DLL function, without knowing its exact dimensions.

Pointers are at the heart of C programming, yet they are a sore spot for VB programmers. However, you don't really need to master all aspects of pointers (they can get quite nasty, as you can have pointers to pointers and pointers to functions and other beasts) in order to write a few simple DLLs to speed a segment of your VB application. You've seen how to pass numeric variables and arrays from a VB application to a Visual C++ function. Later in this chapter, you'll learn how to pass arrays of characters back and forth, and we don't think you need to learn more about pointers.

Although this procedure is valid, on occasions problems can occur. For more on this, see the section "When an Int Is Not an Int," later in this chapter.

When you choose Draw DLL ➤ Mandelbrot (Array), the program displays the time it takes to calculate the color values of the pixels and the time it takes to display these values. It takes 3 seconds to calculate the entire Mandelbrot set and nearly 7 seconds to display it. The DLLMandelbrot() function is very fast. By decoupling the calculations from the manipulation of the display, we were able to pinpoint the major source of delay.

If you are using Visual Basic to design applications that do a lot of drawing on the screen, you have already noticed that Visual Basic isn't extremely fast when it comes to drawing operations. It's almost puzzling, but on a fast Pentium it takes longer to display the pixels than to calculate them. Let's see how much more we can improve the Fractal application by moving the painting of the pixels from the VB application to the DLL. Our last attempt is to design a Visual C++ procedure that not only calculates the fractal, but draws it on the screen as well.

Using Direct Paint

The DLLPaintMandelbrot function accepts a pointer to the device context handle for the PictureBox control on the VB Form. Along with the device context, this function is called with the limit values for the region to be explored. With this much information, the DLLPaintMandelbrot function attempts to perform all the calculations and the paint operations by calling the SetPixelV function.

Code 4.x: Calculating and Painting the Mandelbrot Set

```
EXPORT int CALLBACK DLLPaintMandelbrot( HDC *pDC,
                                        double dXStart, double dYStart,
                                        double dXEnd,   double dYEnd )
{
    double  dXStep, dYStep;
    int     nIndex, nXSize, nYSize;
```

```
nXSize = nYSize = 1001;
dXStep = ( dXEnd - dXStart ) / nXSize;
dYStep = ( dYEnd - dYStart ) / nYSize;
for( int i=0; i<nXSize; i++ )
{
    for( int j=0; j<nYSize; j++ )
    {
        nIndex = DLLMandelbrot( dXStart + i * dXStep,
                                dYStart + j * dYStep );
        if( nIndex < 15 )
            SetPixelV( *pDC, i, j, PALETTEINDEX( nIndex ) );
    }
}
return TRUE;
}
```

To test the new implementation of the Mandelbrot algorithm, run the Fractal application and choose Draw DLL ➤ Mandelbrot (Paint). When executed from within the IDE, the Mandelbrot set takes 5.25 seconds to complete. With the compiled version of the application, the Mandelbrot Set takes 4.5 seconds to complete. The VB compiler can't help this procedure significantly, because nearly all the work (both the calculation and the display of the fractal) is done by the DLL.

The two numbers you should compare are the time it takes for Visual Basic to calculate and display the Mandelbrot set, 13 seconds, and the time it takes for the Visual C++ DLL to display the same image, which is only 4.25 seconds. The function MandelbrotPaint(), implemented in Visual C++, is nearly three times faster than the equivalent VB code. Our effort to build a DLL in Visual C++ certainly paid off.

Another Approach

Visual C++ isn't much faster than Visual Basic when it comes to drawing operations. This shouldn't surprise you, because both languages call the same API function. Instead of using either the PSet or SetPixelV operations—both of which are inherently slow—you can write the pixel values to the pixel data elements within a bitmap (or any other image format) to achieve a major improvement in speed.

Another Approach (continued)

Once the image is written—the memory-addressing operations are inherently fast—you can use the Visual C BitBlt or StretchBlt functions or their equivalents in VB to copy the image from memory to the window. In this fashion, the actual process of transferring the image becomes effectively instantaneous.

This particular approach, however, is not a simple undertaking, especially for a VB programmer. Our goal is to show you how to enhance your Visual Basic applications by implementing relatively simple algorithms in Visual C++. Writing DLLs that bypass Visual Basic entirely is beyond the scope of this book.

Calling DLL Functions from Visual Basic

Now that we've created a dynamic-link library and have provided several exported functions, the next step is to call these functions from within a Visual Basic program.

The Fractal application includes the Draw Direct and the Draw DLL menus. The Draw Direct menu contains two items:

- Mandelbrot
- Mandelbrot (Zoom)

Both draw views of the Mandelbrot set on the PictureBox control using only Visual Basic code (the first command draws the entire Mandelbrot set; the second draws a detail of the Mandelbrot set).

The Draw DLL menu contains four items:

- Mandelbrot
- Mandelbrot (Zoom)
- Mandelbrot (Array)
- Mandelbrot (Paint)

The first two commands are equivalent to the commands of the Draw Direct menu, only they use the DLLMandelbrot function. The other two commands call the DLLMandelbrotArray and DLLPaintMandelbrot functions. To compare the times required for internal and external calculations and drawing operations on the Visual Basic side of the application, a timer receives the system clock information before drawing the set and then compares times with the system clock when the drawing operation is complete. The difference, which is the elapsed time, is then reported through a dialog box.

A similar dialog box reports on each of the menu items. Choosing Draw DLL ➢ Mandelbrot (Zoom) displays an enlarged view, as shown in Figure 4.7.

FIGURE 4.7:

A zoomed view into the Mandelbrot set

The zoomed region, magnified 100 times, shows features that are similar to the set as a whole. This recursion of similarities can be found along the shores of the fractal sea at almost any location and any magnification.

External Function Declarations

Just as the C/C++ DLL has a .H header file with declarations for both local and exported functions, the Visual Basic program also requires forward declarations for the DLL-accessible functions. For the VB-version, however, a .H header is not compatible. Instead, the forward declarations for the Fractal.DLL exported functions appear at the top of the code section of the `Fractal.frm` file as:

```
Private Declare Function DLLMandelbrot Lib "Fractal.DLL"
     ( ByVal XPos As Double, ByVal YPos As Double ) As Integer
```

The DLLMandelbrot procedure is declared as a function, meaning that it returns a value or result. The function name, DLLMandelbrot, is used in the dynamic-link library for the desired function. The term `Lib` following the function name indicates that the function is located in an external library, and the name `"Fractal.DLL"` identifies the library itself.

In this case, the assumption is that the dynamic-link library (the DLL file) is located in the `\Windows\System` directory (or somewhere else in the current path where it will be found without difficulty). As an alternative, the specification can also include an explicit path or drive/path for the DLL file.

Following the DLL name is a list of the calling parameters in parentheses. These parameters, of course, have been translated from Visual C/C++ into Visual Basic terminology, as has the return value for the function following the closing parenthesis.

Translating parameter arguments from C/C++ to Visual Basic is an excellent way to generate serious errors that may or may not be caught by the compiler. The DLLMandelbrot function there doesn't appear to present much opportunity for error; two doubles are passed, by value, as arguments, and an integer value is returned. So what can go wrong? In this case, not much. The difference is unimportant since the return value is a color index that is easily contained in either a long or a short int.

NOTE Do take a look at the sidebar "When an Int Is Not an Int," later in this chapter. The integer expected on return may not be precisely the same as the integer returned by the DLL function.

The next two declarations are not quite as forgiving:

```
Private Declare Function DLLPaintMandelbrot Lib "Fractal.DLL" _
     ( ByRef hDC As Any, _
       ByVal nXSize As Integer, ByVal nYSize As Integer, _
       ByVal dXStart As Double, ByVal dYStart As Double, _
       ByVal dXEnd As Double,   ByVal dYEnd As Double) As Integer
```

In the DLLPaintMandelbrot declaration, the first argument is a handle to a device context, and handles must be passed by reference, not by value. However, since VB doesn't really have a "type" for this, we used the type Any as a catchall.

Two integer values are being passed that are actually short integers (2-byte), but the DLL function is expecting long integers (4-byte). In this case, no conflict occurs because the arguments are passed by value.

In the DLLMandelbrotArray function, however, we find another potential for an error in translation. The declaration for this DLL function—from the Fractal.H header—indicates that the first parameter is expected to be a pointer to an integer:

```
EXPORT int CALLBACK DLLMandelbrotArray( int*, int, int,_
        double, double, double, double );
```

In the Visual Basic code, again there is no exact equivalent type, so the forward declaration again uses the type Any and passes the parameter by reference (ByRef), the VB equivalent of a pointer:

```
Private Declare Function DLLMandelbrotArray Lib "Fractal.DLL" _
    ( ByRef A As Any, _
      ByVal nXSize As Integer, ByVal nYSize As Integer, _
      ByVal dXStart As Double, ByVal dYStart As Double, _
      ByVal dXEnd As Double,   ByVal dYEnd As Double) As Integer
```

Okay, a pointer is a pointer, right? There's no problem here, right? Well, yes and no. The declaration is perfectly correct, but the form of the declaration, as we will discuss in a moment, can inadvertently disguise a more serious problem.

Passing Parameters by Value

By default—that is, if not otherwise specified—arguments in VC++ applications are passed by value. Not only is this convenient, but it allows the operating system to mask what could otherwise be conflicts between types. As long as arguments are only exchanged as values, the raw value data is translated into the expected format without conflict if a short integer is passed to a function expecting a long integer.

On the other hand, if a long integer is being translated as a value to a short integer, information can be lost because the short int will contain only the data from the low word of the long value.

In most cases, the worst that you can expect is a loss of data, but the Visual Basic defaults are not the same as the defaults used by 32-bit C/C++ compilers. Get in the habit of specifying the ByVal keyword in front of the arguments you pass to your DLLs (the same is true with nearly all the Windows API function declarations).

Passing Parameters by Reference

Although passing parameters by value is the simple choice and, in many cases, is perfectly appropriate, in a number of circumstances parameters must be passed by reference.

For example, to call the DLLPaintMandelbrot function from the DLL, the handle to the device context must be passed by reference, not by value. Here, the value of the handle is irrelevant; it is simply an identifier that the operating system uses. What's important is that there is only one device context, and, by passing a pointer to the handle to the DLL, the device context is being shared, giving the DLL access to the original device context.

When you call the DLLMandelbrotArray function from your VB application, another parameter must also be passed by reference (although, this time, for a slightly different reason). Here, a pointer is being passed to the first element in an array so that the DLL can fill in the million-plus array elements with individual values (it wouldn't make a lot of sense to copy the million-plus array elements and pass them by value, not to mention that the values stored in the array by the function wouldn't make it back to the VB application).

If the array is passed by value, the DLL function receives a copy of the array, but any values entered in the copy are not returned to the calling function. The copy is strictly local and is lost (discarded from memory) when the called function returns.

Alternatively, you could treat an array as a structure and pass it by reference to the entire array. This, however, requires a fixed array size and, of course, needs identical definitions in both VB and VC (which in turns means that every time you want to change the size of the fractal image, you must change the DLL's code and recompile). Instead, by passing a reference to the first element of the array only, the called function can calculate a value to be written to that address and then offset the address to the next element in the array. In this fashion, a two-dimensional array (or even a one-dimensional array) of any size can be filled because the array size has been passed separately. And, because the array belongs to the calling application (only an address is being passed), the resulting values remain available even after the DLL-supplied function terminates.

Of course, when you're working with arrays, you also need to keep in mind the following:

- Different languages can mean quite different things even when the terms are the same (for more on this, see the "When an Int Is Not an Int" section, later in this chapter).

- Visual Basic and C/C++ differ subtly in how arrays are dimensioned (for more on this, see the "Array Dimensions in VB versus VC" section later in this chapter).

As long as you avoid these two conflicts (and there are probably others that are less apparent), passing parameters by reference is a useful way to make it possible for a DLL (or any other remote procedure) to return values more complex than a simple integer or a double.

Problems and Conflicts between Visual Basic and C/C++

When you mix languages—for example, when you use a DLL written in Pascal or C/++ with Visual Basic—some conflicts will not show up in the compile/build operation. And, in some cases, the problems may not show up at all, at least, in a form that can be conveniently identified and debugged. Other problems will make themselves entirely too apparent by causing a compiler crash, and debugging them can be annoying. Here are a couple of these types of conflicts.

When an Int Is Not an Int

Visual Basic defines an integer as a 2-byte or WORD value. In contrast, Visual C/C++ (the current, 32-bit version) defines an integer as a 4-byte value (a DWORD or double WORD). In most cases, this difference does not affect development, even when you use a VC-developed DLL with a VB application. When Visual Basic passes an integer parameter (2-bytes) to a DLL that is expecting an integer argument (4-bytes), the translation is automatic.

Likewise, when the VC DLL returns an integer (4-byte) value, the VB application "sees" is a 2-byte integer without a conflict. Of course, if the returned value is greater than 0xFFFF (65535), the data that the Visual Basic program recognizes will not correspond to what the DLL intended to return because the high word value will be lost in translation.

One solution, of course, is for the VB application to always pass INT values as LONG when the DLL is expecting integers and to expect a LONG return when the DLL is returning an integer result. This accommodation, rather obviously, is a shortcoming in Visual Basic, which has simply not fully entered the world of 32-bit operations. When passing arguments by value, this is not a problem, as Visual Basic performs the necessary conversions. When passing arguments by reference, however, you are responsible for providing the proper variable types. In some circumstances, however, no automatic accommodation is possible, and serious results can easily eventuate from such discrepancies in sizes. For example, in the DLLMandelbrotArray function in the Fractal.DLL library, the first parameter expected is the address of an array of integers, and the second and third parameters are the dimensions of the array, arguments passed as integers (2-byte) and expected as integers (4-byte).

As we mentioned earlier, these second and third parameters are passed and accepted without conflict. The first parameter, however, is passed as an address (ByRef) and does have potential for error—a serious error—if the Visual Basic application declares an array of integer as:

```
Private Sub MandelbrotArray_Click()
    Dim A(1000, 1000) As Integer
```

and then passes the address of the array to the DLL's DLLMandelbrotArray function as:

```
bResult = DLLMandelbrotArray( A(0, 0), ...
```

Initially, when the DLL is called, there is no obvious problem. However, within the DLL, the array is recognized only as an address of the first element of an array, and the DLL enters values in the array by incrementing the address to reach successive elements of the array. The address pointer is incremented, however, as if the elements in the array were 4 bytes in size.

Two errors result:

- The DLL is only writing results to every second element in the original array supplied by the Visual Basic application.

- Once the original array is exhausted, the DLL will be writing additional information to an area beyond the array.

In most cases, this addressing error will simply result in the VB application crashing *after* the DLL returns, but, in a worst-case scenario, the result could be the corruption of the system (that is, a system crash).

The solution, of course, is simple. When the DLL expects an array of integers, the VB application should declare an array of Long:

```
Private Sub MandelbrotArray_Click()
    Dim A(1000, 1000) As Long
    bResult = DLLMandelbrotArray( A(0, 0), ...
```

The point, however, is not as simple as the solution shown here. Because VB is not fully 32-bit compliant, be very sure when using a DLL that you know what you are passing as arguments and what you are expecting returned. Even though it is called an integer in both cases, an integer is not the same in both languages.

Array Dimensions in VB versus VC

Visual Basic and Visual C/C++ also differ in the way that they dimension arrays.

WARNING Be aware that passing the wrong array variable or attempting to access nonexisting elements of the array from within the Visual C++ code will frequently lead to crashes.

In Visual Basic, when an array is declared as:

```
Dim A(10) As Long
```

the array actually has 11 elements. In this example, VB allocates and numbers elements as A(0), A(1), A(2), A(3), A(4), A(5), A(6), A(7), A(8), A(9) and A(10).

In C/C++, the corresponding declaration would be:

```
int A[10];
```

but this array has only 10 elements, allocated and numbered as A[0], A[1], A[2], A[3], A[4], A[5], A[6], A[7], A[8], A[9]. There is no A[10] (eleventh) element.

Therefore, if you tell a DLL function that you have passed a pointer to an array with dimensions of (1000, 1000), the DLL will expect the array to include only 1,000,000 elements when the actual array contains 1,002,001 elements (1001 to the square), a discrepancy of 2,001 elements. The solution, obviously, is to always declare the actual array dimensions (1001, 1001) and not the index limits.

Code 4.3: **Visual C++ Program Listing for Fractal DLL**

Fractal.DEF

```
; Fractal.def : Declares the module parameters for the DLL.
LIBRARY      "Fractal"
DESCRIPTION  'Fractal Windows Dynamic Link Library'
EXPORTS
```

```
; Explicit exports can go here
DLLMandelbrot                @1
DLLMandelbrotArray           @2
DLLPaintMandelbrot           @3
```

Fractal.H

```
#define EXPORT extern "C" __declspec( dllexport )
EXPORT int CALLBACK DLLMandelbrot( double, double );
EXPORT int CALLBACK DLLMandelbrotArray( int*, int, int, double, double,
double, double );
EXPORT int CALLBACK DLLPaintMandelbrot( HDC*, int, int, double, double,
double, double );
```

Fractal.CPP

```
#include <windows.h>
#include <math.h>
#include "fractal.h"

int WINAPI DllMain( HINSTANCE hInstance, DWORD dwReason, PVOID
pvReserved )
{
    return TRUE;
}

EXPORT int CALLBACK DLLMandelbrot( double dXPos, double dYPos )
{
    double      dXIter, dYIter, dXTemp;
    int         nSteps, nLimit = 100;
    bool        bDone;

    dXIter = 0.0;
    dYIter = 0.0;
    bDone  = FALSE;
    nSteps = 0;
    do
    {
        dXTemp = pow( dXIter, 2 ) - pow( dYIter, 2 ) + dXPos;
        dYIter = 2 * ( dXIter * dYIter) + dYPos;
        dXIter = dXTemp;
        nSteps++;
        if( sqrt( pow( dXIter, 2 ) + pow( dYIter, 2 ) ) >= 2.0 )
            bDone = TRUE;
```

```
            if( nSteps >= nLimit )
                bDone = TRUE;
    }
    while( ! bDone );
    if( nSteps < nLimit )
        return( nSteps % 15 );
    else
        return( 15 );
}

EXPORT int CALLBACK DLLMandelbrotArray( int *pA, int nXSize, int
nYSize, double dXStart, double dYStart, double dXEnd, double dYEnd )
{
    double     dXStep, dYStep;

    dXStep = ( dXEnd - dXStart ) / nXSize;
    dYStep = ( dYEnd - dYStart ) / nYSize;
    for( int j=0; j<nYSize; j++ )
        for( int i=0; i<nXSize; i++ )
        {
            *pA = DLLMandelbrot( dXStart + i * dXStep, dYStart + j *
dYStep );
                pA++;
        }
    return TRUE;
}

EXPORT int CALLBACK DLLPaintMandelbrot( HDC *pDC, int nXSize, int
nYSize, double dXStart, double dYStart,     double dXEnd, double dYEnd
)
{
    double     dXStep, dYStep;
    int        nIndex;

    SetMapMode( *pDC, MM_ANISOTROPIC );
    SetWindowExtEx( *pDC, nXSize, nYSize, NULL );
    SetViewportExtEx( *pDC, nXSize, nYSize, NULL );

    RealizePalette( *pDC );

    dXStep = ( dXEnd - dXStart ) / nXSize;
    dYStep = ( dYEnd - dYStart ) / nYSize;
```

```
for( int i=0; i<nXSize; i++ )
{
    for( int j=0; j<nYSize; j++ )
    {
        nIndex = DLLMandelbrot( dXStart + i * dXStep, dYStart +
j * dYStep );
        if( nIndex < 15 )
            SetPixelV( *pDC, i, j, PALETTEINDEX( nIndex ) );
    }
}
return TRUE;
}
```

Fractal Images and Palettes

The Fractal application we used in the previous sections to demonstrate how to build DLLs in Visual C++ produces 16-color fractals (not the most exciting images). It's certainly possible to modify the code to produce fractals with many colors and smooth coloring schemes. In the Ch04\Fractals\Palette folder on the CD, you will find another project, also named Fractal, that draws smoothly colored fractals. This fractal application uses 236 iterations in calculating each pixel's color and is significantly slower than the version of the Fractal application we use in this chapter to demonstrate the Fractal DLL. The new Fractal project, which uses palettes to color the fractal images, is implemented in Visual Basic so that it can be used by those of you who would rather experiment on fractal images without resorting to Visual C++.

If you open this project in the Visual Basic IDE, you will see that the line:

```
Picture1.PSet (i, j), QBColor(nSteps Mod 16)
```

is replaced by the line:

```
Picture1.PSet (i, j), &H1000000 + nSteps + 20
```

The color expression in the above statement corresponds to an entry in the current palette. Because the first 20 colors in a palette are reserved for system use, we skip them and use the remaining 236 colors of the palette. The number of iterations is mapped to a palette color that is used to paint the current pixel.

Fractal Images and Palettes (continued)

The fractals shown below were produced by the revised Fractal application and show a few details of the Mandelbrot set. You can experiment by trying different palettes to see which one is best suited for each image.

Manipulating Strings with Visual C++

C/C++ DLLs can be particularly helpful in sorting or ordering large blocks of data. For example, the ReverseString function in the Reverse.DLL accepts a string that can be a maximum of 100Kb. First, the string is reversed entirely, and then, in a second operation, the individual words are re-reversed (restored). Thus, the following sentence:

The quick red fox jumped over the lazy brown dog

becomes:

dog brown lazy the over jumped fox red quick The

Although this example is rather trivial, it is by no means without a practical value, and it does illustrate how to handle character strings in a VC++ DLL. The Visual Basic Instr() function locates instances of a string in a longer string, but it always starts from the beginning of the long string. A function that locates the same instances in the reverse order (starting from the end of the string) would also be useful, but to implement it efficiently, you would have to reverse both strings and then perform a search with the Instr() function.

The Visual Basic routine to reverse the string in place would look something like this:

```
For i = 1 To Len(AString) / 2
    tmpChar = Mid(AString, Len(AString) - i + 1, 1)
    Mid(AString, Len(AString) - i + 1, 1) = Mid(AString, i, 1)
    Mid(AString, i, 1) = tmpChar
Next
```

All this routine does is reverse the original string, character for character:

god nworb yzal eht revo depmuj xof der kciuq ehT

You can reverse a 30Kb string in approximately 0.6 seconds, as you may recall from the section "Manipulating Strings Efficiently," earlier in this chapter.

Alternatively, the ReverseString function in the Reverse.DLL is called in a slightly different fashion. First, the declaration of the function appears as:

```
Private Declare Function ReverseString Lib "Reverse.DLL" (ByVal Str As
Any, ByVal StrLen As Integer) As String
```

The string argument is passed by value, not by reference, and here it is passed as a type Any, although actually it makes little difference whether the type is identified as Any or as String.

Next, to call the external function, the local variable TempStr receives a copy of the string to be modified. This is important because if you try to pass Text1, your application will malfunction with a page fault error.

Also, we supply a size argument StrLen that contains the length of the string. This is necessary because, as you will see in a moment, the ReverseString function has no knowledge of the size of the string or even that it is looking at a string:

```
Private Sub Command1_Click()
    Dim T1 As Single
    Dim T2 As Single
    Dim Msg
    Dim TempStr As String

    TempStr = Text1
    StrLen = Len(TempStr)
    T1 = Timer
    Text2 = ReverseString(TempStr, StrLen)
    T2 = Timer - T1
    Msg = Format(T2, "###0.000")
    Debug.Print "Elapsed time = " & Msg & " seconds to reverse string
(dll)"
End Sub
```

These provisos aside, the ReverseString function returns the modified text string in a form that can be copied to the Text2 member for display. What is not immediately apparent here is that the TempStr argument itself has also been altered, and the value returned by the ReverseString function is actually a pointer to the TempStr member, which has been used as a buffer for the transfer both to and from the external function.

Most important, using the same 30Kb text file as the sample to be processed, the execution time becomes approximately 0.050 seconds. It is more than 10 times faster while executing a more complex operation (it reverses the order of the words in the string, not just the characters). The ReverseString() function ignores punctuation, but you can easily modify the C code for various types of sequential character manipulation.

The Reverse project, shown in Figure 4.8, demonstrates the ReverseString function implemented in REVERSE.DLL.

NOTE   You'll find the Reverse project in the Ch04/REVERSE folder on the CD that comes with this book.

FIGURE 4.8:

The Reverse project demonstrates the ReverseString function, which is implemented in REVERSE.DLL.

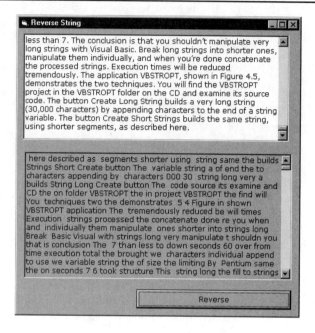

To test this function, copy a large segment of text from another application and paste it in the TextBox control on the Form. Then click the Reverse button.

The first time you click the Reverse button, the operation will complete in almost a second. Visual Basic needs the additional time to load the DLL. After the DLL is loaded, the string is reversed in practically no time.

The Magic Black Box

Now, let's look inside the magic black box, the DLL function. C/C++ does not have particularly sophisticated string-handling functions although, more recently, the MFC CString class has introduced a variety of member functions that parallel the Visual Basic string functions. These CString members, however, are not what we will be using here. Instead, we will rely on much more primitive (and faster) mechanisms.

Neither does C/C++ have a string data type. Instead, strings are simply arrays of characters (char data type in C). In VB, strings are also arrays of characters, but VB's strings are not readily accessible as arrays, whereas C/C++ strings are only accessible as indexed arrays.

The ReverseString function does not actually accept a string argument even though that is what the Visual Basic operation has passed. Instead, the ReverseString function accepts a pointer to type char that essentially is the address of the first character in the string. In this fashion, the ReverseString function does not begin with a copy of the original string but, instead, has a pointer to the memory address for the string that belongs to the Visual Basic application:

```
EXPORT char* CALLBACK ReverseString( char* pStr, int nStrLen )
{
```

Because the string is not local, the ReverseString function needs to know the length of the string. (Granted, we could scan from the address to find the end of the string by searching for nulls, but passing the length, which VB already knows, is simpler.)

Internally, ReverseString declares two arrays of char, each 100Kb in size. Although it's possible to allocate these dynamically, according to the size information provided by nStrLen, this static declaration is simpler for the present example. You might keep this alternative in mind, however, because other types of sort and order operations may well need to use dynamic allocation for buffer space.

```
char strTemp1[102400], strTemp2[102400];
char *pTemp;
int  i, j, k, n;
```

Next, before taking any actions, it is only prudent to clear the two buffers. Unlike Visual Basic, C/C++ does not automatically clear allocated memory, and you must explicitly set the entire range of memory to zeros:

```
//=== clear both buffers
memset( strTemp1, '\0', 102400 );
memset( strTemp2, '\0', 102400 );
```

Next, reverse the entire string. Because the source information is not in a local array and we have only a pointer to the data, we begin by duplicating the pointer. We do this because we will need the original pointer (address) again later:

```
pTemp = pStr;
```

Now that the pTemp pointer points to the same memory location as pStr (the string passed to the function by VB), we can set up a loop that will scan the original array of characters backward and append each character to the end of a new string (strTemp1):

```
// copy remote buffer (incoming) to local buffer in reverse order
for( i=nStrLen-1; i>=0;  )
```

```
        {
            strTemp1[i-] = *pTemp;
            pTemp++;
        }
```

After copying each character, we also increment the pointer **pTemp**. Notice that the loop counter is not decremented in the For statement. Instead, this operation takes place in the loop. The expression i-- does the following: First, it uses the current value of the variable *i* to address an element of the character array strTemp, and after the value is copied, the variable is decremented. Earlier, we discussed problems that can arise when VB and C/C++ don't correctly understand array types. This problem, however, does not arise here, and we can simply increment the address without concerns.

If, however, we were doing this for other types of arrays—such as an array of structures, for example—we would need to make appropriate provisions for incrementing the address pointer according to the size of the structure.

But, once we have our local array, which is now in reverse order, our next task is to re-reverse the individual words to put them in forward order, that is, to restore *sdrawkcab* to *backwards*. We'll begin with several index variables, initializing three of these as zero:

```
        i = j = n = 0;
```

Next, we'll use a Do…While loop to terminate when our index i reaches **nStrLen**:

```
        do
        {
```

Within the Do…While loop, we execute another While loop to look for a non-alphanumeric character, using the isalnum() function to test each character in the array and incrementing i until a space, punctuation, or other nonalphanumeric character is found:

```
            while( isalnum( strTemp1[i] ) ) i++;
```

The isalnum() function is only one of the character-test functions supplied by C/C++. C/C++ provides a variety of useful tests, and we could also include punctuation or exclude numbers or whatever our test required.

In this case, however, as soon as we find a nonalphanumeric character, we've reached the end of the word, and we need another loop to re-reverse the characters belonging to the word:

```
            for( k=i-1; k>=j; k- )
                strTemp2[n++] = strTemp1[k];
```

We've used i-1 to exclude the space (or punctuation or other characters) at the end of the word. But, of course, we need a separator between words, so we'll insert a space.

```
strTemp2[n++] = ' ';
```

Each time we write a char to the strTemp2 array, we're incrementing the n index.

And, last, we increment the i index before copying the value to the j index. (The expression ++i says that i is incremented before anything else happens. If the expression is i++, i is incremented last, after it is used in the operation.)

```
        j = ++i;
    }
    while( i < nStrLen );
```

Now, when our original Do…While loop finishes, we have a copy of the original text that is in reverse word order. (We've also dropped all punctuation, but that's not important here.)

However, this reverse-order copy is a local copy, and, once the ReverseString function exits, these local arrays will be lost, freed from memory, which means that their contents will also be lost. Therefore, our last operation is to copy the data from the local array back to the buffer maintained by the Visual Basic application that called ReverseString. And this is also why we've been careful to maintain our original address pointer. Now we need it again:

```
// write changed buffer (local) back to original buffer (remote)
pTemp = pStr;
```

However, since we still aren't done with the original pointer, we assign pTemp to the same initial address again. And then we initiate another loop to copy the indexed element from strTemp2 back to the memory location addressed by pTemp before incrementing pTemp to the next address:

```
for( i=0; i<nStrLen; i++ )
{
    *pTemp = strTemp2[i];
    pTemp++;
}
```

And, finally, we'll return the pStr pointer to the calling application:

```
    return pStr;
}
```

Remember, pStr is the same pointer that the calling application supplied as the address of the local buffer containing the original data. In this last loop, we've copied the local array back to the original string (TempStr) and then returned the address of the original string to the calling application where it is assigned to a new string member (Text2).

And, because we're changing the string that was passed as an argument, we have another reason for passing a copy (TempStr) rather than the real original (Text1). Now that you have seen the code of the ReverseString function, let's review all the operations it performs on a 30Kb string. First, it copies the string to a local array, reverses all characters, then reverses each word in the string, and finally copies the processed array back to another string, which is returned to the VB application. All these operations don't take more than a few dozen milliseconds, which is really impressive. Visual C++ is extremely efficient when it comes to handling characters, and you should consider a Visual C++ DLL for operations that manipulate strings extensively. One thing to keep in mind is that Visual Basic can handle small strings very fast too, but it slows down quickly as the strings grow large.

Code 4.3:   Visual C++ Program Listing for Reverse DLL

Reverse.DEF

```
; Reverse.def : Declares the module parameters for the DLL.

LIBRARY        "Reverse"
DESCRIPTION    'Reverse Windows dynamic-link libraries'

EXPORTS
    ; Explicit exports can go here
    ReverseString            @1
```

Reverse.H

```
#define EXPORT extern "C" __declspec( dllexport )

EXPORT char* CALLBACK ReverseString( char*, int );
```

Reverse.C

```
#include <windows.h>
#include "reverse.h"

int WINAPI DllMain( HINSTANCE hInstance, DWORD dwReason, PVOID
pvReserved )
{
```

```
        return TRUE;
}

EXPORT char* CALLBACK ReverseString( char* pStr, int nStrLen )
{
    char strTemp1[102400], strTemp2[102400];
    char *pTemp;
    int  i, j, k, n;

    //=== clear both buffers
    memset( strTemp1, '\0', 102400 );
    memset( strTemp2, '\0', 102400 );

    //=== copy remote buffer (incoming) to local buffer in reverse
order
    pTemp = pStr;
    for( i=nStrLen-1; i>=0;  )
    {
        strTemp1[i-] = *pTemp;
        pTemp++;
    }

    //=== now re-reverse each word in the strTemp buffer
    i = j = n = 0;
    do
    {
        while( isalnum( strTemp1[i] ) ) i++;
        for( k=i-1; k>=j; k- )
            strTemp2[n++] = strTemp1[k];
        strTemp2[n++] = ' ';
        j = ++i;
    }
    while( i < nStrLen );

    //=== write changed buffer (local) back to original buffer (remote)
    pTemp = pStr;
    for( i=0; i<nStrLen; i++ )
    {
        *pTemp = strTemp2[i];
        pTemp++;
    }
    return pStr;
}
```

PART II

Object Programming

Object Programming with Visual Basic

- Understanding objects

- Using components to develop software

- Creating object variables

- Creating controls at run time

- Binding variables

- Using the Object Browser

- Using collections

As a term, *object-oriented programming* has been around for a quite a while now. At one time, object-oriented versions of popular programming languages, such as C and Pascal, promised to help developers solve many problems, especially with large applications or for projects on which teams of programmers worked. The catch with object-oriented languages and with the object-oriented approach to programming is that developers must learn and master new concepts and get accustomed to a new programming philosophy.

No wonder most developers worked with object-oriented versions of C in a fashion similar to the way they had worked with non–object-oriented languages. The way they worked was determined (to a large extent) by each programmer's education. Object-oriented programming didn't come naturally to those who went to school before the introduction of object-oriented programming or to those who didn't have a degree in computer science. It's a new approach to application development, and, unlike the traditional approach to programming, it's an acquired taste.

So why bother with object-oriented programming? Because you can't go very far without it. Current programming is object oriented, and you must master the object-oriented techniques necessary for developing software with development tools such as Visual Basic. Some of the benefits include the ability to:

- Write code that can be used in multiple applications

- Update objects throughout their life cycle, without breaking the applications that use them

- Coordinate among multiple programmers working on the same project

Much has been written about object-oriented programming, but the bottom line is this: *Object-oriented programming won't simplify your life instantly.* Actually, you'll be hard-pressed to understand topics such as inheritance, encapsulation, and polymorphism and then apply them to your projects. Down the road, however, the object-oriented approach will simplify your life. But not everyone will make the transition.

NOTE   Visual Basic is a unique environment that over the past seven years gradually and in subtle ways introduced programmers to the principles of object-oriented programming. Those of you who have worked with Visual Basic since version 1 (it may look arcane now, but it was an extraordinary environment for developing early Windows applications) have been using objects for many years.

The environment of Visual Basic and its approach to programming was carefully crafted so that developers don't have to be aware of features such as encapsulation or polymorphism. Visual Basic literally incorporated the complexity of Windows into a simple language. The average VB developer needn't know that TextBoxes are objects derived from the TextBox class. They are boxes that can be dropped on a Form, and, once there, they carry with them the functionality of a text editor. The same programmer doesn't have to know that objects expose properties and methods and that they communicate with the operating system via events. The Properties window displays all the properties you can set to adjust the appearance of the object, and the methods are like commands that you once had to memorize. The truth is, TextBoxes are objects, and they behave like objects on a Form.

So, how do you explain the principles of object-oriented programming? We'll do it gradually, starting with simple topics, such as how to manipulate objects from within your applications. We won't show you how to set properties or how to program with events or deal with other techniques you have mastered already. Instead, we'll focus on a few rather advanced topics, such as:

- How to create object variables
- The early and late binding of variables
- How to create new instances of existing objects

NOTE
Starting with the next chapter, you'll learn how to build your own objects, how to build your own ActiveX controls, and how to extend the Visual Basic editor with your own add-ins. This chapter is a compendium of information on manipulating objects, which is a prerequisite for the following chapters.

The Characteristics of Objects

When you program with Visual Basic, you are actually programming objects. The ActiveX controls you place on a Form are objects, and programming in Visual Basic consists of manipulating their properties and calling their methods. All the action takes place in the events of the objects, which are raised when certain conditions are met. Objects are units of code and data, which can be used as black boxes. Developers don't need to know how each object is implemented. All they need to know is:

- Which properties the object exposes
- Which methods the object provides
- Which events the object can raise

Properties and methods constitute the object's interface. This isn't a graphical interface, and it doesn't have visual elements, but nevertheless, it's an interface: It stands between you and the object, as you can't access the object's code or data directly.

For example, you can add the functionality of a text editor on your application's user interface by placing a TextBox control on the Form and setting its basic properties through the Properties window (whether the TextBox can display multiple lines of text, the font to use, and so on). In your code, you can program how the TextBox reacts to user actions by providing a subroutine (handler) to the events to which it must react. The properties, methods, and events of the TextBox constitute its interface, and you can bring the functionality of this control to your application, without knowing anything about the code that implements the control. Figure 5.1 shows how this works.

The Change event is raised when the user changes the contents of the control. As a developer, you don't have to monitor the mouse or the keyboard to find out when the text changes. The TextBox control itself will notify your program through an event, and all you have to do is provide the code to react to this event. If you don't provide an event handler for the Change event, the control won't react when the text is changed.

Finally, the TextBox control provides a few methods that you can call from within your code to manipulate the control. The SetFocus method lets you move the focus to a TextBox control from anywhere in your code and make it the active control. The Refresh method refreshes the control's contents. The TextBox control is in effect an object that you can manipulate at a high level. You don't have access to its code, and you can neither enhance its operation nor break it. Actually, you can enhance its default operation by programming certain events, but still you don't have to touch its code.

For example, you can capture certain keystrokes and react differently to them. You can think of the TextBox control as an application that exposes a user interface, which consists of properties, methods, and events. Just as users of your application can control it through its user interface, you can only control the objects of your application through the members of the interface they expose.

FIGURE 5.1:

Applications communicate with objects through the properties and methods they expose and the events they raise.

Setting a Property
Text1.ForeColor = RGB(0, 255, 255)

Reading a Property
Comments = Text1.Text

Calling a Method
Text1.SetFocus

Reacting to Events
Private Sub Text1_KeyDown(KeyCode, Shift)
If KeyCode = vbKeyF5 Then
    Text1.SelText = Date
End If
End Sub

NOTE
Restricting access to the code of a control (or any other object) isn't just a strict rule. It serves a practical purpose: It prohibits developers from breaking the control by "enhancing" it. Once users learn what they can do with a TextBox control, they can handle any TextBox, in any application. This consistency in the user interface is a fundamental characteristic of Windows, and objects are designed to enforce this consistency.

Hiding the inner workings of an object is called *encapsulation* or *abstraction*. The object encapsulates (abstracts) complicated operations, such as the breaking of multiple lines, the insertion of new characters, and so on. These are low-level details that you don't have to deal with. Instead, you can concentrate on your application, its user interface, and its operation. In this chapter, we are going to discuss the Visual Basic objects at large and the various techniques for working with them. Objects encapsulate complicated operations into a black box, which you can access through its user interface.

Encapsulation is the first buzzword in object-oriented programming, and you more than likely understand it by now. If you had to describe object-oriented programming with a single word, *encapsulation* would be it.

NOTE   Encapsulation is the ability to wrap code and data in a single unit that can be accessed by a well-defined interface. Developers can carry the functionality of an object to their applications and manipulate it through this interface, but they can't enhance or break the object because they can't alter the code or make it perform illegal operations.

Encapsulation is often referred to as *abstraction* because it abstracts complicated operations. If you have used the Data Access Objects, you understand how this abstraction works. Data in a database are stored in a database file (with the extension MDB). This file, however, has a complicated (undocumented, as far as we know) structure, and you never access it directly. Instead, you specify the information you're interested in and use the DAO (Data Access Objects) to retrieve them. Information is presented in the form of rows and columns, which are easy to understand, visualize, and work with. The database file contains the data, index files, pointers, and all kinds of animals that you don't want to deal with. The DAO interface knows how to extract and/or save the desired information to the database.

Component Software Development

The concept of encapsulation leads to another important development in software design methodology: *component software*. What happens when you're designing applications with Visual Basic? You borrow functionality built in to Windows itself and place it on your Forms by dropping controls from the Toolbox onto the Form. Your code is the glue that holds together these "pieces of functionality." And, considering what you can do with a few lines of VB code, the code you provide is really minimal. Most of the functionality of your application is concentrated in the controls.

NOTE   As operating systems and languages evolve, the code behind the applications will become less and less, but today you can't do much better than VB. It's the most compact of all major programming languages in the Windows environment.

Building applications with Visual Basic isn't unlike building a computer with components that you purchase separately. The sure way to build your dream computer is to purchase the components you need and connect them yourself. (Don't try this if you are not a computer whiz, but the best computers we've seen are custom built.) To build your own computer, you must purchase the components you need and put them together. Things may get a bit nasty when time comes to install drivers for SCSII interfaces and huge hard disks, CD-ROM units, or an inexpensive video capture card. But if you know what you're doing, you'll end up with a powerful computer. When a faster processor comes along, you can replace yours with the new processor. Power surge problem? The trip to the local computer store will take you longer than actually replacing the power supply.

The components you put together to build a custom computer encapsulate characteristics, just like the characteristics of programming objects. You don't have to know anything about power supplies, except for the input they require (110 volts, 220 volts, or switching) and the output they provide. All you have to do is make sure that the power supply provides the voltage required by the motherboard. Hard disk? Just find the one with the capacity and performance that suits your needs. They are all designed to fit in a standard bay, and if they don't, use a couple of brackets. These characteristics are the component's properties.

Hardware components have methods too, which are used by the system software. Methods such as GetThisCluster and WriteThatCluster allow the operating system (and the applications) to use the disk. The glue that makes all the components work together is the BIOS and the operating system. Fortunately, both come ready to use, and you don't have to do anything, short of setting a few parameters.

Here we are again. The operating system itself is another object, which encapsulates an incredible amount of functionality. You can adjust certain characteristics of the operating system with the applications provided in the Control Panel or even through the Registry. As a programmer, you know already that you can access the Registry's functions and use them from within your applications, as we discussed in the first part of this book.

When components are designed according to a set of standards that allow them to work in tandem, they can be put together to build a larger system with a minimum effort. As far as software development goes, one of the standards that allows components to interact is ActiveX (formerly OLE). Every component you build with Visual Basic supports ActiveX, and you don't have to know much about the ActiveX specifications. A software component designed according to ActiveX will work not only with Visual Basic applications, but with any programming language, such as Visual C++, and even with HTML. You can actually embed ActiveX controls on a Web page by inserting a few lines of code in the page's HTML code and turn static documents into interactive applications.

To summarize, software objects have two characteristics:

1. They encapsulate certain functionality and allow developers to access their functionality through their interface.

2. They interact, which means that they can be placed together on a Form and cooperate.

What this means to you is that you can:

1. Select all the components you need for your application or develop some of them if you can't find off-the-shelf components for your application.

2. Put them together by manipulating them with VB code, using the interface components they provide (properties and methods).

This is how current software is developed, and you've been doing it with Visual Basic for many years.

Before we show you how to create your own objects, we are going to review how built-in objects are manipulated. In the rest of this chapter, we will review a few advanced topics, such as how to create new Forms and objects at run time and how to use type libraries, and then we'll introduce object-oriented programming with the built-in objects. Visual Basic provides a large number of objects, and most of you have been using them in your applications. If you plan to exploit object-oriented programming with Visual Basic, you should take a quick look at the examples in this chapter.

Objects Come from Classes

The controls you see on the Toolbox are actually classes, from which the objects you use on your Forms are derived. The class is a *prototype,* and the object is an *instance* of this prototype. When you place a TextBox control on a Form, Visual Basic creates a new object based on the TextBox class. Because of the way we use ActiveX controls in building an application's user interface, this distinction between classes and objects isn't quite obvious. It will become clear when we build our own classes, and then we'll create new objects based on these classes.

Objects Come from Classes (continued)

The classical analogy between classes and objects is that of the cookie cutter and the cookies. All cookies cut with the same cutter are identical (at least as far as their shape and size is concerned). Each TextBox you place on your Form with the TextBox tool of the Toolbox is identical. They all come from the same class, or prototype. Once on the Form, each TextBox can be adjusted, and you can make them all look different. You can change their background and text colors, the font used for rendering the text, and so on. The basic functionality of each TextBox object, however, is the same, and it's determined by the TextBox class.

Creating Object Variables

To access the functionality of a class, you must first create an object variable. Objects are classes (prototypes) that can't be accessed directly. To access the functionality of an object, you must create a special variable that can store a reference to the object. In this section, we'll review the basics of creating object variables to manipulate objects.

Normally, the objects you place on a Form to create the user interface are manipulated from within code through their name (Text1, Command1, and so on). So why create variables to access them? As you will see shortly, on occasions you'll want to be able to access objects through a variable. For example, not all objects can be placed on a Form. If you have done any database programming with Visual Basic, you know that there are two approaches: the simple and limited, no-code approach (through the Data Control), and the serious approach (through the Data Access Objects). To access the objects exposed by the DAO—objects such as recordsets, fields, and so on—you must create variables that represent these objects, just as you create variables to represent integer values or strings.

The Purpose of Object Variables

Object variables can be of two types:

- Generic, which can store all types of objects

- Specific, which can store objects of the same type only

Generic object variables are declared as Object type:

```
Dim myObject As Object
```

The *myObject* variable can store any type of object. The type Variant can also store objects, but this type requires more overhead than other types.

Finally, if you need an object variable to store references to controls, use the Control type:

```
Dim myControl As Control
```

The *myControl* object variable can store references to any control, but no other types of objects. If you know the type of object you want to store in an object variable, use this control's name in the declaration, as in the following statements:

```
Dim TBox As TextBox
Dim OKCancel As CommandButton
```

When an object variable is created, it contains nothing. To assign something to the object variable, you must use the Set statement to reference an existing object. The following statement allows you to use the *TBox* variable to access the Text1 TextBox:

```
Set TBox = Text1
```

Both *TBox* and *Text1* reference the same object, the Text1 TextBox. You can change the Bold attribute of the control with either of the following statements:

```
TBox.Bold = True
Text1.Bold = True
```

Both statements turn on the Bold attribute of the text in the Text1 control.

The Set statement creates a reference to an existing object; it doesn't create a copy of the object. With a regular assignment operation, such as:

```
amount = totalDue
```

a copy of the value of the *totalDue* variable is created, and it's accessed by the name amount. Because the two objects are distinct, changing one of the variables has no effect on the other.

NOTE   When you know the type of object you are going to store in an object variable, you should use a specific type in the Dim statement. This will make your program run faster and also simplify coding. For more details on the effect of object variable declarations, see the section "Early and Late Binding of Variables," later in this chapter.

If you don't need the object variable any longer, release it by setting it to *Nothing:*

```
Set myControl = Nothing
```

One common use for a Control type variable is to access variables on a different Form. If you need to access the Font property of a control on another Form frequently and if the required statement is:

```
Form3!txtName.Font.Bold
```

you can simplify the code by creating an object variable that points to the control on another Form:

```
Dim TBox As Control
Set TBox = Form3!txtName
TBox.Font.Bold = True
```

You could also create an object variable that references the Font object directly:

```
Dim TBoxFont As Object
Set TBoxFont = Form3!txtName.Font
TBoxFont.Bold = True
```

The New Keyword

The object variables we created in the previous section refer to existing objects. To create a new instance of an existing object, you must use the New keyword, either in the Dim statement or in the Set statement. You can declare that an object variable create a new object with the statement:

```
Dim myObject As New Object
```

and then specify the object with a Set statement:

```
Set myObject = anotherObject
```

Or, you can declare it and then assign a new instance of an object to it:

```
Dim myObject As Object
Set myObject = New anotherObject
```

NOTE   You can use the New keyword either when you declare the object variable (Visual Basic prepares an object for storing a new instance of the object) or when you assign an object instance to the variable with the Set statement.

With the New keyword, you specify that the object variable will not reference an existing instance of the control, but will create a copy of the specified object. As you will see, you can create new instances of just about any object, including Forms, but you can't create new instances of controls. To create new controls at run time, you must use the Load statement, which is described in the section "Creating Controls at Run Time," later in this chapter.

Let's see now how these statements are used and what they can do for your application. In the following sections, we'll discuss a few of Visual Basic's built-in objects and see how and when object variables are used.

The Font Object

Objects represent programming entities, which can be as simple as fonts or as complicated as databases. In object-oriented programming terminology, objects encapsulate, or abstract, the entities they represent. The Font object represents the font used by a Form, by another object, or by the printer. As a programmer, you don't have to know how a font is stored in its file or how the object that uses the font reads this file. If you want the text on a Form to appear in bold, you must set the Bold property of the Font object to True:

```
Font.Bold=True
```

To print in bold on the printer, you can use this statement:

```
Printer.Font.Bold=True
```

To display text in bold on a Form, you can use this statement:

```
Form.Font.Bold=True
```

The Font object encapsulates (or abstracts) the font being used. Since both the Form and the Printer objects use a font, they provide a Font property, and you can change the attributes of the font by manipulating the Font object.

Creating a Font Object Variable

Let's create a Font object variable and make it represent the font of a specific control. You must declare an object variable that represents a font with the Font type. The variable *thisFont*, which is declared with this statement:

```
Dim thisFont As StdFont
```

is a Font object variable. You can use this variable to create a new Font property for a Form. This statement:

```
Set thisFont = Form1.Font
```

makes the *thisFont* variable refer to the Font property of Form1. To change the characteristics of the font being used to render the text on the Form1 Form, you can use statements such as the following:

```
thisFont.Name = "Comic Sans MS"
thisFont.Size = 12
thisFont.Bold = True
thisFont.Italic = False
```

Notice the use of the Set statement. When you want an object variable to refer to an existing object of the same type, you must use the Set statement. The Set statement tells Visual Basic to create an object that refers to the Font property of Form1.

You can also create a new Font object, with the following declaration:

```
Dim thisFont As New StdFont
```

This object variable refers to a new Font object. You can set its properties with statements such as the following:

```
thisFont.Name = "Courier"
thisFont.Size = 10
thisFont.Bold = False
thisFont.Italic = False
```

At this point, you can assign the *thisFont* object variable to the Font property of an existing object. The statement:

```
Form1.Font = thisFont
```

will cause the text on Form1 to be rendered in regular Courier typeface, at 10 point.

The FontObject Project

The FontObject project demonstrates the two distinct methods of using object variables.

NOTE   You'll find the FontObject project in the Ch05\FontObj folder on the CD that comes with this book.

The main Form of the project, shown in Figure 5.2, contains two Label controls. The top label's font is Verdana 14 point, and the second label has the default font (MS Serif, 8 point). Clicking the Manipulate Font button changes the attributes of the font of the top label by manipulating its Font property.

FIGURE 5.2:

The FontObject project, after clicking the Create Font button, which manipulates the bottom Label's Font property.

Load the FontObj program to see how object variables can be used to access existing fonts or represent new fonts. The Manipulate Font button manipulates the font of the first Label control through an object variable.

Code 5.1:   The Manipulate Font Button

```
Private Sub Command1_Click()
Dim thisFont As StdFont

' Get original font,
    Set thisFont = Label1.Font
' set its attributes
    thisFont.Bold = True
    thisFont.Italic = True
' and size
    thisFont.Size = 1.5 * thisFont.Size
' Clear object variable
    Set thisFont = Nothing

End Sub
```

The last statement in this subroutine releases the object variable when it's no longer needed by setting it to Nothing. The Nothing keyword is not equivalent to setting a string, an empty string, or a numeric variable to zero. It releases the object variable *thisFont* and returns the resources allocated to the object variable when it was created.

TIP

It's solid programming practice to release any object variable when it's no longer needed.

This subroutine starts by assigning the Font property of the Label1 control to the object variable *thisFont*. It then manipulates the font of the Label control by setting the attributes of the *thisFont* variable. As each statement is executed, the appearance of the font on the Label control changes. You don't need a statement that will assign the new settings of the *thisFont* property to the Font object of the Label control, because the variable *thisFont* and the property Label1.Font refer to the same object. If you want, you can single step through the code (by pressing F8) to see the effect of each statement on the appearance of the text on the control.

The Create Font button modifies the font of the lower label. It starts by creating a new Font object, initializes it to the value of the Font property of the first label, changes a few attributes, and then assigns the new Font object to the Font property of the second Label control.

Code 5.2: The Create Font Button

```
Private Sub Command2_Click()
Dim thisFont As New StdFont

' Use Name and Size properties of the original font
' The Bold and Italic attributes are not inherited
    thisFont.Name = Label1.FontName
    thisFont.Size = 1.5 * Label1.FontSize
    thisFont.Underline = True
    Set Label2.Font = thisFont
    Set thisFont = Nothing

End Sub
```

The object variable *thisFont* is created with the New keyword, when the variable is declared, and it doesn't refer to an existing object. Therefore, it can't affect the appearance of the text on the Label control, unless you specifically assign this object variable to the Font property of the Label control. If you single-step this application and click the Create Font button, nothing will change on the Form until the second to last statement is reached. This statement assigns the characteristics of the object variable to the label's Font property.

Again, you assign the *thisFont* object variable to the Font property of the Label control with the Set statement. Every time you assign an object to another, you must use the Set statement. Simple assignment statements such as the following don't work with objects:

```
Label2.Font = thisFont
```

The Screen and Printer Objects

Two useful built-in objects are the Screen and Printer objects, which represent the monitor and the current printer. You can use these objects to find out the properties of the monitor (its resolution, the fonts it can display, and so on) and of the printer. The Screen object has a Fonts property, which returns the names of the fonts that can be displayed on the screen (they are not necessarily the same as the fonts that can be used on the Printer object, which also supports the same property). If you had to display the names of the fonts in a ListBox control, you'd use a loop like this one:

```
For i = 0 To Screen.FontCount - 1
    List1.AddItem Screen.Fonts(i)
Next i
```

The Printer object is quite similar and supports many of the same properties and methods. The Screen and Printer objects demonstrate what we call encapsulation, or abstraction. As a developer, you don't have to know how the Printer and Screen objects really work. All you care about is that both objects support the Font property. The implementation details are hidden from the developer, who's free to focus on his or her application, and not on the specifics of the various display adapters or printer models.

This is what abstraction is all about: the ability to tell an object to do something or the ability to change a characteristic of an object without having to know how each specific object carries out its operation. The ScreenPrinterObjects project, discussed later in this chapter, demonstrates how you can simplify your code by exploiting the methods that are common to these two objects.

Simple Tricks with Default Properties

If you attempt to assign the *thisFont* object variable to the Font property of the Label2 control without the Set statement, the text on the label won't change, and you won't get an error message either. What's going on?

The Font object, like all other objects, has a default property, which is the Name property. The statements:

```
Label12.Font.Name = "Courier"
```
and
```
Label12.Font = "Courier"
```

Forms Are Classes

Forms are classes that can be created with the Dim statement, and you can control them from within your code. Visual Basic provides four methods for manipulating Forms:

Load loads a new Form in memory, but doesn't show it.

Show displays a Form that has already been loaded or loads and then displays a new Form.

Unload hides a loaded Form and unloads it from memory.

Hide hides a Form, but doesn't unload it from memory

These methods work on Forms that have already been designed and that exist in the current project. It is also possible to create new Forms at run time and display them as part of the application's user interface with the statement:

```
Dim myForm As Form
```

This statement creates a new Form object variable, which you can use in your code to reference an existing Form or to create a new Form. For example, you can set the *myForm* variable to an existing Form:

```
Set myForm = Form1
```

or to a new instance of the Form1 object:

```
Set myForm = New Form1
```

Form1 is an existing Form, but *myForm* is a new instance of Form1 and can be loaded and displayed with the statement:

```
myForm.Show
```

The Forms Project

If you need one or more special Forms in your application, you can design a prototype and then use it in your application. This prototype can have its own properties and methods and can even raise custom events.

The Forms project is a simple example of a special Form that displays a gradient on its background.

NOTE   You'll find the Forms project in the Ch05\Forms folder on the CD that comes with this book.

We will design a Form with a custom method, the BackGradient method, which accepts a single argument, the direction of the gradient. The gradient's direction can be horizontal or vertical. You can call it as follows:

```
myForm.BackGradient(gradient)
```

The value of gradient can be:

- 0 (no gradient)
- 1 (horizontal gradient)
- 2 (vertical gradient)

To design a Form with the BackGradient method, start a new project and add a new Form to it. Name the new Form GradForm, and enter the following code in the Form's Code window.

Code 5.3:   **Drawing Gradients**

```
Enum Gradients
    None = 0
    Horizontal = 1
    Vertical = 2
End Enum
```

```
Public Sub BackGradient(GradientDirection As Integer)

    If GradientDirection = None Then
        Me.BackColor = RGB(128, 128, 128)
        mGradient = None
        Exit Sub
    End If
    If GradientDirection = Horizontal Then
        For i = 0 To Me.ScaleWidth - 1
            GrComponent = Int(i * 255 / Me.ScaleWidth)
            RGBColor = RGB(GrComponent, GrComponent, GrComponent)
            Me.Line (i, 0)-(i, Me.ScaleHeight - 1), RGBColor
            GrComponent = GrComponent + Me.ScaleWidth / 255
        Next
        mGradient = Horizontal
    End If

    If GradientDirection = Vertical Then
        For i = 0 To Me.ScaleHeight - 1
            GrComponent = i * 255 / Me.ScaleHeight
            RGBColor = RGB(GrComponent, GrComponent, GrComponent)
            Me.Line (0, i)-(Me.ScaleWidth - 1, i), RGBColor
            GrComponent = GrComponent + GradForm.ScaleHeight / 255
        Next
        mGradient = Vertical
    End If

End Sub
```

The Enum type at the beginning of the code allows us to refer to the gradient's direction with a descriptive name instead of with a number. The BackGradient() subroutine is declared as public, which makes it a method of the Form. To create a new instance of this Form from within another Form's code, you must first create an object variable such as the following:

```
Dim myForm As GradForm
Set myForm = New GradForm
```

After you create the *myForm* instance of the GradForm class, you can display it with the statement:

```
myForm.Show
```

You can then access its BackGradient method as follows:

```
myForm.BackGradient 1
```

To use the GradForm, create a new Form, the MainForm, and make it the project's Startup object. The MainForm for the Forms project is shown in Figure 5.3. This Form contains a TextBox control and three buttons, which show one instance of the GradForm each. Each time you click one of these buttons, the gradient on the corresponding Form changes (from horizontal to vertical and back).

The instances of the GradForm are created with object variables, which are declared in the Main form as follows:

```
Dim Sleepy As GradForm
Dim Sneezy As GradForm
Dim Dopey As GradForm
```

Any part of the application can access these variables. When the main Form is loaded, it executes the following code.

FIGURE 5.3:

The Forms project

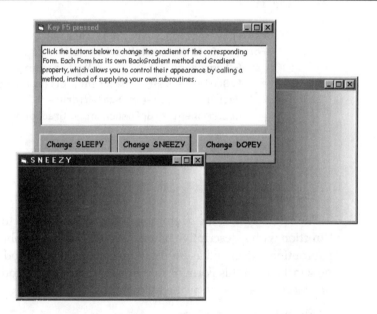

Code 5.4:   Loading the Custom Forms

```
Private Sub Form_Load()

Set Sleepy = New GradForm
Load Sleepy
With Sleepy
    .Top = 2000: .Left = 4000
```

```
        .Caption = "S L E E P Y"
End With
Set Sneezy = New GradForm
Load Sneezy
With Sneezy
        .Top = 3000: .Left = 7000
        .Caption = "S N E E Z Y"
End With
Set Dopey = New GradForm
Load Dopey
With Dopey
        .Top = 3000: .Left = 2000
        .Caption = "D O P E Y"
End With
End Sub
```

Code 5.5 creates three new instances of the GradForm object and places them on the monitor at different locations. The code behind each button changes the gradient's direction on the corresponding Form and shows it, just in case it was covered by another Form.

Code 5.5:   The Change Sleepy Button

```
Private Sub bttnSleepy_Click()
    Sleepy.BackGradient (Sleepy.Gradient Mod 2) + 1
    Sleepy.Show
End Sub
```

Forms with Events

In addition to custom methods, Form classes can raise custom events. Let's say you want to capture certain keystrokes and react to each one differently. To add a new event to the Form, you declare the event's name at the beginning of the code and then use the RaiseEvent statement to raise the custom event from within the new Form:

```
Event SpecialKey(KeyCode As Integer, Shift As Integer)

Private Sub Form_KeyUp(KeyCode As Integer, Shift As Integer)
    If KeyCode >= vbKeyF1 Or KeyCode <= vbKeyF16 Then
        RaiseEvent SpecialKey(KeyCode, Shift)
    End If
End Sub
```

The SpecialKey event is raised from within the Form's KeyUp event, which examines the code of the key pressed. If it corresponds to a function key, it raises the SpecialKey event and lets the main Form of the application handle the keypress.

Custom events introduce a slight complexity to the project. To declare a Form that raises events, you use the WithEvents keyword in the Dim statement, as follows:

```
Dim WithEvents myForm As GradForm
```

The keyword WithEvents tells Visual Basic to raise the events that occur on the object so that you can handle them from within your code. If you omit this keyword, Visual Basic creates a new Form based on the GradForm class, but it does not report the events to the object variable that represents the new Form. Now you can create a new instance of the GradForm Form with the statements:

```
Set myForm = New GradForm
myForm.Show
```

To process the special keystrokes, you provide an event handler for the SpecialKey event of the custom Form. Follow these steps:

1. Open the Objects drop-down list in the main Form's Code window, and select the Sleepy object.

2. In the Events drop-down list, you will see the name of the custom event, SpecialKey. Select it and enter the following code in the event's handler:

```
Private Sub Sleepy_SpecialKey(KeyCode As Integer, Shift As
Integer)
    Me.Caption = "Key F" & Chr(KeyCode - 63) & " pressed"
End Sub
```

3. Now run the project, display the Sleepy Form by clicking the Change Sleepy button, and press a function key.

The main Form's caption displays the key that was pressed on the Sleepy Form. This arrangement allows you to handle certain events of the GradForm's instances from within the main Form's code. The GradForm object will handle other keystrokes or mouse events, and the main Form will never know.

Events Belong to Classes, Not to Objects

If you open the Code window of the GradForm Form, you will see that it doesn't have a SpecialKey event, and you can't program this event for the GradForm Form itself. The SpecialKey event can be raised by the instances of the GradForm you created in your code. This is a strange behavior, but there's a simple explanation.

The GradForm was created when you added it to the project by choosing Project ➤ Add Form. At that point, the Form didn't have the SpecialKey event, so its name doesn't appear in the Events drop-down list of the Form's Code window.

Creating Controls at Run Time

You have seen how to create object variables that represent existing or new objects, such as Forms and fonts. You might expect that it's possible to use the New keyword to create controls at run time, similar to the way that you create Forms. This is not the case, however. If you declare an object variable as:

```
Dim myButton As CommandButton
```

you can then set it to reference an existing command button, but you can't create a new instance of the CommandButton class. The statement:

```
Set myButton = New Command1
```

will cause a run-time error. You can still use a statement like the following one:

```
Set myButton = Command1
```

which creates a reference to the Command1 button on the Form. If you change the Caption property of the myButton object, you are in effect changing the Caption of the Command1 object.

To create new instances of controls and manipulate them from within your code, you use control arrays. Declaring a *Control* object variable with the New keyword isn't going to do the trick. Creating new instances of ActiveX controls at run time is the topic of the next section.

Control Arrays to the Rescue

To create multiple instances of new controls at run time, you use a control array. Did you notice that each time you are about to paste a control you have previously copied from a Form, Visual Basic asks whether you want to create a control array? Every time you place multiple instances of the same control on a Form, you have the option of creating an array of controls. All the elements of the array share the same name, and they are distinguished from one another with the help of the Index property.

If you have three Command Buttons on a Form, you can create the array ThreeButtons. The first Command Button is ThreeButtons(0), the second one is ThreeButtons(1), and the last one is ThreeButtons(2). The Index property of the first element in the array need not be zero. You can start indexing the array at any value.

> **NOTE**
>
> The simplest way to create a control array at design time is to copy an existing control and paste it on the same Form. The first time, Visual Basic asks whether you want to create a control array. After that, every time you paste the same control or create a new one with the same name, it is appended to the existing control array. At run time, you must use the Load method, which is explained next.

You use control arrays when two or more controls have similar code that can be simplified with the use of the Index property. If you have the array ThreeButtons with the three elements, you need not provide three different handlers for each Command Button's Click event. All the elements of the control array share common event handlers. The Click event handler for an array of controls is:

```
Private Sub ThreeButtons_Click(Index As Integer)
End Sub
```

In your code, you can distinguish the various controls based on their index. When the first Command Button is clicked, the Index argument has the value 0, and so on. For example, here is an event handler that changes the caption of the button that was clicked:

```
Private Sub ThreeButtons_Click(Index As Integer)
    ThreeButtons(Index).Caption = "I was clicked!"
End Sub
```

Let's return now to the topic of creating new controls at run time. First, you must create the control you want to repeat and assign the value zero to its Index property. It's also customary to make this control invisible. To create another instance of this control, use the Load method, with a new index value. Assuming that you have created an invisible Command Button on the Form with Name=CButton and Index=0, the following statement will create three instances of this control and display them on the Form:

```
For i = 1 to 3
    Load CButton(i)
    CButton(i).Visible = True
Next
```

When a new control is created at run time, it is initially invisible. That's why you must also set its Visible property.

The CtrlLoad Project

The CtrlLoad project demonstrates how to create new controls using index arrays by creating a Form that can accept a variable number of data points.

NOTE   You will find the CtrlLoad project in the Ch05\CtrlLoad folder on the CD that comes with this book.

When you first run the application, you will see the Form shown in Figure 5.4. Click the New Data Set button, and you'll be prompted to enter the number of data points in the new set. Enter a small number, such as 10, and the Form will be stretched vertically and filled with as many TextBox controls as needed for the entry of the data values. If you specify 6 data values, the Form of the CtrlLoad application will look like the one in Figure 5.5.

FIGURE 5.4:

The initial state of the CtrlLoad application's main Form

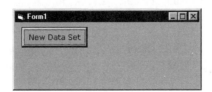

FIGURE 5.5:

The CtrlLoad Form after adding six TextBox controls at run time

To implement the Form of the CtrlLoad project, start a new project and place the following items on the Form:

- A Command Button
- A Label
- A TextBox control

Because the Label and TextBox controls should be invisible when the application starts, set their Visible property to False. At run time, we want to be able to add new instances of these controls on the Form by creating new elements in the control array. The two controls placed on the Form are the first elements in the control array, and you must set their Index property to zero. At run time, you'll be able to add new elements to the array with the Load command and a new index value.

Clicking the New Data Set button executes the following code.

Code 5.6: Adding Controls on a Form at Run Time

```
Private Sub Command1_Click()
Dim sum As Double, avg As Double

        If Command1.Caption = "New Data Set" Then
        dataCount = InputBox("How many data values?")
        If Not IsNumeric(Count) Then
            MsgBox "please enter a valid numeric value"
            Exit Sub
        End If
        For i = 1 To dataCount
            Load Label1(i)
            Load Text1(i)
```

```
                    Label1(i).Top = Label1(i - 1).Top + 1.25 * Label1(i).Height
                    Text1(i).Top = Text1(i - 1).Top + 1.25 * Text1(i).Height
                    Label1(i).Visible = True
                    Label1(i).Caption = "Value #" & i
                    Text1(i).Visible = True
                Next
                Me.Height = Text1(dataCount).Top + 2.5 *
        Text1(dataCount).Height
                Command1.Caption = "Calculate Now"
            Else
                For i = 1 To dataCount
                    If IsNumeric(Text1(i).Text) Then
                        sum = sum + Text1(i).Text
                    End If
                Next
                avg = sum / dataCount
                MsgBox "The average is " & avg
                For i = 1 To dataCount
                    Unload Text1(i)
                    Unload Label1(i)
                Next
                Me.Height = 2000
                Command1.Caption = "New Data Set"
            End If

        End Sub
```

This code first prompts the user for the number of data points in the data set and then creates that many instances of the Label1 and Text1 controls. It positions each new instance on the Form with respect to the previous instance (the placement of the elements Label1(0) and Text1(0) determines the appearance of the Form). In addition to creating and placing the necessary controls for entering data on the Form, the Command Button changes its Caption to Calculate Now. Clicking the Calculate Now button calculates the average of the values entered and removes the controls from the Form with the Unload statement.

NOTE   When new elements are added to a control array, their Visible property is False, and you must manipulate this property from within your code to make them visible. In the CtrlLoad project, the new elements will be invisible anyway, because the initial elements of the array are invisible, but you should always set the Visible property of new control instances to True from within your code.

Manipulating Controls at Run Time

Visual Basic provides a few objects and statements for the manipulation of controls at run time. Let's start with the Control object. We mentioned that, although you can't create new controls at run time by declaring object variables, these variables are frequently used in programming controls. The Control type represents any control on a Form, and you can create variables of Control type with statements such as the following:

```
Dim aControl As Control
```

and then assign instances of other controls to the *aControl* variables with the Set statement:

```
Set aControl = Text1
```

and perhaps later in the code:

```
Set aControl = Command1
```

You can use the *aControl* object variable to manipulate the properties of the Command1 control. For example, you can change the Command Button's Caption property with a statement such as:

```
aControl.Caption = "Click me!"
```

You may be wondering, Why use object variables to manipulate controls and the control names? In some situations, you don't have direct access to a control. Instead, you can access only a variable that represents the control. For example, in programming drag-and-drop operations, you don't have access to the control being dropped. As you will see in the next section, the DragDrop event subroutine passes a reference to the control that was dropped on another control, and not to the control itself. To program the DragDrop event, you must know how to handle object variables that represent controls.

Control Types

Sometimes, you need to know the type of control an object variable represents from within your code. An object variable can store references to any type of control, which is helpful should you need to determine the type of control being referenced within your code. To find out the type of the control referenced by an object variable, use the TypeOf statement, as in the following:

```
If TypeOf aControl Is TextBox Then
```

The keyword TypeOf is followed by the name of the object variable whose type you are seeking, followed by the keyword Is, which is followed by the name of a control's class. TypeOf is not a function that returns the type of the variable; instead, it compares the type of the control to a specific control type and returns a True/False value, which can be used in an If structure, like the one shown here. The TypeOf statement is used frequently in programming drag-and-drop operations to find out the type of the control that was dropped on another control. The following project provides a simple example.

The DragDrop Project

The DragDrop project demonstrates the use of the TypeOf ... Is statement with drag-and-drop operations.

NOTE   You'll find the DragDrop project in the Ch05\DragDrop folder on the CD that comes with this book.

The Form shown in Figure 5.6 contains a TextBox, a Label, and a PictureBox control. The contents of the first two controls can be dragged, so you must set their DragMode property to True. The PictureBox control can't be dragged, but other objects can be dropped on it. All controls can react to the drop of another control, which means you must provide a DragDrop handler for each control.

FIGURE 5.6:

The DragDrop project demonstrates the use of the TypeOf ... Is statement in drag-and-drop operations.

First, we must decide what happens when a control is dropped on another one. When the TextBox and Label controls are dropped on each other, the source's text (Text or Caption property) is copied to the target control. When either control is dropped on the PictureBox control, it is assumed that the text is the path name of an image file, which must be displayed on the control. If the text doesn't correspond to an image file or if, for any reason, the image can't be displayed, an error message is displayed on the PictureBox control, as shown in Figure 5.7.

FIGURE 5.7:

When the string dropped onto the PictureBox control isn't a valid image file name, an error message is displayed.

Let's start with the DragDrop events of the TextBox and Label controls.

Code 5.7:   The DragDrop Events of the TextBox and Label Controls

```
Private Sub Text1_DragDrop(Source As Control, X As Single, Y As Single)
    If TypeOf Source Is Label Then
        Text1.Text = Label1.Caption
    End If
End Sub

Private Sub Label1_DragDrop(Source As Control, X As Single, Y As
Single)
    If TypeOf Source Is TextBox Then
        Label1.Caption = Source.Text
    End If
End Sub
```

The *Source* argument represents the control being dropped, and we can use it to access any of the properties of this control. However, we must first examine the type of the control, to avoid calling a property name not supported by the Source control.

The DragDrop event handler of the PictureBox control is quite similar, but instead of copying the Text or Caption property, it attempts to display the specified file.

Code 5.8: The DragCrop Event of the PictureBox Control

```
Private Sub Picture1_DragDrop(Source As Control, X As Single, Y As
Single)
Dim imgName
    If TypeOf Source Is TextBox Then
        imgName = Source.Text
    Else
        imgName = Source.Caption
    End If
On Error GoTo NOIMAGE
    Picture1.Picture = LoadPicture(imgName)
    Exit Sub

NOIMAGE:
    Picture1.Cls
    Picture1.Font.Bold = True
    Picture1.Print imgName
    Picture1.Font.Bold = False
    Picture1.Print "Can't display file"
End Sub
```

In addition to the event handlers shown here, the DragDrop project contains the DragOver handler for the various controls, which changes the pointer's shape to indicate whether the current control can accept the control being dragged.

The Controls Collection

It is also possible to access from within your code all the controls on a Form through the Controls object. The Controls object is another built-in object, or actually a collection of objects. Each element of the Controls collection is a control. We'll discuss collections in detail in the section "Creating and Using Collections" later in this chapter, but we'll discuss here how you can use the Controls object to access the controls on the current Form.

The Controls object need not be initialized. It's built in to Visual Basic, and you can access it directly. The Count property of the Controls object returns the number of controls it contains. To scan its elements, you can set up a For ... Next loop such as the following one:

```
For i = 0 To Controls.Count - 1
    { process element Controls(i) }
Next
```

There is, however, a better structure for scanning the elements of a collection, namely the For Each statement, whose syntax is:

```
For Each iControl In Controls
{ process element iControl }
Next
```

The *iControl* object variable is declared as Control type. At each iteration of the loop, the *iControl* variable is automatically assigned the next control in the collection. If this control has a Caption property, you can access it with the expression iControl.Caption.

Since all controls have a Name property, you can safely use the expression iControl.Name. Not all properties, however, apply to all controls, and you should use the TypeOf statement to find out whether the current control supports a property. For example, you can change the Text property of all TextBox controls or the Caption property of all Label controls with a loop such as the following:

```
For Each iControl In Controls
    If TypeOf iControl Is TextBox Then
        iControl.Text = "Text Changed"
    Else If TypeOf iControl Is Label Then
        iControl.Caption = "Caption Changed"
    End If
Next
```

The Controls Project

The Controls project demonstrates how to use the Controls collection and object variables to manipulate the controls on a Form from within your code.

NOTE
You'll find the Controls project in the Ch05\Controls folder on the CD that comes with this book.

The main Form of the application, shown in Figure 5.8, contains two TextBox controls and a Label control, whose colors change when the Command Button is clicked.

FIGURE 5.8:

The Controls application demonstrates the use of the Controls collection.

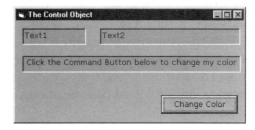

The code behind the Command Button (Change Color) scans each element of the Controls collection and examines its type. If it's a TextBox control, it sets the control's background color to yellow. The other elements in the Controls collection are not processed.

Code 5.9:   The Change Color Button

```
Private Sub Command1_Click()
Dim iControl As Control

For Each iControl In Controls
    If (TypeOf iControl Is TextBox) Or (TypeOf iControl Is Label) Then
        iControl.BackColor = RGB(200, 200, 0)
        iControl.ForeColor = RGB(0, 0, 200)
    End If
Next
End Sub
```

An alternative approach is to use a For ... Next loop to scan all the elements of the collection:

```
For i = 0 To Controls.Count
    Set iControl = Controls(i)
    iControl.BackColor = RGB(200, 200, 0)
    iControl.ForeColor = RGB(0, 0, 200)
Next
```

Early and Late Binding of Variables

In this section, we are going to discuss an important topic in programming with object variables: their binding. As you do with regular variables, you should declare object variables before they are used. The more Visual Basic knows about a variable's type, the more efficiently it will handle it. If you don't declare the variable, Visual Basic automatically creates a variant, which is good for storing all types of data values, even objects. Because of their flexibility, variants can't be processed as quickly. Visual Basic must convert them to the proper type before using them.

The same is true for object variables. For example, if Visual Basic knows in advance that a specific object variable will be used to store a reference to a Font object, it will allocate a structure where information about a Font object can be stored and recalled efficiently. If it doesn't know the type of the object variable, it must set up a structure that can accommodate any type of object. In addition, it must execute a number of lines of code at run time, when an object is assigned to the object variable.

So far, we have seen two ways to declare object variables:

- As objects
- As a specific object type

When the type of the variable is known at design time, Visual Basic will not only protect you from mistakes (such as using nonexistent property names), it will also display the properties and methods that apply to the specific object variable—if you have the Auto List Members feature turned on. Most of the mistakes in your code will be caught by the editor itself as you enter the code or by the compiler before you execute the program. This is called *early binding*. The compiler knows the type of variable and will not compile lines that reference nonexistent properties or methods.

For example, if you declare an object variable as:

```
Dim myBox As TextBox
```

and then attempt to set its Caption property with a statement such as the following:

```
myBox.Caption = "This is a special box"
```

you will get an error message when you compile the application. This error simply can't go undetected. A statement that assigns a value to the *myBox* variable's Text property will compile just fine.

When you declare an object variable as Object, it can be assigned any type of object, and the editor (and the compiler) cannot validate the property names you are using. If you declare an object variable with the following statement:

```
Dim thisFontObject As Object
```

it can store any object. You can even store different objects in the same object variable at run time. When you declare a variable without a specific type, it's created the first time it's referenced, which is when you assign an object instance to it. That is also when the exact type of the variable becomes known.

To create an instance of the *thisFont* object variable, you should use a statement such as:

```
Set thisFontObject = Label2.Font
```

If you go back to the FontObject project and change the declaration of the *thisFont* object variable to:

```
Dim thisFont As Object
```

the rest of the code will work just as well. However, the revised application is slower. When the Visual Basic compiler runs into a statement such as:

```
thisFont.Name = Label1.FontName
```

it must generate additional statements, which find out whether the object supports the Name property. These statements must be executed at run time, and if the object doesn't support the Name property, a run-time error message is generated. Had the object variable been declared with a specific type, these statements would never have been introduced. Any attempt to refer to a nonexistent property name, such as thisFont.TypeFace, would be caught at compile time.

The main advantage of declaring variables with a specific type is that Visual Basic knows at design (or compile) time whether the object represented by the variable supports a property or a method you call in your code and generates optimal executable code. If the object's type isn't known in advance, Visual Basic generates a lot of overhead code, which is executed at run time, making the program slower. In other words, it generates code to contact the object to find out whether it supports a specific property or method. Only when Visual Basic is sure that the object supports this member does it call the member. You can avoid this overhead by declaring object variables with a specific type.

And this brings us to the second advantage of declaring variables with exact types: You can write applications that run better because many potential errors can be caught at design or compile time. These two methods of declaring variables are known as *early binding* (object variables of exact type) and *late binding* (generic object variables). When an object variable's type is known at compile time, the compiler produces shorter, faster-executing code. Of course, a few object variable declarations won't make your code crawl, but when you're trying to squeeze every drop of performance out of your code, it's good to know all the tricks.

To get a feel for the difference that early and late binding can make in your code, let's revise the FontObject application. Let's repeat the code of the Manipulate Font button 10,000 times with a loop and measure the elapsed time.

Code 5.10:   The Revised FontObject Project

```
Private Sub Command1_Click()
Dim thisFont As StdFont

StartTime = Timer
For i = 1 To 10000
' Get original font,
    Set thisFont = Label1.Font
' set its attributes
    thisFont.Bold = True
    thisFont.Italic = True
' and size
    thisFont.Size = 1.001 * thisFont.Size
' Clear object variable
    Set thisFont = Nothing
Next
Debug.Print "10,000 repetition took : " & _
    Format(Timer - StartTime, "#.00") & " seconds"
End Sub
```

On a Pentium 75, the elapsed time was 5.77 seconds. Now change the declaration of the *thisFont* object variable to:

```
Dim thisFont As Object
```

and run it again. With late binding, the 10,000 iterations take 7.91 seconds. Granted, not many applications create and release object variables 10,000 times at run time, but this difference would increase with more complicated objects, such as Database objects.

Notice that we changed the line

```
thisFont.Size = 1.5 * Label1.FontSize
```

to

```
thisFont.Size = 1.0 * thisFont.Size
```

The factor 1.5 would result in an overflow after a small number of iterations.

The effect of early binding on speed can be even more dramatic if the object variable has properties that are also objects. Here's an example. An add-in is an extension to the Visual Basic integrated development environment (IDE) that manipulates the various objects of the IDE, such as the controls and code of a Form. The collection VBProjects, which we'll look at in Chapter 8, can have multiple components (Forms, modules, and so on). A Form may contain multiple controls, which are accessed through the Controls collection.

As you will see in Chapter 8, expressions such as:

```
thisForm.VBControls.Item(i).Properties("Index")
```

are common in developing add-ins. This expression represents a control on a specific Form (the variable *i* goes from 1 to the total number of controls on the Form). If Visual Basic doesn't know the exact type of the object variable *thisForm*, it generates code to find out whether the object represented by the variable supports the VBControls property. VBControls, in turn, is a collection. If Visual Basic doesn't know it, it will generate additional code to find out whether the *VBControls* object variable supports the Item property.

The expression up to the last dot represents a control. If Visual Basic doesn't have this information at compile time, it generates even more lines to make sure that the object represented by the expression *thisForm.VBControls.Item(i)* has a Properties property. And only if it does, will it attempt to read the value of the Index property. As you can see, expressions involving object variables can get quite messy, and the more Visual Basic knows about these variables, the better it can handle them—both at design time and at run time.

Dynamic Object Variables

Previously, we mentioned the significant advantages of early binding:

- Code is shorter.

- Code executes faster.

- There are fewer run-time errors.

The run-time errors we are talking about are actually program errors and can't be corrected at run time, as opposed to user errors or unusual conditions, which can be corrected at run time. For example, if your code detects an error with the printer or an invalid data item, it can prompt the user to check the printer connection or re-enter some data. If your code calls a property that a specific object doesn't support, there's nothing to be done about it. A statement that calls a nonexistent property, such as the following :

```
thisFont.Typeface
```

will produce a run-time error that must be caught at design (or compile) time; error trapping isn't going to help you at all. Distributing a program that contains this statement is simply going to embarrass you. Yet, you can avoid this type of error easily by declaring the *thisFont* object variable with an exact type.

This doesn't mean that generic object variables are useless. Because they can be assigned all types of objects at run time, these variables are *dynamic*. You must simply make sure that you don't attempt to access any nonexistent properties or methods.

The ScreenPrinterObjects Project

Let's look at an example of what you can do with late-bound variables. The ScreenPrinterObjects project demonstrates a common programming technique and shows the solution to a problem you may have already faced.

NOTE   You'll find the ScreenPrinterObjects project in the Ch05\ScrPrn folder on the CD that comes with this book.

Most commercial applications generate output for the screen and the printer. You are already familiar with the methods that produce shapes and text on a Form or a PictureBox control. The same methods apply to the Printer object. The problem is how to redirect the program's output to the screen or the printer. Should you use statements such as the following:

```
If PrinterOutput Then
     Printer.Line (X, Y) - (X + 100, Y + 100)
Else
     Form1.Line (X, Y) - (X + 100, Y + 100)
End If
```

or is there a more elegant method?

There is indeed a more elegant method, and it uses an object variable to draw on. If the object variable represents a Form object, the output is sent to the screen. If it represents the Printer object, the output is sent to the current printer.

The ScreenPrinterObjects project draws a few simple shapes, as you can see in Figure 5.9. The project's main Form contains two option buttons (with their Style property set to Graphical so that they look like buttons) that you can select to specify the output. You can then click the Draw Now button to produce the output.

FIGURE 5.9:

The output of the ScreenPrinterObject project can be redirected to the screen or the printer, depending on the status of the option buttons.

The program starts by declaring an object variable, *OutputObject*, which is set to the Form1 object or to the Printer object, depending on the status of the option buttons:

```
Dim OutputObject As Object

If Option1 Then
    Set OutputObject = Form1
Else
    Set OutputObject = Printer
End If
```

You can then call the graphics methods, which are common to both objects, to produce the desired output. The sample shapes in Figure 5.9 were produced with the following lines:

```
OutputObject.DrawWidth = 2
OutputObject.ForeColor = RGB(255, 0, 0)
OutputObject.Circle (2000, 2000), 800
OutputObject.DrawWidth = 1
```

```
OutputObject.Line (1000, 1000)-(3000, 3000), , B
OutputObject.ForeColor = RGB(0, 0, 255)
OutputObject.CurrentX = 1500
OutputObject.CurrentY = 2400
OutputObject.Print "Graphics methods"
```

Error-Trapping Considerations

The program also contains an error trap, intended for systems without a printer. If you attempt to direct the output to the printer and there's any problem with your printer, the program won't crash.

We were careful not to include any lines that call properties or methods that don't apply to both objects. What if you wanted to change the background color of the Form before printing on it? The statement:

```
OutputObject.BackColor = RGB(230, 230, 0)
```

will work while the *OutputObject* variable refers to the Form1 object, but it will produce a run-time error when the object it refers to is the Printer object. To make sure that the code won't fail, regardless of the current output object, use an If structure, such as the following:

```
If TypeOf OutputObject Is Form Then
    OutputObject.BackColor = RGB(230, 230, 0)
End If
```

Late-bound object variables may have disadvantages over early-bound ones, but if you need to manipulate the object variables dynamically from within your code, you must declare them as late bound (without an exact type).

Using the Object Browser

Where do all these objects come from and how do you know at any point which objects are available and the properties and methods they provide? Each object, whether it's built in to Visual Basic or you build it, has a type library. A *type library* is a catalog of the object's properties, methods, and events, which you can consult at any time. Each object, including your custom ActiveX controls and ActiveX components (in EXE or DLL format) has a type library, which can be displayed in the Object Browser. Fortunately, you don't have to take any special action in order to display your component's members. The Object Browser will pick up their definitions from the executable file (you must provide their descriptions, however). You will find more information on this in the following two chapters.

The type libraries of the available objects are displayed in the Object Browser, which is shown in Figure 5.10. We'll demonstrate how to use the Object Browser by building a simple application that manipulates a few of the objects exposed by the Database object. As you will see, you don't have to know every object and every property of these objects in order to use them. A basic understanding of databases and their structure is all you need to program them with the help of the Object Browser.

FIGURE 5.10:

The Object Browser for a simple VB project

The Object Browser isn't a substitute for the help files or other reference material, but even experienced programmers can't possibly remember the structure of complicated objects such as the Database object. The Object Browser simplifies the task of programming database applications with the Database object, and you will use much of the information in this chapter as you work through the examples in Part III.

The Purpose and Structure of the Object Browser

Every class available within Visual Basic or within other applications that expose objects is described in the Object Browser. The Object Browser is an application that gets these descriptions from the corresponding EXE or DLL files and displays them in an easy-to-visualize and navigate fashion. Objects can be as simple as a Form or as complex as an application such as Microsoft Excel or Microsoft Word. Let's explore the Object Browser by starting with a simple project.

Start a new project and click the Object Browser button, or choose View ➤ Object Browser (or simply press F2) to open the Object Browser. At the top of the Object Browser window you see two drop-down boxes. The first contains the available object libraries, from which you can select one. The second contains previous search arguments, which you can activate for new searches. For a new project (a project to which no special objects have been added), the Object Libraries shown in Table 5.1 are available:

TABLE 5.1: The Default Type Libraries

Library	Description
Project1	This is the current project's name. It contains the current project's classes.
Stdole	The type libraries of the standard OLE classes, such as the StdFont class.
VB	The Visual Basic type library. It contains the type libraries for the ActiveX controls that appear in the Visual Basic Toolbox.
VBA	The VBA type library.
VBRUN	The Visual Basic run-time library. It contains the classes that are available at run time only.

If you select Project1 in the Type Library drop-down box, you will see the only class in the project, which is the main Form, Form1 (you already know that, unlike controls, Forms are classes). In the Classes pane, along with the name of the Form, you will see the entry *globals*. If the project had global variables, their names would appear in the Members pane.

Select the Class Form1, and in the Classes pane you will see all the members of the Form1 class: the properties, methods, and events that the Form1 Form recognizes, as well as any event handlers or procedures you've written. Even the code you entered in the project becomes a member of the Form1 Class, because you can access the Form1 object through the functions and event handlers it provides.

The Object Browser displays in a compact format all the functionality in a project, whether it was brought into the project by Visual Basic (through its built-in objects) or by the developer (through custom components and controls).

Add a couple of controls on the Form and a couple of event handlers. You can place a couple of Command Buttons on it and enter a simple MsgBox function in their Click event. If you open the Object Browser again, you will see that the names of the controls are displayed as properties of the Form1 Class in the Members pane. The event handlers of the Click event for the two Command Buttons are also listed in this pane as methods of the Form1 Class. Something wrong here? Click is an event name for the Command1 and Command2 controls. The subroutines Command1_Click() and Command2_Click(), however, are methods, as they can be called from any other subroutine in this Form. If you click the name of the subroutine Command1_Click(), you will see in the description pane that this subroutine is a member of the Class Project1.Form1.

Using the Data Access Object

In this section, we are going to discuss an advanced topic, the Data Access Object. If you are not familiar with database programming, this section should be of particular interest. Later, in Part III, we cover database programming in detail.

Calling All Database Programmers...

Even if you are experienced with programming the Data Access Object, don't skip this section. Our goal is not to explain the Data Access Object, but to show how to use the Object Browser to find out the members of various objects and use them.

If you have any open projects in the Visual Basic editor, close them and start a new Standard EXE project. To use the Data Access Object, you must first add a reference to it, as this class isn't added by default to every project. Follow these steps:

1. Choose Project ➤ References to open the Reference dialog box, which displays a list of all the available objects you can add to your projects:

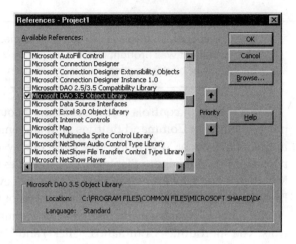

In this dialog box, you see the names of all available classes on your system. Some were installed with Windows itself; others, by programming languages or applications. (In the next chapter you will learn how to add your own classes.) The components referenced in the project are checked.

2. Scroll down the list, locate the entry Microsoft DAO 3.5 Object Library, and check the box in front of its name. Then click OK to close the References dialog box.

You have just added a reference to the Data Access Object to your project.

3. Open the Object Browser window again, and open the Type Library drop-down list. This time you will see a new object, DAO.

4. Select DAO and take a look at the classes it exposes in the Classes pane.

In the next section, we'll show you how to use these classes.

Using the DAO Object

The DAO object has many classes, one of them being the Database class. The Database class represents a database: a structure for storing information in forms of tables. To work with a database, you must first select a table or a set of records, which are stored in a structure called a recordset.

A recordset is a collection of records, such as the invoices issued to customers in California or the best-selling products.

If you scroll down the Classes list in the Object Browser, you will see the Recordset entry. Select the Recordset entry, and you'll see the description of a recordset at the bottom of the window: "A representation of the records in a base table or the records that result from a query" (the last few words are missing, but we had to complete the sentence anyway).

In the Members pane, you will now see the members of the Recordset class. The BOF property, for example, becomes True when the first record is reached, and the EOF property becomes True when the last record is reached. You use the methods FindFirst, FindLast, FindNext, and FindPrevious to locate records in a recordset according to criteria you specify.

To access the members of a Database object, you must first open a database and assign it to an object variable. The function for opening a database does not appear anywhere in the Object Browser, because it's not a member of the Database object. A Database object variable doesn't exist before you actually open the database and assign it to the variable. Therefore, the method for opening the database can't be a member of the Database object. OpenDatabase is a method of the DAO object; however, you don't need to prefix it with the name of the DAO object.

To open a database and assign it to an object variable, you first declare the variable as follows:

```
Dim DB As Database
```

and then open a database and set the DB variable to the database:

```
Set DB = OpenDatabase("C:\PROGRAM FILES\DEVSTUDIO\VB\NWIND.MDB")
```

We assume that the NWIND database is in the default VB folder. If you installed VB in another folder, change the path in the last statement accordingly.

The OpenDatabase() function accepts other optional arguments, and its complete syntax is:

```
OpenDatabase(Name, [Options,] [Read-Only,] [Connect])
```

The arguments in square brackets are optional. The Options argument can be True or False, indicating whether the database will be opened exclusively or will be shared. The Read-Only argument is another True/False argument, indicating whether the database can be written to or is read-only. The last argument sets connection parameters, such as the user name and password.

Selecting Records in Recordsets

The next step is to create a recordset with the records we want to work with. Let's say we want to explore the Customers table, which contains the names of all customers in the NWIND database. Locate the Recordset class of the DAO object, and in the Members pane locate the OpenRecordset method. The description of this method is "Creates a new Recordset object," as shown in Figure 5.11.

FIGURE 5.11:

Locating the
OpenRecordset
method of the
Recordset class

The syntax of the method is:

```
OpenRecordset(Name As String, [Type], [Options], [LockEdit]) As
Recordset
```

The *Name* entry is the name of the table we want to open or a SQL statement that retrieves the desired records from the database. For the purposes of our example, we'll use the name of the Customers table. You could also specify a SQL statement, such as the following, to retrieve selected customers only:

```
SELECT * FROM Customers WHERE Country = 'Germany'
```

The *Type* argument specifies the type of recordset we want to create. You should know the various types of recordsets you can create, but if you need to be reminded of the constants that describe them, locate the class RecordsetTypeEnum and select it. In the Members pane, you will see all possible values for the Type argument:

dbOpenDynamic opens a dynamic recordset (similar to an ODBC dynamic cursor).

dbOpenDynaset opens a Dynaset-type recordset.

dbOpenForwardOnly opens a forward-only recordset (it's faster than a Dynaset).

dbOpenSnapshot opens a Snapshot recordset, which you can use to read but not write back to the database.

dbOpenTable opens a Table recordset.

If you want to find out the constants that can be assigned to an argument, locate a class whose name ends with *Enum* in the Classes pane (the name should resemble the name of the argument), and then look up its values in the Members pane. The last argument determines the type of locking for the recordset, which we will not use in this example. If you want to find out the possible values of this argument, select the LockTypeEnum class in the class pane, and you'll see its values in the Members pane.

To create the recordset with the names of all customers, you declare a *Recordset* object variable and then assign a newly created recordset to it:

```
Dim RS As Recordset
Set RS = DB.OpenRecordset("Customers", dbOpenSnapshot)
```

The recordset type is dbSnapShot, because this type gives the fastest possible access. We don't want to change the Customers table; we only want to read its records.

Exploring the Recordset's Structure

So far we've created a recordset with the rows of the Customers table. What can we do with this recordset? In this example, we want to find out the structure of each field, as well as the values of selected fields. If you select the Recordset class in the Classes pane and look at the members of the class, you will see that it has a property called Fields, as shown in Figure 5.11, earlier in this chapter. The icon in front of the Fields member is similar to the icon for properties with a little dot above it. This means that Fields is a collection.

This make sense, because the recordset contains multiple records. To access the first field, use the expression RS.Fields(i), where *i* goes from zero to the number of fields (columns) in the recordset minus one. The number of fields in the recordset is given by the property Fields.Count. Don't remember the name of the property? Select the Fields class in the Classes pane, as usual, and look it up in the Members pane.

The following loop scans all the fields in the recordset and displays their names in a ListBox:

```
maxFields = RS.Fields.Count
For i = 0 To maxFields - 1
    List1.AddItem RS.Fields(i).Name
Next
```

Now we'll turn our attention to the rows of the recordset. Each row is a record, with data about a different customer. The first piece of information we need is the number of rows in the recordset. Again, select the Recordset class in the Classes pane, and search in the Members pane for a property named RecordCount. Its description is "Returns the number of records accessed in a Recordset." This is the property we need, but there is a detail you should be aware of here. The Object Browser won't be of much help. The RecordCount property won't return the number of records in the recordset because it hasn't seen more than the first record. You must first go to the last record in the recordset with the MoveLast method, and then call the RecordCount property to find out the actual number of records in the recordset. (You'll find much more on this in Part II.)

The recordset's rows can't be accessed through a collection, similar to the Fields collection. Instead, you must use the MoveNext method to move to the next record. The loop for scanning the rows of the RS recordset is:

```
Do
    {process fields of current row}
      RS.MoveNext
Loop While Not RS.EOF
```

To process the fields of the current row, you must know the names of the fields. We're interested in the fields ContactName and CompanyName. Their values can be accessed with the Value property of the Fields Collection of the RS object. The following code displays the values of the fields ContactName and Company name:

```
Do
    List2.AddItem RS.Fields("ContactName").Value & ",  " _
        & RS.Fields("CompanyName").Value
    RS.MoveNext
Loop While Not RS.EOF
```

Now, let's summarize what we have done so far and then build an application.

1. We opened a database and assigned it to a Database object variable.

2. Then, we called the DB object's OpenRecordset method to create a recordset with the rows of the Customers table to the RS object variable.

3. Finally, with two loops we extracted the columns (field names) and rows (field values) of the recordset.

Now we can put it all together and build a small application.

The ObjectLibrary Project

The ObjectLibrary project does the following:

- Opens a database and selects a table—the Customers table
- Displays the names of the fields in the upper ListBox control
- Displays all the values of two fields in the recordset in the lower ListBox control

The application's main Form is shown in Figure 5.12.

NOTE   You'll find the ObjectLibrary project in the Ch05\ObjLib folder on the CD that comes with this book.

FIGURE 5.12:

The ObjectLibrary project's Form

The code starts by declaring two object variables:

```
Private DB As Database
Private RS As Recordset
```

When the Form is loaded, the program opens the NWIND database and assigns it to the *DB* object variable. The statement that opens the NWIND database is:

```
Set DB = OpenDatabase("c:\program files\devstudio\vb\nwind.mdb")
```

NOTE   NWIND is a sample database that comes with Visual Basic 5, and we'll be using it a lot in this book's examples. The database's path used in the code segments is the default one. If you installed it in a different folder, you must adjust the code accordingly.

After this statement is executed, the *DB* variable refers to the NWIND database. The following line creates the recordset with the rows of the Customers table:

```
Set RS = DB.OpenRecordset("Customers", dbOpenSnapshot)
```

After the two object variables are created, the code proceeds with the two loops we presented earlier to populate the lists:

```
List1.Clear
List2.Clear
maxFields = RS.Fields.Count
For i = 0 To maxFields - 1
    List1.AddItem RS.Fields(i).Name
Next

Do
    List2.AddItem RS.Fields("ContactName").Value & ",   " & _
        RS.Fields("CompanyName").Value
    RS.MoveNext
Loop While Not RS.EOF
```

Another event handler in the ObjectLibrary project is the Click event handler of the List1 control, which holds the names of the fields. When you click a field name in the upper list, its characteristics are displayed in three Label controls next to the field names list, as shown in Figure 5.12, earlier in this chapter.

Using Collections

The last topic we'll discuss in this chapter is collections. In some situations, you will want to store multiple object variables in a tablelike structure. An array would do, but you'd have to keep track of the indices and the objects to which they refer. A collection is a simple structure that works just like an array, but it allows you to access its elements (or items, as the members of a collection are called) with the help of a key.

Let's start with a simple example, a structure for storing city names and temperatures. The simplest structure for storing this type of information is a two-dimensional array, with statements such as the following:

```
Temperatures(1,1) = "Atlanta"
Temperatures(1,2) = 67
Temperatures(2,1) = "Charlotte"
Temperatures(2,2) = 58
```

The problem with this approach is that you must keep track of the city names or scan the entire array to locate a given city. You can also maintain the array sorted so that you can quickly locate a city name. Ideally, you should be able to read the temperature in Atlanta with a statement such as the following:

```
Temperatures("Atlanta")
```

In other words, use the name of the city as an index, or a key, to access the temperature. This is exactly what collections do for you. They allow you to specify a key for each item and recall the item's value with this key.

To use a collection, you must first declare it with a statement such as the following:

```
Dim Temperatures As New Collection
```

The New keyword tells Visual Basic to set up a new collection and name it Temperatures. Temperatures is not array. You don't have to specify its size (there are no parentheses after the collection's name), and you can't assign new elements with an assignment operator. Temperatures is an object, and you must use its members to access it.

The Members of a Collection

Collections expose three methods and one property:

- Add method
- Item method
- Remove method
- Count property

Let's examine these members in detail.

The Add (item, key, before, after) Method

To add a new element to a collection, assign its value to the *item* argument, and assign its key to the *key* argument. To place the new item in a specific location in the array, specify one of the arguments before or after (but not both). To insert the new item before another item whose key (or index) you will specify, use the *before* argument. To place a new item after another one, specify this item's key (or index) with the *after* argument.

For example, to add the temperature for the city of San Francisco to the Temperatures collection, use the following statement:

```
Temperatures.Add 78, "San Francisco"
```

The number 78 is the value to be stored (temperature), and the string "San Francisco" is the new item's key. To insert this item immediately after the temperature of Santa Barbara, use this statement:

```
Temperatures.Add 78, "San Francisco", , "Santa Barbara"
```

The extra comma denotes the lack of the *before* argument. The Add method supports named arguments, so the previous statement could also be written as follows:

```
Temperatures.Add 78, "San Francisco", after:= "Santa Barbara"
```

Collections aren't sorted; neither do they have a method to automatically sort their items. To maintain an ordered collection of values (or objects), use the *before* and *after* arguments of the Add method. In most practical situations, however, you don't care about sorting a collection's items. You sort arrays to simplify access of their elements. Because collections can be accessed with the help of a key, however, there is no reason to keep them sorted.

The Remove (index) Method

The Remove method removes an item from a collection. The index argument can be either the position of the item you want to delete or the item's key. To remove the city of Atlanta from the Temperatures collection, use this statement:

```
Temperatures.Remove "Atlanta"
```

Or, if you know the city's index in the collection, specify the index in place of the key:

```
Temperatures.Remove 3
```

The Item (index) Method

The Item method returns the value of an item in the collection. As with the Remove method, the index argument can be either the item's position in the collection or its key. To recall the temperature in Santa Barbara, use one of the following statements:

```
T1 = Temperatures.Item("Santa Barbara")
T1 = Temperatures.Item(3)
```

The Item method is the default method of the collection object, so you can omit it when you access an item. The previous example could also be written as:

```
T1 = Temperatures("Santa Barbara")
```

TIP

Collections maintain their indices automatically as items are added and deleted. The index of a given item, therefore, changes during the course of a program, and you shouldn't save index values and expect to use them to retrieve the same element later in your program. Use keys instead.

The Count Property

The Count property returns the number of items in the collection. To find out how many cities have been entered so far in the Temperatures collection, use the following statement:

```
Total = Temperatures.Count
```

You can also use the Count property to scan all the elements of the collection with a For ... Next loop, such as the following:

```
For city = 1 To Temperatures.Count
    {process item}
Next
```

Processing a Collection's Items

To scan all the items in a collection, Visual Basic provides the For Each ... Next structure, whose syntax is:

```
For Each Item In Collection
    {process item}
Next
```

The *Item* variable is the loop's counter, but you don't have to initialize it. You should, however, declare it with the same type as the items of the collection. At each iteration, the *Item* variable holds the current item's value. In the case of city temperatures, it's an integer (or single) value. If the collection contains objects, the *Item* variable is an object variable that represents the current object.

In Chapter 8, you will see that Visual Basic returns the controls on a specific Form as a collection of Control objects. If the counter variable *iControl* is declared as a Control object variable:

```
Dim iControl As Control
```

the following structure scans all the controls on a Form and displays their names in the Immediate window:

```
For Each iControl In thisForm.VBControls.Count
    Debug.Print iControl.Properties("Name")
Next
```

The VBControls object is a property of the object variable *thisForm* (which represents a Form). This object happens to be a collection, which contains all the controls on the given Form. The variable *iControl*, therefore, represents a control, and its properties can be accessed with the Properties property.

For example, the Documents collection exposed by Word represents the currently open documents. To find out the name of the first open document, you use a statement such as the following:

```
Documents(1).FullName
```

The Selection object, also exposed by Word, supports a number of properties that are also collections. The Words collection contains all the words in the current selection, the Sentences collection contains all the sentences in the current selection, and the Paragraphs collection contains all the paragraphs in the current selection. The first word in the selection is:

```
Selection.Words(1)
```

and the last word in the selection is:

```
Selection.Words(Selection.Words.Count)
```

Many of the objects we will discuss in the following chapter expose properties that are collections. A collection is a simple structure for storing sets of similar objects and is used extensively in Visual Basic programming. You can, however, also store dissimilar objects in a collection. If you do, you must use the appropriate If statements to find out the type of the object before attempting to access any of its properties or methods.

Building ActiveX Components

- Understanding modules and class modules

- Working with the Crypto class

- Working with the Stats class

- Encapsulating database operations

- Building out-of-process servers

- Dealing with synchronous and asynchronous processing

In the last chapter, we discussed how to use the built-in Visual Basic objects and introduced the concepts you need in order to create your own custom objects. This chapter discusses in depth how to build custom ActiveX components and use them within your applications or distribute them to other developers.

An ActiveX component can be any of the following:

- A code component
- An ActiveX control
- An ActiveX document

Code components are server applications that expose their functionality through an interface consisting of properties, methods, and events. The difference between ActiveX controls and code components is that ActiveX controls have a visible interface and are integrated into the Visual Basic IDE. Code components are classes that can be accessed through properly declared object variables with the CreateObject() function.

ActiveX documents are applications that can be hosted in containers such as Internet Explorer and the Office Binder. At this time, there aren't many ActiveX documents on the Internet (at least, we haven't seen any), and it seems it will be a while before they catch up. Developing ActiveX documents for Office Binder is even more questionable. In this book we won't cover ActiveX documents, which are really simple compared with ActiveX code components and ActiveX controls.

We'll start our exploration of ActiveX components with the so-called code components. Code components provide a functionality similar to that of ActiveX controls, but they aren't as integrated with the development environment (for example, you can't drop a code component on a Form as you can a control), and they don't have a visible interface. Instead, they must be accessed in the same way that built-in objects are accessed, as we discussed in the last chapter, with the help of object variables.

ActiveX components are implemented as classes. They are prototypes that you use to create objects. We'll start our discussion of ActiveX code components with a short presentation of classes, class modules, and the two types of code components.

Modules and Class Modules

Classes are implemented in Visual Basic as class modules. Modules have existed in Visual Basic since the earliest versions. They store variable declarations and code (functions and subroutines) that are available to all other components of an application. For example, if the function ConvertTemperature(degrees As Double) or the function Encrypt(Text As String, Key As String) will be called from several places in your code and from within multiple Forms, implement the function in a module.

Procedures stored in a module can be called from any part of an application. You can think of these procedures as methods of the module, only you don't have to prefix a procedure with the name of the module when you call it. You can also think of the public variables you store in a module as properties of the module. Therefore, a module is not unlike a class, and classes are implemented as special types of modules, called *class modules*.

TIP   Why bother with classes when a module can provide the functionality you need in your application? If you need only a few procedures and global variables for a single project, you're probably better off dumping them in a module. If you plan to use the same procedures in multiple projects, however, you should build a class module.

Let's say you've implemented several functions in a module, tested them with Project A, and are satisfied with them. Later, you build Project B, which uses the same module. You realize that the functions in the module need some tweaking, so you introduce a few additional public variables. Now, although the module works well with Project B, you've inadvertently broken Project A. Even if you're disciplined enough not to touch the module, what if you belong to a group working on a common project? Allowing many programmers to access the same module from within their projects is an accident waiting to happen. One of them will inevitably tweak the code and break some of the existing projects.

If you believe in reusable software, classes are your best friends. To implement a class, you must first design its members so that they address the needs of multiple projects. For example, if your project needs a function that converts degrees Celsius to Fahrenheit, a class should contain a function that converts temperatures from any system to any other system. In the place of the function ConvertTemperature(degrees As Double), implement the function ConvertTemperature(degrees As Double, fromUnits As Integer, toUnits As Integer), which allows the developer to specify the temperature to be converted, as well as the units. You then test the function (which is a method of the class), and finally you cast it in concrete by building a DLL.

Other developers can add a reference to this class in their projects, use the method ConvertTemperature(), and use any other method of the class, but they will never see the code and won't be able to change it. Should conditions necessitate changes in the ConvertTemperature() function (unusual conditions, such as the introduction of a new temperature unit), you can carefully revise the class so that it won't break any code that already works.

Classes exhibit the two most important benefits of object-oriented programming:

Abstraction: The users of the class that exposes the ConvertTemperature method need not know anything about the intricacies of temperature conversion (well, you get the point). In the last chapter, you saw how classes abstract the complexity of objects such as a Database. In this chapter, you'll learn how to hide the complexity of custom operations and give developers simple ways to access them.

Reusability: A class is a real reusable component, at the binary level. As you will see, classes are reusable components on another level too. You can implement new classes that use the features of existing classes, without having to recode them. This is called *polymorphism*, but more on this later.

Implementing In-Process and Out-of-Process Servers

A class module is a server—an application that provides its services to the client application. When you create an object variable to access the properties and methods of a class, you are actually invoking an executable file (DLL or EXE) that runs in the background and waits to be contacted. Every time you set or read a property value or call a method, this executable is activated, it performs some action, and, optionally, it returns some result to your application.

You can implement servers as ActiveX DLL or ActiveX EXE components. The difference between the two is how the server is executed. An ActiveX DLL is an *in-process server*. The DLL is loaded in the same address space as the executable that calls the server, and it runs on the same thread as the client. At any given moment, however, either the client application or the DLL is running. The benefit of DLLs is that they are faster, because, in effect, they become part of the application that uses them.

An *out-of-process server* runs as a separate process. When a client application creates an object provided by an EXE server for the first time, the server starts running as a separate process. If another client application creates the same object, this object is provided by the running EXE server. In other words, a single EXE server can service multiple clients. Out-of-process servers seem to be more efficient in terms of resource allocation, but exchanging information between servers is a slow process. Therefore, in terms of execution speed, in-process servers are faster.

NOTE The communication between two processes is complicated and is known as *marshaling*.

What we have here is a client/server model. Your application is the client, which makes requests. The ActiveX Component is the server, which services the request. It's hard to think of ActiveX DLLs as servers, since they run in the same process as the client, but this is what they are. ActiveX EXE servers are separate processes, which can also service multiple clients. But more on this in the second half of the book.

This distinction between server types has ramifications in testing the components. You can easily test an ActiveX DLL by adding a test project to the ActiveX DLL project. Since both the server component and the test application run in the same process (the current instance of Visual Basic), you don't need two different executables. To test an ActiveX EXE component, however, you need two distinct processes—one instance of Visual Basic with the server and another with the test project. You can't have both the test application and the EXE server running in the Visual Basic environment.

The first few projects in this chapter are in-process servers (ActiveX DLL projects). In the second half of the book, you will see how to design and test out-of-process servers. Out-of-process servers are more difficult to implement because they should be designed so that they can provide their services to multiple clients.

Adding Methods to Class Modules

Adding a method to a class is as simple as declaring a Public function or subroutine. Any procedure that can appear in your code can become a method of a class if you enter it in a class module and declare it as Public. Let's add a really simple method to the class, one that returns its name. We'll call this method ClassName and implement it as a function:

```
Public Function GetClassName() As String
    GetClassName = "why should you care?"
End Function
```

The class module now contains a method, GetClassName, which always returns the string "why should you care?" Of course, you could implement GetClassName as a property, whose value is set by the class, and the application can read it (we'll discuss class properties shortly).

Should It Be a Method or a Property?

You can implement some members both as methods and properties, and it isn't always easy to figure out which is best. Fortunately, it's not extremely important either.

You should try to follow the paradigm of the built-in, or third-party, controls. For example, if the class were an ActiveX control, a member you would like to see in the Properties window, implement it as a property (the opposite isn't necessarily true). Methods should correspond to actions, and properties are attributes.

The naming scheme is also important. A name such as GetClassName suggests a method, and a name such as ClassName suggests a property.

Class modules can also contain private procedures. These procedures can be called from within the class's code, but other applications that use the class can't call them. If you want to track how many times a method is called during the course of an application, you can include a function such as the following:

```
Private Function CallCounter() As Integer
Static Popularity As Integer
    Popularity = Popularity + 1
    CallCounter = Popularity
End Function
```

This function can be called from within the class's code, but any application that uses this class can't see the CallCounter() function. Because CallCounter() is private, it's not a method of the class. It's a regular function in the class's code.

Declaring Friend Members

In addition to private and public members, classes have a third type of scope modifier, which is called Friend. A Friend member is public for the entire project, and all the classes in the project can access it. In a Standard EXE application, all other modules and Forms can access public variables. In a standard EXE application, however, this is the broadest scope a variable can have.

With ActiveX components, whose public members can also be accessed from other applications, there has to be another type that makes members accessible from anywhere in the project, but not from outside.

NOTE   Only procedures (functions or subroutines) and properties can be declared as Friend. Variables are either private or public. This means that the classes of an ActiveX component can communicate by calling Friend methods and Friend properties.

Adding Properties to Class Modules

Implementing properties for classes requires some extra programming. You can still create properties by declaring public variables. Any variable you declare as public is accessible from outside the class, and other applications can set and read it. If you add the following declaration to the current class module:

```
Public IntProperty As Integer
```

you can access this property from an application and read its value, or you can assign a new value to it, with statements such as the following:

```
Count = Class1.IntProperty
Class1.IntProperty = 999
```

But what if the user attempts to assign an invalid value? A statement such as the following would result in a run-time error:

```
Class1.IntProperty = 99000
```

Implementing properties as public variables can lead to erratic behavior. The application that uses the class is responsible for trapping all possible errors, because your class never has an opportunity to validate the value assigned to the variable-property. Visual Basic provides special procedures for accessing class variables through code: the Property Let and Property Get procedures. The proper method for implementing a property in your class is to add the following procedures:

```
Private m_IntProperty
Public Property Let IntProperty(newValue As Integer)
    m_IntProperty = newValue
End Property

Public Property Get IntProperty() As Integer
    IntProperty = m_IntProperty
End Property
```

The private variable *m_IntProperty* is a local copy of the property's value. Every time an application sets this property's value, the Property Let procedure is automatically invoked, and the value specified is passed as an argument. In other words, the line:

```
IntProperty = 100
```

invokes the following procedure in your class:

```
Property Let IntProperty(100)
```

Assignments to property values trigger a special event, which causes a Property Let procedure (the one with the same name as the property) to execute. The new value is stored in the *m_IntProperty* variable. Likewise, when an application requests the value of the IntProperty property, the value of the local variable *m_IntProperty* is passed to it. In the Property Let procedure, you can insert all the validation code you see fit. For example, here's how you would implement an Age property:

```
Private m_Age
Public Property Let Age(newValue As Integer)
    Select Case newValue
    Case < 0: m_Age = 0
    Case > 100 : m_Age = 100
    Else m_Age=newValue
    End Select
End Property

Public Property Get Age() As Integer
    Age  = m_Age
End Property
```

If the application specifies an invalid age value, the class takes an action that will prevent some serious errors later in the code. The amount of validation code depends on the nature of the property, and you can insert as little or as much validation code in the Property Let procedure as you like.

You can also raise errors from within your Property Let procedure, which can be trapped by the application's code. For example, you could implement the Age property as follows:

```
Public Property Let Age(newValue As Integer)
    If newValue < 0 or newValue > 100 Then
    Err.Raise 1999, "Invalid Age", _
    "Age must be greater than zero and less than 100"
    Else
            m_Age = newValue
End Property
```

The error is passed back to the application, and it will either generate a run-time error or be trapped by the application's code.

TIP
You will find more information on raising errors from within a class in the section "Raising Errors in a Class," later in this chapter.

You might think about displaying a message with the MsgBox() function. This isn't such a good idea, for two reasons.

1. The message box may not be displayed on the user's monitor. If the class resides on a server and is used remotely by an application on a network (or the Internet), the message box will be displayed on the server, not on the client computer. Since the user of the application never sees the message box, he or she will never get a chance to click the OK button. As a result, the application will freeze.

2. Because the ActiveX component generates the error, it can offer the user only a generic message such as "Please enter a valid value." This action must take place in the application's code, and the best way to react to errors in classes is to raise errors to the calling application.

It is possible, however, to display message boxes from within a class; you can even display an entire Form or a dialog box and request user input. Just remember that the class's visible user interface may become invisible, if the class is executed remotely.

Providing Property Set Procedures

The Property Let procedure is invoked every time the application assigns a new value to a property of a simple data type (Integer, String, and so on). As we saw in Chapter 5, some properties may themselves be objects. If a property is an object, such as Font, the application can't set it with a simple assignment statement like the following:

```
Class1.Font = newFont
```

or

```
Class1.Font = Text1.Font
```

You assign values to object variables with the Set statement:

```
Set Class1.Font = Text1.Font
```

For properties that are set in the code, you must provide a Property Set procedure in place of the Property Let procedure. The Property Set procedure is simply a variation of the Property Let procedure and doesn't require any special coding. For example, here's a Property Set procedure that sets the Font property:

```
Private m_Font As Font
Public Property Set Font (newFont As Font)
    If newFont.Size > 36 Then newFont.Size = 36
    Set m_Font = newFont
End Property
```

This code segment makes sure that the font's size isn't unreasonable. Object properties are read with the Property Get procedure, as usual.

> **NOTE**
> Of course, there's very little use for setting a Font property in a class because it doesn't have a visible user interface, but you will be setting Font properties in the next chapter, in which we will discuss ActiveX controls.

You've now seen the basics of building classes, which are basically applications without a visible user interface. They do, however, have an interface, which is made up of the properties, methods, and events they provide. Actually, you haven't seen how to raise events, but we'll discuss this topic in the section "Asynchronous Methods and Properties," later in this chapter. As you recall from the previous chapter, events are raised with the RaiseEvent method. But it's about time to put together the information presented so far to build an actual ActiveX component.

Developing the Crypto Class

In this section, we will develop a class that encrypts text based on a password. Any application that must encrypt text can add a reference to this class and call its Encrypt method. With a class such as Crypto, you'll never have to provide your own encryption procedures, and all your applications can use a consistent encryption method. The same method will also decrypt previously encrypted messages.

The cryptography engine used by the Crypto class is fairly simple, yet it will prevent most occasional intruders. If you need a truly safe encryption, you must tweak the code, and we'll give you a few ideas about how to do this at the end of this section. To simplify the code and focus on the mechanics of implementing a class, we'll implement a simple cryptography engine. (Actually, it's not that simple. Many commercial products use similar methods.)

All encryption techniques are based on the XOR operator, which has the following unique property: If you XOR a character with another character, you'll get an encrypted version of the original character. If you XOR this character with the same key character once again, you will get the original one. For example, if you XOR the value 132 with the value 45, you'll get 169. If you XOR the new value, 169, with 45, you will get the number you started with, 132. This unique feature of the XOR operator is used extensively with drawing methods. You can place a shape over a bitmap and then remove it, using the XOR drawing mode.

To encrypt a string, we'll XOR its first character with the first character of the password, the second character of the string with the second character of the password, and so on, until we run out of characters in the password. Then, we must start with the first character of the password again. Figure 6.1 shows which characters will be XORed with each other in encrypting the message "Attack before dawn" with the password TORA.

FIGURE 6.1:

Encrypting by XORing strings with a key. The first line is XORed with the second line to yield the encrypted message, which is then XORed with the fourth line to yield the original message.

Code 6.1:   Encrypting the Message

```
Message = "Attack before dawn"
Key = "TORA"
For i = 1 To Len(Message)
    textChar = Mid(Message, i, 1)
    keyChar = Mid(Key, (i Mod Len(Key)) + 1)
    encryptedChar = Asc(textChar) Xor Asc(keyChar)
    EncryptedMessage = EncryptedMessage & Chr(encryptedChar)
Next
Debug.Print EncryptedMessage
```

The encrypted message is:

```
&55,9a6*4.&*r%58<
```

(The first character is unprintable and, therefore, left blank in the text.) If you run the previous lines using the encrypted text as a message, you'll get back the original string.

TIP

> To test the previous lines, place them in the Click event of a Command Button. If you want to test them in the Immediate window, be sure that the entire For ... Next loop is entered on a single line, using the colon (:) to separate successive statements.

This code segment is the core of the encryption engine we are going to implement in our Crypto class. Before you start coding the class, however, you must design its interface: its properties and methods. In other words, you must decide how to access the functionality of the class. The Crypto class provides three properties and a method, as shown in Table 6.1.

TABLE 6.1: The Crypto Class Members

Member	What It Is
Text	The text to be encrypted
Key	The encryption key (password)
EncryptedText	The encrypted text
Encrypt	The method that performs the encryption by XORing the Text and Key properties

Building the Crypto Class

To build a new class, start an ActiveX DLL project. Visual Basic will add a folder named Class Modules, with a class module in it. Change the name of the class module to CryptoClass, and change the project name to Crypto. Then save the components of the project in a new folder.

The Crypto Project on the CD

The components of the Crypto project on the CD are named `Crypto.vbp` and `Crypto.cls`. The file `Crypt.vbp` contains the class, and the file `TestProj.vbp` contains the test project. To open both the class and the test project and test them at once in the IDE, open the file `Crypto.vbg`.

The first time you open this project from the CD (as well as all other projects in this chapter), you will get the following error message:

```
Unable to set the version compatible component
```

This only means that the project can't find the class on your computer. Click the OK button to open the project, and then run the project. The class will be registered on your system.

The class's Encrypt method doesn't accept any arguments. It acts on the values of the properties Text and Key and stores the result of the encryption in the EncryptedText property. First, add the declarations of the private variables that hold the values of the properties in the class module:

```
Private mvarText As String
Private mvarKey As String
Private mvarEncryptedText As String
```

The next step is to write the Property Let and Property Get procedures for each property. Notice that the EncryptedText property is read-only. It doesn't make sense to set the encrypted text from outside the class, so we omit the Property Let procedure for the EncryptedText property. Later, you'll see how you can raise an error message when the application attempts to set the value of a read-only property.

Code 6.2: **The Property Procedures for the Class's Properties**

```
Public Property Get EncryptedText() As String
    EncryptedText = mvarEncryptedText
End Property
```

```
Public Property Let Key(ByVal vData As String)
    mvarKey = vData
End Property

Public Property Get Key() As String
    Key = mvarKey
End Property

Public Property Let Text(ByVal vData As String)
    mvarText = vData
End Property

Public Property Get Text() As String
    Text = mvarText
End Property
```

The Property Let procedures don't validate the property values at their assignment. The validation will take place when the Encrypt method is called. Code 6.3 shows the implementation of the Encrypt() function in its simplest form.

Code 6.3:   The Encrypt() Function

```
Public Function Encrypt() As Integer
Dim textChar As String * 1
Dim keyChar As String * 1
Dim encryptedChar As Integer

    mvarEncryptedText = ""
    For i = 1 To Len(mvarText)
        textChar = Mid(mvarText, i, 1)
        keyChar = Mid(mvarKey, (i Mod Len(mvarKey)) + 1)
        encryptedChar = Asc(textChar) Xor Asc(keyChar)
        mvarEncryptedText = mvarEncryptedText & Chr(encryptedChar)
    Next
    Encrypt = 1
End Function
```

You declare the Encrypt() function as public, and it automatically becomes a method of the class. When it's called, it encrypts the value of the *mvarText* local variable with the key stored in the *mvarKey* local variable and assigns the result to another local variable, *mvarEncryptedText*. The application must then read the EncryptedText property's value to retrieve the encrypted text.

Raising Errors from within a Class

The simple code we presented here doesn't protect the developer from possible errors. What if the key or the text hasn't been specified? The Encrypt method must make sure that the Text and Key properties have valid values, before it attempts to encrypt the text. If it detects an abnormal condition, it must notify the developer by raising an error. The class shouldn't display error messages or prompt the user to enter the missing data. The Crypto class doesn't have a visible interface, and it should notify the client application by raising an error.

Although it is possible for the class to display message boxes and request user input with the InputBox() function and even to display Forms and dialog boxes, we generally avoid giving a class a visible user interface, because the class may be running on a remote computer. In that case, any dialog boxes will appear on the server computer, and not on the client. Besides, the responsibility for the client application's user interface lies with the developer, not with the class itself. You must, therefore, offer the means for the developer to detect from within code any unusual conditions and react to them as he or she sees fit. The best way to detect unusual conditions from within your class and yet leave the responsibility for handling them to the developer is via trappable errors.

To raise an error from within your code, you can call the Raise method of the Err object. The Raise method causes a run-time error, and its syntax is:

```
Err.Raise number, source, description, helpfile, helpcontext
```

The number parameter is a Long Integer that identifies the nature of the error. Visual Basic errors (both Visual Basic–defined and user-defined errors) are in the range 0–65536. When setting the Number property to your own error code in a class module, you must add the vbObjectError constant to this error's number. For example, to generate the error number 1099, assign vbObjectError + 1099 to the Number property.

TIP
The numbers you choose for your class's errors are up to you. We suggest, however, that you use consecutive numbers and add the vbObjectError constant to them.

The remaining arguments are optional. The source argument is a string naming the object or application that generated the error. When you raise errors from within classes, you usually set this property to "project.class" ("Crypto.CryptoClass" for this project). If you omit the source argument, the programmatic ID of the current

Visual Basic project is used. The next argument, `description`, is another string that describes the error. If this is unspecified, Visual Basic examines the value of the Number property, and if it corresponds to an existing run-time error, Visual Basic displays this error's description. If no Visual Basic error corresponds to the specified number, the string "Application-defined or object-defined error" is displayed as the error's description.

The last two arguments let you specify additional help. The path to the Microsoft Windows Help file with information about this error is `helpfile`. If this is unspecified, Visual Basic uses the fully qualified drive, path, and file name of the Visual Basic Help file. The context ID of a topic within *helpfile* that provides help for the specific error is *helpcontext*.

The Encrypt method may discover two error conditions:

- Unspecified text
- Unspecified encryption key

Let's use the numbers 100 and 101 for these two errors and the descriptions "Can't encrypt null text" and "Encryption key not specified." Code 6.4 shows the complete code of the Encrypt() function, which validates the data before acting on them.

Code 6.4:   The Complete Encrypt() Function

```
Public Function Encrypt() As Integer
Dim textChar As String * 1
Dim keyChar As String * 1
Dim encryptedChar As Integer

    If mvarText = "" Then
        Err.Raise vbObjectError + 100, _
            "Crypto.Encrypt", "Can't encrypt null text"
        Encrypt = 0
        Exit Function
    End If
    If mvarKey = "" Then
        Err.Raise vbObjectError + 101,_
            "Crypto.Encrypt", "Encryption key not specified"
        Encrypt = 0
        Exit Function
    End If

    mvarEncryptedText = ""
```

```
        For i = 1 To Len(mvarText)
            textChar = Mid(mvarText, i, 1)
            keyChar = Mid(mvarKey, (i Mod Len(mvarKey)) + 1)
            encryptedChar = Asc(textChar) Xor Asc(keyChar)
            mvarEncryptedText = mvarEncryptedText & Chr(encryptedChar)
        Next
        Encrypt = 1
    End Function
```

After you enter the complete code, you are ready to test the class. Save all the components of the project (the class module and the project itself), and then choose File ➣ Make Crypto.dll. If you saved the class with a different file name, this file name with the extension DLL will appear in the File menu. Select this command and create the DLL in the same folder where you saved the project.

Handling Errors at Design Time

When you are testing a class module with an application that resides in the same project group, errors raised by the class are not passed to the host application. The Encrypt method, for example, raises two errors. If you are testing the class with the test project in the same project group, the program will stop at the line that raises the error, in the class's code.

If you run the test project separately, the code won't break in the class module (developers don't have access to the class's code anyway). To change this behavior, choose Tools ➣ Options to open the Options dialog box:

Handling Errors at Design Time (continued)

In the Error Trapping section, check the Break on Unhandled Errors option. This causes the class to pass the error to the host application, where it's supposed to be handled by an error-trapping routine. The code will break only if an error is received by a procedure that calls a method or a property of the class and doesn't have its own error handler.

Creating Object Variables

In the last chapter, you saw how to access an object through object variables. You also saw two ways to declare object variables:

1. Declare an object variable with the New keyword:

   ```
   Private objectVar As New objectType
   ```

2. Declare an object variable and then set it to the object you want to access:

   ```
   Private objectVar As objectType
   Set objectVar = New objectType
   ```

Both methods require that Visual Basic know the *objectType*. You can expect Visual Basic to know about Forms, controls, and other types of built-in objects. But how about your custom objects? Visual Basic doesn't know anything about the objects you create; you must tell it that a specific project must access an object by adding a reference to this object to your project. For example, if you want to add the Crypto class to a project, choose Project ➤ References to open the References dialog box:

Locate the object you want to reference from within your code, check its box, and click OK.

If you open the Object Browser dialog box after adding a new reference to your project, you will see the Type Library of the recently added object. Select it in the Type Library box to see the classes it exposes in the Classes pane. The Crypto project exposes a single class, the Crypto class. Click the name of the class to see its members.

Unless you add a reference to a specific object to your project, you won't be able to declare variables of this type. You can also declare object variables with the CreateObject function, which requires that you supply the application and class name. First, declare an object variable, and then assign an object instance to it:

```
Private cryptoObject As Object
Set cryptoObject = CreateObject("Crypto.CryptoClass")
```

You usually place the Set statement in the Form_Load event or in the procedure that needs to access the object. You can change the declaration of the object variable *cryptoObject* in the test application with the CreateObject method, as shown here. The rest of the code remains the same.

Testing the Crypto Class

To test the Crypto class, you create a new project, add a reference to the class to the new project, and then create an object variable that represents the Crypto class, as discussed in the previous section. Through this object variable, you can access the class's properties and methods. The test project we'll use for the Crypto class is the TestPrj.vbp project. The test project's main Form is shown in Figure 6.2.

NOTE   You'll find the TestPrj.vbp project in the Ch06\Crypto folder on the CD that comes with this book.

FIGURE 6.2:

The main Form of the test project for the Crypto class

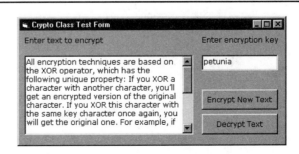

This Form contains two TextBox controls: a multiline one in which the text to be encrypted appears, and a smaller one in which the key is displayed. The Encrypt New Text button encrypts the text in the multiline TextBox with the specified key. The result is stored in a private variable, and clicking the Decrypt Text button decrypts it.

NOTE

The encrypted text isn't displayed in the TextBox, because it's possible for an encrypted character to have the ASCII value zero. This character signifies the end of the text in the TextBox and would truncate the encrypted text in the TextBox control. The test project maintains a Form wide private variable, the *secretText* variable, in which the last encrypted text is stored. The Decrypt Text button uses this variable's value to decrypt the text.

Code 6.5:   **The TestPrj.vbp Project**

```
Private CryptoObj As New CryptoClass
Private secretText As String

Private Sub Command1_Click()
On Error GoTo EncryptionError

    CryptoObj.Key = Text2.Text
    CryptoObj.Text = Text1.Text
    Call CryptoObj.Encypt
    secretText = CryptoObj.EncryptedText
    MsgBox Len(CryptoObj.Text) & " characters encrypted successfully."
    Text1.Text = ""
    Exit Sub

EncryptionError:
    MsgBox Err.Description
End Sub

Private Sub Command2_Click()
On Error GoTo DecryptionError

    CryptoObj.Key = Text2.Text
    CryptoObj.Text = secretText
    Call CryptoObj.Encypt
    Text1.Text = CryptoObj.EncryptedText
    Exit Sub
```

```
DecryptionError:
     Debug.Print Err.Number
     MsgBox Err.Description
End Sub
```

You declare the *CryptoObj* variable with the New keyword, so you don't have to set it in the code. The object variable is created not at the moment it's declared, but the first time it's referenced in the code. Notice that the *CryptoObj* object variable is declared in the Form so that both event handlers can access it. Because it was declared with the New keyword and we don't have to set this variable in the code, it doesn't make any difference which event handler will instantiate the variable. The user can click either button for the first time.

NOTE   It doesn't make much sense to decrypt a string that hasn't been encrypted yet. However, you can try clicking both buttons for the first time and see that this doesn't make any difference to the creation of the object variable.

Code 6.6:   **The Decrypt Text Button**

```
Private Sub Command2_Click()
On Error GoTo DecryptionError

    CryptoObj.Key = Text2.Text
    CryptoObj.Text = secretText
    Call CryptoObj.Encypt
    Text1.Text = CryptoObj.EncryptedText
    Exit Sub

DecryptionError:
     MsgBox Err.Description
End Sub
```

As explained earlier, the encrypted text is stored in the *secretText* variable, which is declared at the Form level. The decryption is performed by the same method that encrypted the text and with the same key.

Developing More Robust Encryption Schemes

The encryption engine we implemented for the CryptoClass class isn't terribly secure. The problem with this scheme is that it uses a fixed-length key. If the original text contains a (not so unusual) pattern of asterisks, dashes, or other special characters, the length of the key will become evident. If you encrypt the string:

```
******************************
```

with the key abcd, you'll get the following encrypted string:

```
HINKHINKHINKHINKHINKHINKHINKH
```

One can easily spot a pattern in the encrypted text. This pattern reveals the length of the key. In addition, if you XOR the encrypted text with a pattern consisting of special symbols, you'll come up with the encryption key. Let's pretend that we don't know what the original string is, but that we do know that it's made up of a long run of identical characters. If you XOR the encrypted text with several patterns (runs of dashes, spaces, asterisks, and so on), you will eventually discover the encryption key.

One simple trick to make this encryption scheme more secure is to blend the key with the text as you move along. When you run out of characters in the key, you wrap the key and start with its first character again. But you can replace it with a new key, based on the text characters you've encrypted already. For example, instead of using the first character of the key for a second time, you can XOR its first character with the first character of the text and use the result of the operation as the first character of the key. This process is reversible, because when you run out of characters in the encryption key, the first few characters of the original text will be available.

You can also use really convoluted operations between the key and the string to totally eliminate patterns. The new encryption scheme isn't unbeatable, but it will serve the needs of a typical programmer (which is to secure some files on a local area network).

TIP   If you plan to transmit sensitive information over the Internet, look into more advanced encryption schemes, which are readily available.

Setting Project Properties

At this point we'll take a break to discuss the Project Properties dialog box. Most of the entries in this dialog box are obvious, but some aren't. Also, some seemingly obvious options may have ramifications you must be aware of. You can skip this section if you want and come back to it when you need this information. In the Project Properties dialog box, shown in Figure 6.3, you select a project type and set various options for the project.

FIGURE 6.3:

The Project Properties
dialog box

The General Tab

As you can see in Figure 6.3, the General tab of the Project Properties dialog box is selected by default. This dialog box contains the options described in the following sections.

Project Type   This drop-down list box contains the types of projects, as they appear in the File Open dialog box. The following project types are available:

- Standard EXE

- ActiveX DLL

- ActiveX EXE

- ActiveX control

Changing the project type at will isn't always feasible or simple, but many times it is. Switching between ActiveX DLL and ActiveX EXE projects is possible and fairly easy. Let's say you want to build an ActiveX DLL. To simplify the testing and debugging process, you can start a Standard EXE project and add a class module to the project. When the class is working in the context of the current project, you can remove the project's Forms and change the type of the project from Standard EXE to ActiveX DLL.

Startup Object   You use this drop-down list box to specify what will happen when the project is run. You can't execute ActiveX control projects; you must place the ActiveX control on a Form of a Standard EXE project, which is then executed. For Standard EXE projects, the Startup object can be a Form or the subroutine Main. The Main subroutine must reside in a standard module of the project, and it must display the first visible Form of the application. Code components can't start by displaying Forms. The Startup object of an ActiveX EXE or DLL component must be None or the subroutine Main. If you change the type of a project during its design, you must also change the Startup object.

You can set a different Startup object for each project in a project group. To specify the Startup project, right-click the project's name in the Project window and select Set As Startup.

Project Name   This property is the component's name in the Object Browser. In other words, this is how developers will locate your component in the Object Browser and look up its members. It's important to set a proper project name in this field. If you don't, you'll have to differentiate among various Project1 components on your disk. If the component's name is MyComponent and it exposes a class called MyClass, the code can create an object variable to reference the class with the following statement:

```
Set Object1 = CreateObject("MyComponent.MyClass")
```

As you can see, changing the project's name (or the class's name for that matter) after the fact requires that the code be revised too. Use descriptive project names, and avoid generic names such as Test, Example, Server, and so on. ActiveX components are registered to the system; they aren't just files that live in a folder.

Help File Name, Project Help Context ID   You use these two fields to specify the help file for the project and the ID. Although we won't discuss help files in this book, any component you plan to release (especially ActiveX controls) must have a help file.

Project Description   This is the project's description and appears in the Object Browser when a user selects your component.

Upgrade ActiveX Controls   Check this option if you want Visual Basic to automatically upgrade ActiveX controls to newer versions when the user upgrades one or more of the controls in the project.

Require License Key   This field enables you to protect your components with a license key. When you develop and distribute an ActiveX component (or control), some developers will use it in their applications. The users of these applications should be able to use your components at run time, but you may not want to allow them to use your components in designing new projects. This would be equivalent to distributing your components for free. To protect your software, you can use license keys. If a developer attempts to use your control in the design of an application and doesn't have a license key, Visual Basic won't permit the installation of the control. If you are protecting your components with license keys, check this option.

Unattended Execution   The options in this section apply to multithreaded servers, and we discuss them in the second half of this chapter.

The Make Tab

Now click the Make tab. As you can see, this tab contains mostly developer information, such as version numbers and conditional compilation arguments.

Version Number   Here you can set the version of your component, or you can check the Auto Increment box (which increments the component's version number each time you build a new EXE or DLL file). You should set the version number manually before releasing the component. Releasing a new control with version number 16 isn't the best idea.

Application   Here you can specify the name of the application and select an icon for its executable file.

Version Information Enter comments, copyright notices, trademark notes, and other types of information in this section.

Command Line Arguments Enter any command line arguments for Standard EXE projects here.

Conditional Compilation Arguments In this field, you can enter the values of the conditional compilation arguments.

The Compile Tab

Now, click the Compile tab. You use it to specify the various compilation options.

Compile to P-Code, Compile to Native Code These two options let you select how the Visual Basic compiler will optimize the executable file. With older versions of Visual Basic, you could only produce p-code, but now there's a real compiler. Go for native code and optimize for fast code, right? Not so simple.

Native code isn't necessarily faster than p-code (it's not slower either). A typical application spends most of its time waiting for user input and performs tasks that take much less than a second. Optimizing speed beyond a threshold is really unnecessary, especially if you consider that the natively compiled files are larger. P-code is quite efficient, and you should prefer it, unless your application contains many computationally intensive procedures. If you are using double-precision math, go ahead and select Compile Native Code and Optimize for Fast Code. But with most applications, you won't see any difference between p-code and native code. Don't forget that Visual Basic applications spend a lot of time executing what's known as *support code* (for example, an ActiveX server must be loaded first and then executed). When you are accessing a database through the Data Access Objects (DAO), the compiler isn't going to make any difference. The DAO is an executable, and it can't be made any faster or any slower. So, if the benchmark is how fast you can retrieve records, you can't count on Visual Basic's compiler. If you need faster response, you'll probably have to do something more drastic, such as porting the database to the SQL Server.

Advanced Optimizations   Click the Advanced Optimizations button to open the Advanced Optimizations dialog box, in which you can set a number of options (listed below) that will marginally improve the speed of the executable. You can turn off some or all of these checks by checking the appropriate checkbox.

WARNING   Enabling these optimizations may prevent the correct execution of your program. You must understand what each option does and be sure that your application doesn't require any of the options you turn off.

Assume No Aliasing: This option tells the compiler that your program does not use aliasing. Aliasing is a technique that lets your code refer to the same variable (memory location) by more than one name. We don't use this technique in this book, so you can safely turn on this option.

Remove Array Bound Checks: By default, Visual Basic checks an array's bounds every time your code accesses the array to determine if the index is within the range of the array. If the index is not within array bounds, a run-time error is generated (which can be trapped from within the code). Select this option to turn off the array bound checking and speed up applications that use arrays. However, the code that will ensure that the array's bounds are not exceeded may cost more in execution time. If an array bound is exceeded, the results will be unexpected.

Remove Integer Overflow Checks: By default, Visual Basic checks every calculation for integer-style data types—Byte, Integer, and Long—to ensure that the value is within the range of the data type. If the magnitude of the value being put into the data type is incorrect, a run-time error is generated. Select this option to turn off the error checking and speed up integer calculations. If data-type capacities are overflowed, you will get incorrect results.

Remove Floating Point Error Checks: By default, Visual Basic checks every calculation of a Floating Point data type—Single and Double—to be sure that the value is within range for that data type and that there are no divide-by-zero or invalid operations. If the magnitude of the value being put into the data type is incorrect, an error occurs. Select this option to turn off the error checking and speed up floating-point calculations. If data-type capacities are overflowed, no error handling occurs, and you may get incorrect result.

Allow Unrounded Floating Point Operations: When this option is selected, the compiler uses floating-point registers more efficiently, avoids storing and loading large volumes of data to and from memory, and does floating-point comparisons more efficiently

Remove Safe Pentium FDIV Checks: Checking this option removes the safety checking so that the code for floating-point division is faster. You may, however, get slightly incorrect results on Pentium processors with the FDIV bug.

The Component Tab

Now, select the Component tab. This tab contains a few options for ActiveX servers and lets you specify the version compatibility, a handy way to ensure that each time you update a component, all projects that used the previous version will be updated as well.

Start Mode   In this section, you can specify whether an ActiveX EXE server will start as a standalone application or as an ActiveX server. This option applies to ActiveX EXE components only, and the default is ActiveX Component (it will start when an application contacts the server).

Remote Server   When this option is selected, Visual Basic creates a file with a VBR file name extension and the same file name as the DLL file. This VBR file contains information needed by the Windows Registry to run an ActiveX Server on a remote computer.

Version Compatibility   The options in this section allow you to set the level of version compatibility: how newer versions of ActiveX components and controls will affect existing projects.

> **No Compatibility:** Compatibility is not enforced.
>
> **Project Compatibility:** If you select this option, the Location dialog box is activated, and you can use it to search for the file with which this project is to be compatible. If this option is not selected, the Location dialog box is not available. If you design an ActiveX control or a code component to be used with a specific project, select this option, and select the name of the project in the last field. By default, this option is selected for all ActiveX projects; so every time you change the control or component's code, the project is also updated.
>
> **Binary Compatibility**: Select this option to maintain compatibility among projects that have been compiled using your component.

Developing the RunningStats Class

The Crypto class is as simple as it gets. Our next project, the RunningStats class, demonstrates a class that processes its properties by calculating running statistics. It calculates the basic statistics (average and standard deviation) of a data run. The main feature of this class is that it calculates the so-called running statistics; it doesn't require that all the data be supplied at once. As each new data value becomes available, the statistics are updated, and the application can retrieve their values at any time. The Stats project is a Standard EXE project that has a Form and a class module, to which we added a class module. Figure 6.4 shows the Stats project at design time.

NOTE You'll find the Stats projects in the Ch06\Stats folder on the CD that comes with this book.

FIGURE 6.4:

The Stats project at design time

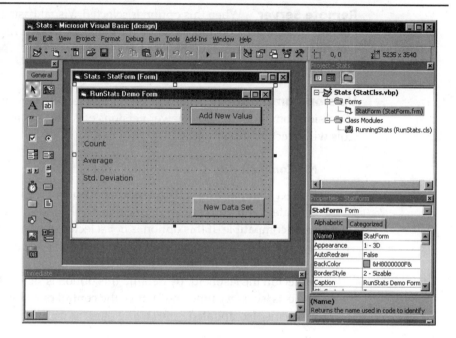

The benefit of this approach is that you can implement and test the class with a single project. Since the class module was added to the project, it became immediately part of the project, and you don't have to add a reference to the RunningStats class through the References dialog box. Yet, the class can be made available for use by other projects too. To do so, however, you must:

1. Change the project type from Standard EXE to ActiveX DLL

2. Set the Instancing property to MultiUse

The Instancing property of a class module is discussed in the following section. Let's return to the Stats project. Table 6.2 lists and describes the members of the RunningStats class.

TABLE 6.2: The Members of the RunningStats Class

Member	Description
NewValue	New data value to be appended to the current data set. Each time a new data value is added to the current data set, all statistics are recalculated.
RunningCount	The number of data values in the data set.
RunningAverage	The current average of the data set.
RunningDeviation	The current standard deviation of the data set.
NewDataSet	This method resets the data set.

The average is calculated as the sum of all values in the run, divided by their count. Therefore, we need a private variable that holds the running sum, which is the *m_Sum* variable. At any point, the average can be calculated as:

```
m_Sum / m_var_RunningCount
```

The local variable *m_var_RunningCount* implements the RunningCount property.

The standard deviation is calculated according to a standard formula. It's the square root of the difference between the sum of squares minus the square of the average multiplied by the number of data values and divided by the square of the count of the data points. It's implemented with a fairly long line, as you'll see, but if you aren't interested in statistics, you can ignore the calculations. The deviation is an important attribute of the data set that describes the dispersion of the values around their mean value.

Code 6.7:   The RunningStats Class

```
Option Explicit
Private m_var_RunningCount As Long
Private m_var_RunningAverage As Double
Private m_var_RunningDeviation As Double
Private m_Sum As Double
Private m_SumSquares As Double

Public Property Get RunningAverage() As Double
    RunningAverage = m_var_RunningAverage
End Property
```

```
Public Property Get RunningCount() As Long
    RunningCount = m_var_RunningCount
End Property

Public Property Get RunningDeviation() As Double
    RunningDeviation = m_var_RunningDeviation
End Property

Public Property Let NewValue(vNewValue As Double)
    m_var_RunningCount = m_var_RunningCount + 1
    m_Sum = m_Sum + vNewValue
    m_var_RunningAverage = m_Sum / m_var_RunningCount
    m_SumSquares = m_SumSquares + vNewValue ^ 2
    If m_var_RunningCount > 1 Then m_var_RunningDeviation = _
        Sqr(m_SumSquares - m_var_RunningCount * _
        m_var_RunningAverage ^ 2) / (m_var_RunningCount * _
        (m_var_RunningCount - 1))
End Property

Public Sub NewDataSet()
    m_var_RunningAverage = 0
    m_var_RunningCount = 0
    m_var_RunningDeviation = 0
    m_Sum = 0
    m_SumSquares = 0
End Sub
```

The Form's code is simple too. First, we create an object variable that references the RunningStats object:

```
Private StatObj As New RunningStats
```

and then we use it from within the Add New Value button's code to add a new value to the data set and retrieve the updated statistics:

```
Private Sub Command1_Click()
    If IsNumeric(Text1.Text) Then
        StatObj.NewValue = Text1.Text
        Text1.Text = ""
        lblCnt.Caption = StatObj.RunningCount
        lblAvg.Caption = StatObj.RunningAverage
        lblDev.Caption = StatObj.RunningDeviation
    End If
End Sub
```

This class is useful in maintaining running statistics of large data sets, especially if they can be updated from many places in an application. However, it doesn't keep track of the data values. It is possible to build a class that maintains a list of data values (which need not be numeric, by the way) and report them to the application. We'll look at this in the next section.

Array Properties

The Stats class can report the running statistics at any time, but not the data supplied to the class. If the calling application doesn't store them in an array or another structure, the data values will be lost. Of course, the purpose of the Stats class is to avoid keeping track of the data points. As each new data point becomes available, the running statistics are updated, and the value is discarded. Keeping track of the data points in a statistics application requires some careful design, as each run may contain many thousands of data points.

Let's assume that you will use the Stats class to calculate the statistics of a small data run and that it's feasible to maintain an array with the values passed to the class. Storing the data values isn't a problem; a simple array structure will do. But how about retrieving the data values? To access the data values, you need a property such as DataValue, which must accept as an argument an index value, which will be the order of the desired data value in the DataValue array. The Stats1 class demonstrates how to implement array properties.

The Stats1 project is similar to the Stats project, but it implements an additional property, Datapoints. The data values are stored in a collection, which is declared at the beginning of the code as follows:

```
Private Datapoints As New Collection
```

It would probably be more efficient to use an array of Doubles to store the data values, but the additional code for redimensioning the array when the data values exceed its declared size wasn't worth it for this example. We assume that the class is used with a small number of data values and only for demonstration purposes. Storing an enormous collection of data values in a class isn't a good idea, but in situations where the potential number of data values is limited by the nature of the application, this approach will work nicely.

In the NewValue property, you must add the following line, which appends a new item to the collection:

```
Datapoints.Add vNewValue
```

In the NewDataSet method, which resets the running statistics in preparation for a new data run, you must remove all the elements of the collection:

```
For cItem = Datapoints.Count To 1 Step -1
    Datapoints.Remove cItem
Next
```

The Property Get procedure that implements the array property is shown next:

```
Public Property Get DataValue(Index As Long)
    DataValue = Datapoints(Index)
End Property
```

To test the Stats1 server, you can add a button for displaying all the data values passed to the server so far in the Immediate window. Here's the code for this button:

```
Dim i As Long
For i = 1 To StatObj.RunningCount
    Debug.Print StatObj.DataValue(i)
Next
```

Open the Stats1 project to see the full implementation of the class and the test application.

The Class's Instancing Property

As you have noticed, classes have two properties:

- Name
- Instancing

The Instancing property determines whether applications can use the class and how. Its possible settings are described below.

Private   Only components in the same applications can access Private objects. If you are developing a class that can't be used in other projects or if you don't want to make a class available to other developers, set its Instancing property to Private.

SingleUse   This setting applies to ActiveX EXE code components only, which we will discuss in the second half of the book. An ActiveX EXE server is an executable file (an application) that can service one or more clients. If the server's Instancing property is SingleUse, a new instance of the server is started for every client that calls the class's objects. This setting is an inefficient method for creating and using objects, and it's usually avoided. If you need a new instance of the server for each client, you might as well implement the server as an ActiveX DLL.

TIP
For more information on the two types of servers, see the section "Building Out-of-Process Servers" later in this chapter.

MultiUse   This setting is the opposite of Private and can be used only with code components. It allows a single instance of the server to provide as many objects as required by the client applications. Every new ActiveX EXE or ActiveX DLL project you start has its Instancing property set to MultiUse by default.

GlobalSingleUse   This setting creates a global object with SingleUse characteristics. If you are going to implement a global object, make it SingleUse so that all clients that call it can be serviced by a single instance of the server. It's also available with ActiveX EXE and ActiveX DLL components.

GlobalMultiUse   This setting is available with ActiveX EXE and ActiveX DLL projects and should be used rarely. The objects exposed by the GlobalMultiUse component are available to the entire system and can be accessed by any application, as if they were system components. Visual Basic provides its systemwide objects, which are called global objects. The Screen and Printer objects, for example, are global objects because you need not add a reference to them in the applications that use them. If you think you have an object that's important for the rest of the system (and not just the application that needs it) to know about, set its Instancing property to GlobalMultiUse.

PublicNotCreatable   The objects of a class with this setting can be accessed by other applications, but can't be created. Now, what good is this? The objects of a PublicNotCreatable class must first be created by another component in the same object and must be accessed through this component's objects. For example, let's say you have a class that implements database operations. One of the objects exposed by the class represents the database. Another class in the project represents a table of the database. If you allow the developer to access the second object directly, there's a chance he or she may attempt to open a table without first opening the database. If you make the class that exposes the Database object Public, but the class that exposes the Table object PrivateNotCreatable, you can then create a reference to the object that represents the table as soon as the database is opened. The developer can access the Table object directly, but only after it has been created.

For an example of PrivateNotCreatable and MultiUse classes, see the DBClass project in the following section.

Registering a Code Component

Classes are registered automatically on the system on which they are designed. When you create the DLL or EXE file that implements the class, Visual Basic registers it as well. But what if you want to make the class available to other developers who are working on different systems? If the component is an EXE server, you can distribute the EXE file. Once it is run on the target computer, the class is registered automatically. No messages or Forms are displayed. You simply execute the server, and it registers itself.

If the file you want to distribute is a DLL server, it must be registered with the REGSVR32 utility, which comes with Visual Basic (it's in the `Tools/RegUtils` folder on the Visual Basic 5 CD). RegServer is a program that allows you to register and unregister servers. Being able to unregister out-of-process servers is just as important. For example, removing the DLL files that implement the code components isn't enough. You must also unregister the components from the Registry, which you can do with the REGSVR32 utility.

To register a DLL, follow these steps:

1. Copy the file to your Windows System folder, or copy it to any other folder in the path.

2. Open a Command Prompt window (a DOS window), switch to the folder where the DLL resides, and issue the following command (`filename.dll` is the file that implements the server):

    REGSVR32 filename.dll

You can use several options with the REGSVR32 utility. The /u option uninstalls a previously registered DLL. To unistall the file `filename.dll`, use the following command:

    REGSVR32 /u MyServer.dll.

When a new DLL is registered, the REGSVR32 utility reports the results of the operation in a message box. To suppress this message box, use the /s (silent) option.

Using REGSVR32 is the simplest way to distribute DLL servers. All you have to do is write a small application that copies the DLL file to a folder and then run the REGSVR32 utility on the target computer to register it.

Encapsulating Database Operations

The classes we developed so far are fairly straightforward. The essence of a class is to encapsulate fairly complicated data and operations and allow the developer to perform complex tasks with a few statements. In this section, we are going to develop a class that encapsulates database operations. But this is what the DAO does, isn't it? The DAO abstracts many of the low-level details of manipulating databases, but to use its objects, you need a solid understanding of recordsets, SQL statements, and so on. By abstracting certain operations on a database, you can provide simple tools to other programmers, who can build applications using your classes instead of the DAO itself.

Let's say you have a number of programmers in a corporate environment writing code to display customer names or invoices for their applications. Visual Basic provides the data-bound Grid control, which can be easily connected to a database. But this requires that programmers know how to access a database with the Data Access Objects.

Suppose, however, that you offer programmers a simple class that retrieves customer names and provides them through the following methods:

- GetFirstCustomer
- GetLastCustomer
- GetNextCustomer
- GetPreviousCustomer

The programmer using your class need not know anything about recordsets (not even that these methods are actually implemented directly on the recordset). All a programmer has to know is how to set up a small program that scans the customer names (which are already sorted somehow) to display them on a Grid and add them to a ListBox control or to any other control. The fields of the current record are accessed as properties of this class as well. The developer types the name of the object that represents this class and then a period, and the available field names appear in the Auto List Members box.

This class simplifies the task of developing database applications by allowing programmers to access databases without getting into the complexities of DAO. Debugging is also simplified because your class is tested separately, before other applications use it.

The Classes of the DBClass Project

The DBClass project contains four classes. The project is based on the NWIND sample database that comes with Visual Basic, and it implements three classes for retrieving customers, invoices, and invoice details with simple methods, designed specifically for the type of records retrieved by each class.

> **NOTE** You'll find the DBClass project in the Ch06/DBClass folder on the CD that comes with this book.

The class that retrieves customer records, for instance, provides the following methods:

- GetFirstCustomer
- GetNextCustomer
- GetPreviousCustomer
- GetLastCustomer

The current record's fields are properties of the class. The developer using this class need not know how customer records are stored in the database or anything about accessing databases with the Data Access Objects (DAO). In the sections that follow, we'll look at the members of each class.

DefinitionsClass

This class opens the NWIND database and makes it available to the other classes and exposes the following members:

DatabaseName, which must be set to the database's path, and a single method.

SetDatabase, which opens the specified database. The user need specify only the path of the database, not its name.

CustomersClass

This class exposes the properties and methods for accessing the Customers table in the database and exposes the following members:

> **OpenCustomers:** This method retrieves the customer data. The records are stored in a recordset in the class and can be accessed with the following methods:

> > **GetFirstCustomer, GetLastCustomer, GetNextCustomer, GetPrevious-Customer:** These four methods allow the programmer to move to another record, similar to the MoveFirst, MoveLast, MoveNext, and MovePrevious methods of the Recordset object. Contrary to the equivalent methods of the Recordset object, the methods of the CustomersClass don't require that the developer know anything about the EOF and BOF properties and their role in scanning the records. These methods return a True/False value, which indicates that the desired record exists (if True) or the records have been exhausted (if False).

> > **CustomerID, CompanyName, ContactName, ContactTitle:** These properties return the values of the fields by the same name in the current record. These properties are read-only to protect the developer from overwriting the data. You can also make them settable if you want to allow the developer to change the data.

InvoicesClass

This class has the same structure as the CustomersClass and exposes the following members:

> **OpenInvoices CustID:** This method retrieves the invoices issued to a specific customer, whose ID is passed to the method as an argument. The records are stored in a recordset in the class and can be accessed with the following methods:

> > **GetFirstInvoice, GetLastInvoice, GetNextInvoice, GetPreviousInvoice:** These are the InvoiceClass's navigational methods.

> > **InvoiceID, CompanyName, OrderDate, ShippedDate, SubTotal:** These properties return the values of the fields by the same name in the current record. They are all read-only.

DetailsClass

This class has the same structure as the two previous ones and exposes the following members:

> **OpenDetails InvID:** This method retrieves the lines of a specific invoice, whose ID is passed to the method as an argument.
>
> **GetFirstLine, GetLastLine, GetNextLine, GetPreviousLine:** These are the DetailsClass's navigational methods.
>
> **ProductID, ProductName, ProductPrice, Quantity, Units, Discount, ExtendedPrice:** These properties return the values of the fields by the same name in the current record. They are all read-only.

As you can see, the classes for accessing customer names, invoices, and invoice lines have the same structure:

- A method that opens a recordset with the appropriate records
- Four navigational methods
- A number of properties that return field values

Their implementation is also quite similar, so we need not present all three of them in detail. Before we look at the implementation of these classes, however, let's see how the developer can use them from within a client application.

Using the DBClass Objects

Figures 6.5 and 6.6 show a few typical examples of using the DBClass objects. The grid in Figure 6.5 contains the list of customers, and each time the user clicks a customer name, the invoices issued to the specific customer are displayed on another grid. The two Forms in this figure are among the test Forms used in the DBClass project.

Figure 6.6 is a similar application, which displays the invoices for a specific customer. When you select an invoice with the mouse, the corresponding lines are displayed in the smaller grid. These are also among the test Forms of the DBClass application.

FIGURE 6.5:

Displaying customers
and invoices with the
CustomersClass and
InvoicesClass objects of
DBClass

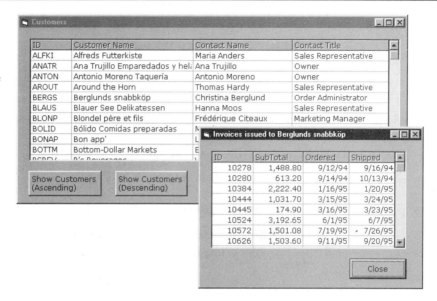

FIGURE 6.6:

Displaying invoices and
their details with the
InvoicesClass and
DetailsClass objects of
DBClass

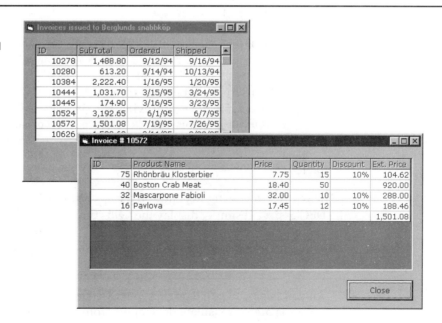

To use the classes exposed by the DBClass server, the developer must first create an object variable to reference the DataBase class and then open the database:

```
Dim DBObject As New DefinitionsClass
```

```
DBObject.DatabaseName = "c:\program files\devstudio\vb\nwind.mdb"_
    DBObject.SetDatabase
```

The *DBObject* variable lets you access the database. To retrieve the customer names, declare another object variable, *CustObject*, which will be used to reference a recordset with customer data:

```
Dim CustObject As New CustomersClass
```

```
CustObject.OpenCustomers
```

The customer names are stored in a tabular structure, which can be scanned with the CustomersClass navigational methods. The current record's fields can be read with the same object's properties. Here's a loop structure that scans the customer records:

```
Dim CustObject As New CustomersClass
CustObject.OpenCustomers
If CustObject.GetFirstCustomer Then
    {process first record using the properties:
        CustObject.CustomerID, CustObject.CompanyName,
        CustObject.ContactName & CustObject.ContactTitle }

    While CustObject.GetNextCustomer
        {process first record using the properties:
            CustObject.CustomerID, CustObject.CompanyName,
            CustObject.ContactName & CustObject.ContactTitle }
    Wend
End If
```

The type of processing depends on the application. In the test application for the DBClass, we'll simply display the fields on a Grid control. In your code, you could access the InvoicesClass class to process the invoices issued to each customer, calculate statistics for products sold to each customer, and so on.

TIP

If you think you could do this with SQL statements, remember that this class is meant to isolate developers from complicated database operations. It's meant to be used by developers who aren't familiar with the DAO object. For instance, you could provide this class along with your application to allow your customers to write simple customer reports, without having complete access to the database itself.

The loops for scanning the invoices issued to a specific customer or for scanning the lines of an invoice are quite similar. The basic difference is that the customers recordset is opened without an argument. To open the invoices recordset, you must call the OpenInvoices method, passing the customer's ID as an argument:

```
InvObjectClass.OpenInvoices(customerID)
```

The customerID argument is read from the customers recordset (it's the CustomerID property of the CustObject object). Similarly, the OpenDetails method of the Details object requires the invoice's ID as an argument:

```
DetObject.OpenDetails (InvID)
```

In this case, *InvID* is a Long variable that holds the ID of the desired invoice (which will be the InvoiceID property of the InvObject object).

Implementing DBClass

Since all three classes have similar structures, the code is also similar. Therefore, we'll look only at the implementation of the CustomersClass class. First, we declare a recordset where the customer data are stored:

```
Private CustomersRS As Recordset
```

The CustomersRS recordset is populated in the OpenCustomers method's code. This method is called by the client application to retrieve the customer data.

Code 6.8:   The OpenCustomers Method

```
Public Sub OpenCustomers()
Dim SQLString As String

    SQLString = "SELECT CustomerID, CompanyName, ContactName, _
        ContactTitle FROM CUSTOMERS"
    Set CustomersRS = DB.OpenRecordset(SQLString)

End Sub
```

The code of the other two classes uses more complicated SQL statements, but the principle is the same: Build an SQL statement, use it to open a recordset on the DB database, and then assign it to the *CustomersRS* object variable.

The Class navigation methods use the equivalent navigation methods of the recordset to move the record pointer in the recordset.

Code 6.9: The GetFirstCustomer Method

```
Public Function GetFirstCustomer() As Integer
Dim SQLString As String
On Error GoTo FirstCustomerError

    If CustomersRS.RecordCount > 0 Then
        CustomersRS.MoveFirst
        SetFields
        GetFirstCustomer = 1
    Else
        GetFirstCustomer = 0
    End If
    Exit Function

FirstCustomerError:
    Err.Raise vbError + 1027, "Customers", _
        "Error in reading first customer's data"
    End Function
```

Code 6.10: The GetNextCustomer Method

```
Public Function GetNextCustomer() As Integer
On Error GoTo NextCustomerError

    CustomersRS.MoveNext
    If Not CustomersRS.EOF Then
        SetFields
        GetNextCustomer = 1
    Else
        GetNextCustomer = 0
    End If
    Exit Function

NextCustomerError:
    Err.Raise vbError + 1027, "Customers", _
        "Error in reading next customer's data"
    End Function
```

Notice how these navigation methods handle the EOF property to detect whether the end of the recordset has been reached. The developer need not be concerned with these details. All he or she has to do is examine the value returned by the method and, if it's True, access the fields of the current record.

Each time the pointer is moved to another record, the SetFields subroutine is called. This subroutine extracts the values of the current record's fields and assigns them to private variables, which are later used to implement the class's properties.

Code 6.11:   The SetFields Subroutine

```
Private Sub SetFields()
On Error GoTo 0
    mvarCustomerID = CustomersRS.Fields("CustomerID")
    mvarCompanyName = CustomersRS.Fields("CompanyName")
    mvarContactName = CustomersRS.Fields("ContactName")
    mvarContactTitle = CustomersRS.Fields("ContactTitle")
End Sub
```

Finally, here's the implementation of a few of the class's properties:

```
Public Property Get CompanyName() As String
    CompanyName = mvarCompanyName
End Property

Public Property Get CustomerID() As String
    CustomerID = mvarCustomerID
End Property
```

The properties are read-only, and there are no equivalent Property Let procedures.

Using the members of the DBClass is certainly simpler than using the Data Access Object. Besides isolating developers from the complexity of the DAO, the DBClass offers developers a solid foundation for accessing the database. Should you decide to port the database to the SQL Server, all you have to do is rewrite the class's code; the application programmer may not even notice the difference. However, the test application contains quite a lot of code for placing the record fields on the grid, sizing the grids' columns, and so on.

NOTE   In the following chapter, we'll come back to this project and implement it as an ActiveX control. When the Forms of the DBClass application are converted to ActiveX controls, the developer simply places them on a Form and calls a method to display the data. The appearance of the control is handled internally, and the application's code is reduced to a few method calls.

Building Out-of-Process Servers

In this section, we are going to explore out-of-process servers, which are implemented as ActiveX EXE code components. We'll start by building a simple server that performs complicated calculations, and we'll explain the process step by step because out-of-process servers aren't simple to test (they require that you keep two instances of VB running at the same time and switch back and forth). We will add features to the simple EXE server, and by the end of the chapter you will know how to build an asynchronous server that notifies the client when an operation (such as a method or a property call) has completed. In the meantime, the application can go about its business instead of freezing the client window.

The SERVER1 Project

Start a new ActiveX EXE project. When the class module appears in the Project window, rename the project to SRVREXE, and change the name of the class module from Class1 to EXESRV1. Let's start by implementing a method that performs a few simple calculations, but repeats them many times. We simply need a method that takes a few seconds to complete. Enter the following code in the class module's Code window:

```
Public Function CalculateLong(Iterations As Long) As Double
Dim i As Long
    Randomize(Time)
    For i = 1 To Iterations
        a = a + Cos(32.33)
        b = b + Sin(0.3233)
    Next
    CalculateLong = a / b
End Function
```

The number of iterations is passed to the method as an argument. The result is a double value that depends on the number of iterations. Any math functions will do; you can even use the Rnd() function. We use an argument to specify the number of iterations so that you can adjust the loop's duration according to your computer's speed.

Let's implement another method, the CalculateShort method, which returns almost instantly:

```
Public Function CalculateShort(Iterations As Long) As Double
Dim i As Long
Dim a As Double, b As Double
```

```
For i = 1 To Iterations
    a = a + i
Next
CalculateShort = a
```

```
End Function
```

Our sample server contains two methods. You can add more methods or properties, but these two are adequate for our purposes. Now, let's build a client application to test our server. As you may have guessed, we'll examine the behavior of the two methods and discuss ways to execute them asynchronously so that the CalculateLong method won't hold the execution of the client application until it completes its execution.

The EXETest Client Application

The test application has two Command Buttons, one for each of the server's methods. A Label, at the top left section of the Form, displays the time and it's updated every second (to see how the server application affects the execution of the client). The PictureBox on the right reacts to the Click event, by drawing a gradient. This is another CPU intensive operation that will help us observe how the client and server applications share the CPU (which one executes and when, as well as how to steal cycles from the server application to execute the client application).

To build the test application (Figure 6.7 shows its Form), follow these steps:

1. Start another instance of VB, and create a new Standard EXE project. Place the controls you see on the Form in Figure 6.7, plus a Timer control, which we'll use to update the time every second.

In order to call the server's methods, we must create an object variable that references the SERVER1 class. First add to the project a reference to the server.

2. Choose Project ➤ References to open the References dialog box, and search for the entry SERVER1.

There is no such component in the list of available references. Don't bother browsing for the EXE component, as we have neither saved the ActiveX EXE project nor created the SERVER1.EXE component. The EXE component isn't available because it doesn't exist yet.

FIGURE 6.7:

The EXETest client
application's Form at
design time

3. Switch to the instance of VB with the SERVER1 project, and press F5 to run it.

4. Now, switch back to the test project, and open the References dialog box again. This time, you will see the name of the SERVER1 component in the list.

5. Check the checkbox in front of SERVER1, and click the OK button.

Now you've added a reference to the SERVER1 server to your application.

6. Open the client application's Code window, and enter the following lines:

```
Dim CObject1 As New EXESRV1
Dim CObject2 As New EXESRV1
```

If you have the Auto List Members feature on, as soon as you type the word *New*, you will see the list of object types available to the project. Select the EXESRV1 entry in this list.

7. Enter the following lines in the Command Button's Click event:

```
Private Sub Command1_Click()
    MsgBox CObject1.CalculateLong(100000)
End Sub
```

8. Now, enter the following lines in the second Command Button:

```
Private Sub Command2_Click()
    MsgBox CObject2.CalculateShort(30000)
End Sub
```

9. Run the application to get a feel for how fast the server responds.

The 100,000 iterations cause a delay of a few seconds on our system. If you start the client application by pressing F8 (to single-step through the code), you will be switched to the EXE Server project when the line that calls the CalculateLong() method is reached. Single-step through a few commands, and then press F5 to continue the program's execution. When the calculations complete, you will be taken back to the instance of VB with the test project. This is an interesting approach. It allows you to single-step through the code of the server and see how the server interacts with the client.

While the server is busy calculating, the client application is frozen. The time display isn't updated, and you can't press any button on the Form or draw the gradient on the PictureBox control. This doesn't happen because the CalculateLong method doesn't yield control to the processor. Insert the following line in the CalculateLong method's main loop:

```
If (i Mod 100) = 0 Then DoEvents
```

This statement breaks the execution of the loop and gives Windows a chance to attend to other application needs (process keystrokes, refresh windows, and so on). Start the server, and run the client; you won't notice any difference in its behavior.

This leads us to the question: If a server takes too long to respond to a method call, couldn't we let the server go about its business without freezing the client application and notify us with an event when the result is available? Imagine calling a method that downloads an image from a server on the Internet. Would we have to wait for the transmission to complete before allowing the user of the client to press another button on the Form or even move the Form? And what if the user decides not to wait for the download to complete? At the very least, the user should be able to press a Cancel button. (In the next chapter, you will see that it's possible to start a download process with the AsyncRead method and be notified about the file's arrival with the AsyncReadComplete event.) This is indeed possible, but it's a bit involved.

We'll explain the process in detail so that you'll be able to apply the technique in more complicated situations. The server we are building in this section, however, is not what you call a "textbook" example. Many useful servers perform complicated calculations or access databases, format the results (for instance, in HTML format), and notify the clients asynchronously when the data is available.

Synchronous versus Asynchronous Processing

When an application makes a procedure call (which can be a function call, a sub-routine call, or a call to a method exposed by an object), it's blocked until the call returns. In other words, no matter how long the procedure takes to complete its task, the code can't proceed past the line that made the call; it just has to wait. This is how programming languages work. They execute one statement at a time, and you can safely assume that all previous statements have been executed. Consequently, the results of the previous lines are assumed to be known and available when a new line is executed.

> **NOTE** Parallel computers, which rely on a large number of processors working in parallel, follow a different programming paradigm that allows program lines to be executed out of order. But writing code for parallel computers is an entirely different story and the topic of another book.

The same is true when an application calls a method of an ActiveX component. While the method executes, the application has to wait. This type of processing is called *synchronous* because the two processes are synchronized. The advantage of synchronous processing is that the developer need not take any special action to synchronize the application with the server. If the method called must perform time-consuming math calculations, the application must wait. In some situations, however, the application doesn't require the results immediately. For example, in a printing operation the application has no reason to wait for the completed printout. The user should be able to initiate a printing operation and then move about his or her business. And from your experience with Windows, you know that printing doesn't freeze the application.

Under Windows, it is possible for a method to return control to the calling application immediately, without any results. In the mean time, the component continues its calculations and notifies the client application that the result is available. This type of processing is called *asynchronous*, because the two programs need not be synchronized. The client and server applications work independently of each other, and when the task is complete, the component notifies the client that the result is ready. It is possible to implement an asynchronous server, but to do so, we must solve two problems:

- How to return immediately from a method call and defer the execution of the code

- How to notify the client that the results are available when the calculations are complete

Asynchronous Methods and Properties

For the client application to continue operation, the CalculateLong method must return immediately. And for this to happen and yet carry out its calculations, the server must queue the request and process it in its own good time. We'll now revise the EXESRV1 class so that it queues requests instead of processing them immediately. When it's done with the calculations, it must trigger an event that will let the client know that the results are available (or that some action has taken place). The revised project is called EXESRV2.

> **NOTE**
>
> You'll find the EXESRV2 project in the Ch06\EXESRV2 folder on the CD that comes with this book. If you don't want to repeat all the instructions listed here, open the server project in one instance of Visual Basic, and open the test application (the client) in another instance of Visual Basic. Start the server, and then start the client.

To queue the calls to the methods, we need the services of a Timer control—some external event that will remind the server to poll the queue and process the next method. When clients make requests, the server queues them in a collection (it's the simplest structure for the purpose in terms of coding, but you can use an array if you prefer and if you don't mind writing the code to keep track of the array's size at any moment). Then, from within a Timer event, the server examines the queue. If there are queued calls to methods, it processes the oldest one and removes it from the queue. In the next Timer event, it repeats the same process, until all suspended calls have been removed from the queue.

The SERVER2 Project

This sounds simple in principle, but how do you add a Timer to a class module? We must add a Form to the project, place a Timer control on the Form, and reference it from within our code. The Form will never be displayed or receive any events, so it doesn't violate the requirement that EXE servers shouldn't have a visible user interface. Let's assume you have declared the *Tmr* object variable, which receives the Timer's Timer event. Let's also assume that you have declared a new collection, the Queue collection with the following statement:

```
Private Queue As New Collection
```

The client application will no longer call the CalculateLong method. Instead, it will call the StartCalculations method, which will queue the call:

```
Public Function StartCalculations(Iterations As Long) As Double
    Queue.Add Iterations
End Function
```

Since the CalculateLong method requires a single argument, we store it in the collection. Normally, you would create an object (or a custom data type) with all the arguments required by the method and append this object to the collection.

In the Tmr object's Timer event, we must call the CalculateLong function (which now is private to the class) and pass it the value of the argument stored in the Queue collection. At the same time, we must remove this value from the queue.

Code 6.12:   The Timer Event

```
Private Sub Tmr_Timer()
Dim results As Double
Dim CalcIterations As Long
    If Queue.Count = 0 Then
        Exit Sub
    End If
    CalcIterations = Queue.Item(Queue.Count)
    Queue.Remove Queue.Count
    results = CalculateLong(CalcIterations)
    RaiseEvent Done(results)
End Sub
```

If no requests are pending, the code exits. Or, it extracts the argument value stored in the Queue collection's current item, passes it to the CalculateLong() function, and then returns the result of the function through the Done event to the client application. The Done event is another member of the class. So far, our project is simple and does nothing out of the ordinary.

Incorporating the functionality of the Timer control, which resides on another Form, is a bit more complicated. Follow these steps:

1. Choose Project ➤ Add Form to add a Form to the project.

2. Now, place a Timer control on the Form, set its Enabled property to True, and set its Interval value to 1000 (1 second).

At this point, the IDE should look like the one shown in Figure 6.8.

FIGURE 6.8:

The EXESRVR2 project after the addition of a Form with a Timer control on it

Next, you must add the code to load the Form when the server is initialized and create an instance of the Timer control. You must create two object variables that represent the Form and the Timer objects.

3. Place the following lines in the class's declarations section:

```
Private Frm As Form
Private WithEvents Tmr As Timer
```

Notice the WithEvents keyword in the *Tmr* variable's declaration. Without it, your code would have access to the Timer control, but wouldn't be able to receive any events.

4. While editing the declarations, add the following event declaration:

```
Event Done(result As Double)
```

5. In the class's Initialize event, enter the following lines:

```
Private Sub Class_Initialize()
    Set Frm = New Form1
    Load Frm
    Set Tmr = Frm.Timer1
End Sub
```

The first two lines create an instance of the Form and load it (the Load method loads the Form into memory, but doesn't display it). Once the Form is loaded, you can create an object variable to access the Timer control on it. The Tmr object will receive the Timer event of the Timer control, and the Tmr_Timer event handler we discussed earlier will be activated every second.

You must also release any object variables when the server is terminated. When the last client application releases all references to the server's objects, the *Frm* and *Tmr* object variables will be released automatically.

NOTE   It's a good practice to release any unneeded resources to the system. Not all programs end in an orderly manner.

Code 6.13:   The Class's Terminate Event

```
Private Sub Class_Terminate()
    Set Tmr = Nothing
    Unload Frm
    Set Frm = Nothing
End Sub
```

The last step is to revise slightly the CalculateLong procedure. It is no longer a method of the server; it's a private function, whose declaration is as follows:

```
Public Function CalculateLong(Iterations As Long) As Double
Dim i As Long
Dim a As Double, b As Double
    Randomize (Time)
    For i = 1 To Iterations
        a = a + Cos(32.33)
        b = b + Sin(0.3233)
    Next
    CalculateLong = a + b
End Function
```

Switch to the client application to test the new server. Open the References dialog box before you run the application. You should see that the component SERVER1 has been replaced with the component SERVER2. If not, add a reference to the component SERVER2 manually. Change all instances of the class EXESRV1 to EXESRV2 in the client's code.

When VB Can't Find the Server Application

When you add a new component to the server project and then attempt to start the client application, you will see the message:

```
Connection to type library or object library to remote process has been lost. Press OK for dialog to remove reference.
```

Click the OK button to open the References dialog box, which lists the reference to the SRVREXE object as:

```
MISSING:SRVREXE
```

Clear the checkmark in this box to remove the reference from the list, and then locate the SRVREXE entry and select it. Your project is up-to-date. However, it is important to understand what happened.

The server is running in another instance of Visual Basic and is available only if this instance of Visual Basic is in run mode. Had you created an EXE file, the client application would start the server automatically, by simply requesting one of its objects.

To use the new server, we must further revise the client application. For one thing, it must call the StartCalculations method instead of the CalculateLong method, and we must provide a handler for the Done event. Change the declarations of the objects CObject1 and CObject2 to:

```
Private WithEvents CObject1 As EXESRV2
Private WithEvents CObject2 As EXESRV2
```

The new objects can raise events, and in order for the client application to receive these events, the variables must be recognized with the WithEvents keyword. You can't use the New keyword with the WithEvents keyword. The two object variables must be instantiated explicitly. Enter the following lines in the Form's Load event:

```
Private Sub Form_Load()
    Set CObject1 = New EXESRV2
    Set CObject2 = New EXESRV2
End Sub
```

You must also change the first button's code to call the StartCalculations method instead of the CalculateLong method:

```
Private Sub Command1_Click()
    CObject1.StartCalculations (300000)
End Sub
```

361

The test client application (EXETest) in the EXESRVR2 folder on the CD is identical to the test application of the EXESRVR1 project, except for a TextBox control, where you can specify how many times the CalculateLong() function will repeat the calculations. This will help you observe the behavior of the server application with asynchronous notifications, regardless of the speed of your CPU.

Asynchronous Notification

Finally, you must add the two event handlers for the Done events of the *CObject1* and *CObject2* variables. Because we declared these object variables with the WithEvents keyword, they appear in the Object drop-down list of the Code window. Select CObject1 in this list, and the editor creates the definition of the Done event and places the pointer in it. Enter the following lines:

```
Private Sub CObject1_Done(result As Double)
    MsgBox result
End Sub
```

The code for the CObject2_Done event is identical. Now run the application to see how the new server behaves. Press the Calculate Long button to start the calculations. If your computer is really fast, change the argument to the StartCalculations method. Be sure this method takes a while to complete.

While the calculations take place, the window isn't frozen. The time is updated every second, and you can click the PictureBox to draw another gradient.

> **NOTE**
>
> While the gradient is being drawn, the time isn't updated, but that's because the client's code is tight. It has nothing to do with the server.

If you click the Calculate Long button twice in succession, you will see the message box with the results twice, as soon as each deferred invocation of the method completes its execution. If you click the Calculate Long button and then click the Calculate Short button, you will see first the result of the lengthy method and then the result of the short method. That's expected; results arrive in the order in which they were queued by the server.

This leads to another question: What if we have 10 clients, each connecting to the server to request a different method? For example, suppose 9 clients need a quick result from the CalculateShort method, and the tenth client calls the CalculateLong method. Delaying the client that requested the services of the lengthy method for a second (perhaps less than that) wouldn't make any difference to the speed perceived by the users of the client application. They would have to wait for the lengthy calculations to complete anyway and only then see the results. It could, however, frustrate the users of the client applications that call the CalculateShort method because they (usually) know whether they've requested a lengthy or a trivial calculation.

One approach to this problem is to prioritize the queued requests: Examine the contents of the queue and execute the ones that take the least time. But in a more practical situation, you aren't going to have methods that take either a fraction of a second or several seconds. Prioritizing the events is rather inflexible, because once a method starts its execution, it must complete it before another one can start.

Let's do another experiment. Stop the test application, and then stop the EXE server application. If you stop them in reverse order, the server instance issues a warning to the effect that another application is accessing the server. Even if the code in the server's method isn't executing, the object variables *CObject1* and *CObject2* in the test application are still alive. Had you set it to Nothing, you would be able to stop the server before the application.

Switch to the server application, and insert a call to the DoEvents statement, right in the loop that performs the calculations.

Code 6.14:   The Revised CalculateLong Function

```
Public Function CalculateLong(Iterations As Long) As Double
Dim i As Long
Dim a As Double, b As Double
    Randomize (Time)
    For i = 1 To Iterations
        a = a + Cos(32.33)   ' rnd()
        b = b + Sin(0.3233)  ' rnd()
' Remove this line and requests will be serialized
        If (i Mod 100) = 0 Then DoEvents
    Next
    CalculateLong = a + b
End Function
```

The If line is actually commented out in the EXESRV2 application on the CD. We don't want to call the DoEvents statement frequently, because it can really slow the process. Depending on the nature of the calculations, you can call it more or less frequently. Run the server, switch to the client application, and test it again. Click the Calculate Long button, and then click the Calculate Short button. The client application will first receive the results from the CalculateShort method and then receive the results from the CalculateLong calculations.

You now have a server application that works nicely and balances short and lengthy methods. Why didn't we implement a method like StartCalculations that would queue calls to the CalculateShort method? Queuing a method that takes less than a second to complete actually makes it slower (the Timer event itself, which would trigger the execution of the function that implements the method, is triggered every second). A method such as CalculateShort takes so little time that we can let it interrupt the CalculateLong function, but not the other way around.

Testing the Executables

Now, stop both projects, and save the components of the EXE Server application. Choose File ➤ Make SRVREXE2.EXE to build an executable file, which any client application can then use. This action generates the EXE file that implements the server and registers it on the system. You can start the RegEdit application to see the ClassID of the newly created server. Close the VB instance with the server application, as we no longer need it.

Switch to the instance of VB with the client application. We are going to make an executable file and test it outside Visual Basic's environment. You will not only test the application in "real conditions," you will also be able to run multiple instances of the client and see how they are serviced by a single server.

Start by removing the reference SRVREXE from the project, and then add the reference SERVER2 by checking it in the References dialog box. This is the reference that has become a permanent part of the system. The SRVREXE component won't be there the next time you run the client application. Thus far, it was maintained by Visual Basic itself, but this instance of Visual Basic doesn't exist anymore.

Run the project one last time in Visual Basic's environment to make sure it works (if it doesn't, be sure you have added a reference to the newly created EXE server and not to an old instance of it). Now, follow these steps:

1. Choose File ➤ Make EXETest.exe to create an executable file.

2. Save the executable file in the same folder as the EXESRV2 project.

3. Close the Visual Basic window, and run the EXETest program by double-clicking its icon.

4. Start two or more instances of the client application, and monitor the behavior of the client application under all conditions.

You can start as many instances of the client application as you wish, but one copy of the server is running. To verify this, press Ctrl+Alt+Enter to open the Close Program dialog box, shown in Figure 6.9. Notice the three instances of the EXETest application and the single instance of the EXESrv2 server.

To simplify the testing of the executables, we added a TextBox control on the test Form, in which you can enter the argument of the method StartCalculations (the number of iterations for the lengthy calculations). Enter the number of desired iterations, and then click the Calculate Long button, as shown in Figure 6.10. You can also click this button several times, using different arguments, before the first result becomes available.

FIGURE 6.10:

The EXETest application lets you specify how many times the calculations will be repeated.

Building ActiveX Controls

- Understanding the types of ActiveX controls

- Exploring the UserControl object

- Using the ActiveX Control Interface Wizard

- Designing and using Property Pages

- Developing the LensEffect control

- Working with Internet-enabled controls

- Incorporating interconnected controls in your projects

The single most important feature introduced with Visual Basic 5 is the ability to author ActiveX (formerly OLE) controls. Until now, developing custom ActiveX controls was a task for seasoned C++ programmers. Not only did you have to use a difficult language, but the process was complicated. The latest version of Visual Basic has simplified one of the most difficult programming tasks.

Developing an ActiveX control with Visual Basic is strikingly similar to developing any application, and Microsoft has done a marvelous job of hiding much of the complexity of ActiveX development. The ActiveX Control Interface Wizard takes care of the trivial parts of the code and generates a working skeleton, to which you can add the code that implements the unique functions.

Developing ActiveX controls is also similar to developing classes. ActiveX controls are basically classes that have a visible user interface. Implementing the interface of the control (its properties, methods, and events) is similar to writing code for a class. The design of the visible interface is similar to the design of the interface of a standard VB application.

> **NOTE**
>
> As you will see, you will need to master a few basic concepts that are unique to ActiveX controls, but the process of developing ActiveX controls is similar to developing VB applications. Many of the steps unique in developing ActiveX controls are taken care of by the ActiveX Control Interface Wizard.

We'll start this chapter with a general discussion about the process of developing ActiveX controls, and we'll explain how it differs from developing standard applications. Then, we'll go through the steps of developing an ActiveX control with the ActiveX Control Interface Wizard, and we'll examine the code that the Wizard generates, which is the foundation of any ActiveX control. We'll highlight the shortcomings of this Wizard-created control and see how they can be overcome. By then, you will be able to use the Wizard as your starting point and then adjust the code manually to get the functionality you want from the control. Finally, we'll present in detail a few practical ActiveX controls that you can use as they are in your projects.

The Types of ActiveX Controls

You can design three types of ActiveX controls:

- User-drawn controls
- Enhancements to existing Visual Basic controls
- New controls built with constituent controls

The techniques for authoring all ActiveX controls are the same. Which type you build, however, depends on what you want to do and how much of the functionality that you want to include in your control already exists. So, before you start designing, you need to consider which type suits your needs.

User-Drawn Controls

These are the controls you author from scratch. You are responsible for designing the control's interface, and you are in control of its appearance and interface. You place the code for drawing the control's interface in the Paint event, which is invoked every time the control must be redrawn. You can also call the Paint event handler from within your code to redraw the control in reaction to certain user actions or property changes.

User-drawn controls are the most difficult to implement because you have to code every bit of functionality you need—from the control's interface to its appearance. They are also the most flexible though, because you don't have to put up with the limitations of other controls.

Existing Visual Basic Controls

The simplest type of custom ActiveX control you can develop is one that's based on an existing control and enhances its operation. You can keep most or all of the original control's functionality and then add custom members.

One built-in control that programmers frequently enhance from within their code is the ComboBox control. When the Style property of the ComboBox is set to 0 (DropDown Combo) or 1 (Simple Combo), the user can enter a new field value in the edit box of the control, but the new entry isn't appended to the list of available choices. To allow users to add new items to the ComboBox, all you have to do is capture the Enter key and, when the user presses Enter, add the entry in the Edit box to the list of options. Actually, you need some more code, as some users may use the Enter key to make a selection, in which case you must avoid adding multiple instances of the same option.

Programmers have been adding code to enhance the operation of the ComboBox control on their Forms with previous versions of Visual Basic. Now, you can implement a new control that enhances the ComboBox control, call it SuperCombo or something else, and use this one in your projects instead of the standard ComboBox control.

Constituent Controls

If most of the functionality you want to include in your custom control exists already, you can design a new control that includes other controls. The controls that are part of your custom control are called *constituent* controls. Although you can't alter the appearance of a constituent control, you can choose which of its members to expose. Most of the custom controls you will be authoring will make use of some constituent controls, because much of the functionality required by a typical control is already available in the form of existing controls.

Most controls are user-drawn and use constituent controls as well. In this chapter, you will see examples of this mixed approach, as well as controls based on constituent controls.

WARNING When designing custom controls with constituent controls, you must be sure you have the appropriate license to distribute these controls. You can freely distribute the controls that come with Visual Basic, but you should mention in the About box the original control on which they are based. Most third-party controls are also royalty free, but before you decide to distribute a control, read the product's documentation or contact the control's manufacturer.

The UserControl Object

An ActiveX control is similar to a class, in the sense that it provides properties and methods and triggers events, through which developers can program your control. If you can add properties and methods to a class, you can add these members to a custom ActiveX control. Methods are nothing more than public procedures (subroutines or functions); you add properties with the public Property Let and Get procedures, and events are triggered with the RaiseEvent statement.

NOTE   If you've read the previous chapter, you are ready to build your first custom control. Most of the information in Chapter 6 also applies to ActiveX controls.

Unlike classes, controls have a visible interface. An ActiveX control isn't accessed through an object variable, but is placed on a Form and can be edited through the Properties window. The visible interface of an ActiveX control is drawn on an object called *UserControl*, which is similar to the Form object. As you will see, the UserControl object supports nearly all the properties and methods of the Form object. If you are designing a user-drawn control, all the drawing must take place on the UserControl object. If you are designing a custom control based on constituent controls, they must all be placed on the UserControl object as well. So, designing the visible interface of a custom control is a lot like designing a new Form.

As you can guess, there are some fundamental differences between UserControl and Form objects. A UserControl object can only exist when placed on a Form. You can't display an ActiveX control in its own window, and you can't run an ActiveX control. You must place it on a Form and then run the project to which the Form belongs.

Actually, ActiveX controls must be placed on containers, which are not necessarily Forms. ActiveX controls can be placed on an HTML layout, which in turn is placed on a Web page and displayed by Internet Explorer. They can also be placed directly on Web pages. In this chapter, we are going to limit our discussion to using ActiveX controls with Visual Basic applications, and we'll focus on Forms as containers.

Design-Time and Run-Time Behavior

You design Forms in the Visual Basic IDE, and then you test them by running a test application right in the IDE, similar to developing and testing standard VB applications. The process of designing a Form is:

You repeat these steps as many time as required to get your application working. In the process, you can add new ActiveX controls on your Form and incorporate them in your design. When you add ActiveX controls to a Form, they have two distinct modes of operation:

- Design-time behavior
- Run-time behavior

A Timer control won't issue any Timer events in design mode, even if it's enabled and its Interval property has been set. It will start triggering Timer events as soon as it's placed in run mode.

Another example is the Scrollbar control. In design mode, you can't move its button to adjust the control's value. To change the position of the Scrollbar control, you must set the Value property accordingly. If you attempt to move the bar's button with the mouse, you'll end up moving the entire control on the Form. At run time, you can change the Scrollbar's value with the mouse.

Your custom ActiveX controls must support both operational modes. In addition to these two modes, ActiveX controls have their own design mode. When you design an ActiveX control, you can't test it by pressing F5. To test an ActiveX control, you must follow these steps:

1. Create a new project.

2. Add the ActiveX control on a Form.

3. Test the control's behavior both at design time and at run time.

As you will see, testing your custom control at design time is an important part of the process. Even when the test project is in design mode, the control's code is running. That's why you can change the control's properties while you're designing the Form. For example, as you change the BackColor property, the actual background color of the control changes in response to the property change in the Properties window. This means that the control's code is in run mode, even though the test project is in design mode.

To change the control's code, you must stop the test application and switch back to the ActiveX control project. Visual Basic simplifies the design of ActiveX controls by allowing you to add a test project to the ActiveX control project and switch between the two. You open the ActiveX control to change the code, close this project, and switch to the test project. Because the two projects live together in the IDE, switching between designing and testing the control doesn't require that you close a project to open another one.

We will explain th[...] ActiveX control as we build the sample projects later [...]ique characteristic of ActiveX controls, and you must k[...]sign and test an ActiveX control. The control's design mode is [...]nguish. While you work with the UserControl object, the control is in design mode. When testing it, the control is running. In your code, you may have to distinguish between the design-time and run-time modes of the project the control belongs to and react differently. For example, there are design-time and run-time–only properties, and your code must know at any time which can be set and which can't.

Designing a Simple Control

To create a custom ActiveX control, you draw its user interface by placing as many constituent controls as you need on the UserControl object. You then implement properties with the Property Let and Property Get procedures, you implement methods as public procedures (functions and subroutines), and you raise events with the RaiseEvent method. As with classes, you store properties in local variables, and you declare events at the beginning of the code.

If the custom control contains constituent controls, you can expose many of their properties by mapping them to the properties of the constituent controls or to the equivalent property of the UserControl. This is best done with the ActiveX Control Interface Wizard, which we'll discuss briefly in the next section. For example, if your custom control provides a text property and you provide a TextBox constituent control where users can enter the text, you can map the custom control's Text property (or the SecretText or whatever you want to call this property) to the Text property of the TextBox control.

To start the design of an ActiveX control, you create a new ActiveX control project. A new ActiveX control project has a folder named UserControls, which contains a UserControl object. Contrast this with a new Standard EXE project, which has a folder named Forms and a Form object in it.

Your first step is to add a new project, which is the test project we discussed earlier, and create a project group. The reason for doing so is to simplify the testing of the control. Without the test project, you'd have to close the ActiveX control project, open a test project, and then switch back to the control project to make changes and then repeat the process all over. To simplify the process of developing custom components, Visual Basic 5 allows you to create project groups and switch from one project to the other with a mouse click.

To add the te[...]

1. Choose File [...] Standard Exe as the project type. A new
   folder is added [...] ow, which contains an empty Form.

2. Rename the components of the project.

TIP

Do step 2 early in the process to avoid scattering custom controls with
names such as Project1 all over your hard disk.

In this book, we will use a separate folder for each project and name the test project of each control TestProject. The CD production process requires that file names
follow the 8.3 scheme, so we are using the name TestPrj for the test project.

Control and Project Names

The name of a custom ActiveX control is important because this is what developers will see in the Components dialog box when they open it to add your control
to their projects. You should change the default names before you start coding.

WARNING

If you don't rename controls, you risk creating (and registering) controls
with totally meaningless names such as Project1. Even worse, you may
end up with many Project1 controls on your computer. It's possible to
have multiple controls with the same name, as long as they are implemented by different OCX files, but this is a very bad practice.

To rename the components of a project, follow these steps:

1. In the new ActiveX control project, change the name of the UserControl
   object to MyControl, and change the project's name to DemoControl.

2. Now, change the name of the test project to TestProject, and the name of its
   Form to TestForm. Save all the components of the project to a new folder.

3. Select the DemoControl project in the Projects window, and then open the
   File menu to see the command:

   ```
   Make DemoControl.ocx
   ```

TIP

TIP   By default, the name of the OCX file in which the control's code is stored is named after the project. Instead of changing the name of the OCX file, we suggest that you change the name of the project.

4. Select the Make DemoControl.ocx command, and in the Save As dialog box, select a folder in which to store the OCX file (create the folder where the project will be stored and store the OCX file there). The DemoControl.ocx file will be created and registered automatically.

5. Close the control's designer window, and open the test project.

In the Toolbox, you will see the generic icon of a custom control. This is your new ActiveX control. If you move the pointer over the icon, its name will appear in a ToolTip box. The new control isn't named after the OCX file, but after the UserControl object, MyControl.

You have actually designed your first ActiveX control by doing nothing! The control doesn't do anything on the Form, but it's been integrated into the environment of Visual Basic, and you can add it to any project through the Components dialog box. You can actually open the Components dialog box at this point and see the entry that corresponds to your new ActiveX control.

As you can see in Figure 7.1, the name of the control is DemoControl. Now, you may find this confusing. If you do, name the OCX file after the UserControl object when you create it so that the control has the same name in the Toolbox and the Components dialog box. It is also common to prefix the name of the control, as it appears in the Components dialog box, with a company name.

How does the system know about your custom control? As with ActiveX components, every time you create a new component by choosing File ≻ Make, the component is automatically registered in the system and is assigned a ClassID. You can find out the control's ClassID by searching the Registry (run the program RegEdit from the Start menu) for the entry DemoControl. The question now is, How will the control be registered to another system so that it can be used by developers? The answer is with the help of a proper setup program. To create a setup program for your custom control, run the Application Setup Wizard (it comes with VB5) to create an installation and setup program that will install and register the control on the target computer. If the ActiveX control is part of an application, the application's setup program will also install the control along with the application.

FIGURE 7.1:

Once a custom
ActiveX control has
been registered, its
name will appear
automatically in
the Components
dialog box.

NOTE   We don't discuss the Application Setup Wizard in this chapter, but it's a
straightforward application. It locates all the components of the application
for which you want to prepare an installation program and dumps
them into one or more CAB files, which can then be distributed. In the
case of ActiveX controls, it also includes the necessary code for any constituent controls.

The Extender and Ambient Objects

So far, we haven't added any members to the MyControl custom control. Yet, if
you place the control on a Form and select it, you will see a number of properties
in the Properties window (see Figure 7.2). Where did they come from? If you
examine these properties carefully, you will realize that they are not determined
by the control itself. The developer determines the Width and Height properties,
as well as the Top and Left properties, when placing the control on a Form. Your
control can't decide about its location on the Form.

Each custom control displays a number of properties, which you don't have to code. The Extender object provides these properties.

Likewise, the control can't set its own Index property. If the developer decides to build an array of controls, he or she will determine the Index property. The same is true for the TabIndex property. Your control doesn't know how many controls exist on the Form and can't set its own TabIndex property. Visual Basic automatically assigns this property a value when the control is placed on the Form, and the developer can change it manually.

The properties you see in the Properties window of a minimal control like the one we just designed are provided by the *container*. The container is the Form on which the control is placed. In Visual Basic or Visual C++, the container of the control is a Form. If you are going to use this control on a Web page, the container is Internet Explorer or whatever browser is used to view the page.

You can access the container object's properties from within the control's code through the Extender object, which represents the container. However, because not all containers are identical and you can't be sure that every container supports the same properties, you must always use error-trapping code when accessing the Extender object.

When you develop the control's code, you don't know the control's Name property. Even though its default name will be something like MyControl1, MyControl2, and so on, the developer can name the control anything he or she pleases. To find out the Name of your control at run time from within your code, use the expression Extender.Name. Likewise, you can find out the location of your control on the Form with the properties Extender.Top and Extender.Left.

The DragMode property is also an Extender object property. You don't have to provide any code to your control for dragging it around. Visual Basic provides this functionality, as long as the developer has set the DragMode property to Automatic (1). You can't prohibit the dragging of your control from within its code either. But if you want to take some special action for controls that can be dragged, you can check the value of the Extender.DragMode property to find out whether the control can be dragged.

The Extender object lets you access the properties of your control that are provided by the container, and you can only read the settings of these properties. You can access another group of properties from within your code—the properties of the container on which the control is sited. For example, we always try to make the default font of a control the same as the font of the Container control. The properties of the container are accessed through an object property named Ambient. To find out the Font and BackColor properties of the container, use the expressions Ambient.Font and Ambient.BackColor. Figure 7.3 shows how this works.

FIGURE 7.3:

The Ambient and Extender objects give you access to the properties of the container and the custom control's properties that are maintained by the container.

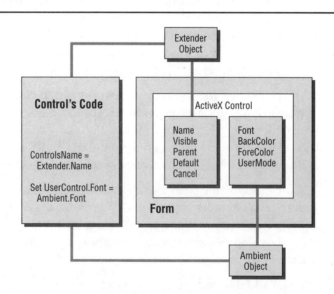

If your control manipulates color palettes, you may want to find out the container's palette. To do so, use the Ambient.Palette property. The developer sets this property for the Form at design time, and it applies to all controls on the Form (which means that you can't use a different palette for your custom control).

The most important property of the Ambient object is the UserMode property, which returns True if the project that contains the control is in run mode. Once placed on a container, your custom control is always in run mode. However, we frequently want to distinguish between the project's design mode and run mode, and the UserMode property of the Ambient control lets you find out the project's status. We use this property to distinguish between run-time and design-time properties or assign a different appearance to the control at design and run time.

As you will see in the examples that follow, when we want to make a property settable at design time only, we use an If statement such as the following:

```
If Ambient.UserMode = False Then Err.Raise 382
```

This statement raises the trappable error 382 if the developer attempts to set the property at run time. Likewise, to make a property settable at run time only, we use the following statement:

```
If Ambient.UserMode Then Err.Raise 393
```

You will see how the ActiveX Control Interface Wizard manipulates run-time and design-time properties in the first example in this chapter.

With the basics of ActiveX control design out of the way, we can now look at a few actual, working ActiveX controls. We'll start our discussion with the ActiveX Control Interface Wizard, which automates the process of ActiveX control design.

Opening This Chapter's Sample Apps

When you open the sample applications in this chapter, you'll get a warning to the effect that Visual Basic can't locate a compatible component. This simply means that the ActiveX control used in the project isn't registered on your computer. Here's what to do:

1. Continue loading the project, and then open it.

2. Delete the PictureBox control. (When Visual Basic can't find the OCX file of a control on a Form, it replaces the instance of this control with a PictureBox control.)

3. Select the Custom control on the Toolbox, and draw an instance of this control on the test Form.

Opening This Chapter's Sample Apps (continued)

Let's say you open the DemoControl project. On the test Form, you will see a PictureBox control named DemoControl1 instead of the DemoControl ActiveX control. Delete the PictureBox control, select the custom ActiveX control on the Toolbox (it's the new icon of a grid with a pen), and then draw an instance of the custom ActiveX control in place of the PictureBox control. Now you're ready to test the DemoControl project.

The ActiveX Control Interface Wizard

The ActiveX Control Interface Wizard takes you through the steps of setting up a custom control's interface. Using the Wizard, you can specify the control's properties, methods, and events, and the Wizard generates the skeleton of the control's code. Of course, the Wizard can only generate the trivial code; the actual code that makes the control do something special is your responsibility. Even so, the Wizard generates a lot of code and frees you from trivial tasks, such as mapping properties of the control to properties of the UserControl object or to properties of the constituent controls.

For example, if your control has a Font property that you want to map to a Label control on the custom control or to the Font property of the UserControl object itself, you can count on the Wizard to produce all the required code. It will also generate the necessary code for design-time and run-time–only properties or for read-only and write-only properties. Trivial, error-prone tasks are best left to the Wizard. However, if you want to implement a custom property that requires special code, provide the code yourself. The Wizard will generate the necessary declarations, but you must insert some real code in the Property Let and Property Get procedures.

Let's start by implementing a simple control. Follow these steps:

1. Place two Label controls and a TextBox control on the UserControl object of the DemoControl project.

2. Assign the strings TransparentLabel and OpaqueLabel to the two labels, and set them to a large, bold font (we used 28 point, Comic Sans MS). The TextBox control's name is Text1, and the names of the two Label controls are lblOpaque and lblTransparent.

3. Make the UserControl object large enough to contain its constituent controls, as shown in Figure 7.4.

FIGURE 7.4:

Designing the DemoControl project

4. Choose Add-Ins ➣ ActiveX Control Interface Wizard to generate the control's code.

TIP

If this Wizard doesn't appear in your Add-Ins menu, select Add-In Manager to install the ActiveX Control Interface Wizard. When you run the Wizard for the first time, you will see a welcome screen, which you can disable for the future by checking the checkbox at the bottom of the window.

5. Click Next to see the first window of the Wizard, which is the Select Interface Members window, shown in Figure 7.5. In this window, you can select the members of the UserControl object and the constituent controls that you want to become part of your control's user interface. The UserControl's background color will most likely become your control's BackColor property.

FIGURE 7.5:

The Select Interface
Members window
of the Wizard

The Available Names list contains the names of all members of the UserControl object itself and the constituent controls. It's likely that you will need many of these members, so the Wizard displays them all. It also suggests a few members in the Selected Names list. These are the common members of a typical ActiveX control, such as its background and foreground colors, the mouse and keyboard events, and so on. We are going to keep the suggested members and add one more property, the Picture property.

6. Select the Picture member in the Available Names list, and click the right-arrow button to add it to the Selected Names list.

7. Click Next to open the Create Custom Interface Members window, in which you can specify the custom members of the control:

8. To add a new member, click New to open the New Member dialog box. Here, you can enter the new member's name and its type: whether it's a property, an event, or a method. Methods are implemented either as public subroutines or as public functions (if they return a value), and you must check the appropriate Option button in the New Member dialog box.

9. Add the custom members shown in Table 7.1 to the DemoControl control (they are all properties).

TABLE 7.1: The DemoControl Control's Custom Members

Member	What It Is
TransparentCaption	The transparent Label's caption
OpaqueCaption	The opaque Label's caption
Text	The TextBox control's text
DesignTime	A string property available at design time only
DTimeReadOnly	A read-only string property available at design time only
RunTime	A string property available at run time only
RTReadOnly	A read-only string property available at run time only
RTWriteOnly	A write-only string property available at run time only

10. Click Next to open the Set Mapping window of the Wizard, shown in Figure 7.6.

FIGURE 7.6:

The Set Mapping window of the Wizard

In this window, you can map the control's properties to the equivalent properties of the UserControl object or to the properties of the constituent controls. Map properties such as BackColor, ForeColor, Font, and Picture, as well as the events, to the UserControl object. Map custom properties to the equivalent properties of the constituent controls. You will map the OpaqueCaption property to the Caption property of the lblOpaque control, you will map the TransparentCaption property to the Caption property of the lblTransparent control, and you will map the ControlText property to the Text property of the Text1 control (as shown in Figure 7.6).

11. Select all the members of the control in the Public Name list except for the custom members (use the Shift and/or Control key to select multiple items in the list with the mouse). With the members selected in the left list, expand the Control drop-down list in the section Maps To, and select UserControl. The selected members will be mapped to the members of the UserControl object with the same name.

You must manually map the remaining members to the appropriate members of the constituent controls.

12. Now select one member in the Public Name list at a time, and map it to a property of one of the constituent controls according to Table 7.2.

TABLE 7.2: The Constituent Controls of the DemoControl project

Property Name	Constituent Control	Property
ControlText	Text1	Text
OpaqueCaption	LblOpaque	Caption
TransparentCaption	LblTransparent	Caption

You can't map the remaining properties to any existing properties. The Wizard will generate the declaration of the properties, but will not add any lines of code in them.

13. Now click the Next button to open the Set Attributes window:

In this window, you can set the attributes of the properties, the arguments, the return types of methods (if they are implemented as functions), and the arguments of the event procedures.

You can't set the attributes of multiple properties here, so you must select the members one at a time in the Public Name list and set their attributes according to Table 7.3.

TABLE 7.3: The Attributes of the DemoControl Project's Properties

Property Name	Data Type	Default Value	Run Time	Design Time
DesignTime	String	"Design Time"	Not Available	Read/Write
DtimeReadOnly	String	"Design Time, Read Only"	Not Available	Read Only
RunTime	String	"Run Time"	Read/Write	Not Available
RTReadOnly	String	"Run Time, Read Only"	Read Only	Not Available
RTWriteOnly	String	"Run Time, Write Only"	Write Only	Not Available

NOTE   You can't have write-only properties at design time. It wouldn't make much sense to be able to set a property at run time, but not be able to read its value.

After setting the properties of the five variables shown in Table 7.3, click Next again to see the last window of the Wizard, which prompts you to click Finish to generate the code. Click Finish, and after the Wizard generates the control's code according to your prompts in the various windows we examined in this section, it will display a text window with simple instructions as to how to proceed. Close this window, and open the ActiveX designer's Code window.

The Wizard's Code

Let's examine the code generated by the Wizard. Your custom ActiveX controls, even if you develop them manually from scratch, will have the same structure. In examining the code generated by the Wizard, we will also discuss the structure of a typical ActiveX control. Code 7.1 shows the beginning of the code, which contains the necessary declarations.

Code 7.1: Declarations and Constants

```
'Default Property Values:
Const m_def_DesignTime = ""
Const m_def_DTReadOnly = ""
Const m_def_RunTime = ""
Const m_def_RTReadOnly = ""
'Property Variables:
Dim m_DesignTime As String
Dim m_DTReadOnly As String
Dim m_RunTime As String
Dim m_RTReadOnly As String
'Event Declarations:
Event Click() 'MappingInfo=UserControl,UserControl,-1,Click
Event DblClick() 'MappingInfo=UserControl,UserControl,-1,DblClick
Event KeyDown(KeyCode As Integer, Shift As Integer)_
     'MappingInfo=UserControl,UserControl,-1,KeyDown
Event KeyPress(KeyAscii As Integer) _
     'MappingInfo=UserControl,UserControl,-1,KeyPress
Event KeyUp(KeyCode As Integer, Shift As Integer)_
     'MappingInfo=UserControl,UserControl,-1,KeyUp
Event MouseDown(Button As Integer, Shift As Integer, X As Single,_
Y As Single) _
     'MappingInfo=UserControl,UserControl,-1,MouseDown
Event MouseMove(Button As Integer, Shift As Integer, X As Single,_
Y As Single) _
```

```
        'MappingInfo=UserControl,UserControl,-1,MouseMove
Event MouseUp(Button As Integer, Shift As Integer, X As Single,_
Y As Single)_
        'MappingInfo=UserControl,UserControl,-1,MouseUp
```

These declarations are outside any procedure so that all procedures can access them. The constants are the default values for the various custom properties, and the property variables are private variables that store the values of the custom properties.

NOTE   The naming scheme used by the Wizard makes the code really easy to read.

After the variable declarations come the event declarations. All the events raised by the control must be declared, even though they are mapped to the equivalent events of the UserControl object.

Then come the Property procedures for the various properties of the control. The BackColor property, for instance, is implemented with the procedures in Code 7.2.

Code 7.2:   **The BackColor Property**

```
Public Property Get BackStyle() As Integer
    BackStyle = UserControl.BackStyle
End Property

Public Property Let BackStyle(ByVal New_BackStyle As Integer)
    UserControl.BackStyle() = New_BackStyle
    PropertyChanged "BackStyle"
End Property
```

As you can see, mapping a property is simple. The new setting of the property is assigned to the equivalent property of the UserControl object, in the Property Let procedure. When the value of a mapped property is read, the Property Get procedure returns the value of the same UserControl property. As you can see, mapped properties are not stored in local variables. The name of a mapped property need not be the same as the name of the property to which it maps. The Property procedures for the OpaqueCaption property, which is mapped to the Caption property of the opaque Label control, are:

```
Public Property Get OpaqueCaption() As String
    OpaqueCaption = lblOpaque.Caption
End Property
```

```
Public Property Let OpaqueCaption(ByVal New_OpaqueCaption As String)
    lblOpaque.Caption() = New_OpaqueCaption
    PropertyChanged "OpaqueCaption"
End Property
```

Some properties, like the Font property, are set with the Property Set procedure. These properties are objects and can't be set with the assignment operator (see the discussion of the Set operator and the Font object in Chapter 5).

Code 7.3: The Font Property Procedures

```
Public Property Get Font() As Font
    Set Font = UserControl.Font
End Property

Public Property Set Font(ByVal New_Font As Font)
    Set UserControl.Font = New_Font
    PropertyChanged "Font"
End Property
```

Raising Events

The control's events are raised from within the equivalent events of the UserControl object. You can raise events from anywhere in the control's code—just call the RaiseEvent method. The Click and DblClick events of the custom control are raised from within the UserControl object's Click and DblClick events.

Code 7.4: The Click and DoubleClick Events of the UserControl Object

```
Private Sub UserControl_Click()
    RaiseEvent Click
End Sub

Private Sub UserControl_DblClick()
    RaiseEvent DblClick
End Sub
```

By default, the host application does not see the events of the UserControl object. You can insert your own code in these events and handle user actions from within the control's code. To pass these events to the host application, you call the RaiseEvent method, as shown in these examples. If the events pass arguments, you must pass them to the host application as well. MouseMove is an example of an event with an argument.

Code 7.5: **The Event Handler for the MouseMove Event of the UserControl Object**

```
Private Sub UserControl_MouseMove(Button As Integer, Shift As Integer,
X As Single, Y As Single)
    RaiseEvent MouseMove(Button, Shift, X, Y)
End Sub
```

In processing events from within your custom control, you have three options.

- Process them locally and never let the host application see them (simply don't call the RaiseEvent method).

- Process them locally, and then pass them to the host application with the RaiseEvent method. In this case, any local processing must take place before passing the event to the host application

- Ignore an event altogether, as you do with most events in programming VB applications anyway.

The Custom Properties

Now we can look at the Property procedures for the custom properties, which are available at design time or run time only and are read-only or write-only.

Code 7.6: **The DesignTime Only Property**

```
Public Property Get DesignTime() As Variant
    If Ambient.UserMode Then Err.Raise 393
    DesignTime = m_DesignTime
End Property

Public Property Let DesignTime(ByVal New_DesignTime As Variant)
    If Ambient.UserMode Then Err.Raise 393
    m_DesignTime = New_DesignTime
    PropertyChanged "DesignTime"
End Property
```

The procedures of properties that are available at design time only examine the value of the Ambient.UserMode property to determine whether the control is in run mode. If so, they raise error 393:

```
Get not supported at run time.
```

If the property is available at run time only, the corresponding Property procedures raise the error 382 if the developer attempts to set these properties at design time.

Code 7.7:   The RunTime Property

```
Public Property Let RunTime(ByVal New_RunTime As String)
    If Ambient.UserMode = False Then Err.Raise 382
    m_RunTime = New_RunTime
    PropertyChanged "RunTime"
End Property

Public Property Get RTReadOnly() As String
    RTReadOnly = m_RTReadOnly
End Property
```

As you will see, run-time properties don't even appear in the Properties window and therefore can't be set at design time. To exclude a property from the Properties window, you must change its attributes, as explained in the section "Displaying Properties in the Properties Window," later in this chapter.

Key Events in the Control's Life Cycle

Before we examine the behavior of the minimal control that the Wizard generated, we must discuss the key events in the life cycle of the control. This is another important aspect of the custom-control authoring process, and you must be aware of these events while developing custom controls. If you want to experiment with the order of these events, start a new ActiveX control object, add a test project, and then follow these steps:

1. Set the control's BackColor property to red so that you can distinguish it from the Form when you place it there. The control doesn't contain any constituent controls, although you can add some.

2. Locate the following events, and place Print statements as shown here:

    ```
    Private Sub UserControl_Initialize()
        Debug.Print "INITIALIZE"
    End Sub

    Private Sub UserControl_InitProperties()
        Debug.Print "INITPROPERTIES"
    End Sub
    ```

```
Private Sub UserControl_ReadProperties(PropBag As PropertyBag)
    Debug.Print "READPROPERTIES"
End Sub

Private Sub UserControl_Terminate()
    Debug.Print "TERMINATE"
End Sub

Private Sub UserControl_WriteProperties(PropBag As PropertyBag)
    Debug.Print "WRITEPROPERTIES"
End Sub
```

3. Now switch to the test project, and add an instance of the new control on the test Form. Read the messages printed in the Immediate window.

4. Run the application by pressing F5, and read the messages displayed in the Immediate window

5. Stop the application, and see which messages are now printed in the Immediate window.

Let's see when the various events are triggered and how they are used.

When the Control Is Sited on a Form

When you site an instance of an ActiveX control on a Form, the following events are triggered, in the order in which they are listed:

Initialize: A new instance of the control is created and initialized. This event is the first one received by your control, and it is triggered every time the control is placed on the Form, as well as every time the project is placed in run mode. Place your control's initialization code here.

InitProperties: The InitProperties event follows the Initialize event when the control is placed on the Form. This event isn't triggered when the project starts running. In this event, we place the code for initializing the control's private variables.

When the Project Switches to Run Mode

When the test project switches from design mode to run time mode (that is, when you press the F5 key), the following events are triggered, in the order in which they are listed:

WriteProperties: The control triggers this event to give you a chance to save the values of its properties. As you will see, the design instance of the control will be terminated before a new, run-time instance is created. In between, the values of the properties must be stored somewhere so that the run-time instance of the control can read them. The property values are stored in an object called PropertyBag (we'll discuss it shortly). The property values are stored for another good reason. During the execution of the application, properties can change value, usually through code or user actions. When the project returns to design mode, these values are discarded, and the control's properties take on the values they had before the application was switched to run mode.

Terminate: The current (design time) instance of the control is terminated.

ReadProperties: This event tells your code that it's time to read the values of its properties from the PropertyBag object, where they were stored from within the WriteProperties event. You'll see shortly how the property values are read from the PropertyBag object.

When the Project Switches Back to Design Mode

When the test project switches from run-time mode to design-time mode (that is, when you choose Run ➤ End), the following events are triggered, in the order in which they are listed:

Initialize: When the project's execution is terminated, the run-time instance of the control is terminated too. A new design instance of the control is created, which is initialized again.

ReadProperties: This event tells your code that it must read the values of the properties from the PropertyBag object. These are the values stored before the previous design-time instance of the control was terminated. In effect, the design-time instance of the control must have the same property values as it did before it was placed in run time. Any changes made to the property values at run time are discarded.

The Wizard generated the listing in Code 7.8 and 7.9 for these key events. If you created the project to follow these events, now open the Demo project again.

- The Initialize event contains no code. Normally you use this event to initialize module-level variables and properties of the constituent controls. However, you should not access the Extender and Ambient objects from within this event because the control hasn't been sited on the Form yet. When the Initialize event is triggered, the control knows nothing about its environment.

- The InitProperties event initializes the private variables that hold the property values, which is done by assigning the constants declared at the beginning of the code to the private variables, also declared at the beginning of the code.

Code 7.8: **The InitProperties Event's Handler for the DemoControl**

```
Private Sub UserControl_InitProperties()
    Set Font = Ambient.Font
    m_DTReadOnly = m_def_DTReadOnly
    m_RunTime = m_def_RunTime
    m_RTReadOnly = m_def_RTReadOnly
    m_DesignTime = m_def_DesignTime
    m_DesignTime = m_def_DesignTime
    m_RTWriteOnly = m_def_RTWriteOnly
End Sub
```

- The Terminate event is also empty. If your control creates any object variables in the Initialize event, this is the place to release them and return the allocated resources to the system.

- The WriteProperties event handler stores the property values in the PropertyBag object. Every property, including the properties of the UserControl object and its constituent controls, must be written to the PropertyBag object.

- The ReadProperties event handler reads the property values from the PropertyBag object and assigns them to the corresponding properties.

The PropertyBag Object

PropertyBag is a complicated object that is used for storing all types of property values. Some properties are as simple as numbers, others are strings, and some can be objects (such as the Font property). Fortunately, all the complexity of the PropertyBag object is hidden from you. To access it, you need two methods:

- The WriteProperty method, to store a property value
- The ReadProperty method, to read a property value

The syntax of the WriteProperty method is:

```
UserControl.WriteProperty(PropertyName, Value[, DefaultValue])
```

The *PropertyName* argument is the name of the property you want to save, and *Value* is the property's value (usually the local variable that holds the property value). Although the last argument is optional, you should always supply a default value for every property you save to the PropertyBag object because properties with default values are not saved. This makes the PropertyBag object smaller and faster to access. If you don't supply a default value, Visual Basic will be wasting time saving default values that are (or should be) known to your program.

The syntax of the ReadProperty method is:

```
PropertyValue = UserControl.ReadProperty(PropertyName[, DefaultValue])
```

The *PropertyName* argument is the name of the property whose value you are reading, and *DefaultValue* is the value to be returned if no value has been stored in the PropertyBag object. If you specified a default value in the WriteProperty method, you must supply this default value to the ReadProperty method as well. If you do not, the method wouldn't know what value to return.

Now that we have looked at how property values are stored to and read from the PropertyBag object, we can look at the code generated by the Wizard for the WriteProperties and ReadProperties events.

Code 7.9:   **The WriteProperties and ReadProperties Events**

```
Private Sub UserControl_WriteProperties(PropBag As PropertyBag)
    Call PropBag.WriteProperty("BackColor", UserControl.BackColor,_
        &H8000000F)
    Call PropBag.WriteProperty("Font", Font, Ambient.Font)
    Call PropBag.WriteProperty("TransparentCaption", _
        lblTransparent.Caption, "TransparentLabel")
    Call PropBag.WriteProperty("OpaqueCaption", lblOpaque.Caption,_
        "OpaqueLabel")
    Call PropBag.WriteProperty("DTReadOnly", m_DTReadOnly, _
        m_def_DTReadOnly)
End Sub

Private Sub UserControl_ReadProperties(PropBag As PropertyBag)
    UserControl.BackColor = PropBag.ReadProperty("BackColor",
&H8000000F)
    Set Font = PropBag.ReadProperty("Font", Ambient.Font)
    lblTransparent.Caption = _
PropBag.ReadProperty("TransparentCaption",_
        "TransparentLabel")
    lblOpaque.Caption = PropBag.ReadProperty("OpaqueCaption", _
```

```
     "OpaqueLabel")
     m_DTReadOnly = PropBag.ReadProperty("DTReadOnly", m_def_DTReadOnly)
End Sub
```

We only show selected lines in the two subroutines. The actual code contains many more lines, which are quite similar to the ones shown here.

This is the code produced by the Wizard. Our control doesn't do much yet, because we have not added any code; it contains the code generated by the Wizard, which is too trivial for a meaningful operation. Now we can examine the behavior of the control from a developer's point of view. As you can see, the Wizard took care of many trivial details for you, and you can step in to add the actual code. A good segment of the code of an ActiveX control is similar to the code of a class. Unlike classes, however, ActiveX controls have a visible interface and behave differently at design time and run time. Once you understood the implications of these differences, you'll start building ActiveX controls with the same ease as you build VB applications.

NOTE As you may have noticed, all Property procedures call the PropertyChanged method, followed by the name of the property that changed value. The PropertyChanged method notifies Visual Basic that a property value has changed and that it must be saved. The same method is also used to update the setting of a property in the Properties window when another property is changed from within the control's code. You should always call the PropertyChanged method from within any Property Let or Property Set procedure.

Design-Time Behavior of the Demo Control

Once your custom control is placed on a Form, it's actually in run mode. The code you've entered is executed. When the BackColor property of the control is changed through the Properties window, the Property Let Background() procedure is actually called to change the control's background color. The test project, however, is still in design mode. This means that none of the run-time properties we added to the control will be available.

To test the code, you must take off your control author hat and put on your VB programmer hat. While testing the control, you have no access to the control's code, just like a developer using your control. To make any changes, you must switch back to the control project and assume your control author attributes again.

Displaying Properties in the Properties Window

Close all the windows of the ActiveX control project, switch to the test project, and place an instance of the DemoControl custom control on the test Form.

TIP   If the icon of the custom control isn't enabled on the Toolbox, you haven't closed all the windows of the ActiveX control project.

Select the DemoControl control on the Form, and look at the Properties window. Although the RunTime property has a Property Let procedure, it's not displayed in the Properties window. Actually, none of the run-time properties appear in the Properties window. Why is that? There's a place where you can specify whether a property appears in the Properties window. Follow these steps:

1. Switch back to the control project, open the Code window, and choose Tools ➢ Procedure Attributes.

2. In the Procedure Attributes dialog box, click the Advanced button, and you will see the full window, shown in Figure 7.7.

FIGURE 7.7:

In the Procedure Attributes dialog box, you specify a number of attributes for the control's custom properties.

3. Expand the Name drop-down list, and select the RunTime property.

In the Attributes section, the Don't Show in Property Browser option is checked (this option is cleared by default; it is checked in the Demo project). This is how you control which properties are not displayed in the Properties window. The

Hide This Member option has a similar effect. It prevents the property from show-ing up in the Properties window, but it also prevents the member from showing up in the control's type library. This feature allows you to implement "undocu-mented" features in your controls. The average developer will never know that a member exists, because it doesn't appear in the Object Browser. However, you can write applications that access this member through code.

The User Interface Default option lets you specify that the selected member is the default property of the control. If you make the OpaqueCaption property the default for the custom control, the developer can also access the property DemoControl1.OpaqueCaption as DemoControl.

Enumerated Properties

You may have noticed a small flaw in the (automated) design of the custom control. Properties with a small number of valid settings normally display a list with the pos-sible settings in the Properties window. This didn't happen with the BackStyle prop-erty. The BackStyle property is declared as Integer in the code, and you can enter any integer value in the BackStyle field of the Properties window. If you attempt to enter an invalid value, such as 9, the following message will appear:

```
Invalid property value
```

This message doesn't convey much information to the developer. You must declare a property such as BackStyle as an Enumerated type so that the developer won't be able to set it to an invalid value.

To do so, open the Demo control's Code window and enter the following lines in the declarations section:

```
Enum BackgroundStyles
    Transparent
    Opaque
End Enum
```

An Enumerated type maps strings to integers. The first string, Transparent, cor-responds to the value zero. The second string corresponds to the value 1, and so on. Now locate the property procedures of the BackStyle property, and change the type Integer to BackgroundStyles. The revised procedures are:

```
Public Property Get BackStyle() As BackgroundStyles
    BackStyle = UserControl.BackStyle
End Property
```

```
Public Property Let BackStyle(ByVal New_BackStyle As BackgroundStyles)
    UserControl.BackStyle() = New_BackStyle
    PropertyChanged "BackStyle"
End Property
```

If you switch back to the test Form, select the Demo control on the Form, and try to set its BackStyle property, you will see a drop-down list in its field in the Properties window. If you expand this field, you will see the values "0 - Transparent" and "1 - Opaque." Developers simply can't set them to an invalid value. Not only that, but if you enter the control's BackStyle property name in the editor's window, as soon as you type the equals sign, you will see the Auto List Members list with the valid settings of this property (provided that you have turned on the Auto List Members feature of the editor):

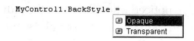

Enumerated properties display their members automatically in the Auto List Members list.

Transparency Issues

The lblOpaque constituent control is transparent, which means that the text is displayed on the UserControl object. Change the background color of the control to see how the two Label controls are displayed. You can't change the second Label's background color.

Now change the BackStyle property of the Demo control to zero (transparent). The top label's caption will be displayed directly on the Form. Constituent controls are made transparent with respect to the control to which they belong. To make them completely transparent, you must also set the UserControl object's BackStyle property to zero (transparent). Place a Picture on the test Form, and you will see the bitmap through the letters of the transparent Label's caption.

Caption and Text Properties

As you design Forms with the Demo control, you will notice another shortcoming: The text properties (ControlText, OpaqueCaption, and TransparentCaption) are not updated on the control as you enter their new values. With the built-in controls, the Text and Caption properties behave differently: The control is updated as you enter its new value in the corresponding field box in the Properties window.

To make a text property behave like the standard Text and Caption properties, you must assign the Caption Procedure ID (or Text Procedure ID) to the property. To do so, follow these steps:

1. In the Procedure Attributes dialog box, select the ControlText property in the Name drop-down list, and click the Advanced button:

2. In the Procedure ID list, select the entry Text.

    The control's ControlText property will be handled in a way similar to the Text property of the TextBox control. As the developer changes the setting of the property in the Properties list, the control is updated automatically.

3. Select the OpaqueCaption property, and set its Procedure ID to Caption. The OpaqueCaption property will behave like a Label's Caption property.

4. Return to the test Form, and experiment with the new attributes of the text and caption properties by changing their settings in the Properties window.

If you have more than one text or caption property on the control, you won't be able to assign the same Procedure ID to more than one of them. Each procedure ID can be assigned to a single property. If you assign the same Procedure ID to a second property, the first property's Procedure ID is reset to None.

The last drop-down list in the Procedure Attributes dialog box, the Property Category list, contains the various categories of properties, as displayed in the

Properties window when you select the Categorized tab. To specify the category to which a property belongs, follow these steps:

1. Select the property's name in the Name list.

2. Select the category in the Property Category list.

3. Finally, supply a short description for each member of the Demo control in this dialog box. The description will appear in the Properties window when the property is selected, as well as in the Object Browser.

The Run-Time Behavior of the Demo Control

Now, let's test the control in run time. Press F5 to start the test project, and you will see the window shown in Figure 7.8. The top label is transparent and lets the control's background show through. Since the control's background is also transparent, the Form on which the control is sited shows through. For Figure 7.8, we assigned an image to the Form's Picture property. If your control isn't transparent, set its BackStyle property to 1 (Transparent).

FIGURE 7.8:

The Transparent control lets the underlying image show through, even between the Label's characters.

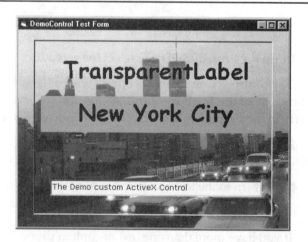

Raising Events from Constituent Controls

To test the Click event, enter the following code on the test Form (stop the application and double-click the Form to open its Code window):

```
Private Sub Form_Click()
    MsgBox "Form clicked"
End Sub
```

```
Private Sub MyControl1_Click()
    MsgBox "ActiveX Control clicked"
End Sub
```

These two messages let you know which object you clicked. When you click the Form, the "Form clicked" message is displayed, as you might expect. To see the "ActiveX Control clicked" message, though, you must click the UserControl's object, outside any of the constituent controls. The constituent controls receive the Click event, but they don't pass it to the control. To receive a Click event when the Label control is clicked, you must raise the Click event from within this control's Click event. Stop the project, switch to the Code window of the control project, and enter the following code in the lblOpaque and lblTransparent controls' Click events:

```
Private Sub lblOpaque_Click()
    RaiseEvent Click
End Sub
```

```
Private Sub lblTransparent_Click()
    RaiseEvent Click
End Sub
```

Now run the application again, and click the Form, the Demo control, and the constituent controls. The messages tell you which control was clicked.

NOTE   If you click the transparent label, but outside the text, you will receive a Click event from the Form. If you click the transparent label's text, you will receive the Click event from the Demo control. The TextBox constituent control doesn't raise the Click event.

Unique Properties of the UserControl Object

The UserControl object supports nearly all the properties of the Form object (after all, they have the same role in different environments), but you may have noticed a few new property names in the Properties window. The properties unique to the UserControl object are described next.

Alignable

When this property is set to True, Visual Basic automatically adds the Align property in the control's Properties window, which lets the user specify whether the control will be aligned along one of the edges of the Form on which the control is contained. If you need to know the alignment of the control on its Form, you can access the Align property of the Extender object.

ControlContainer

If this property is set to True, the developer can place other controls on top of your custom control. Custom controls that contain constituent controls aren't commonly used as containers, although it's possible. When a control acts as a container, any control drawn on top of it belongs to the control. In other words, you can't slide the controls with the mouse outside the container control's boundaries, and when you copy the container control, the contained controls are copied with it. This also means that when you delete the container control, all other controls sited on it are also deleted.

You can access the controls contained on your custom control from within its code with the ContainedControls collection. For example, you can align the contained controls automatically, or you can assign common attributes to them. Accessing the ContainedControl collection from within your code is a slow, late-bound process. The contained controls aren't known before run time, and accessing them requires substantial overhead, including serious error-trapping code.

DefaultCancel

When this property is set to True, Visual Basic automatically adds the Default and Cancel properties in the control's Properties window. These two properties are False by default, and the developer can set one of them to True to indicate that the control will function as the default (it will respond to the Enter key) or as the cancel control (it will respond to the Escape key). The Default and Cancel properties are provided by the Extender object, and you can access them as Extender.Default and Extender.Cancel.

EditAtDesignTime

Usually, you can edit controls through the Properties window at design time, and you can manipulate their properties through code at run time. You can edit some controls visually at design time. These controls assume a run-time behavior at design time, simplifying the task of editing the control's appearance. To make a control editable with visual tools at design time, set its EditAtDesignTime property to True. This adds the Edit command to the control's shortcut menu. When you select the Edit command, the control's interface behaves as it would at run time.

Let's say you have a control with a Scrollbar control on it. As you know by now, you can't move the Scollbar's button at design time. If you attempt to move the button with the mouse, you'll end up moving the entire control. You can only change the setting of the Scrollbar through the appropriate property in the Properties window.

If you use the Scrollbar control to adjust another attribute of the control, such as its color, "guessing" its value isn't the most convenient way to adjust the control's appearance. Figure 7.9 shows the ColorDesigner control, which lets the user specify a color by adjusting its red, green, and blue components. This control is similar to the Color common dialog box, but it can be placed directly on a Form, unlike the Color common dialog box, which is displayed in its own window. In addition, you can adjust the color with the mouse at design time, right on the Form to which it belongs. The ColorDesigner control also demonstrates how to extract the three color components of a given color.

NOTE You'll find the ColorDesigner project in the Ch07/C1Design folder on the CD that comes with this book.

FIGURE 7.9:

The Edit command of the ColorDesigner control's shortcut menu lets the developer adjust the color by sliding the scrollbars with the mouse at design time.

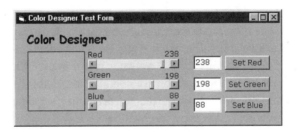

Open the project's test Form and adjust the control's color at design time by scrolling the three scrollbars. We won't present the control's code here; it's quite straightforward, except perhaps for the code that extracts the three basic color components from a long color value. If the variable *SelectedColor* holds a long value representing a color, the following lines extract the red, green, and blue color components:

```
m_RedComponent = SelectedColor And &HFF
m_GreenComponent = (SelectedColor / 256) And &HFF
m_BlueComponent = (SelectedColor / (256 ^ 2)) And &HFF
```

If you experiment with this application, you should notice the following. As you change the color on the control by sliding the scrollbars, the values of the properties RedComponent, GreenComponent, and BlueComponent in the Properties window change as well, to follow the values you specify visually.

EventsFrozen

This interesting event is available at run time only, and it lets your code know whether the Form is receiving events. At certain times, the Form can't receive events from the control. For example, if the Form displays a message box, it won't be able to receive any events. If your control must raise one or more events that can't be missed, it must first read the value of this property. If the EventsFrozen property is True, the event won't be processed; so you shouldn't raise it. Queue the event (store it in a private variable, or store multiple events in an array), and keep checking the EventsFrozen property periodically (possibly with the help of a Timer control). When the EventsFrozen property becomes False again, you can safely raise the queued events. This property is used in special cases, and typical ActiveX controls don't raise events that can be missed.

InvisibleAtRunTime

Some controls remain invisible at run time, but they can communicate with the application via their interface members. One example is the Timer control, which is always invisible, yet it triggers Timer events as specified by the Interval property. Another invisible control is one that provides methods for calculating math expressions. Such a control need not be visible at run time; as long as you can call its methods and properties to carry out the calculations, users need not see a control with which they can't interact.

Public

Something we haven't mentioned so far is that ActiveX controls can be private within executables or other ActiveX controls. To expose an ActiveX control for use by other applications, set its Public property to True (this is the default value). If you want to use a custom control in an application, yet not make it available to the users of your application as a component, set its Public property to False.

ToolboxBitmap

This bitmap appears in the Toolbox when the developer adds your custom control to an application. Assign a bitmap file (BMP) to this property with the icon of the control. The bitmap's dimensions must be 16×15 pixels. We designed a Toolbox icon (DBIcon.BMP) for the DBControl project, which we discuss later in this chapter.

> **NOTE**   You'll find the DBIcon.BMP file in the Chapter7/DBCtrls folder on the CD that comes with this book.

Designing and Using Property Pages

A control that has many properties usually has Property Pages in which users can visually manipulate the control at design time. Related properties are grouped as tabs on the same Property Page, and the user can change the settings on the Property Page and apply the new settings on the selected control(s) on the Form or cancel the editing operation. To display a Property Page, you usually select Properties from the control's shortcut menu. It is also possible to display an ellipsis (a button with three dots) next to a property's box in the Properties window, which invokes the Property Pages for the selected control(s).

To see the Property Pages in action, start a new project and place a FlexGrid, Chart, or ActiveMovie control on it. The Chart control's Property Pages have a total of eight tabs, with which you can set just about any of the Chart control's properties (its type, data, colors, axis, labels, and so on). Many of the properties that you can set through the Chart control's Property Pages don't even appear in the Properties window. Without the Property Pages, you'd need quite a lot of code to determine not only the appearance but the function of the control.

Figure 7.10 shows the Property Pages for the FlexGrid control. All the properties for setting the general appearance of the grid's cells are collected on the General tab. The other tabs contain related properties. As you change the control's settings, you can click the Apply button from time to time to see their effect on the FlexGrid control, which you can see behind the Property Pages in Figure 7.10.

FIGURE 7.10:

The Property Pages for the FlexGrid control contains five tabs with related properties.

The design of a Property Page is straightforward; there's even a Wizard for designing Property Pages. We'll design a Property Page with multiple tabs shortly, but first let's look at the process.

- A Property Page can contain one or more tabs. Each tab contains a group of related properties. When the user selects a new tab, the settings of the controls on the new tab must be set according to the current settings of the properties of the selected control.

- The user can change the selection on the Form while the Property Page is open. The SelectionChanged event reports this, and you must update the current tab's settings from within this event's code.

- The user can also click the Apply button to see the effects of the changes on the current tab. Your code doesn't have access to the Apply button. In other words, you can't insert your own code in the Apply button's Click event. Instead, you must insert the code for updating the selected control(s) on the Form from within the ApplyChanges event, which is triggered when the user clicks the Apply button.

The SelectedControls Collection

The selected controls on the Form are accessed by the collection SelectedControls. The number of selected controls is given by the property SelectedControls.Count, and each control in the collection can be accessed as SelectedControls(0), SelectedControls(1), and so on. To read the Caption property of the first selected control on the Form, use a statement such as the following:

```
CaptionText = SelectedControls(0).Caption
```

To set this property from within the code of a Property Page, use a statement such as the following:

```
SelectedControls(0).Caption = "I'm selected"
```

Because the user may have selected multiple instances of the control on the Form, use a loop such as the following:

```
For selControl = 0 To SelectedControls.Count
    SelectedControls(selControl).Caption = txtCaption.Text
Next
```

In this code, `txtCaption` is the name of the TextBox control on the Property Page where the user enters the new setting of the Caption property. If you want to manipulate multiple selections, you must also check all the selected controls, to find out whether they have a common property setting. If each has a different setting, you disable the control for changing this setting in the Property Page, or you display a string such as "multiple values." In general, it's not uncommon to act on the first selected control and ignore the remaining ones. Actually, this is what the Property Page Wizard does, which acts on the control SelectedControls(0) only.

Designing Property Pages

In this section, we are going to design a Property Page for the DemoControl. To get started, follow these steps:

1. Switch to the ActiveX control project.

2. Choose Project ➤ Add Property Page.

3. In the Add Property Page dialog box, select the VB Property Page Wizard icon.

Before we go through the windows of this Wizard, let's take a look at the Property Page we are about to design. Figure 7.11 shows the DesignTime tab of the DemoControl, and Figure 7.12 shows the Captions tab.

FIGURE 7.11:

The DesignTime tab of the DemoControl Property Page

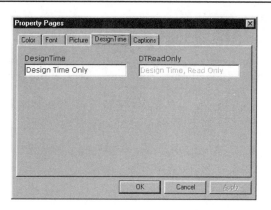

FIGURE 7.12:

The Captions tab of
the DemoControl
Property Page

The Property Page of this control contains three more tabs, which are standard tabs that you have seen many times:

- The Color tab lets you specify the control's background color.

- The Font tab lets you specify the control's Font.

- The Picture tab lets you specify the picture to be displayed on the UserControl object's background.

The Wizard automatically creates these tabs; you don't have to supply a single line of code.

When you add one or more Property Pages to an ActiveX control project, a new folder, the Property Pages folder, is added to the Project window. The Property Pages folder contains the custom tabs of the control's Property Pages.

The simplest way to design a Property Page is with the help of the Wizard. Follow these steps:

1. In the Add Property Page dialog box, select VB Property Page Wizard to open the Wizard's first window, a welcome page.

2. Click Next to open the Select the Property Pages window:

It initially contains the three standard tabs shown in Figure 7.13:

- StandardColor
- StandardFont
- StandardPicture

FIGURE 7.13:

The three standard tabs of a Property Pages

If the control contains a Color, a Font, or a Picture property, the corresponding standard tab is checked automatically. To omit this tab from your control's

Property Page, clear the checkbox in front of the corresponding entry. The last two tabs (DesignTime and Caption) will not appear on the dialog box initially. You must add them with the Add button. Click the Add Button to open the Property Page Name dialog box in which you can enter the name of the tab.

3.   Click the Next button to open the Add Properties window:

In this window, you can select a tab in the Available Property Pages section and add the properties that will appear on them. Add the properties shown in Table 7.4.

TABLE 7.4: The Properties for the Tabs of the DemoControl's Property Page

Tab	Property
StandardColor	BackColor, ForeColor
StandardFont	Font
StandardPicture	Picture
DesignTime	DTReadOnly, DesignTime
Captions	TransparentCaption, OpaqueCaption, ControlText

After you specify the properties and their tabs, click Next to open the last window of the Wizard. Click the Finish button to generate the Property Page and the corresponding code. The Wizard will produce some really primitive pages, which you must edit a little. Figure 7.14 shows the two custom tabs produced by the Wizard—after a little editing. As you can see, the tabs don't have the OK, Cancel, and Apply buttons that appear in the Property Page. Visual Basic itself manages these buttons.

FIGURE 7.14:

The two custom tabs of the DemoControl Property Page

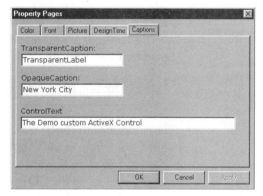

Let's examine the code that the Wizard produced for the DesignTime tab.

Code 7.10:   The DesignTime Tab

```
Private Sub txtDesignTime_Change()
    Changed = True
End Sub

Private Sub txtDTReadOnly_Change()
    Changed = True
End Sub

Private Sub PropertyPage_ApplyChanges()
    SelectedControls(0).DesignTime = txtDesignTime.Text
End Sub
```

```
Private Sub PropertyPage_SelectionChanged()
    txtDesignTime.Text = SelectedControls(0).DesignTime
    txtDTReadOnly.Text = SelectedControls(0).DTReadOnly
End Sub
```

The Change event of the two TextBox controls sets the Changed property, which is used to enable the Apply button in the Property Page. If no settings have changed, the Apply button is disabled. Clicking the Apply button triggers the ApplyChanges event, which sets the value of the DesignTime property on the selected control. Finally, when the user selects a new instance of the DemoControl on the Form, the SelectionChanged event is triggered. This event's handler reads the settings of the DesignTime and DTReadOnly properties on the selected control and updates the TextBox controls on the DesignTime tab.

NOTE
The TextBox for entering the value of the DTReadOnly property is locked so that the user can't edit its contents. The property is read-only, so it's displayed on the tab, but can't be changed. That's why the corresponding line is missing from the ApplyChanges event handler.

The Captions tab contains three TextBox controls, with which the user can change the settings of the ControlText, OpaqueCaption, and TransparentCaption properties. The code is quite similar, and we need not repeat it here. If you open the Demo project on the CD (in the Demo folder), you will see that the standard tabs don't appear in the Property Pages folder. Visual Basic maintains these tabs, and you cannot access their code. If you don't like their appearance, you can replace them with custom tabs, which you must design yourself.

Now that we've explored the techniques for building ActiveX controls and designing Property Pages, it's time to look at some examples that are more complicated and more practical. We'll start with a control that implements a lens-over-image effect. The LensEffect control can display any bitmap and magnify a small section of it, as if you were examining the image with a magnifying lens. You can move the lens around with the mouse, or you can program it to slide around.

The next example, OnLine, demonstrates how to download property values over the Internet and display them on a custom control. The OnLine control shows you how to use the UserControl object's methods and events for downloading data over the Internet asynchronously.

In the last section of this chapter, we'll build three interconnected controls that can perform quite complicated tasks with only a few lines of code. We will also present three ActiveX controls that implement the functionality of the DBClass classes (see Chapter 6), but they are far easier to use in an application.

The LensEffect Control

The LensEffect control is an example of the most common type of ActiveX control: a user-drawn control that uses constituent controls. The control we are going to build in this section implements a lens-over-image effect. The UserControl object accepts a bitmap, as shown in Figure 7.15. A small rectangular area of the image is enlarged. This is the area of the image under a magnifying lens. You can move the lens around with the mouse, or you can program it to slide around.

FIGURE 7.15:

The LensEffect control displaying an image and a magnifying glass over a small area of the bitmap

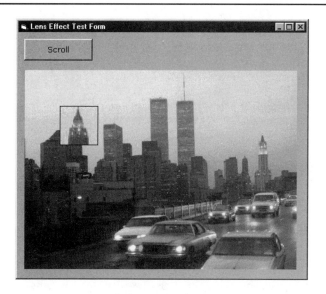

The implementation of the control is quite simple in principle: The rectangular lens is a borderless PictureBox control that displays a small area of the bitmap under it in magnification. The lens's dimensions are 64 × 64 pixels, and it displays an area of the bitmap with dimensions 16 × 16 pixels. This area of the bitmap is centered around the center of the lens. The magnification is performed by the PaintPicture method, which copies the 16 × 16 pixel bitmap to the PictureBox control that implements the lens.

> **NOTE**   You'll find the LensEffect project in the Ch07Lensfx folder on the CD that comes with this book.

The test Form of the project, shown in Figure 7.15, has a Command Button too, which starts sliding the lens around and bouncing on the edges of the control. If you click the Scroll button, its Caption becomes Pause , and you must click it again to stop the sliding of the lens. You can then slide the lens around with the mouse.

A More Realistic Lens Control

A more realistic lens control would implement a round lens and would magnify the underlying bitmap unevenly. The magnification at the center should be stronger, and the magnification around the lens's circumference would be smaller.

This operation, however, requires a lot of math and trigonometric operations, and the result would be a slow-moving lens. Our goal is to demonstrate how to build a control with constituent controls, and not to explain the math involved (and lose our readers in the process).

Those of you who are mathematically inclined and would enjoy experimenting with math and graphics can find a description of the transformations involved at:

www.neutralzone.org/home/faqsys/docs/lens.txt

The lens effect is implemented with a single line of code, which copies a rectangular area of the bitmap on the UserControl on to the PictureBox control that implements the lens:

```
Picture1.PaintPicture UserControl.Picture, 0, 0, _
Picture1.ScaleWidth, Picture1.ScaleHeight, _
m_LensX + Picture1.ScaleWidth / 4, m_LensY + Picture1.ScaleHeight / 4, _
Picture1.ScaleWidth / 2, Picture1.ScaleHeight / 2, &HCC0020
```

The variables *m_LensX* and *m_LensY* are the coordinates of the lens's upper-left corner. The coordinates of the upper-left corner of the rectangular area of the bitmap to be copied are:

```
(m_LensX + Picture1.ScaleWidth / 4,  m_LensY + Picture1.ScaleHeight / 4)
```

The dimensions of this rectangle are one-half the dimensions of the lens (Picture1 control); so the magnification is 400%.

The actual implementation of the control is straightforward, but the required code is quite lengthy. Let's start with the members of the control's interface. The LensEffect control exposes the members in Table 7.5.

TABLE 7.5: The Members of the LensEffect Control

Member	Description
WidthInPixels, HeightInPixels	The dimensions of the image on the control's background. The control isn't autoresized, so the image may be smaller or larger than the available display area.
LensX, LensY	The coordinates of the lens's upper-left corner in pixels. The origin is the control's upper-left corner.
LensWidth, LensHeight	The lens's dimensions.
MoveTo(X, Y)	Method that moves the lens to the specified coordinates.

If you open the project, you'll see that it was designed with the ActiveX Interface Wizard. Most of the control's properties are mapped to the UserControl object. Next, we'll describe the custom members.

When you set the coordinates of the lens's upper-left corner, the code must make sure that the specified values are valid (in other words, it won't allow the developer to move the lens outside the control's visible area).

Code 7.11: **The Property Let and Get Procedures for the LensX Property**

```
Public Property Get LensX() As Integer
    LensX = m_LensX
End Property

Public Property Let LensX(ByVal New_LensX As Integer)
    If ((New_LensX < (UserControl.ScaleWidth - Picture1.ScaleWidth)) _
        And (New_LensX > 0)) Then
            m_LensX = New_LensX
            UserControl_Paint
            PropertyChanged "LensX"
    End If
End Property
```

The Property procedures for the LensY property are similar. The WidthInPixels and HeightInPixels properties are mapped to the control's ScaleWidth and ScaleHeight properties, which aren't available directly to the developer (the code relies on the PicturePaint method, which assumes that the source and destination bitmaps are measured in pixels). Moreover, we made these properties read-only by omitting the Property Let procedures.

Code 7.12:   The Property Procedures for the LensY Property

```
Public Property Get WidthInPixels() As Integer
    WidthInPixels = Int(UserControl.ScaleWidth)
End Property

Public Property Get HeightInPixels() As Integer
    HeightInPixels = Int(UserControl.ScaleHeight)
End Property
```

As expected, the code for drawing a user-drawn control resides in the UserControl's Paint event.

Code 7.13:   The UserControl's Paint Event

```
Private Sub UserControl_Paint()
Picture1.Move m_LensX, m_LensY
On Error Resume Next
Picture1.PaintPicture UserControl.Picture, 0, 0, _
   Picture1.ScaleWidth, Picture1.ScaleHeight, _
   m_LensX + Picture1.ScaleWidth / 4, m_LensY + Picture1.ScaleHeight / 4, _
   Picture1.ScaleWidth / 2, Picture1.ScaleHeight / 2, &HCC0020
End Sub
```

The Paint event contains a single line that copies part of the original bitmap to the Picture1 control and magnifies it in the process, as we explained earlier.

Moving the Lens

The most interesting code in this project is in the mouse events of the UserControl. This code captures the movement of the mouse and slides the Picture1 control in the direction of the mouse movement. All three mouse events use the following variables, which are declared on the UserControl object, outside any event:

```
' Program local variables
Private MovingLens As Boolean
```

```
Private XStart As Integer
Private YStart As Integer
```

When you press the left mouse button while the pointer is over the Picture1 control, the *MovingLens* variable is set to True in the MouseDown event to indicate that the control can be moved. This variable is examined in the MouseMove event and reset to False in the MouseUp event. Likewise, the variables *XStart* and *YStart* are set to the coordinates of the point where the mouse button was pressed initially. These variables are used in the MouseMove event as well.

Code 7.14:   The Event Handler of the MouseDown Event of the Picture1 Control

```
Private Sub Picture1_MouseDown(Button As Integer, Shift As Integer, _
        X As Single, Y As Single)
    If Button = vbLeftButton Then
        XStart = X
        YStart = Y
        MovingLens = True
    End If
End Sub
```

In the MouseMove event of the Picture1 control, we monitor the movement of the mouse and displace the Picture1 control by the difference between the current coordinates of the mouse and the coordinates XStart and YStart where the mouse was pressed initially. The code contains more lines that make sure the lens is not moved outside the visible area of the control.

Code 7.15:   The MouseMove Event

```
Private Sub Picture1_MouseMove(Button As Integer, Shift As Integer, _
        X As Single, Y As Single)
    If Button = vbLeftButton And MovingLens Then
        If Picture1.Left + (X - XStart) > 0 And _
                (Picture1.Left + (X - XStart)) < _
                (UserControl.ScaleWidth - Picture1.ScaleWidth) Then
            m_LensX = Picture1.Left + (X - XStart)
        End If
        If Picture1.Top + (Y - YStart) > 0 And _
                (Picture1.Top + (Y - YStart)) < _
                (UserControl.ScaleHeight - Picture1.ScaleHeight) Then
            m_LensY = Picture1.Top + (Y - YStart)
        End If
```

```
            UserControl_Paint
      End If
End Sub
```

After the Picture1 control is moved to its new location, the Paint event is called to redraw the control. Finally, in the MouseUp event we reset the MovingLens variable to False.

Code 7.16: **The MouseUp Event**

```
Private Sub Picture1_MouseUp (Button As Integer, Shift As Integer, _
      X As Single, Y As Single)
   If Button = vbLeftButton And MovingLens Then
      MovingLens = False
   End If
End Sub
```

The rest of the code is rather trivial; at least, it was created with the ActiveX Interface Wizard.

Internet-Enabled Controls

With the domination of the Internet and the merging of the Desktop and the Web—demonstrated by the Active Desktop and the latest release of Internet Explorer—ActiveX controls should be able to connect to the Internet and download information from HTTP servers. No matter how much information you provide along with your control, there will always be more, up-to-date information on a server. An interesting, nearly necessary feature you may want to add to your controls is the ability to connect to HTTP servers and download information on request.

The ActiveX controls you design with Visual Basic support asynchronous downloading of property values. To download a file from a URL, you can use the AsyncRead method, whose syntax is:

```
UserControl_AsyncRead Target, AsyncType [, PropertyName]
```

The Target argument is a string specifying the location of the data, and it can be a URL to a remote HTTP server or the path to a file on a local or network disk. A URL would look something like this:

```
http://www.servername.com/Updates/Latest.txt
```

And a path to a local file would look something like this:

```
file://m:\Software\Updates\Latest.txt
```

You specify the type of the file to be downloaded with the AsyncType argument, which can be one of the constants in Table 7.6.

TABLE 7.6: The Possible Settings of the AsyncType Argument of the AsyncRead Method

Constant	Description
VbAsyncTypeFile	The data is provided in a file that Visual Basic can open later.
VbAsyncTypeByteArray	The data is provided as a byte array. The application must handle the elements of the array.
VbAsyncTypePicture	The data is provided in a Picture object.

The last, optional argument is the name of the property to be downloaded. This name is simply an identifier, which you can use later to retrieve the value of the property downloaded or to cancel the downloading of the data. In our examples, we are going to use the PropertyName argument to distinguish among multiple properties that are downloaded simultaneously. The PropertyName argument can be any arbitrary name, since it's only function is to act as an identifier for this particular data request. The value in PropertyName is used to identify the particular asynchronous read to cancel in the CancelAsyncRead method. It is also used to identify the particular asynchronous read that has completed in the AsyncReadComplete event.

Once the data is requested with the AsyncRead method, control is relinquished to the application, which can continue with other tasks. The download may take a while, so the AsyncRead method performs an asynchronous operation. When the download is complete, the AsyncReadComplete event is raised. The code for handling the downloaded data goes into the AsyncReadComplete event handler.

The AsyncReadComplete event's definition is:

```
Sub UserControl_AsyncReadComplete(PropertyValue As AsyncProperty)
```

The PropertyValue argument is an object that has the properties shown in Table 7.7.

TABLE 7.7: The Properties of the AsyncProperty Object

Property	Description
Value	A variant containing the results of the asynchronous download.
PropertyName	The property name, as specified with the last argument in the AsyncRead method.

TABLE 7.7 (CONTINUED): The Properties of the AsyncProperty Object

Property	Description
AsyncType	An integer specifying the type of the data in the Value property. It takes the same values as the AsyncType argument of the AsyncRead method, described earlier.

The AsyncReadComplete event will be raised even if an error occurred during the transmission. If the download wasn't completed successfully, a run-time error will occur when you access the Value property of the AsyncProperty object.

> **TIP**
>
> Always include an On Error statement in the AsyncReadComplete event handler to trap download errors.

It is possible to cancel the asynchronous download by calling the CancelAsyncRead method. Its syntax is:

```
UserControl.CancelAsyncRead PropertyName
```

PropertyName is the name of the property being downloaded (the last argument of the AsyncRead method). If PropertyName is not supplied (because no such property was specified in the AsyncRead method), the last AsyncRead method invocation that was called without a PropertyName will be canceled.

The OnLine Project

The asynchronous downloading of property values over the Internet is demonstrated in the OnLine project, which is shown in Figure 7.16. The OnLine control has two panes, the left one being a ListBox control and the right one a TextBox control. The control connects to a user-specified URL and downloads a list of topics, which are displayed in the left pane. When the user clicks a topic, the control connects to the same URL and downloads a text file, which is displayed in the pane on the right (the TextBox control).

Start a new ActiveX control project, and design a UserControl object like the one shown in Figure 7.16. Place a narrow ListBox control on the left and a TextBox control on the right. Since the developer must have the option to resize the control at will, in the Resize event we must resize the two controls according to the control's dimensions.

FIGURE 7.16:

The OnLine control downloads and displays text files over the Internet from an HTTP server.

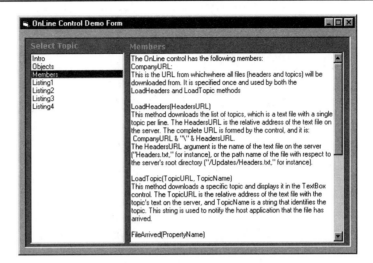

Code 7.17: The Resize Event

```
Private Sub UserControl_Resize()
    If UserControl.Height < 3000 Then UserControl.Height = 3000
    List1.Height = UserControl.Height - (4 * Label1.Top +
Label1.Height)
    If UserControl.Width < 6000 Then UserControl.Width = 6000
    Text1.Height = List1.Height
    Text1.Width = UserControl.Width - Text1.Left - 2 * List1.Left
End Sub
```

This code doesn't resize the two constituent controls proportionally. It simply adjusts the width of the TextBox control. It also enforces a minimum size for the control.

WARNING   Don't make a control such as this one too small; it would be practically useless. Enforce a minimum size from within the control's Resize event.

The OnLine control has the following members:

CompanyURL: This is the URL from which all files (headers and topics) will be downloaded. It is specified once and used by both the LoadHeaders and LoadTopic methods.

LoadHeaders(HeadersURL): This method downloads the list of topics, which is a text file with a single topic per line. The HeadersURL is the relative address of the text file on the server. The complete URL is formed by the control, and it is:

```
CompanyURL & "/" & HeadersURL
```

The HeadersURL argument is the name of the text file on the server (Headers.txt, for instance) or the path name of the file with respect to the server's root directory (/Updates/Headers.txt, for instance).

LoadTopic(TopicURL, TopicName): This method downloads a specific topic and displays it in the TextBox control. The *TopicURL* argument is the relative address of the text file with the topic's text on the server, and *TopicName* is a string that identifies the topic. This string is used to notify the host application that the file has arrived.

FileArrived(PropertyName): This event is triggered from within the AsyncReadComplete event and notifies the host application that a download has completed.

OnLineError(ErrorNumber, ErrorDescription): This event is also triggered from within the AsyncReadComplete event, to notify the application that an error has occurred.

TopicClick(TopicName): This event is raised when a topic in the Topics list is selected by the user. The OnLine control starts the downloading of the selected topic automatically and also notifies the host application that a new topic was selected.

Header: This property returns the selected header (if any) in the left pane.

TopicText: This property returns the text displayed in the right pane.

Using the OnLine Control

Before examining the actual code of the control, let's see how it's used in the test project. The test project consists of a single Form that contains an instance of the OnLine control only.

When the Form is loaded, it assigns the URL of the server on which all the files reside to the CompanyURL property. It then calls the LoadHeaders method to load the list of topics and display them in the left pane.

```
Private Sub Form_Load()
    OnLine1.CompanyURL = "http://127.0.0.1"
    OnLine1.LoadHeaders ("headers.txt")
End Sub
```

The test project need not do anything more. The rest is up to the OnLine control. After the headers are downloaded and displayed, every time the user clicks a topic, the corresponding text file is displayed in the right pane. The test project uses the URL 127.0.0.1, the URL of the local computer.

To test this project successfully, you must set up a Web server on your computer and copy all the text files from the OnLine folder on the CD to the Web server's root folder or to a subfolder underneath. You can create a folder named Online and change the CompanyURL property to the following:

```
http://127.0.0.1/online
```

Under this project folder on the CD, you will find the WEBSrvr folder, which contains a few files you must place in your server's root folder to experiment with the OnLine and DLImage projects. If you don't want to set up your own server, you can copy the files to your own folder on your ISP's computer and change the CompanyURL accordingly. The simplest approach is to set up your own Web server, since we are going to use it with other projects in Part IV of this book.

TIP
If you are not familiar with the Personal Web Server, see Chapter 16 for details.

The test project displays the error message (should an error occur) from within the OnLineError event:

```
Private Sub OnLine1_OnLineError(Number As Integer, Description As
String)
    MsgBox Description
End Sub
```

Finally, it prints messages to the Immediate window for demonstration purposes:

```
Private Sub online1_FileArrived(Name As String)
    Debug.Print Name & " arrived"
End Sub
```

```
Private Sub online1_TopicClick(topic As String)
    Debug.Print topic & " requested"
End Sub
```

The FileArrived event is triggered every time a new file is downloaded. This applies to both the headers file and the topics file.

The OnLine Control's Code

We used the ActiveX Interface Wizard to add the standard properties of the control. We are going to focus on the procedures that download the headers and the topics. The names of the files with the headers are passed to the method LoadHeaders as an argument.

Code 7.18:   The LoadHeaders() Method

```
Public Sub LoadHeaders(HeadersURL As String)
Dim HURL As String
On Error GoTo HeadersError

    HURL = m_CompanyURL & HeadersURL
    AsyncRead HURL, vbAsyncTypeFile, "Headers"
    Exit Sub


HeadersError:
    RaiseEvent OnLineError(1024, "Could not download list of topics.")

End Sub
```

Notice that the complete URL for the headers file is formed by concatenating the company URL and the name of the file. The local variable *m_CompanyURL* stores the CompanyURL property. Before calling the LoadHeaders method from the host application, you must set this property.

The LoadTopic method is similar. It accepts two arguments:

- The relative path of the topic file (TopicURL)

- A property name (topic)

Code 7.19:   The LoadTopic Method

```
Private Sub LoadTopic(TopicURL As String, topic As String)
On Error GoTo TopicURL
    If List1.ListIndex >= 0 Then
        AsyncRead TopicURL, vbAsyncTypeFile, topic
    End If
    Exit Sub
```

```
TopicURL:
    RaiseEvent OnLineError(1025, "Could not download topic " & topic)
End Sub
```

The interesting action takes place in the AsyncReadComplete event of the UserControl object.

Code 7.20: **The AsyncReadComplete Event**

```
Private Sub UserControl_AsyncReadComplete(AsyncProp As AsyncProperty)
Dim FileName As String

On Error GoTo DLoadError
    If AsyncProp.PropertyName = "Headers" Then
        FileName = AsyncProp.Value
        LoadTopicsList (FileName)
        RaiseEvent FileArrived("Headers")
    Else
        For i = 0 To List1.ListCount - 1
            If AsyncProp.PropertyName = List1.List(i) Then
                    FileName = AsyncProp.Value
                    Label2.Caption = AsyncProp.PropertyName
                    LoadTopicText FileName
                    RaiseEvent FileArrived(AsyncProp.PropertyName)
                    Exit For
            End If
        Next
    End If
    Exit Sub

DLoadError:
    RaiseEvent OnLineError(1028, "Error in Downloading topic " &
List1.List(i))

End Sub
```

This event is triggered no matter which file has completed downloading, so the code must first figure out whether it's the headers file or a topic file. If the property's name is Headers, the code opens the file just downloaded and displays its lines in the ListBox control. When the AsyncRead method downloads a file, the AsyncProp object's Value property is the name of the file that stored the text on the local disk. It has nothing to do with the actual file name on the server. It's a unique file name created by the system in the Temporary Internet Files folder. The LoadTopicsList subroutine uses the name of the file to display the headers in the ListBox.

Code 7.21:   **The LoadTopicsList Subroutine**

```
Sub LoadTopicsList(FileName As String)
Dim FNum As Integer
Dim topic As String
    FNum = FreeFile
    List1.Clear
On Error GoTo LoadTopicsError
    Open FileName For Input As FNum
    While Not EOF(FNum)
        Input #FNum, topic
        List1.AddItem topic
    Wend
    Exit Sub
LoadTopicsError:
    RaiseEvent OnLineError(1029, "Couldn't load topics")

End Sub
```

This is straightforward VB code that opens a text file and appends its lines to the List1 ListBox control.

Back to the AsyncReadComplete event. If the downloaded file isn't the Headers file, the code scans each topic in the left pane to see which topic name matches the property name of the downloaded file. Once a match is found, the subroutine calls the LoadTopicText subroutine, which opens the text file and displays it in the right pane.

WARNING   Notice the error-trapping code in all subroutines. When downloading information from the Internet, any number of things can go wrong. The HTTP server may be down, files may be rearranged on the server, transmission errors can occur, and so on. These errors must be trapped and dealt with in a robust manner.

You might want to add to this project a feature that keeps track of the property being downloaded and prevents the host application from initiating another download of the same property while it's being downloaded. Our code will give a generic error message:

```
Could not download headers
```
or
```
Could not download topic
```

The AsyncRead method can be called to download a file while another one is being downloaded, but it can't download the same file twice simultaneously.

Downloading Image Properties

The AsyncRead method can also download picture properties. You can download pictures as binary files and display them with the LoadPicture method. Visual Basic can also create a device context and store the downloaded bitmap there. The DLImage project (in the DLImage folder on the CD) is a variation of the OnLine control, which downloads images. The headers are image names, and each time a new image name is selected in the left pane, it is downloaded and displayed in the right pane, as shown in Figure 7.17.

The DLImage control downloads images from an HTTP server and displays them.

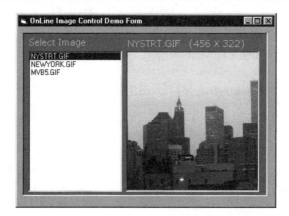

The DLImage project is quite similar to the OnLine project, except that it uses the vbAsyncTypePicture constant in the AsyncRead method. Also, the pane in which the selected image is displayed is a PictureBox control. To build this project, copy the components of the projects to a new folder and rename them accordingly.

The data downloaded are stored in a bitmap structure, which can be manipulated like the Image property of the PictureBox control or the Form object. The ShowImage subroutine displays the image on the PictureBox control. The image is displayed progressively, one line at a time, starting from the top of the image. The code uses the PaintPicture method of the PictureBox control to copy an increasingly wider stripe of the downloaded image.

Code 7.22:   The ShowImage Subroutine

```
Private Sub ShowImage(Image As StdPicture)
Dim irow
On Error GoTo DisplayError

    For irow = 1 To Picture1.ScaleHeight - 1
        Picture1.PaintPicture Image, 0, 0, _
        Picture1.ScaleWidth, irow, 0, 0, Picture1.ScaleWidth, irow
    Next
    ScrollImage = False
    OldXStart = 0
    OldYStart = 0
    If ScaleX(Image.Height, vbHimetric, vbPixels) >
Picture1.ScaleHeight_
        Or ScaleY(Image.Width, vbHimetric, vbPixels) >
Picture1.ScaleWidth_
        Then
            ScrollImage = True
    End If
    Exit Sub

DisplayError:
    RaiseEvent OnLineError(1030, "Couldn't display image")

End Sub
```

An interesting feature of this control is that, if the image's dimensions exceed the dimensions of the PictureBox control, the user can scroll the image around with the mouse. *ScrollImage* is a Boolean variable that indicates whether the image can be scrolled. If the image fits in the PictureBox control, the *ScrollImage* variable is set to False to prohibit the movement of the image in the control.

Moving the Image

The code for moving the image around in the PictureBox control is located in the three mouse events of the PictureBox control. You can also use this code as your starting point to implement a control that can display large images and allow the user to scroll them with the mouse and bring any portion of the image into view (see Figure 7.18). One shortcoming of the PictureBox control is that it doesn't provide scrollbars that would allow the user to select any part of the image.

FIGURE 7.18:

As the user drags the image around in the control's right pane, the pointer assumes a cross-arrow shape.

The scrolling starts in the MouseDown event of the PictureBox control.

Code 7.23:   The MouseDown Event of the PictureBox Control

```
Private Sub Picture1_MouseDown(Button As Integer, Shift As Integer, _
      X As Single, Y As Single)
    If Button = vbLeftButton And ScrollImage Then
        Screen.MousePointer = 5
        ScrollNow = True
        XStart = X - OldXStart
        YStart = Y - OldYStart
    End If
End Sub
```

The MouseDown event stores the coordinates of the location at which the mouse was clicked for the first time in the variables *XStart* and *YStart*. The variables *OldXStart* and *OldYStart* are the coordinates of the location at which the mouse was released the last time. It is necessary to subtract these values so that the image won't jump back to its initial position when the user releases the mouse, moves it to another location, and starts sliding the image again.

To see the effect that these two variables have on the movement of the image, comment them out temporarily. The image will jump back to its initial position every time the user starts dragging it. The correct behavior of the program is to continue scrolling the image from its current position. We also change the pointer's shape to a cross-arrow to indicate that the image can be scrolled in all four directions.

In the MouseMove event, we copy the appropriate portion of the Bitmap image (the downloaded image) to the PictureBox control. We also check the coordinates of the mouse to make sure that the image won't be scrolled beyond its boundaries.

Code 7.24:   The MouseMove Event of the PictureBox Control

```
Private Sub Picture1_MouseMove(Button As Integer, Shift As Integer, _
        X As Single, Y As Single)
Dim X1 As Integer, Y1 As Integer

    If Button = vbLeftButton And ScrollNow Then
        X1 = XStart - X
        Y1 = YStart - Y
        If X1 < 0 Then X1 = 0: XStart = X
        If Y1 < 0 Then Y1 = 0: YStart = Y
        If X1 > ScaleX(Bitmap.Width, vbHimetric, vbPixels) _
Picture1.ScaleWidth Then _
            X1 = ScaleX(Bitmap.Width, vbHimetric, vbPixels) _
Picture1.ScaleWidth
        If Y1 > ScaleY(Bitmap.Height, vbHimetric, vbPixels) _
Picture1.ScaleHeight Then _
            Y1 = ScaleY(Bitmap.Height, vbHimetric, vbPixels) _
Picture1.ScaleHeight
        Picture1.PaintPicture Bitmap, 0, 0, _
            Picture1.ScaleWidth, Picture1.ScaleHeight, _
            X1, Y1, Picture1.ScaleWidth, Picture1.ScaleHeight
    End If

End Sub
```

Finally, in the MouseUp event we reset the *ScrollNow* variable to False, we set the pointer back to its normal shape, and we set the variables *OldXStart* and *OldYStart* so that they can be used again by the MouseDown event if the user continues scrolling the image.

Code 7.25:   The MouseUp Event of the PictureBox Control

```
Private Sub Picture1_MouseUp(Button As Integer, Shift As Integer, _
        X As Single, Y As Single)
    Screen.MousePointer = vbDefault
    ScrollNow = False
    OldXStart = (X - XStart)
    OldYStart = (Y - YStart)
End Sub
```

The three mouse events track the movement of the mouse and respond by sliding the image around in the PictureBox (if the image is larger than its container). The code is similar to the code we used in the LensFX control.

Interconnected Controls

In some situations, one control isn't enough. For instance, multiple controls are common in a user interface. Visual Basic's file system controls are typical. To build a custom file selection Form, you must place all three controls (DriveListBox, DirectoryListBox, and FileListBox) on the Form. These controls are not connected by default, but they are designed so that you can connect them with a few statements. These controls have been replaced for the most part by the Common Dialogs controls, but let's look at a simple example. Figure 7.19 shows a typical Form that combines the three File System controls (DriveListBox, DirectoryListBox, and FileListBox).

FIGURE 7.19:

A typical Form that combines the three File System controls

The controls on this Form are connected with the following simple statements:

```
Private Sub Dir1_Change()
    File1.Path = Dir1.Path
End Sub

Private Sub Drive1_Change()
    Dir1.Path = Drive1.Drive
End Sub
```

When the user selects a new drive, the DirectoryListBox control is updated to display the current folder in the new drive. When the user selects a new folder, the FileListBox control is updated to display the files in the selected folder. Put these three controls together on a UserControl object along with a few lines of code, and you have an ActiveX control for cruising the local disk(s). The FileOpen common dialog control offers much more flexibility, but some situations call for custom dialog boxes. The point we want to make here is that the File System controls are designed to work with one another on a Form; all you have to do is add the code that connects them. All the functionality you need is built into the controls themselves.

> **NOTE**
>
> The File System controls are not officially called interconnected, and you won't find the term *interconnected controls* in Microsoft's documentation (at least, we haven't run into this term yet). We're using it here to describe a group of controls that can be tied to one another with a few simple statements. Once connected, they practically work on their own, and they are adequate for building an elaborate user interface.

In this section, we are going to convert the DBClass class we developed in Chapter 5 into a group of ActiveX controls that will not only retrieve records from the NWIND database, but display them in Grid controls. Figure 7.20 shows the three interconnected controls:

- CustomersControl
- InvoicesControl
- DetailsControl

The statements between them connect them. What you don't see in Figure 7.20 are the events that contain these lines. As you have probably guessed, these events indicate that a new selection was made in the corresponding control.

NOTE The three interconnected controls were developed in a common project, which you will find in the Ch07/DBCtrls folder on the CD.

FIGURE 7.20:

The three intercon-
nected controls and
the statements that
connect them

Let's start with the test project to see how the interconnected controls interact on a Form. Figure 7.21 contains the three controls.

FIGURE 7.21:

The CustTest test project for the DBControls ActiveX controls

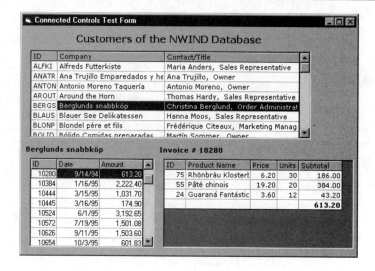

On the top is the CustomersControl control, which displays the customer names. When the Form is first loaded, the following code is executed:

```
Private Sub Form_Load()
    Me.Show
    DoEvents
    Me.Caption = "Opening NWIND database..."
    Me.MousePointer = vbHourglass
    CustomersControl.SetDatabase "c:\program files\devstudio\vb"
    Me.Caption = "Loading Customers Table..."
    CustomersControl.GetCustomers
    Me.MousePointer = vbDefault
    Me.Caption = "Connected Controls Test Form"
End Sub
```

As you can see, most of this code deals with the shape of the pointer and setting the Form's Caption to reflect the current operation. The two lines of interest here are the following:

```
CustomersControl.SetDatabase "c:\program files\devstudio\vb"
CustomersControl.GetCustomers
```

The first line opens the NWIND database. It calls the CustomersControl's SetDatabase method with the path of the database. The name of the database isn't specified, because all three interconnected controls operate on the same database(which is the NWIND sample database). Well, this may raise some eyebrows, but wait. The interconnected controls may apply to a single database, but they are quite flexible. As you will soon see, they can be used in many projects that manipulate this database.

NOTE   Not all ActiveX controls you will develop will be distributed in the millions. If you work as part of a programming team for a corporation, you will save yourself and your team many hours of work by providing a few controls that address common programming tasks. How many report or invoice-entry screens are designed in a corporation? Every programmer who needs to display customers or invoices could use your controls.

The second line populates the CustomersControl by calling the control's GetCustomers method. This method doesn't have to specify any arguments; the control knows how to populate the Grid.

To display the invoices issued to a customer, the user must click a customer's name. The CustomersControl issues the CustomerSelected event every time the user clicks a customer's name.

Code 7.26:   The Event Handler of the CustomersControl

```
Private Sub CustomersControl_CustomerSelected(customerID As String)
    Me.MousePointer = vbHourglass
    InvoicesControl.ClearGrid
    DetailsControl.ClearGrid
    Label2.Caption = ""
    InvoicesControl.GetInvoices (customerID)
    Label1.Caption = CustomersControl.CompanyName
    Me.MousePointer = vbDefault
End Sub
```

Again, most of this code sets up the appearance of the Form. It changes the shape of the pointer while the invoices are read from the database, it displays the name of the selected customer in a Label on top of the InvoicesControl, and so on. Only one line of code is needed to connect the CustomersControl to the InvoicesControl:

```
InvoicesControl.GetInvoices (customerID)
```

This line calls the InvoicesControl's GetInvoices method, which retrieves the invoices issued to a single customer. The selected customer's ID is passed as an argument and used by the GetInvoices method, which not only retrieves the records, but displays them on the Grid as well. It also calculates the total and displays it after the last invoice.

You've probably guessed what happens when the user clicks an invoice. The program calls another method that displays the lines of the invoice in the DetailsControl.

Code 7.27:   The InvoiceSelected Event Handler of the InvoicesControl

```
Private Sub InvoicesControl_InvoiceSelected(InvoiceID As Long)
    Me.MousePointer = vbHourglass
    DetailsControl.ClearGrid
    Label2.Caption = "Invoice # " & InvoiceID
    DetailsControl.GetDetails (InvoiceID)
    Me.MousePointer = vbDefault
End Sub
```

The InvoiceSelected event reports to the host application the ID of the selected invoice, which is later used by the GetDetails method of the DetailsControl to retrieve and display the lines of the selected invoice. Again, a single line of code connects the InvoicesControl to the DetailsControl.

Practically, all the work is done by the interconnected controls. All you have to do is detect certain events that let you know that the user has made a new selection and call the method that updates another control. The developer can use the three interconnected controls to set up an elaborate report screen in no time. With some additional effort, you can allow editing of the records. This example isn't suited for editing operations, as invoices shouldn't be edited after the fact. You must void an invoice and issue another one, but all the work will take place in the control, and developers don't need to add a single line of code (short of setting a property that allows a control's contents to be edited).

You may think that the interconnected controls are good enough for a single operation, namely display the Form shown in Figure 7.21. Why not package the entire Form as an ActiveX control? Because the interconnected controls can be used in other projects too, on their own. The InvoicesControl has a GetInvoicesByDate method that retrieves the invoices issued on a single date. Figure 7.22 shows a second test Form for the same controls. It's called DateTest. This test project uses a date as its starting point and doesn't use the CustomersControl at all.

NOTE   You'll find the DateTest Form in the Ch07/DBCtrls folder on the CD that comes with this book. To display this Form, set it as the project's Startup object.

FIGURE 7.22:

The second test Form
for the interconnected
controls retrieves
invoices by date.

The DateTest Form contains three ComboBox controls, in which the user can specify a date. You could probably use a more elaborate Calendar control in their place, but we're avoiding using controls that may not exist on every system. The Form's Load event handler sets up the ComboBox control and the appearance of the Form. The following one line relates to the interconnected controls:

```
InvoicesControl.SetDatabase "c:\program files\devstudio\vb"
```

This line opens the NWIND database. Clicking the Command Button executes the following lines:

```
Private Sub Command1_Click()
Dim thisDate As String
    InvoicesControl.ClearGrid
    DetailsControl.ClearGrid
    Me.MousePointer = vbHourglass
    thisDate = MonthBox.Text & "/" & DayBox.Text & "/" & YearBox.Text
    If IsDate(thisDate) Then
        InvoicesControl.GetInvoicesByDate (thisDate)
    Else
        MsgBox "Invalid date selected"
    End If
    Me.MousePointer = vbDefault
End Sub
```

The code clears the two controls and then populates the InvoicesControl with this line:

```
InvoicesControl.GetInvoicesByDate (thisDate)
```

It also makes sure that the user hasn't specified an invalid date with the IsDate() function. The GetInvoicesByDate method accepts an argument, which is a date. It retrieves the invoices issued on the specific date and populates the control. When another invoice is selected in the InvoicesControl, the InvoiceSelected event is triggered. This event's code is the same as that in the CustTest project. It calls the GetDetails method of the DetailsControl to populate the second control with the details of the selected invoice.

Figure 7.23 shows a simplified diagram of how the InvoicesControl and DetailsControl are connected. To populate the InvoicesControl, we call the GetInvoicesByDate method of the Invoices control. When the user selects an invoice by clicking it, the GetDetails method of the DetailsControl is called, which populates the Details control with the lines of the selected invoice.

FIGURE 7.23:

These statements connect the InvoicesControl and DetailsControl ActiveX controls when viewing invoices by date.

As you can see, the three interconnected controls do all the work for retrieving and displaying customer data, invoices, and invoice details. The developer simply drops them on the Form and enters a few lines of code to connect them, and the controls do their work.

TIP

Although these controls operate on a single database, you can use them in many projects. This will reduce development time in a team environment, and it will also ensure a consistent user interface among multiple applications.

Coding the DBControls Project

Now we can look at the code of the DBControls project. The first peculiarity of this project is that it implements three controls in a single project. The project has three UserControl objects in its User Controls folder, and the OCX file it produces will have three controls in it. When you add the ConnectedControls ActiveX control to a project, you will see three new icons in the Toolbox. Although the appearance of the three icons is the same, each has a different name. The icon names are displayed in a ToolTip box when the pointer rests over them, as shown in Figure 7.24.

FIGURE 7.24:

The Connected-Controls component will place three different controls in your Toolbox.

NOTE

You should design a different icon for each control, but it's difficult to create icons that are similar yet different enough to convey information about the controls they represent.

The DBCtrls project is fairly lengthy, but we are going to concentrate on the core of the code. For this project, we didn't use the ActiveX Interface Wizard. As you will see, the three controls have the same structure and few properties. Sometimes it's faster to start typing than to go through the steps of the Wizard to define a few methods.

To implement the DBControls custom controls, start a new ActiveX project, and add two more UserControl objects to the project. Name the three UserControl objects as follows:

CustomersControl, which displays customer data

InvoicesControl, which displays invoices

DetailsControl, which displays an invoice's lines

In addition to the three UserControl objects, the DBControls project has a module. Add a new module, name it DatabaseModule, and enter the following declaration in it:

```
Public DB As Database
```

The *DB* variable is set to the NWIND database when it's opened with the OpenDatabase method.

Let's examine the structure of the CustomersControl. The control uses a single variable and raises an event. Their declarations are:

```
Event CustomerSelected(CustomerID As String)
Dim CustomersRS As Recordset
```

The *CustomersRS* argument is a recordset in which the selected records will be stored. The records are selected with a SQL statement in the GetCustomers method.

Code 7.28:   The GetCustomers Method

```
Public Sub GetCustomers()
Dim SQLString As String
Dim row As Integer
    SQLString = "SELECT CustomerID, CompanyName, ContactName, _
        ContactTitle FROM CUSTOMERS"
    Set CustomersRS = DB.OpenRecordset(SQLString, dbOpenSnapshot)
    CustomersRS.MoveLast
    Customers.Rows = CustomersRS.RecordCount + 1
    CustomersRS.MoveFirst
    row = 1
    While Not CustomersRS.EOF
        Customers.TextMatrix(row, 0) = CustomersRS.Fields("CustomerID")
        Customers.TextMatrix(row, 1) = _
            CustomersRS.Fields("CompanyName")
        Customers.TextMatrix(row, 2) = _
            CustomersRS.Fields("ContactName")& _
            ",  " & CustomersRS.Fields("ContactTitle")
        row = row + 1
        CustomersRS.MoveNext
    Wend
End Sub
```

This code builds the CustomersRS recordset and then places each record in a new row of the Customers MSFlexGrid control. You could replace the MSFlexGrid control with a data-bound Grid control, which would simplify the code considerably, but we want to show how to populate non–data-bound controls with records. In addition, the MSFlexGrid control offers additional features, such as the display of totals after the last row of data, automatic calculations based on the values of the fields, flexibility to color rows and columns and set fonts, and so on. The other two controls of the DBCtrls project are also based on the MSFlexGrid control.

The CustomersControl provides a few properties too, which are the values of the fields of the selected row.

Code 7.29:   Field Values As Properties

```
Public Property Get CustomerID() As String
On Error GoTo CustIDError
    CustomerID = Customers.TextMatrix(Customers.RowSel, 0)
    Exit Property
CustIDError:
    CustomerID = ""
End Property

Public Property Get CompanyName() As String
On Error GoTo CompanyError
    CompanyName = Customers.TextMatrix(Customers.RowSel, 1)
    Exit Property
CompanyError:
    CompanyName = ""
End Property

Public Property Get ContactName() As String
On Error GoTo ContactError
    ContactName = Left(Customers.TextMatrix(Customers.RowSel, 2),_
        InStr(Customers.TextMatrix(Customers.RowSel, 2), ","))
    Exit Property
ContactError:
    ContactName = ""
End Property
```

The values of the fields are read from the Grid control, not from the recordset itself. There is no simple way to go from the selected row of the Grid control to the corresponding recordset row.

The CustomerSelected event is raised when the user clicks a row of the Grid control. The code highlights the selected row (in blue) and then retrieves the CustomerID field of the selected row. If this key field is not empty, the CustomerSelected event is raised to notify the host application that a new selection was made.

Code 7.30:   The Click Event of the Customers Control

```
Private Sub Customers_Click()
Dim custID As String * 5
    Customers.Col = 0: Customers.ColSel = 2
```

```
        custID = Customers.TextMatrix(Customers.RowSel, 0)
        If custID <> "" Then
            RaiseEvent CustomerSelected(custID)
        End If
    End Sub
```

Similarly, the InvoicesControl has a GetInvoices method, which accepts as an argument a customer's ID and retrieves the invoices issued to that customer. The subroutine that implements the GetInvoices method builds the appropriate SQL statement and then uses it with the OpenRecordset method of the *DB* object variable to retrieve the invoices.

Code 7.31:   The GetInvoices Method

```
Public Sub GetInvoices(custID As String)
Dim SQLString As String
Dim row As Integer
Dim totAmount As Currency

On Error GoTo InvoicesError

    SQLString = "SELECT DISTINCTROW [Order Subtotals].Subtotal AS_
        SaleAmount, Orders.OrderID,"
    SQLString = SQLString & " Customers.CompanyName,
Orders.ShippedDate,_
        Orders.OrderDate"
    SQLString = SQLString & " FROM Customers INNER JOIN (Orders INNER _
        JOIN [Order Subtotals] ON Orders.OrderID = [Order _
        Subtotals].OrderID)"
    SQLString = SQLString & " ON Customers.CustomerID =
Orders.CustomerID"
    SQLString = SQLString & " WHERE Orders.CustomerID=" _
        & Chr(34) & custID & Chr(34)
    Set InvoicesRS = DB.OpenRecordset(SQLString, dbOpenSnapshot)
    InvoicesRS.MoveLast
    Invoices.Rows = 1
    Invoices.Rows = InvoicesRS.RecordCount + 2
    InvoicesRS.MoveFirst
    row = 1
    totAmount = 0
    While Not InvoicesRS.EOF
        If Not IsNull(InvoicesRS.Fields("OrderID")) Then _
            Invoices.TextMatrix(row, 0) = InvoicesRS.Fields("OrderID")
        If Not IsNull(InvoicesRS.Fields("OrderDate")) Then _
```

```
            Invoices.TextMatrix(row, 1) =
InvoicesRS.Fields("OrderDate")
        If Not IsNull(InvoicesRS.Fields("SaleAmount")) Then _
            Invoices.TextMatrix(row, 2) = _
            Format(InvoicesRS.Fields("SaleAmount"), "#,###.00")
        totAmount = totAmount + InvoicesRS.Fields("SaleAmount")
        row = row + 1
        InvoicesRS.MoveNext
    Wend
    Invoices.TextMatrix(Invoices.Rows - 1, 2) = _
        Format(totAmount, "#,###.00")
    Invoices.row = Invoices.Rows - 1: Invoices.Col = 2
    Invoices.CellFontBold = True
    Exit Sub

InvoicesError:
    If Err.Number = 3021 Then
        Exit Sub
    Else
        Err.Raise Error.Number, "GetInvoices", Err.Description
    End If
End Sub
```

In addition to the GetInvoices method, the control provides another method, GetInvoicesByDate, which accepts a date as an argument and returns the invoices issued on that date (regardless of customer). The GetInvoicesByDate method is identical to the GetInvoices method, except for the SQL statement. Here are the lines that build the SQL statement which retrieves invoices by date:

```
SQLString = "SELECT DISTINCTROW [Order Subtotals].Subtotal AS
SaleAmount,_
        Orders.OrderID, Customers.CustomerID,"
SQLString = SQLString & " Customers.CompanyName, Orders.ShippedDate, _
        Orders.OrderDate"
SQLString = SQLString & " FROM Customers INNER JOIN (Orders INNER JOIN
_
        [Order Subtotals] ON Orders.OrderID = [Order
Subtotals].OrderID)"
SQLString = SQLString & " ON Customers.CustomerID = Orders.CustomerID"
SQLString = SQLString & " WHERE Orders.OrderDate=#" & invDate & "#"
```

In the previous lines, invDate is the date passed to the method as an argument. Although the two subroutines fill the grid's rows, they keep track of the sum of the invoice totals, which they display after the last row.

Similar to the CustomersControls, the InvoicesControl provides a number of properties that return the values of the fields in the selected row. We need not repeat these Property procedures here; you can open the project and examine the code. The event that signals the selection of an invoice on the InvoicesGrid is called InvoiceSelected and is raised from within the Click event of the Invoices control.

Code 7.32:   The Click Event of the Invoices Control

```
Private Sub Invoices_Click()
Dim InvID As Long
    Invoices.Col = 0: Invoices.ColSel = 2
    If Invoices.TextMatrix(Invoices.RowSel, 0) <> "" Then
        InvID = Invoices.TextMatrix(Invoices.RowSel, 0)
        RaiseEvent InvoiceSelected(InvID)
    End If
End Sub
```

This code is quite similar to the code of the Click event of the Customers control.

The third of the interconnected controls, the DetailsControl, is implemented along the same lines. It uses a SQL statement (which incorporates the invoice's ID) to build a SQL statement that retrieves and then displays the lines of the specified invoice. It also provides a number of properties that return the values of the fields on the selected row on the grid, but it doesn't raise any event to signify the selection of an invoice line.

TIP

If you design similar controls frequently, you might want to consider developing a code generator. The controls contain similar statements (only the names of the fields change), which makes them ideal targets for a code generator.

It's been a lengthy project, but we hope we've demonstrated a useful technique for designing ActiveX controls that encapsulate complicated operations. You can incorporate the three interconnected ActiveX controls in many projects that use the NWIND database. If you are working as a programmer in a corporate environment, you know very well how much code is duplicated in designing Forms to display customers, invoices, and invoice lines. With some additional effort, you can adjust these controls to allow the editing of their contents as well.

Another benefit of this approach is that the developer doesn't need to know how to build SQL statements or how to manipulate recordsets. The most important aspect of the three controls is that you can change their implementation without worrying about breaking the application's code. As long as the new implementation provides the same interface members, the applications that use it will work. For example, you could redesign these controls around the Remote Data Object to access the NWIND database over the Internet.

Extending the IDE with Add-Ins

■ Understanding add-ins

■ Exploring the VBIDE class

■ Building an add-in

■ Programming the Demo add-in project

■ Manipulating the IDE menu

■ Detecting IDE events

8

One major strength of Visual Basic is its environment. In Visual Basic's Integrated Development Environment (IDE), you can develop, test, and debug all types of projects, from Standard EXE projects to ActiveX controls and ActiveX documents. And as you know by now, the IDE is extended and enhanced with each new version of Visual Basic.

You can also enhance the IDE by incorporating new commands and even new menus with the help of add-ins. *Add-ins* are components that must be installed on the developer's system, and when developers need the functionality of a specific add-in, they add it to the IDE.

One of the project types you can create with Visual Basic is the Add-In project, which is an application you can hook into the environment to enhance the IDE itself. Using add-ins, you can extend the functionality of the Visual Basic IDE and streamline the design process. Add-ins can be as simple as programs that ensure that all TextBox controls on a Form are aligned or that all data-entry controls use the same font name and size. They can also be complete applications that design Forms and generate code automatically (the so-called Wizards), manipulate databases (such as the Visual Data Manager), and so on.

The proper term for adding an add-in to the environment is *connecting*. When the add-in is no longer needed, it must be *disconnected*. You connect an add-in to the IDE with the help of the Add-In Manager. The process is similar to adding references or components to a project. Here are the steps:

1. Choose Add-Ins ➤ Add-In Manager to open the Add-In Manager dialog box:

2. To select an add-in, check the box in front of its name.

The add-in's name is added to the Add-Ins menu, and you can activate it from there.

Manipulating Visual Basic's IDE is complicated. Even using it isn't always simple. For example, you have to know the difference between in-process and out-of-process servers. You can test in-process servers in the same instance of Visual Basic, but you must test out-of-process servers in a second instance of Visual Basic. In the last chapter, you saw that the behavior of an ActiveX control depends on whether the test project is running in design mode or in run-time mode. However, the ActiveX control is running in both modes. As you can see, the environment of Visual Basic consists of many interacting components, and when manipulating one of them, you must consider the state of other components.

The same is true for an add-in. While a project is in design mode, the add-in's code is running in the background. Testing add-ins isn't as simple as running the project. You need two instances of Visual Basic running at once—one with the add-in, and another with a project with which you'll be testing the add-in.

NOTE   Add-ins are not project components. They are used by the IDE and only in design mode. The project contains no references to the add-ins you have connected to the IDE. Moreover, if you connect the add-ins while a project is open and then open another project or start a new one, the add-ins will remain connected.

Who Needs Add-Ins?

Most of you have managed without building custom add-ins, and chances are that you don't have any compelling reasons to do so now. The add-in market is also small. You can design really useful add-ins to simplify the development process, but marketing them isn't easy. You're better off selling custom ActiveX controls. The add-ins you're using come with Visual Basic itself, and, as you know by now, they are life-savers. Imagine how many lines of code you would have to enter manually to create a simple control that delegates the members of its constituent controls. The ActiveX Control Interface Wizard is basically an application, capable of affecting the IDE itself. You provide the specifications for the interface of a new ActiveX control, and the Wizard creates the skeleton of the control (it generates the trivial part of the code and creates the placeholders, where you'll enter your own code).

Another example of a useful add-in is the Visual Data Manager, which is a totally separate application that can be called from within the Add-In menu. The Visual Data Manager allows you to design and manipulate databases while the

Visual Basic window is open. You can move back and forth to look up field names and their definitions, perhaps to add a new index to a table according to your application's needs, and so on.

As far as the integration between the Visual Basic IDE and the add-in is concerned, there is none (short of being able to start the add-in from within the IDE). As a proof, you can end Visual Basic, and the Visual Data Manager will remain active. As you probably guessed, this is the simplest type of add-in you can develop. You may claim it's simpler to develop something like the Visual Data Manager as a separate application, which users can start by double-clicking its icon. You're probably right. Personally, we can't think of many add-ins like the Visual Data Manager, although here's an idea for a useful add-in that functions independently of Visual Basic.

Most of us resort to the online help files to get information about constants, especially the ones we need to set up a common dialog box such as the File Open dialog box. You can design a Form that lets the user set all the available options visually and displays the common dialog box that corresponds to these settings. When the developer gets the desired dialog box, the program generates the statements that produce the dialog box and copies them to the clipboard, from where you can paste them anywhere in your code. Turning a VB Form into an add-in isn't difficult, as you'll see, and you can turn many "helper" applications that you use at design time into add-ins.

The Data Form Wizard is an excellent example of the functionality of an add-in. This Wizard walks you through a series of dialog boxes where you specify the type of Form you want to create, the fields that will appear on the Form, their organization on the Form, and other optional information. It then creates the corresponding Form, including its visual interface and the supporting code. With a few mouse clicks, you can create elaborate data-entry or report Forms for your applications. Figure 8.1 shows a data-entry Form with the familiar editing buttons.

FIGURE 8.1:

A simple data-entry Form designed with the Data Form add-in

Here's a short segment of the code generated by the add-in:

```
Private Sub cmdDelete_Click()
  With datPrimaryRS.Recordset
    .Delete
    .MoveNext
    If .EOF Then .MoveLast
  End With
End Sub

Private Sub cmdRefresh_Click()
  'This is only needed for multi user apps
  datPrimaryRS.Refresh
End Sub
```

This code doesn't depend on the application. It's generic and performs basic operations in a data-entry application that uses the Data control. If you want additional validation tests or more specific error messages, you can tweak the code generated by the Wizard. The data-entry Form is automatically added to your project, and you can test and edit it as usual.

Designing Forms automatically (in other words, placing the appropriate controls on a Form, aligning them, and assigning initial values to them), as well as generating code for these controls, is one of the most useful things you can do with an add-in, and you will see an example of how this is done in the section "A Form Generator," later in this chapter. But first, we must explore the structure of the objects you will use when designing add-ins.

The VBIDE Class

To allow developers to enhance the development environment, Visual Basic provides the VBIDE class, which represents this environment. VBIDE stands for Visual Basic Integrated Development Environment, and it exposes all the objects needed to access the integrated environment's components (the various windows, menus, project components, the controls on a Form and the corresponding code, and so on). Every object you work with while designing an application can be accessed and manipulated through the properties and methods of the VBIDE class.

To see the objects exposed by the VBIDE class, follow these steps:

1. Start a new project, and then add a reference to the Microsoft Visual Basic 5.0 Extensibility class through the References dialog box.

2. Start the Object Browser.

3. Select the VBIDE Type Library, and you'll see its classes and their members, as shown in Figure 8.2.

FIGURE 8.2:

The Contained-VBControls class of the VBIDE object and its members

Figure 8.2 shows the members of the ContainedVBControl class, which represents a collection of VB controls that may reside on a Form or on a container control (for example, a Frame control). Its Add member is a method that allows you to add a control to this collection. Writing the code to manipulate the controls on a Form is rather easy, considering all the help provided by the Object Browser. However, you can't enter a few lines of code in the Immediate window or in a Command Button's Click event to test the objects of the VBIDE class. You must first generate an add-in project. It's similar to developing an ActiveX EXE server. You must first create it and then test it from within another instance of Visual Basic.

At this point, we should probably describe how you create an add-in, integrate it into the Visual Basic IDE, and then make it do something. Creating an add-in requires a few steps that are quite unique. Instead of getting into the details of building your "first add-in" and then examining the objects exposed by the IDE (which you need in order to program the add-in), we will start with an introduction to this object model. This discussion will help you understand what your add-ins can do. It will also help you understand the structure of the objects that allow you to access the IDE's components and its functionality and give you ideas for useful add-ins, which will streamline your development efforts. Then, we'll put these objects together to build many examples that manipulate the environment (add new commands to Visual Basic's menus, manipulate Forms and controls, react to events such as the deletion of a control on a Form, and so on). Some of these examples are lengthy, but you can use many of them as starting points for your add-in projects.

As we mentioned in Chapter 2, the Object Browser can practically replace the documentation, as long as you are familiar with the structure of an object model. If you are familiar with the concepts of relational databases, you can use the Object Browser to locate the objects of the DAO class you need and then locate their members. The same is true for the objects exposed by the VBIDE, but first you need to get acquainted with the VBIDE object model.

> **NOTE**
>
> In the following sections, you will see code segments demonstrating the most important aspects of the VBIDE object model. Unfortunately, you won't be able to test them immediately. The process of creating an add-in and integrating it in a Visual Basic project (which is the only way to test it) is rather involved. VBIDE is a complicated object, and, instead of presenting long lists of step-by-step procedures to carry out on your own, we will explain the basic principles of programming Visual Basic's environment through the object of the VBIDE object. Then, we are going to look at a number of useful examples. So, bear with us, and you will soon learn about building add-ins and incorporating them into your favorite development environment.

Using the Demo Add-In Project

All the examples we'll discuss in the first part of this chapter will be used later in the Demo add-in. If you want to use these examples and modify them as you go along, follow these steps:

1. Open the Demo project.

> **NOTE**
>
> You'll find the Demo project in the Chapter8/Demo folder on the CD that comes with this book.

2. Press F5 to run the project.

3. Break the project and enter the following line in the Immediate window:

```
AddToIni
```

4. Press F5 to resume execution.

The add-in has been registered, and you can connect it to another project.

5. Start another instance of VB5, and create a new Standard EXE project.

6. Choose Add-Ins ➤ Add-In Manager to open the Add-In Manager dialog box.

7. Check the My Add-In add-in, and click OK.

The Demo add-in has been added to the second instance of VB5, and you can activate it by clicking its name in the Add-Ins menu.

If you want to edit the add-in's code, to experiment with additional objects or properties, disconnect the add-in and then switch to the add-in project and interrupt it. At this point, you can edit the code or enter statements in the Immediate window. When you are done, resume execution by pressing F5 again, switch to the second instance of VB5, and connect the add-in again. (Why is it called My Add-In and not Demo? It's a bug in Visual Basic, which we explain in the sidebar "Changing Add-In Names," later in this chapter. You'll find a work-around in the same sidebar.)

Some Add-In Tips

As you're working with add-ins, here are some things to keep in mind:

- If you interrupt the execution of the add-in while it's connected, its name remains in the Add-Ins menu, but the add-in isn't connected. If you connect it again, its name will appear twice in the Add-Ins menu. Only the last instance of its name in the menu can be activated. The other one hangs there, but It won't react to the Click event. It will be removed when you shut down this instance of Visual Basic and start a new one.

- The add-in won't react in the test project's environment if the add-in project isn't running. Watch for this when you're troubleshooting and testing your add-ins.

- If you display message boxes from within your add-in or prompt the user for input with the InputBox function, the corresponding dialog boxes won't show up in the test project. Instead, you will get a warning that the other application isn't reacting. You must switch to the other instance of VB5 (the add-in project) to see the message box or input box and close it.

In general, testing and troubleshooting add-ins can be confusing. Use Debug.Print statements in the add-in's code instead of displaying message boxes, and be sure that the add-in is disconnected from the test project before you stop the add-in project. When the add-in is compiled to an EXE or a DLL file, you no longer need to run the add-in in a separate instance of Visual Basic, and these problems won't be an issue. But for this to happen, you must first make sure the add-in works.

If things get really messy, you can always shut down both instances of Visual Basic and start them again. In nearly all cases, when we had to restart add-in projects, it wasn't Visual Basic's fault. There was always a good explanation for why things went wrong—adding a new command to the wrong menu or leaving behind dead add-in commands on the Add-Ins menu. Knowing what caused the problem was, however, little consolation. When you are working with add-ins, you will make mistakes as usual, but because they affect the very environment in which you work, they will seem more catastrophic than the effects of mistakes you make in developing ActiveX components or regular VB applications.

VBInstance: The Environment Variable

To understand the objects exposed by the VBIDE class and their members, consider for a moment what an add-in should be able to do:

- It must expose the objects needed to manipulate the Visual Basic environment.

- It should provide objects that represent the various windows (the Code window, the Properties window, the Toolbox, and so on), the components of a project, and so on.

All these objects are properties of the root object, which represents the environment itself (just like every item in a database is accessed via an object variable that represents the open database).

The root component of every add-in is the *VBInstance* object variable, which represents the current instance of Visual Basic. All the components of the VBIDE object are accessed through the *VBInstance* variable. The name *VBInstance* isn't mandatory, but we have yet to see an add-in that doesn't use it. The *VBInstance* object variable is set by the add-in's code and only when the add-in is attached to a project. In the examples in the following sections, we'll use the *VBInstance* variable to access all the classes and members exposed by the VBIDE object, but we won't show you yet how this variable is created. It's the one variable that must exist in every add-in, and, for now, take it for granted.

The Window Object and the Windows Collection

The most obvious components of the Visual Basic IDE are its windows. The VBIDE class exposes an object that represents the various windows (the Code window, the Properties window, the Toolbox, and so on) and methods to manipulate these windows (change their location, make visible a specific line in the Code window, and so on), the Window objects. All these windows are members of the Windows collection, which is made up of Window objects. If you've opened the Object Browser window for the VBIDE class, scroll down to the last two classes:

Window, a class that represents a window in the environment

Windows, a collection of Window objects

If you look at the members of these two classes, you'll see that the Window object has a number of properties. The Caption, Width, Height, Top, and Left properties need not be explained any further. These properties let you rearrange the various windows of the IDE on the screen. The SetFocus method lets you move the focus to a specific window. One of the most useful properties of the Window object is the Type property, which returns the window's type. The declaration of this property in the Object Browser's description section is:

```
Property Type As vbext_WindowType
```

All constants of the VBIDE object begin with the prefix *vbext*. Scroll up the Classes list to locate the entry vbext_WindowType, and select it. It's an enumerated type with the following values:

vbext_wt_Browser

vbext_wt_CodeWindow

vbext_wt_ColorPalette

vbext_wt_Designer

vbext_wt_Find

vbext_wt_FindReplace

vbext_wt_Immediate

vbext_wt_LinkedWindowFrame

vbext_wt_Locals

vbext_wt_MainWindow

vbext_wt_Preview

vbext_wt_ProjectWindow

vbext_wt_PropertyWindow

vbext_wt_Toolbox

vbext_wt_ToolWindow

vbext_wt_Watch

The constant names are self-explanatory. The vbext_wt_Designer signifies that the window is a designer (a Form's or UserControl's design window). In this type of window, you can add new instances of controls. As you can see, you indeed have access to all the windows the user can open in the IDE, and you can figure out the type of each window by examining its Type property.

If you look at the members of the Windows class, you will see that it contains two of the standard members of a collection:

- Count
- Item

The Window object is special in the sense that you can't create new Window objects and add them to the Windows collection with the Add method; nor can you remove existing windows with the Remove method. This is why the Add and Remove methods aren't exposed. (Sure, you can close certain windows, but you can't remove them from Visual Basic's environment.)

To access the windows in the current instance of the Visual Basic IDE, you must set up a loop such as the following:

```
Dim iWindow As VBIDE.Window
For Each iWindow In VBInstance.Windows
    If Not iWindow.Visible Then iWindow.Visible = True
Next
```

Alternatively, you can use a For...Next loop such as the following:

```
For iWindow =1 To VBInstance.Windows.Count
    If Not Windows.Item(iWindow).Visible Then _
        Windows.Item(iWindow).Visible = True
Next
```

Notice here that the Item property is the default member of a collection, so you can omit it. In other words, the element Windows.Item(iWindow) can also be accessed as Windows(iWindow). In this book, we'll use the explicit notation. You can also examine the type of a window by comparing its Type property with the constants listed earlier.

So, can you access an application's code through the Code window? You can indeed access an application's code, but not through the Windows collection (see the CodeModule object, later in this chapter).

The current, active window in the IDE can be read by the MainWindow property of the VBE object. To find out the type of the active window, use an If statement such as the following one:

```
Dim currentWin As Window
Set currentWin = VBE.MainWindow
If currentWin.Type = vbext_wt_Designer Then ...
```

This If statement ensures that the current window is a designer window, which means you can place controls on it.

The AddIn Object and AddIns Collection

The AddIn object represents an add-in in the development environment. The add-ins can be accessed through the AddIns collection, which has the same members as the Windows collection (basically you can add new add-ins and disconnect add-ins already connected to the IDE).

We won't discuss this object any further in this book. It's a rather advanced topic and not really needed in developing typical add-ins. You can use it from within an add-in's code during initialization to find out whether another, related add-in has already been connected. To access the add-ins already connected to an application (in other words, the add-ins whose names appear in the Add-Ins menu), use a loop similar to the one we presented for the Windows collection and then examine its Connect property.

The VBProject Object and VBProjects Collection

VBProject is one of the top-level objects of the VBIDE class, and it represents a Visual Basic project. If the current instance of the Visual Basic IDE contains a project group, the VBProjects collection can access each project in the group. To scan the VBProjects collection, use a loop such as this:

```
Dim iProject As VBProject
For Each iProject In VBInstance.VBProjects
    Debug.Print iProject.Name
Next
```

The VBProject object has a number of properties, including:

- Name, which is the project's name

- Type, which returns the type of the project

- IsDirty, which returns a Boolean value that indicates whether a project was edited after the last time it was saved

- VBComponent, which represents a project's component, such as a Form, a module, and so on

As you have guessed, the components of a project can be accessed through the VBComponents collection. The VBComponent object is one of the most commonly used objects in programming the IDE, and we'll examine it in detail.

If you look at the members of the VBProjects collection in the Object Browser, you will see that this collection has an Add member. Using the Add member, you can add a new project to the current project group. Creating an entire project in code is quite a task, so the common way to add a new project to a project group is with the AddFromFile method, which adds a project already stored on disk to the current project group. The VBProjects collection contains a number of properties that are not related to collection. The StartProject property, for instance, returns (or sets) the project that will start executing when the F5 key is pressed. Finally, the VBProjects collection recognizes four events, which are shown in Table 8.1.

TABLE 8.1: The Events of the VBProjects Collection

Event	What It Does
ItemActivated	Notifies the add-in that a project was activated
ItemAdded	Notifies the add-in that a project was added
ItemRemoved	Notifies the add-in that a project was removed
ItemRenamed	Notifies the add-in that a project was renamed

All these events pass a VBProject object as an argument. This is the project that was activated, added, or deleted. When a project is renamed, the ItemRenamed event passes two arguments: the project being renamed and the old name of the project (they are both string values).

Finally, the FileName property of the Projects collection specifies the full path name of the project's VBG file on the disk. To save the project to another folder, use the SaveAs method. If the project hasn't been saved yet, the FileName property is a blank string. In this case, you must either create a new file name (you will most likely base the file name on the project's name) or activate the Save As command in the File menu to prompt the user for a location and file name for the project. (Yes, you can access the menu commands too and activate them from within your code.)

The active project in a project group is returned by the ActiveVBProject property of the *VBInstance* object variable. The name of the active project is given by the property VBInstance.ActiveVBProject.Name and is the name specified in the Project window. If the user hasn't changed it, it's something like Project1, Project2, and so on.

NOTE   There is no object that represents a project group.

The VBComponent Object and VBComponents Collection

The VBProject object represents a single project, but each project has a number of components (Forms, classes, Property Pages, and so on). To access the components of a VBProject object, you use the VBComponents collection. Each member of the VBComponents collection is a VBComponent object, whose members you can look up in the Object Browser. They are similar to the members of the VBProjects collection. This shouldn't surprise you because a project group has multiple components (projects) just as a project can have multiple components. That's why the two collections have similar members and even support the same events. The VBComponents collection supports two more events, which are shown at the bottom of Table 8.2 (the events unique to the VBComponents collection are the last two in the table).

TABLE 8.2: The Events of the VBComponents Collection

Event	What It Does
ItemActivated	Notifies the add-in that a project component was activated
ItemAdded	Notifies the add-in that a project component was added
ItemRemoved	Notifies the add-in that a project component was removed
ItemRenamed	Notifies the add-in that a project component was renamed

TABLE 8.2: The Events of the VBComponents Collection (continued)

Event	What It Does
ItemReloaded	Notifies the add-in that a project component was reloaded from disk
ItemSelected	Notifies the add-in that a project component was selected (became the active component)

The VBComponents collection also supports the StartupObject property, which returns the startup component of the current project. The Startup component is usually a Form, but it could be the Main subroutine or even None. The programmer can specify the startup component of each project in the Project Properties dialog box (choose Project ➤ Project Properties). From within the add-in's code, you can set the value of the StartupObject property to the name of a startup component (which is usually a Form).

You can examine all the components of the active project with a loop such as the following:

```
Set thisProject = VBInstance.ActiveVBProject
pComponents = thisProject.VBComponents.Count
For i = 1 To pComponents
    MsgBox "VB Component " & _
        thisProject.VBComponents.Item(i).Name
 ' The component type is given by the property
 ' thisProject.VBComponents.Item(i).Type
 ' and its name by the property
 ' thisProject.VBComponents.Item(i).Name
 ' is the startup object the current component?
 ' If thisProject.VBComponents.Item(i).StartupObject = _
 '     thisProject.VBComponents.Item(i).Name

Next
```

The object variable *thisProject* must be declared with type VBProject and is assigned the current project in the current instance of VB. The number of components in the active project is given by the property VBComponents.Count. The Type property of the VBComponent object can have one of the following values:

vbext_ct_ActiveXDesigner

vbext_ct_ClassModule

vbext_ct_DocObject

vbext_ct_MSForm

vbext_ct_PropPage

vbext_ct_RelatedDocument

vbext_ct_ResFile

vbext_ct_StdModule

vbext_ct_UserControl

vbext_ct_VBForm

vbext_ct_VBMDIForm

As usual, the names of the constants are self-explanatory, and they reflect the types of components you can add to a project through the Project menu. Visual Basic can handle all these components (for example, return the controls on a Form, as you will see shortly, or the code for an event handler), with the exception of the Resource File component. Resource Files are created with the Resource Editor, outside Visual Basic, and you can't access their contents from within your add-in.

The expressions that represent the components of a project (or any objects under the root object, for that matter) can be lengthy. To shorten these expressions in your code, you can declare object variables, such as the *thisComponent* variable, which will hold a reference to a project component:

```
Dim thisComponent As VBComponent
```

You can then assign a project component to this variable by using the following statement:

```
ThisComponent = thisProject.VBComponents.Item(i)
```

You can also use the name of the *thisComponent* variable in place of the object expression that represents a component.

The SelectedVBComponent Object

As you recall, the current project is given by the property VBInstance.ActiveVBProject. You can also access the currently selected component in the active project, only the property you must use this time doesn't have the word *active* in its name. It's the

SelectedVBComponent of the *VBInstance* object variable. The following statement prints the name of the active project and the name of the selected component in the active project:

```
Debug.Print "The selected project is " & _
    VBInstance.ActiveVBProject.Name & vbCrLf & _
    "The selected component is " & VBInstance.SelectedVBComponent.Name
```

Let's look at a code segment that puts together the properties discussed in this and the last section to print the names of all the components in a project and the name of the selected component. The code uses a loop to scan all the projects in the Project window of the IDE (there is no property that represents a project group) and a nested loop to scan all the components of the current project. Here's the listing:

```
Dim thisProject As VBProject
Dim nProjects As Integer, nComponents As Integer
Dim i As Integer, j As Integer
Dim projectName As String

nProjects = VBInstance.VBProjects.Count
For i = 1 To nProjects
    Set thisProject = VBInstance.VBProjects.Item(i)
    projectName = VBInstance.VBProjects.Item(i).Name
    nComponents = thisProject.VBComponents.Count
    For j = 1 To nComponents
        MsgBox "PROJECT " & projectName & vbCrLf & "Component #" & _
        j & "    " & thisProject.VBComponents.Item(j).Name
    Next
Next
MsgBox "The selected project is " & VBInstance.ActiveVBProject.Name & _
        vbCrLf & "The selected component is " & _
        VBInstance.SelectedVBComponent.Name
```

This code segment is straightforward. If you have programmed with objects before, you can certainly understand how the VBIDE objects are used to scan the components of a project group (the outer loop) and the components of each project (the inner loop). Here's the structure of a test project, whose components will be listed in the Immediate window. Figure 8.3 shows the Project window of the test project with the components listed in Table 8.3.

FIGURE 8.3:

A test project with all the types of components you can add to a VB project

TABLE 8.3: The Components of the Test Project

PROJECT1

Forms	Form1, Form2
Modules	Module1
Class Modules	Class1, Class2
User Controls	UserControl1
Property Pages	PropertyPage1

PROJECT2

Forms	Form1, Form2, Form3
Modules	Module1, Module2
Class Modules	Class1, Class2, Class3
Designers	UserConnection1

The code segment we just presented printed the following lines in the Immediate window. Notice that some of the components in the second project are out of order. The order in which the components are printed reflects the order in which they were added to the project. The last two lines print the name of the active project and the name of the currently selected component in this project.

```
PROJECT Project1
Component #1  Form1
PROJECT Project1
Component #2  Form2
PROJECT Project1
Component #3  Module1
PROJECT Project1
Component #4  Class1
PROJECT Project1
Component #5  Class2
PROJECT Project1
Component #6  UserControl1
PROJECT Project1
Component #7  PropertyPage1
PROJECT Project2
Component #1  Form1
PROJECT Project2
Component #2  Form2
PROJECT Project2
Component #3  Form3
PROJECT Project2
Component #4  Module1
PROJECT Project2
Component #5  Class1
PROJECT Project2
Component #6  Module2
PROJECT Project2
Component #7  Class2
PROJECT Project2
Component #8  Class3
PROJECT Project2
Component #9  UserConnection1

The selected project is Project2
The selected component is Module2
```

The VBControls and ContainedVBControls Collections

OK, we've worked our way from the Visual Basic environment down to the project components. If we can access the controls on each Form (or UserControl object) and the code behind each component, we'll be ready to develop Wizards such as the ones that come with Visual Basic. To access the controls on a Form, you use the VBControls collection (made up of VBControl objects) or the ContainedVBControls collection (also made up of VBControl objects). To access the code, you use the CodeModule object, which is described in the next section.

The VBControl object represents a VB control (built-in or custom) object. To access the controls on a Form, use the VBControls collection, which contains a VBControl object for each control on the current component (Form or UserControl object). As expected, this collection exposes the standard collection members (Add, Remove, Count, and Item) and recognizes the three events shown in Table 8.4.

TABLE 8.4: The Events of the VBControls Collection

Event	What It Does
ItemAdded	Notifies the add-in that a new control was added to the current component
ItemRemoved	Notifies the add-in that a control was removed from the current component
ItemRenamed	Notifies the add-in that a control on the current component was renamed

If the object variable *thisForm* represents a Form in the current project, the following loop will scan all the controls on the Form with the help of the VBControls collection and print their names:

```
For iControl = 1 To thisForm.VBControls.Count
    Debug.Print_
        thisForm.VBControls.Item(iControl).Properties("Name")
Next
```

The VBControls collection contains all the controls on a Form. But as you know, not all controls may be sited directly on the Form. Some controls may reside on other controls, called *containers*. A typical container control is the Frame control, which is commonly used to group Option buttons. If you want to know not only all the names of the controls that live on the Form, but the control they belong to, you must use the ContainedVBControls collection. The ContainedVBControls collection is made up of VBControl objects too, but it contains only the controls on a container. If the object variable *thisForm* represents a Form, the following loop will print the names of the controls on the Form:

```
For iControl = 1 To thisForm.ContainedVBControls.Count
    Set thisControl = _
        thisForm.ContainedVBControls.Item(iControl)
    Debug.Print thisControl.Properties("Name")
Next
```

If the Form contains the Frame1 control, which in turn contains a few Command Buttons, this loop prints the name of the Frame1 control, but not the names of the controls on the Frame control. Just like the members of the VBComponents collection, the controls are printed in the order in which they were placed on the container. The object variable *thisControl* must be declared with type VBControl.

In programming the Visual Basic environment, we commonly need to access controls, grouped according to the control to which they belong. The code for scanning the controls on a Form and then the controls contained on each control, to any level, isn't complicated, but it is recursive. Let's revise the previous code so that it examines each control on the Form for a contained control. The previous code segment remains as is, but after printing the name of the current control, we'll call a subroutine, the ShowContainedControls() subroutine, that scans for contained controls. This subroutine must accept as an argument a *VBControl* object variable, which represents the current control. Here is the main loop's code:

```
For iControl = 1 To thisForm.ContainedVBControls.Count
    Set thisControl = thisForm.ContainedVBControls.Item(iControl)
    Debug.Print thisControl.Properties("Name")
    ShowContainedControls thisControl
Next
```

The ShowContainedControls() subroutine accepts as an argument the control whose name was just printed and scans it for contained controls. In its simplest form, it is:

```
Sub ShowContainedControls(thisControl As VBControl)
Dim iControl As Integer

    If thisControl.ContainedVBControls.Count = 0 Then Exit Sub
    For iControl = 1 To thisControl.ContainedVBControls.Count
        Debug.Print thisControl.ContainedVBControls.Item_
            (iControl).Properties("Name")
    Next

End Sub
```

This subroutine prints the names of the controls contained on the control *thisControl*, but not any controls contained by its container control. Now, that's a bit unusual, but because it is possible to nest contained controls at more than two levels, we should call another subroutine, from within this loop, to display the names of any controls that are possibly contained within the current control. This subroutine exists already. It's ShowContainedControls(), which must be called recursively. Here's the code of the subroutine that will scan contained controls in any level:

```
Sub ShowContainedControls(thisControl As VBControl)
Dim iControl As Integer
Dim newControl As VBControl

    If thisControl.ContainedVBControls.Count = 0 Then Exit Sub
    For iControl = 1 To thisControl.ContainedVBControls.Count
        Debug.Print thisControl.ContainedVBControls.Item_
            (iControl).Properties("Name")
        Set newControl = _
            thisControl.ContainedVBControls.Item(iControl)
        ShowContainedControls newControl
    Next
End Sub
```

This code is quite simple, as long as you are familiar with recursive procedures. The ShowContainedControls() subroutine calls itself to carry out an identical task. Each time, however, it is called with a different argument (the *newControl* object variable). The actual code in the Demo project contains a few additional lines, to indent the contained controls under the name of the control that contains them. Here, we've skipped these lines to make the code of the subroutine easier to read.

Figure 8.4 shows a Form with several container controls and containers within containers. The names of the controls are the default ones, so they are identical to their captions (some controls have the same caption, which means they are members of a control array). We are going to see how the controls on this Form can be accessed with the VBControls and ContainedVBControls collections.

FIGURE 8.4:

A Form with controls contained within other controls in three levels

Let's look at the list of control names that the two code segments will print in the Immediate window. The code segment that uses the VBControls collection will print all the controls of the Form, regardless of whether they are sited directly on the Form or on another control:

```
Frame1(1)
Text1(1)
Text1(2)
Text1(3)
Text1(4)
Label1(1)
Label1(2)
Label1(3)
Label1(4)
Option4(0)
Option4(2)
Option4(1)
Picture1
Check1
Check3
Check2
Option3
Option2
Option1
Command2
Command1
```

The code segment that uses the ContainedVBControls collection (and calls the ShowContainedControls()) subroutine will display all the controls too, but contained controls will be listed under their container's name (they are indented in the following listing). If you omit the call to the ShowContainedControls() subroutine, the second code segment prints only the names of the controls sited directly on the Form.

The button All ContainedControls of the Demo add-in would also print the names of controls sited on other controls that are contained already, and it would indent them properly as shown here. Besides the grouping of the controls according to their container, they are not otherwise ordered within the group to which they belong.

```
Frame1(1)
    Text1(1)
    Text1(2)
    Text1(3)
```

```
        Text1(4)
        Label1(1)
        Label1(2)
        Label1(3)
        Label1(4)
    Picture1
        Option4(0)
        Check1
        Option4(2)
        Option4(1)
        Check3
        Check2
    Option3
    Option2
    Option1
    Command2
    Command1
```

The CodeModule Object

And we've come to the last component of a project you can access through the VBIDE object: the project's code. As you know, the project's code is scattered in the various events of the controls and procedures. Each component's code is separate from any other component's code, so you must access each code module in the component to which it belongs. In the context of this discussion, a code module is the smallest, self-sufficient piece of code in the Code window. It could be a variable declaration, an event handler, a general procedure, or a Property procedure.

To access the code modules in the current project, use the CodeModule object of the VBIDE. CodeModule is also a property of the VBComponent object and represents the code behind the component. The CodeModule object exposes many properties and methods for accessing the code's modules (declarations, events, methods, and so on). First, it exposes the Members collection, which is made up of CodeModule objects that represent the code module contained in the current component's Code window. All variable declarations, event handlers, property procedures, and general procedures (functions and subroutines) of a component can be accessed through the CodeModule object. Because CodeModule is not a collection, the individual modules must be accessed via the Members property, and not via the Item property.

This may confuse you at first, but CodeModule is an object, not a collection. To access the individual code modules, you must use the CodeModule's Members property, which is a collection.

Let's say you have created a variable that represents the current project:

```
Set thisProject = VBInstance.ActiveVBProject
```

The first component of the current project is:

```
thisProject.VBComponents.Item(1)
```

To access the controls of this component, you have to make sure that it is a Form component and then use the ContainedVBControls or VBControls collection, as discussed in the last section. To access the code behind the module, you use the CodeModule property:

```
thisProject.VBComponents.Item(1).CodeModule
```

This expression represents the code of the module—the entire code on a Form or a class module, for example. To access each of the components, you use the Members property, which is a collection of CodeModule objects. According to the documentation, Members is not a collection. But it looks and behaves like a collection, so we are going to use the term *collection* to describe it. The number of code modules in the first component of the project is given by the property:

```
thisProject.VBComponents.Item(1).CodeModule.Members.Count
```

Before we proceed with any examples, let's take a look at the basic properties and methods of the Members collection of the CodeModule object. Each object of this collection is a CodeModule object, so its members are listed under the CodeModule class. The basic properties of the CodeModule object are listed in Table 8.5, and the basic methods are listed in Table 8.6.

TABLE 8.5: The Basic Properties of the CodeModule Object

Property	Description
CountOfDeclarationLines	The number of lines of code in the declarations section in a code module.
CountOfLines	The number of lines of code in a code module.
Lines(startLine, count)	This property acts like a method and returns the specified block of lines (returns *count* lines starting at *startLine*).
ProcBodyLine(procedureName, procedureType)	Returns the first line of the specified procedure.
ProcCountLines(procedureName, procedureType)	Returns the number of lines in the specified procedure.

TABLE 8.5: The Basic Properties of the CodeModule Object (continued)

Property	Description
ProcStartLine(procedureName, procedureType)	Returns the line in which the specified procedure begins.
ProcOfLine(Line, procedureType)	Returns the name of the procedure that contains the specified line.

TABLE 8.6 : The Methods of the CodeModule Object

Method	What It Does
DeleteLines(startLine, count)	Deletes *count* lines in the code module, starting at *startLine*.
InsertLine(lineNumber, codeLine)	Inserts one or more code lines at the location specified by the *numberLine* argument.
ReplaceLine(lineNumber, codeLine)	Replaces the specified line of code with the line(s) *codeLine*.
Find()	Searches a specified module for a specific string. See the members description in the Object Browser for an explanation of its arguments.
CreateEventProc(eventName, objectName)	Creates the specified event procedure for the specified object.

Using the members of the CodeModule, you can access the code of a project, edit it, and even create new procedures from within your add-in. We will create a complete add-in that places controls on a Form and code in the Form's code module. The examples here are simple, and they are meant to clarify a few points about using the CodeModule object. You will see more practical examples in the section "A Form Generator," later in this chapter.

Let's start with the basic loop structure that examines each member of the code module of a component.

```
' Set up an array with member type names
Dim MemberType(5) As String
MemberType(vbext_mt_Event) = "EVENT    "
MemberType(vbext_mt_Method) = "METHOD   "
```

```
MemberType(vbext_mt_Const) = "CONSTANT"
MemberType(vbext_mt_Property) = "PROPERTY"
MemberType(vbext_mt_Variable) = "VARIABLE"
''''''''''''''''''''''''''''''''''''''''''''''
Set thisProject = VBInstance.ActiveVBProject
pComponents = thisProject.VBComponents.Count
For i = 1 To pComponents
    Debug.Print "VB Component " & thisProject.VBComponents.Item(i).Name
    pMembers = _
thisProject.VBComponents.Item(i).CodeModule.Members.Count
    For j = 1 To pMembers
        Set thisCodeModule = _
thisProject.VBComponents.Item(i).CodeModule
        Debug.Print MemberType(thisCodeModule.Members.Item(j).Type) &_
          "  " & thisProject.VBComponents.Item(i).CodeModule._
          Members.Item(j).Name
    Next
Next
```

The first line after the assignment sets the object variable *thisProject* to the active project. The code then sets up a loop (the outer loop) that scans each component in the project and prints the name of each component and the number of code lines in the component's code module. Then, for each project component, the program calculates the number of code members and sets up a nested loop, which prints each code component's type and name. Notice the lines at the beginning of the code segment that set up an array with the names of the CodeModule's Type property values. The Type property is an enumerated variable and can have one of the values in Table 8.7.

TABLE 8.7: The Possible Types of a CodeModule Object

Value	What It Is
vbext_mt_Const	Constant declaration
vbext_mt_Variable	Variable declaration
vbext_mt_Event	Event declaration
vbext_mt_Method	Method declaration
vbext_mt_Property	Property declaration (Let, Get, or Set property procedure)

The section "Listing a Project's Code Components" demonstrates how to use this property when accessing code components.

The number of code components in a project component is given by the following expression:

```
thisProject.VBComponents.Item(i).CodeModule.Members.Count
```

This is the number of items in the Members collection. To access each code component, you must access a specific item of the collection and read its Type property. The full expression is:

```
thisProject.VBComponents.Item(i).CodeModule.Members.Item(j).Type
```

Object expressions can get really long. Surprisingly, these long expressions are easier to write—especially if you have the Auto List Members option turned on—than they are to read. To keep code lines shorter, you can create intermediate object variables. For the specific example, we can use the *thisCodeModule* object variable, which is of CodeModule type and is set with the following statement:

```
Set thisCodeModule = thisProject.VBComponents.Item(i).CodeModule
```

You can then access individual code components with an expression such as the following:

```
thisModule.Members.Item(i)
```

This object represents a CodeModule, and not the module's code (the actual text). To access the code, you must use one of the properties listed in Table 8.5 or one of the methods listed in Table 8.6 to edit the module's lines. In the following sections, you will see examples that scan the procedures and declarations of a code module, and you will see examples of how to edit a project's code.

Now that we have looked at the major objects of the VBIDE class, we are ready to look at a few examples. First, we'll examine the structure of an add-in. Next, we'll go through the steps that are unique in building and testing add-ins, and then we'll work through a few practical add-ins.

Building an Add-In

Building an add-in isn't much different from building regular VB applications. Basically, an Add-In project type creates the skeleton of an add-in, which you can flesh out with your own code. Unlike VB projects, however, add-ins have special requirements, and you must understand them in order to develop your own add-ins that can be smoothly integrated into the Visual Basic environment.

As we mentioned at the beginning of this chapter, add-ins are displayed in the Add-Ins menu. To add an add-in to this menu, you choose Add-Ins ➤ Add-In Manager to open the Add-In Manager dialog box. You then select the name of the add-in. Something similar happens with ActiveX controls: The user selects the desired control in the Components dialog box. The difference is that ActiveX controls don't require any special code to appear in the Toolbox; neither do you have to provide any code to be executed every time the user clicks the control's icon.

With add-ins, you must supply the code to append the add-in's name to the Add-Ins menu yourself, and you must supply the code to react to the click of the add-in's name (after all, it's a menu command). Not only that, but you must register your add-in manually. These extra steps require some lines of code, which may even throw you off if you haven't developed add-ins in the past. Since the structure of an add-in is always the same, we'll start by examining the default Add-In project type. We'll build a simple add-in that connects and disconnects itself to the IDE and displays a Form when selected in the Add-Ins menu.

The AddIn Project Template

Start a New project, and in the New Project window, select AddIn. Visual Basic will add three folders in the Project window:

> **Forms**, which contains the Forms that will be displayed by the add-in (if any)
>
> **Modules,** which contains the add-in module that in turn contains a single function that adds the add-in to the VBADDIN.INI file
>
> **Class Modules**, which contains the Connect class module in which all the code for connecting the add-in to the IDE and disconnecting it from the IDE resides

These are the three basic components of an add-in. The Connect class module contains the code that connects and disconnects the add-in. The AddIn module contains an API function declaration and the AddToIni function (explained in the next section). Finally, the frmAddIn Form is the add-in's visible interface (if the add-in has one).

You can change the default names. In this book, we'll use the default names for the AddIn Module and the Connect Class Module, since they appear in every add-in, and we'll use a different name for the Form.

The AddIn Module

Let's start with the AddIn module.

Code 8.1:	The AddIn Module

```
Option Explicit
Declare Function WritePrivateProfileString& Lib "Kernel32" Alias
"WritePrivateProfileStringA" (ByVal AppName$, ByVal KeyName$, ByVal
keydefault$, ByVal FileName$)


'====================================================================
'this sub should be executed from the Immediate window
'in order to get this app added to the VBADDIN.INI file
'you must change the name in the 2nd argument to reflect
'the correct name of your project
'====================================================================
Sub AddToINI()
    Dim ErrCode As Long
    ErrCode = WritePrivateProfileString("Add-Ins32",
"MyAddIn.Connect",_
                "0", "vbaddin.ini")
End Sub
```

This function adds the add-in to the VBADDIN.INI file. This file contains information about the available add-ins, and Visual Basic reads this file each time the user selects the Add-In Manager command to connect a new add-in. The VBADDINI.INI file contains one line per add-in, and it resides in the Windows folder. It's a text file that you can open with a text editor. Here are the contents of a typical VBADDIN.INI file:

```
[Add-Ins32]
VBSDIAddIn.Connect=0
DataToolsAddIn.Connect=0
AppWizard.Wizard=0
WizMan.Connect=0
ClassBuilder.Wizard=0
```

```
AddInToolbar.Connect=0
ControlWiz.Wizard=0
DataFormWizard.Wizard=0
ActiveXDocumentWizard.Wizard=0
PropertyPageWizard.Wizard=0
APIDeclarationLoader.Connect=0
Demo.Connect=1
DelCode.Connect=0
```

The last two lines in this sample file correspond to two custom add-ins we are going to build later in this chapter, the Demo and Code Remover add-ins. The value following the name of the add-in determines whether the add-in will be activated automatically as soon as its loaded (if its value is 1) or only if the user selects it in the Add-Ins menu (if its value is 0).

You must manually call the AddToINI() function to add the add-in's name to the VBADDIN.INI file. If you plan to distribute the add-in, you must either write a simple application that appends a line such as the following to the VBADDIN.INI file:

```
DelCode.Connect=0
```

or you must create a setup program for the add-in with the Application Setup Wizard.

The first argument of the AddToIni() function must be the string "Add-Ins32" for all add-ins. The second argument is the name of the add-in project, followed by the name of the class module that implements the class. All the examples in this chapter use the name *Connect* for the add-in's class module. The third argument specifies whether the add-in will be activated as soon as it's connected or only when the user clicks its name in the Add-Ins menu, and the last argument is the same as the numeric value stored in the VBADDIN.INI file.

The Add-In template uses the name *MyAddIn* as the name of the add-in (which is the project name), and you should change it. If you do not change it before the add-in is registered on your system, you will have to remove the corresponding entries manually from the Registry. *Connect* is the name of the class module that contains the initialization code.

Changing Add-In Names

Changing the name of the add-in in the Project window won't have any effect on the add-in's name as it appears in the Connect Add-In dialog box. This is probably a bug in Visual Basic; it seems there's no simple way to change an add-in's default name (MyAddin) from within the development environment.

The only way we know to change an add-in's name is to manually edit its entry in the Registry. After you create an add-in's EXE or DLL file, follow these steps:

1. Open the Registry (choose Start ➤ Run, and type **RegEdit** in the Open box).

2. Locate the first instance of the string "My Add-In." You will see the key (Default) in the right pane of the Registry Editor's window.

3. Right-click the key's name, and from the shortcut menu, select Modify to open the Edit String dialog box.

4. Now, enter the new name of the add-in and click OK.

5. Repeat the same process until no more instances of the string "My Add-In" are found.

6. Press F5 to activate the changes.

7. Switch to Visual Basic, and choose Add-Ins ➤ Add-In Manager.

Now, at last, you will see your add-in with its proper name.

If you have created many add-ins and haven't changed their default names, you can find out whether an add-in registered as My Add-In is the one you are interested in by examining the value of its LocalServer32 key (it appears under the Default key). This is the name of the EXE or DLL that implements the add-in, and it will help you decipher whether it's the add-in you want to rename.

The Connect Class Module

The Connect class module is the most important part of an add-in, and most of you will not be familiar with it. The Connect class exposes various members, just as any class does. The minimum Connect class must provide three procedures, one to do each of the following:

- Initialize the add-in
- Disconnect it from the IDE
- React when the user clicks the name of the add-in in the Add-Ins menu

The third procedure isn't really required, but it's disconcerting for users to click a menu command and receive no feedback.

> **NOTE**
>
> The Connect class module implements an interface for the IDTExtensibility class, and you can't omit any of its members, even if they contain no code. Some methods are usually blank, but you must still insert a comment line. If you do not, the editor will remove them.

The Connect class starts with the following declarations:

```
Option Explicit

Implements IDTExtensibility

Public FormDisplayed As Boolean
Public VBInstance As VBIDE.VBE
Dim mcbMenuCommandBar As Office.CommandBarControl
Dim mfrmAddIn As New frmAddIn
Public WithEvents MenuHandler As CommandBarEvents
```

The following line:

```
Implements IDTExtensibility
```

adds a new interface to the project (procedures you must code explicitly). *Form-Displayed* is an auxiliary variable, used by add-ins that display Forms. *VBInstance* is an object variable that represents the Visual Basic IDE. Later in the code, we'll use this variable to access the active project (VBInstance.ActiveVBProject), the components of the active project (VBInstance.ActiveVBProject.VBComponents), and so on. The *mcbMenuCommandBar* is another object variable that represents a command in the IDE's Command Bar. This variable will be used to add the add-in's name to the Add-Ins menu. (We will discuss later how to manipulate the menus of the IDE and how to intercept menu commands.)

The *mfrmAddIn* variable represents the add-in's Form (many add-ins don't have a visible user interface). Finally, the *MenuHandler* object variable will be used to program the Click event of the command that corresponds to the add-in.

Then comes the code required to initialize and install the add-in. We will examine the basic procedures of an add-in in an order different from that in which they appear in the class module.

NOTE   The Connect class contains all the methods required to connect and disconnect the add-in. The IDTExtensibility_OnConnection() procedure, for example, is a method of the class. To you, the VB programmer, it looks like an event, but it's a method of the IDTExtensibility class. Visual Basic doesn't generate an OnConnection event; it simply calls the OnConnection method of the IDTExtensibility object, and you must provide all the members of the Connect class, even if this means placing a single comment line in them.

Connecting the Add-In

The OnConnection method of the IDTExtensibility class is called when Visual Basic installs the add-in, and it contains the code needed to initialize and install the add-in.

Code 8.2:   **The Default Implementation of the OnConnection Method**

```
Private Sub IDTExtensibility_OnConnection(ByVal VBInst As Object, ByVal
ConnectMode As vbext_ConnectMode, ByVal AddInInst As VBIDE.AddIn, cus-
tom() As Variant)

    On Error GoTo error_handler

    'save the vb instance
    Set VBInstance = VBInst

    'this is a good place to set a breakpoint and
    'test various addin objects, properties and methods
    Debug.Print VBInst.FullName
```

```
    If ConnectMode = vbext_cm_External Then
        'Used by the wizard toolbar to start this wizard
        Me.Show
    Else
        Set mcbMenuCommandBar = AddToAddInCommandBar("My AddIn")
        'sink the event
        Set Me.MenuHandler =
            VBInst.Events.CommandBarEvents(mcbMenuCommandBar)
    End If

    If ConnectMode = vbext_cm_AfterStartup Then
        If GetSetting(App.Title, "Settings", "DisplayOnConnect", "0") =
            "1" Then
            'set this to display the form on connect
            Me.Show
        End If
    End If

    Exit Sub

error_handler:

    MsgBox Err.Description

End Sub
```

Visual Basic passes a reference to the current instance of the IDE to this event with the argument VBInst. This reference is saved in the *VBInstance* public variable so that all other parts of the code can use it. The second argument, ConnectMode, determines how the add-in was connected. Table 8.8 shows its values.

TABLE 8.8: The Values of the ConnectMode Argument of the OnConnection Method

Value	Description
vbext_cm_AfterStartup	The add-in was started with the project.
vbext_cm_Startup	The add-in was started before any project was opened.
vbext_cm_External	The add-in was started by another program.

The third argument is another object variable that represents the add-in itself. The last argument, custom(), is an array that contains user-defined data.

The code examines the value of the ConnectMode argument to figure out how the add-in was started. If it was started by another add-in, it displays the Form. If not, it adds the name of the add-in (you must replace My AddIn with your add-in's name) to the Add-Ins menu with the AddToAddInCommandBar() function. This is not a built-in function. You can find it later in the code, but you need not change it either. Even if the add-in contains no visible interface, you must place its name in the Add-Ins menu so that users know that the add-in has been installed.

Handling the Add-Ins Menu Events

The AddToAddInCommandBar() function returns an object that represents a menu command. A reference to this object is stored in the *mcbMenuCommandBar* public variable, which is used later in the code to monitor the Click event of the add-in's name. The following line:

```
Set Me.MenuHandler = VBInst.Events.CommandBarEvents(mcbMenuCommandBar)
```

prepares the *MenuHandler* object to detect the events of the *mcbMenuCommandBar* object (it reports the Click event only). If you open the Objects list in the Code window, you will see the name of the MenuHandler object. Select it, and then open the Events list, which contains a single event, Click.

Code 8.3:   The Click Event

```
Private Sub MenuHandler_Click(ByVal CommandBarControl As Object, _
        handled As Boolean, CancelDefault As Boolean)
    Me.Show
End Sub
```

The Click event displays the add-in's Form. If your add-in has no visible interface, you could use this event to display a message box or an About box with information about the add-in. This is how an add-in's name is added to the Add-Ins menu and how the add-in handles the Click event, which is triggered every time the user selects it. You'll be using the same code for nearly every add-in you build. (We'll discuss the CommandBarControl object in detail later in this chapter.)

The first argument of the event represents the menu command or Command Button that was clicked. The second argument is a Boolean variable, indicating whether the event has been handled already by another add-in. Even if it was handled, your add-in will be notified about the event. If the event has been handled by another add-in, the CancelDefault argument is True, which indicates that your handler's code won't be executed. If you want to handle an event from within your add-in and prohibit other add-ins from handling the same event, set the CancelDefault argument to True.

Disconnecting the Add-In

When the user disconnects the add-in, the IDTExtensibility OnDisconnection method is called. This method (which also looks like an event to you) accepts two arguments:

- The RemoveMode, which determines how the add-in was disconnected
- The custom() array, which holds the same custom data with the last argument of the OnConnection method

Table 8.9 lists and describes the values of the RemoveMode argument.

TABLE 8.9: The Values of the RemoveMode Argument of the OnDisconnection Method

Value	Description
vbext_dm_HostShuDown	The add-in was closed by the host application.
vbext_dm_UserClosed	The add-in was closed by the user, through the Add-Ins dialog box.

The code of the OnDisconnection method deletes the mcbMenuCommandBar menu command (which in effect removes the add-in's name from the Add-Ins menu) and then unloads the Form. If your add-in doesn't display a Form, you need to keep only the line that removes the add-in's name from the Add-Ins menu.

Code 8.4:   The OnDisconnection Method

```
Private Sub IDTExtensibility_OnDisconnection(ByVal RemoveMode As
vbext_DisconnectMode, custom() As Variant)

    On Error Resume Next

    'delete the command bar entry
    mcbMenuCommandBar.Delete

    'shut down the Add-In
    If FormDisplayed Then
        SaveSetting App.Title, "Settings", "DisplayOnConnect", "1"
        FormDisplayed = False
    Else
        SaveSetting App.Title, "Settings", "DisplayOnConnect", "0"
```

```
End If

Unload mfrmAddIn
Set mfrmAddIn = Nothing
```

End Sub

The OnStartupComplete method is called as soon as the add-in has been successfully connected. It examines the value of the DisplayOnConnect parameter (set by the AddToIni() procedure) to determine whether it should display the add-in automatically. Although the Add-In template project displays the Form by default, most add-ins don't start automatically.

Code 8.5:   The OnStartupComplete Method

```
Private Sub IDTExtensibility_OnStartupComplete(custom() As Variant)
    If GetSetting(App.Title, "Settings", "DisplayOnConnect", "0") _
        = "1" Then
        'set this to display the form on connect
        Me.Show
    End If
End Sub
```

The OnAddInsUpdate is another method that's called every time the Add-In Manager command is executed. Use this command to find out whether another add-in has been connected or disconnected and whether your add-in's behavior should change, depending on the presence of another add-in. This method is usually empty and contains a single comment line:

```
Private Sub IDTExtensibility_OnAddInsUpdate(custom() As Variant)
    '
End Sub
```

This is the general structure of an add-in. The code that does something is usually placed in the buttons of a Form, although some add-ins don't display any Forms. Later in this chapter, you will see an add-in that detects when the user deletes or renames controls on a Form. The Code Remover add-in prompts the user each time he or she removes a control as to whether it should remove the control's event handlers. The code for this add-in is contained in the class module.

In the next section, we are going to build a working add-in that demonstrates many of the topics discussed so far in this chapter. You can use this add-in as the starting point for many add-ins and experiment with the objects of the IDTExtensibility model. We are going to build more advanced, and practical, add-ins later in the chapter.

Testing an Add-In

Testing an add-in is similar to testing an out-of-process ActiveX component. You can compile an add-in into an EXE or a DLL file just as you can compile an ActiveX component into either of those file types. When you create the executable file, the add-in is added to the Registry and is available to the system. To register the component to another system, you must either run the executable (if it's an EXE file) or use the REGSVR32 utility to register it manually or from within a batch file (if it's a DLL file).

In either case, the name of the add-in isn't added automatically to the VBADDIN.INI file, and Visual Basic doesn't know at startup that another add-in is available. To add a reference to your new add-in to this file, you must either write a small program that appends a new line to the VBADDIN.INI file or create a proper setup program for the add-in.

When you design and test an add-in, you don't have to manually add the add-in reference to the VBADDIN.INI file. You can run the AddToIni() function in the IDE's Immediate window, and that's all it takes. Once a reference to the add-in is appended to the VBADDIN.INI file, every new instance of VB5 you start will see the add-in and add it to the list of available options in the Add-In Manager dialog box.

To test and debug the add-in, you must first connect it. Follow these steps:

1. Run the add-in project, and then start another instance of Visual Basic.

2. Choose Add-Ins ➢ Add-In Manager to open the Add-In Manager dialog box.

3. Select the add-in you want.

If you haven't changed the Registry entries for the new add-in, its name will be My Add-In. Once the add-in is added to the list of connected add-ins in the Add-Ins menu, you can activate it by clicking its name. When an error occurs in the add-in's code, Visual Basic will switch you immediately to the add-in's instance of VB5, at the line of the error. You can change the code, press F5 to resume execution, and then switch to the add-in. (In most cases, Visual Basic will take you back to the test project automatically.)

Changing the add-in's code (for example, adding new variables) may necessitate restarting the project. Visual Basic will warn you with a message like the one in Figure 8.5. If the test project is running, you must cancel the edits, switch to the test project, and disconnect the add-in. Then come back to the add-in project and edit it.

FIGURE 8.5:

If an add-in is used by
another project, Visual
Basic will warn you
when you try to end the
add-in's execution.

When you switch to the add-in, however, you won't be able to disconnect it. You will see another warning, indicating that the current operation can't complete because another application isn't responding. We usually move the current line pointer (the arrow that indicates the line where execution was interrupted) in the add-in project's Code window to the end of the offending procedure and press F5. The add-in's project will finally respond, and we can disconnect the add-in from the test project. This trick may not work in some situations, and you'll have to end the add-in project. In this case, you won't be able to remove the add-in's name from the Add-Ins menu without shutting down the test project and restarting it.

Another common situation in add-in design and testing is to attempt to connect an add-in, without having started the add-in. In this case, Visual Basic displays a message box telling you that it couldn't locate a component. It will ask whether you want to remove it from the list of the available add-ins (the VBADDIN.INI file). Click the Yes button, and then follow these steps:

1. Cancel the connection to the new add-in.

2. Switch back to the add-in project and start it.

3. Switch to the test project and connect the add-in.

The usual debugging aids apply to add-in projects as well. You can set breakpoints in the add-in project's Code window and single-step the add-in to see what each statement does. While the add-in project is in break mode, you can issue commands in the Immediate window and examine the structure of the various objects of the VBIDE object model and their properties and methods. Because you can't declare variables in the Immediate window and because the objects of the VBIDE are usually manipulated through object variables, declare all the variables that you may need later in the Immediate window as public in the add-in's code.

Developing add-ins isn't a complicated process, but the object model that allows you to access the IDE is complex, and the expressions can get quite lengthy. If you want to develop custom add-ins, spend some time experimenting with the examples in this chapter to get the hang of the process, and soon you'll be able to apply your VB knowledge to building add-ins.

The Demo Add-In Project

In this section, we are going to put together all the examples we discussed in the first half of the chapter (where we introduced the basic objects of the IDTExtensibility class) and build an add-in. You can use the add-in to experiment with these objects and explore additional objects and their properties and methods. When first connected, and each time its connected thereafter, the Demo add-in displays the Form shown in Figure 8.6. The buttons on this Form perform many of the operations we've discussed in this chapter. In the previous sections, we focused on the basic lines that carry out each task. Now you are going to see the complete implementation of these examples, including the declarations of the variables and error-trapping code (as needed).

FIGURE 8.6:

The Demo add-in's Form

Here is what each button on this Form does:

Project Components displays the current project's components.

Save Project in Folder saves these components to a new folder.

All Controls displays all the controls on the components of the project.

ContainedVBControls displays only the controls sited directly on the Form.

All ContainedVBControls displays the names of all controls on the project's Forms, grouped according to their container.

Comment Code inserts comment lines in the project's procedures.

Code Components displays all methods and event handlers in the project, along with each procedure's starting line and length.

CommandBar Controls prints the IDE's menu structure (with all its submenus).

Add MOVE Command adds a MOVE custom command to the File menu.

Remove MOVE Command removes the MOVE custom command from the File menu.

In the following sections, we'll discuss the code behind each of these Command Buttons in detail.

Listing a Project's Components

The Project Components button demonstrates the VBComponents collection, which returns information about all components in a project. You have already seen the core of this add-in in the section "The VBComponents Collection and the VBComponent Object," earlier in this chapter. The Click event handler of this button prints the names of the projects in the Project window, and under each project's name it prints the names of all its components (Forms, class modules, and so on). The last section of the code displays the name of the active project and the name of the selected component in the active project.

Code 8.6: The Project Components Button

```
Private Sub Command5_Click()
Dim thisProject As VBProject
Dim nProjects As Integer, nComponents As Integer
Dim i As Integer, j As Integer
Dim projectName As String
Dim msg As String

    nProjects = VBInstance.VBProjects.Count        ' # of projects
    List1.Clear
    For i = 1 To nProjects                          ' scans each project
        Set thisProject = VBInstance.VBProjects.Item(i)
        projectName = VBInstance.VBProjects.Item(i).Name
        nComponents = thisProject.VBComponents.Count
        List1.AddItem "PROJECT " & projectName
        For j = 1 To nComponents   ' scans each component
                                   ' of the selected component
            List1.AddItem Space(15) & "Component #" & j & "   " & _
                   thisProject.VBComponents.Item(j).Name
        Next
    Next

On Error GoTo NoSelectedComponent ' in case no component is selected
    msg = "The selected project is   " &
VBInstance.ActiveVBProject.Name _
            & vbCrLf
    msg = msg & "The selected component is " _
            & VBInstance.SelectedVBComponent.Name
    MsgBox msg
    Exit Sub

NoSelectedComponent:
    MsgBox "No component is selected"

End Sub
```

The subroutine extracts the number of projects in the project group (property Count of the VBProjects collection) and then sets up a loop that scans the components of each project. This loop starts by setting the object variable *thisProject* to the current project, to shorten the expressions required to access each component. In the rest of the code, the expression VBInstance.VBProjects.Item(i) or VBInstance.VBProjects(i) is replaced by the name of the variable *thisProject*. (You can also shorten the expression that represents the current component by introducing a new object variable, *thisComponent*. You must declare it as VBComponent.)

Each project has a number of components that can be accessed through the VBComponents collection. The code sets up a nested loop that scans the components of the current project. The number of components is given by the property Count of the VBComponents collection. The names of each project's components are printed in the ListBox control, following the name of the project they belong to, as shown in Figure 8.7.

FIGURE 8.7:

The Project Components button of the Demo add-in displays the names of the projects in the current project group, followed by the names of the components in each project.

Through the VBComponents collection, you can manipulate the components of the project. You can add a new component to the project with the Add and AddFile methods (the AddFile method adds a component that exists on the disk). The Remove method removes a component from the project. Finally, you can specify the project's startup object by assigning its name to the VBComponents collection's StartUpObject property.

Once you know how to access each project component, you can also manipulate them through the properties and methods of the VBComponent object. Each member of the collection is a VBComponent object, and you can access an individual component either with the Item property of the collection or with an index value. The Properties property returns the value of any of the properties listed in the Properties window when this component is selected. You can also save the component in a disk file with the SaveAs method or force the IDE to reload it with the Reload method.

NOTE For the syntax of the methods mentioned in this section, consult the Object Browser.

Listing a Project's Controls

The All Controls, ContainedVBControls, and All ContainedVBControls buttons demonstrate three methods to access the controls on all (or selected) Forms in the current project. (We discussed all three methods in the section "The VBControls and ContainedVBControls Collections," earlier in this chapter.) The VBControls collection returns all the controls on a Form and on any container controls on the Form (if any), and the ContainedVBControls collection returns only the controls sited directly on the Form. If some of these controls contain other controls, the contained controls must be accessed by the ContainedVBControls of the container control. The All ContainedVBControls button demonstrates a recursive routine for scanning each container's contained controls, to any depth.

Let's start with the code of the All Controls button, which is simpler than the others.

Code 8.7:   The All Controls Button

```
Private Sub Command7_Click()
Dim thisComponent As VBComponent
Dim thisProject As VBProject
Dim thisForm As VBForm
Dim iProject As Integer, iComponent As Integer, iControl As Integer
Dim thisControl As VBControl
Dim allControls As VBControls

    List1.Clear
    For iProject = 1 To VBInstance.VBProjects.Count        ' scans each
project
        Set thisProject = VBInstance.VBProjects.Item(iProject)
        ' the following loop scans each component of the current pro-
ject
        For iComponent = 1 To thisProject.VBComponents.Count
        ' and examines its type.
            If thisProject.VBComponents.Item(iComponent).Type = _
                vbext_ct_VBForm Or _
                thisComponent.Type = vbext_ct_UserControl Then
        ' thisForm is an object variable referencing the design window
                Set thisForm = _
                    thisProject.VBComponents.Item(iComponent).Designer
        ' The following loop scans each control on the current Form
                For iControl = 1 To thisForm.VBControls.Count
                    Set thisControl =
thisForm.VBControls.Item(iControl)
        ' If the control belongs to a control array, its index value
        ' must be listed along with the control's name
                    If thisControl.Properties("Index") >= 0 Then
                        List1.AddItem thisControl.Properties("Name") & _
                            "(" & thisControl.Properties("Index") & ")"
                    Else
                        List1.AddItem thisControl.Properties("Name")
                    End If
                Next
            End If
        Next
    Next
End Sub
```

This code sets up a loop that scans all the projects and a nested loop that scans all the components of the current project. For each component, it examines its Type property, and if the component's type is Form (constant vbext_ct_Form) or UserControl (constant vbext_ct_UserControl), it prints all the components on the Form. This takes place from within another nested loop, which scans the elements of the VBControls collection and prints the value of the Name property of each control. The program examines the control's Index property, and if the control belongs to a control array, it displays the index value as well. Figure 8.8 shows the output generated by the All Controls button. The project used to create Figure 8.8 is called TestProj.

NOTE   You'll find the TestProj project in the TestForm folder under the Demo project's folder (Chapter8/Demo/TestForm) on the CD that comes with the book.

FIGURE 8.8:

The All Controls button of the Demo add-in displays the names of the controls on all Forms in the current project, as well as controls placed on container controls.

Listing Contained Controls

The ContainedVBControls button uses the ContainedVBControls collection to access the controls on the application's Forms. The output generated by the ContainedVBControls button is shown in Figure 8.9. This list contains only the controls that are directly sited on the Form, and not the controls they contain. The Form with the controls that produced the output in Figure 8.9 is shown in Figure 8.10.

FIGURE 8.9:

The Contained-VBControls button of the Demo add-in displays the names of the controls on all Forms in the current project.

FIGURE 8.10:

The test Form used to produce the list of controls in Figure 8.9

The code behind the ContainedVBControls button is similar to the code of the All Controls button. It uses the same three loops to scan projects, components, and controls. However, instead of using the VBControls collection, it uses the ContainedVBControls collection.

Code 8.8:   The ContainedVBControls Button

```
Private Sub Command2_Click()
Dim thisComponent As VBComponent
Dim thisProject As VBProject
Dim thisForm As VBForm
Dim iProject As Integer, iComponent As Integer, iControl As Integer
```

```
        List1.Clear
        For iProject = 1 To VBInstance.VBProjects.Count        ' scans each
project
            Set thisProject = VBInstance.VBProjects.Item(iProject)
            List1.AddItem thisProject.Name
            ' the following loop scans each component of the current project
            For iComponent = 1 To thisProject.VBComponents.Count
                Set thisComponent =
thisProject.VBComponents.Item(iComponent)
                List1.AddItem Space(10) & thisComponent.Name
            ' and examines its type.
            ' If the control belongs to a control array, its index value
            ' must be listed along with the control's name
                If thisComponent.Type = vbext_ct_VBForm Or
thisComponent.Type_
                        = vbext_ct_UserControl Then
                    Set thisForm = thisComponent.Designer
            ' The following loop scans each control on the current Form
                    For iControl = 1 To thisForm.ContainedVBControls.Count
                        List1.AddItem Space(20) & _
        thisForm.ContainedVBControls.Item(iControl).Properties("Name")
                    Next
                End If
            Next
        Next
    End Sub
```

The list of all controls, shown in Figure 8.9, doesn't have a particular structure. They are not listed in any order. The list of contained controls, shown in Figure 8.10, has a better structure, but it doesn't contain all the controls on the Form. Ideally, we would like a list of all controls on the Form and the controls they may contain, to any depth, as shown in Figure 8.11. The arrays of the Label and TextBox controls sited on the Frame1(1) container control are listed under the name of the control that contains them, appropriately indented. The list in Figure 8.11 was generated with the All ContainedVBControls button.

The code behind the All ContainedVBControls is interesting. Basically, it uses the same structure to access the components of the project's Forms. After printing the name of each control on the current Form, it calls the ShowContainedControls(), subroutine, passing to it as an argument an object variable representing the current control. The ShowContainedControls() subroutine displays the contained controls. This subroutine, in turn, calls itself recursively for each control it prints in the list.

Let's start with the code behind the All ContainedVBControls button, and then we'll examine the implementation of the ShowContainedControls() subroutine.

FIGURE 8.11:

The All Contained-Controls button of the Demo add-in displays the names of the controls and their contained controls on all Forms in the current project.

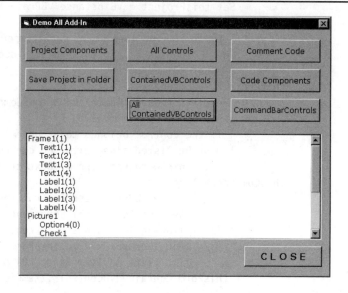

Code 8.9:   The All ContainedVBControls Button

```
Private Sub Command8_Click()
Dim thisComponent As VBComponent
Dim thisProject As VBProject
Dim thisForm As VBForm
Dim iProject As Integer, iComponent As Integer, iControl As Integer
Dim thisControl As VBControl

    List1.Clear
    For iProject = 1 To VBInstance.VBProjects.Count        ' scans each
project
        Set thisProject = VBInstance.VBProjects.Item(iProject)
        ' the following loop scans each component of the current project
        For iComponent = 1 To thisProject.VBComponents.Count
            If thisProject.VBComponents.Item(iComponent).Type = _
                vbext_ct_VBForm Then
                Set thisForm =_
                    thisProject.VBComponents.Item(iComponent).Designer
        ' The following loop scans each control on the current Form
                For iControl = 1 To thisForm.ContainedVBControls.Count
                    Set thisControl = _
```

```
                                thisForm.ContainedVBControls.Item(iControl)
                  If thisControl.Properties("Index") >= 0 Then
                      List1.AddItem thisControl.Properties("Name") & _
                          "(" & thisControl.Properties("Index") & ")"
                  Else
                      List1.AddItem thisControl.Properties("Name")
                  End If
          ' Now scans the controls contained on the current control (if
any)
                  ShowContainedControls thisControl
              Next
          End If
      Next
    Next
End Sub
```

The ShowContainedControls() subroutine uses the ContainedVBControls collection of the control passed as an argument to display the names of the controls contained on this control. If the current control is a container for additional controls, it calls itself again to print any controls sited on it. (It's quite unlikely that a Form contains multiple levels of container controls, but the code will work anyway.)

Code 8.10:   The ShowContainedControls() Subroutine

```
Sub ShowContainedControls(thisControl As VBControl)
Dim iControl As Integer
Dim newControl As VBControl
Static indentLevel As Integer
Dim indentSpace As String

    If thisControl.ContainedVBControls.Count = 0 Then Exit Sub
    indentLevel = indentLevel + 5
    indentSpace = Space(indentLevel)
    For iControl = 1 To thisControl.ContainedVBControls.Count
        Set newControl = thisControl.ContainedVBControls.Item(iControl)
        If newControl.Properties("Index") >= 0 Then
            List1.AddItem indentSpace & newControl.Properties("Name") &_
                "(" & newControl.Properties("Index") & ")"
        Else
            List1.AddItem indentSpace & newControl.Properties("Name")
        End If
        ShowContainedControls newControl
    Next
```

```
        indentLevel = indentLevel - 5

End Sub
```

Most of this code deals with formatting the list (indenting the contained controls under their container). Here, however, is the core of this subroutine:

```
If thisControl.ContainedVBControls.Count = 0 Then Exit Sub
For iControl = 1 To thisControl.ContainedVBControls.Count
    Set newControl = thisControl.ContainedVBControls.Item(iControl)
    {DISPLAY CONTROL'S NAME}
    ShowContainedControls newControl
Next
```

First, the program checks the number of contained controls on the current control. If there are no contained controls, the subroutine exits. If there are contained controls, the code scans each element of the ContainedVBControls collection, displays its name on the list, and then calls itself, again passing the current control as an argument (in case this one is also a container control).

NOTE   The ContainedVBControls collection is used in the event handler of the ContainedVBControls button and in the event handler of the All ContainedVBControls button. In the first case, it's a property of the VBForm class (thisForm.ContainedVBControls), and it contains all the controls on the Form. In the second case, it's a property of the VBControl class (thisControl.ContainedVBControls), and it contains all the controls sited on the control represented by the *thisControl* object variable.

Examining and Setting Control Properties

Through the VBControls and ContainedVBControls collection, you can access the properties of the controls on the Forms and set them. We have used the expression newControl.Properties("Index") in our code to access the Index property of the current control. To set the BackColor property of the same control, you would use a statement such as the following:

```
thisForm.ContainedVBControls.Item(i).Properties("BackColor") = _
    RGB(255, 0, 0)
```

To change a property on multiple selected controls, use a statement such as the following:

```
thisForm.SelectedVBControls.Item(i).Properties("BackColor") = _
    RGB(255, 0, 0)
```

The Properties property lets you manipulate a control in any way you like. Use it to access the Left and Top properties to align it with other controls, to access the Width and Height properties to resize it, and so on.

The examples in this section demonstrate how to access all the controls on a Form or on a container control. Using the same structure you can read or set any of the properties of the controls and manipulate them from within your add-in. For example, you can write an add-in that makes sure that all contained controls have the same background color or font as the control that contains them. To access the properties of the container control (or Form, which is usually the case), use the ContainerControl property. The following expression:

```
thisForm.SelectedVBControls.Item(i).ContainerControl
```

returns a VBControl object that represents the container control. Use this object to find the properties of the control that contains the control with which you are working.

All properties that appear in the Properties window when a specific control is selected can be accessed through the Properties property of the VBControl object. Just make sure that the selected control supports the property you want to read (or set) before attempting to access it. Read the control's type first (ClassName property) and then access a property. If you can't be sure that the selected control is a text control, use an If statement such as the following:

```
Set thisControl = thisForm.SelectedVBControls.Item(1)
If thisControl.ClassName = "TextBox" Then
    thisControl.Property("Text") = "I'm a Textbox"
ElseIf thisControl.ClassName = "Label" Then
        thisControl.Property("Caption") = "I'm a Label"
End If
```

The VBControl object doesn't have a Type property, as do most objects. It has a ControlType property, which returns one of the values shown in the Table 8.10.

TABLE 8.10: The Values of the VBControl Object's ControlType Property

Value	What It Does
vbext_ct_Container	Returns True if it's a container control
vbext_ct_Light	Returns True if it's a light-weight control
cvext_ct_Standard	Returns True if it's a standard control

The VBControl object's InSelection property returns True if the specific control belongs to the current selection; however, you can't change the selection by setting this property. You can also change the control's Zorder by assigning a value to the ZOrder property.

You'll see more examples of how to manipulate the properties of the controls on a Form and how to place new instances of controls on a Form from within an add-in in the section "Developing a Form Generator," later in this chapter. Actually, you already have all the information you need to develop an application generator that will create a Form from scratch and place the required code in the event handlers.

Listing a Project's Code Components

The Code Components button on the Demo add-in's Form prints the code components of a component, through the Members collection of the CodeModule object. The list generated by the Code Components button for a typical project (it's the TabOrder add-in demo that comes with Visual Basic) is shown in Figure 8.12. Notice that variable and constant declarations are also code components and that you can access them individually.

FIGURE 8.12:

The Code Components button of the Demo add-in prints the names of all procedures in a project's code, along with their location and size.

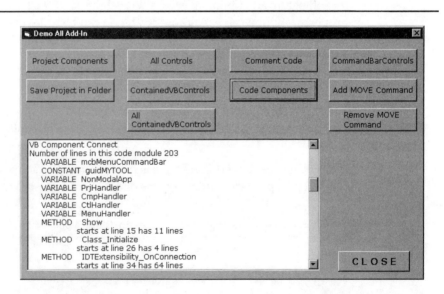

To access the code of a component, use the CodeModule object of the VBComponent object. The CodeModule object exposes several properties and methods that you can use to manipulate the component's code, as discussed in the section "The CodeModule Object," earlier in this chapter. Now we are going to see how to read the code and edit it. In the section "Developing a Form Generator," you will see how to create code modules entirely from within your add-in's code.

As usual, we set up a loop that scans each component in the active project and a nested loop that scans each member of the current component's CodeModule collection. The structure of the two loops is shown next:

```
Set thisProject = VBInstance.ActiveVBProject
pComponents = thisProject.VBComponents.Count
For i = 1 To pComponents
    pMembers = thisProject.VBComponents(i).CodeModule.Members.Count
    For j = 1 To pMembers
        Set thisCodeModule = thisProject.VBComponents(i).CodeModule
        {process current CodeModule object}
    Next
Next
```

NOTE   We use a slightly different notation to access the elements of the collection in this segment (we omit the Item property and apply the index directly to the collection's name). The only reason for doing this is to avoid long lines of code that break on the printed page.

Each element in the Members collection represents a declaration line, an event handler, a general procedure, or a Property procedure. The methods that extract the member's starting line and its length require that you know the member's type, which is returned by the Type property. If the member's type is an event or a method, you must call the ProcBodyLine property (which returns the location of the first line) as follows:

```
thisCodeModule.ProcBodyLine(thisProject.VBComponents.Item(i).CodeModule
.Members.Item(j).Name, vbext_pk_Proc)
```

WARNING   The syntax of the ProcBodyLine property requires that you specify the member's name and its type. Things get a bit complicated when you want to access Property procedures. The Type property of the Members collection returns the constant vbext_mt_Property. Yet, in the ProcByLine method you must specify one of the constants vbext_pk_Get, vbext_pk_Let, or vbext_pk_Set. If you look at the code, you'll see that we try to extract all three types of Property procedures. If one or more are missing (the Set Property procedure is usually missing), the code uses an error handler to skip the corresponding lines.

The rest of the code is straightforward. First, it sets up an array with the names of the member types:

```
' Set up an array with member type names
Dim MemberType(5) As String
MemberType(vbext_mt_Event) = "EVENT    "
MemberType(vbext_mt_Method) = "METHOD   "
MemberType(vbext_mt_Const) = "CONSTANT"
MemberType(vbext_mt_Property) = "PROPERTY"
MemberType(vbext_mt_Variable) = "VARIABLE"
```

The elements of this array are then used to display the type of the member (EVENT, METHOD, and so on), along with its name:

```
MemberType(thisCodeModule.Members.Item(j).Type) & "  " &
thisProject.VBComponents.Item(i).CodeModule.Members.Item(j).Name
```

Finally, we call the ProcBodyLine and ProcCountLines methods to extract the member's starting line and length (in number of lines) and display them on the ListBox control. Take a closer look at the lines that handle Property procedures. The code tries to read all three types of Property procedures (Get, Let, and Set), but if one of them is missing, a run-time error is generated. Notice also the long If statement that skips the code if the current component's type isn't one of the following:

- Class Module
- Property Page
- Standard Module
- UserControl
- Form
- MDI Form
- Document Object

Basically, this statement skips the resource files that Visual Basic can't handle.

Code 8.11:   The Code Components Button

```
Private Sub Command3_Click()
Dim thisProject As VBProject
Dim thisCodeModule As CodeModule
```

```
Dim pComponents As Integer
Dim pMembers As Integer
Dim i As Integer, j As Integer
Dim line1 As Integer, line2 As Integer
Dim compType As Integer
' Set up an array with member type names
Dim MemberType(5) As String
MemberType(vbext_mt_Event) = "EVENT   "
MemberType(vbext_mt_Method) = "METHOD  "
MemberType(vbext_mt_Const) = "CONSTANT"
MemberType(vbext_mt_Property) = "PROPERTY"
MemberType(vbext_mt_Variable) = "VARIABLE"
'''''''''''''''''''''''''''''''''''''''''''
    Set thisProject = VBInstance.ActiveVBProject
    pComponents = thisProject.VBComponents.Count
    List1.Clear
    For i = 1 To pComponents
        List1.AddItem "VB Component " & _
            thisProject.VBComponents.Item(i).Name
        compType = thisProject.VBComponents.Item(i).Type
        ' the following line examines the component's type
        ' so that the program won't attempt to read code
        ' in modules that have none.
        If Not (compType = vbext_ct_ClassModule Or compType = _
                vbext_ct_PropPage Or compType = vbext_ct_StdModule Or _
                compType = vbext_ct_UserControl Or _
                compType = vbext_ct_VBForm Or _
                compType = vbext_ct_VBMDIForm Or _
                compType = vbext_ct_DocObject) Then
            GoTo NextLoop
        End If
        pMembers = _
thisProject.VBComponents.Item(i).CodeModule.Members.Count
        List1.AddItem "Number of lines in this code module " & _
            thisProject.VBComponents.Item(i).CodeModule.CountOfLines
        For j = 1 To pMembers
            Set thisCodeModule = _
                thisProject.VBComponents.Item(i).CodeModule
            List1.AddItem Space(5) & _
                MemberType(thisCodeModule.Members.Item(j).Type) & _
                "  " & thisProject.VBComponents.Item(i)._
                CodeModule.Members.Item(j).Name
```

```
                line1 = 0: line2 = 0
                If thisCodeModule.Members.Item(j).Type = vbext_mt_Event Or _
                    thisCodeModule.Members.Item(j).Type = vbext_mt_Method _
Then
                    line1 =  _
                    thisCodeModule.ProcBodyLine _
                    (thisCodeModule.Members.Item(j).Name, vbext_pk_Proc)
                    line2 = _
                        thisCodeModule.ProcCountLines _
                        (thisCodeModule.Members.Item(j).Name, _
                        vbext_pk_Proc)
                    If line1 <> 0 And line2 <> 0 Then
                        List1.AddItem Space(20) & "starts at line " & _
                            line1 & " has " & line2 & " lines"
                    End If
                ElseIf thisCodeModule.Members.Item(j).Type =_
                            vbext_mt_Property Then
                    On Error GoTo PropertySET
                    line1 = 0: line2 = 0
                    line1 = _
                        thisCodeModule.ProcBodyLine _
                        (thisCodeModule.Members.Item(j).Name, _
vbext_pk_Get)
                    line2 = _
                        thisCodeModule.ProcCountLines _
                        (thisCodeModule.Members.Item(j).Name, _
vbext_pk_Get)
                    If line1 <> 0 And line2 <> 0 Then
                        List1.AddItem Space(20) & "GET Procedure starts at _
                            line " & line1 & " has " & line2 & " lines"
                    End If
PropertySET:
On Error GoTo PropertyLET
                    line1 = 0: line2 = 0
                    line1 = _
                        thisCodeModule.ProcBodyLine _
                        (thisCodeModule.Members.Item(j).Name, _
vbext_pk_Set)
                    line2 = _
                        thisCodeModule.ProcCountLines _
                        (thisCodeModule.Members.Item(j).Name, _
vbext_pk_Set)
```

```
                    If line1 <> 0 And line2 <> 0 Then
                        List1.AddItem Space(20) & "SET Procedure starts at _
                            line " & line1 & " has " & line2 & " lines"
                    End If
PropertyLET:
On Error GoTo EndProp
                    line1 = 0: line2 = 0
                    line1 = _
                        thisCodeModule.ProcBodyLine _
                        (thisCodeModule.Members.Item(j).Name, _
vbext_pk_Let)
                    line2 = _
                        thisCodeModule.ProcCountLines _
                        (thisCodeModule.Members.Item(j).Name, _
vbext_pk_Let)
                    If line1 <> 0 And line2 <> 0 Then
                        List1.AddItem Space(20) & "LET Procedure starts at _
                            line " & line1 & " has " & line2 & " lines"
                    End If
EndProp:
            End If
NextLoop:
            Next
        List1.AddItem " "
    Next
End Sub
```

If you look at the first few lines displayed by the Code Components button for
a typical project, you will see that they are the declarations of the module's variables and constants. If the module contains API function declarations, they are
listed as METHODS. Figure 8.13 shows the first few lines of the output generated
by the Code Components button for the TabOrder project (you will find it in the
Samples\CompTool\Addins\TabOrder folder on the VB5 CD). PostMessage is
not a method of the project; it's an API function whose declaration (and not its
implementation) appears in a module.

FIGURE 8.13:

The first four METHODS in this project are API function declarations, incorrectly classified by Visual Basic as methods.

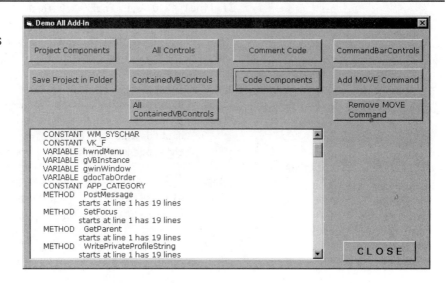

The entry:

```
METHOD PostMessage
        Starts at line 1 has 19 lines
```

corresponds to the following declaration in the code:

```
Private Declare Sub PostMessage Lib "user32" Alias "PostMessageA"_
    (ByVal hwnd&, ByVal msg&, ByVal wp&, ByVal lp&)
```

This declaration doesn't start at line 1, and it certainly doesn't have 19 lines. The problem is that Visual Basic (incorrectly) thinks that this is a method, but in reality it's a declaration. Actually, it's a Sub declaration, but nevertheless a declaration. (It contains the keyword Declare and doesn't have a matching End Sub.)

And how about the incorrect line numbers? When the code extracts the first line and length of this method (because this is the component type returned by the Type method), it reads the first line and the length of the entire declarations section. A small bug you must live with. You can actually bypass it by reading the number of declaration lines with the CountOfDeclarationLines property and then classifying as a declaration all the methods that start at line 1 and have CountOfDeclarationLines lines of code.

Editing a Module's Code

In addition to reading the code of a module, you can edit it. In fact, this is how you can build a code generator, which is the core of a Wizard application. The Comment Code button is a simple example that inserts a copyright notice after the name of each method and event handler. The button's code uses the Insert Lines method of the CodeModule object, which inserts a string (that may contain multiple lines separated by a carriage return/line feed combination) at a specified location in the Code window. The code is a bit more complicated than that, as it first makes sure the copyright notice isn't already there. Figure 8.14 shows the Code window of a test project before and after the insertion of the copyright notice.

FIGURE 8.14:

The Comment Code button inserts a copyright notice after each procedure's definition line.

```
Private Sub Command1_Click()
Rem *** Software Unlimited Inc***
Dim sum As Double, avg As Double

        If Command1.Caption = "New Data Set" Then
        dataCount = InputBox("How many data values?")
        If Not IsNumeric(Count) Then
            MsgBox "please enter a valid numeric value"
            Exit Sub
        End If
        For i = 1 To dataCount
            Load Label1(i)
            Load Text1(i)
            Label1(i).Top = Label1(i - 1).Top + 1.25 * Label1(i).Height
            Text1(i).Top = Text1(i - 1).Top + 1.25 * Text1(i).Height
```

The code finds the location of the first line of a code component and reads the first line of code in the module with the Lines method of the CodeModule object. It then compares it to the copyright message, and if they don't match, the copyright notice is inserted in the code. This step is necessary to avoid filling the code module with copyright notices if the user clicks this button more than once. The rest of the code, which has the same structure as the code of the Code Components button, is shown next.

Code 8.12:   The Comment Code Button

```
Private Sub Command4_Click()
Dim thisProject As VBProject
Dim thisCodeModule As CodeModule
Dim pComponents As Integer
Dim pMembers As Integer
```

```
Dim i As Integer, j As Integer
Dim line1 As Integer, line2 As Integer
Dim cpRightLine As String
Const cpRightNotice = "REM *** Software Unlimited Inc***"

    Set thisProject = VBInstance.ActiveVBProject
    pComponents = thisProject.VBComponents.Count
    ' scan each component in the active project
    For i = 1 To pComponents
        pMembers = thisProject.VBComponents.Item _
                (i).CodeModule.Members.Count
        For j = 1 To pMembers
            Set thisCodeModule = _
                    thisProject.VBComponents.Item(i).CodeModule
            If thisCodeModule.Members.Item(j).Type = vbext_mt_Event _
                Or thisCodeModule.Members.Item(j).Type _
                = vbext_mt_Method Then
                line1 = _
                 thisCodeModule.ProcBodyLine_
                 (thisProject.VBComponents.Item(i)._
                 CodeModule.Members.Item(j).Name, vbext_pk_Proc)
                 cpRightLine = thisCodeModule.Lines(line1 + 1, 1)
                 If StrComp(Trim(cpRightLine), Trim(cpRightNotice),_
                        vbTextCompare) Then
                    thisCodeModule.InsertLines line1 + 1, cpRightNotice
                End If
            End If
        Next
    Next
End Sub
```

In the next section, you will see an add-in that first creates a Form with user-specified controls on it and then inserts the code for selected event handlers. If you spend a good deal of time developing applications with similar interfaces and/or code, you should consider building an add-in or a Wizard that generates the Forms for you, instead of copying Forms and modifying their existing controls and code.

Developing a Form Generator

In this section, we are going to show you how to develop an application generator as an add-in. It's not just a code generator, but a real application generator that can produce applications with multiple Forms and the code behind them. A complete application generator should have the format of a Wizard and guide the user through a sequence of windows that collect the required information and then build the application.

In this section, we are going to examine the code of the application generator. We'll look at how to create Forms and add controls on them from within the add-in's code and at how to add code to the events. Most of the information we'll present here isn't new to you. We'll use the objects discussed already, and you'll see that building an application generator is a straightforward process, although it requires a lot of typing. From within your code, you must set every property of the controls you place on the Form, including the position and size properties.

First, you must decide what type of application you want the add-in to create. Obviously, you can't write a code generator that can produce all types of applications. Application generators are best suited for data-entry and report screens and for other programs that are used in multiple projects, with small variations— data-entry screens for tables in a database, reports based on different recordsets, and so on. It won't pay to write an application generator for a program that will be used in a single project. If you examine the Wizards that come with Visual Basic, you'll get a good feel for the type of programs that you can streamline with the help of an application generator.

Another good use for an application generator is building Class Modules, such as the ones we looked at in Chapter 6 or the interconnected ActiveX controls we looked at in Chapter 7. The classes we designed in Chapter 6 to access the customers and invoices of the NWIND database had an identical structure and differed only in the names of the properties in which the various fields are stored. If you plan to use the approach shown in the last two chapters with other databases, you can save yourself a lot of time and trivial coding by building an add-in to automatically generate these applications.

Adding Controls on a Form

One of the basic operations a Form generator must perform is the placement of new controls on a Form, and we haven't discussed yet how to do it. To add a control on a Form, you use the Add method of the ContainedVBControls collection. The syntax of the Add method is:

```
ContainedVBControls.Add(ProgID As String, [RelativeVBControl As_
    VBControl], [Before As Boolean])
```

The ProgID is the programmatic ID of the control you want to add ("Label" for a Label control, "TextBox" for a TextBox control, and so on). The following arguments are optional and are usually omitted in similar applications. The RelativeVBControl is another control on the same Form, relative to which the new control will be inserted. If you specify this argument and omit the last one, the new control is placed after the specified control. If the last argument, Before, is True, the new control is placed before the specified control. These two arguments are useful in inserting controls in control arrays.

The Add method returns a VBControl object, which represents the newly added control. You can use this object to manipulate the control from within the code. To place a Label control on the current Form and set some properties, use statements such as the following:

```
Set thisControl = thisForm.ContainedVBControls.Add("Label")
thisControl.Properties("AutoSize") = True
thisControl.Properties("Caption") = "VB5 Developer's Handbook"
thisControl.Properties("Top") = currentTop + _
    1.5 * thisControl.Properties("Height")
thisControl.Properties("Left") = 1000
Set thisControl = Nothing
```

You declare the *thisControl* object variable as VBControl, and it's created as soon as you set it with the Add method of the VBControls or ContainedVBControls collection. You can then set any of the properties of the Label control through the Properties property. After you are done, release the object variable by setting it to Nothing.

Sizing Controls

You rarely can set the width of a TextBox or a Label control in twips or other absolute units. The control's size usually depends on its contents. The simplest way to size text controls (such as TextBoxes, Labels, and ListBoxes) is to create a Label control with its AutoSize property set to True. (In Code 8.13 in the next section, this Label control is called templateLabel.) Then assign the text control's Text or Caption property to this auxiliary control and make the text control's Width property equal to the Label's Width property.

Because the Label is placed on the same Form as the other text controls, by default it will have the same font as the other controls, and their sizes will match perfectly. As a result, you won't have to deal with font sizes and use the TextWidth property to set the widths of the controls (a rather complicated process).

Prompting the User for Data

The first thing a Form generator will do is prompt the user for the data needed to design the Form. When you invoke the Form Generator add-in by choosing Add-Ins ➤ Form Generator, it starts by displaying the Form shown in Figure 8.15.

FIGURE 8.15:

The Form Specification Data dialog box of the Form Generator add-in

The user can enter the data needed to build the data-entry Form. Each line in the multiline TextBox corresponds to a separate field, and the fields are placed on the Form in the same order as they appear in the Form Specification Data window. Each line must contain the field's title (which becomes the Caption of the Label control in front of it). Optionally, you can specify two more arguments, which are separated by a comma:

- The name of the field

- The field's length in number of characters

The minimum requirement for a field is its title (UserID or Address, for instance). By default, the name of the TextBox is the field's title, prefixed by the string "fld." If you specify only the field's title, the TextBox in which the field is entered will be named fldUserID or fldAddress. If you want to use another name, append it to the field's title, using a comma to separate the two entities (for instance, "UserID, UIDfield").

Finally, you can specify a length for the field, with a line such as the following:

```
"UserID, UIDfield, 12"
```

You can't omit the field name and specify a length in its place. The specification "UserID, 12" will attempt to create a TextBox control named 12, and you'll end up receiving an error message.

NOTE   This add-in doesn't contain any error-trapping code. Our goal is to demonstrate the basics of building a Wizard-style add-in, and we didn't include any code to deal with common user errors. You can add the required logic for trapping all types of errors and inform the user with your own error messages.

Placing the Controls on the Form

When the user clicks the OK button, the code starts by cleaning all the controls and the code on the Form. The user has presumably selected a new Form in the project or wants to use the specific Form to create a data-entry window. The lines of the TextBox control are then saved in a collection (the Entries collection), where it's easier to read them later in the code.

The code adds one Label control and one TextBox control for each field. The Label's Caption is set to the field's title, and the TextBox control is initially empty. The Label controls are automatically resized to the dimensions of their captions, and their right edges are aligned. The TextBox controls are left-aligned and sized indirectly, through the templateLabel control. The templateLabel's Caption is set to the string:

```
String(length, "M")
```

in which *length* is the field's length (20 characters if not specified). The Label is resized automatically around its caption, and this length is assigned to the Length property of the corresponding TextBox control. Figure 8.16 shows the Form that corresponds to the specifications shown in Figure 8.15.

FIGURE 8.16:

This Form was generated by the Form Generator add-in, based on the specifications of the dialog box shown in Figure 8.15.

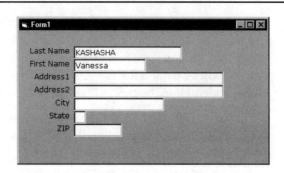

Code 8.13:   Placing the Controls on the Form

```
' Create and place new controls on the Form
    currentTop = 300
    For i = 1 To Entries.Count
        ' Set up a template Label control
        ' to calculate each TextBox's width
        Set templateLabel = thisForm.ContainedVBControls.Add("Label")
        templateLabel.Properties("AutoSize") = True
        templateLabel.Properties("Top") = 0
        ''''''''''''''''''''''''''''''''''''''''''''''''''''''''''''''
        Set thisControl = thisForm.ContainedVBControls.Add("Label")
        thisControl.Properties("Name") = "lbl" & _
                MakeControlName(Entries.Item(i))
        thisControl.Properties("AutoSize") = True
        thisControl.Properties("Caption") = _
                MakeFieldTitle(Entries.Item(i))
        If Len(thisControl.Properties("Caption")) > longestLabel Then _
                longestLabel = Len(thisControl.Properties("Caption"))
        thisControl.Properties("Top") = currentTop + 1.5 * _
                thisControl.Properties("Height")
        thisControl.Properties("Left") = 1000
        cHeight = thisControl.Properties("Height")
        cTop = thisControl.Properties("Top")
        Set thisControl = Nothing

        Set thisControl = thisForm.ContainedVBControls.Add("TextBox")
        thisControl.Properties("Name") = "txt" & _
                MakeControlName(Entries.Item(i))
        thisControl.Properties("Text") = ""
        thisControl.Properties("Height") = cHeight
        templateLabel.Properties("Caption") = _
                String(GetFieldLength(Entries.Item(i)), "M")
        thisControl.Properties("Width") = _
                Val(templateLabel.Properties("Width"))
        thisControl.Properties("Top") = cTop
        thisControl.Properties("Left") = 2000
        currentTop = cTop

    Next
```

Each control is placed on the Form as soon as the Add statement of the corresponding VBControl object is set. Initially, the control has the default size and is placed at the same location on the Form, as if you had double-clicked its icon in the Toolbox. The code then uses the object variable returned by the Add method (which represents the new control) to manipulate the properties of the control in order to size and align it on the Form. Although the controls are placed on the Form, we can't align them to their final positions because we need to know the longest caption. The lengthiest caption is stored in the variable *longestLabel*, which is used by another loop that aligns the right edges of the Label controls and the left edges of the TextBox controls.

Code 8.14:   Aligning the Controls on the Form

```
' Now arrange controls on the Form according to their lengths
    controlRight = 500 + longestLabel * 10 * Screen.TwipsPerPixelX
    For i = 1 To thisForm.ContainedVBControls.Count
        If thisForm.ContainedVBControls.Item(i).ClassName = "Label" _
Then
            thisForm.ContainedVBControls.Item(i).Properties("Left") = _
                controlRight - thisForm.ContainedVBControls._
                Item(i).Properties("Width")
        Else
            thisForm.ContainedVBControls.Item(i).Properties("Left") = _
                controlRight + 100
        End If
    Next
```

You can edit this code segment to align the controls in any way you see fit for the application. If you want to resize the Form, use the Properties property of the Form variable itself (*thisForm*).

WARNING When you test the Form Generator add-in, the TextBox controls will all have the same width if the add-in's Form covers the templateLabel control. If a control is covered by another, Visual Basic doesn't redraw the Label control when its Caption changes, and the control won't be resized as expected. The workaround is to minimize the Form Specification Data dialog box when the OK button is clicked. The project on the CD doesn't minimize the window, so you will have to move it completely outside the Form on which the controls are placed.

Adding Code to the Form

An application generator should not only place the controls on a Form, but program them as well. If the add-in we are developing in this section were an actual data-entry window connected to a database, we would have to add the code to validate the field values, store them to the database, and then read the next record (just like the Data Form Wizard). Our example is certainly less ambitious, but the same logic applies to other situations too. The idea is to create a long string with the required code and insert it in the Form's CodeModule.

The Form Generator add-in uses the CodeModule's AddFromString method to add code in the Form's Code window. The application's code is generated on the fly, although you could read it from a file, use constants, and in general use any VB technique with which you're more familiar. In this example, we'll insert a simple handler for the LostFocus event, which will turn the field's value to uppercase. You must place the following lines of code in the loop that places the controls on the Form, just before the Next statement:

```
txtCode = "Private Sub " & thisControl.Properties("Name") &
"_LostFocus()"
txtCode = txtCode & vbCrLf & "    " & thisControl.Properties("Name") &_
          ".Text =  UCase(" & thisControl.Properties("Name") & ")"
txtCode = txtCode & vbCrLf & "End Sub"
VBInstance.SelectedVBComponent.CodeModule.AddFromString txtCode
```

Executing these lines for a control named fldCity inserts the following text in the Form's code:

```
Private Sub fldCity_LostFocus()
    fldCity.Text = UCase(fldCity)
End Sub
```

You can create long strings for all the events of the current control, as well as general procedures, variable and constant declarations, and so on. Even though it's simple in principle, getting the code (along with line breaks and proper indention) to a string variable can be tricky. If the code you want to insert is complicated, first test it with a Standard EXE project, and then embed it in the add-in, making sure you replace the references to control names with the appropriate expressions.

TIP

Remember, the expression Chr(34) inserts a double quote in the text.

The last few lines in the OK button's code generate a message, asking if the user wants to run the project. These lines are commented out in the actual project on the CD, and they are meant to demonstrate how you can invoke the IDE's commands from within your add-in's code.

```
Dim reply As Integer
reply = MsgBox("Do you want to run the application now?", vbYesNo)
If reply = vbYes Then
VBInstance.CommandBars(1).Controls("Run").Controls("Start").Execute
End If
```

To execute a menu command, call the Execute method of the object variable that represents the specific command. As you will see in the next section, the first-level menu options can be accessed through the CommandBars(1).Controls collection. Each element in this collection is another collection that contains the commands in the specific submenu.

You can extend this example by adding more Forms to prompt the user for more data. Organize the data you need in order to build an add-in, place related data on the same Form, and you have built a Wizard.

The VB Wizard-Building Wizard

Actually, Visual Basic provides a Wizard for building Wizards! It's the VB Wizard Manager add-in, and it will create much of the standard code for your add-in. For example, it will generate the code for the navigation buttons that take the user to the previous or next screen, the procedures for connecting and disconnecting the add-in, and much more.

The VB Wizard Manager produces a lot of code, but the information in this chapter will help you work your way through it and build the proper Wizard for your applications.

Manipulating the IDE Menu

So far, you've read about the objects that represent projects (their components, the controls and the code of the components, and so on). In the last part of this chapter, we are going to discuss a few objects that represent the environment itself.

These objects allow you to intercept many user actions from within an add-in and react to them. You'll learn how to add new commands to the menu bar, detect events during the design of an application, and so on.

The VBIDE class provides a collection that gives your add-ins access to the commands of the Visual Basic menus. You can find out the state of individual menu commands, add new commands to the menu structure, and even invoke menu commands from within your add-in. This collection is the CommandBars collection, which is made up of Control objects. The CommandBars collection represents the command bars of the environment (the Edit command bar, the Format command bar, and so on). The first element of this collection represents the Visual Basic window's main menu, which is the only one we are going to examine in this chapter. The techniques for accessing the other command bars are identical; only the indices will differ.

To access the main menu of the Visual Basic window, you can use one of the following expressions:

```
VBInstance.CommandBars.Item(1)
VBInstance.CommandBars(1)
```

This expression returns an object of type Office.CommandBarControl. This is a type like all others, but it has a rather odd name. This object was originally designed to allow Visual Basic to control the menus of Office applications. The Count property of this collection returns the number of commands on the Visual Basic menu bar (the first-level commands)—File, Edit, Project, and so on. Each one of these commands leads to a submenu.

The Controls Collection

To access a command's submenu, you use another collection, the Controls collection. Each element in this collection represents an entire submenu. The expression:

```
VBInstance.CommandBars(1).Controls(1)
```

represents the entire File menu. Unlike other collections, the elements of the Controls collection can be indexed by name. The File submenu can also be accessed as:

```
VBInstance.CommandBars(1).Controls("File")
```

And now we need yet another collection to access the elements of a submenu. A collection for accessing the members of a menu exists already, and it's the Controls collection. To access the third command in the File menu, you can use the expression:

```
VBInstance.CommandBars(1).Controls("File").Controls(3)
```

Or, if you know the name of the command, you can use the following equivalent expression:

```
VBInstance.CommandBars(1).Controls("File").Controls("Add Project")
```

This expression represents a menu command or a Command Button. You can find out the name of the command by reading the Caption property, and you can find out its state by reading the Enabled property. In short, the properties of a menu option are also properties of the Controls collection.

The Controls collection is not listed in the Object Browser, and its members won't be listed in the Auto List Member window. Because it represents a menu command, however, it has a few members. Its most important properties are Caption and Enabled (there may be more that we haven't discovered yet). The Execute method invokes the command, as if it were clicked with the mouse. To invoke the Paste command of the Edit menu, use the following statement:

```
VBInstance.CommandBars(1).Controls("Edit").Controls("Paste").Execute
```

and to execute the third command of the File menu, use the following statement:

```
VBInstance.CommandBars(1).Controls("File").Controls(3).Execute
```

Besides reading the commands of Visual Basic's menus, you can also add and remove methods with the Add and Delete methods of the Office.CommandBar-Control control. The Add method's syntax is:

```
CommandBars(i).Control(j).Add([Type], [Id], [Parameter], [Before],
[Temporary])
```

Notice that all arguments are optional. The Add method returns a CommandBars-Control object, which represents the newly added command. The *Type* argument determines the type of command and can have one of the following values:

- msoBarTypeMenuBar
- msoBarTypeNormal
- msoBarTypePopUp

The *Id* argument is a long value, which you can use to refer to the new command. The *Before* argument is the position of the command, after which the new one will be inserted. The Add method returns an Office.CommandBarControl type object, which represents the newly added command. You can use this variable to access the properties of the command (set its Caption, for instance). To remove a command from a menu, you first create an object variable that represents the command, and then you issue the Delete method of the object variable.

Adding and Removing Menu Commands

The next example demonstrates how you can add new commands to the Visual Basic IDE menu. Later, you will see how to add the code to carry out a task when the new command is clicked. The Demo add-in has two Command Buttons, the Add MOVE Command and the Remove MOVE Command, that add and remove a Move Project command in the File menu. This command copies all the components of a project to a new folder.

NOTE   Saving the project to another folder doesn't move the files there. To move an entire project to another folder, you must manually save each component to this folder.

We'll look at the implementation of the Move Project command later in this chapter. In this section, we'll look at the code for adding and removing commands to the various menus of the Visual Basic IDE.

Let's start by looking at the code behind the Add MOVE Command button. The event handler, shown below, scans the commands in the File menu to make sure that the Move Project command isn't already there (in which case, it doesn't add it again). If the command isn't found in the File menu, it adds the Move Project command with the Add method of the Controls collection.

Code 8.15:   The Add MOVE Command Button

```
Private Sub Command6_Click()
Dim MoveCommand As Office.CommandBarControl
Dim i As Integer
```

```
        For i = 1 To _
VBInstance.CommandBars.Item(1).Controls("File").Controls.Count
            If _
VBInstance.CommandBars.Item(1).Controls("File").Controls(i).Caption =
"Move Project" Then
                Exit Sub
            End If
        Next

        Set MoveCommand = _
VBInstance.CommandBars.Item(1).Controls("File").Controls.Add(1, , , 3)
        MoveCommand.Caption = "Move Project"

End Sub
```

A few explanations are necessary here. The expression VBInstance .CommandBars.Item(1) represents the main menu bar. Each command in this menu is accessed through the Controls collection. The File menu is the first one, so the object VBInstance.CommandBars.Item(1).Controls("File") represents the File menu. To access the commands of this menu, you must use the Controls collection of this object. You can also declare an object variable, *fileMenu*, set it to the File submenu, with the following statement:

```
Set fileMenu = VBInstance.CommandBars.Item(1).Controls("File")
```

You can then replace the entire expression VBInstance.CommandBars.Item(1) .Controls("File") with the name of the *fileMenu* object variable.

To add a new command to a menu, use the Add method. The last argument of this method is the position of the new command in the menu. Our Move Project command is added right after the New Project and Add Project commands on the File menu. Click the Add MOVE Command Button in the Demo project, and then open the File menu (it should look like the one shown in Figure 8.17).

To remove the command, we must create an object variable that references the Move Project command and then call this variable's Delete method.

FIGURE 8.17:

The File menu after the addition of the Move Project command

The Remove MOVE Command Button

```
Private Sub Command10_Click()
Dim MoveCommand As Office.CommandBarControl

    Set MoveCommand =_
        VBInstance.CommandBars.Item(1).Controls("File").Controls(3)
    If MoveCommand.Caption = "Move Project" Then MoveCommand.Delete

End Sub
```

This code removes the third item in the File menu, but not before it examines its Caption (in case the command has already been removed).

NOTE   The code shown here isn't quite robust. Another add-in might have added a command before the Move Project command. In this case, the Move Project command won't be at the same position in the File menu, as when we added it there. You should use a loop identical to the one in the event handler of the Add MOVE Command Button, which will actually locate the command in the File menu and then remove it.

The add-in's code protects you from adding the same command twice, but it doesn't remove the command from the File menu when the add-in is disconnected. The place to insert the code for adding and removing a menu command is not in a Command Button on the add-in's Form, but in the OnConnection and OnDisconnection methods (you'll see shortly how this is done). So, as long as you are experimenting with the Demo add-in, don't forget to remove the Move Project command by clicking the Remove MOVE Command Button.

Handling Menu Events

You've seen how to add and remove commands in the Visual Basic IDE menu bar, but what good is it if you can't detect the Click event for the new command and handle it from within your add-in? In this section, we'll set up an object that receives the Click event of the new command. This object will be added to the Objects list in the Code window, and you'll be able to program its Click event handler.

You already know how to add an event handler for the Click event of a menu command; the Add-In template contains an event handler for the Click event of the add-in's entry in the Add-Ins menu. In your code, you may have to create event handlers for your own custom commands and here are the steps:

1. In the OnConnection method of the add-in, declare an object variable of Office.CommandBarControl type (it represents a menu command) with the following statement:

    ```
    Dim NewCommand As Office.CommandBarControl
    ```

2. Declare another object variable of type CommandBarEvents, which will be used to access the events of the custom command. You must declare this variable in the Class Module's declarations section, as:

    ```
    Public WithEvents NewCommandHandler As CommandBarEvents
    ```

TIP

Notice the keyword WithEvents; without it, the object variable won't recognize any events, and you won't be able to program it.

3. Create a new command with the Add method of the CommandBars.Control collection, as explained earlier:

    ```
    Set MoveCommand =
    VBInstance.CommandBars.Item(1).Controls("File").Controls.Add(1, , , 3)
        NewCommand.Caption = "New Command"
    ```

This code segment inserts a new command in the third place of the File menu. The command's caption is New Command.

Now you are ready to create the object variable that will detect the events of the new command (the one represented by the *NewCommand* variable) with the following statement:

```
Set Me.NewCommandHandler =
VBInst.Events.CommandBarEvents(NewCommand)
```

4. Open the Connect Class Module's Code window, expand the Objects list, and select NewCommandHandler. In the Events list, the Click event will be selected automatically. Enter the code that implements the new command in this event handler.

5. When the add-in is disconnected, you must remove the custom command from the File menu. Declare the *NewCommand* object variable in the OnDisconnection method of the add-in with a statement such as the following:

```
Dim NewCommand As Office.CommandBarControl
```

6. Add the following code, which actually disconnects the custom command:

```
Set NewCommand =
VBInstance.CommandBars.Item(1).Controls("File").Controls(3)
    NewCommand.Delete
```

The process is straightforward, and you can duplicate it for as many new commands as you wish. Notice that the *NewCommand* object variable isn't public. It's declared in the methods that add the command to and remove it from the IDE's menu. Also notice that a menu command can't be accessed directly; you must first create an object variable that references the command and then call the variable's Delete method.

In the section "The Project Mover Add-In," we are going to build an add-in that adds a custom command to the File menu, which moves an entire project to a new folder. But first, we are going to look at a couple of simpler examples that manipulate menu commands through the CommandBarControl object.

Listing the IDE Menu Commands

The CommandBarControls button of the Demo add-in displays the names of the commands in each of the IDE's submenus, as shown in Figure 8.18.

FIGURE 8.18:

The CommandBar-Controls button displays the name and status of all the first level submenus of the Visual Basic IDE.

Each submenu is a member of the CommandBars collection of the current instance of the IDE. The first element of the CommandBars collection is another collection that represents the commands in the main menu. The first-level menu commands (File, Edit, and so on) are accessed with the elements of the collection VBInstance.CommandBars.Item(1).Controls. The File menu is the element VBInstance.CommandBars.Item(1).Controls.Item(1) or VBInstance.CommandBars(1).Controls(1), if you prefer this latter notation.

To access the commands of the File menu, the code assigns this menu to the variable *currentMenu* and then uses this object to access the command through the currentMenu's Controls collection. The code scans each element of the main menu and all its commands. It displays each command's caption, along with the designators V and E, which stand for Visible and Enabled. If the command is enabled and/or visible, the corresponding digit appears in front of its name.

Code 8.17:   The CommandBarControls Button

```
Private Sub Command1_Click()
Dim mcbMenuCommandBar As Office.CommandBarControl
Dim cmenus As Integer
Dim i As Integer, j As Integer
Dim currentMenu As CommandBarControl
Dim menuProp As String
```

```
    List1.Clear
' The first element in the CommandBars collection corresponds
' to the File menu
    cmenus = VBInstance.CommandBars.Item(1).Controls.Count
    For i = 1 To cmenus
        Set currentMenu = VBInstance.CommandBars.Item(1).Controls(i)
' Add menu name to the lise
        List1.AddItem "MENU    " & currentMenu.Caption
' Scan all items in the menu, examine their Visible and Enables proper-
ties
        For j = 1 To currentMenu.Controls.Count
            menuProp = ""
            If currentMenu.Controls(j).Visible Then
                menuProp = "V"
            Else
                menuProp = "  "
            End If
            If currentMenu.Controls(j).Enabled Then
                menuProp = menuProp & "E"
            Else
                menuProp = menuProp & "  "
            End If
    and add them to the list
            List1.AddItem "      " & menuProp & "    " & _
                    currentMenu.Controls(j).Caption
        Next
    Next

End Sub
```

As you know, some menu commands lead to submenus. Most of the commands in the Format menu, for example, lead to submenus, which won't be printed by the previous subroutine. Accessing second-level submenus is a bit trickier (in all honesty it's quite simple, but undocumented). To access a first-level command menu, we used the expression VBInstance.CommandBars.Item(1).Controls(i) (i goes from 1 to the number of menus on the menu bar). This menu is assigned to the *currentMenu* object variable, and each command in this menu can be accessed through the *currentMenu* variable's Controls collection. If *currentMenu* represents the Format menu, the following expression:

```
currentMenu.Controls(2)
```

represents the command Make Same Size. This command is a submenu whose elements can be accessed by another Controls collection.

The three commands of the Make Same Size submenu are:

- Width
- Height
- Both

The command Width can be accessed with the expression currentMenu.Controls(2).Controls(1). This looks confusing, and we need to simplify it.

You can create a new object variable to reference the Make Same Size submenu, as follows:

```
Set currentSubMenu = currentMenu.Controls(2)
```

You can then access the commands of the Make Same Size submenu with the following expression:

```
currentSubMenu.Controls(k)
```

in which k goes from 1 (for the Width command) to 3 (for the Both command).

To display the second-level submenus, you need another nested loop that scans each command's submenu.

Code 8.18:   Displaying the Second-Level Submenus

```
For k = 1 To currentSubMenu.Controls.Count
    If currentSubMenu.Controls(k).Visible Then
        menuProp = "V"
    Else
        menuProp = "  "
End If

    If currentSubMenu.Controls(k).Enabled Then
        menuProp = menuProp & "E"
    Else
        menuProp = menuProp & "  "
    End If
    List1.AddItem "            " & menuProp & "    " & _
            currentSubMenu.Controls(k).Caption
Next
```

If you insert this loop in the code, you will get an error message for all commands that don't lead to submenus. One would expect the expression currentSubMenu.Controls.Count to be zero for these commands. But this isn't the case.

Attempting to access the Count property of an object variable that represents a submenu generates a run-time error. To avoid this error message (without inserting unneeded error handlers), you must examine the value of the current command's Type property.

TIP

A menu command's Type property is normally 1, unless it leads to a submenu, in which case it's 10. These values don't correspond to any constants, and you won't find them in the Object Browser (at least, we couldn't locate the settings of a menu command's Type property in any of the obvious places). Code 8.19 figures out whether a command leads to a submenu, in which case it executes the inner loop.

Code 8.19:   The CommandBarControls Button

```
Private Sub Command1_Click()
Dim mcbMenuCommandBar As Office.CommandBarControl
Dim cmenus As Integer
Dim i As Integer, j As Integer, k As Integer
Dim currentMenu As CommandBarControl
Dim currentSubMenu As CommandBarControl
Dim menuProp As String

    List1.Clear
' The first element in the CommandBars collection corresponds
' to the File menu
    cmenus = VBInstance.CommandBars.Item(1).Controls.Count
    For i = 1 To cmenus
        Set currentMenu = VBInstance.CommandBars.Item(1).Controls(i)
        List1.AddItem "MENU     " & currentMenu.Caption
        For j = 1 To currentMenu.Controls.Count
            menuProp = ""
            If currentMenu.Controls(j).Visible Then menuProp = "V" Else_
                menuProp = "   "
            If currentMenu.Controls(j).Enabled Then menuProp = _
                menuProp & "E" Else menuProp = menuProp & "   "
            List1.AddItem "       " & menuProp & "   " & _
                currentMenu.Controls(j).Caption
            Set currentSubMenu = currentMenu.Controls(j)
            If currentSubMenu.Type = 10 Then
                For k = 1 To currentSubMenu.Controls.Count
```

```
                            If currentSubMenu.Controls(k).Visible Then menuProp
                               ="V" Else menuProp = "  "
                            If currentSubMenu.Controls(k).Enabled Then menuProp
                               =menuProp & "E" Else menuProp = menuProp & "  "
                            List1.AddItem "          " & menuProp & "    " & _
                               currentSubMenu.Controls(k).Caption
                        Next
                    End If
                Next
            Next
        End Sub
```

This trick will work unless there are third-level submenus. The Visual Basic IDE doesn't have nested submenus, but if you create an add-in that implements submenus with commands that lead to other submenus (rather unlikely), you should write a recursive routine that scans each command's submenus. See the section "Listing a Project's Controls," earlier in this chapter, for the description of a similar recursive routine.

Figure 8.19 shows how the CommandBarControls button displays the commands of the Format menu.

FIGURE 8.19:

The output of the CommandBarControls button of the Demo add-in

The Project Mover Add-In

In this section, we'll put together much of the information presented in the last few sections to build an add-in that installs a new command on the File menu and detects the Click event on this command. The command's name is Move Project, and every time the user clicks this command, the current project's components are copied to a new, user-specified folder. The project is called Project Mover.

NOTE   You'll find the Project Mover project in the `Chapter8/MoveProj` folder on the CD that comes with this book.

A VB project consists of several to many components that may reside in a number of folders on the hard disk. The Visual Basic project file (VBP) contains a list of the components, including the files' path names. These path names are usually relative to the folder of the project file. When you save the current project with the Save Project or Save Project As command, only the project file is saved. You must save its components separately.

TIP   A simple way to save all the components of a project is to start a new project. Visual Basic will ask whether you want to save the components that have changed since the last save. Click the Yes button, and in the New Project dialog box, click Cancel to return to your project.

It would be useful to have a command that saves the entire project to a new folder, especially if you add existing files to the project. Such a command isn't available on the File menu, so an add-in that implements this operation could be useful to many developers. We'll build a simple add-in that saves all the components in the current project to a user-specified folder. The original files, no matter where they reside initially, will be copied to the new folder. The original files won't be removed from their folders. It's a good practice, however, to maintain a single version of each project, so you might consider adding the code to delete the original files after they have been copied to their destination folder.

WARNING   The examples in this book are meant to demonstrate the topics discussed, so you should test the Project Mover add-in exhaustively before you implement this change in the code.

529

To build the add-in from scratch, start a new Add-In project and then follow these steps:

1. Remove the frmAddin Form from the project, add a new, blank Form, and name it frmSelect (we'll design this Form later).

2. Remove the code that shows and hides the frmAddin Form from the OnConnection and OnDisconnection methods of the add-in. You can open the MoveProject's Connect class module in a Notepad window and compare the code in the two windows to see which lines manipulate the Form.

3. Declare the *MoveCommandHandler* object variable in the module's declarations section, with the following line:

```
Public WithEvents MoveCommandHandler As CommandBarEvents
```

4. Add the following declarations to the module's declarations section:

```
Implements IDTExtensibility

Public VBInstance As VBIDE.VBE
Dim mcbMenuCommandBar As Office.CommandBarControl
Public WithEvents MenuHandler As CommandBarEvents
```

Code 8.20: The OnConnection Method of the Add-In

```
Private Sub IDTExtensibility_OnConnection(ByVal VBInst As Object, ByVal
ConnectMode As vbext_ConnectMode, ByVal AddInInst As VBIDE.AddIn, cus-
tom() As Variant)
Dim MoveCommand As Office.CommandBarControl

    On Error GoTo error_handler

    'save the vb instance
    Set VBInstance = VBInst

    Set mcbMenuCommandBar = AddToAddInCommandBar("Move Project")
    'sink the event
    Set Me.MenuHandler =
VBInst.Events.CommandBarEvents(mcbMenuCommandBar)

    Dim i As Integer
    For i = 1 To VBInstance.CommandBars.Item(1).Controls_
            ("File").Controls.Count
        If VBInstance.CommandBars.Item(1).Controls_
            ("File").Controls(i).Caption = "Move Project" Then
```

```
                Exit Sub
            End If
        Next
        Set MoveCommand = _
                VBInstance.CommandBars.Item(1).Controls(_
                "File").Controls.Add(1, , , 3)
        MoveCommand.Caption = "Move Project"
        Set Me.MoveCommandHandler = _
                VBInst.Events.CommandBarEvents(MoveCommand)
        Exit Sub

    error_handler:

        MsgBox Err.Description

    End Sub
```

This code is identical to the outline we presented in the last section, except for the loop that scans the commands of the File menu. This loop makes sure that the File menu doesn't contain a Move Project command already. If it does, the code exits and doesn't add it again.

If you compare the OnDisconnection subroutine with the one supplied by the template, you'll see that it doesn't contain the lines that hide the Form and that it contains a few additional lines for removing the Move Project command from the File menu.

Code 8.21:   The OnDisconnection Method

```
    Private Sub IDTExtensibility_OnDisconnection(ByVal RemoveMode As
    vbext_DisconnectMode, custom() As Variant)
    Dim MoveCommand As Office.CommandBarControl

        On Error Resume Next
        Set MoveCommand =
    VBInstance.CommandBars.Item(1).Controls("File").Controls(3)
        MoveCommand.Delete

        'delete the command bar entry
        mcbMenuCommandBar.Delete

        'shut down the Add-In
        SaveSetting App.Title, "Settings", "DisplayOnConnect", "0"

    End Sub
```

Coding the Project Mover Add-In

We have implemented all the code for adding a new custom command to the existing menu structure of the Visual Basic IDE. Now, we must provide the code that makes the command do something. This is straight VB code that manipulates the objects of the VBIDE class. The code in this section demonstrates how to access the components of a VB project, find out their type and the names of the files in which they are stored, and how to save them in a different folder.

The first issue we must deal with is how to allow the user to select the destination folder to which the project will be moved. We must display a dialog box from within our code that will allow the user to select a drive and a folder on the selected drive. This dialog box is shown in Figure 8.20. Add a new Form to the project, and place on it the controls you see in Figure 8.20. The FileListBox control is not really needed; neither can you act on the names of the existing files, but they are displayed to help you locate the desired folder. (Be sure it doesn't contain another project with file names that conflict with the file names of the current application, for example.)

FIGURE 8.20:

The Select Target Folder dialog box allows the user of the Project Mover add-in to select the project's destination folder.

The code behind the controls of the frmSelect Form is trivial, with one exception. The name of the selected folder is a property of the Form so that the add-in can read it (the add-in can't set this property, although it wouldn't be a bad idea to let the add-in select an initial folder).

Code 8.22:   The FrmSelect Form

```
Private Sub Dir1_Change()
    File1.Path = Dir1.Path
End Sub

Private Sub Drive1_Change()
    Dir1.Path = Drive1.Drive
End Sub
```

When you click the OK button, the code hides the Form and assigns the name of the selected path to the private variable *m_newFolderName*, which stores the value of the NewFolderName Form's property. This is a read-only property, implemented with the following Property Get procedure:

```
Property Get newFolderName() As String
    newFolderName = m_newFolderName
End Property
```

Once the user selects the destination folder, the program can extract its path by reading the frmSelect Form's newFolderName property. In the following section, we are going to look at the code that moves the components of the current project to a new folder.

Saving a Project's Components

Before we look at the code that actually saves the project's components, we must discuss a special requirement of this add-in. If a component has been saved already, we must use the same file name. If not, we must either create a new name, based on the name of the component, or prompt the user for a file name. Since the Project Mover add-in is meant to move projects with components in various folders, we opted for the first approach. If the component UserControl1 hasn't been saved already, we'll use the name UserControl1.ctl for its file name.

When creating file names based on the component name, we must also supply an extension. The extension is based on the component's type, which is returned by the component's Type property. The Type property is an integer, and we use it to build an array of possible extensions, as shown here:

```
' SET UP FILE TYPE EXTEXNSIONS
extNames(vbext_ct_ClassModule) = ".cls"
extNames(vbext_ct_PropPage) = ".pag"
extNames(vbext_ct_StdModule) = ".cls"
```

```
extNames(vbext_ct_ClassModule) = ".bas"
extNames(vbext_ct_ResFile) = ".res"
extNames(vbext_ct_UserControl) = ".ctl"
extNames(vbext_ct_VBForm) = ".frm"
extNames(vbext_ct_VBMDIForm) = ".mdi"
extNames(vbext_ct_DocObject) = ".doc"
```

These extensions are then used to create the default file names, with two statements such as the following:

```
ext = extNames(thisProject.VBComponents.Item(j).Type)
FName = thisProject.VBComponents.Item(j).Name & ext
```

in which j is the index of the current component. The property thisProject .VBComponents.Item(j).Type returns one of the constants we used to build the array.

The add-in's core code uses two loops (a structure you're so accustomed to by now). The outer loop scans the projects in the current project group, and the inner loop scans the components of each project and saves them to a new folder.

Code 8.23:   The Move Project Command

```
Private Sub MoveCommandHandler_Click(ByVal CommandBarControl As Object,
handled As Boolean, CancelDefault As Boolean)
'     MsgBox "Ready to save the project's files"
Dim thisProject As VBProject
Dim i As Integer, j As Integer, k As Integer
Dim fileCount As Integer, projectsCount As Integer
Dim newFolderName As String

Dim SepPos As Integer
Dim PName As String, FName As String
Dim ext As String
Dim extNames(10) As String
' SET UP FILE TYPE EXTEXNSIONS
extNames(vbext_ct_ClassModule) = ".cls"
extNames(vbext_ct_PropPage) = ".pag"
extNames(vbext_ct_StdModule) = ".cls"
extNames(vbext_ct_ClassModule) = ".bas"
extNames(vbext_ct_ResFile) = ".res"
extNames(vbext_ct_UserControl) = ".ctl"
extNames(vbext_ct_VBForm) = ".frm"
extNames(vbext_ct_VBMDIForm) = ".mdi"
extNames(vbext_ct_DocObject) = ".doc"
```

```
''''''''''''''''''''''''''''''''''''''''''''''''''''''''''''''''''
' Show Form and exit if no folder is selected
    frmSelect.Show vbModal
    newFolderName = frmSelect.newFolderName
    If newFolderName = "" Then
        Beep
        Exit Sub
    End If
' THE SAVE FEATURE
    projectsCount = VBInstance.VBProjects.Count
    For i = 1 To projectsCount
' Get project name first
        PName = ""
        ext = ".vbp"
        PName = VBInstance.VBProjects.Item(i).FileName
        If Len(PName) > 0 Then
            SepPos = InStr(PName, "\")
            While SepPos > 0
                PName = Mid(PName, SepPos + 1)
                SepPos = InStr(PName, "\")
            Wend
        Else
            PName = VBInstance.VBProjects.Item(i).Name & ext
        End If
        Set thisProject = VBInstance.VBProjects.Item(i)
        fileCount = thisProject.VBComponents.Count
        For j = 1 To fileCount
            If thisProject.VBComponents.Item(j).Type <>_
                    vbext_ct_ResFile Then
                ext = extNames(thisProject.VBComponents.Item(j).Type)
                FName = thisProject.VBComponents.Item(j).FileNames(1)
                If Len(FName) > 0 Then
                    SepPos = InStr(FName, "\")
                    While SepPos > 0
                        FName = Mid(FName, SepPos + 1)
                        SepPos = InStr(FName, "\")
                    Wend
                Else
                    FName = thisProject.VBComponents.Item(j).Name & ext
                End If
                If Dir(newFolderName & "\" & FName) <> "" Then Kill_
                    newFolderName & "\" & FName
                thisProject.VBComponents.Item(j).SaveAs newFolderName _
                    & "\" & FName
```

535

```
                    Debug.Print "Saving " & newFolderName & "\" & FName
                End If
            Next
    ' Now save project
            If Dir(newFolderName & "\" & PName) <> "" Then Kill _
                newFolderName & "\" & PName
            VBInstance.VBProjects.Item(i).SaveAs newFolderName & "\" &
    PName
            Debug.Print "Saving " & newFolderName & "\" & PName
        Next

    End Sub
```

This code examines the file name under which the project (VBInstance.VBProjects .Item(i).FileName) or the component (thisProject.VBComponents.Item(j) .FileNames(1)) is saved. If the project or the component hasn't been saved yet, this property returns a blank string. In this case, the program creates a new file name, based on the component's name, using an extension based on the component's type.

If the component has been saved already, the FileName property returns the full path name of the file, and the code parses it (with the While...Wend loop) to extract the file name. Whether the file name exists or is generated by the code, the component is saved with the Save method of the VBProjects collection or the VBComponents collection. If the file exists already in the destination folder, the add-in overwrites it. We don't ask the user about overwriting the files because this Move Project command is used just once for a project, and it usually saves the project's components to a new folder.

Detecting IDE Events

Like Visual Basic applications, add-ins can't do much without events. The most useful add-ins are those that detect user actions and react to them. In programming the IDE, events are triggered each time the user selects a menu command or adds or removes components to a project and each time controls are added, deleted, or renamed.

You know already how to detect and program the Click event of any menu command. The IDTExtensibility model provides more events, which you can access through the Events class. The Events class exposes six objects that detect the events shown in Table 8.11.

TABLE 8.11: The Elements of the Events Class

Element	What It Does
CommandBarEvents	Detects the Command Bar's events
FileControlsEvents	Detects when the user adds/removes file components
ReferencesEvents	Detects when the user adds/removes references to the current project
VBControlsEvents	Detects when the user adds/removes/renames controls on the Form
SelectedVBControlsEvents	Detects when the user changes the current selection on the Form
VBComponentsEvents	Detects when the users selects/reloads/activates/adds/deletes a component

Detecting and programming all the categories of events provided by the IDE is similar, and we'll focus on the VBControlsEvents and SelectedVBControls events. These events are generated constantly in the design process, and you can use them to write add-ins that work in tandem with the user to streamline the design process. We'll limit our discussion to these two categories of events, because they are the most commonly used. The same techniques apply to all other categories of events. To find out the names of the supported events and the arguments passed, consult the Object Browser.

During the design of a Form, the events shown in Table 8.12 are triggered to notify the add-in about user actions related to the design of the user interface:

TABLE 8.12: The Events of the VBControlsEvents Object

Event	Is Triggered
ItemAdded	When a new control is placed on the Form
ItemRemoved	When a control is deleted
ItemRenamed	When a control is renamed

These events are members of the VBControls collection. The first two events are also members of the SelectedVBControls collection. Since you can't rename multiple controls at once, the ItemRenamed event isn't triggered for the SelectedVBControls collection. As with the Command Bar's events, you must first create an object variable that you will use to program these events. This variable must be of VBControlsEvents type. The declaration:

```
Private WithEvents ctrlHandler As VBControlsEvents
```

must appear in the declarations section of the class module or Form. Later in the code, you must tell Visual Basic which events to look for. The *ctrlHandler* variable is set with a line such as the following:

```
Set ctrlHandler = VBInstance.Events.VBControlsEvents(thisProject,_
thisForm)
```

The first argument tells Visual Basic to detect the events on the Form referenced by the *thisForm* variable, of a specific project, referenced by the object variable *thisProject*. If the project *thisProject* has other Forms, their control-related events won't be detected by the *ctrlHandler* variable. To detect these events on every Form of the project, set the second argument of the VBControlsEvents property to Nothing. To detect all events on all Forms, set both arguments to Nothing. If you set the *ctrlHandler* variable with the following line:

```
Set ctrlHandler = VBInstance.Events.VBControlsEvents(thisProject,_
thisForm)
```

it will detect all the control-related events in the project. In terms of coding, though, this isn't as convenient as you may think. You must provide the code to detect on which Form the event originated and react accordingly. It's easier to start by deciding which events and on which Forms you want to monitor and then create object variables for these Forms.

The ctrlHandler is an object that recognizes events, so its name will appear in the Objects list of the Code window, and the events it recognizes will appear in the Events list of the same window. To program a handler for any of the supported events, select the ctrlHandler object in the Objects list, and select the name of the event in the Events list, as shown in Figure 8.21. Unlike controls themselves, the IDE provides only a few control-related events.

You can program the ctrlHandler object's events as usual. You can access the entire VBIDE object model from within the event's code and perform all the actions you deem appropriate. In the following section, you will see how you can program the events generated by the IDE every time the user deletes a control on a Form, to remove any event handlers left behind. The same add-in detects the events triggered when controls are renamed too so that you can modify the code automatically.

FIGURE 8.21:

The events recognized
by object variables
declared as
VBControlsEvents

```
Demo - frmAddIn (Code)                                    _ □ ×
ctrlHandler                    ▼    ItemRemoved                      ▼
                                    ItemAdded
    Private Sub ctrlHandler_ItemRemov  ItemRemoved
    Dim reply As Integer               ItemRenamed
    Dim msg As String
    Dim thisModule As VBIDE.CodeModule
    Dim pMembers As Integer
    Dim ctrlName As String
    Dim firstLine As String
    Dim i As Integer
    Dim line1 As Integer, line2 As Integer

        If DontPrompt Then
            DontPrompt = False
            Exit Sub
        End If
        ctrlName = VBControl.Properties.Item("Name")
        msg = "Remove code for " & ctrlName
        If VBControl.Properties.Item("Index") >= 0 Then msg = msg & "("
        reply = MsgBox(msg, vbYesNo)
```

The Code Remover Add-In

The last example in this chapter demonstrates an add-in that detects events during the design cycle of a Form and handles them silently. This add-in doesn't have a visible interface, and it doesn't install any command in the IDE's menu. When connected, it installs an event handler that detects when the user deletes controls on the Form and prompts the user to delete the corresponding code.

Normally, when a control is deleted during the design of an application, the IDE doesn't remove the event handlers already entered in the Code window because the user might need these procedures for another control. They are simply listed under the General category in the Objects list of the Code window. If you plan to permanently remove a control from your Form, however, you should also remove the associated code. The Code Remover add-in automates the deletion of unneeded code.

This add-in doesn't display any Forms when invoked. Actually, the Code Remover command in the Add-Ins menu does nothing; it simply indicates that the add-in has been installed. The add-in is automatically invoked every time the user deletes or renames a control on the Form and asks the user whether he or she wants to remove the associated code.

To implement the add-in, start a new AddIn project, remove the frmAddIn Form, and then remove the code that shows and hides the Form from its Connect class module. The *ctrlHandler* object variable is declared in the class module, from within the OnConnection method with the following line:

```
Set ctrlHandler = VBInstance.Events.VBControlsEvents(thisProject, thisForm)
```

All the action takes place from within the ctrlHandler's ItemRemoved and ItemRenamed events.

Code 8.24:   The Standard Class Module

```
Implements IDTExtensibility

Public VBInstance As vbide.VBE
Private mcbMenuCommandBar As Office.CommandBarControl
' Detects the RemoveItem/RenameItem events
Private WithEvents ctrlHandler As VBControlsEvents


'_____

'this method adds the Add-In to VB
'_____

Private Sub IDTExtensibility_OnConnection(ByVal VBInst As Object, ByVal
ConnectMode As vbext_ConnectMode, ByVal AddInInst As vbide.AddIn, cus-
tom() As Variant)

    On Error GoTo error_handler

    'save the vb instance
    Set VBInstance = VBInst

    'this is a good place to set a breakpoint and
    'test various addin objects, properties and methods
    Debug.Print VBInst.FullName

    Set mcbMenuCommandBar = AddToAddInCommandBar("Code Remover")

' Set up the MenuHandler object variable to detect the Edit > Paste
' command selection
    Dim thisProject As VBProject
    Dim thisForm As VBForm

    Set thisProject = VBInstance.ActiveVBProject
    Set ctrlHandler = VBInstance.Events.VBControlsEvents(_
        thisProject, thisForm)
```

```
    Exit Sub

error_handler:

    MsgBox Err.Description

End Sub

'_____
'this method removes the Add-In from VB
'_____
Private Sub IDTExtensibility_OnDisconnection(ByVal RemoveMode As
vbext_DisconnectMode, custom() As Variant)

    On Error Resume Next
    'delete the command bar entry
    mcbMenuCommandBar.Delete
    'shut down the Add-In
    SaveSetting App.Title, "Settings", "DisplayOnConnect", "0"

End Sub

Private Sub IDTExtensibility_OnStartupComplete(custom() As Variant)
    '
End Sub

Private Sub IDTExtensibility_OnAddInsUpdate(custom() As Variant)
    '
End Sub

Function AddToAddInCommandBar(sCaption As String) As
Office.CommandBarControl
    Dim cbMenuCommandBar As Office.CommandBarControl   'command bar
object
    Dim cbMenu As Object

    On Error GoTo AddToAddInCommandBarErr

    'see if we can find the Add-Ins menu
    Set cbMenu = VBInstance.CommandBars("Add-Ins")
    If cbMenu Is Nothing Then
        'not available so we fail
```

```
        Exit Function
    End If
Set cbMenuCommandBar = cbMenu.Controls.Add(1)

    'add it to the command bar
'set the caption
    cbMenuCommandBar.Caption = sCaption

    Set AddToAddInCommandBar = cbMenuCommandBar

    Exit Function

AddToAddInCommandBarErr:

End Function
```

After these procedures, you can insert the code that reacts to the ItemRemoved and ItemRenamed events. In the Code Remover add-in, we have implemented the ItemRemoved event only.

```
Private Sub ctrlHandler_ItemRemoved(ByVal VBControl As vbide.VBControl)
Dim reply As Integer
Dim msg As String
Dim thisModule As vbide.CodeModule
Dim pMembers As Integer
Dim ctrlName As String
Dim firstLine As String
Dim i As Integer
Dim line1 As Integer, lineCount As Integer
Dim currentLine As Integer

    ctrlName = VBControl.Properties.Item("Name")
    msg = "Remove code for " & ctrlName
    If VBControl.Properties.Item("Index") >= 0 Then msg = msg & "(" & _
        VBControl.Properties.Item("Index") & ")"
    reply = MsgBox(msg, vbYesNo)
    If reply = vbYes Then
        Set thisModule = VBInstance.SelectedVBComponent.CodeModule
        pMembers = thisModule.Members.Count
        For i = pMembers To 1 Step -1
```

```
            If thisModule.Members.Item(i).Type = vbext_mt_Method Then
                line1 = _
                    thisModule.ProcBodyLine(_
                    thisModule.Members.Item(i).Name, vbext_pk_Proc)
                firstLine = thisModule.Lines(line1, 1)
                If InStr(firstLine, "Sub " & ctrlName & "_") Then
                    currentLine = line1
                    lineCount = 1
                    While Trim(thisModule.Lines(currentLine, 1)) <>_
                        "End Sub"
                        currentLine = currentLine + 1
                        lineCount = lineCount + 1
                    Wend
                    thisModule.DeleteLines line1, lineCount
                    Debug.Print "deleted " & line1 & ", " & lineCount & _
                        " in " & firstLine
                End If
            End If
        Next
    End If

End Sub
```

The ItemRemoved event's handler asks the user whether the event handlers of the deleted control should be removed. If so, the program scans all the items of the CodeModule collection, looking for event handlers. If one is found, it sees if the deleted control's name is in the first line, along with the word *Sub* and followed by an underscore (these characteristics uniquely characterize the definition of an event handler). If the current item is an event procedure of the deleted control, the code removes all lines up to the line End Sub.

TIP

Why didn't we use the ProcCountLines property of the CodeModule method to find out the number of lines in the module and then delete them with the DeleteLines method? The ProcCountLines property doesn't count empty lines at the beginning of the module, and some special action is required to fix this behavior. The approach here is the simplest, and it will work even if this behavior of the ProcCountLines property is changed in the future. Because it goes through all the lines in the code, however, it's not the most efficient implementation, at least for projects with very long code listings.

The code for changing the program listing when a control is renamed isn't included in the listing. To implement it, you must locate all the instances of the string "Sub oldCtrlName_" (where OldCtrlName is the control's name) and change it to "Sub newCtrlName_" (where newCtrlName is the control's new name). This action will make the event handlers for the original control match the new name of the control.

In addition, you must search the entire code for references to the old control name. If the control Command1 is renamed to OKButton, all instances of the string "Command1." must be changed to "OKButton."

TIP

The period ensures that we change only instances of the control that were renamed, and not another control whose name partially matches the control's old name (like OKButton2, for instance).

In the CodeDel project on the CD you will find the outline of the ctrlHandler_ItemRenamed procedure, which shows how to use its arguments. The outline of this procedure is:

```
Private Sub ctrlHandler_ItemRenamed(ByVal VBControl As vbide.VBControl,
ByVal OldName As String, ByVal OldIndex As Long)
Dim reply As Boolean
Dim msg As String

    If VBControl.Properties("Index") >= 0 And OldIndex = -1 Then Exit
Sub
    msg = "Revise code for " & OldName
    If OldIndex >= 0 Then msg = msg & "(" & OldIndex & ")"
    reply = MsgBox(msg, vbYesNo)
    If reply = vbYes Then
        ' INSERT CODE TO RENAME ALL INSTANCES OF RENAMED CONTROL
    End If

End Sub
```

With the discussion of the IDE events, this chapter comes to an end. You have seen nearly all the objects of the IDTExtensibility model and many examples that will help you experiment with this object model. We designed these examples so that you can use them as starting points for many new add-ins. We skipped a few objects that aren't quite as useful or are not used commonly in add-in design, but you will find all the information you need about them in the Object Browser.

PART III

Database Programming

Client/Server Programming

- Understanding the difference between the file-server and the client/server models

- Introducing three-tiered applications

- Deciding to adopt the client/server model

- Looking at the Visual Basic 5 data access options

- Exploring the client/server tools in the Enterprise Edition of Visual Basic 5

Client/server is not a type of computer hardware, nor is it a feature of a software application. Client/server is a computer methodology. In general, the term *client/server computing* means connecting a single-user client machine to a multiuser server machine and sharing the processing load between the two. The client requests services, and the server provides services.

To take full advantage of the client/server relationship, the client should request data, and the server should respond with only the data needed. The client presents the data to the user, and the server processes the data. The client does little processing.

Today, most applications provide some type of data access. More and more developers are adopting the client/server model as the basis for their applications—not because they want to, but because they have to. For the most part, the client/server approach fulfills an important need: The application requires the user interface to connect to an intelligent server database engine, and client/server provides that connection. A well-designed client application does not have hard-coded SQL statements, and it does not care where or how the data is stored or managed; nor does it perform data manipulation. Instead, the client requests raw data at a higher level. The server then processes that data and returns processed records to the client, which then presents them to the user.

The distributed client/server model has both logical and physical partitioning that allows the database tier to be distributed across one or more physical computers to enhance processing speed, increase accessibility, and take advantage of specialized machines.

NOTE   Microsoft SQL Server version 6 introduced the distributed client/server methodology.

As more and more developers use the Microsoft Access Database (MDB) to store data, it is important to understand that, even though the MDB supports multiuser access, it is not a true client/server implementation—it is a file server. In the next section, we'll look at these differences in more detail. Then in the rest of the chapter, we'll look at when and why you should adopt the client/server model, the data access options you can choose from, and the Visual Basic 5 client/server tools you can use in developing client/server applications.

File-Server versus Distributed Client/Server

In a file-server configuration, no intelligent processing takes place at the server level. All intelligent processing takes place on the individual workstation. When your application needs data, it is the responsibility of the software on the workstation to determine which tables should be read and how to access the network drive. All the data in the database tables must be sent from the server to the workstation, resulting in slower access and increased network traffic.

After the table or file is retrieved, a query can then be run against it to retrieve the needed records. In other words, when a SQL statement is called against an MDB, all the processing takes place on the client side, and only a file request is sent across the network to retrieve the required tables. No logic is executed on the server side, except that needed to provide the tables. Figure 9.1 shows a typical file-server configuration.

FIGURE 9.1:

A typical file-server configuration

In a distributed client/server environment, the server is responsible for intelligently servicing a client's request for data. The workstation does not request data at a file or table level, but sends a request to the server to execute a query and return specific records. This is a vast improvement over the file-server approach.

For example, if you are looking for a set of address records for the state of Texas, the client sends a SQL statement to the server. The server processes the query and then returns a resultset of Texas addresses only, instead of the entire address file or table. This results in improved access time and reduces network traffic. Figure 9.2 shows a typical client/server configuration.

FIGURE 9.2:

A typical client/server configuration

Engine requesting data from database

Database Engine

Database Engine

Database Engine

Engine passing querry results of server

Database server returning rows to local database engine

Network Server

Database

The client/server concept we have been discussing thus far is a two-tiered application—the client and the server. As advanced business methods and technologies are unfolding, however, a new approach is being used in corporate enterprise computing—three-tiered architecture, which we'll look at briefly in the next section. In Chapter 15, we'll look at this topic in depth and present a sample three-tiered application.

Three-Tiered Applications

Three-tiered architecture partitions an application into three logical tiers, or services:

- User services (the front end)
- Business services (the middle)
- Data services (the back end)

Figure 9.3 shows how this works. Using three-tiered architecture, the developer can separate user access, business rules, and data access into separate modules. These tiers do not necessarily correspond to physical locations on the network; they are conceptual tiers and help the developer to create robust component-based applications. Separate project teams can develop these reusable services, or components, which can be physically located anywhere on the network.

FIGURE 9.3:

The components in a three-tiered application

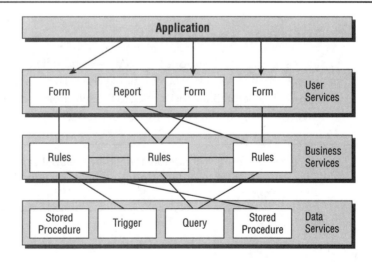

Building the application in tiers also addresses the issue of scalability. The traditional two-tier application can falter as the transaction load increases. With three-tiered applications, the workload is split among the services.

The three-tiered application development method provides many benefits and advantages, including:

Flexibility: Work can be moved from desktop machines to more powerful servers.

Reusability: Many applications can share and reuse code that is written as a component or a service.

Manageability: Large, complex applications can be divided into smaller components.

Maintenance: Maintaining business rules and databases is much easier when they are deployed on central servers rather than on multiple desktop machines.

Tier 1: User Services

User services, commonly referred to as the front end, provide the user interface for presenting information and gathering data. In our case, this service is a Visual Basic application that provides a graphical interface between the user and the business rules. It is responsible for gathering requirements from the user and presenting data in response to a question or query.

Tier 2: Business Services

Business services are the bridge between user and data services. They respond to requests from the user services for data services. The business services, or middle services, apply defined business rules to the selection of data to narrow the retrieval so that only pertinent data are returned to the user services.

> **NOTE** A *business rule* is a condition defined by the application, such as selecting the correct parts to order or printing only the new customers on a customer report.

Tier 3: Data Services

Data services, commonly referred to as the back end, maintain, access, and update data. They also manage and satisfy requests to manipulate data that are initiated by business services. Data services may be supplied by a particular database management system—such as Microsoft SQL Server, Oracle, or Sybase—or by a collection of databases that may reside on multiple platforms. Separating data services allows the data structure and access mechanisms to be maintained, modified, or even re-architected without affecting business or user services.

As you can see, three-tiered applications are ideally suited to the client/server model of separating the client, or first tier, from the server, or the third tier. In the next section, we will look at what drives developers to build client/server applications.

Why Adopt the Client/Server Method?

Today, developers are adopting the client/server methodology more than ever before. Why? What drives developers to move to this type of system? We believe they are doing so for three primary reasons:

The need for enterprisewide access to corporate data: As technology advances and computers become less expensive, smaller, more powerful, and easier to use, information is becoming more widely distributed across the enterprise. Client/server technology provides flexible links to access and manipulate this data regardless of its location or storage format.

The inadequacy of multiuser file-server applications: Client/server applications provide the performance, reliability, and security needed to drive enterprisewide computing into the next century. As database applications grow and become more complex, developers need the assurance that they are on a proven path that can keep pace with the ever-increasing demands and plan for the needs of tomorrow.

The downsizing of mainframe and minicomputer database applications: Companies are aggressively moving away from text-based applications and file-server applications to provide their users with an easier, friendlier graphical user interface. The power inherent in the client/server model is the basis for this enterprisewide reengineering movement. Reengineering is happening now because it can. Downsizing, however, is more difficult and more expensive, both in capital costs and in resource costs. This makes the move from mainframes to the client/server arena a priority.

Once you decide to move from a file-server to a client/server approach, you'll find that you can use a plethora of Visual Basic data access options, as you will discover in the following sections.

Data Access Options

As we have already discussed, the majority of applications being developed today provide some type of data access. Visual Basic provides a variety of options when it comes to accessing remote client/server databases. In this section, we will explore the following alternatives for client/server data access through the Enterprise Edition of Visual Basic 5:

Data Access Objects (DAO), which communicates with Microsoft Access and other ODBC-compliant data sources through the JET database engine.

Data Control, which binds data-aware controls to Microsoft Access or other ODBC data sources.

ODBCDirect, which allows you to access ODBC data sources through the RDO (Remote Data Objects) with DAO objects, bypassing the JET database engine.

Remote Data Objects (RDO), which provide a framework for using code to create and manipulate components of a remote ODBC database system.

Remote Data Control (RDC), which binds controls to an ODBC remote database.

Open Database Connectivity (ODBC), which is an API call interface to the Open Database Connectivity libraries and drivers to provide data access to Microsoft SQL Server and other databases that provide an ODBC driver.

Visual Basic Library for SQL Server (VBSQL), which is an implementation of the DB_Library API specifically designed to provide access to SQL Server through a Visual Basic application.

Active Data Objects (ADO), which is a programming model that eliminates the need to choose from among DAO and RDO and all the other data access methods and that is being designed to provide a common bridge between different databases, file systems, and e-mail servers.

Figure 9.4 summarizes these data access models. In the sections that follow, we'll look at each of them in detail.

FIGURE 9.4:

The data access models available in the Enterprise Edition of Visual Basic 5

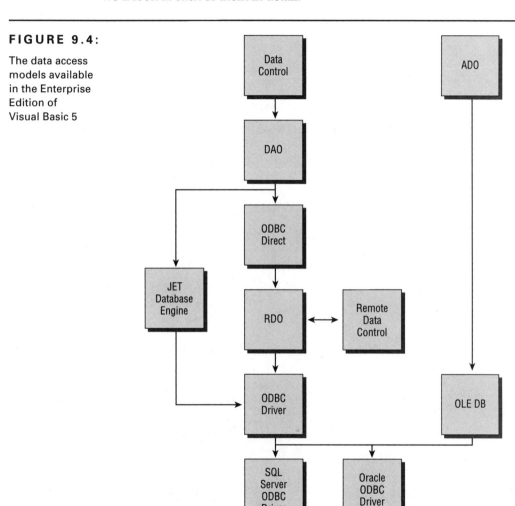

Data Access Objects

Data Access Objects (DAO) communicate with Microsoft Access and other ODBC-compliant data sources through the JET engine. The DAO model is a collection of object classes that model the structure of a relational database system. They provide properties and methods that allow you to perform all the operations necessary to manage such a system, including the ability to do the following:

- Apply referential integrity
- Create databases
- Define tables, fields, and indexes
- Establish relations between tables
- Navigate and query the database, and so on

Figure 9.5 shows a typical remote data access using DAO and the JET engine.

FIGURE 9.5:

Remote data access using DAO and the JET engine

The JET database engine translates these operations on data access objects into physical operations on the database files themselves, handling all the mechanics of interfacing with the different supported databases. This approach simplifies access to the database and insulates you from the underlying mechanics of retrieving and updating data. It affords you great flexibility because the same objects, properties, and methods can be used with a wide variety of supported database formats.

Through DAO and the JET engine, Visual Basic recognizes three categories of databases, and these are summarized in Table 9.1.

TABLE 9.1: Database Categories for DAO and the JET Engine

Category	Description
Visual Basic Databases	Also called native databases, these database files use the same format as Microsoft Access. These databases are created and manipulated directly by the JET engine and provide maximum flexibility and speed.
External Databases	These are Indexed Sequential Access Method (ISAM) databases in several formats, including Btrieve, dBASE III, dBASE IV, Microsoft FoxPro versions 2 and 2.5, and Paradox versions 3.x and 4.
ODBC Databases	These include client/server databases that conform to the ODBC standard, such as Microsoft SQL Server. To create true client/server applications in Visual Basic, you can use ODBCDirect to pass commands directly to the external server for processing.

The DAO programming model provides the following features:

- Advanced resultset management.

- An object-oriented programming model that does not require API functions

- A pass-through implementation that allows the JET query processor to be bypassed

- A universal programming model that can access any ODBC database regardless of the ODBC compliance level

- Keyset, static, and forward-only scrolling snapshot cursor implementation

- The ability to fetch and join heterogeneous data from multiple ODBC or ISAM sources

- The ability to create updatable cursors against complex resultsets created as a join product

- Universal error management

> **NOTE**
>
> Visual Basic version 5 includes only the 32-bit JET 3.5 database engine. The 16-bit version of the JET engine is no longer included in Visual Basic, but the JET 3.5 engine can read and write JET version 1 through version 2.5 (16-bit) databases.

Data Control

A data control binds data-aware controls to Microsoft Access or to other ODBC data sources, enabling you to move from record to record and to display and manipulate data from the records in bound controls.

> **NOTE**
>
> A *bound control* is a control that is assigned to a field in a database.

You can perform most data-access operations with a data control without writing any code. You set the database name and record source—a table, a view, or a SQL statement—of the data control at run time or at design time. When a Form that has a data control is opened, the data control is automatically populated with the data from the data control's database and record source properties, and the bound controls are loaded with the data from the first record. Figure 9.6 shows the data control and DAO with bound controls.

ODBCDirect

ODBCDirect allows you to access ODBC data sources through the RDO with DAO objects, bypassing the Microsoft JET database engine. Originally, DAO was tied to the JET engine, but with DAO 3.5, the DAO object interface was separated from the JET engine, giving developers an alternative—to create ODBCDirect workspaces without the JET engine. When your code opens a DAO Recordset object, the ODBCDirect interface creates an RDO ResultSet to retrieve the data. Figure 9.7 shows remote data access using ODBCDirect.

FIGURE 9.6:

The data control,
DAO, and bound
controls

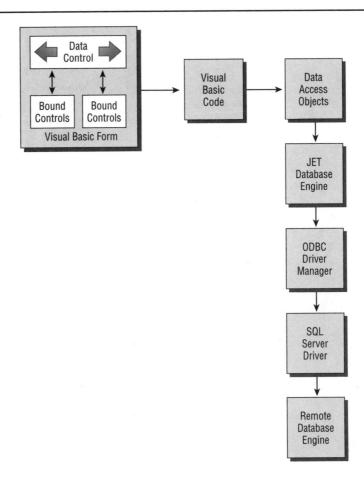

The ODBCDirect programming model is associated with the following advantages:

- It bypasses the JET database engine.

- It reduces resource requirements. Since you don't have to load the Microsoft JET database engine, your application requires fewer resources at the workstation.

- It provides a DAO interface to the RDO libraries.

FIGURE 9.7:

Remote Data
Access using
ODBCDirect

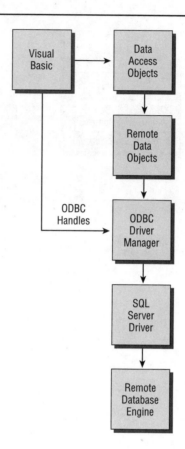

- Your application can access ODBC data sources directly, making the server responsible for all query processing.

- It provides improved access to server-specific functionality.

- You can execute a query and perform other operations without waiting for the query to finish. You can then check properties to keep track of the query's execution. This provides greater possibilities for your application in terms of concurrency and optimized performance.

- You can cache recordset changes locally and then submit these changes to the server in a single batch.

- You can handle output parameters and return values from stored procedures.

Remote Data Objects

Remote Data Objects (RDO) and collections provide a framework for using code to create and manipulate components of a remote ODBC database system. Because RDO is a thin object-model layer over the ODBC API, it does not impact data access times. RDO is Visual Basic's flagship interface to relational ODBC data sources. Figure 9.8 shows a typical remote data access using RDO.

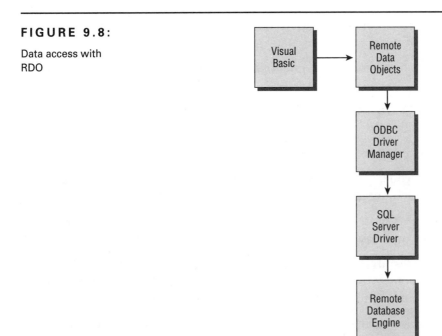

RDO is specifically designed to deal with remote intelligent data sources such as SQL Server and Oracle, as opposed to ISAM databases. RDO can execute ordinary table-based queries, but it is especially good at building and executing queries against stored procedures and at handling all types of resultsets. RDO 2 is so adept at providing control over remote data sources that you need not code an ODBC interface, except in unusual cases.

RDO includes a number of objects, properties, and methods specifically designed to work with stored procedures and their arguments, input and output parameters, and return values. RDO will trigger events during and after the completion of an operation, so you no longer have to poll for the status. This allows the developer to leverage the ability of Windows 95 and Windows NT to run multiple threads of execution. RDO can also handle multiple resultsets generated by a single query.

The following advantages are associated with the RDO programming model:

- It is a universal programming model that can access any 32-bit Level II ODBC data source.

- It can access virtually all Microsoft SQL Server and Oracle remote database engine features.

- It is an object-oriented programming model that does not require the use of APIs.

- Keyset, static, dynamic, and forward-only cursors are implemented on the server side.

- Its operations are fully asynchronous and event-driven.

- It gives you the ability to create standalone rdoQuery and rdoConnection objects and to associate queries with connections at design time.

- It supports synchronous, asynchronous, and event-driven connections, queries, and resultset population methods.

- It provides advanced resultset management, including the ability to limit the number of returned rows, to manage multiple resultsets, and to handle the input, output, and return value arguments of stored procedures.

- It provides universal error management that exposes not only ODBC error messages but also native errors and messages.

Today, most developers consider RDO the primary data access method when working with SQL Server, Oracle, or any relational database that is exposed with an ODBC driver.

NOTE For a complete discussion of RDO including code samples, see Chapter 11.

RemoteData Control

The RemoteData Control (RDC) binds controls to an ODBC remote database. The RemoteData Control is similar to the data control, except that it creates and manipulates RDO objects. By using RDO and the RemoteData Control, you can access ODBC data sources through data-aware, or bound, controls without going through the JET engine, resulting in significantly higher performance and greater flexibility when accessing remote data sources. Figure 9.9 shows a typical RDO/RemoteData Control providing access to a remote data source.

FIGURE 9.9:

A typical RDO/RDC data access

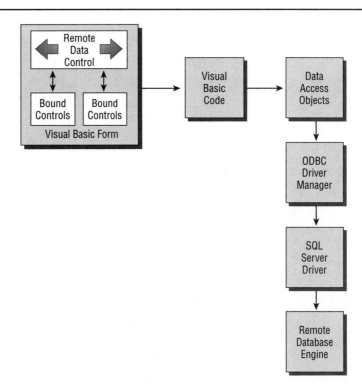

You can perform most remote data access operations using the RDC without writing any code at all. Data-aware controls bound to an RDC automatically display data from one or more columns for the current row or, in some cases, for a set of rows on either side of the current row. RemoteData Controls perform all operations on the current row. The RemoteData Control automatically handles a number of contingencies, including empty resultsets, adding new rows, editing and updating existing rows, converting and displaying complex data types, and handling some types of errors.

NOTE You'll find a complete discussion of the RemoteData Control, including example code, in Chapter 11.

Open Database Connectivity

Open Database Connectivity (ODBC) is an API call interface to the Open Database Connectivity libraries and drivers to provide data access to Microsoft SQL Server and other databases that provide an ODBC driver. Figure 9.10 shows a typical ODBC API access to a remote data source.

FIGURE 9.10:

Typical ODBC API access to a remote data source

The ODBC API is designed to provide an interface to database front ends that need a fast, small footprint and a relatively stable platform with which to connect to client/server systems. ODBC provides API calls that can expose the application to specific features of the data source.

Generally, there are two approaches to using the ODBC API:

Extending RDO with the ODBC API: Remote Data Objects (RDO) are, for the most part, object interfaces to the ODBC API. Using ODBC handles provided by the object-level interfaces to call ODBC API functions can be an effective way to control aspects of your rdoEnvironment, rdoConnection, rdoQuery, or rdoResultset objects.

Coding directly to the ODBC API: It is possible to create an application using the ODBC API that does not depend on RDO or other object-style interfaces to allocate handles, open connections, create and manage cursors, or perform complex data retrieval, binding, and update operations. The ODBC API can perform all these functions. Although you might gain some speed in data access, it is far more difficult to code and maintain when compared with using RDO.

The ODBC API programming model provides the following features:

- A native interface to Microsoft SQL Server
- A flexible programming model that can access most database architectures
- Access to virtually all SQL Server features
- Advanced resultset management
- Complete post-call error management
- Fewer API functions than required by VBSQL
- Intelligent handling of stored procedure parameters
- Keyset, dynamic, static, and forward-only cursors
- Support of server-side cursors on Microsoft SQL Server starting with version 6

As the complexity and flexibility of remote data source platforms has evolved, the complexity of using Visual Basic with the ODBC API programming model has also increased. Although it is possible to create applications using the ODBC API from Visual Basic, it no longer affords sufficient benefit over using the Remote Data Object interface or other object-model interfaces.

Visual Basic Library for SQL Server

The Visual Basic Library for SQL Server (VBSQL) is an implementation of the DB-Library API specifically designed to provide access to SQL Server through a Visual Basic application. VBSQL exposes virtually all the DB-Library API functions and is supported as a native interface to SQL Server. Figure 9.11 shows VBSQL accessing the SQL Server.

Use VBSQL when your application needs to connect only to Microsoft SQL Server. You can use VBSQL to open one or more connections, submit queries, create cursors, process resultsets, execute stored procedures, and execute bulk copy operations. This set of functions invokes equivalent functions in the DB-Library DLL, which is specifically designed to access Microsoft SQL Server.

FIGURE 9.11:

VBSQL accessing the
SQL Server

The VBSQL and the OBDC API functions are similar in that they both provide the broadest flexibility and, in some cases, better data access performance than RDO when accessing SQL Server. VBSQL does not support bound controls, so you will have to write all the code to connect, populate, and maintain Form-based controls. VBSQL provides the following features: Access to virtually all SQL Server features except two-phase commit.

- Access to Microsoft SQL Server

- A native interface to Microsoft SQL Server

- Bulk copy (BCP) interface

- Complete interrupt-driven error and message handlers

- Fully asynchronous operations

- Keyset, dynamic, static, and forward-only scrolling cursors

- 'N' Row buffer resultsets

- Server-side cursor support on SQL Server starting with version 6

- Specific API functions to address all SQL Server features

Active Data Objects

Over the next year or so, Active Data Objects (ADO) will emerge as another data access alternative that will, over time, replace the need for other interfaces. Version 1 of ADO exposes only a subset of RDO 2 functionality; however; ADO 2 will eventually provide a superset of RDO 2 functionality and provide a far more sophisticated data access interface and an easier programming model. Figure 9.12 shows an ADO connection to a remote data source.

FIGURE 9.12:

An ADO connection to a remote data source

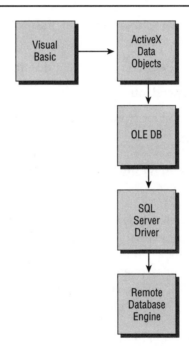

ADO enables you to write a client application to access and manipulate data in a database server through a provider. ADO's primary benefits are ease of use, high speed, low memory overhead, and a small disk footprint.

In ADO, the object hierarchy is deemphasized. Unlike Data Access Objects (DAO) or Remote Data Objects (RDO), ADO allows you to create objects independently; you no longer have to navigate through a hierarchy to create objects. This allows you to create and track only the objects you need. The ADO model also results in fewer objects, which allows for a smaller working set.

ADO is designed to eventually negate the need for all other interfaces. ADO is not specifically designed for ISAM or relational database access, but as an object interface to any data source. ADO is built around a set of core functions that all data sources are expected to implement.

The ADO programming model provides the following features:

- Advanced recordset cache management

- Batch updating

- Different cursor types, including the potential for support of back-end–specific cursors

- Free-threaded objects for efficient Web server applications

- Independently created objects

- Support for stored procedures with in/out parameters and return values

- Support for limits on the number of returned rows and other query goals

- Support for multiple recordsets returned from stored procedures or batch statements

ADO version 1 is not included with Visual Basic 5, but Visual Basic can host it. This integration will be provided in subsequent versions of VB. So, should you use ADO today? It is possible to implement ADO in Visual Basic 5, but it might not make sense given ADO's current level of implementation when compared with RDO 2. For example, ADO 1 does not currently expose any of the following features as implemented in RDO 2:

- Asynchronous operations

- Enhanced batch-mode error and contingency handling

- Events on the Engine, Connection, ResultSet, and Column objects

- Queries as objects

- Tight integration with Visual Basic 5, as in the Query Connection designer and TSQL debugger

---

TIP   ADO is available from Microsoft and can be downloaded from www.microsoft.com/data/ado. Be sure to also download the ADO help file.

Client/Server Tools Available in the Enterprise Edition of Visual Basic

The Enterprise Edition of Visual Basic 5 presents a design strategy for building component-based solutions based on the three-tiered services model. This section introduces some of the software tools and utilities provided by the Enterprise Edition to assist in building these distributed solutions.

The tools and utilities described here enable developers to connect to a data source, design queries and stored procedures, graphically design and maintain databases, and debug stored procedures.

The following sections briefly introduce and summarize the uses and benefits of each of these tools:

The UserConnection Designer uses Visual Basic's new ActiveX designer architecture to provide design-time support for stored procedures and query objects. It allows you to create connection and query objects based on the RDO rdoConnection and rdoQuery objects at design time.

Visual Database Tools is available as an add-in from your development environment to help create and manage data-driven applications that rely on live connections to databases.

The T-SQL Debugger is a stored procedure debugger that is fully integrated with the UserConnection designer and allows you to interactively debug remote stored procedures written in Microsoft SQL Server's Transact SQL dialect, from within the Visual Basic 5 development environment.

The UserConnection Designer

As you write client/server applications, you will find that it will become increasingly difficult to stay aware of and maintain your stored procedures and queries. You will have stored procedures on the server and query objects in your VB code, but how do you track all of them?

The UserConnection Designer uses Visual Basic's new ActiveX designer architecture to provide design-time support for stored procedures and query objects. It allows you to create connection and query objects based on the RDO rdoConnection and rdoQuery objects at design time. These connections and queries become project-level objects. You can pre-set properties, define new properties, methods, and parameters, and write code behind the objects.

571

This provides a simplified method for responding to events raised from connections and queries, as well as for calling stored procedures and client-defined queries at run time.

Here are the basic steps involved in using the UserConnection Designer:

1. Choose Projects ➤ Components to open the Components dialog box, and then select the Designers tab and check Microsoft UserConnection to enable the UserConnection Designer.

2. Choose Project ➤ Add ActiveX Designer ➤ Microsoft UserConnection to insert the UserConnection designer into the project.

3. Use the UserConnection object's Property Page to establish connection information and specify settings for properties that can be set at design time.

4. Create new Query objects for the connection by selecting stored procedures from the target database or by inserting SQL code for user-defined queries.

5. Configure each Query object by setting properties on its Property Page.

6. Write Visual Basic code that creates an instance of the new UserConnection class and calls any of its queries as methods.

Inserting a UserConnection Object

Before you can use the UserConnection designer, you must add it to your project. To insert and configure a new UserConnection object, follow these steps:

1. Choose Project ➤ References to open the References dialog box, and then check the Remote Data Object 2.0 Library.

2. Choose Project ➤ Components to open the Components dialog, and then select the Designers tab and check Microsoft User Connection.

3. Choose Project ➤ Add ActiveX Designer ➤ Microsoft UserConnection to insert the UserConnection designer into the project. A Designers entry is added to your project tree, the UserConnection1designer window opens, and the UserConnection1 Properties dialog box opens, as shown in Figure 9.13.

FIGURE 9.13:

The UserConnection1
Properties dialog box

The UserConnection Properties Dialog Box

You use the UserConnection Property Page to set the properties for your User-Connection to communicate with SQL Server. This Property Page has three tabs:

- Connection

- Authentication

- Miscellaneous

The Connection Tab You use the options on the Connection tab (shown in Figure 9.13) to establish and monitor connections to the server during design time. These are maintained in the new UserConnection object so that you do not have to specify connection information when the class is created at run time. The options you set in this tab also provide connection information for Microsoft Visual Data tools.

The Use ODBC Datasource option is selected by default; so select the Pubs database from the drop-down list. If you prefer to supply all the connection information in your code, select the Use DSN-Less Connection String option.

NOTE If you choose to use a DSN-less connection, you *must* include the name of the server and driver along with any other user-specific information in the connect string. However, if you choose this option, you can *only* use the default OEMTOANSI (Off), NETWORK (named pipes), and other settings that can only be set when creating a DSN.

We describe the Microsoft Visual Data tools in the next section.

The Authentication Tab   In this tab (shown in Figure 9.14), you supply the information that is needed for connecting to the data source specified in the Connection tab. In the Authentication Information section enter your Server's SA (server administrator) user name in the User Name text box, and enter your password in the Password text box.

FIGURE 9.14:

The Authentication tab

Two levels of persistence are available for the UserConnection object's Authentication properties. By default, both properties are turned off so that caching and persistence of authentication does not occur. If you check the *Save Connection Information for new Run-mode Class* checkbox, the user name and passwords are stored in the properties of the actual class and are persisted in the built executable or DLL. If you check the Save Connection Information for Design Time checkbox, the user name and password persist only during design time and do not become part of the executable or DLL.

The Miscellaneous Tab   You use this tab (shown in Figure 9.15) to adjust the Timeout properties for Login and Query execution and to select a cursor library. For purposes of this example, accept the defaults and then click OK to save the changes and close the UserConnection1 Property Page.

FIGURE 9.15:

The Miscellaneous tab

The UserConnection Designer Form

Now, it's time to set up the UserConnection Form, as shown in Figure 9.16.

FIGURE 9.16:

The UserConnection Form

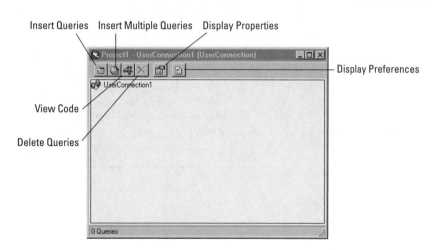

First, we'll insert a query based on the BYROYALTY stored procedure included with the sample Pubs database. Follow these steps:

1. Click the Insert Query button to open the Query1 Property Page. The General tab is selected by default, and the Query Name field is preset to Query1.

2. Select the Based on Stored Procedure option button, and then select the BYROYALTY stored procedure from the list box. You can also select the Based on User-Defined SQL option and enter a SQL statement for the query. If you then click the Build button, the designer launches MS_Query, where you can create a query. When you return to Visual Basic, Microsoft Query has copied the SQL statement into the dialog box.

For this example, we will accept the defaults for the Parameters and Advanced tabs, but let's take a look at them for future reference.

NOTE   If you click the Build button without entering a SQL statement, you will get an error. Simply enter something like **Select * from authors**.

---

3. Now select the Parameters tab:

In the Parameters tab, you adjust the properties for each parameter in the current query. You cannot change, delete, or add to the parameters in the Parameters list box; the source query automatically determines them. You can change the Name, Direction, ODBC Binding Data Type, and Visual Basic Data Type properties.

Now select the Advanced tab:

In the Advanced tab, you fine-tune the query by setting limits and thresholds. The ODBC Call Syntax edit box lets you change the call syntax that RDO uses to call the stored procedure. You can edit this to adjust the number of parameters and the presence of the return value. The values are preset defaults, but you can change them or later.

Using the UserConnection Object in Your Code

Now that we've set up all the dialog boxes, it's time to add some code and test the UserConnection. You insert the UserConnection object into your Visual Basic code just as you would insert any class. You can use Code 8.1 to execute the BYROYALTY stored procedure through the UserConnection class.

Code 8.1:   Establishing a UserConnection

```
Private Sub Form_Load()
    Dim ucnTest As New UserConnection1
    Dim rs As rdoResultset

    ucnTest.EstablishConnection

    ucnTest.Query1 (25)

    Set rs = ucnTest.LastQueryResults

    Do Until rs.EOF
        Debug.Print rs![au_id]
        rs.MoveNext
    Loop
End Sub
```

Code 8.1 creates a new UserConnection1 as uncTest and then establishes a connection to it. The Query is executed, and the rdoResultset is set to the LastQueryResults. Finally, the author id numbers (au_id) are written to the Debug window.

As you can see, the UserConnection can become a repository for your queries and stored procedures. It is also a great vehicle to use in working with queries and stored procedures that require parameters.

Visual Database Tools

Visual Database Tools, as shown in Figure 9.17, is a VB add-in that you can use to help create and manage data-driven applications that rely on live connections to databases.

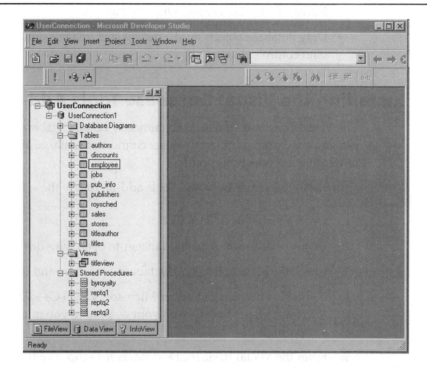

Visual Database Tools is tightly coupled with the UserConnection that we discussed in the previous section. Visual Database Tools uses the UserConnection to set its default WorkSpace. The Query Designer enables you to use visual tools to build SQL statements that retrieve data or modify the contents of tables. The interface of the Visual Database Tools is similar to that of Microsoft Access. The Database Designer graphically represents tables and their relationships and lets you create and modify the database objects on which your application relies. All this can be done while you are connected to the underlying database. You can design, query, and populate your databases from within the design environment that you use to build your application. With Microsoft Visual Database Tools, you can:

- Add, update, and delete data stored in database tables.

- Create and modify Microsoft SQL Server 6.5 databases using database diagrams.

- Connect to and explore any ODBC-compliant database.

- Design, execute, and save complex queries.

- Design objects—such as tables, triggers, and stored procedures—in Microsoft SQL Server and Oracle databases.

- Drag database objects onto a design surface form and then drag and drop to bind controls to those objects.

Installing the Visual Database Tools Add-In

The Visual Database Tools add-in launches Visual Database Tools and, if the project you are working in contains user connections, makes available the databases to which the connections point.

To install the Visual Database Tools add-in, follow these steps:

1. Open a Visual Basic 5 project.

2. Choose Add-Ins ➤ Add-In Manager to open the Add-In Manager dialog box.

3. Check the Microsoft Visual Database Tools box, and then choose OK.

4. If you haven't installed either Microsoft Visual C++ 5.0 Enterprise Edition or Microsoft Visual InterDev on your computer, you must run an additional setup program.

5. From the Visual Basic 5 CD-ROM, run `setup.exe` (it's in the `\Tools\DataTool` folder) and follow the installation instructions.

The Microsoft Visual Database Tools menu item now appears on the Add-Ins menu.

The Components of Visual Database Tools

Microsoft Visual Database Tools is made up of four components:

Data View provides a graphical environment for creating, viewing, and editing the database objects that reside on a remote database server. Data View is your starting point for managing your database objects, such as database diagrams, tables, triggers, views, and stored procedures.

The Database Designer is used to create, edit, or delete database objects for Microsoft SQL Server 6.5 databases while you're directly connected to the database in which those objects are stored.

The Query Designer is used to create SQL statements to query or update databases. It automatically creates joins and graphically shows table relationships.

Source Code Editor for Stored Procedures and Triggers is used to create, edit, and debug stored procedures and triggers.

This combination of database design tools provides a complete, tightly integrated database-development and administration tool for developers.

Data View

The Data View component, shown in Figure 9.18, provides a visual interface to live connections to the databases in each project and to objects available in each database, organized into folders, including the following:

Database Diagrams, which is a graphical representation of any portion of a database schema. A database diagram can be either a whole or a partial picture of the structure of a database; it includes objects for tables, the columns they contain, and the relationships among them.

Tables, which can be viewed as a set of rows and columns, similar to the rows and columns of a spreadsheet. In a relational database, the rows are called *records,* and the columns are called *fields.*

Stored Procedures, a precompiled collection of Transact-SQL statements and optional control-of-flow statements that are stored under a name and processed as a unit. Stored procedures are kept within a database, can be executed with one call from an application, and allow user-declared variables, conditional execution, and other powerful programming features. The stored procedures that SQL Server supplies are called *system stored procedures.*

Triggers, which is a special type of stored procedure that is activated when data in a specified table is modified. Triggers are often created to enforce referential integrity or consistency among logically related data in different tables.

Views, which is another way of looking at data from one or more tables in the database. A view is usually created as a subset of columns from one or more tables. The tables from which views are derived are called *base tables.*

A view looks almost exactly like any other database table, and you can display it and manipulate it almost as you can any table.

FIGURE 9.18:

The Visual Data Tools
Data View

Double-clicking a table, a view, or a stored procedure in Data View opens the object in a window. The data source permitting, you can edit and delete rows or add new rows. Give it a try. Double-click the Employee table in Data View, and the table will open as shown in Figure 9.19.

FIGURE 9.19:

Data View with an
open table

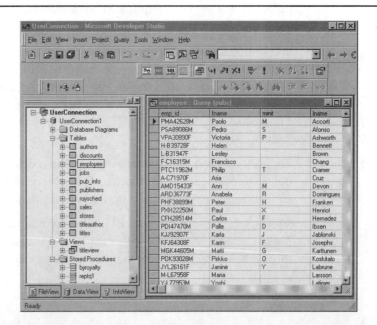

The Database Designer

You use the Database Designer, shown in Figure 9.20, to create, edit, or delete database objects for Microsoft SQL Server 6.5 databases while you're directly connected to the database in which those objects are stored.

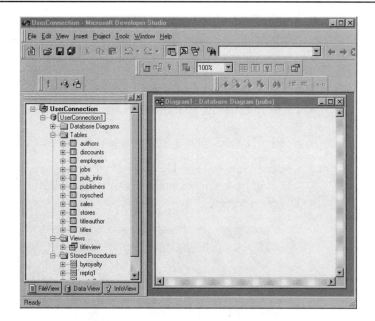

The Database Designer provides a graphical environment in which you can do the following:

- Create and modify the structure of Microsoft SQL Server databases

- Create, modify, or delete database objects such as tables, relationships, indexes, and constraints

- Experiment with the design of your Microsoft SQL Server database without affecting the database until you choose to save your new design

You interact with the server database using Database Diagrams, which graphically represent tables, the columns they contain, and the relationships among them.

Creating and Managing Database Diagrams   You can use Database
Diagrams to do the following:

- Alter the structure of your database

- Create new objects and relationships

- Experiment with database changes without modifying the underlying
  database

- Manipulate database objects without writing Transact-SQL code

- Provide different views of complex databases

- Perform complex operations to alter the physical structure of your database

To create a Database Diagram, follow these steps:

1. Choose View ➤ New Database Item to open the Insert Database Item dialog
   box, and then select Database Diagram. You'll see a blank Database
   Diagram screen:

2. Drag a table from Data View and drop it in the Database Diagram.

Saving Changes When you modify a database object through a Database Diagram, the modifications you make are not saved in the database until you save the table or the Database Diagram. Thus, you can experiment with what-if design scenarios without permanently affecting the existing design or data. The tables represented in your diagrams are merely references to tables that reside on the server.

A table that appears in multiple Database Diagrams actually exists only in the server database itself. When you modify a table in a diagram, your modifications are immediately applied to that table in every other diagram in which it appears.

When you save a Database Diagram, all the tables in your diagram and their related objects are saved in the server database. You can choose to select only certain tables in your diagram and save them without affecting the others.

You can then do one of the following:

- Save the changes to selected tables or the Database Diagram and have the changes modify the server database

- Cancel and discard your changes

- Save the Transact-SQL code generated by your changes to the diagram in a change script

You control the timing, type, and extent of the changes to your database by choosing how changes to the Database Diagram affect the server database.

The Query Designer You can use the Query Designer, shown in Figure 9.21, to create SQL statements to query or update databases. It automatically creates joins and graphically shows table relationships. It is similar to the Query tab in Microsoft Access. With the Query Designer you can do the following:

- Drag tables from the Data View into the query and use graphical controls to manipulate the query definition

- Use a criteria grid to specify search criteria, sort order, and output columns

- Use a SQL pane to type SQL statements or let the Query Designer generate the SQL for your queries

- Browse and edit live views of data in your database tables

You can copy and paste the SQL statements that the Query Designer creates into your Visual Basic application. This can be especially helpful if your query has a lot of complex joins.

FIGURE 9.21:

The Query Designer

The Diagram pane

The Grid pane

The SQL pane

The Results pane

If you are familiar with SQL, you can also do the following:

- Enter SQL statements directly or edit the SQL statements created by the Query Designer

- Create back-end specific SQL statements to take advantage of the features of a particular database

- Execute Microsoft SQL Server stored procedures

NOTE

You can also copy SQL statements that you code in your Visual Basic applications into the Query Designer and execute them. This is a great way to check your SQL syntax.

Query Designer Layout   The Query Designer consists of four panes (as shown in Figure 9.21). Table 9.2 lists and describes each pane.

TABLE 9.2: The Query Designer Panes

Pane	Description
The Diagram pane	Displays the input sources (tables or views) that you are querying. Each input source appears in its own window, showing the available data columns as well as icons that indicate how each column is used in the query. Joins are indicated by lines between the input source windows. Double-click the join lines to get additional information on the join.
The Grid pane	Contains a spreadsheetlike grid in which you specify query options, such as which data columns to display, how the results should be sorted, and what rows to select.
The SQL pane	Displays the SQL statement for the current query. You can edit the SQL statement, or you can enter your own SQL statement. If you edit the SQL statement, the diagram pane is updated to reflect the changes after you run the query.
The Results pane	Shows a grid with the results of the most recently executed query. You can edit the values, add rows, and delete rows from this grid.

Using Different Panes to Create Queries   You can create a query by working in some or all the panes. You can specify a column to display by choosing it in the Diagram pane and entering it into the Grid pane.

The Diagram, Grid, and SQL panes are synchronized, so when you make a change in one pane, the Query Designer updates the other panes to reflect the change. This allows the Query Designer to represent your query by displaying graphics in the Diagram and Grid panes and displaying text in the SQL pane.

Running the Query   If you are creating a Select query, the results are displayed in the Results pane. The Query Designer enables you to begin viewing rows immediately by running the query in small batches.

The Query Designer dims the contents of the Results pane if the current query changes to indicate that it no longer reflects the current query.

Creating Queries in the SQL Pane   In addition to creating queries in the Diagram and Grid panes, you can enter SQL statements directly into the SQL pane. When you move to another pane, the Query Designer parses the SQL statement and synchronizes the other panes to reflect the new statement. This is a great way to check the syntax of SQL statements in your Visual Basic application. You can copy from VB, paste into the SQL pane, and run the query. The Query Designer displays any errors that occur.

If you create a SQL statement that cannot be represented in the Diagram and Grid panes, the Query Designer dims those panes to indicate that they no longer reflect the state of the current query.

As you can see, the Query Designer can be a useful tool, helping you create, test, and debug SQL statements.

The Source Code Editor

You can use the Source Code Editor, shown in Figure 9.22, to do the following:

- Edit stored procedures and triggers
- Execute stored procedures and view their results

FIGURE 9.22:

The Source Code Editor

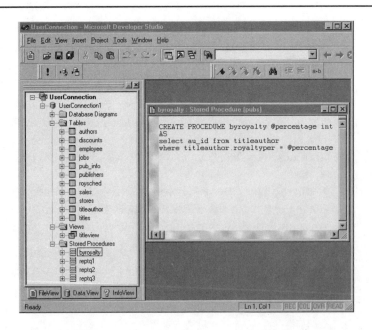

Editing Stored Procedures and Triggers   You can open a procedure stored in your Microsoft SQL Server or Oracle database to view or edit its text. Stored procedures are written in SQL. Follow these steps to open and edit a stored procedure or trigger:

1. In Data View, expand the `Stored Procedures` folder.

2. Right-click the name of the stored procedure that you want to open.

3. Double-click the stored procedure to open it in a text editor that you can use to edit the SQL statements.

4. Choose File ➤ Save to save the stored procedure or trigger.

NOTE   Stored procedures must have unique names in the database. If the name beside CREATE PROCEDURE in the procedure text is already assigned to another database object, the Server Error(s) dialog box prompts you to choose another name for the stored procedure.

Running Stored Procedures and Triggers   If you are using Microsoft SQL Server, in addition to creating queries, you can execute stored procedures. This feature enables you to take advantage of precompiled queries and system procedures. The project workspace displays a list of stored procedures available in the current database.

To see a list of available stored procedures in Data View, expand the name of your project, expand the name of the data connection you are querying, and then display the Stored Procedures node.

You can execute a stored procedure in two ways:

- Directly from Data View. This method does not require you to have the Query Designer open.

- In the SQL pane of the Query Designer.

Executing a Stored Procedure in Data View   Follow these steps to execute a stored procedure from Data View:

1. In Data View, expand the Stored Procedures node.

2. Right-click the stored procedure you want to execute, and then choose Run from the shortcut menu. If the stored procedure requires parameters, the Run Stored Procedure dialog box prompts you for parameter values:

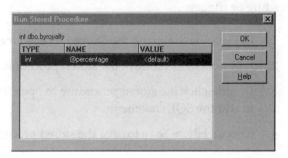

The results are displayed as text in the project's Output pane. The display lists any rows produced by the stored procedure and the return value.

Executing a Stored Procedure in the SQL Pane   Follow these steps to execute a stored procedure in the SQL pane:

1. Enter the stored procedure command in the SQL pane using this syntax:

```
EXECUTE procedure_name [parameter [, parameter ] ...]
```

NOTE   To execute stored procedures in other databases or stored procedures belonging to other owners, you can qualify the name of the stored procedure.

2. Select the Run option to execute the stored procedure.

Any returned rows appear in the Results pane, where you can copy them individually or as a column. However, the Results pane does not display the return value explicitly.

The T-SQL Debugger

As you create client/server applications, you will no doubt compile quite a set of stored procedures. Trying to keep these procedures current could become a full-time job. Well, Visual Basic includes a tool, the T-SQL Debugger (shown in Figure 9.23), that can help cut this job down to size.

FIGURE 9.23:

The T-SQL Designer

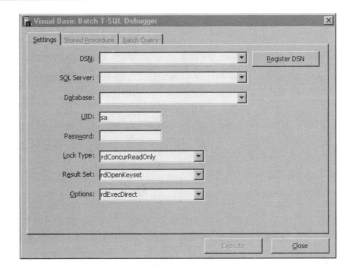

The T-SQL Debugger is a stored procedure debugger that is fully integrated with the UserConnection Designer and allows you to interactively debug remote stored procedures written in Microsoft SQL Server's Transact SQL dialect, from within the Visual Basic 5 development environment. The T-SQL Debugger allows you to do the following:

- Create stored procedures
- Display the SQL code, local variables, and parameters for stored procedures
- Set and manage breakpoints in the SQL statement
- View and modify local variables and parameters
- View global variables

Setting Up the Debugger

To use the T-SQL Debugger, you must have SQL Server Version 6.5 with at least Service Pack 1 installed and available as a server.

NOTE   Service Pack 3 for Microsoft SQL Server is now available from the Microsoft Web site. You can download it from www.microsoft.com/sql.

The debugger uses the functionality exposed by SQL Server's Sdi.dll and Remote Automation.

The Client-Side Setup   The client-side components are installed when you choose to install the Enterprise tools with Visual Basic. Follow these steps to make the debugger available from within VB.

1. Choose Add-Ins ➢ Add-In Manager.

2. Select the T-SQL Debugger option from the list of available add-ins.

The debugger will be initialized, and a dialog box will notify you that it is ready to use.

The Server-Side Setup   For server-side setup, be sure that you have at least Service Pack 1 installed. This is when support for the debugger is added. Follow these steps to set up the server:

1. Set the Remote Procedure Call (RPC) Service and locator to Automatic if they are not already so that they start when your system boots.

2. On Windows NT, run the application Sdi_nt4.exe from the \Tools\SrvSetup directory.

NOTE   For setup on Windows NT Server 3.51, you must manually copy and register the necessary files. Consult the Readme.txt file located in the \CliSrv\Tsql\SrvSetup directory.

Using the T-SQL Debugger

You can invoke the T-SQL Debugger in three ways:

- At design time
- From within the UserConnection object
- While debugging Visual Basic code

Let's take a look at each method, using the sample UserConnection project that we used previously in the "UserConnection Designer" section.

Debugging at Design Time   To debug a stored procedure or a batch query at design time, follow these steps:

1.   Choose Add-Ins ➤ T-SQL Debugger to open the Visual Basic Batch T-SQL Debugger, as shown in Figure 9.23 earlier in this chapter. The Settings tab is selected by default.

2.   From the DSN drop-down list box, select the Pubs database.

3.   In the UID text box, enter your UserId, and in the Password text box, enter your password.

4.   Now select the Stored Procedure tab:

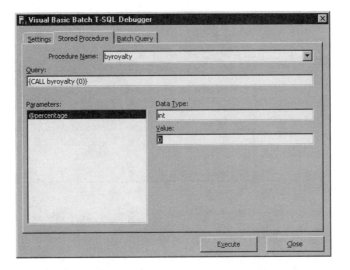

NOTE

The parameters are set by default to the Query1 object you created with the UserConnection in the previous section. All you have to do is provide the Percentage Parameter value.

5.   In the Parameters text box, enter **25,** and then click the Execute button to display the T-SQL Debugger screen showing the stored procedure SQL statement.

6.   Click the Go tool on the toolbar to run the stored procedure. The results are displayed in the Results pane at the bottom of the Debugger.

Debugging from within the UserConnection Object   To debug a stored procedure from within the Visual Basic UserConnection object, follow these steps:

1.   Right-click Query1, and select Debug Stored Procedure from the short-cut menu.

2.   If the query has parameters, the T-SQL Debugger displays the Enter Unassigned Parameters dialog box:

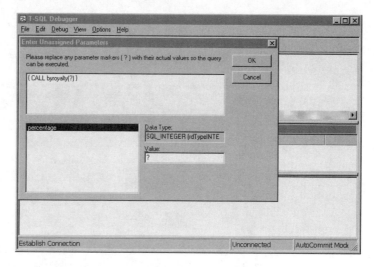

3.   Supply the parameters, and then click OK. The Debugger displays the SQL statements. You can click the Run tool to run the query.

Debugging from within Visual Basic Code   To debug from within your Visual Basic code, follow these steps:

1.   Choose Tools ➢ T-SQL Debugger Options to open the T-SQL Debugging Options dialog box:

2. The *Automatically step into Stored Procedures through RDO connections* option button is selected by default. With this option selected, the Debugger is called whenever you press F8 in an RDO method that executes a stored procedure.

3. Select the *Use Safe Mode (transaction rollback) for Stored Procedure calls* option. This automatically rolls back any design-time queries that you debug.

4. In the *Limit SQL output to the following number of lines per resultset* box, enter the number of rows that you want to appear in the Debugger's output window.

5. In the *Login Timeout value for retrieving stored procedure text* box, set the login timeout value that the debugger uses to connect to the database.

If you press F8 on a line of code that executes a stored procedure while running your code with the *Automatically step into Stored Procedures through RDO connections* option selected, the debugger automatically opens. You can then step through the stored procedure code.

Using SQL Server

- ■ What's new in SQL Server 6.5

- ■ Installing SQL Server 6.5

- ■ Using the tools in SQL Server 6.5

- ■ Creating Database objects in SQL Server 6.5

- ■ Creating and executing stored procedures and triggers

Most applications being developed today provide some type of data access. With its built-in data replication, powerful management tools, Internet integration, and open system architecture, Microsoft SQL Server 6.5 is a scalable, high-performance database management system designed specifically for distributed client/server computing.

As businesses streamline processes, decentralize decision-making, and depend increasingly on technology to bring users and information together, distributed client/server computing becomes the bridge between data and informed business decisions.

Building on Microsoft SQL Server 6, the first relational database management system (RDBMS) designed particularly for distributed client/server computing, SQL Server 6.5 extends performance, reliability, and scalability to satisfy today's business challenges. By providing advanced, graphical-based management tools and powerful, server-based job scheduling, SQL Server 6.5 gives you visual control over multiple servers and the capability to automate remote operations.

The enhanced, built-in data replication feature provides a powerful and reliable way to disseminate accurate information throughout your enterprise, not only across Microsoft SQL Server databases, but across Oracle, IBM DB2, Sybase, and other databases as well.

SQL Server 6.5, designed with the Internet and intranets in mind, also provides high-performance access to information on your company's Web site. Using the new Web Assistant, you can populate your Web server with SQL data through a variety of methods, allowing distribution of your company's data on a private intranet or worldwide on the Web.

The Distributed Transaction Coordinator in SQL Server 6.5 makes distributed applications easier to create by automating the management of transactions across multiple servers. And now, locking is configurable between row-level and page-level, with automatic deadlock resolution.

What's New in SQL Server 6.5

Whether you're new to SQL Server or you have been using it all along, it is important to take a look at some of the new and improved features that affect

Visual Basic developers. SQL Server 6.5 includes new features and components for the server and the client. The new features can be grouped into six categories:

Setup: Installing or upgrading SQL Server.

Administrators: SQL Server administration.

Transact_SQL: An enhanced version of Structured Query Language (SQL). SQL is a high-level language for relational database systems.

OLE Automation Stored Procedures: Stored procedures that allow you to use standard OLE Automation objects within a Transact_SQL statement.

SQL_DMO: A custom component that provides 32-bit COM objects which can be used by 32-bit Visual Basic programs and 32-bit C++ programs.

DB_Library for Visual Basic: Enhanced functions for the DB_Library for Visual Basic.

In the sections that follow, we will discuss these new features and how they relate to Visual Basic developers.

What's New and Improved in Setup

The SQL Server program automates much of the setup process. Since SQL Server is an intelligent database system, you can begin using the SQL Server right after it is set up. To automate the setup task even more, the setup program includes some new and updated features.

Keywords and Character Sets

As SQL Server improves, the upgrade from version 6 to version 6.5 has seen some changes in keywords and character sets. The following words, reserved in SQL Server 6, are now keywords in SQL Server 6.5:

AUTHORIZATION

CASCADE

CROSS

DISTRIBUTED

ESCAPE

FULL

INNER

JOIN

LEFT

OUTER

PRIVILEGES

RESTRICT

RIGHT

SCHEMA

WORK

In an effort to make SQL Server available to more developers and users, several character sets have been added. This is good news for developers of international applications, because now the server can be maintained in a wider language spectrum. The following is a list of the new character sets:

- CP1250: Central European
- CP936: Chinese (simplified)
- CP949: Korean
- CP950: Chinese (traditional)

Platform Support

You can install SQL Server 6.5 on a Windows 3.51 system. But to take advantage of SQL Server features that require the server to access the network, such as generating Web pages, the SQL Server must be set up to log on under a user account.

What's New and Improved for Administrators

Administrators are responsible for overseeing and maintaining SQL Server. SQL Server provides powerful tools for enterprisewide administration, data replication, scalability to very large databases, and Web and mail support. This section summarizes some of the new and improved features that make the administrator's job a little easier.

NOTE In some situations, especially on small projects, the administrator and the developer might be the same person.

The Database Maintenance Plan Wizard

You use the Database Maintenance Plan Wizard to set up and schedule the core maintenance actions for a database, which include the following:

- Logging transactions
- Backing up the database
- Checking data links
- Checking index links and allocation
- Optimizing data

You can preset maintenance on a daily or weekly schedule.

You can run this new Wizard from SQL Enterprise Manager, or you can run the sqlmaint command-line utility. You can even generate a report about database maintenance that can be e-mailed to a designated mail account.

External Tools Support

You can launch any Windows NT application from SQL Enterprise Manager, and you can add and run external applications from the Tools menu and from the Tools bar.

You can add, change, or remove external applications with SQL Enterprise Manager. External tools can be run from the Tools menu or from the floating, dockable Tools bar.

Adding Visual Basic as an External Tool

Follow these steps to add Visual Basic as an external tool:

1. Start SQL Enterprise Manager from the SQL Server 6.5 program group.

2. Choose Tools ➢ External Tools to open the External Tools dialog box:

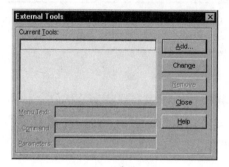

3. Click the Add button to open the Add External Tool dialog box:

   In the Command box, type the path and the file name of the application. Or click the Browse button and complete the Open dialog box. In this case, we are looking for vb5.exe.

4. In the Parameters box, type the parameters to pass to the application each time it is launched. (This is an optional entry.)

5. Click OK.

6. Click Close.

To change an external tool, follow these steps:

1. In the External Tools dialog box (as shown earlier), select a tool from the Current Tools list.

2. In the Menu Text box, type the change.

3. In the Command box, type a command. Generally, the command is a fully qualified path and includes the filename of an application.

4. In the Parameters box, type the parameters to pass to the application each time it is launched. (This is an optional entry.)

5. Click Change. The changed tool name will appear on the Tools menu and on the floating, dockable Tools bar.

Removing an External Tool

Follow these steps to remove an external tool:

1. In the External Tools dialog box, select a tool from the Current Tools list box.

2. Click Remove.

The convenience of running applications from within SQL Executive will prove to be a big plus as you use the SQL Executive to perform maintenance on your servers.

Print Support

The SQL code for stored procedures, triggers, and views can now be printed directly from SQL Enterprise Manager. To print the information from these windows, choose the Print icon or choose File ➤ Print. Now, with this print support, you no longer have to copy the SQL code and paste it into Notepad to print it. This is a convenient and time-saving feature.

Backup and Recovery

Today's hardware and software components are several times more reliable than those of the not-so-distant past; however, they will never be perfect, and there is always the possibility of having some type of failure. You should periodically make a backup copy of your database to protect against a catastrophic failure or user error that could result in data loss. Data can be restored from a backup with minimal user disruption and inconvenience.

SQL Server 6.5 maintains a history of database backups. It also supports point-in-time recovery, which enables transaction logs to be recovered through a specific date and time. And now, you can back up and restore individual tables (using table dump and load).

Fallback Support

Most enterprises rely heavily on their database solutions, so it important to have databases available all the time. However, in these situations, there is the concern that hardware or system failure could render the databases unavailable.

Fallback support enables a separate computer running SQL Server to automatically assume control of the crucial databases and devices of a primary server that is experiencing hardware or software failure. A fallback server can provide active fallback support for three primary servers simultaneously while holding databases from many other primary servers. Fallback support ensures that databases will be accessible even if an equipment failure occurs.

SQL Mail

SQL Server 6.5 includes extended stored procedures that allow mail messages to be sent and received through the built-in mail application programming interface (MAPI). SQL Mail is enhanced in SQL Server 6.5 and is now compatible with Microsoft Exchange Server. Enhancements also provide the ability to do the following:

- Stop and start SQL Mail from the Server Manager window of SQL Enterprise Manager

- Assign a mail logon name and password from SQL Enterprise Manager

- Set SQL Mail to impersonate a client for security purposes

SNMP Enhancements

SNMP (Simple Network Management Protocol) is part of the TCP/IP (Transmission Control Protocol/Internet Protocol) suite and was originally developed in the Internet community to monitor and troubleshoot routers and bridges. SNMP transports management information and commands between a management system and an SNMP agent. The SNMP agent sends status information to one or more hosts when the host requests it or when a significant event occurs.

Communication between SNMP clients and SQL Server is enabled in SQL Server 6.5. You can use SNMP applications to do the following:

- Monitor the status of SQL Server installations
- Monitor performance information
- Access databases
- View server and database configuration parameters
- Set conditions that initiate an alert message to be sent to workstations that are running SNMP monitoring applications

Remote Server Management

A *remote server* is a SQL Server on the network that users can access by using their local server. When a server is set up as a remote server, users can use the system procedures and the stored procedures on it without explicitly logging on to it.

The Remote Servers and Logins Manager interface in SQL Enterprise Manager centralizes administrative tasks and makes it easy for one person to manage many servers. You can also set distribution options for replication and configure ODBC subscribers from this interface.

NOTE A lot of new and improved tools are available for the administrator. We'll discuss these later in this chapter in the "Tools in SQL Server 6.5" section.

What's New and Improved in Transact-SQL

Transact-SQL is an enhanced version of Structured Query Language (SQL), a high-level language for relational database systems. With Transact-SQL you can retrieve data from a database, create databases and database objects, and add, delete, and update individual data records.

ANSI-Standard Null Handling

The American National Standards Institute (ANSI) provides standards throughout the trade and communications industries to promote compatibility among products and establish common behavior in related products.

Microsoft SQL Server 6.5 complies with ANSI standards and retains backward compatibility with configuration options that can be switched on or off by using the SET statement.

NOTE You'll find a complete listing of the ANSI-Standard null-handling configuration options in Appendix C, which is on the CD that comes with this book.

Catalog Stored Procedures

Catalog stored procedures provide a uniform catalog interface for accessing database gateways, as well as SQL Server, from the same application. These stored procedures are compatible with the catalog interface for the Microsoft Open Database Connectivity (ODBC) API.

NOTE You'll find a list of the improved catalog stored procedures in SQL Server 6.5 in Appendix C, which is on the CD that comes with this book.

The CUBE Operator

New to SQL Server 6.5 is aggregate operator called CUBE that can be used to produce resultsets that are typically used for reports.

CUBE operations are accessed by a switch in the GROUP BY clause in the SELECT statement. Columns included in the GROUP BY clause are cross-referenced to produce a superset of groups. The aggregate function specified in the select_list is applied to these groups to produce summary values for the additional super-aggregate rows.

Extended Stored Procedures

Extended stored procedures provide a way to dynamically load and execute a function within a dynamic-link library (DLL) in a manner similar to that of a stored procedure, seamlessly extending SQL Server functionality. Actions outside SQL Server can be easily triggered and external information returned to SQL Server. Return status codes and output parameters.

Extended stored procedures are implemented as DLLs, rather than as separate processes because a separate process would require a context switch and add additional security overhead. The DLL does not have direct access to or know of SQL Server data structures.

NOTE SQL Enterprise Manager includes the Extended Stored Procedures Manager. With it, you can add extended stored procedures to or drop existing extended stored procedures from SQL Server. You can use the Extended Stored Procedures Manager only when the *master* database is the current database. Appendix C, which is on the CD that comes with this book, provides a list of the extended stored procedures that have been added to SQL Server 6.5.

Functions

Functions return special information from the system about users, expressions, a database, or database objects. Aggregate functions return summary values. Other built-in functions perform various operations and are often used on their own or as part of a stored procedure. When used in SQL statements, functions can be used anywhere an expression is allowed.

NOTE Appendix C, which is on the CD that comes with this book, lists the new functions added in SQL Server 6.5.

Joins

Joining two or more tables is the process of comparing the data in specified columns and using the comparison results to form a new table from the rows that qualify.

NOTE
Appendix C lists the joins added and enhanced in SQL Server 6.5 and summarizes the ANSI-Standard joins supported in SQL Server 6.5. We discuss joins in more detail in Chapter 11.

Replication Stored Procedures

Replication stored procedures are the stored procedures that enable you to replicate or copy table schemas and data and have been added for use by SQL Enterprise Manager; however, you can manually set up replication through these new stored procedures.

NOTE
You'll find a list of replication stored procedures that have been added or enhanced in Appendix C, which is on the CD that comes with this book.

SQL Executive Stored Procedures

SQL Executive stored procedures give system administrators the ability to create tasks for replication, schedule events, and manage alert notification. The SQL Executive stored procedures are rarely executed directly; they are usually manipulated by SQL Enterprise Manager. It is recommended that you use SQL Enterprise Manager to configure your alert and scheduling infrastructure.

NOTE
You'll find the new SQL Executive stored procedures highlighted in Appendix C, which is on the CD that comes with this book.

System Stored Procedures

SQL Server system stored procedures are provided for your convenience and make it easy to retrieve information from the administrator databases and system tables and to perform other tasks that involve updating system tables.

System stored procedures are created in the master database during installation, and the system administrator owns them. The names of all system stored procedures begin with sp_, and all stored procedures for which documentation is provided are for regular system use. Additional stored procedures exist in the master database for internal use only, and you can view and use them as examples for writing your own procedures. However, they are not guaranteed to be included in future releases.

You can run system stored procedures from any database, but if a system stored procedure is executed from a database other than the master database, any non-qualified references to system tables are mapped to the database from which the procedure is being run. For example, if the database owner of the Pubs database runs sp_adduser from pubs, the new user is added to pubs..sysusers.

NOTE You'll find the new and enhanced system stored procedures for SQL Server 6.5 listed in Appendix C, which is on the CD that comes with this book.

Statements

SQL Server 6.5 has several new and improved statements. These statements make it easier for you to create and alter database structures and to add, update, and delete data.

NOTE You'll find all these statements outlined in Appendix C, which is on the CD that comes with this book.

Tables

A table is a collection of rows (records) that have associated columns (fields). The master database and each user database contain system tables of information about SQL Server as a whole and about each user database.

All the SQL Server–supplied tables in the master database are considered system tables. Each user database is created with a subset of those system tables.

The master database and its tables are created when you install SQL Server, and the system tables in a user database are automatically created when the database is created. The names of most system tables begin with sys. Several system tables have been added or improved in SQL Server 6.5.

NOTE You'll find a summary of additions and enhancements to the SQL Server 6.5 system tables in Appendix C, which is on the CD that comes with this book.

Utilities

SQL Server contains several command-line utilities, such as isql and SQLMAINT, for performing certain maintenance, administration, and debugging tasks.

The isql utility is a command-line query tool that is used for MS-DOS–based connectivity and batch processing.

SQLMAINT is a command-line utility for running automated consistency checks and backups. For example, it can create status reports and send them to an e-mail account.

What's New for OLE Automation Stored Procedures

OLE Automation stored procedures allow you to use standard OLE Automation objects within a Transact-SQL statement batch. These OLE objects reside and run on the SQL Server computer and behave as OLE extended stored procedures. You can use existing OLE Automation objects, such as the SQL Distributed Management Objects (SQL-DMO) or Microsoft Visual Basic (32-bit only) to create your own OLE Automation objects.

> **NOTE**
> You'll find a list of the new OLE Automation stored procedures in Appendix C, which is on the CD that comes with this book.

What's New For SQL-DMO

Microsoft SQL Server Distributed Management Object (SQL-DMO) is a Component Object Model (COM) object representation of the standard SQL Server internal objects. SQL-DMO is an in-process OLE server that exposes representations of Microsoft SQL Server database objects. Using these new OLE server objects, you can now manipulate any SQL Server database object from Visual Basic or any OLE Automation controller.

Physically, SQL-DMO is a set of dynamic-link libraries (DLLs) with a type library and can be used just like any other OLE server. SQL-DMO objects have been added and enhanced to support SQL Server 6.5 features, including ConnectionPoint events, which can be used to write COM objects that are notified by SQL-DMO when certain events occur.

What's New for DB-Library for Visual Basic

DB-Library for Visual Basic is a set of functions and routines for building front-end applications for Windows that interact with Microsoft SQL Server. DB-Library for Visual Basic is built on and is a subset of the SQL Server client library for C programmers.

SQL Server 6.5 includes a new DB-Library for Visual Basic OLE custom control, a 32-bit OLE custom control for creating DB-Library for Visual Basic projects using Visual Basic 5.

DB-Library for Visual Basic includes the same enhancements as DB-Library for C, except for Microsoft Distributed Transaction Coordinator (MS DTC) support. It also includes the new SqlCursorRowStatus function for returning the row fetch status value for a row in the cursor fetch buffer.

NOTE You'll find a summary of the new features for DB-Library on SQL Server 6.5 in Appendix C, which is on the CD that comes with this book.

As you can see, SQL Server 6.5 has a lot of interesting new features; however, since the database server provides the basic building blocks for business applications, it will continue to require constant improvements in an effort to respond to the ever-increasing demands of today's developers and users. In the next section, we will install SQL Server 6.5.

Installing SQL Server 6.5

Microsoft SQL Server 6.5 is distributed on a single CD-ROM that contains the setup program and server software for computers with:

- Alpha AXP microprocessors
- Intel 32-bit x86-based microprocessors
- MIPS microprocessors

Also included on the CD are the SQL Server client software and client software setup programs.

SQL Workstation

Microsoft also provides a version of SQL Server 6.5 known as the SQL Workstation. SQL Workstation 6.5 has the same features and functionality as Microsoft SQL Server except it is a single-user licensed product that supports a maximum of 15 simultaneous database connections. It includes the Microsoft SQL Server Programmer's Toolkit (PTK). SQL Workstation is primarily intended as a development platform.

SQL Server 6.5 Setup

Follow these steps to set up SQL Server 6.5:

NOTE   The setup procedures for SQL Workstation differ slightly, and we'll note these differences as we go through the steps.

1. Insert the SQL-Server 6.5 CD-ROM, and select Setup.exe from the appropriate subdirectory containing the software compatible with your hardware.

2. In the Welcome dialog box, click Continue to begin the installation process.

NOTE   For this example setup, we are installing SQL Server on an Intel-based Pentium computer, so we will run Setup.exe from the I386 subdirectory.

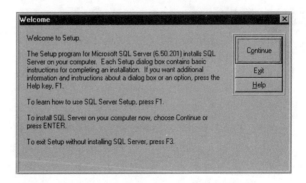

3. In the Enter Name and Organization dialog box, fill in three fields:

   Name: Enter the name of the user. This entry is required.

   Company: Enter the name of your company or organization. This entry is optional.

   Product ID: This is an identifier provided by Microsoft. It can be found on the CD case. This is an optional entry, but it is a good idea to enter it, as it will be used for product support.

   Click Continue.

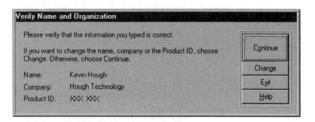

4. In the Verify Name and Organization dialog box, you can change your entries or accept them and then click Continue.

5. In the Microsoft SQL Server 6.5 - Options dialog box, you have the following options:

   Install SQL Server and Utilities: This is the default option. Selecting it installs all the server software and the utility applications.

   Upgrade SQL Server: Select this option if you are upgrading from a previous version of SQL Server.

Install Utilities Only: Select this option to install the Administrator utilities only.

Click Continue to accept the default option.

6. In the Choose Licensing Mode dialog box, select the type of licensing you purchased, and then click Continue.

NOTE   If you are installing the SQL Workstation, the Choose Licensing Mode dialog box notifies you that the SQL Workstation is licensed to a single user and is limited to 15 simultaneous database connections.

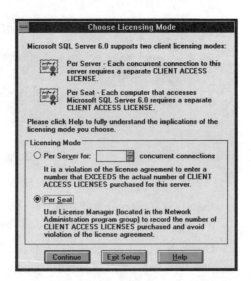

7. In the SQL Server Installation Path dialog box, set the installation path as shown. This will set the drive and directory for your server software.

8. In the MASTER Device Creation dialog box, the default device size is set to 25MB. You can accept this value or increase it.

NOTE To allow the new devices more room, let's set them to 35MB. You can change this value later in SQL Administrator.

---

9. In the SQL Server Books Online dialog box you have the following options (SQL Server Books Online gives you on-screen access to the entire set of SQL Server 6.5 documentation):

   Install on Hard Disk: This option uses 15MB of space; however, if you consult Books Online often and have the space, choose this option.

Install to Run from CD: This option uses 1MB of space and requires the CD to be in the CD player to access Books Online.

Do Not Install: Choose this option if you don't want to install Books Online.

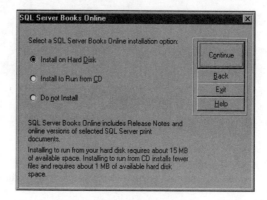

10. In the Installation Options dialog box, you have the following options:

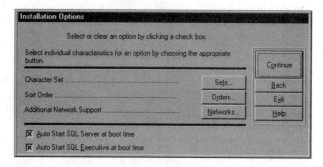

Character Set: A set of 256 uppercase and lowercase letters, numbers, and symbols. The character set you select determines the type of characters that SQL Server recognizes in your database. You have the following choices:

ISO 8859-1 (Latin 1 or ANSI): This is the default character set. It is compatible with the ANSI characters used by Microsoft Windows and Windows NT.

Code page 850 (Multilingual): This set includes all characters for most European, North American, and South American languages. Use this character set when you have MS-DOS–based client applications that use extended characters.

Code page 437 (U.S. English): Although this is the most commonly used character set in the United States, it includes many graphics characters not usually stored in databases. Unless you have an overriding reason to select this character set, choose Code page 850, which provides more compatibility with languages other than U.S. English.

Sort Order: A set of rules that determines how SQL Server collates and presents data in response to database queries. You have the following options:

- Dictionary order, case-insensitive (the default)
- Binary order
- Dictionary order, case-sensitive
- Dictionary order, case-insensitive, uppercase preference
- Dictionary order, case-insensitive, accent-insensitive
- Strict compatibility with version 1.*x* case-insensitive databases
- Alternate dictionary order, case-sensitive
- Alternate dictionary order, case-insensitive
- Alternate dictionary order, case-insensitive, uppercase preference
- Alternate dictionary order, case-insensitive, accent-insensitive
- Scandinavian dictionary order, case-sensitive
- Scandinavian dictionary order, case-insensitive, uppercase preference

Additional Network Support: Microsoft SQL Server 6.5 uses network libraries, known as Net-Libraries, to pass network packets back and forth between clients and a SQL Server. The Net-Libraries, implemented as dynamic-link libraries (DLLs), perform the network operations required to communicate using specific interprocess communication (IPC) mechanism protocols. During installation, the setup program gives you the option of setting up one or more of the following Net-Libraries on the server:

Multi-Protocol: The Multi-Protocol Net-Library takes advantage of the powerful remote procedure call (RPC) facility of Windows NT. Unlike other Net-Libraries, Multi-Protocol Net-Library need only be selected as an option from the Select Network Protocols dialog box; it does not require the entry of any configuration parameters.

TCP/IP Sockets: This Net-Library allows SQL Server to communicate using standard Windows sockets as the IPC method across the TCP/IP protocol.

Banyan VINES: SQL Server supports Banyan VINES Sequenced Packet Protocol (SPP) as the IPC method across Banyan VINES IP network protocol. Banyan VINES support for Windows NT-based clients and servers is available only for SQL Server on the Intel platform; it is not currently available on the MIPS or Alpha AXP platforms.

NOTE   Before you can configure SQL Server to listen on Banyan VINES, you must install the Banyan VINES software (available from Banyan).

AppleTalk ADSP: For Intel-, MIPS-, and Alpha AXP–based computers, server-side AppleTalk (ADSP) Net-Libraries are provided for use with Microsoft SQL Server. The server-side AppleTalk Net-Library allows Apple Macintosh-based clients to connect to SQL Server via native AppleTalk (as opposed to TCP/IP).

DECnet: For Intel-, MIPS-, and Alpha AXP–based computers, server-side DECnet sockets Net-Libraries provide connectivity with PATH-WORKS networks by allowing clients running on VMS to connect to Microsoft SQL Server via DECnet sockets.

Auto-Start Options: By default, SQL Server is installed so that SQL Server and SQL Executive are not started when NT starts. To change this option, select the Auto-Start options at the bottom of the screen.

NOTE   If you use SQL-Server regularly and your hardware will support it, it is nice to have the server start up with NT. This way your server is always available.

After you complete the Installation Options dialog box, click Continue to open the SQL Executive Log On Account dialog box:

The option you select in this dialog box indicates whether SQL Executive runs under a Windows NT user account (the default) or under the server's Local System account. If you select the default, you must provide an account name and a password. When you click Continue, SQL Server begins copying files to your installation directory. After the files are copied, you will be prompted to reboot the computer.

After you reboot, SQL Server is set up, and you can begin using it. Before we do so, however, we need to take a look at the tools available in SQL Server 6.5.

Tools in SQL Server 6.5

SQL Server 6.5 provides a wealth of tools that make it easier to set up, configure, and maintain servers, devices, and databases. Table 10.1 summarizes these tools, and we'll provide details throughout the rest of this section.

TABLE 10.1: The Tools in SQL Server 6.5

Tool	Description
ISQL/w	Allows you to enter Transact-SQL statements and system stored procedures in a graphical query interface.
Ms Query	Provides a query interface to relational databases. With SQL Server 6.5, Microsoft Query is installed by the SQL Server setup program. It is always installed with the server and can be optionally installed on 32-bit clients with the utilities option.
SQL Client Configuration Utility	Sets the default Net-Library and server connection information on clients, displays the DB-Library version number, and searches for multiple copies of DB-Library and Net-Library in your path.

TABLE 10.1 (CONTINUED): The Tools in SQL Server 6.5

Tool	Description
SQL Enterprise Manager	Provides easy, enterprisewide management from a server or a workstation. It allows you to configure servers, manage databases and database objects, schedule events, and configure and manage replication.
SQL Performance Monitor	Integrates Windows NT Performance Monitor with SQL Server, providing real-time activity and performance statistics.
SQL Security Manager	Allows you to manage user accounts for SQL Servers that are using security integration with Windows NT.
SQL Server Books Online	Provides online access to the Microsoft SQL Server documentation set. Includes the same full-text search capability that is in Visual Basic Books Online.
SQL Server Web Assistant	Allows you to generate standard Hypertext Markup Language (HTML) files from SQL Server data. The SQL Server Web Assistant uses Transact-SQL queries, stored procedures, and extended stored procedures to generate HTML files that can be viewed using any HTML browser. HTML files, or Web pages, are resources for displaying information on the World Wide Web (WWW) and on internal networks.
SQL Service Manager	Allows you to start, pause, continue, and stop SQL Server and SQL Executive.
SQL Trace	Monitors and records SQL Server 6.5 database activity.
SQL Transfer Manager	Provides a graphical way to transfer objects and data from one SQL Server to another. You can transfer from a Microsoft-based SQL Server or a non–Microsoft-based SQL Server to a Windows NT–based Microsoft SQL Server.
SQL Setup	Allows you to reconfigure the server. You can use the setup program to change network support options, rebuild the master database, change the character set or sort order, set server options, add a language, set security options, and remove SQL Server.

ISQL/w

ISQL/w (shown in Figure 10.1) provides a graphical way to query SQL Server, to analyze the execution plan of a query, and to view statistics information about an executed query. You can execute multiple queries simultaneously with ISQL/w.

FIGURE 10.1:

The ISQL/w tool

To start ISQL/w, choose Programs ➤ Microsoft SQL Server 6.5 ➤ ISQL_w.

Working With Queries

When you open ISQL/w, the Query tab is selected by default. Here you can type a query, execute it, save the query, start a new query, or open an existing query. The results are displayed in the Results tab. The Queries box maintains a list of queries run in the session, and you can switch among the queries at any time.

Enter the following code in the Query tab.

Code 10.1:   Testing ISQL/W

```
Use pubs
Select * From authors
```

Choose Query ➤ Execute or press Ctrl+E to run the query. The code changes to the Pubs database and selects all the fields from the Authors table. The results are displayed in the Results tab:

Using Graphical Statistics I/O

Graphical Statistics I/O depicts the amount of disk input/output required to access data for a query. You must execute the query to generate Statistics I/O information and verify that the No Execute option is off.

You can also generate a textual description of the Statistics I/O. The I/O statistics are scan count, logical reads, and physical reads.

Follow these steps to use Graphical Statistics I/O:

1. In the Microsoft ISQL/w window, type a query in the Query tab. (You can use the example query from Code 10.1.)

2. Choose Query ➤ Statistics I/O.

3. Click the Execute button, or press Alt+X or Ctrl+E.

4. Select the Statistics I/O tab.

The I/O statistics are graphed in the Statistics I/O tab, as shown in Figure 10.2.

As you become more familiar with SQL Server 6.5 and Transact-SQL, you will find ISQL/w to be a powerful, flexible, and useful tool indeed.

FIGURE 10.2:

The results graphed
in the Statistics I/O tab

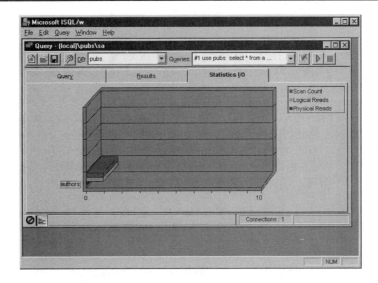

SQL Enterprise Manager

Microsoft SQL Enterprise Manager is a graphical tool, included as part of Microsoft SQL Server 6.5, that provides an intuitive way to administer SQL Servers enterprisewide:

SQL Enterprise Manager supplies powerful administration tools for managing multiple servers. A new scheduling engine enables you to schedule tasks to run automatically and completely unattended at a specified time. A new alert engine enables you to set alerts for various SQL Server events to notify someone, through e-mail or paging or to automatically execute a task.

If you have access to SQL Server 6.5, you also have access to SQL Enterprise Manager. However, access to the objects and tasks within SQL Enterprise Manager is controlled by the permissions allowed through logon identification. System administrators (SAs) can access all tasks and objects; database owners (DBOs) can access those tasks and objects for which they have permission; and users can access all objects they created and perform whatever other tasks they have permission for.

With SQL Enterprise Manager you can do the following:

- Configure SQL Server
- Back up and restore databases
- Create and manage devices and databases
- Create and schedule tasks
- Execute and analyze queries
- Generate SQL scripts
- Manage database objects (everything from tables and views to user-defined data types)
- Manage object and statement permissions
- Manage server logon IDs and database users
- Monitor current server activity
- Start, pause, resume, and stop servers
- Set up alerts
- Set up and manage replication
- View object dependencies
- View the SQL Server error log

NOTE
We will use SQL Enterprise Manager in the next sections to create devices, databases, and database objects.

SQL Server Books Online

SQL Server Books Online (shown in Figure 10.3) provides on-screen access to the entire SQL Server 6.5 documentation set. A notable and powerful feature is its full-text search capability, which allows you to quickly search for a word or a phrase. You can search through the entire documentation set or through selected books or topics.

As you saw earlier, when you install server software or client software on 32-bit or 16-bit Windows-based computers, the setup program gives you the option of installing SQL Server Books Online. If you select this option, the SQL Server Books Online icon is added to the Microsoft SQL Server 6.5 program group.

SQL Server Books Online contains the most up-to-date information about SQL Server 6.5, including information that has been revised or was unavailable at the time the SQL Server 6.5 documentation was printed. Here is a list of the books that are included and a description of what each contains:

Microsoft SQL Server System Administrator's Companion incorporates configuration, administration, and troubleshooting topics. It describes server and client configuration and explains system administration tasks, such as managing devices and databases, backing up and recovering data, performing replication, scheduling tasks, and managing security. It also describes error conditions and gives troubleshooting procedures.

Microsoft SQL Server Database Developer's Companion provides an overview of Transact-SQL and discusses managing data and database objects.

Microsoft SQL Server Transact-SQL Reference explains the use of Transact-SQL statements to access databases and provides syntax and descriptions for Transact-SQL statements, system procedures, utility programs, and system tables.

Microsoft SQL Server Setup provides instructions for installing SQL Server 6.5 servers and clients.

Microsoft SQL Server Programming SQL Distributed Management Objects provides syntax and reference information for the SQL Distributed Management Objects. These are used to write scripts and programs that can administer multiple SQL Servers distributed across a network.

Microsoft SQL Server Programming DB-Library for C provides syntax and reference information for the DB-Library API, which is used to write C/C++ client programs.

Microsoft SQL Server Programming DB-Library for Visual Basic provides syntax and reference information for the DB-Library API, which is used to write Microsoft Visual Basic client programs.

Microsoft SQL Server Programming Open Data Services provides syntax and reference information for the Microsoft Open Data Services API, which is used to write C/C++ server and gateway programs.

SQL Server Web Assistant

Today, as companies rush to establish a presence on the Internet, they are discovering the Internet's architecture to be both an internal corporate network and an external publication platform. And, as they explore new ways to leverage the Internet, they are quickly realizing that most of the business content they would like published is already available and being managed by relational database management systems.

Microsoft SQL Server 6.5 allows you to exploit the power of the Internet by enabling you to build active Web sites that publish real-time information and conduct business on the Internet securely and reliably.

The SQL Server Web Assistant is a tool that you can use to generate standard Hypertext Markup Language (HTML) files from SQL Server data. The SQL Server Web Assistant uses Transact-SQL queries, stored procedures, and extended stored procedures to generate HTML files that can be viewed with any HTML browser. HTML files, or Web pages, are resources for displaying information on the World Wide Web (WWW) and on internal networks.

With the SQL Server Web Assistant, you can generate an HTML file on a one-time basis or as a regularly scheduled SQL Server task. An HTML file can be updated by using a trigger whenever relevant data changes.

Let's give it a try. In this example, we will create a simple Web page from the Authors table in the Pubs database.

NOTE The Pubs database is a sample database installed with SQL Server.

Logging In

Choose Start ➤ Programs ➤ Microsoft SQL Server 6.5 ➤ SQL Server Web Assistant to open the SQL Server Web Assistant - Login dialog box:

Follow these steps to log in to SQL Server:

1. Enter a SQL Server name.

2. Enter your login ID.

3. Enter your password.

Or, if your network administrator has set up NT security, choose *Use Windows NT security to log in instead of entering a login ID and/or password*. Click Next to continue.

NOTE   To get help with the Web Assistant dialog boxes, click the More Info button at the bottom of each screen.

Creating SQL Server Web Assistant Queries

You can use the SQL Server Web Assistant in three ways:

- To build a query from a database/table hierarchy.
- To create a query with free-form text.
- To use an existing stored procedure.

Let's take a closer look at each of these options.

Building a Query from a Database/Table Hierarchy   In the SQL Server Web Assistant - Query dialog box, the *Build a query from a database hierarchy* option is selected by default:

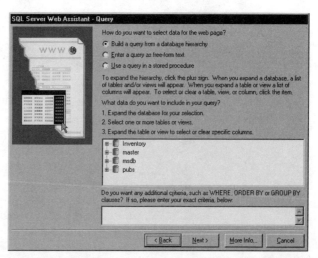

With this option selected, you can select a database, a table, and fields interactively. Follow these steps to build a query:

1. Select and expand the Pubs database by clicking the plus sign (+) icon.

2. Select and expand the dbo.authors table by clicking the plus sign (+) icon.

3. Click the au_id, au_lname, and au_fname fields. The icons to the left of the field names change color to indicate that they are selected. This creates a query that selects the Author's ID Number, Last Name, and First Name fields from the Authors table in the Pubs database.

That's all there is to it, but let's not leave this dialog box just yet. Let's take a look at the other two options available for building Web queries.

Entering a Query As Free-Form Text   Selecting the *Enter a query as free-form text* option opens the second SQL Server Web Assistant - Query dialog box:

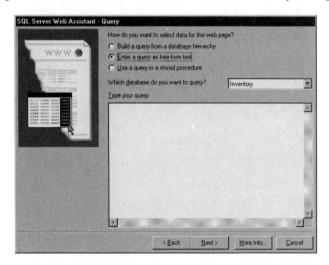

Here you can enter a Transact-SQL statement that will be used to create the query. The following SQL statement builds the query from the previous step:

```
Select au_id, au_lname, au_fname From authors
```

This statement creates a query that selects the Author's ID Number, Last Name, and First Name fields from the Authors table in the Pubs database.

Using a Query in a Stored Procedure   The last option is to use a stored procedure as the basis for a query. Select *Use a query in a stored procedure* to open the third SQL Server Web Assistant - Query dialog box:

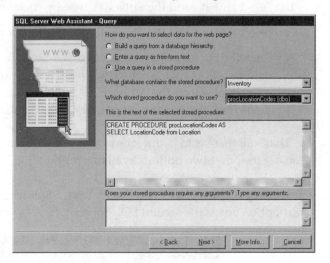

Follow these steps to use a stored procedure:

1. Select a database from the *What database contains the stored procedure?* combo box.

2. Select a stored procedure from the *Which stored procedure do you want to use?* combo box.

3. The text of the stored procedure is shown in the next box, and you can enter any parameters for the stored procedure in the last box.

Scheduling SQL Server Web Assistant Queries

Now that we have looked at the query options, select the *Build a query from a database hierarchy* option to return to the Pubs query we created at the beginning of this section. Your selections should still be on the screen. Click the Next button to open the SQL Server Web Assistant - Scheduling dialog box:

You can choose to create a Web page at different times. Table 10.2 lists the options available to you in the drop-down list box.

TABLE 10.2: Scheduling Options for Creating Web Pages

Scheduling option	Description	Arguments
Now	The default. An immediate, one-time execution.	None
Later	A scheduled, one-time execution.	Date, time
When Data Changes	An automatic, triggered execution.	Table(s), column(s) from expandable list
On Certain Days of the Week	A scheduled execution.	Days, time
On a Regular Basis	A scheduled execution.	Every *n* hours, days, or weeks

Follow these steps to schedule the creation of a Web page:

1. Select the scheduling option from the combo box. You may be asked for more information, depending on your selection. For our example, accept the default option Now.

2. Click Next button to open the SQL Server Web Assistant - File Options dialog box:

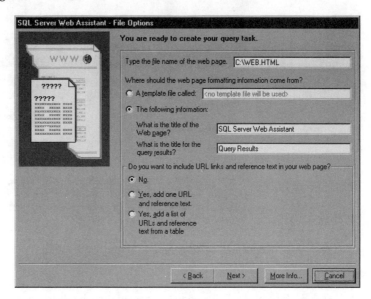

Using the SQL Server Web Assistant File Options

You use the SQL Server Web Assistant - File Options dialog box to actually locate and create your query task. Table 10.3 explains the options.

TABLE 10.3: The SQL Server Web Assistant File Options

Option	Description
Type the file name of the Web page	The full path specification to reference the generated HTML file. This file name is relative to where SQL Server is running. The default file specification is C:\WEB.HTML. You must have adequate privileges to create files in the specified directory.
A template file called	The full path specification used to reference an HTML template file. This file name is relative to where SQL Server is running. The default is <no template file will be used>. If you use a template file, *The following information* option does not apply.
The following information	Specifies whether to use Web page formatting options.

TABLE 10.3 (CONTINUED): The SQL Server Web Assistant File Options

Option	Description
What is the title of the Web page?	Specifies the title used by your browser when displaying the Web page. The default title is SQL Server Web Assistant.
What is the title for the query results?	Specifies the title for the results data. The default results title is Query Results.
Do you want to include URL links and reference text in your Web page?	Specifies whether to include one or more URL links to a home page or other location.

Selecting the More Info… button here provides information on using URL links:

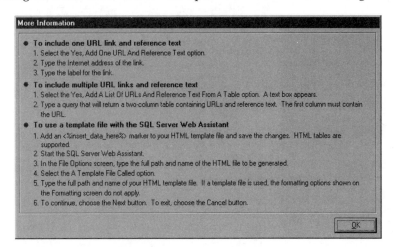

Our example Web page will use the defaults, so click Next to open the SQL Server Web Assistant - Formatting dialog box.

Using SQL Server Web Assistant Formatting Options

If you do not choose to use a template file from the previous dialog box, and for our example we did not, you can use the SQL Server Web Assistant - Formatting dialog box to add some basic font characteristics to the results title and the results data portions of the Web page:

Follow these steps to apply formatting options:

1. From the *How do you want the results title to look?* drop-down list box, select a formatting option for the query results title.

2. Select a formatting option for the query results data. Your choices are:

   - Fixed font

   - Proportional font

   - Bold

   - Italic

3. Select or clear the *Insert an update date/time stamp at the top of the page* option.

4. Select or clear the *Include column or view column names with the query results* option.

5. Select or clear the row limit option.

6. Click Finish.

The SQL Server Web Assistant compiles your answers and creates a Web page. The page is stored in the location you specified. The default is `C:\WEB.HTML`. Using Windows Explorer, locate and open this file to see the completed Web page displayed in Internet Explorer, as shown in Figure 10.4.

The completed Web
page produced with
the SQL Server Web
Assistant

As you can see, publishing dynamic Web pages is a snap with the help of the SQL Server Web Assistant.

Now, it's time to turn our attention to creating devices and databases in SQL server. In the next sections, we will use some SQL Server 6.5 tools to build a sample device and a database.

Creating a Database

Databases are the heart and soul of SQL Server. A relational database management system is made up of related, interacting databases. Each database stores and manages a segment of the business. In this section, we'll focus on using the SQL Enterprise Manager to create a database on SQL Server 6.5. Table 10.4 lists the major parts of a database on SQL Server 6.5.

TABLE 10.4: The Major Parts of a SQL Server 6.5 Database

Part	Description
Device	The operating system files that store databases, transaction logs, and their backups.
Database	A repository for data.
Table	A set of rows and columns, similar to the rows and columns of a spreadsheet. In a relational database, the rows are called records, and the columns are called fields.
Key	A field or fields in a table that is indexed for fast retrieval.
Index	Specifies the order of records accessed from database tables and whether duplicate records are accepted, providing efficient access to data.
View	A virtual table derived from one or more tables in a database.
Stored Procedure	A precompiled set of instructions written in Transact_SQL.
Trigger	A special kind of stored procedure that is executed automatically when a user attempts to modify data (insert, update, or delete) in the specified table.

Understanding Devices

A *device* is a physical disk file where all SQL Server database and transaction logs reside. You provide both a logical and a physical name when you create a database device. SQL Server uses the *logical name* to identify the database device. You refer to the database device by it's logical name when you use SQL Enterprise Manager and Transact-SQL statements. The *physical name* is an operating-system file name that includes the full path to the physical location of the file on the server's drive.

There are two types of devices:

- Database
- Backup

A *database device* is a file that stores databases. A device can store many databases, and a database can be stored in several devices. A *backup device* is a file that stores backups of databases. SQL Enterprise Manager supports local and network disk backup devices. A *local disk backup device* is created on a disk drive that is attached to the local computer; a *network disk backup device* is created on a shared network directory. SQL Enterprise Manager also supports *local tape backup devices* (tape drives attached to the local computer).

> **NOTE** If you don't specify a database device when you create a database, that database is placed on a default database device selected by SQL Server. Default database devices are used in alphabetic order, and one is filled before another one is used. Only database devices can be default devices.

Creating a Database Device

In the examples that follow, we'll create a database device and an inventory database for TeleVision, a fictitious company that distributes TVs and VCRs! Follow these steps to create a database device:

1. Choose Start ➤ Programs ➤ SQL Server 6.5 ➤ SQL Server Enterprise Manager to open the Server Manager:

2. From the list, select a server.

3. Choose Manage ➢ Select Database Devices to open the Manage Database Devices dialog box:

4. Click the New Devices icon to open the New Database Device dialog box:

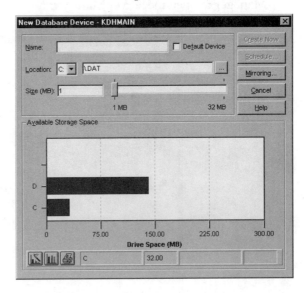

5. Assign the values for the new database device according to Table 10.5.

TABLE 10.5: New Database Device Values

Field	Value	Description
Name	MAIN	The logical database device name.
Drive	C:	The disk on which the database will reside. Change the C, if necessary, to an appropriate disk for your installation.
Size (MB)	10	The size of the device in megabytes.

6. Click the Create Now button to add the new device.

NOTE　A message box will notify you if the device is added successfully.

Creating a Backup Device

A backup device, referred to as a dump device in previous versions of SQL Server, does not have to reside solely on a disk. It can be stored on a floppy disk, on tape, or on other network servers. To create a backup device, follow these steps:

1. Open the Server Manager, and right-click the Backup Device folder to open the pop-up menu:

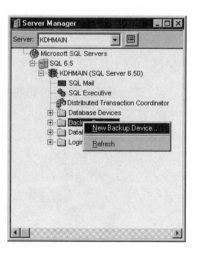

2. Click New Backup Device to open the New Backup Device dialog box:

3. Enter **BackupMAIN** in the Name field.

4. Click the Create button to create the backup device.

NOTE   A message box will notify you if the device is created successfully.

Now that we have created a database device and a backup device, let's move on to the database.

Creating a Database

Databases store and manage business data. For TeleVision, our fictitious company, we are going to create an inventory database. Follow these steps:

1. Choose Start ➤ Programs ➤ SQL Server 6.5 ➤ SQL Server Enterprise Manager to open the Server Manager.

2. Choose Manage ➤ Databases to open the Manage Databases dialog box:

3. Click the New Databases icon to open the New Database dialog box:

4. Assign the values for the new database according to Table 10.6.

TABLE 10.6: New Database Values

Field	Value	Description
Name	Inventory	The name of our new database.
Data Device	MAIN	The data device that will hold our new database.
Size (MB)	7	The size of the new database in megabytes.
Log Device	MAIN	The data device that will hold our new log.
Size (MB)	3	By default, this value is set to 3; accept this value.

5. Click the Create Now button to create the inventory database.

The inventory database is created, and the Manage Databases dialog box shows the new database:

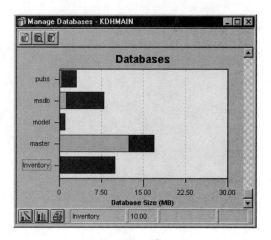

That's all it takes to create a new database in SQL Server 6.5 using SQL Enterprise Manager. In the next section, we will create and populate two tables for it.

Creating a Table in Server Manager

Now that we have created our inventory database, we are ready to create two tables:

- The OnHand table, which will hold the current inventory for TeleVision

- The Location table, which will define the possible locations where the parts can be stored

Creating the OnHand Table

Follow these steps to create the OnHand table:

1. Click the Inventory folder in the Server Manager.

2. Choose Manage ➤ Tables to open the Manage Tables dialog box. Assign the values listed in Table 10.7.

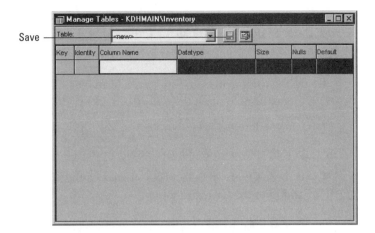

Save

TABLE 10.7: Values for the OnHand Table

Column Name	Data Type	Size	Nulls
PartNumber	char	5	No
QuantityOnHand	int		No
ReorderPoint	int		No
LocationCode	char	3	No
Comment	char	255	Yes

NOTE

You cannot enter a value in the Size column for int type fields. A value of 4 is automatically entered when the table is saved.

3. Click the Save icon to open the Specify Table Name dialog box:

4. In the New Table Name box, enter **OnHand** and click OK.

5. Close the Manage Tables dialog box.

Now that the OnHand table has been created, we need to populate it with some test data. To do so, we'll use the OnHand.SQL script from the Ch10\OnHand folder on the CD that comes with this book. Follow these steps:

1. In the Microsoft SQL Enterprise Manager dialog box, choose Tools ➤ SQL Query Tool to open the Query screen.

2. Choose File ➤ Open to open the File Open dialog box.

3. Select the OnHand.SQL file from the Ch10 folder on the CD.

4. Choose Query ➤ Select Execute to run the SQL script. Five records will be added to the OnHand table.

The other table in the Inventory database is the Location table, and we will create it in the next section.

Creating the Location Table

The Location table holds the valid locations for parts to be stored. Follow these steps to create the table:

1. In Server Manager, select the Inventory folder.

2. Choose Manage ➤ Tables to open the Manage Tables dialog box. Assign the value listed in Table 10.8.

TABLE 10.8: Values for the Location Table

Column Name	Data Type	Size	Nulls
LocationCode	char	3	No
Description	char	255	Yes

3. Click the Save icon to open the Specify Table Name dialog box.

4. In the New Table Name box, enter **Location** and click OK.

The table will be saved and your screen should look like this:

Location table

Now that the Location table has been created, we need to populate it with some test data. Do so by running the SQL script Location.SQL from the Ch10 folder on the CD that comes with this book. This script adds five records to the Location table.

NOTE　　See the earlier section, "Creating the OnHand Table," for the steps required to run a SQL script.

Understanding Keys in SQL Server 6.5

There are two types of keys in SQL Server 6.5:

- Primary
- Foreign

Most tables are designed to have one column or a combination of columns whose values uniquely identify each row of data in the table. This column or combination of columns is the *primary key*.

A primary key ensures that the key value is not null and that duplicate values do not exist in a table. You can create a primary key by defining a PRIMARY KEY constraint when the table is created. There can be only one primary key per table.

If you define a PRIMARY KEY constraint for a table, this constraint automatically creates an *index*. This index enforces uniqueness in the table and permits quick access to data when you use the primary key in queries.

If you look at the sample data in our OnHand table, you will see that the PartNumber column is a good candidate to be the primary key.

A *foreign key* is a column or a combination of columns whose values match the primary key of another table. A foreign key does not have to be unique. However, foreign key values must be copies of the primary key values; no value in the foreign key except NULL can exist unless the same value exists in the primary key of the referenced table. This sets the basis for referential integrity. There can be an unlimited number of foreign keys per table. A foreign key can be NULL, but if any part of a composite foreign key is NULL, the entire foreign key must be NULL.

Creating a Primary Key

You can create a primary key by defining a PRIMARY KEY constraint when you create or alter a table.

Creating a Primary Key for the OnHand Table

To create a primary key on the PartNumber field of the OnHand table that we created earlier, follow these steps:

1. Choose Start ➤ Programs ➤ Microsoft SQL Server 6.5 ➤ Microsoft SQL Server 6.5 Utilities ➤ SQL Enterprise Manager.

2. Select the server that contains our sample Inventory database.

3. Expand the Databases folder to expose the databases.

4. Expand the Inventory database folder to expose its subfolders.

5. Expand the Objects folder.

6. Expand the Tables folder to show the OnHand and Location tables.

7. Double-click the OnHand Table folder to display the OnHand table.

8. Click the Advanced Features icon to display the Advanced Features section of the OnHand table in the Manage Tables dialog box:

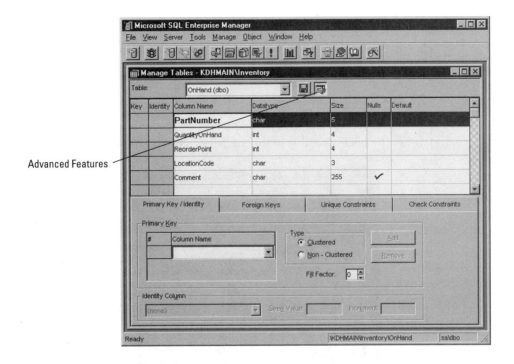

Advanced Features

9. Select PartNumber from the list of non-null fields in the Column Name combo box.

10. Click the Add button to create the primary key.

11. Close the Manage Tables dialog box and choose Yes from the Apply Changes message box.

The PartNumber is added as the primary key for the OnHand table.

Creating a Primary Key for the Location Table

To create a primary key on the LocationCode field of the Location table that we created earlier, follow these steps:

1. Choose Start ➤ Programs ➤ Microsoft SQL Server 6.5 ➤ Microsoft SQL Server 6.5 Utilities ➤ SQL Enterprise Manager.

2. Select the server that contains our sample Inventory database from the list of servers.

3. Expand the Databases folder to expose the databases.

4. Expand the Inventory database folder to expose its subfolders.

5. Expand the Objects folder.

6. Expand the Tables folder to show the OnHand and Location tables.

7. Double-click the Location Table folder to display the Location Table.

8. Click the Advanced Features icon to display the Advanced Features section of the Location table in the Manage Tables dialog box:

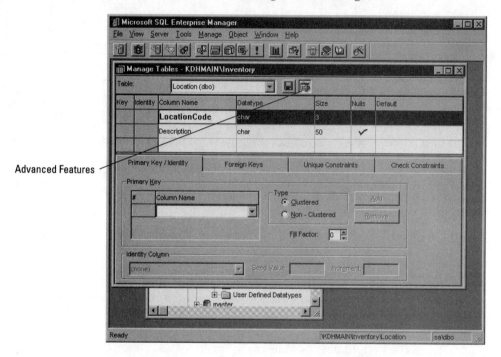

9. Select LocationCode from the Column Name combo box.

10. Click the Add button to create the primary key.

11. Close the Manage Tables dialog box and choose Yes from the Apply Changes message box.

The LocationCode is added as the primary key for the Location table. In the next section, we will create a foreign key to set up referential integrity on the OnHand and Location tables.

Creating a Foreign Key for the OnHand Table

When a new PartNumber record is added to the OnHand table, we want SQL Server to verify the LocationCode field against the LocationCode field in the Location table. We should not be able to add a PartNumber to a LocationCode that does not exist. We will enforce this rule by adding a foreign LocationCode key to the OnHand table.

Follow these steps to create a foreign key for the OnHand table:

1. Choose Start ➤ Programs ➤ Microsoft SQL Server 6.5 ➤ Microsoft SQL Server 6.5 Utilities ➤ SQL Enterprise Manager.

2. Select the server that contains our sample Inventory database from the list of servers.

3. Expand the Databases folder to expose the databases.

4. Expand the Inventory database folder to expose its subfolders.

5. Expand the Objects folder.

6. Expand the Tables folder to show the OnHand and Location tables.

7. Double-click the Location Table folder to display the Location Table.

8. Click the Advanced Features icon to display the Advanced Features section of the Location table in the Manage Tables dialog box.

9. Select the Foreign Keys tab to display the foreign key fields.

> **NOTE**
>
> The Referenced Table field should already be filled in with the Location table.

10. Select LocationCode from the list of Foreign Key Columns.

11. Click the Add button.

12. Close the Manage Tables dialog box and choose Yes in the Apply Changes message box.

13. A dialog box will ask if you want to check constraints and foreign keys against existing table data. Choose Yes. SQL Server will verify that the data in the existing tables does not break the new foreign key rules.

The foreign key and constraint has now been added, linking the LocationCode field in the OnHand table to the LocationCode field in the Location table. If a new PartNumber record is added to the OnHand table, the LocationCode must already exist in the Location table; however, if it does not already exist, you will get an error message, and the record will not be added. Also, you cannot delete a LocationCode from the Location table if a record exists in the OnHand table with the same value in the LocationCode field.

Indexes in SQL Server 6.5

An *index* is a table structure that SQL Server 6.5 uses to provide quick access to rows of a table based on the values of one or more columns. Properly planned indexes provide the most important performance improvement that can be made to your database tables.

SQL Server 6.5 uses an index in much the same way that you use the index of a book; it searches the index to find a particular value and then follows the pointer to locate the row containing the value.

In SQL Server 6.5, there are two types of indexes:

- Clustered

- Nonclustered

In a *clustered index*, the physical order of rows is the same as the indexed order of rows. You can create only one clustered index per table. UPDATE and DELETE operations require a large amount of reading, so they are often accelerated by clustered indexes. Typically, if a table has at least one index, that index should be a clustered index; if a table has more than one index, at least one should be clustered.

In a *nonclustered index,* the logical ordering of a table is specified. The physical order of the rows is not the same as their indexed order. You can have multiple nonclustered indexes per table.

To be effective, indexes must be created for the fields that will be used to assess the data. In our TeleVision example, the PartNumber is the index because it is unique in each record. Most of the time, when you need to look up a particular part, you will know the PartNumber. You might think, therefore, that you should index every field. Although that would certainly speed your query searches, it would slow the database because too many indexes would need to be updated.

NOTE
Indexes are not considered part of the logical database design; they can be dropped, added, and changed without affecting the database schema. Experimenting with indexes will not damage the database; it will affect only the performance of a database or an application.

It's good to keep in mind the type of data access and searches that you will require and to plan your indexes accordingly.

SQL Server 6.5 automatically creates an index for the PRIMARY KEY and UNIQUE constraints that you create in your tables. If you want to add more indexes, you will have to create them yourself.

Creating a New Index on the OnHand Table

The OnHand table is currently indexed on the PartNumber field. SQL Server 6.5 set this index to the primary key field when you created the table. In addition to the PartNumber field, it would be helpful to have an index on the LocationCode field. It would seem logical to allow the users of the database to be able to search for all the parts in a specific location, and an index would speed the searches.

Follow these steps to add an index to the LocationCode field of the OnHand table:

1. Choose Start ➣ Programs ➣ Microsoft SQL Server 6.5 ➣ Microsoft SQL Server 6.5 Utilities ➣ SQL Enterprise Manager.

2. Select the server that contains our sample Inventory database from the list of servers.

3. Expand the `Databases` folder to expose the databases.

4. Expand the `Inventory` database folder to expose its subfolders.

5. Expand the `Objects` folder.

6. Expand the `Tables` folder to show the OnHand and Location tables.

7. Click the OnHand table to select it.

8. Choose Manage ➣ Manage Indexes to open the Manage Indexes dialog box:

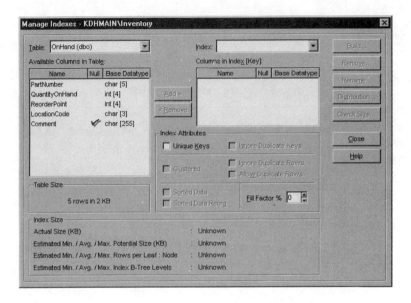

9. Select (New Index) from the Index combo box.

10. In the Index combo box, enter **ndxLocationCode** as the name for this index.

11. Click the LocationCode field in the Available Columns in Table list box to highlight it.

12. Click the Add button to add the LocationCode to the Columns in Index [Key] list box on the right.

13. Click the Build button to create the index.

14. In the Index Build dialog box, click the Execute Now button to process the new index:

15. Close the Manage Indexes dialog box.

Understanding Views in SQL Server 6.5

A *view* is a virtual table whose contents are defined by a query and that looks like a real table with a set of named columns and rows of data. A view, however, does not exist as a stored set of data values in a database. Instead, the rows and columns of data in a view come from database tables and are produced by the query that defines the view.

Views provide data security by controlling the data that users can see. Views allow users to work with a database in the form they are used to, and they restrict data access without the burden of creating a security layer on top of the database. If, for example, employees must access an Employee Records table, you might create a view that does not include the Salary field.

A view looks and acts exactly like any other database table. You can display, update, and delete data on it just as you can on any other table. Transact-SQL enhances standard SQL so that there are no restrictions on querying through views and that there are few restrictions on modifying them.

Creating a View

Let's create a view in our sample Inventory database. Let's say we need to access and manipulate data on the OnHand table, but we do not want the clerks to see or change the QuantityOnHand or the ReorderPoint fields. In addition, we want the clerks to see the description of the LocationCodes from the Location table.

Although we could do all this with a query, we would have to rerun the query every time a clerk wanted to access the data. By creating a view, we can satisfy all our requirements.

Follow these steps to create the sample view:

1. Choose Start ➢ Programs ➢ Microsoft SQL Server 6.5 ➢ Microsoft SQL Server 6.5 Utilities ➢ SQL Enterprise Manager.

2. Select the server that contains our sample Inventory database from the list of servers.

3. Choose Manage ➢ Views to open the Manage Views dialog box:

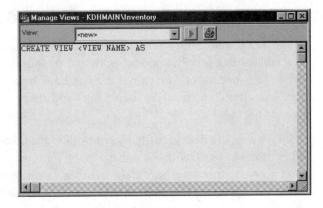

4. Enter the following SQL code:

```
CREATE VIEW vwLocate
(PartNumber, LocationCode, Comment, Description)
AS
SELECT a.PartNumber, a.LocationCode, a.Comment, b.Description
FROM OnHand a, Location b
Where a.LocationCode = b.LocationCode
```

This SQL statement combines the PartNumber, LocationCode, and Comment fields in the OnHand table with the Description field from the LocationCode table. The combination is based on the common field LocationCode. Table 10.9 lists and explains the code lines.

TABLE 10.9: The vwLocate View Code

Line Number	Code	Explanation
1	Create View vwLocate	Names the view vwLocate.
2	(PartNumber, LocationCode, Comment, Description)	Selects the fields to be used to make up the view.
3	SELECT a.PartNumber, a.LocationCode, a.Comment, b.Description	Tells SQL Server from which tables to retrieve the data. (The prefix assigned in line 4 identifies the table.)

TABLE 10.9 (CONTINUED): The vwLocate View Code

Line Number	Code	Explanation
4	FROM OnHand a, Location b	Provides alias names for the tables. You could enter the third line as SELECT OnHand. PartNumber, ONHand.LocationCode... but it is much easier to set the OnHand table to "a" and the LocationCode table to "b". This way you do not have to refer to them by their full names.
5	Where a.LocationCode = b.LocationCode	Tells SQL Server to fetch all the rows from the OnHand and Location tables where the values in the LocationCode fields are equal.

5. Choose File ➤ Save or press Ctrl+E to save the view.

Now that the view has been created and saved, let's create a query to look at its contents.

Querying a View

In the previous section you created the vwLocate view that includes data from the OnHand and Location tables. To create a query that lists the records in the vwLocate view, follow these steps:

1. Choose Start ➤ Programs ➤ Microsoft SQL Server 6.5 ➤ Microsoft SQL Server 6.5 Utilities ➤ SQL Enterprise Manager.

2. Select the server that contains our sample Inventory database from the list of servers.

3. Open the Databases folder.

4. Select the Inventory database and choose Tools ➤ SQL Query Tool to open the Query dialog box:

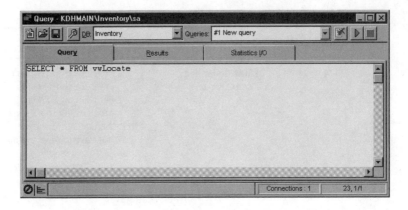

5. Enter the following SQL statement:

   ```
   SELECT * FROM vwLocate
   ```

6. Press Ctrl+E to run the query. The results are displayed in the Results tab. You should see 5 records.

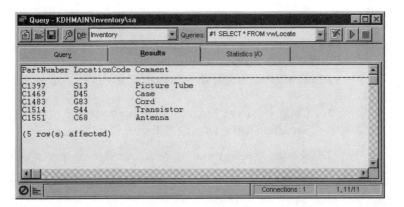

Views are a good vehicle for controlling data security by limiting who can access and manipulate data.

The next section provides an introduction into stored procedures in SQL Server 6.5.

SQL Server 6.5 Stored Procedures

Stored procedures, which we have discussed throughout this chapter, are compiled SQL statements that are stored in the database. SQL Server stores the executable stored procedure so that it does not have to be re-created each time the query is executed.

There are two basic types of stored procedures:

- Precompiled
- User-defined

Precompiled stored procedures are special-use stored procedures that are included with SQL Server 6.5. Here are some examples:

- Catalog stored procedures, which provide a uniform catalog interface for accessing database gateways, as well as SQL Server, from the same application
- Extended stored procedures, which provide a way to dynamically load and execute a function within a dynamic-link library
- System stored procedures, which make it easy to retrieve information from the administer databases and system tables

User-defined stored procedures are written by the developer in Transact_SQL code. These procedures can be used to perform almost any type of data access and manipulation. Here are some examples:

- Select all records from a Customer table for a mailing list.
- Provide a list of all orders placed last month from a Sales table.
- List the top five sales areas for the last quarter, show the top salesperson in each area, and give each of them a 5 percent salary increase.

Running a Precompiled Stored Procedure

Let's say you want a list of all the columns in the OnHand table and the type of data that can be stored in each column in our test Inventory database. How can you get it? An easy way is to use the sp_columns system stored procedure.

The sp_columns stored procedure returns column information for a single object that can be queried in the current environment. The returned columns belong to a table or a view. The syntax for sp_columns is:

```
sp_columns object_name [, object_owner][, object_qualifier] [,
column_name]
```

Table 10.10 explains the parts of the sp_columns stored procedure.

TABLE 10.10: The Parts of the sp_columns Stored Procedure

Part	Description
object_name	Required. Specifies the name of the table or view used to return catalog information.
object_owner	Optional. Specifies the object owner of the table or view used to return catalog information.
object_qualifier	Optional. Specifies the name of the table or view qualifier.
column_name	Optional. Specifies a single column and is used when only one column of catalog information is desired. If column_name is not specified, all columns will be returned.

Follow these steps to execute the sp_columns stored procedure from SQL Enterprise Manager:

1. Choose Start ➢ Programs ➢ Microsoft SQL Server 6.5 ➢ Microsoft SQL Server 6.5 Utilities ➢ SQL Enterprise Manager.

2. Select the server that contains our sample Inventory database from the list of servers.

3. Expand the Databases folder to expose the databases.

4. Expand the Inventory database folder to expose its subfolders.

5. Choose Tools ➢ SQL Query Tool to open the Query dialog box:

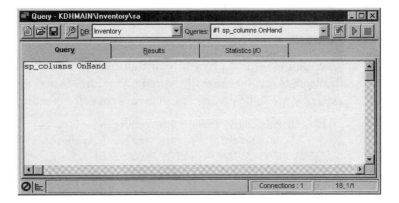

6. Enter the following code:

   ```
   sp_columns OnHand
   ```

7. Choose Query ➤ Execute or press Ctrl+E to execute the stored procedure. The procedure will run, and the results will be displayed in the Results tab of the Query dialog box:

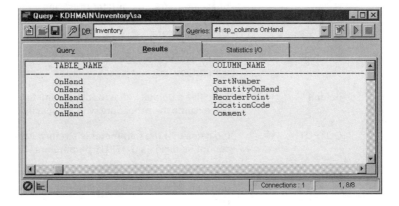

This is just one example of the hundreds of precompiled stored procedures included in SQL Server 6.5 to help you create, examine, and maintain your servers.

Creating and Executing a User-Defined Stored Procedure

User-defined stored procedures are stored procedures that you write yourself in Transact-SQL. You can write stored procedures to access or create almost every part of your SQL Servers. The general syntax for creating a stored procedure is:

```
CREATE PROCedure [owner.]procedure_name[;number]
    [(parameter1 [, parameter2]...[parameter255])]
[{FOR REPLICATION} | {WITH RECOMPILE}
    [{[WITH] | [,]} ENCRYPTION]]
AS sql_statements
```

Table 10.11 lists and defines the parts of the stored procedure syntax.

TABLE 10.11: The Parts of the Stored Procedure Syntax

Part	Description
Parameter	Specifies a parameter in the procedure. One or more parameters can optionally be declared in a CREATE PROCEDURE statement. The value of each declared parameter must be supplied by the user when the procedure is executed. A stored procedure can have a maximum of 255 parameters.
Datatype	Specifies the data type of the parameter. All data types except *image* are supported.
default	Specifies a default value for the parameter. If a default is defined, a user can execute the procedure without specifying a value for that parameter.
OUTPUT	Indicates that the parameter is a return parameter. *Text* parameters cannot be used as OUTPUT parameters.
FOR REPLICATION	Is mutually exclusive of the WITH RECOMPILE option. Stored procedures created for replication cannot be executed on the subscribing server.
number	An optional integer used to group procedures of the same name so that they can be dropped together with a single DROP PROCEDURE statement.
procedure_name	The name of the new stored procedure. Procedure names must conform to the rules for identifiers and must be unique within the database and its owner.
RECOMPILE	Indicates that SQL Server does not cache a plan for this procedure and that the procedure is recompiled each time it is executed.

TABLE 10.11 (CONTINUED): The Parts of the Stored Procedure Syntax

Part	Description
ENCRYPTION	Encrypts the *syscomments* table entry that contains the text of the CREATE PROCEDURE statement.
AS *sql_statements*	Specifies the actions the procedure is to take. Any number and type of SQL statements can be included in the procedure.

Let's create a user-defined stored procedure that lists the Location codes from the Location table in our test Inventory database.

Creating the procLocationsCode Stored Procedure

Follow these steps to create the stored procedure:

1. Choose Start ➣ Programs ➣ Microsoft SQL Server 6.5 ➣ Microsoft SQL Server 6.5 Utilities ➣ SQL Enterprise Manager.

2. Select the server that contains our sample Inventory database from the list of available servers.

3. Expand the Databases folder to expose the databases.

4. Select the Inventory database and choose Manage ➣ Stored Procedures to open the Manage Stored Procedures dialog box:

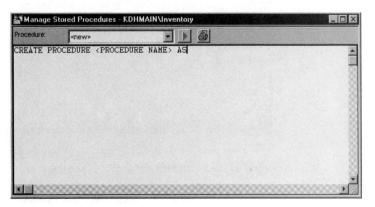

5. Enter the following code:

```
CREATE PROCEDURE procLocationCodes AS
SELECT LocationCode from Location
```

Table 10.12 explains this code.

TABLE 10.12: The procLocationCodes Stored Procedure Code

Line Number	Code	Explanation
1	Create Procedure procLocationCodes	Names the view procLocationCodes.
2	SELECT LocationCode from Location	Selects the LocationCodes field from the Location table.

6. Choose File ➢ Save or press Ctrl+E to compile and save the procedure. The procedure is compiled, saved, and listed in the Stored Procedure folder in the SQL Enterprise Manager dialog box.

7. Close the Manage Stored Procedures dialog box.

8. Select the procLocationCodes stored procedure, and choose Tools ➢ Manage Stored Procedures to display the new procedure in the Manage Stored Procedures dialog box. Notice that some code has been added to your procedure. This code deletes the procedure, if it exists, before it is run.

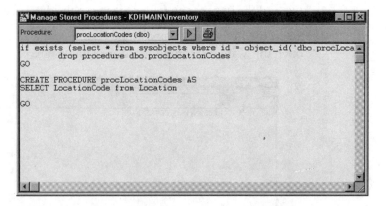

9. Close the Manage Stored Procedures dialog box.

Executing the procLocationsCode Stored Procedure

Now that you have created, compiled, and saved the procedure, let's run it and see the results. Follow these steps:

NOTE
If you have just created the procedure, continue here. Otherwise, follow the steps outlined in the previous section to create and save the procLocationCodes stored procedure.

1. Choose Tools ➤ SQL Query Tool to open the Query dialog box.

2. Enter the following code:

    ```
    procLocationCodes
    ```

3. Choose Query ➤ Execute or press Ctrl+E to run the procedure. The results, a list of the location codes, will be displayed in the Results tab:

You can use stored procedures to access and manipulate almost any data that you store in your databases. Stored procedures can be thought of as automatic code runners. Triggers, a special kind of stored procedures, also run code automatically. In the next section, we will take a look at how triggers fit into SQL Server 6.5 to help you keep your data in sync.

Using Triggers in SQL Server 6.5

Triggers are special stored procedures that are automatically executed when an Insert, Update, or Delete is performed. A trigger validates data in response to an action statement against a table. A trigger can apply to only one table and can call a maximum of 16 stored procedures. The syntax for a trigger is:

```
CREATE TRIGGER [owner.]trigger_name
ON [owner.]table_name
FOR {INSERT, UPDATE, DELETE}
[WITH ENCRYPTION]
AS sql_statements
```

Or, using the IF UPDATE clause:

```
CREATE TRIGGER [owner.]trigger_name
ON [owner.]table_name
FOR {INSERT, UPDATE}
[WITH ENCRYPTION]
AS
IF UPDATE (column_name)
[{AND | OR} UPDATE (column_name)...] sql_statements
```

Table 10.13 explains the parts of the trigger's syntax.

TABLE 10.13: The Parts of a Trigger's Syntax

Part	Description
trigger_name	Specifies the name of the trigger.
table_name	Specifies the table on which the trigger will be executed.
INSERT, UPDATE, DELETE	Specifies the trigger type and which data modification statements will activate the trigger. Any combination (in any order) of these are allowed in a trigger.
ENCRYPTION	Encrypts the text entries of the CREATE TRIGGER statement.
AS sql_statements	Specifies trigger conditions and actions.

The following SQL statements are not allowed in a trigger:

- All CREATE statements (DATABASE, DEFAULT, INDEX, PROCEDURE, RULE, TABLE, TRIGGER, and VIEW)
- All DISK statements
- All DROP statements
- ALTER TABLE and ALTER DATABASE

- GRANT and REVOKE

- LOAD DATABASE and LOAD TRANSACTION

- RECONFIGURE

- SELECT INTO (triggers cannot create tables)

- TRUNCATE TABLE

- UPDATE STATISTICS

WARNING   If a trigger is defined for an operation (INSERT, UPDATE, or DELETE) that already has a trigger, the existing trigger is replaced without a warning message.

Creating a Trigger

In this section, you will create a trigger on the LocationCode table in our test Inventory database. The trigger, named tgrNewLocation, will print a message notifying the clerks that a new inventory location is available for parts storage.

Follow these steps to create the test tgrNewLocation:

1. Choose Start ➣ Programs ➣ Microsoft SQL Server 6.5 ➣ Microsoft SQL Server 6.5 Utilities ➣ SQL Enterprise Manager. Select the server that contains our sample Inventory database from the list of available servers.

2. Expand the **Databases** folder to expose the databases.

3. Select the Inventory database and choose Manage ➣ Triggers to open the Manage Triggers dialog box:

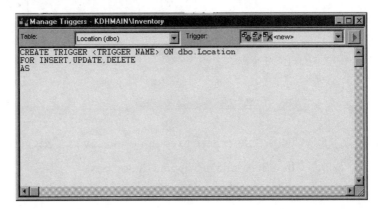

4. Select the OnHand table from the Table combo box at the top of the dialog box.

5. Enter the following code:

```
CREATE TRIGGER tgrNewLocation
ON dbo.Location
FOR INSERT AS
RAISERROR ("A new location code has been added", 0, 1)
```

Table 10.14 explains this code.

TABLE 10.14: The tgrNewLocation Trigger Code

Line Number	Code	Explanation
1	CREATE TRIGGER tgrNewLocation	Names the trigger tgrNewLocation.
2	ON dbo.Location	The name of the table for the trigger.
3	FOR INSERT AS	Defines the trigger as an Insert trigger. The trigger will execute when a new record is added to the Location table.
4	RAISERROR ("A new location code has been added", 0, 1)	The message that will print when the trigger is executed.

The Manage Triggers dialog box should look like this:

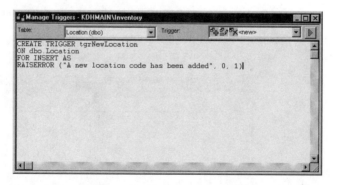

6. Choose File ➤ Save to compile and save the trigger.

7. Close the Manage Triggers dialog box.

Executing a Trigger

Now that your trigger has been compiled and saved, let's execute it by adding a new Location record to the Location table. Follow these steps:

1. Choose Tools ➢ Query Tool to open the Query dialog box.

2. Enter the following code:

```
INSERT INTO Location VALUES ('R48', 'Room 8 on the 4th floor')
```

3. Choose Query ➢ Execute or press Ctrl+E to insert the new record into the Location table and execute the tgrNewLocation trigger.

The new record will be inserted into the Location table, and you should see the message "A new location code has been added" in the Results tab of the Query dialog box:

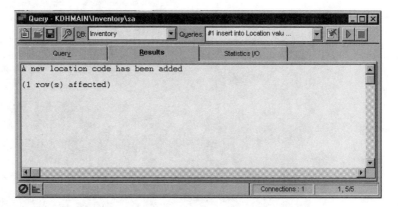

Although this has been a very simple test of a trigger's uses, it serves to demonstrate how easy it is to create and execute your own triggers.

The RDO Object

- Creating an ODBC data source

- Exploring the RemoteData Control

- Understanding the Remote Data Object

- Using parameter queries

- Executing stored procedures

- Using transactions with RDO

- Working with ActiveX Data Objects

The Data Access Object (DAO) has been the basic mechanism with which we have created and accessed databases since Visual Basic 3, and most VB programmers have learned and mastered this valuable tool. It is, in a sense, the parent of all data access models. The DAO, however, was designed primarily for the Microsoft Access JET engine, and with the advent of the Internet and corporate intranets and the proliferation of SQL Server applications, the time has come to replace the DAO.

The Remote Data Object (RDO) follows a similar paradigm, but it's smaller and provides fewer objects. Not that RDO does less than DAO; quite the contrary. The RDO was introduced with Visual Basic 4 to address the needs of client/server developers. It performs better than DAO and provides support for features such as batch cursors and optimistic updates. It is also simpler to use than the DAO because it uses fewer objects. In effect, it's a friendlier interface to the Open Database Connectivity Application Programming Interface (ODBC API). In Visual Basic 5, we use RDO2, the current version of RDO.

In this chapter, we're going to look at how you connect RDO to a Visual Basic application with a standalone connection and with the aid of the RemoteData Control so that your applications can take advantage of all the speed, flexibility, and reliability of SQL Server, Oracle, and any other ODBC database.

Creating an ODBC Data Source

You connect RDO to a Visual Basic application through an ODBC data source. ODBC is Microsoft's standard data access interface that relies on specific drivers to access any relational database. It is the layer that sits between the database management system and whatever access mechanism you are using. Its function is to interface DAO and RDO with the actual database.

All the Database Management System (DBMS)-dependent code is placed in a driver, usually supplied by the database's manufacturer, and developers can access the database through a simple, object-based interface.

The sample code and projects in this chapter are based on the Pubs sample database that ships with SQL Server 6.5.

NOTE   This section shows you how to create a new data source using ODBC 3.5. If you are using a different version, your steps will vary.

Before you can connect RDO to your Visual Basic application, you must create a data source. If you do not already have one, follow these steps to create a data source for the Pubs database using the ODBC Data Source Administrator:

1. Choose Start ➣ Settings ➣ Control Panel to open the Control Panel.

2. Double-click the ODBC32 icon to open the ODBC Data Source Administrator dialog box:

3. Select the System DSN tab, and then click the Add button to open the Create New Data Source dialog box:

4.   Select SQL Server, and then click Finish to open the Create a New Data Source to SQL Server dialog box:

5.   In the Name box, enter **Pubs,** and in the Description box, enter **Pubs Test.** From the Server drop-down list box, select the server where the Pubs database is located, and click Next to open the next screen:

This screen gathers login and connection information. The *How should SQL Server verify the authenticity of the login ID?* section tells the data source how to verify the login ID and password.

6.   If you want to use your NT login, select the *With Windows NT authentication using the network login ID* option. If you want to enter a login ID and password for the server, select the *With SQL Server authentication using a login ID and password entered by the user* option.

Clicking the Client Configuration button launches the SQL Client Configuration utility. If you specified a new name in the Server box on the first screen of the ODBC Data Source Administrator, you may need to create an Advanced entry in the SQL Client Configuration utility. To do so, select the Advanced tab. The name you specify for the Advanced entry must match the name in the Server box on the first screen of the ODBC Data Source Administrator.

7. Check the *Connect to SQL Server to obtain default settings for the additional configuration options* checkbox to tell the SQL Server driver to obtain initial settings from the SQL Server for the options on the following screens of the Wizard. The SQL Server driver connects to the SQL Server named in the Server box on the first screen. If you do not select this option, the driver uses standard defaults as the initial settings for the options on the following screens.

8. Enter a login ID and password. This only applies to the connection made to determine the server default settings; it does not apply to subsequent connections made using the data source after it has been created.

9. Click the Next button to open the next screen, in which you select a database and set options for stored procedures, quoted identifiers, and nulls:

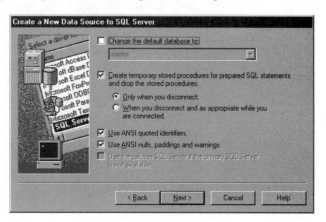

10. Click the *Change the default database to* checkbox and select Pubs from the list of available databases.

11. Check the *Create temporary stored procedures for prepared SQL statements and drop the stored procedures* checkbox. This tells the SQL Server driver to create temporary stored procedures to support the SQLPrepare ODBC function.

12. Check the *Only when you disconnect* checkbox to specify that SQL Server should drop temporary stored procedures created for SQLPrepare when the SQLDisconnect ODBC function is called. This allows the driver to reuse stored procedures and not delete them while the application is running.

13. For our test, accept the default settings *Use ANSI quoted identifiers* and *Use ANSI nulls, paddings, and warnings.* These options specify that QUOTED_IDENTIFIERS be set to on when the SQL Server ODBC driver connects and that the ANSI_NULLS, ANSI_WARNINGS, and ANSI_PADDINGS be set to on when the SQL Server driver connects.

14. Click the Next button to continue and display the screen that allows you to choose a language, define character set translation, and display regional settings:

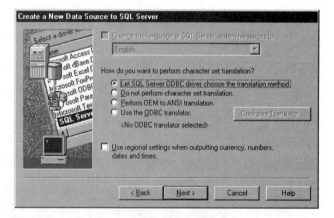

15. If your server is set up with multiple languages, select the language from the drop-down list box.

16. Accept the default choice *Let SQL Server ODBC driver choose the translation method.* This tells the SQL Server driver to automatically configure itself for any needed character-set translations when a connection is made.

17. Leave the *Use regional settings when outputting currency, numbers, dates, and times* checkbox unchecked. Select this option for applications that only display data, not for applications that process data. This specifies that the driver use the regional settings of the client computer for formatting currency, numbers, dates, and times in character output strings.

18. Click the Next button to display the screen that allows you to save query and statistical information to log files:

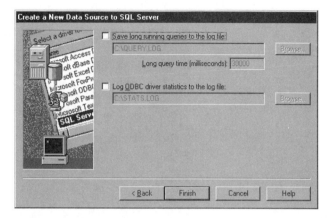

19. The *Save long running queries to the log file* checkbox notifies the driver to log any query that takes longer than the Long query time value. We will not run any long queries for our samples, so accept the unchecked default for this checkbox.

20. The *Log ODBC driver statistics to the log file* checkbox specifies that statistics be logged. Accept the unchecked default.

22. Click the Finish button to display the ODBC summary screen, which recaps your choices and gives you an opportunity to test the new data source connection:

23. Click the Test Data Source button to test the connection. SQL Server will attempt to connect to the database using the options you set. You will see the SQL Server ODBC Data Source Test screen:

If all went as planned, you will see the message "Tests Completed Successfully."

24. Click OK to Close the SQL Server ODBC Data Source Test screen.

25. Click OK to Close the Microsoft SQL Server Setup screen. You will see the ODBC Data Source Administrator dialog box.

26. Click OK to close the ODBC Data Source Administrator dialog box and save the new Pubs data source.

Phew! Now that's done, let's take a look at the RemoteData Control.

The RemoteData Control

We first discussed the RemoteData Control (RDC) in Chapter 9. The RemoteData Control binds data-aware controls to an ODBC remote database. You can perform most remote data access operations using the RDC without writing any code at all. Data-aware controls bound to an RDC control automatically display data from one or more columns for the current row. The RDC automatically handles a number of contingencies, including the following:

- Empty resultsets

- Adding new rows

- Editing and updating existing rows
- Converting and displaying complex data types
- Handling some types of errors

Adding the RemoteData Control 2 Component to Your Project

To use the RDC in an application, you must first add the Microsoft RemoteData Control 2 component to your project. Follow these steps:

1. Choose Project ≻ Components to open the Components dialog box.

2. Choose the Microsoft RemoteData Control 2.0 component from the list of available components.

3. Click the OK button to close the dialog box and add the RDC to your project.

   Now that you have a test data source and the RDC added to your Toolbox, let's look at the process of making the actual connection.

Connecting the RDC

At this point, you have a Visual Basic project, a data source, and an RDC, but they are not connected. The RDC provides a Connect property that can be set at design time or at run time to connect the RDC to a data source. Table 11.1 lists the parameters of the Connect property.

TABLE 11.1: The RDC Connect Elements

Parameter	Specifies	Example
DSN	Registered ODBC data source by name.	DSN=pubs; (If specified when establishing a DSN-less connection, DSN must be the last argument.)
UID	User name of a recognized user of the database.	UID=sa;
PWD	Password associated with the user name.	PWD=;

TABLE 11.1: The RDC Connect Elements (continued)

Parameter	Specifies	Example
DRIVER	Description of the driver. (Driver names that include spaces must be enclosed in brackets.)	DRIVER={SQL Server};
DATABASE	Default database to use once connected.	DATABASE=Pubs;
SERVER	Name of the remote server.	SERVER=local;
WSID	Workstation ID (your system's Net name).	WSID=AFG-003
APP	Application name. At design time, this is set to your project name. At run time, this is your EXE name.	APP=Lab

NOTE   All parameters are not required for all data sources.

You could use the following Connect string for an RDC for the Pubs data source:

```
DSN=pubs;UID=sa;PWD=;DATABASE=pubs;
```

This string uses the Pubs data source; as the user ID, the password is blank, and the database is set to Pubs. Notice that the parameters are separated by a semicolon.

In addition to the Connect property, you also must supply a SQL string to use to populate the RDC. This can be any valid SQL String, such as:

```
SELECT * FROM authors
```

The RDC has its pros and cons, as do all tools and components. The RDC is great if you need to display data from different tables, because you do not have to know the data type. Thus, it's a good choice for conversion programs in which you need to convert data from one table to another. It is designed to display and update data, as it is in a database. However, if you need to manipulate the data, perform calculations, or base decisions on the data, the RDC might not be the best choice. And it would not be a good idea to build a complete application with the RDC and bound controls, as you would likely find yourself fighting with the RDC instead of taking advantage of its strong points. Remember, the RDC is a great tool; it is not an application.

Chapters 12 and 13 include some good examples of using the RDC with bound controls.

The Remote Data Objects

To use the Remote Data Objects in an application, you must first add a reference to the RDO object library in the References dialog box. Follow these steps:

1. Choose Project ➤ Project Properties to open the References dialog box.

2. Check the Microsoft Remote Data Objects 2.0 checkbox.

You can now open the Object Browser to look at the objects exposed by the RDO and their members.

The RDO consists of objects and collections that form a framework for manipulating components of a remote ODBC database system. The relationships among objects and collections represent the logical structure of the database system.

The RDO is supported only on 32-bit operating systems. (You can't create 16-bit applications with Visual Basic 5 anyway.)

The process of accessing a database through the RDO is straightforward. First, you create an rdoConnection object to the database. Once you establish a connection and open the database (which is usually a data source), you can execute SQL statements and stored procedures against the database. The results are returned in an rdoResultset object, which is similar to a Recordset object. With the rdoResultset object's methods and properties, you can access the qualified records, edit them (if the type of the resultset permits editing), and save them back to the database. In the following section, we will discuss these steps and the objects involved in detail.

Establishing a Connection

An rdoConnection object represents an open connection to a data source and a specific database of that data source. You can also create an rdoConnection object without specifying a connection and establish a connection as needed in the code.

For example, the following statement creates a new standalone rdoConnection object:

```
Dim RDOConn as new rdoConnection
```

Once the rdoConnection object is created, you can set its properties and then establish the actual connection with the EstablishConnection method. You can create multiple connections in an application, which you can access through the rdoConnections collection. New connections are not automatically added to the rdoConnections collection. You use the Add or Remove method of the rdoConnections collection to add or delete standalone rdoConnection objects to or from the collection. It is not necessary, however, to add an rdoConnection object to the rdoConnections collection before it can be used to establish a connection.

The syntax of the EstablishConnection method is:

```
rdoConnection.EstablishConnection prompt, readonly, options
```

All arguments of the EstablishConnection method are optional. The *prompt* argument determines the ODBC prompting characteristic (whether the user will be prompted to log in to the database). It can have one of the following values:

- rdDriverPrompt, which asks the user to select or verify a driver and database.

- rdDriverNoPrompt, which uses the specified driver and database.

- rdDriverComplete, which is the connection string you provide that includes the DSN keyword that the driver manager uses to connect; otherwise, it behaves as it does when rdDriverPrompt is specified.

- rdDriverCompleteRequired, which is the same as rdDriverComplete except that the driver disables the controls for any information not required to complete the connection.

You will see how this argument is used in the examples in this section.

The *readonly* argument is a Boolean value that you should set to True if you are going to use the connection to read records only. The *options* argument can have the value rdAsyncEnable, which determines that the operation will be executed asynchronously, or it can be omitted.

The rdoConnection object supports a number of cursors. Here are the most important:

CursorDriver: This property returns or sets the type of cursor to be created. It affects only connections that have not yet been established and is read-only on existing connections. The type of cursor driver can have a significant impact on the overall performance of your application. Here's a short description of the cursor types:

Server-Side maintains the keyset on the server, which eliminates the need to transmit the keyset to the workstation where it consumes needed resources. However, this cursor driver consumes disk space on the server. A limitation of server-side cursors is that they cannot contain more than one SELECT statement.

ODBC Client-Side copies the keyset on the workstation. As a result, it causes heavy network traffic when the keyset is initially created. This option gives better performance for small resultsets, but degrades quickly for larger resultsets.

Client-Batch deals with the special requirements of optimistic batch updates. Use a client-batch cursor if you want to connect to the server, transfer the keyset to the client, and disassociate the connection. After processing the data, you can reestablish the connection, and RDO will transfer only the records that were modified. This type of processing conserves bandwidth, which could be extremely valuable with dial-up connections.

No-Cursor creates a forward-only, read-only resultset with a RowsetSize set to 1. The main limitation of this option is that you cannot update the records. If you need to fetch rows quickly or perform action queries against the database without the overhead of a cursor, you can choose to instruct RDO to bypass creation of a cursor.

The CursorDriver property can have one of the values shown in Table 11.2.

TABLE 11.2: The Values of the CursorDriver Property

Value	Description
rdUseIfNeeded	The ODBC driver will choose the appropriate style of cursor.
rdUseOdbc	RDO will use the ODBC cursor library.
rdUseServer	RDO will use server-side cursors.
rdUseClientBatch	RDO will use the batch-cursor library.
rdUseNone	Results are not returned as a cursor.

Here is a typical example of establishing an rdoConnection object with the EstablishConnection method:

```
Dim RDOConn As New rdoConnection
RDOConn.Connect = "uid=sa;pwd=;DSN=pubs;"
RDOConn.CursorDriver = rdUseOdbc
RDOConn.EstablishConnection rdDriverNoprompt
```

Establishing the connection takes a while. During this time, you shouldn't attempt to use the database (perform queries or update records). When connections are made synchronously, the EstablishConnection method will not return control to the program before the connection has been established or has failed for some reason.

Another way to establish a connection is with the RDO Environment object's OpenConnection method. This method accepts a number of arguments, as shown below. Only the first argument is mandatory, which is the name of the data source to which you want to connect:

```
Set RDOConn = RDO.OpenConnection(dsName, prompt, readonly, connect, _
    options)
```

The other arguments are optional, and they are the same as the EstablishConnection method's arguments.

Specifying Additional Parameters

You can specify additional parameters a connection string. The simplest way to create connection strings is to use the UserConnection Designer. It will step you through creating the connection string. To open the UserConnection Designer, follow these steps:

1. Choose Project ➤ Add ActiveX Designer.

2. From the submenu, choose Microsoft UserConnection.

For more information on using the UserConnection Designer, see Chapter 9.

Asynchronous Connections

Both the EstablishConnection and OpenConnection methods support synchronous, asynchronous, and event-managed operations. By setting the rdAsyncEnable option, control returns to your application before the connection is established. Once the StillConnecting property returns False, the connection has either been made or failed to complete. You can also detect the completion of a connection with the help of the Connect event. This event's syntax is:

```
Private Sub RDOConn.Connect(ErrorOccurred As Boolean)

End Sub
```

In the Connect event, you can insert code to perform some initial queries or to enable parts of the interface that won't function without a connection, such as a Command Button that makes a query.

To use the Connect event or other rdoConnection events in your application, you declare the Connection object with the WithEvents keyword:

```
Dim WithEvents RDOConn As rdoConnection
```

Once the *RDOConn* object variable is declared with the WithEvents keyword, the RDOConn object's name will appear in the Objects list of the Code window, and the Events list will display the events (shown in Table 11.3).

TABLE 11.3: Events of the rdoConnection Object

Event	Description
BeforeConnect	Occurs just before RDO attempts to establish a connection to the server.
Connect	Occurs after a connection to the server is established.
Disconnect	Occurs after a connection is closed.
QueryComplete	Occurs after a query returns the resultset.
QueryTimeout	Occurs if a query didn't complete in the specified timeout period. You can cancel the query from within this event.
WillExecute	Occurs before the execution of a query. You can cancel the query from within this event.

As you may have guessed by looking at the list of events of the rdoConnection object, it is possible to issue queries on this object.

After you request an asynchronous connection to the server, you should always check to see whether the operation has completed successfully. Here is the typical, but overly simplified, code of the Connect event:

```
Private Sub RDOConn_Connect(ByVal ErrorOccurred As Boolean)
    If ErrorOccurred Then
        MsgBox "Could not open connection"
    Else
        RunqueryButton.Enabled = True
    End If
End Sub
```

You can also find out the status of an asynchronous connection attempt by examining the value of the rdoConnection object's StillConnecting property. A similar property, StillExecuting, indicates the status of an asynchronous query.

Executing SQL Statements

After you establish a connection, you can execute queries on the database. The simplest way to run queries against a database is to call the OpenResultSet method of the Connection object. The OpenResultSet method creates an rdoResultSet object, which contains the results of the query. The rdoResultSet object is similar to the DAO RecordSet object, but it's more flexible (see the discussion of the rdoResultSet object, later in this chapter).

Before using the OpenResultSet method, you must create an object variable of rdoResultSet type:

```
Dim RS As rdoResultSet
```

The syntax of the OpenResultSet method is:

```
Set RS = rdoConn.OpenResultSet(name, type, locktype, option)
```

The *name* argument, which is mandatory, is a string that specifies the source for the new rdoResultSet object. This argument can specify the name of an rdoTable object, the name of an rdoQuery object, or a SQL statement that will be executed on the server. The remaining arguments are optional. The *type* argument is a constant that specifies the type of cursor that will be created by the data source to manage the qualified records, and it can have one of the following values (not all ODBC data sources support all types of cursors):

rdOpenForwardOnly (the default) opens a forward-only type resultset. You can use only the MoveNext method to scan the resultset forward, and you can't update it or use bookmarks. It is the most limited type of result-set, but very efficient if you need to read only a small number of records.

rdOpenKeyset opens a keyset-type resultset. This is similar to a Dynaset-type DAO recordset. It can be scanned forward and backward with the Move methods, supports bookmarks, and can be updated. However, once the keyset is built, the application won't see any changes made to the records by other users.

rdOpenDynamic opens a dynamic-type resultset, which is the most expensive type of resultset. It supports all the features of a keyset, but also lets the application see changes made by other users. Because it must check the state of the retrieved records constantly, it generates a lot of traffic on the network.

rdOpenStatic opens a static-type resultset, which consists of all the qualified records, not just their keys, and resides on the server. It can be scanned forward and backward, but can't be updated and doesn't reflect changes made by other users.

The *option* argument can be set to rdAsyncEnable to perform the query asynchronously. Control returns to your application as soon as the query is issued without waiting for the resultset to become available. To test for completion of the query, use the StillExecuting property or the QueryComplete event, as discussed in the previous section.

The *lockType* argument determines how other users can access the data in the resultset. Table 11.4 shows the valid values, which are constants, of the lockType argument.

TABLE 11.4: The Values of the lockType Argument

Value	Description
rdConcurReadOnly	Read-only (the default)
rdConcurLock	Pessimistic concurrency
RdConcurRowVer	Optimistic concurrency based on row ID
RdConcurValues	Optimistic concurrency based on row values
rdConcurBatch	Optimistic concurrency using batch mode updates

Use read-only concurrency when you're opening resultsets that will not be updated. Other users are allowed to read or edit records while the application is using them. The optimistic concurrency control is the most common; it locks the entire page containing the record being edited, but only while the record is being updated. In other words, users can access the record between the Edit and Update operations. The pessimistic concurrency control is used less frequently and is the strictest and safest form of concurrency control; it locks the page that contains the current record and frees it only after the application moves to a record in another page.

Another option you can use is the rdExecDirect constant. If you don't want to create a temporary stored procedure and then execute it, set the option argument to rdExecDirect (or rdExecDirect plus rdAsyncEnable). This option will speed the individual query, but only if it's going to be executed once. Queries that are executed many times should be stored as procedures on the server the first time they are issued and then executed. This will speed the execution of reissuing the resultset. This option is mandatory for queries that create temporary tables for use by subsequent queries.

Here's a typical example of using the OpenResultset method to run a query against a database through the rdoConnection object:

```
Dim rsResultset As rdoResultset
Set rsResultset = rdoConn.OpenResultset("SELECT au_fname, au_lname _
FROM authors")
rsResultset.Close
```

A second way to execute SQL queries through the rdoConnection object is with the object's Execute method, whose syntax is:

```
rdoConnection.Execute source, option
```

Here's a typical example of using the Execute method to delete a record from the Authors table:

```
Dim ssql as String
ssql = "DELETE FROM authors WHERE au_id = '123-46-3756'
rdoConn.Execute ssql
```

The *source* argument is the SQL statement, and the *option* argument can take the same values as the option argument of the OpenResult method. For an example of the Execute method of the rdoConnection method, see the section "The RdoObject Project," later in this chapter.

NOTE

The Execute method of the rdoConnection object does not return a result-set; neither does it append an rdoResultSet object to the rdoResultSets collection. It behaves like a subroutine that submits the SQL statement to be executed to the database driver. Therefore, you can't execute SELECT queries with the Execute method; only ACTION queries can be executed with this method.

Manipulating the rdoResultset Object

The results of a query performed with the Remote Data Object's methods are returned in an rdoResultSet object. The rdoResultSet object is similar to a Recordset object; it consists of rows (records) and columns (fields).

To navigate among the rows of the rdoResultset, you can use the Move navigation methods (MoveFirst, MoveLast, MoveNext, and MovePrevious), bookmarks, and the AbsolutePosition property, which determines the absolute row number of an rdoResultset object's current row. Forward-only rdoResultset objects can be scanned forward only (using the methods MoveNext and MoveLast).

The number of rows in the rdoResultset is given by the property RowCount, but its value reflects the number of records accessed already. To find out the total number of records in the rdoResultset, you must access the last record (it can't be a forward-only rdoResultset) and then use the RowCount property.

NOTE

Actually, you can move to the last record of a forward-only rdoResultSet and find out the proper number of records, but you won't be able to process them because you can't move backward.

You can use the following code to find the last record in the rdoConn ResultSet:

```
While Not rdoConn.EOF
    'Move to the last record
    rdoConn.MoveLast
Wend
```

To process the current record, you need to access its columns (fields). To do so, use the rdoColumns property, which is a collection. It contains one rdoColumn object for each column. The total number of columns (selected fields in the query) is given by the property rdoColumns.Count. To access each field, use the rdoColumns collection with an index value or the name of the field you want to access. To access all the fields of the rdoConn Resultset, set up a loop such as the following:

```
For i = 0 To rdoConn.rdoColumns.Count - 1
    Debug.Print rdoConn.rdoColumns(i)
Next
```

The rdoColumn object has more properties than the DAO Recordset object, including:

- The SourceTable property, which returns the name of the table from which the field comes

- The OriginalValue, which is the value of the field as fetched from the database—a handy feature for programming canceling operations for edits

---

NOTE   Use the Object Browser to find a list of the rdoColumn object's properties.

In programming with the RDO, you will also find useful the rdoColumn object's DataChanged event, which is triggered when the value of a column changes value.

In the next section, we will create a sample project that uses the Pubs data source and RDO to access and manipulate the Authors table.

The RdoObject Project

The RdoObject project (shown in Figure 11.1) uses the RDO to access and manipulate the records in the Authors table. The project consists of one Form with the fields from the Authors table, a scrollbar that can be used to navigate among the records, and three Command Buttons:

- Clicking the New button adds new records.

- Clicking the Update button updates record changes.

- Clicking the Delete button deletes records.

NOTE   You'll find the RdoObject project in the Ch11\RdoObject folder on the CD that comes with this book.

FIGURE 11.1:

The RdoObject
project

Code 11.1:	**Connecting to the Pubs Data Source**

```
Public Sub ConnectToDSN()
    On Error GoTo ErrorRoutineErr

    Dim connectstring As String

    Set rdoEnv = rdoEnvironments(0)
    connectstring = "UID=sa;PWD=;Database=Pubs;DSN=Pubs;"
    Set rdoConn = rdoEnv.OpenConnection("Pubs", rdOpenKeyset, _
        False, connectstring, rdAsyncEnable)

ErrorRoutineResume:
    Exit Sub
ErrorRoutineErr:
    MsgBox "Project1.Form1.ConnectToDSN" & Err & Error
    Resume Next
End Sub
```

The OpenConnection method is used with the rdOpenKeySet cursor to allow for editing.

NOTE   The major reason that a resultset is not updatable with ODBC is that the table does not have a unique nonnull index. When you build your tables, be sure to define a nonnull unique index field.

To load the first record and to refresh the resultset after updates, the RefreshResultset subroutine is called.

Code 11.2: Refreshing the Resultset

```
Public Sub RefreshResultset()
    On Error GoTo ErrorRoutineErr

    'Declare variables
    Dim i
    Dim ssql As String
    Dim rdoErr As Object

    'Clear rdo errors
    RDO.rdoEngine.rdoErrors.Clear

    'Set the sql
    ssql = "SELECT * FROM Authors "

    'Build the resultset
    Set rdoRs = rdoConn.OpenResultset(ssql, rdOpenKeyset)

    'Check for errors
    If RDO.rdoEngine.rdoErrors.Count > 0 Then
        'An error has occurred
        For Each rdoErr In rdoErrors
            Debug.Print rdoErr
        Next
    ElseIf rdoRs.EOF = True Then
        'Record not found
        MsgBox "No records match"
    Else
        'No errors
        'Clear all except ID
        For i = 0 To 7
            txtFields(i) = ""
        Next
        chkFields(8) = 1

        'Fill results
        For i = 0 To 7
            txtFields(i) = rdoRs.rdoColumns(i)
```

```
            Next
            If rdoRs.rdoColumns(8) = True Then
                chkFields(8).Value = 1
            Else
                chkFields(8).Value = 0
            End If

    End If
    dataChanged = False
ErrorRoutineResume:
    Exit Sub
ErrorRoutineErr:
    MsgBox "Project1.Form1.RefreshResultset" & Err & Error
    Resume Next
End Sub
```

In this code, first, the rdoErrors are cleared so that we do not get an old error. Next, the SQL statement is defined, and then the resultset is built with the OpenResultset method. Notice the use of the rdOpenKeyset type of cursor. This assures that, if it is supported, the recordset will be updatable. The fields are loaded with the value from the rdoColumns property. The fields on the Form are actually a control array of text boxes indexed from 1 to 7. This matches the rdoColumns index except for the checkbox control for the contract field. This is set after the text fields. Finally, the *dataChanged* variable that holds whether a change has been made is reset to False.

The ScrollBar control allows you to move from record to record.

Code 11.3: Moving from Record to Record with the ScrollBar Control

```
Private Sub HScroll1_Change()
    Dim i
    If dataChanged Then
    Dim reply
        reply = MsgBox("Save changes?", vbYesNo)
        If reply = vbYes Then
            Call UpdateRecord
        End If
    End If
    dataChanged = False
    Call rdoMove(HScroll1.Value)
End Sub
```

First, the dataChanged flag is checked. If it is True, a message box is displayed asking if you want to save your changes. If you reply by clicking Yes, the record is saved, and the new record is displayed.

Records are updated in the UpdateRecord subroutine. This subroutine is called from the ScrollBar click event if you move to a new record without saving your changes or if you click the Update button. An interesting aspect of the Update code is how it deals with fields that contain quote marks, such as in O'Leary. If you attempt to execute the update method on a field with a single quote in it, SQL Server will return an error. You cannot have unclosed quotes in a SQL string. To get around this problem, the function CheckForQuote is called with the value from the fields. If an embedded quote is found, a second quote is added to the value: O'Leary becomes O''Leary. SQL Server will then store "O'Leary" as the value for the string. Later in this chapter, you will see how parameter queries deal with this problem.

Code 11.4:   Updating a Record

```
On Error GoTo ErrorRoutineErr

    'Declare variables
    Dim ssql As String
    Dim rdoErr As Object
    Dim slCurRecord
    Dim i

    'Clear rdo errors
    RDO.rdoEngine.rdoErrors.Clear

    'Build the SQL statement
    'The Function CheckForQuotes checks for a single
    'quote in the field and replaces it with two quotes
    ssql = "UPDATE Authors SET " _
    & "au_lname = '" & CheckForQuote(txtFields(1)) & " '," _
    & "au_fname = '" & CheckForQuote(txtFields(2)) & " '," _
    & "phone = '" & CheckForQuote(txtFields(3)) & "'," _
    & "address = '" & CheckForQuote(txtFields(4)) & "'," _
    & "city = '" & CheckForQuote(txtFields(5)) & "'," _
    & "state = '" & CheckForQuote(txtFields(6)) & "'," _
    & "Zip = '" & CheckForQuote(txtFields(7)) & "'," _
    & "contract = " & chkFields(8).Value & "" _
    & "WHERE au_id = '" & txtFields(0) & "' "
```

```
        'Save the position
        slCurRecord = rdoRs.AbsolutePosition

        'Save the changes
        rdoConn.Execute ssql

        'Check for errors
        If RDO.rdoEngine.rdoErrors.Count > 0 Then
            'An error has occurred
            For Each rdoErr In rdoErrors
                Debug.Print rdoErr
                Exit Sub
            Next
        End If


        'Refresh the resultset
        Call RefreshResultset
        rdoRs.AbsolutePosition = slCurRecord
        'Fill results
        For i = 0 To 7
            txtFields(i) = rdoRs.rdoColumns(i)
        Next
        If rdoRs.rdoColumns(8) = True Then
                chkFields(8).Value = 1
            Else
                chkFields(8).Value = 0
        End If
        'Reset the dataChanged flag
        dataChanged = False

ErrorRoutineResume:
    Exit Sub
ErrorRoutineErr:
    MsgBox "Project1.Form1.UpdateRecord" & Err & Error
    Resume Next
```

This code clears the rodError object and builds the SQL statement incorporating the CheckForQuote function. The record is updated by calling the Execute method, and if there are no errors, the resultset is refreshed, and the Form is filled in with the newly updated record.

Code 11.5:   Checking for Embedded Quotes

```
Public Function CheckForQuote(str As String)
    Dim slPos1
    slPos1 = InStr(1, str, "'")
    If slPos1 > 0 Then
        CheckForQuote = Mid(str, 1, slPos1) & "'" & _
        Mid(str, slPos1 + 1, Len(str) - slPos1)
    Else
        CheckForQuote = str
    End If
End Function
```

In this code sample, a value is passed in, such as O'Leary. If a quote character is located in the string, a second quote is added, changing O'Leary to O''Leary. This is what SQL Server expects to see, and it will treat it as a text string.

Let's start the RdoObject project and give it a try.

Testing the RdoObject Project

Press F5 to start the RdoObject, as shown in Figure 11.2, and follow these steps to test the project:

1. Click the right arrow on the scrollbar to move to the next record.

2. Click the left arrow on the scrollbar to move to the previous record.

3. Change the state field to TX, and click the right arrow on the scrollbar. Notice that a message box is displayed asking you if the change should be saved. Choose Yes to save the changes.

4. Change the Zip field to 77444, and click the Update button. This will save the changes.

5. Enter new values in the fields, and click the New button to add a new record.

6. Click the Delete button to delete the current record. You will be prompted to confirm your delete request.

Now that you have a good working knowledge of the RDO, let's take a look at the rdoQuery object.

FIGURE 11.2:

Running the
RdoObject project

The rdoQueries Collection and the rdoQuery Object

Another way to issue SQL statements against a database with RDO is to create an rdoQuery object, specify the SQL statement, as well as any other required parameters, and then execute the query with the OpenResultSet of the rdoQuery object. Use this method to execute queries that require user input or stored procedures. The rdoQuery object provides the following properties:

ActiveConnection returns or sets an rdoConnection object with which this query should be associated.

SQL is a string value that holds the SQL statement to be executed.

CursorType indicates the type of cursor to be created. It is similar to the *Type* argument of the OpenResultSet method.

LockType returns or sets a value indicating the type of concurrency handling. It can take the same values as the *lockType* argument of the OpenResultSet method.

StillExecuting returns True if the server hasn't completed the query.

RowsetSize determines how many rows are buffered when building a cursor. It is also the number of records locked when using pessimistic locking.

KeysetSize determines the number of rows in the keyset for a Keyset or Dynamic cursor. If it's zero (the default value), the cursor is populated with keys. If it's greater than zero, the cursor is mixed (it contains as many keys as specified by the property and is dynamic outside the keyset). If KeysetSize is greater than RowsetSize, its value defines the number of rows in the keyset that are to be buffered by the driver.

MaxRows sets or returns the maximum number of rows to be returned by a query.

RowsAffected returns the number of rows affected by an action query.

QueryTimeout indicates how long the driver will wait before pausing a query and triggering the QueryTimeout event.

Updatable is set to True if the resultset generated by the query can be updated.

To execute a query specified with the rdoQuery object, use the OpenResultset method of the rdoQuery object. Here's a simple SQL query executed on the server through an rdoQuery object (the *RDOConn* variable represents an open connection):

```
Dim qry As New rdoQuery
Dim RSet As New ResultSet
Set qry.ActiveConnection = RDOConn
qry.SQL = "SELECT * FROM authors"
qry.LockType = rdConcurReadOnly
qry.Type = rdOpenForwardOnly
Set RSet = qry.OpenResultset
```

The OpenResultset method is equivalent to the rdoConnection object's Execute method. No matter how you execute a query, its results are returned in an rdoResultset object.

Using the CreateQuery Method

Another type of rdoQuery method is the CreateQuery method. The CreateQuery method creates a new rdoQuery object for this connection and adds it to the rdoQueries collection. The following code sample sets up and creates an rdoQuery using the CreateQuery method and executes the query with the Execute method.

Code 11.6:   **The CreateQuery Method**

```
Dim ssql As String
Dim slQuery As rdoQuery
Dim lvRecordset As rdoResultset

ssql = "Update titles set type = '" & Text1.Text & _
    "' WHERE title_ID = '" & Text2.Text & "'"
```

```
Set slQuery = rdoConn.CreateQuery("", ssql)

'Run the query
slQuery.Execute

Debug.Print slQuery.RowsAffected
```

This code defines a query and a recordset and creates a SQL statement that takes two values from text boxes. The first value, from Text1, is the new type, and the second value, Text2, is the existing type to be replaced. The query, named slQuert, is then added to the rdoQuery object with the Set statement and executed with the Execute method. Finally, the number of rows affected is printed to the Immediate window with the Debug statement.

This type of query is a good choice if you know the data types and if the parameters do not change often, but what if you are not sure of the data types? Another type of query supported by RDO is the Parameter query, and we'll explore it in the next section.

Parameter Queries

Parameter queries are special rdoQueries that employ placeholders to insert values into parameters in queries. You are already familiar with queries that use concatenated strings, such as:

```
Select * FROM authors WHERE au_id = '" & Text1.Text & "'"
```

This type of query constructs the author's ID by piecing together the single quote, the value from a text box, and finally, another single quote.

With Parameter queries, you do not have to enclose text strings in quotes. RDO takes care of the data types for you. All you have to do is construct a query that uses a question mark (?) as a parameter placeholder.

Although this query is usually a SELECT statement, it could be an Action query (INSERT, UPDATE, or DELETE) as well. The following example illustrates how to code a simple SELECT query with a single parameter. The query looks up employees by employee ID from the Pubs sample database.

Code 11.7: Creating a Parameter Query

```
Dim ssql As String
Dim slQuery As rdoQuery
Dim lvRecordset As rdoResultset

ssql = "SELECT * FROM employee WHERE emp_ID = ?"

Set slQuery = rdoConn.CreateQuery("", ssql)

slQuery.rdoParameters(0) = Text1.Text

'Run the query
Set lvRecordset = slQuery.OpenResultset()
```

First, set up a SQL query that marks each parameter using the ? parameter marker. Next, create an rdoQuery object to manage the query and its parameters with the Set statement. Then, use the rdoParameter parameter to replace the placeholder with the value. Notice that you do not have to supply quotes in the value. RDO takes care of this for you. Next, create an rdoResultset to fetch the qualifying rows (those whose emp_ID match the parameter value). Finally, run the query with the OpenResultset method.

If the user changes the parameter value in Text1.Text, you can reapply the new parameter and reexecute the query by using the Requery method against the rdoResultset (lvRecordset) without having to rebuild the rdoQuery object, as shown in the following code:

```
SlQuery.rdoParameters(0) = Text1.Text
lvResordset.Requery
```

The rdoParameters object can be implied here, as it is the default collection of the rdoQuery object. The equivalent code would be:

```
slQuery(0) = Text1.Text
```

When RDO executes the Requery method, it refreshes the parameter value(s) in the rdoParameters collection bound to the query parameters, flushes the current resultset, sends the query to the data source for execution, and creates a new rdoResultset.

Keep in mind that when the query is first created, RDO and the ODBC layers create a temporary stored procedure on the remote server designed to accept the parameters. Each time the query is executed, this temporary query is simply passed the new argument(s) and executed.

In the next section, we will look at the RdoQuery project and see the rdoQuery in action.

Creating the RdoQuery Project

The RdoQuery project (shown in Figure 11.3) is the same project as the RdoObject project, except that it employs rdoQueries to access and manipulate the records in the Authors table. The project consists of one Form with the fields from the Authors table, a scrollbar that can be used to navigate among the records, and three Command Buttons:

- Clicking the New button adds new records.

- Clicking the Update button updates record changes.

- Clicking the Delete button deletes records.

NOTE You'll find the RdoQuery project in the Ch11\RdoQuery folder on the CD that comes with this book.

FIGURE 11.3:

The RdoQuery project

NOTE Since this project is structurally the same as the RdoObject project shown earlier in this chapter, we'll explain only the rdoQuery code here.

Adding New Records with a Parameter Query

The Add button is used to add new records to the Authors table. When you click the Add button, a Parameter query is built, the parameters are loaded, and the query is executed as demonstrated in the following code taken from the cmdNew_Click subroutine.

Code 11.8: **Adding a Record with a Parameter Query**

```
'Declare variables
    Dim ssql As String
    Dim rdoErr As Object

    'Clear rdo errors
    RDO.rdoEngine.rdoErrors.Clear

    'Construct Parameter SQL statement
    ssql = "INSERT INTO Authors(au_id,au_lname," _
        & "au_fname,phone,address,city,state,zip,contract)" _
        & "VALUES (?, ?, ?, ?, ?, ?, ?, ?, ?)"

    Set slQuery = rdoConn.CreateQuery("", ssql)

    'The Function CheckForQuotes checks for a single
    'quote in the field and replaces it with two quotes
    slQuery.rdoParameters(0) = txtFields(0)
    slQuery.rdoParameters(1) = CheckForQuote(txtFields(1))
    slQuery.rdoParameters(2) = CheckForQuote(txtFields(2))
    slQuery.rdoParameters(3) = CheckForQuote(txtFields(3))
    slQuery.rdoParameters(4) = CheckForQuote(txtFields(4))
    slQuery.rdoParameters(5) = CheckForQuote(txtFields(5))
    slQuery.rdoParameters(6) = CheckForQuote(txtFields(6))
    slQuery.rdoParameters(7) = CheckForQuote(txtFields(7))
    slQuery.rdoParameters(8) = chkFields(8).Value

    'Save the changes
    slQuery.Execute ssql
```

This code is similar to the listing in Code 11.6 from the RdoObject project. First, the rdoErrors are cleared. Then, an INSERT SQL statement is constructed with question mark placeholders. Next, the slQuery query object is added to the rdoQuery collection with the Set statement, and the parameters are loaded from the text boxes on the Form. The Execute method is called to add the new record.

As you can see, the result is the same whether you use the rdoObject, an rdoQuery, or a Parameter query.

Updating Records with a Parameter Query

Using a Parameter query to update records is, in most cases, easier than using the rdoObject or regular query code because you do not have to concern yourself with data types. RDO takes care of them for you. Code 11.9 employs a Parameter query to update records on the Authors table taken from the Update subroutine.

Code 11.9:   Updating Records with a Parameter Query

```
'Declare variables
    Dim ssql As String
    Dim rdoErr As Object
    Dim slCurRecord
    Dim i

    'Clear rdo errors
    RDO.rdoEngine.rdoErrors.Clear

    'Build the Parameter SQL statement
    ssql = "UPDATE authors SET " _
    & "au_lname = ?, " _
    & "au_fname = ?, " _
    & "phone = ?, " _
    & "address = ?, " _
    & "city = ?, " _
    & "state = ?, " _
    & "Zip = ?, " _
    & "contract = ? " _
    & "WHERE au_id = ? "

    Set slQuery = rdoConn.CreateQuery("", ssql)

    'The Function CheckForQuotes checks for a single
    'quote in the field and replaces it with two quotes
    slQuery.rdoParameters(0) = CheckForQuote(txtFields(1))
    slQuery.rdoParameters(1) = CheckForQuote(txtFields(2))
    slQuery.rdoParameters(2) = CheckForQuote(txtFields(3))
    slQuery.rdoParameters(3) = CheckForQuote(txtFields(4))
    slQuery.rdoParameters(4) = CheckForQuote(txtFields(5))
    slQuery.rdoParameters(5) = CheckForQuote(txtFields(6))
```

```
slQuery.rdoParameters(6) = CheckForQuote(txtFields(7))
slQuery.rdoParameters(7) = chkFields(8).Value
slQuery.rdoParameters(8) = txtFields(0)

'Save the position
slCurRecord = rdoRs.AbsolutePosition

'Save the changes
slQuery.Execute ssql
```

The steps are about the same as in the Add subroutine. First, the rdoErrors are cleared. Then, an UPDATE SQL statement is constructed with question mark placeholders. Next, the slQuery query object is added to the rdoQuery collection with the Set statement, and the parameters are loaded from the text boxes on the Form. The Execute method is called to update the record.

Deleting a Record with a Parameter Query

Deleting a record with a Parameter query is just as easy. The following code, taken from the cmdDelete_Click subroutine, demonstrates how to delete a record with a Parameter query.

Code 11.10:   Deleting a Record with a Parameter Query

```
'Clear rdo errors
RDO.rdoEngine.rdoErrors.Clear

'Confirm the delete request
Msg = "Delete the current Author's record?"
Style = vbYesNo + vbQuestion + vbDefaultButton1
Title = "Confirm Delete"
Response = MsgBox(Msg, Style, Title)
If Response = vbYes Then
    'Construct Parameter SQL statement
    ssql = "DELETE authors   " _
        & "WHERE au_id = ?"

    Set slQuery = rdoConn.CreateQuery("", ssql)

    'Set the parameter value
    slQuery.rdoParameters(0) = txtFields(0)

    'Delete the record
    slQuery.Execute ssql
```

```
Else
     'no action
     Exit Sub
End If
```

As in the previous code samples, the rdoErrors are cleared, and then the slQuery is added to the rdoQuery collection. Next, the SQL statement is constructed, the parameter is loaded from the first text box with the author's ID number, and the Execute method is called to delete the record.

Let's take the RdoQuery project for a quick test drive.

Testing the RdoQuery Project

Press F5 to start the RdoQuery project as shown in Figure 11.4 Follow these steps to test the project:

1. Click the right arrow on the scrollbar to move to the next record.

2. Click the left arrow on the scrollbar to move to the previous record.

3. Change the state field to NY, and click the right arrow on the scrollbar. Notice that a message box is displayed asking you if the change should be saved. Choose Yes to save the changes.

4. Change the Zip field to 04324, and click the Update button. This will save the changes.

5. Enter new values in the fields, and click the New button to add a new record.

6. Click the Delete button to delete the current record. You will be prompted to confirm your delete request.

FIGURE 11.4:

Running the RdoQuery project

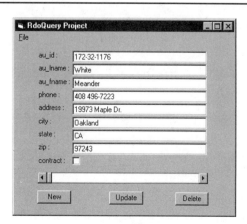

As you can see, Parameter queries can save some time over regular concatenated strings or regular queries if the query changes every time it is run. In the next section, we will see how to run a stored procedure with RDO.

Executing Stored Procedures

The SQL statements executed most frequently on a database should be attached to the database itself as stored procedures. Stored procedures execute faster than SQL statements submitted at run time, and you can make them quite flexible by means of arguments. Essentially, they are small, powerful programs. That's why they are called stored procedures rather than stored SQL statements.

The previous version of RDO supported an object called PreparedStatement, which is outdated. PreparedStatement objects were query definitions (SQL statements), similar to the rdoQuery objects. In version 2, they were replaced by stored procedures.

The name of the stored procedure must be passed as an argument to the OpenResultSet method of the rdoQuery object. To execute the Catalog stored procedure on the Pubs database, call the Execute method as follows:

```
slQuery.SQL = "{ Call Catalog }"
Set RS = slQuery.OpenResultset(rdOpenForwardOnly, rdConcurReadOnly)
```

The QRY object has been set already, as explained in the previous section.

This is a simple stored procedure that doesn't accept any arguments. Stored procedures are usually called with parameters, whose values are supplied by the application. If a stored procedure expects three parameters, you must append a pair of parentheses to the name of the procedure and insert as many question marks in it as there are parameters. To call the BYROYALTY stored procedure and pass one parameter value to it, use the following SQL property:

```
slQuery.SQL ={ Call byroyalty (?) }
```

Then, to specify the values of the parameters, use the rdoParameters collection of the rdoQuery object:

```
slQuery.rdoParameters(0).Value = 40
```

The rdoParameters is the default collection of the rdoQuery object, and Value is the default property of the rdoParameter object, so the previous line could have also been written as:

```
slQuery(0) = 40
```

In the next section, we will look at the RdoStoredProcedure project and see a stored procedure in action.

The RdoStoredProcedure Project

The RdoStoredProcedure project (shown in Figure 11.5) calls and displays the results of the BYROYALTY stored procedure that is included with the Pubs sample database. The project consists of one Form with an MSFlexGrid control and a Command Button. The Command Button displays an input box that you can use to supply the Percentage parameter required by the stored procedure and then runs the BYROYALTY stored procedure.

> **NOTE**
>
> You'll find the RdoStoredProcedure project in the Ch11\RdoStoredProcedure folder on the CD that comes with this book.

FIGURE 11.5:

The RdoStored-
Procedure project

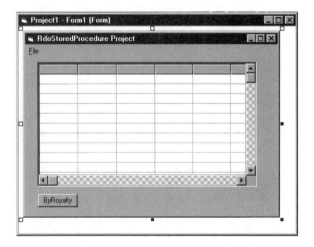

Examining the BYROYALTY Stored Procedure

The BYROYALITY stored procedure displays the author's ID number for all authors that have their Royaltyper field equal to the value you enter in the input box.

Code 11.11:   The BYROYALTY Stored Procedure

```
CREATE PROCEDURE byroyalty @percentage int
AS
select au_id from titleauthor
where titleauthor.royaltyper = @percentage
```

As you can see, this is a simple stored procedure. The SQL statement selects all au_id fields from the Titleauthor table where the Royaltyper field is equal to the percentage parameter.

The RdoStoredProcedure Project Code

The code in the RdoStoredProcedure project is straightforward. First, a connection is made to the Pubs data source as it has been in all the projects in this chapter. The following code shows the connection.

Code 11.12:   Connecting to the Pubs Data Source

```
Public Sub ConnectToDSN()
    On Error GoTo ErrorRoutineErr

    Dim connectstring As String

    Set rdoEnv = rdoEnvironments(0)
    connectstring = "UID=sa;PWD=;Database=Pubs;DSN=Pubs;"
    Set rdoConn = rdoEnv.OpenConnection("Pubs", rdOpenKeyset, _
        False, connectstring, rdAsyncEnable)

ErrorRoutineResume:
    Exit Sub
ErrorRoutineErr:
    MsgBox "Project1.Form1.ConnectToDSN" & Err & Error
    Resume Next
End Sub
```

The *rdoEnvironment* and *connectstring* variables are set. Then, the OpenConnection method is used to make the connection to the data source. In the next section, we will call the BYROYALTY stored procedure and fill the grid with the results.

Calling the Stored Procedure and Filling the Grid

The ByRoyalty button's code on the Form creates the SQL statement and displays an InputBox for you to enter a test percent. An rdoQuery object is then created with the results of the stored procedure.

Code 11.13:   Calling the BYROYALTY Stored Procedure

```
Private Sub cmdRunSP_Click()
    On Error Resume Next

    'Declare variables
    Dim i
    Dim ssql As String
    Dim rdoErr As Object

    'Clear rdo errors
    RDO.rdoEngine.rdoErrors.Clear

    'Set the sql
    ssql = "{Call byroyalty (?)}"

    Set slQuery = rdoConn.CreateQuery("", ssql)

    slQuery.rdoParameters(0) = _
        InputBox("Enter a royalty amount")

    'Run the query
    Set rdoRs = slQuery.OpenResultset _
        (rdOpenDynamic, rdConcurLock)

    'Check for errors
    If RDO.rdoEngine.rdoErrors.Count > 0 Then
        'An error has occurred
        For Each rdoErr In rdoErrors
            Debug.Print rdoErr
        Next
    ElseIf rdoRs.EOF = True Then
        'Record not found
        MsgBox "No records match"
    Else
        DisplayData rdoRs
        rdoRs.Close
    End If
End Sub
```

The code that displays the records on the grid is fairly straightforward. First, it scans the resultset's columns to display the field names on the top row. It then scans each row of the resultset, one at a time. For each row, it displays the column values in consecutive rows on the grid.

Code 11.13:   Displaying the Data

```
Private Sub DisplayData(ResSet As rdoResultset)
    Dim cl As rdoColumn
    Dim MaxLen As Integer
    Dim Rows As Variant
    Dim i, j

    On Error GoTo DisplayDataError

    Grid.Cols = ResSet.rdoColumns.Count
    Grid.Row = 0
    For Each cl In ResSet.rdoColumns
        Grid.Col = cl.OrdinalPosition - 1
        Grid = cl.Name
        MaxLen = ResSet.rdoColumns(cl.OrdinalPosition - 1) _
        .Size + 4
        Grid.ColWidth(Grid.Col) = TextWidth(String(MaxLen, "n"))
    Next cl

    ResSet.MoveLast
    Grid.Rows = ResSet.RowCount + 1
    ResSet.MoveFirst
    Grid.Row = 1
    Grid.Col = 0
    With Grid
        For i = 1 To ResSet.RowCount
            .Row = i
            For j = 0 To ResSet.rdoColumns.Count - 1
                .Col = j
                .Text = "" & ResSet.rdoColumns(j)
            Next
            ResSet.MoveNext
        Next
        .Row = 1
    End With
    Exit Sub
```

```
DisplayDataError:
    MsgBox "Could not display data: " & Err.Description
    Exit Sub

End Sub
```

The resultset's type was set to Dynamic, not because we are going to edit the records from within the application, but because we want to be able to move back and forth in the resultset (go to the last record to find the number of records and then return to the beginning). You can use a Forward-Only resultset, but this type of resultset can only be scanned forward. Since you don't know the number of rows in advance, you must increase the size of the grid as you go along, by adding more rows.

With everything in its place, let's test the RdoStoredProcedure project.

Testing the RdoStoredProcedureProject

Press F5 to start the project, as shown in Figure 11.6, and follow these steps to test the project:

1. Click the ByRoyalty button to start the BYROYALTY stored procedure code.

2. Enter the value **40** in the input box, and click the OK button. The BYROYALTY stored procedure will display all author ID numbers that match the criteria.

FIGURE 11.6:

Running the Rdo-StoredProcedure project

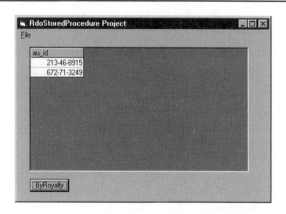

Up to this point, we have looked at applications and samples that process one query or action at a time. In the next section, we will discuss how RDO uses transactions to enable you to run two or more action queries and cancel or roll back a query if an error occurs.

Using Transactions with RDO

So far in this chapter we have discussed actions that affect only one record or table in one database. It is possible and very probable that, at some time, you will need to update multiple records in multiple tables, and for this, you use transactions.

A *transaction* is a recoverable set of changes that you make to a resultset. You use transactions when you want to verify changes before they are committed to the database. If you decide the changes are correct, you can commit them, but if you find that something went wrong, you can undo the changes. This is called *transaction processing*.

For example, an Inventory application supports the creation of new purchase orders. The process involves adding data to two separate tables:

- The Header table stores the header data such as the purchase order number, company name, and the purchase order date.

- The Detail table holds the detail records for each part that is ordered.

In the update process, you first add a record to the Header table and then add the detail records to the Detail table for each part that you want to order. This all works great until something happens in one of the updates.

Let's say that the update to the Header record works as expected, but an error occurs while adding one of the Detail records. Now you have a problem. The Header record is already in the database, but the Detail record is not. You could simply rerun the operation to add the Detail record, but that would also again add the Header record. This looks like a job for transaction processing.

When you first open a database and no transactions are pending, the transaction state is *auto-commit*. This means that all changes to the database happen immediately and cannot be reversed. When this action is not desirable, you can use transactions to control the timing of your changes.

Visual Basic includes three statements that control transaction processing:

- BeginTrans
- CommitTrans
- RollbackTrans

When you use transactions, they apply to all open databases, even databases that are opened after the transaction begins. The CommitTrans and RollbackTrans statements affect all pending transactions, regardless of the database.

Beginning a Transaction

The BeginTrans statement marks the beginning of a transaction and takes the next sequence of operations out of auto-commit mode. Once you begin a transaction, you must commit the transactions with the CommitTrans statement or roll them back with the RollbackTrans statement before you close the database or end the program. If you attempt to close a database that has uncommitted transactions, an error will occur. All uncommitted transactions are automatically rolled back when your program ends.

Committing Changes

The CommitTrans statement saves all resultset changes made since the transaction was opened with the BeginTrans statement. The CommitTrans statement saves all changes, ends the transaction, and returns the database state to auto-commit.

Undoing Changes

Calling the RollbackTrans statement reverses all the changes in the current transaction, ends the transaction, and returns the state to auto-commit.

A Transaction Example

The following example shows the process of using transactions to update two tables. If an error occurs in either operation, the transaction is reversed with the RollbackTrans statement. It is assumed that a connection called rdoConn is active to a data source.

Code 11.14:   Creating a Transaction

```
'Declare variables
    Dim ssql As String
    Dim rdoErr As Object

    'Clear rdo errors
    RDO.rdoEngine.rdoErrors.Clear

    'Begin the transaction
    rdoConn.BeginTrans

    'Build the SQL statement
    ssql = "INSERT INTO Header VALUES " _
        & "(145, 'Acme Inc.', '11/01/1997')"

    'Create the header record
    rdoConn.Execute ssql

    'Check for errors on the header record
    If RDO.rdoEngine.rdoErrors.Count > 0 Then
        'An error has occurred
        For Each rdoErr In rdoErrors
            'Notify the user of the error
            MsgBox " An error has occurred in the Header " _
            & rdoErr
            'Roll back the transaction
            rdoConn.RollbackTrans
            Exit Sub
        Next
    End If

    'If no errors, create the detail record
    'Build the SQL statement
    ssql = "INSERT INTO Detail VALUES " _
        & "(150, 'Case', 'CA1397')"

    'Create the header record
    rdoConn.Execute ssql

    'Check for errors on the header record
```

```
If RDO.rdoEngine.rdoErrors.Count > 0 Then
    'An error has occurred
    For Each rdoErr In rdoErrors
        'Notify the user of the error
        MsgBox " An error has occurred in the Detail " _
        & rdoErr
        'Roll back the transaction
        rdoConn.RollbackTrans
        Exit Sub
    Next
End If


'No errors, so commit the records
rdoConn.CommitTrans
```

This code is a good example of transaction processing. After the rdoErrors are cleared out, the SQL statement is built to add the Header record and is executed with the Execute method. Next, we check for errors. If an error is found, we undo the transaction with the RollbackTrans statement. If no errors are found, we build the SQL statement for the Detail record and execute it. Again we check for errors. If we find some, we must undo the transactions with the RollbackTrans statement. If all goes as planned, we commit the new records with the CommitTrans statement.

You can think of transaction processing as a safety net that will save you from making incorrect changes to your database. In the next section, we will take a short look at ActiveX Data Objects, the future of data access.

ActiveX Data Objects

The RDO addresses many client/server issues, but it works with ODBC, and ODBC isn't Microsoft's final standard. ODBC will also be replaced by another standard, the OLE DB (OLE for Databases), which is more in line with COM (Component Object Model). Instead of rewriting RDO for OLE DB, Microsoft introduced yet another data access mechanism, the ActiveX Data Objects (ADO). The ADO is destined to replace both DAO and RDO, and it will be around for a while. At the moment, ADO is Microsoft's vision of the ultimate object model for accessing databases. It uses a simple object model and few methods to access the data. DAO, for example, provides many methods that are specific to the JET engine. The new data access objects (RDO and ADO) are not dependent on specific databases and can be used to connect to any database.

The ADO is based on the Component Object Model and is a brand-new component. It lacks many features of the RDO, especially asynchronous operations, but it's a work in progress. The next version of ADO will be a superset of DAO and RDO and will eventually replace both objects.

So why bother with either DAO or RDO? Each has advantages, not the least of which is that many applications use these components today. Converting applications based on the DAO or RDO model isn't a trivial task, and you shouldn't convert a working application if you don't need any of the functionality provided by ADO.

Getting Started with ADO

ADO is not included with Visual Basic, but it certainly works with it. It was not far enough along when VB came out.

Microsoft has three items to help you get started with ADO, and they can be found at:

`www.microsoft.com/data/ado`

This is the official Web site for Microsoft ActiveX Data Objects. At this site, you can download the following:

ADO and SQL Server Developer's Guide. This paper is part of the Microsoft SQL Server Developer's Resource Kit and introduces ADO and the ADO programming model for developers who are building applications with Microsoft SQL Server. It was available as of November 3, 1997.

Microsoft Data Access Components 1.5 Release. The Microsoft Data Access Components (MDAC) are the key technologies that enable Universal Data Access. MDAC 1.5 contains the latest versions of ActiveX Data Objects, including Remote Data Service, formerly Advanced Data Connector, OLE DB Provider for ODBC, ODBC Driver Manager, and updated Microsoft ODBC drivers for Microsoft SQL Server, Microsoft Access, and Oracle. It was available as of October 6, 1997.

ADO Online Help in a Downloadable WinHelp File. You can download the complete ADO reference documentation in a WinHelp file. Copy these files (129Kb compressed, 205Kb uncompressed) to your `Windows\System` or `Winnt\System32` directory.

Advanced SQL Examples

- Reviewing SQL basics

- Using the SQLControl project

- Using SQL statements

- Creating JOINs

- Using SQL's built-in functions

- Changing data with SQL

Structured Query Language (SQL) enables you to communicate with a relational database to define, query, modify, and control the data. With SQL syntax, you can construct a statement that extracts records according to the criteria you specify.

SQL has quickly become the standard relational database language. It is a declarative fourth-generation language that requires you to tell the database management system what you want as opposed to how you want it. SQL is important to the Visual Basic developer because it is the primary means of communication between Visual Basic and the SQL Server Database Engine.

SQL is a published American National Standards Institute (ANSI) standard. Most of the examples in this chapter are geared toward Microsoft's SQL Server 6.5; however, SQL as a language is not database specific. Therefore, the code we use here will work with almost all database engines that support ANSI-standard SQL.

The SQL language is used in client/server, file-server, and standalone environments. Since it is a set-oriented language, it delivers data as a set of records; how the records are used is up to the application . For example, to access all the addresses in Texas from your Customer table, you would request the following:

```
SELECT * FROM Customer WHERE State = 'TX'
```

This request returns only the records in Texas and not the entire Customer table. This set could then be listed, reported, or altered as needed by your application.

SQL programming is extremely flexible and powerful and allows you to do a lot more than construct queries that retrieve data. You can also use SQL to do the following:

- Create, administer, and maintain databases
- Create and maintain tables
- Insert new data
- Update and delete existing data

In this chapter, we'll take a look at SQL from the Visual Basic developer's point of view.

A Refresher Course in SQL

Although this chapter deals with advanced SQL, we thought it would be helpful to take a brief look at some SQL basics. The SQL language is vast and contains hundreds of statements; however, most of them stem from the following few basic statements:

SELECT identifies which tables and columns in the data source are to be used.

ORDER BY applies a sort order to the recordset.

INSERT adds new records to a recordset.

DELETE deletes records from a recordset.

UPDATE modifies the fields of a record.

WHERE applies a filter that narrows the selection and is used in almost all SQL statements.

These statements are versatile, and you can use them to access and manipulate data in a database, or you can expand and combine them to create a flexible and powerful SQL data manipulation tool. First, let's review these statements in their basic form. Later in the chapter, we will unlock their power to create, access, and maintain SQL Server data.

NOTE   Most of the examples in this chapter refer to the Pubs database, which is created when you install SQL Server 6.5. To run the examples in this chapter, you must have access to the Pubs database. If it is not installed on your server or if it has been altered, you can run the Instpubs.sql script included on the CD that comes with this book to install it.

Coding a SQL Select Statement

The most frequently used SQL statement, the SELECT statement, is extremely versatile, and you can use it to retrieve data, compute totals, and create new tables. To use the SELECT statement, you must know what you want to select and where it is located. The syntax for a general SELECT statement is:

```
SELECT [ALL] select list FROM table name WHERE clause ORDER BY sort list
```

NOTE
> By convention, SQL keywords are coded in uppercase; however, this is not required. SQL statements are not case-sensitive. In this book we place keywords in uppercase for clarity and to distinguish them from regular code.

Table 12.1 lists the parts of the SELECT statement.

TABLE 12.1: The Parts of the SELECT Statement

Part	Description
ALL	Retrieves all rows in the results. ALL is the default.
select_list	Specifies the columns to select. The select_list can be an asterisk (*), representing all columns in the table; a list of column names, specified in the order in which you want to see them; a column name and column heading that will replace the default column heading; an expression; the IDENTITYCOL keyword instead of the name of a column that has the IDENTITY property; a local variable assignment; or a local or global variable.
FROM	Indicates the specific table(s) and view(s) for the SELECT statement.
WHERE clause	Specifies the restricting conditions for the rows returned in the result set. There is no limit to the number of conditions that can be included in a SQL statement.
ORDER BY	Sorts the results by columns.

Sample SELECT Statement   To obtain a list of all the first and last names of the authors in the Authors table from the Pubs database sorted by last name, use the following SELECT statement:

```
SELECT au_fname, au_lname FROM authors ORDER BY au_lname
```

NOTE
> If you want data presented in a specific order when returned in a query, you use the ORDER BY keyword. The ORDER BY keyword determines how SQL Server collates and presents data in response to database queries. It also determines how certain queries are resolved, such as those involving WHERE and DISTINCT.

Coding a SQL Insert Statement

You use the SQL INSERT statement to add a new row of data to a recordset. Its general syntax is:

```
INSERT INTO table name VALUES
```

Table 12.2 lists the parts of the INSERT statement:

TABLE 12.2: The Parts of the INSERT Statement

Part	Description
table name	The name of the table in which to insert data.
VALUES	The values to insert into each column in the table.

Sample INSERT Statement To insert a new row in the Authors table in the Pubs database, use the following statement:

```
INSERT INTO authors VALUES
('555-67-8910','Martin','Robert', '408 555-9657', '15415 Main St.',
'Bay Shore', 'TX', '77003', 1)
```

Notice that the test strings are enclosed in single quotes and the numeric values are not. This is a SQL rule. All text strings and date fields must be enclosed in single quotes.

Coding a SQL DELETE Statement

You use the DELETE statement to remove rows from a recordset. Use DELETE alone to delete all rows, or use DELETE with a WHERE clause to limit the rows deleted. The general syntax of the DELETE statement is:

```
DELETE [FROM] table name [WHERE clause]
```

Table 12.3 lists the parts of the DELETE statement.

TABLE 12.3: The Parts of the DELETE Statement

Part	Description
table name	The name of the table from which to delete row(s).
WHERE	Conditions to limit the row(s) to delete.

Sample DELETE Statement   To use the DELETE statement to delete the test row that was added in the previous section, use the following code:

```
DELETE FROM authors WHERE au_id = '555-67-8910'
```

Coding a SQL UPDATE Statement

You use the SQL UPDATE statement to change data in existing rows, either by adding new data or by modifying existing data. The general syntax is:

```
UPDATE table name SET column name = new value WHERE clause
```

Table 12.4 lists the parts of the UPDATE statement.

TABLE 12.4: The Parts of the UPDATE Statement

Part	Description
table name	The name of the table to be used in the UPDATE statement.
column name	The name of the column in which the data will be changed.
WHERE	An optional WHERE clause used to limit the rows updated.

Sample UPDATE Statement   To update the phone number of an author in the Authors table from the Pubs database, use the following code:

```
UPDATE authors SET phone = '418 496-7223'
WHERE au_id = '172-32-1176'
```

Understanding SQL Server 6.5 Data types

Data types specify the data characteristics of columns, stored-procedure parameters, and local variables. It is important to know the data type of the data you are working with so that you can properly code the SQL statements.

Data types in SQL Server come in two varieties:

- System-supplied
- User-defined

Data types are categorized by the type of data stored within the data type. For example, in a column is the data:

- In the form of text that is to be displayed?
- Numbers that are to be added?
- Dates that are to be set?

SQL Server assigns a data type to every column in every database. In addition to system-supplied data types, SQL Server allows user-defined data types, which are based on the system data types. Table 12.5 lists the data types supplied for SQL Server 6.5.

TABLE 12.5: The SQL Server 6.5 Data Types

Data type	Description
BINARY	Holds as many as 255 bytes of fixed-length binary data.
BIT	Holds either 1 or 0. Integer values other than 1 or 0 are accepted but are always interpreted as 1.
CHAR	Holds a character string of fixed-string length. A good data type choice when data in columns will be consistently close to the same size.
DATETIME	Stores date and time in 8 bytes of two 4-byte integers: 4 bytes for the number of days before or after the base date of January 1, 1900, and 4 bytes for the number of milliseconds after midnight. If no value is entered, the default is January 1, 1900.
DECIMAL	Stores numbers as 96-bit (12-byte) unsigned integers scaled by a variable power of 10.
FLOAT	Stores a 4-byte floating point number.
IMAGE	A variable-length data type that can hold as many as 2^{31}, or 1 (2,147,483,647) bytes of binary data.
INT	A data type that holds whole numbers from -2^{31} (-2,147,483,648) through $2^{31} - 1$ (2,147,483,647). Storage size is 4 bytes.

TABLE 12.5 (CONTINUED): The SQL Server 6.5 Data Types

Data type	Description
MONEY	Stores monetary values from -922,337,203,685,477.5808 through +922,337,203,685,477.5807, with accuracy to a ten-thousandth of a monetary unit.
NUMERIC	Stores numbers as 96-bit (12-byte) unsigned integers scaled by a variable power of 10.
REAL	Stores a floating-point column that has 7-digit precision.
SMALLDATETIME	Stores a date and time data type that is less precise than datetime.
SMALLINT	Holds whole numbers from -2^{15} (-32,768) through 2^{15} - 1 (32,767). Storage size is 2 bytes.
SMALLMONEY	Stores monetary values from - 214,748.3648 through +214,748.3647, with accuracy to a ten-thousandth-of-a-monetary-unit.
TEXT	A variable-length data type that can hold as many as 2^{31} - 1 (2,147,483,647) characters.
TIMESTAMP	Is automatically updated every time a row containing a *timestamp* column is inserted or updated. Values in *timestamp* columns are not *datetime* data, but *binary*(8) *varbinary*(8) data, indicating the sequence of SQL Server activity on the row.
TINYINT	Holds whole numbers from 0 through 255. Storage size is 1 byte.
VARBINARY	A variable-length *binary* data type that holds a maximum of 255 bytes of variable-length binary data.
VARCHAR	Holds a maximum of 255 characters. A good data type choice when you expect null values or a wide variation in the length of the stored data.

Using Character Strings and Quotes

Character strings and dates (*char, varchar,* and *datetime* data types) must be enclosed in single quote marks when you search for them, as in the following:

```
SELECT * FROM authors WHERE au_fname = 'Cheryl'
```

You must use two consecutive single quote marks to specify a single apostrophe within a character entry, as in the following:

```
SELECT * FROM authors WHERE au_lname = 'O''Leary'
```

Arithmetic Operators

Operators are symbols used to perform mathematical computations or comparisons on numeric columns. You can compare columns with like data types without any data conversion. Table 12.6 lists the arithmetic operators used in SQL statements:

TABLE 12.6: Arithmetic Operators

Symbol	Operation
+	Addition
/	Division
*	Multiplication
%	Modula
-	Subtraction

You can use arithmetic operators that perform addition, division, multiplication, and subtraction on any column with a numeric data type (DECIMAL, FLOAT, INT, MONEY, NUMERIC, SMALLINT, SMALLMONEY, or TINYINT). You cannot use the modula operator with money data types.

> **NOTE**
>
> A *modula* is the remainder after the division of two integers. For example, 5 % 2 = 1 because 5 divided by 2 equals 2 with a remainder of 1.

Operator Precedence

Operator precedence becomes an issue when multiplying values. It determines the order of computations or comparisons. Operator precedence is based on the following levels:

- Primary grouping: ( )
- Bitwise: ~
- Multiplication: * / %
- Additive: + -

- Bitwise: ^
- Bitwise: &
- Bitwise: |
- NOT
- AND
- OR

The precedence order is from left to right when all operators in a given expression are at the same level. You can change the order of precedence by using parentheses, in which case the most deeply nested expression is evaluated first. Often, the order in which an expression is evaluated can make a difference in the result.

Comparison Operators in SQL Statements

Comparison operators contrast the difference between two expressions and can only be used between variables and columns of similar data types. Table 12.7 lists the valid comparison operators:

TABLE 12.7: The Valid Comparison Operators

Symbol	Meaning
=	Equal to
>	Greater than
<	Less than
>=	Grater than or equal to
<=	Less than or equal to
<>	Not equal

Keywords Used in a WHERE Clause

The SQL language contains many keywords that can be used in a WHERE clause to limit the records selected. Table 12.8 lists them.

TABLE 12.8: Keywords That Can Be Used in a WHERE Clause

Keyword	Use
ANY	Tests for any values.
ALL	Tests for all values.
AND	Tests for multiple conditions.
OR	Tests for one of two conditions.
BETWEEN	Tests for values between two values.
EXISTS	Tests for values that exist.
NOT EXISTS	Tests for values that do not exist.
NOT BETWEEN	Tests for values not between two values.
IN	Tests for values in a range of values.
NOT IN	Tests for values not in a range of values.
LIKE	Tests for values that are like a value.
NOT LIKE	Tests for values that are not like a value.
IS NULL	Tests for null values.
IS NOT NULL	Tests for values that are not null.

Using Wildcards and the LIKE Keyword

You use the LIKE keyword to select rows containing fields that match a specified portion of a character string. LIKE can be used with CHAR, VARCHAR, DATETIME, SMALLDATETIME, and TEXT data types. The LIKE keyword takes one of four wildcard characters as shown in Table 12.9.

TABLE 12.9: SQL Wildcards

Wildcard	Meaning
-	Any single character.
%	Any string of zero or more characters.
[]	Any single character within a specified range ([a-c]) or in a set ([abc]).
[^]	Any single character not in a specified range ([^a-c]) or in a set ([^abc]).

The wildcard and character string must be enclosed in single quotes when it is part of a SQL statement. Here are some examples:

- `LIKE '_heryl'` searches for six-letter words ending in the letters *heryl,* such as Cheryl and Sheryl.

- `LIKE 'St%'` searches for values that begin with *St,* such as Start, Started, and Stop.

- `LIKE '%ob%'` searches for all words that contain *ob,* such as Robert and Robbery.

- `LIKE '[CS]eryl'` searches for Cheryl or Sheryl.

- `LIKE 'C[^o]'` searches for words that start with the letter *C* and do not have the letter *o* in the second position, such as Carpet.

Well, that's a brief review, and now it's time to explore the real power of the SQL language. In the next section, we will take a look at the SQLControl project. The remainder of this chapter is devoted to some really hard-core SQL.

The SQLControl Project

We'll use the SQLControl project, shown in Figure 12.1, as a reference point for the main SQL examples in this chapter. It can also serve as a tool with which you can construct and run SQL statements.

> **NOTE**   You'll find the SQLControl project in the `Ch12\sqlcontrol` folder on the CD that comes with this book.

The SQLControl project has a Windows Explorer–style tree on the left side that has four main branches:

Statements, which are the SQL example SELECT statements

Functions, which hold the sample aggregate, date, mathematical, niladic, string, system, and text and image functions

JOINs, which create queries by joining two or more tables on common columns

Actions, such as SELECT, DELETE, and UPDATE

The SQLControl
application

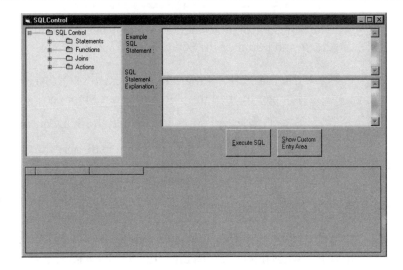

The right side of the SQLControl Form has two text boxes:

- The Example SQL Statement text box displays the example SQL statement for the selected statement.

- The SQL Statement Explanation text box pulls double duty: It provides a description of the current SQL example statement, and it serves as a place for you to enter a SQL statement to be executed.

Below the SQL text box are two Command Buttons:

Execute SQL allows you to execute the current SQL statement.

Show Custom Entry Area allows you to toggle between displaying the current SQL statement and an empty text box in which you can construct a custom SQL statement of your own.

Rounding out the Form is the Results Grid at the bottom. This grid displays the results of the current SQL statement—either the text statement or a custom SQL statement that you enter.

Loading the SQLControl Project

The SQLControl project relies on a SQL Server database. Follow these steps to create and populate the SQLControl database:

1. Choose Start ➤ Programs ➤ Microsoft SQL Server 6.5 ➤ SQL Enterprise Manger to open the SQL Enterprise Manager.

2. Select the server you want to hold the SQLControl database.

3. Choose Tools ➤ SQL Query Tool to display the Query Tool screen.

4. Choose File ➤ Open and select the `instsqlc.sql` file from the Ch12Code subdirectory on the book's CD. This SQL code will create and populate the SQLControl database.

5. Choose Query ➤ Execute or press Ctrl+E to execute the `instsqlc` code.

6. After this code executes, the database is created and populated.

NOTE See Chapter 10 if you need a refresher in using the SQL Enterprise Manager.

Taking the SQLControl Project for a Test Drive

Follow these steps to select and execute the SELECT statement example:

1. Press F5 to start the project. You should see the SQLControl Form as shown in Figure 12.1.

2. Click the plus (+) sign next to the STATEMENTS folder.

3. Click the Execute SQL Command Button to populate the text boxes and the Syntax Grid with the SQL statement syntax. The Results Grid will display the results of the example SQL statement, as shown in Figure 12.2.

FIGURE 12.2:

The SQLControl application displaying results

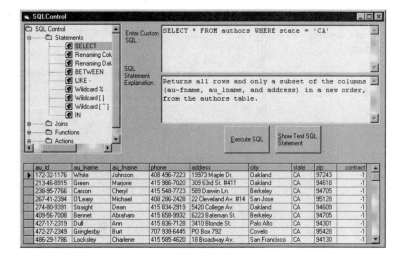

Testing a Custom SQL Statement

As mentioned earlier, the SQLControl Form has a dual role: It presents information about the sample SQL statements in this chapter, and it allows you to enter and execute custom SQL statements. Follow these steps to enter and execute a custom SQL statement:

1. If the SQLControl project is not already running, press F5 to start it. You should see the SQLControl Form as shown in Figure 12.1, earlier in this chapter.

2. Click the Show Custom Entry Area Command Button.

3. Enter the following SQL statement into the Custom SQL Area:

   ```
   SELECT * FROM authors WHERE state = 'CA'
   ```

4. Click the Execute SQL Command Button or press Alt+E to execute the statement. The Results Grid will display the results (a list of authors residing in California), as shown in Figure 12.3.

FIGURE 12.3:

The results of a custom
SQL statement

This example demonstrates the ease of use, versatility, and power of the SQLControl project. The examples in the rest of this chapter are stored in the project. In the next section, we will take a look at some advanced SQL statements that deal with retrieving, presenting, and editing data with queries.

Using SQL Statements

In this section, we will take a look at some advanced SQL statements. For the purposes of this chapter, SQL statements will be considered statements that retrieve, present, and edit data.

Coding the SELECT Statement

In the earlier section "A Refresher Course in SQL," you saw a general SELECT statement. The full syntax of the SELECT statement is:

```
SELECT [ALL | DISTINCT] select_list
    [INTO [new_table_name]]
[FROM {table_name | view_name}[(optimizer_hints)]
    [[, {table_name2 | view_name2}[(optimizer_hints)]
    [..., {table_name16 | view_name16}]]
[WHERE clause]
[GROUP BY clause]
[HAVING clause]
[ORDER BY clause]
```

You must use the clauses in a SELECT statement in the order shown. For example, if you want to list the columns to select, you must do so before you set the sort order with the ORDER BY clause.

You can order a resultset either by the column name as:

```
SELECT * FROM authors ORDER BY au_lname
```

or as:

```
SELECT * FROM Authors ORDER BY 2
```

Both statements return a resultset of the Authors table ordered by the authors' last names. Give this a try in the SQLControl application.

SELECT Statement Examples

The following examples show various options used with the SELECT statement against the Pubs database.

SELECT: All Rows, Subset of Columns   This example returns all rows and only a subset of the columns (au_fname, au_lname, and address) from the Authors table:

```
SELECT au_fname, au_lname, address FROM authors
```

au_fname	au_lname	address
Johnson	White	19973 Maple Dr.
Marjorie	Green	309 63rd St. #411
Cheryl	Carson	589 Darwin Ln.
Michael	O'Leary	22 Cleveland Av. #1
Dean	Straight	5420 College Av.
Meander	Smith	10 Mississippi Dr.
Abraham	Bennet	6223 Bateman St.
Ann	Dull	3410 Blonde St.
Burt	Gringlesby	PO Box 792

SELECT: Renaming Columns   The name given to a column when it is returned in a query is used as the default column heading. Sometimes, as developers, we tend to be cryptic in our naming of objects. If a column holds someone's first name, we might name that column fname. This makes perfect sense to us, but to the user it is just a bunch of letters. As you code SQL statements, you can change the column names to be more user-friendly. You do so by renaming a column's display. For example, the following code renames the authors' first name column from au_fname to Author's First Name and renames the authors' last name column from au_lname to Author's Last Name in the Authors table.

```
SELECT 'Author''s First Name' = au_fname, 'Author''s Last Name' =
au_lname from authors
```

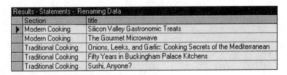

Author's First Name	Author's Last Name
Johnson	White
Marjorie	Green
Cheryl	Carson
Michael	O'Leary
Dean	Straight
Meander	Smith
Abraham	Bennet
Ann	Dull
Burt	Gringlesby

NOTE   Notice the use of double apostrophes in the code. If you want to use an apostrophe in a character entry in a SQL statement, you must use two single apostrophes.

SELECT: Renaming Data   In addition to renaming column headings, you can rename data in a resultset. The following code uses the CASE statement to rename the types from the Titles table.

```
SELECT Section = CASE type WHEN 'mod_cook' THEN 'Modern Cooking'
WHEN 'trad_cook' THEN 'Traditional Cooking'
END, title = title FROM titles WHERE type LIKE '%cook'
```

Section	title
Modern Cooking	Silicon Valley Gastronomic Treats
Modern Cooking	The Gourmet Microwave
Traditional Cooking	Onions, Leeks, and Garlic: Cooking Secrets of the Mediterranean
Traditional Cooking	Fifty Years in Buckingham Palace Kitchens
Traditional Cooking	Sushi, Anyone?

In this example, whenever a record is encountered with a type equal to 'mod_cook', the type is returned as Modern Cooking, and the type 'trad_cook' is returned as Traditional Cooking. These values will make more sense to users and will certainly look better on a printed report.

SELECT: BETWEEN   You use the keyword BETWEEN to select values between two values. The following example returns the sales from January 1, 1993, and December 31, 1993, from the Sales table:

```
SELECT qty, ord_date FROM sales WHERE ord_date BETWEEN '01/01/93' AND
'12/31/93' ORDER BY ord_date [tech changes]
```

When using BETWEEN, the values returned are greater than or equal to the first value, and less than or equal to the second value. In our example, you will get records with an ord_date greater than or equal to "01/01/93" and less than or equal to "12/31/93."

Querying with Wildcards and the LIKE Clause

Wildcards can be very useful in writing SQL queries. If you need to query on a group of records that have one or more characters in common, you can make your coding life easier by incorporating wildcards. Let's take a look at some examples using wildcards with the LIKE clause.

SELECT: LIKE_   You use the LIKE keyword to select rows containing fields that match a specified portion of a character string. The LIKE wildcard "_" replaces any single character in a query. If you want to select all authors with the first name of Cheryl or Sheryl, you can use the LIKE keyword combined with the "_" wildcard as in the following:

```
Select * from authors WHERE au_fname LIKE '_heryl'
```

This query returns two records—one for Cheryl and one for Sheryl.

SELECT: Wildcard %   You use the % wildcard to select any string of zero or more characters. Let's say that you want to find a certain employee in the Pubs database, but you can't remember the employee's name. You believe that it starts with either an *A* or an *M* and that the employee was hired in 1993. You could use the following SQL statement to query the Employee table to narrow your search:

```
SELECT * FROM employee WHERE (fname LIKE 'A%' or fname LIKE 'M%') AND
hire_date BETWEEN '01/01/93' AND '12/31/93' ORDER BY lname
```

emp_id	fname	minit	lname	job_id	job_lvl	pub_id	hire_date
ARD36773F	Anabela	R	Domingues	8	100	0877	1/27/93
MMS49649F	Mary	M	Saveley	8	175	0736	6/29/93

This query returns only those employees hired in 1993 with a first name that starts with an *A* or an *M*. As you can see, it is easy to combine SQL keywords and clauses to create powerful queries.

SELECT: Wildcard [ ]   You can use the wildcard [ ] with the LIKE clause to search for a range of values—for example, you want to find an author that lives in the 415 area code, but you can remember only that the phone number begins with a 5 or an 8. If you want a range, you use [5-8]; simply add a dash between the low and high values. You can retrieve a list of employees with that pattern in their phone numbers with the following SQL statement:

```
SELECT * FROM authors WHERE phone LIKE '415 [58]%'
```

au_id	au_lname	au_fname	phone	address	city	state	zip	contract
238-95-7766	Carson	Cheryl	415 548-7723	589 Darwin Ln.	Berkeley	CA	94705	-1
274-80-9391	Straight	Dean	415 834-2919	5420 College Av.	Oakland	CA	94609	-1
427-17-2319	Dull	Ann	415 836-7128	3410 Blonde St.	Palo Alto	CA	94301	-1
486-29-1786	Locksley	Charlene	415 585-4620	18 Broadway Av.	San Francisco	CA	94130	-1
724-08-9931	Stringer	Dirk	415 843-2991	5420 Telegraph Av.	Oakland	CA	94609	0
756-30-7391	Karsen	Livia	415 534-9219	5720 McAuley St.	Oakland	CA	94609	-1
846-92-7186	Hunter	Sheryl	415 836-7128	3410 Blonde St.	Palo Alto	CA	94301	-1

This query returns records that have 415 in the beginning of the phone field and that have either a 5 or an 8 as the next number.

SELECT: Wildcard [^]   You can use the wildcard [^]with the LIKE clause to search for any single character not specified within a range of values. For example, you would like to find all authors that live in California in the 90000 zip code area, but do not live in the Bay Area. The Bay Area has a 4 in the second space of the zip code. You can query for all zips that start with a 9 and that do not have a 4 in the second space with the following SQL code:

```
SELECT * FROM authors WHERE zip LIKE '9[^4]%'
```

au_id	au_lname	au_fname	phone	address	city	state	zip	contract
172-32-1176	White	Johnson	408 496-7223	19973 Maple Dr.	Oakland	CA	97243	-1
267-41-2394	O'Leary	Michael	408 286-2428	22 Cleveland Av. #14	San Jose	CA	95128	-1
472-27-2349	Gringlesby	Burt	707 938-6445	PO Box 792	Covelo	CA	95428	-1
648-92-1872	Blotchet-Halls	Reginald	503 745-6402	55 Hillsdale Bl.	Corvallis	OR	97330	-1
893-72-1158	McBadden	Heather	707 448-4982	301 Putnam	Vacaville	CA	95688	0

This query will return only those authors from the Authors table that have a zip code that starts with a 9 and that do not have a 4 in the next space.

SELECT: IN   You use the IN keyword to select values that match a list of values. For example, if you want a list authors from the Authors table that live in Berkeley, Nashville, or Oakland, you can use the following statement:

```
SELECT * FROM authors WHERE city = 'Berkeley' OR city = 'Nashville' OR
city = 'Oakland'
```

au_id	au_lname	au_fname	phone	address	city	state	zip	contract
172-32-1176	White	Johnson	408 496-7223	19973 Maple Dr.	Oakland	CA	97243	-1
213-46-8915	Green	Marjorie	415 986-7020	309 63rd St. #411	Oakland	CA	94618	-1
238-95-7766	Carson	Cheryl	415 548-7723	589 Darwin Ln.	Berkeley	CA	94705	-1
274-80-9391	Straight	Dean	415 834-2919	5420 College Av.	Oakland	CA	94609	-1
409-56-7008	Bennet	Abraham	415 658-9932	6223 Bateman St.	Berkeley	CA	94705	-1
527-72-3246	Greene	Morningstar	615 297-2723	22 Graybar House Rd.	Nashville	TN	37215	0
724-08-9931	Stringer	Dirk	415 843-2991	5420 Telegraph Av.	Oakland	CA	94609	0
724-80-9391	MacFeather	Stearns	415 354-7128	44 Upland Hts.	Oakland	CA	94612	-1
756-30-7391	Karsen	Livia	415 534-9219	5720 McAuley St.	Oakland	CA	94609	-1

Or you could use the IN keyword and rewrite the SQL statement as follows:

```
SELECT * FROM authors WHERE city IN ('Berkeley', 'Nashville', 'Oakland')
```

This query returns authors from the Authors table that live in Berkeley, Nashville, or Oakland. The IN keyword is useful if you have a long list. You can save yourself a lot of typing.

The SQL statements we have been looking at thus far have involved only one table. If you need to query data from more than one table, you use the JOIN keyword. In the next section, we will explore the world of SQL JOINS.

Querying Multiple Tables with JOIN

In relational databases, the main theory is that no redundant data should be stored in the database. Simply stated, you would not store the name, address, phone number, and like data for an author in the Titles table. Instead, you would create an identification field in the Authors table and use it in other tables. Then, if you need the author's name from the Titles table, you would join the tables on the identification fields.

In a good database design, referred to as *normalized*, each table stores one type of data—a person, a place, a location, an event, or a thing. JOINS are used to present or select data from multiple tables.

Table 12.10 show the types of ANSI JOINS that are permitted.

TABLE 12.10: ANSI JOINS

JOIN Type	Description
CROSS JOIN	The cross-product of two tables. Returns the same rows as if no WHERE clause were specified.
INNER	Specifies that all inner rows be returned. Discards unmatched rows.
LEFT OUTER	Specifies that all left outer rows be returned, that all rows from the left table that did not meet the condition specified be included in the resultset, and that output columns from the other table be set to NULL.
RIGHT OUTER	Specifies that all rows from the right table that did not meet the condition specified be included in the resultset and that output columns that correspond to the other table be set to NULL.
FULL OUTER	Specifies that if a row from either table does not match the selection criteria, the row is included in the resultset and its output columns that correspond to the other table be set to NULL.

If you are trying to select columns in different tables with the same name, you must use an alias. An *alias* is a value that uniquely identifies each table. If you are not selecting columns from different tables, you can still use an alias.

In the next sections, we will take a look at each type of JOIN.

NOTE In our examples, NULL fields will display blank; they will not show the word *NULL*.

Creating a CROSS JOIN

A CROSS JOIN is the cross-product of two tables and returns the same rows as if no WHERE clause were specified.

This example returns the cross-product of the Authors and Publishers tables. A list of all possible combinations of au_lname rows and all pub_name rows are returned. This is a JOIN in its simplest form.

```
SELECT au_lname, pub_name FROM authors CROSS JOIN publishers
```

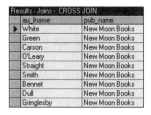

Creating an INNER JOIN

An INNER JOIN specifies that all inner rows be returned, discarding unmatched rows. For example, if you want to query for the titles written by authors Ringer and Green, you INNER JOIN the Authors table with the Titles table.

The Titles table stores the titles, but does not have the authors' names. The Authors table has the authors' names, but does not have the titles. This results in all rows being selected from the Authors table and only rows that match the au_id being selected from the Titles table.

You perform an INNER JOIN on the Authors and Titles tables with the au_id field as in the following:

```
SELECT authors.au_lname, authors.au_fname, titles.title FROM authors
INNER JOIN titleauthor ON authors.au_id = titleauthor.au_id INNER JOIN
titles ON titleauthor.title_id = titles.title_id WHERE au_lname IN
('Ringer', 'Green') ORDER BY title
```

The resulting query returns the first and last names from the Authors table and the titles each has written from the Titles table and then sorts the results by the title.

In the JOINS discussed so far, only matching rows are included in the results. These JOINS eliminate the information in rows that do not match the JOIN criteria.

When you want to retain and display the unmatched rows, you can use an OUTER JOIN. An OUTER JOIN displays all rows from the main table regardless of whether matching data exists in the other table. In the next section, we will explore the ANSI OUTER JOINS.

Creating a LEFT OUTER JOIN

A LEFT OUTER JOIN specifies that all left outer rows be returned, that all rows from the left table that did not meet the condition specified be included in the resultset, and that output columns from the other table be set to NULL.

The following SQL statement selects the order number from the Sales table, the store name from the Stores table, and the title and type from the Titles table. A LEFT OUTER JOIN is performed from the Sales table to the Stores table, returning all rows from the Sales table and setting the store name to NULL if there is not a matching record in the Stores table.

There is also a LEFT OUTER JOIN from the Sales table to the Titles table, returning all rows from the Sales table and setting the values from the Titles table to NULL for any rows that do not match on the title_id. We add a WHERE clause to select only the business and popular_comp type books.

```
SELECT sales.ord_num, stores.stor_name, titles.title, titles.type FROM
sales LEFT OUTER JOIN titles ON sales.title_id = titles.title_id LEFT
OUTER JOIN stores ON sales.stor_id = stores.stor_id WHERE titles.type
IN ('popular_comp', 'business'))
```

Results - Joins - LEFT OUTER JOIN

ord_num	stor_name	title	type
6871	Eric the Read Books	The Busy Executive's Database Guide	business
423LL930	Bookbeat	The Busy Executive's Database Guide	business
P723	Bookbeat	Cooking with Computers: Surreptitious Balance Sheets	business
X999	Fricative Bookshop	You Can Combat Computer Stress!	business
QQ2299	Fricative Bookshop	Straight Talk About Computers	business
QA879.1	Bookbeat	But Is It User Friendly?	popular_comp
A2976	Barnum's	Secrets of Silicon Valley	popular_comp

NOTE An easy way to create and test a JOIN is to use the Visual Database Tools Add-In for Visual Basic. See Chapter 9 for a discussion of this tool.

The resulting query returns all rows from the Sales table and all rows from the Stores and Titles tables.

NOTE No fields are set to NULL. This means that the LEFT OUTER JOIN found a match for the JOIN fields of sales.title_id to titles.title_id for the first LEFT OUTER JOIN and also found a match for the second LEFT OUTER JOIN from the sales.stor_id to stores.stor_id.

Earlier versions of SQL Server LEFT OUTER JOINS (=*) are supported, as in the following example:

```
SELECT authors.au_lname, titleauthor.title_id
FROM authors, titleauthor
WHERE titleauthor.au_id =* authors.au_id
```

Creating a RIGHT OUTER JOIN

A RIGHT OUTER JOIN specifies that all rows from the right table that did not meet the condition specified are included in the resultset and that output columns that correspond to the other table be set to NULL. A RIGHT OUTER JOIN is useful when you want to see all the data from a given table and match it against the data from a related table.

The following example selects all the publishers from the Publishers table with a pub_id greater than 1300 and, with a RIGHT OUTER JOIN, selects all the titles from the Titles table whether a title exists for the publisher or not. If a publisher does not have a title, the query returns NULL.

```
SELECT publishers.pub_id, titles.title, titles.title_id, publishers.state
FROM titles RIGHT OUTER JOIN publishers ON publishers.pub_id = titles.pub_id
WHERE (publishers.pub_id > '1300')
ORDER BY publishers.pub_id
```

pub_id	title	title_id	state
1389	The Busy Executive's Database Guide	BU1032	CA
1389	Cooking with Computers: Surreptitious Balance Sheets	BU1111	CA
1389	Straight Talk About Computers	BU7832	CA
1389	But Is It User Friendly?	PC1035	CA
1389	Secrets of Silicon Valley	PC8888	CA
1389	Net Etiquette	PC9999	CA
1622			IL
1756			TX
9901			

The resulting query returns all publishers from the Publishers table with a pub_id greater than 1300 and all titles, whether data exists or not, from the Titles table.

Earlier versions of SQL Server RIGHT OUTER JOINS (*=) are supported, as in the following example:

```
Select authors.au_lname, titleauthor.title_id
FROM authors, titleauthor
WHERE authors.au_id *= titleauthor.au_id
```

NOTE

Support for the (*=) JOIN symbols may be dropped in future versions of SQL, so we suggest that you use the ANSI-STYLE JOINS instead. You cannot use both OUTER JOIN operators and ANSI-SQL joined tables in the same query.

Creating a FULL OUTER JOIN

A FULL OUTER JOIN specifies that if a row from either table does not match the selection criteria, the row is included in the resultset and its output columns that correspond to the other table be set to NULL.

This example returns the book title and its corresponding publisher in the Titles table for publishers that are not in California or Washington, D.C. It also returns any publishers who have not published books listed in the Titles table and any book titles from a publisher other than the one listed in the Publishers table. The output is sorted by title_id with the ORDER BY clause.

```
SELECT titles.title, publishers.pub_name, publishers.state
FROM publishers FULL OUTER JOIN titles ON titles.pub_id
= publishers.pub_id
WHERE (publishers.state <> 'Ca' AND publishers.state <> 'DC') ORDER BY
titles.title_id
```

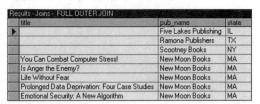

title	pub_name	state
	Five Lakes Publishing	IL
	Ramona Publishers	TX
	Scootney Books	NY
You Can Combat Computer Stress!	New Moon Books	MA
Is Anger the Enemy?	New Moon Books	MA
Life Without Fear	New Moon Books	MA
Prolonged Data Deprivation: Four Case Studies	New Moon Books	MA
Emotional Security: A New Algorithm	New Moon Books	MA

The resulting query selects all the publishers and all the titles, even if a publisher has not published a book or a book title does not have a publisher.

JOINS make it possible for you to select and view data from multiple tables with ease. Built-in functions are another time-saving feature of the SQL language, whether you want to calculate values, manipulate dates, or perform complex mathematical operations. Functions are a great extension to SQL. In the next section, we will take a look at the role of built-in function extensions.

Using SQL's Built-In Functions

Functions return special information in the form of queries. Functions perform various operations and can be used in a SELECT list, a WHERE clause, or anywhere an expression is allowed. SQL has eight types of built-in functions:

Aggregate, which return summary values.

Conversion, which transform one data type to another.

Date, which display information about dates and times.

Mathematical, which perform operations on numeric data.

Niladic, which allow you to insert a system-supplied value into a table when no value is provided.

String, which perform operations on character strings, binary data, or expressions.

System, which return a special piece of information from the database.

Text and Image, which perform operations on text and image data.

In the following sections, we will take a closer look at some of the built-in functions.

Returning Summary Values with Aggregate Functions

Aggregate functions return summary values, such as averages, sums, and counts, from all non-null values in a column. They return a single value for each set of rows to which the function applies. You can have multiple function calls in the same query, and each summary value will be in its own column.

You can use aggregate functions with SELECT clauses such as GROUP BY and with a WHERE clause. With a GROUP BY clause, you receive a summary value for each group.

The syntax for aggregate functions is:

```
aggregate_ function ([ALL | DISTINCT] expression)
```

Table 12.11 lists the parts of the aggregate function syntax, and Table 12.12 lists the aggregate functions.

TABLE 12.11: The Parts of the Aggregate Function Syntax

Part	Description
aggregate_function	Specifies an aggregate function as listed in Table 12.12.
ALL	Default. Applies the aggregate function to all values.
DISTINCT	Eliminates duplicate column values before the function is calculated. DISTINCT cannot be used with COUNT(*) and has no meaning in MIN and MAX functions.
expression	The column name or any combination of columns, a constant, or a function.

TABLE 12.12: Aggregate Functions

Aggregate Function	Description
AVG	Calculates the average of all the values or only the DISTINCT values in the *expression*. AVG can be used with numeric columns only, and Null values are ignored.
COUNT	Adds the number of non-null values in the *expression* or only the DISTINCT number of unique non-null values. COUNT can be used with both numeric and character columns, and null values are ignored.
COUNT(*)	Adds the number of rows. No parameters or the DISTINCT keyword can be used, and COUNT(*) includes rows with null values.
MAX	Returns the maximum value in numeric, character, or datetime columns, ignoring any null values. MAX finds the highest value in the collating sequence for character columns. DISTINCT is available, but it is not meaningful with MAX.
MIN	Returns the minimum value in a numeric, character, or datetime column, ignoring any null values. MAX finds the highest value in the collating sequence for character columns. DISTINCT is available, but it is not meaningful with MIN.
SUM	Returns the sum of all the values or only the DISTINCT values in the *expression*. SUM can only be used with numeric columns and null values are ignored.

In the next sections, we will take a look at some example queries that use the aggregate functions. These examples, like the ones in the previous sections, are available in the SQLControl application under the Functions tree node.

AVG and SUM with GROUP BY Clause   The following example calculates the total sales as the SUM of the qty column and the average sales as the AVG of the qty column from the Sales table. The column SUM(qty) is changed to Total Sales, and the column AVG(qty) column is changed to Average Sales to be more user-friendly. In addition, the values are grouped and sorted by the stor_id column.

```
SELECT 'Total Sales' = SUM(qty), 'Average Sales' = AVG(qty), stor_id
FROM sales
GROUP BY stor_id ORDER BY 'Total Sales'
```

Total Sales	Average Sales	stor_id
8	4	6380
60	20	7896
80	20	8042
90	22	7067
125	62	7066
130	21	7131

The query results in three columns—the SUM(qty) column, which is renamed to Total Sales, the AVG(qty) column, which is renamed to Average Sales, and the stor_id column.

COUNT(*)   This example simply returns the number of rows in the Publishers table.

```
SELECT COUNT(*) FROM publishers
```

Column1
8

The results, 8, is the number of publishers in the Publishers table. Null values, if present, are counted.

The remainder of the aggregate functions work the same way. You specify the function name and include the column in parentheses. In the next section, we will look at the CONVERT function that is used to convert one data type to another.

Converting Data types with the CONVERT Function

The CONVERT function converts an *expression* of one data type to another data type. You can also use it to obtain a variety of special date formats.

SQL Server automatically handles certain data type conversions. You do not need to use the CONVERT functions for the following expressions:

- *char* and *char expressions* of different lengths
- *datetime*

- *smallint*

- *int*

It is never wrong, however, to use the CONVERT function, even when you are comparing two expressions of exactly the same data type.

Here are some general rules to keep in mind when converting data types:

- SQL Server automatically supplies a length of 30 if you do not specify a length for the data type to which the expression is to be converted.

- SQL Server rejects all values it cannot recognize as dates when converting to *datetime* or *smalldatetime*.

- Converting to *bit* changes any nonzero value to 1.

- Integers are assumed to be monetary units when converting to *money* or *smallmoney*.

- Expressions of data types *char* or *varchar* that are being converted to an integer data type must consist only of digits and an optional plus or minus sign. Leading blanks are ignored.

- Expressions of data types *char* or *varchar* that are being converted to *money* can also include an optional decimal point and dollar sign ($).

- Expressions of data types *char* or *varchar* that are being converted to *float* or *real* can also include optional exponential notation (e or E, followed by an optional plus or minus sign and then a number).

- Values that are too long for their new data type are truncated, and SQL Server displays an asterisk (*).

- When converting between data types with a different number of decimal points, the value is truncated.

- You can explicitly convert *text* columns to *char* or *varchar* columns, and you can explicitly convert *image* columns to *binary* or *varbinary* columns, but you are limited to 255 characters as the maximum length of the *character* and *binary* data types. If you attempt a conversion that is not possible, SQL Server displays an error message.

The syntax for the CONVERT function is:

```
CONVERT (data type[(length)], expression [, style])
```

The parts of the CONVERT function syntax are listed in Table 12.13.

TABLE 12.13: The Parts of the CONVERT Function Syntax

Part	Description
data type	Any system data type (for example, *char*(10), *varbinary, int*) into which the expression is to be converted. User-defined data types cannot be used.
length	An optional parameter with *char, varchar, binary,* and *varbinary* data types. The maximum allowable length is 255.
expression	A column name, a constant, a function, a variable, a subquery, any combination of column names, constants, and functions connected by an operator(s) or a subquery.
style	The style of date representation you want when converting *datetime* or *smalldatetime* data to character data.

The following examples demonstrate how to convert data types using the built-in CONVERT function.

CONVERT: Character Data with Select   If you want to perform a string comparison with the LIKE keyword and wildcards, the data type must be of a character type. The following example converts the qty column in the Sales table to *char* so it can be used with LIKE.

```
SELECT stor_id, ord_num, qty FROM sales WHERE CONVERT(char(5), qty)
LIKE '%25%'
```

stor_id	ord_num	qty
7131	N914014	25
7131	P3087a	25
7131	P3087a	25
8042	P723	25

Results - Functions - Character Data with Select

This query returns only those records from the Sales table that have 25 in the qty column.

CONVERT: Different Size   When expressions are converted to a data type of a different size, values too long for the new data type are truncated, and SQL Server displays an asterisk (*). In this example, the CONVERT function converts the ytd_sales column in the Sales table to a four-place character string.

```
SELECT title, CONVERT(char(4), ytd_sales) FROM titles
WHERE type like '%cook'
```

Results - Functions - Different Size	
title	Column2
Silicon Valley Gastronomic Treats	2032
The Gourmet Microwave	*
Onions, Leeks, and Garlic: Cooking Secrets of the Mediterranean	375
Fifty Years in Buckingham Palace Kitchens	*
Sushi, Anyone?	4095

The results of this query show how SQL Server displays an asterisk (*) for fields that are too long for the converted data type.

In the next section we will look at the date functions in SQL.

Manipulating Datetime Values with Date Functions

Date functions manipulate datetime values by adding to and subtracting from dates and by separating dates into parts. The syntax for the Date functions is:

```
date_function (parameters)
```

You can use the Date functions in the SELECT list or in the WHERE clause of a query. Use the *datetime* data type only for dates after January 1, 1753. When entering datetime values, always enclose them in quotation marks. Store as character data for earlier dates. Table 12.14 lists the parts of the Date function syntax, and Table 12.15 lists the built-in Date functions.

TABLE 12.14: The Parts of the Date Function Syntax

Part	Description
date_function	Specifies the date function as listed in Table 12.15
parameters	DATEADD, DATEDIFF, DATENAME, andDATEPART

TABLE 12.15: The Built-In Date Functions

Date Function	Description
DATEADD(datepart, number, date)	Produces a date by adding an interval to a specified date resulting in a datetime value equal to the date plus the number of date parts.
DATEDIFF(datepart, date1, date2)	Returns the number of datepart "boundaries" crossed between two specified dates.
DATENAME(datepart, date)	Returns a character string representing the specified date part (datepart) of the specified date (date).

TABLE 12.15 (CONTINUED): The Built-In Date Functions

Date Function	Description
DATEPART(datepart, date)	Returns an integer representing the specified date part (datepart) of the specified date (date).
GETDATE()	Returns the current system date and time in the SQL Server standard internal format for datetime values. GETDATE does not take any parameters.

Table 12.16 provides a list of the valid date parts, abbreviations, and valid values for the datepart parameter used with the DATEADD, DATEDIFF, DATENAME, and DATEPART functions.

TABLE 12.16: The Date Part Parameters

Date Part	Abbreviation	Values
hour	hh	0–23
minute	mi	0–59
second	ss	0–59
millisecond	ms	0–999
day of year	dy	1–366
day	dd	1–31
week	wk	1–53
weekday	dw	1–7 (Sun.-Sat.)
month	mm	1–12
quarter	qq	1–4
year	yy	1753–9999

NOTE   If the year is given with two digits, <50 is the next century, and >=50 is this century. So 25 is 2025, and 50 is 1950.

The date part weekday or dw returns the text of the day of the week (Sunday, Monday, and so on) when used with datename. It returns a corresponding number (Sunday = 1, Saturday = 7) when used with datepart.

Smalldatetime is accurate only to the minute. When a smalldatetime value is used with either datename or datepart, seconds and milliseconds are always 0.

DATEADD and DATEPART   The following example adds one month to the pubdate in the Publishers table with the DATEADD date function and selects only those records with a pubdate greater than 1991. In addition, it sets the new date column heading to Pub Date + 1 Month.

```
SELECT pubdate, 'Pub Date + 1 Month' = dateadd(month, 1, pubdate) FROM
titles WHERE (datepart(year, pubdate) <> 1991)
```

Results - Functions - DATEADD and DATEPART	
pubdate	Pub Date + 1 Month
10/27/97 4:02:08 PM	11/27/97 4:02:08 PM
6/12/94	7/12/94
10/27/97 4:02:08 PM	11/27/97 4:02:08 PM

This query returns two columns: one with the publication date and another with one month added to the publication date for all publication dates not in 1991.

All the Date functions work in the same general way as this example; you state the desired function and provide the parameters.

In the next section, we will explore the mathematical functions provided in SQL.

Performing Mathematical Operations with the Built-In Mathematical Functions

Mathematical functions perform operations on mathematical data. These functions are not keywords. The syntax for mathematical functions is:

```
function_name(parameters)
```

Table 12.17 lists the parts of the mathematical functions syntax, and Table 12.18 lists the built-in mathematical functions.

TABLE 12.17: The Parts of the Mathematical Functions Syntax

Part	Description
function_name	Specifies a mathematical function as listed in Table 12.18.
parameters	The parameters are either numeric_expr, an expression of the decimal, float, int, money, numeric, real, smallint, smallmoney, or tinyint data type or float_expr expressions of the float data type.

TABLE 12.18: The Built-In Mathematical Functions

Function	Parameters	Result
ABS	*(numeric_expr)*	Absolute value of the numeric expression.
ACOS	*(float_expr)*	Angle (in radians) whose cosine is the specified approximate numeric (*float*) expression.
ASIN	*(float_expr)*	Angle (in radians) whose sine is the specified approximate numeric (*float*) expression.
ATAN	*(float_expr)*	Angle (in radians) whose tangent is the specified approximate numeric (*float*) expression.
ATN2	*(float_expr1, float_expr2)*	Angle (in radians) whose tangent is (*float_expr1/float_expr2*) between two approximate numeric (*float*) expressions.
CEILING	*(numeric_expr)*	Smallest integer greater than or equal to the numeric expression.
COS	*(float_expr)*	Trigonometric cosine of the specified angle (in radians) in an approximate numeric (*float*) expression.
COT	*(float_expr)*	Trigonometric cotangent of the specified angle (in radians) in an approximate numeric (*float*) expression.
DEGREES	*(numeric_expr)*	Degrees converted from radians of the numeric expression.
EXP	*(float_expr)*	Exponential value of the specified approximate numeric (*float*) expression.
FLOOR	*(numeric_expr)*	Largest integer less than or equal to the specified numeric expression.
LOG	*(float_expr)*	Natural logarithm of the specified approximate numeric (*float*) expression.
LOG10	*(float_expr)*	Base-10 logarithm of the specified approximate numeric (*float*) expression.
PI	*( )*	Constant value of 3.141592653589793.
POWER	*(numeric_expr, y)*	Value of numeric expression to the power of y, where y is a numeric data type (*decimal, float, int, money, numeric, real, smallint, smallmoney, or tinyint*).

TABLE 12.18 (CONTINUED): The Built-In Mathematical Functions

Function	Parameters	Result
RADIANS	*(numeric_expr)*	Radians converted from degrees of the numeric expression.
RAND	*([seed])*	Random approximate numeric (*float*) value between 0 and 1, optionally specifying an integer expression (*tinyint, smallint, or int*) as the seed.
ROUND	*(numeric_expr, length)*	Numeric expression rounded off to the *length* (or precision) specified as an integer expression (*tinyint, smallint, or int*).
SIGN	*(numeric_expr)*	Returns the positive (+1), zero (0), or negative (-1) sign of the numeric expression.
SIN	*(float_expr)*	Trigonometric sine of the specified angle (measured in radians) in an approximate numeric (*float*) expression.
SQRT	*(float_expr)*	Square root of the specified approximate numeric (*float*) expression.
TAN	*(float_expr)*	Trigonometric tangent of the specified angle (measured in radians) in an approximate numeric (*float*) expression.

ROUND   This example rounds the number 123.456 to two decimal places.

```
SELECT 'Rounded' = ROUND(123.456, 2)
```

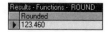

The result of this operation is a column named Rounded with the value 123.460.

SQRT   You can calculate the square root of a number with the SQRT mathematical function. The following example returns the square root of 49:

```
SELECT 'Square Root' = SQRT(49)
```

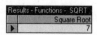

This query returns one column, Square Root, with a value of 7.

The rest of the mathematical functions perform the same operations as these examples; they specify the mathematical function name and the required parameter(s). In the next section, we will examine the built-in string functions.

Performing Operations with String Functions

String functions perform operations on character strings, binary data, and expressions, and you can use them anywhere an expression is allowed. Most string functions can be used only on *char* and *varchar* data types and on data types that implicitly convert to *char* or *varchar*.

Concatenation can be used on *binary* and *varbinary* columns as well as on *char* and *varchar* columns.

String functions can be nested. When you use constants with a string function, enclose them in single quotation marks. The syntax for string functions is:

```
function_name(parameters)
```

Table 12.19 lists the parts of the string function syntax, and Table 12.20 lists the built-in string functions.

TABLE 12.19: The Parts of the String Function Syntax

Part	Desription
function_name	The name of a string function as listed in Table 12.20.
parameters	Parameters of char_expr, which are alphanumeric expression of character data; integer_expt, which is a positive whole number; or float_expr, which is an approximate numeric data type with a decimal point.

TABLE 12.20: The Built-In String Functions

Function	Parameters	Result
+	(expression expression)	Concatenates two character strings, binary strings, column names, or a combination.
ASCII	(char_expr)	Indicates the ASCII code value of the leftmost character of an expression.
CHAR	(integer_expr)	Converts a character from an ASCII code that is a value in the range 0 through 255; otherwise, NULL is returned.

TABLE 12.20 (CONTINUED): The Built-In String Functions

Function	Parameters	Result
CHARINDEX	('pattern', expression)	Returns the starting position of the specified *pattern* in a *char_expr*. The second parameter is an *expression*, usually a column name, in which SQL Server searches for the *pattern*.
DIFFERENCE	(char_expr1, char_expr2)	Shows the difference between the values of two character expressions as returned by the SOUNDEX function. The DIFFERENCE function compares two strings and evaluates the similarity between them, returning a value from 0 through 4, with a 4 signifying the best match indicating that the SOUNDEX values of *char_expr1* and *char_expr2* are identical.
LOWER	(char_expr)	Converts uppercase character data to lowercase.
LTRIM	(char_expr)	Removes leading blanks.
PATINDEX	('%pattern%', expression)	Returns the starting position of the first occurrence of *pattern* in the specified expression or returns zeros if the pattern is not found. You can use wildcard characters in *pattern*, as long as the wildcard character % precedes and follows *pattern* (except when searching for first or last characters).
REPLICATE	(char_expr, integer_expr)	Repeats a character expression a specified number of times.
REVERSE	(char_expr)	Returns the reverse of *char_expr* in a constant, variable, or column.
RIGHT	(char_expr, integer_expr)	Part of a character string starting *integer_expr* characters from the right. If *integer_expr* is negative, a null string is returned.
RTRIM	(char_expr)	Removes trailing blanks.
SOUNDEX	(char_expr)	Returns a four-digit (SOUNDEX) code to evaluate the similarity of two strings. The SOUNDEX function converts an alpha string to a four-digit code to find similar-sounding words or names.
SPACE	(integer_expr)	Returns a string of repeated spaces equal to *integer_expr*. If *integer_expr* is negative, a null string is returned.

TABLE 12.20 (CONTINUED): The Built-In String Functions

Function	Parameters	Result
STR	*(float_expr [, length[, decimal]])*	Converts character data from numeric data for a *length* of the total length, including decimal point, sign, digits, and spaces.
STUFF	*(char_expr1, start, length, char_expr2)*	Deletes *length* characters from *char_expr1* at *start* and then inserts *char_expr2* into *char_expr1* at *start*. If the *start* position or the *length* is negative, a null string is returned.
SUBSTRING	*(expression, start, length)*	Returns part of a character or binary string. The first parameter can be a character or binary string, a column name, or an expression that includes a column name. The third parameter specifies the number of characters in the substring.
UPPER	*(char_expr)*	Converts lowercase character data to uppercase.

String Concatenation   String concatenation is the act of combining two or more string values to make one value. The following example creates one column named Author's Name & Address and concatenates the au_fname, au_lname, address, city, state, and zip columns from the Authors table for authors that do not live in California and sorts the list by the author's city:

```
SELECT 'Author''s Full Name & Address' = (au_fname + au_lname + ', ' +
address + ' ' + city + ', ' + state + ' ' + zip) FROM authors WHERE
state <> 'CA' ORDER BY city
```

```
Results - Functions - String Concatenation
Author's Full Name & Address
Innesdel Castillo, 2286 Cram Pl. #86 Ann Arbor, MI 48105
ReginaldBlotchet-Halls, 55 Hillsdale Bl. Corvallis, OR 97330
MichelDeFrance, 3 Balding Pl. Gary, IN 46403
MeanderSmith, 10 Mississippi Dr. Lawrence, KS 66044
MorningstarGreene, 22 Graybar House Rd. Nashville, TN 37215
SylviaPanteley, 1956 Arlington Pl. Rockville, MD 20853
AnneRinger, 67 Seventh Av. Salt Lake City, UT 84152
AlbertRinger, 67 Seventh Av. Salt Lake City, UT 84152
```

The result of this query is one column made up of the values from the author's first name, last name, address, city, state, and zip columns from the Authors table.

CHARINDEX   This example uses the CHARINDEX string function to locate the position of the string "cook" from the Type column in the Titles table.

```
SELECT CHARINDEX('cook', type), type FROM titles
```

Results - Functions - CHARINDEX	
Column1	type
0	business
0	business
0	business
0	business
5	mod_cook
5	mod_cook
0	UNDECIDED
0	popular_comp
0	popular_comp

The result is a value representing the location of "cook" in the Type column. A zero is returned if the string is not found.

As you can see, string functions can be a big help in performing all types of operations on character data. In the next section, we take a look at the system functions provided in the SQL language.

Retrieving Special Server or Database Information with System Functions

System functions return a special piece of information from the database and help you query the system tables. You can use system functions in SELECT lists, WHERE clauses, or anywhere an expression is allowed. The syntax for system functions is:

```
function_name(parameters)
```

Table 12.21 lists the parts of the system function syntax, and Table 12.22 lists the built-in system functions.

TABLE 12.21: The Parts of the System Function Syntax

Part	Description
function_name	Specifies a function name as listed in Table 12.22.
parameters	The required table name, value, or object.

TABLE 12.22: System Functions

System function	Parameters	Result
COALESCE	*(expression1, expression2, ... expressionN)*	Returns the first non-null expression.
COL_LENGTH	*('table_name','column_name')*	The length of a column.
COL_NAME	*(table_id,column_id)*	The column's name in the specified table.
DATALENGTH	*('expression')*	The actual length of an *expression* of any data type.
DB_ID	*(['database_name'])*	The database identification number.
DB_NAME	*([database_id])*	The database name.
GETANSINULL	*(['database_name'])*	The default nullability for the database. This function returns 1 when the nullability is the ANSI NULL default.
HOST_ID	*( )*	The identification number of the workstation.
HOST_NAME	*( )*	The workstation name.
IDENT_INCR	*('table_or_view')*	The value that is added to the increment value when a new record is added to the table.
IDENT_SEED	*('table_or_view')*	The starting number for an identity column.
INDEX_COL	*('table_name', index_id, key_id)*	The indexed column name.
ISNULL	*(expression, value)*	Replaces NULL entries with the specified value.
NULLIF	*(expression1, expression2)*	The resulting expression is NULL when *expression1* is equivalent to *expression2*.
OBJECT_ID	*('object_name')*	The database object identification number.
OBJECT_NAME	*(object_id)*	The database object name.
STATS_DATE	*(table_id, index_id)*	The date that the statistics for the specified index *(index_id)* were last updated.
SUSER_ID	*(['login_name'])*	The user's login identification number.

TABLE 12.22 (CONTINUED): System Functions (continued)

System function	Parameters	Result
SUSER_NAME	*([server_user_id])*	The user's login identification name.
USER_ID	*(['user_name'])*	The user's database identification number.
USER_NAME	*([user_id])*	The user's database username.

HOST_NAME This system function returns the name of the current workstation. This is an easy way to determine which workstation is currently accessing your application. For example, with this information you can tailor an application to specific user groups—Customer Service, a Help Desk, or clerks. The following example returns the workstation name in a column called Workstation:

```
SELECT 'Workstation' = host_name()
```

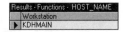

The HOST_NAME system function does not require any parameters. You can, as always, specify the name for the return column.

DATALENGTH This system function returns the length of the data in a column. You supply the column name. This can be a great help if you need to verify whether a text value will fit into a report or print in a given location. You can use the DATA-LENGTH system function and then loop through the values to make sure they will all fit. The following example returns the length of the data for the address column in the Authors table.

```
SELECT 'Data Length' = DATALENGTH(address), address FROM authors
```

```
Results - Functions - DATALENGTH
Data Length | address
        15 | 19973 Maple Dr.
        17 | 309 63rd St. #411
        14 | 589 Darwin Ln.
        20 | 22 Cleveland Av. #14
        16 | 5420 College Av.
        18 | 10 Mississippi Dr.
        16 | 6223 Bateman St.
        15 | 3410 Blonde St.
        10 | PO Box 792
```

The Data Length column is returned with the length of the data for each author's address and the address.

System functions can be a great help in managing a database, its objects, and the data stored in it. In the next section, which will be our last one on built-in functions in the SQL language, we will discuss the Text and Image functions.

Using Text and Image Functions

The Text and Image functions return commonly needed information about text and image data only. Text and image data are stored in binary format. The syntax for the text and image functions is:

```
function_name(parameters)
```

Table 12.23 lists the parts of the Text and Image functions syntax, and Table 12.24 lists the Text and Image functions.

TABLE 12.23: The Parts of the Text and Image Functions Syntax

Part	Description
function_name	The name of the function as listed in Table 12.24.
parameters	A column name or a text pointer.

TABLE 12.24: Text and Image Functions

Function	Parameters	Result
TEXTPTR	(column_name)	The text-pointer value in *varbinary* format. The text pointer is checked to ensure that it points to the first text page.
TEXTVALID	('table_name.column_name', text_ptr)	Checks whether a given text pointer is valid. Returns 1 if the pointer is valid and 0 if the pointer is invalid.

TEXTVALID   This function verifies whether a given text pointer is valid. In this example, we verify the text pointer of the pr_info column, which describes the logo in the pub_info table. A 1 signifies a valid text pointer:

```
SELECT pub_id, 'Valid Text Data = 1'= TEXTVALID('pub_info.pr_info',
textptr(pr_info)) FROM pub_info
```

The previous query returns a 1 in the Valid Text Data = 1 column if the text pointer is valid for the pr_info column.

So far, we have looked at SQL statements and queries that select and return data from databases. In the next section, we will explore action statements in SQL.

Changing Data with SQL

SQL provides INSERT, DELETE, and UPDATE statements for your use to maintain the data in your databases. In this section, you will see how you can use these statements.

Adding Rows with the INSERT Statement

The INSERT statement adds a new row to a table or a view. You can add a row with data in all the columns, or you can add data to some, but not all, of the columns in a row by specifying only those columns and the data for those columns. The following rules apply when inserting rows:

- Inserting an empty string (' ') into a *varchar* or *text* column inserts a single space.

- Inserting a null value into a *text* or an *image* column does not create a valid text pointer and does not create a 2Kb page.

- SQL Server fails and displays an error message if an INSERT statement violates a constraint, a default, or a rule or if the wrong data type is used.

- Trailing spaces are removed from data inserted into *varchar* columns, except in strings that contain only spaces. These strings are truncated to a single space.

The syntax for the INSERT statement is:

```
INSERT [INTO]
{table_name | view_name} [(column_list)]
{DEFAULT VALUES | values_list | select_statement}
```

Table 12.25 lists the parts of the INSERT statement syntax.

TABLE 12.25: The Parts of the INSERT Statement Syntax

Part	Description
INTO	An optional keyword.
table_name	view_name	Specifies the name of the table or view used in the INSERT statement.
column_list	Lists one or more columns to which data is to be added.
DEFAULT VALUES	Inserts the default values for all columns.
values_list	The list of values to be added to the columns.
select_statement	A standard SELECT statement used to retrieve the values to be inserted from an existing table.

All Columns   This example inserts values into all columns of the Jobs table.

```
INSERT INTO jobs
VALUES('Developer', 75, 175)
SELECT * FROM jobs WHERE job_desc = 'Developer'
```

	job_id	job_desc	min_lvl	max_lvl
▶	15	Developer	75	175

Results - Actions - INSERT, All Columns

This query adds one row to the Jobs table. A value is not supplied for the job_id column. This is an Identity column, and SQL Server generates this value. The SELECT statement is used at the end to select the new row and to see if it was added properly. INSERT statements by themselves do not return any rows of data; the rows are simply added to the database

Specify Columns   If you want to insert a row into the Jobs table but you do not know the formal name of the position, you can still insert the row because the job_description field has a default value. When the table was created, the owner created a default value of "'New Position - title not formalized yet'" for the job_desc column. The following example creates a new row in the Jobs table but does not supply a value for the job_desc. In this case, you must tell the server which columns you intend to supply data for.

```
INSERT INTO jobs (min_lvl, max_lvl)
VALUES (55, 95)
SELECT * FROM jobs WHERE job_desc LIKE 'New Position%'
```

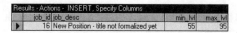

This query inserts a new row in the Jobs table, accepting the default value for the job_desc field, and then selects the new row.

As you can see, the INSERT statement is flexible and allows you to dynamically add rows of data. In the next section, we will explore deleting rows of data with the DELETE statement.

Deleting Rows with the DELETE Statement

You use the DELETE statement to remove rows from a recordset. You can use DELETE alone to delete all rows, or you can use it with a WHERE clause to limit the rows deleted. The DELETE statement removes rows one at a time and places each row deletion in the log. The DELETE statement reclaims the space occupied by the data and its associated indexes.

Here are the rules associated with the DELETE statement:

- DELETE can affect only one base table at a time, so you cannot use DELETE with a view that has a FROM clause naming more than one table.

- If you omit a WHERE clause, all rows in the table are removed. The table itself, along with its indexes and constraints, remains in the database.

- You can use the IDENTITYCOL keyword in place of a *column_name* that has the IDENTITY property.

- Cursor operations affect only the single row on which the cursor is positioned.

The syntax of the DELETE statement is:

```
DELETE [FROM] {table_name | view_name}
    [WHERE clause]
```

Table 12.26 lists the parts of the DELETE statement syntax.

TABLE 12.26: The Parts of the DELETE Statement Syntax

Part	Description
table_name | view_name	Specifies the table or view used in the DELETE statement.
WHERE clause	WHERE {*search_conditions* | CURRENT OF *cursor_name*} is used to perform a searched delete (using *search_conditions*) or a positioned delete (using CURRENT OF *cursor_name*).

Transact-SQL Extensions for the DELETE Statement

In addition to the DELETE syntax shown earlier, Transact-SQL includes a feature that allows you to select data from a table or tables and delete corresponding data from the first-named table.

The Transact-SQL extension syntax is:

```
DELETE [FROM] {table_name | view_name}
    [FROM {table_name | view_name}
           [, {table_name | view_name}]...]
                  [..., {table_name16 | view_name16}]]
[WHERE clause]
```

The FROM clause allows you to name more than one table or view to use with a WHERE clause to specify which rows to delete. The additional FROM clause allows you to delete rows from one table based on data stored in other tables, giving you similar functionality to a correlated subquery (SELECT statement in the WHERE clause).

All Rows This example deletes all rows from the Jobs table.

```
DELETE jobs
```

NOTE This DELETE query is not provided as a sample in the SQLControl application. If you use the DELETE statement without a WHERE clause, all rows are deleted from the table.

Selected Rows If you want to delete selected records from a table, you add a WHERE clause to the DELETE statement. This example deletes the job added in the previous section.

```
DELETE FROM jobs WHERE job_desc = 'Developer'
SELECT * from jobs
```

	job_id	job_desc	min_lvl	max_lvl
▶	1	New Hire - Job not specified	10	10
	2	Chief Executive Officer	200	250
	3	Business Operations Manager	175	225
	4	Chief Financial Officier	175	250
	5	Publisher	150	250
	6	Managing Editor	140	225
	7	Marketing Manager	120	200
	8	Public Relations Manager	100	175
	9	Acquisitions Manager	75	175

Results - Actions - DELETE, Selected Rows

All rows in the Jobs table with the **job_desc** of Developer are deleted with this query.

SQL Extensions Let's say that you want to delete the author records in the Authors table for the mod_cook type of book. You have to create a SELECT statement that goes through the Authors, Titleauthor, and Type tables to join the type to the author. The following example does this:

```
DELETE FROM titleauthor FROM authors a, titles t
WHERE a.au_id = titleauthor.au_id AND  titleauthor.title_id =
t.title_id AND
t.title LIKE '%cook%'
SELECT * FROM titles
```

Results - Actions - DELETE, SQL Extensions

	title_id	title	type	pub_id	price	advance	royalty	ytd_sales	notes
▶	BU1032	The Busy Executive's D	business	1389	19.99	5000	10	4095	An overview of available database
	BU1111	Cooking with Computers	business	1389	11.95	5000	10	3876	Helpful hints on how to use your
	BU2075	You Can Combat Compu	business	0736	2.99	10125	24	18722	The latest medical and psychologi
	BU7832	Straight Talk About Com	business	1389	19.99	5000	10	4095	Annotated analysis of what compu
	MC2222	Silicon Valley Gastronom	mod_cook	0877	19.99	0	12	2032	Favorite recipes for quick, easy, a
	MC3021	The Gourmet Microwave	mod_cook	0877	2.99	15000	24	22246	Traditional French gourmet recipe
	MC3026	The Psychology of Com	UNDECIDE	0877					
	PC1035	But Is It User Friendly?	popular_con	1389	22.95	7000	16	8780	A survey of software for the naive

This example deletes the authors of the cookbooks from the Authors table.

Altering Data with the UPDATE Statement

You use the SQL UPDATE statement to change data in existing rows, either by adding new data or by modifying existing data. Here are some rules to keep in mind for the UPDATE statement:

- All trailing spaces are removed from data inserted into *varchar* columns, except in strings that contain only spaces, and they are truncated to a single space.

- An update does not take place and an error message is returned if a column being updated violates a constraint or a rule or if the wrong data type is used.

- Modifying a *text* column with UPDATE initializes it, assigns a valid text pointer to it, and allocates at least one 2K data page (even if updating the column with NULL).

- Updating a *varchar* or *text* column to a column with an empty string (' ') in it inserts a single space. All *char* columns are right-padded to the defined length.

The syntax for the UPDATE statement is:

```
UPDATE {table_name | view_name}
SET [{table_name | view_name}]
    {column_list
    | variable_list
    | variable_and_column_list}
        [, {column_list2
                | variable_list2
                | variable_and_column_list2}
            ...    [, {column_listN
                        | variable_listN
                        | variable_and_column_listN}]]
[WHERE clause]
```

Table 12.28 lists the parts of the UPDATE statement syntax.

TABLE 12.28: The Parts of the UPDATE Statement Syntax

Part	Description
table_name | view_name	Specifies the name of the table or view used in the UPDATE statement.
SET	A required keyword used to introduce the list of column or variable clauses to be updated. When more than one column name and value pair are listed, separate the names with commas.
column_list =	Specifies a column from the table (table_name) or view (view_name).
WHERE clause	Any valid WHERE clause to limit or define the rows to be updated.

Transact-SQL Extensions for the UPDATE Statement

In addition to the UPDATE syntax shown above, Transact-SQL includes a feature that allows you to select data from a table or tables and update corresponding data in the first-named table. This feature is included in the form of a FROM clause. The extension syntax is:

```
[FROM {table_name | view_name}
    [, {table_name | view_name}]...]
            [..., {table_name16 | view_name16}]]
```

The FROM clause allows you to name more than one table or view to use with a WHERE clause to specify which rows to update. The additional FROM clause allows you to update rows from one table based on data stored in other tables.

WHERE Clause   You can use a WHERE clause in an UPDATE statement to limit the rows that are updated. The following example increases the beg_lvl column in the Jobs table by 10% where the job_desc for all new hires does not have specified titles:

```
UPDATE titles SET price = price * 1.1 WHERE (type = 'business')
SELECT * FROM titles WHERE type = 'business'
```

title_id	title	type	pub_id	price	advance	royalty	ytd_sales	notes
BU1032	The Busy Executive'	business	1389	21.989	5000	10	4095	An overview
BU1111	Cooking with Compu	business	1389	13.145	5000	10	3876	Helpful hints
BU2075	You Can Combat Co	business	0736	3.289	10125	24	18722	The latest m
BU7832	Straight Talk About (	business	1389	21.989	5000	10	4095	Annotated a

This will increase the price for all business titles by 10%.

Multiple Columns   You can change the data in multiple columns with the same UPDATE statement. The following example updates an author's complete address consisting of the address, city, state, and zip columns:

```
UPDATE authors SET address = '19973 Maple Dr.', city = 'Oakland', state
= 'CA', zip = '97243' WHERE au_id = '172-32-1176'
SELECT * FROM authors
```

au_id	au_lname	au_fname	phone	address	city	state	zip
172-32-1176	White	Johnson	408 496-7223	19973 Maple Dr.	Oakland	CA	97243
213-46-8915	Green	Marjorie	415 986-7020	309 63rd St. #411	Oakland	CA	94618
238-95-7766	Carson	Cheryl	415 548-7723	589 Darwin Ln.	Berkeley	CA	94705
267-41-2394	O'Leary	Michael	408 286-2428	22 Cleveland Av. #1	San Jose	CA	95128
274-80-9391	Straight	Dean	415 834-2919	5420 College Av.	Oakland	CA	94609
341-22-1782	Smith	Meander	913 843-0462	10 Mississippi Dr.	Lawrence	KS	66044
409-56-7008	Bennet	Abraham	415 658-9932	6223 Bateman St.	Berkeley	CA	94705
427-17-2319	Dull	Ann	415 836-7128	3410 Blonde St.	Palo Alto	CA	94301

NOTE   Chapter 14 provides advanced SQL examples on creating database objects.

CHAPTER

THIRTEEN

Writing Front Ends

- Selecting a front-end style

- Using data-bound controls

- Incorporating dialog boxes into front-end interfaces

- Accessing menu options with a toolbar

- Developing a front-end application

An application's user interface, or *front end*, is the user's window to the program and is critical to every project. It doesn't matter how technologically advanced, how fast, or how complete an application is if people won't use it. The user must be able to interact comfortably with your application via its interface.

Designing and building a good front end is a difficult task for it must provide all the information that your application needs to function properly and still be appealing, intuitive, and functional for the users.

The tools, controls, and functionality provided in Visual Basic 5 offer the developer a vast array of front-end design solutions to facilitate the task.

While designing an application and considering the interface, you need to answer several key questions:

- Which style should you use?

- How many Forms will you need?

- Which commands will your menus include?

- Will you use toolbars to duplicate and supplement menu functions?

- Will your provide dialog boxes to interact with the user?

Most commercial-quality applications for Microsoft Windows share a familiar and consistent user interface. This improves the usability of the application because the user is not forced to relearn common operations. For example, a user who regularly prints documents from Microsoft Word intuitively looks for a Print option on the File menu when confronted with the task of printing in an unfamiliar application.

Microsoft's user interface services provide a graphical means of displaying information and receiving user input. These services also enable you to interact with the Windows Desktop (shell).

The basic feature of the user interface is *windowing.* Graphical applications use windows, dialog boxes, and property sheets to display information and receive user input. Windows, dialog boxes, and property sheets contain menus to expose commands to users and controls to perform input and output. The common dialog box library contains a set of dialog boxes for performing common tasks. Using the common dialog boxes enables users to take care of common tasks in a consistent manner in every application that uses them.

Users interact with your Visual Basic application through graphical features. They should be able to control the application by choosing menu commands and, optionally, by clicking icons on a toolbar. They receive information from resources such as bitmaps, carets, cursors, and icons.

In this chapter, we will explore the tools that Visual Basic 5 offers and look at some of the design issues and solutions facing you as you develop Visual Basic front-end solutions.

The Developer's and the User's Viewpoint

Designing and building the front end to any application is difficult. The visual nature of Windows makes the job even more difficult.

The front end to a Visual Basic application must pull double duty: It must provide you, the developer, with all the information you need for the inner workings of the application, the business rules, and the database, and it must be visually appealing, functional, and intuitive to your users.

From the developer's point of view, an application's front end must provide:

- Complete access to all data

- The user's answers to business rule issues

From the user's point of view, an application's front end must provide:

- Complete access to all Forms and data

- Access to information in an intuitive, stress-free environment

- A familiar environment

- Complete error trapping

Selecting a Front-End Style

In today's Windows/Visual Basic application environment, there are three main application styles:

Single Document Interface (SDI), as shown in Figure 13.1, which has one main Form and allows the user to open one document at a time. Both Notepad and WordPad are SDI applications.

FIGURE 13.1:

Notepad is an example of an SDI.

Multiple Document Interface (MDI), as shown in Figure 13.2, which maintains multiple Forms within a single container Form. Applications such as Microsoft Excel and Microsoft Word for Windows are multiple-document interface applications.

Explorer Interface, as shown in Figure 13.3, which is a single window containing two *panes*, or regions, usually consisting of a tree or hierarchical view on the left and a display area on the right, as in the Windows Explorer or Windows RegEdit applications. This type of interface lends itself to navigating or browsing large numbers of documents, pictures, or other files.

FIGURE 13.2:

Microsoft Word is an
example of an MDI.

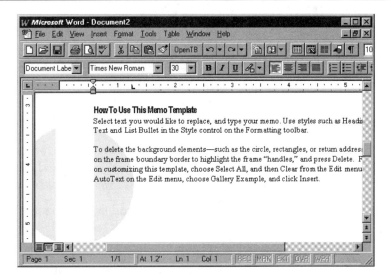

FIGURE 13.3:

Windows Explorer is an
example of an Explorer
Interface.

Visual Basic provides many controls and tools that you can use to create functional and exciting front ends. In the next section, we will look at some of the data-aware bound controls available in the Enterprise Edition of Visual Basic.

Data-Bound Controls

Data-bound controls, which we have discussed throughout this book, are controls that can be bound to a data source. Visual Basic provides a data-bound control for almost every purpose. The common element is the bound data source. In the Enterprise Edition of Visual Basic, it is the RemoteData Control (RDC). In this section, we'll look at the following data-bound controls:

DbCombo, which is a data bound combo box with a drop-down list box that is automatically populated from a field in an attached RDC control. It optionally updates a field in a related table of another RDC control.

DbList, which is a data-bound list box that is automatically populated from a field in an attached RDC control. It optionally updates a field in a related table of another RDC control.

DbGrid, which is a spreadsheetlike bound control that displays a series of rows and columns representing records and fields from a Recordset object.

TextBox, which is the standard text box that can be bound to an RDC control.

Using the DBCombo Control

The DBCombo control is automatically filled with data from a field in the Recordset object of an RDC control to which it is attached. You must populate the standard ComboBox control manually by using the AddItem method. In addition, the DBCombo control has the ability to update a field within a related Recordset object that may reside in a different data control.

The DBCombo control also supports an automated search mode that can quickly locate items in the list without additional code. Figure 13.4 shows the sources for the DBCombo control.

FIGURE 13.4:

The sources for the vbound DBCombo control

As you can see from Figure 13.4, the DBCombo box has two separate data sources. The first source provides the field value from the current record, and the second provides the data for the drop-down list.

The DBCombo control is commonly used to provide lookup values in another table. For example, if you want the user to enter a valid state or zip code, you can provide a list in a DBCombo box from which the user can select. This simplifies data entry and reduces the possibility of a data-entry error.

Table 13.1 lists the properties used to fill and manage the DBCombo or DBList controls and bind the selected data to a data control.

TABLE 13.1: The Properties of the DBCombo and DBList Controls

Property	Description
BoundColumn	The name of a field in the Recordset object specified by the RowSource to be passed back to the DataField once the user makes a selection.
BoundText	The text value of the BoundColumn field. Once a selection is made, this value is passed back to update the Recordset object specified by the DataSource and DataField properties.
DataField	The name of the field that is updated in the Recordset object specified by the DataSource property.
DataSource	The name of the data control or RDC that is updated once the user makes a selection.
ListField	The name of a field in the Recordset specified by the RowSource that is used to fill the drop-down list.
MatchEntry	Defines how the list is searched as the user types characters at run time.
RowSource	The name of the data control or RDC used as a source of items for the list portion of the control.
SelectedItem	The bookmark of the selected item in the Recordset specified by the RowSource property.
Text	The text value of the selected item in the list.
VisibleCount	The number of items visible in the list (fully or partially).
VisibleItems	An array of bookmarks with a maximum number of items equal to the VisibleCount property.

Adding the DBCombo and the DBList Controls to a Project

Follow these steps to add the DBCombo and DBList controls to a project:

1. Start a new Visual Basic project.

2. Choose Project ➤ Components to open the Components dialog box.

3. Select Microsoft Data Bound List Controls 5 from the list of available controls.

The DBCombo and DBList controls are added to your Toolbox, as shown in Figure 13.5.

FIGURE 13.5:

The DBCombo and DBList controls added to the Toolbox

DBList control

DBCombo control

In the next section, with the DBCombo control added to your toolbar, we will create a sample project using the DBCombo control.

The DBCombo Project

The DBCombo project (shown in Figure 13.6) demonstrates how to use a DBCombo control as a table lookup. The sample project includes two RDCs linked to the Pubs database and a DBCombo control that displays the current author's city; it also provides a list of valid cities from the Authors table.

NOTE   You'll find the DBCombo project in the Ch13/DBCombo folder on the CD that comes with this book.

FIGURE 13.6:

The DBCombo project

Creating the DBCombo Project

To create the DBCombo project, start by adding the following to Form1:

- Two RemoteData Controls. One will display the current record from the Authors table, and the other will provide the query for the lookup portion of the DBCombo control

- One DBCombo control.

NOTE   See Chapter 11 for information about adding a RemoteData Control to a Form.

Connecting the RemoteData Controls

Now, you need to set the properties for the RemoteData Control (named MSRDC1). Table 13.2 lists the properties and their values and describes them. Table 13.3 shows the settings for MSRDC2.

TABLE 13.2: The Values for the RemoteData Control (MSRDC1) Property Settings

Property	Value	Description
Connect	DSN=KDHMAIN;UID=sa; PWD=;DATABASE=pubs;	Sets the server connect string
SQL	SELECT * FROM authors	Provides the records for the display portion of the DBCombo control

TABLE 13.3: The Values for the RemoteData Control (MSRDC2) Property Settings

Property	Value	Description
Connect	DSN=KDHMAIN;UID=sa; PWD=;DATABASE=pubs;	Sets the server connect string.
SQL	SELECT au_fname FROM authors ORDER BY au_fname	Sets the recordsource for the RDC control to the author's first name and sorts the records in ascending order.
Visible	False	Makes MSRDC2 invisible at run time.

NOTE   Substitute your DSN in place of KDHMAIN or add a KDHMAIN DSN entry for the Pubs database, and supply a valid UID and PWD for your server.

Now that we've set up the RemoteData Controls, it is time to connect the DBCombo control.

Connecting the DBCombo Control

The DBCombo control will be connected to both of the RemoteData Controls; one provides the author's first name from the current record, and the other provides the list of valid authors from the Authors table. Set the DBCombo properties according to Table 13.4:

TABLE 13.4: The DBCombo Property Settings

Property	Value	Description
DataSource	MSRDC1	Sets the data source of the display portion to the Authors table through the RemoteData Control MSRDC1.
DataField	au_fname	Connects the author's first name from the current record.
RowSource	MSRDC2	Sets the list portion to the names from the Authors table through the RemoteData Control MSRDC2.
ListField	au_fname	Provides the source for the drop-down list portion of the DBCombo control.

Testing the DBCombo Project

Press F5 to run the project. You will see the Form with the DBCombo control and the RDC as shown in Figure 13.6, earlier in this chapter. Click the drop-down arrow on the DBCombo control to see the list of available authors from the Authors table. Change records with the RDC to display the current author's first name in the DBCombo control.

WARNING   If you change the name by selecting a different name from the drop-down list and then change records, the author's name will be changed in the Authors table.

As you can see from the DBCombo project, the DBCombo control is a great tool to help users select values from a list. If you have an application that needs to present a more visible list to the users, however, you can use the DBList control.

Using the DBList Control

The DBList control is automatically filled with data from a field in the Recordset object of an RDC control to which it is attached. You must populate the standard ListBox control manually by using the AddItem method. In addition, the DBList control has the ability to update a field within a related Recordset object that may reside in a different data control.

The DBList control also supports an automated search mode that can quickly locate items in the list without additional code. Figure 13.7 shows how the DBList control is bound to a RDC.

FIGURE 13.7:

The bound DBList control

As you can see from figure 13.7, the DBList control has two separate data sources just as the DBCombo control does. The first provides the field from the current record, and the second provides the data for the list portion.

The DBList control is used, as is the DBCombo box control, to provide a list of data-entry selections for the user. The main difference in the DBCombo control and the DBList control is the way the data is presented to the user. In a DBCombo control, the data is presented in a drop-down list; in the DBList control, the data is presented in a stationary list.

Table 13.1, earlier in this chapter, lists the properties you use to fill and manage the list and to bind the DBCombo or DBList box controls to a data control or to an RDC.

The DBList Project

The DBList project (shown in Figure 13.8) demonstrates a DBList control populated with the names from the Authors table.

FIGURE 13.8:

The DBList project

Creating the DBList Project

To create the DBList project, first add the following to Form1:

- Two RemoteData Controls. One displays the current record from the Authors table, and the other provides the query for the lookup portion of the DBCombo control.

- One DBCombo control.

> **NOTE**
>
> See Chapter 11 for information about adding a RemoteData Control to a Form.

Connecting the RemoteData Controls

Now, set the properties for MSRDC1. Table 13.5 lists and describes the settings for MSRDC1, and Table 13.6 lists and describes the settings for MSRDC2.

TABLE 13.5: The MSRDC1 Property Settings

Property	Value	Description
Connect	DSN=KDHMAIN;UID=sa; PWD=;DATABASE=pubs;	Sets the server connect string
SQL	SELECT * FROM authors	Provides the records for the display portion of the DBCombo control

TABLE 13.6: The MSRDC2 Property Settings

Property	Value	Description
Connect	DSN=KDHMAIN;UID=sa; PWD=;DATABASE=pubs;	Sets the server connect string.
SQL	SELECT au_fname FROM authors ORDER BY au_fname	Sets the recordsource for the RDC control to the author's first name and sorts the records in ascending order.
Visible	False	Makes MSRDC2 invisible at run time.

NOTE Substitute your DSN in place of KDHMAIN or add a KDHMAIN DSN entry for the Pubs database, and supply a valid UID and PWD for your server.

Now that we've set up the RemoteData Controls, it is time to connect the DBList control.

Connecting the DBList Control

The DBList control will be connected to both RemoteData Controls. One provides the author's first name from the current record, and the other provides the list of valid authors from the Authors table. Set the DBList properties according to Table 13.7.

TABLE 13.7: The DBList Property Settings

Property	Value	Description
DataSource	MSRDC1	Sets the data source of the display portion to the Authors table through the RemoteData Control MSRDC1.
DataField	au_fname	Connects the author's first name from the current record.
RowSource	MSRDC2	Sets the list portion to the names from the Authors table through the RemoteData Control MSRDC2.
ListField	aufname	Provides the source for the drop-down list portion of the DBCombo control.

Testing the DBList Project

Press F5 to run the project. The DBList control will be populated with the names from the Authors table, and the current record will be highlighted.

Navigate through the records with the RDC, and the DBList control will follow. As with the DBCombo control, if you select a different name in the DBList control and change records, the author's name will be changed to the new value.

The DBCombo and DBList controls display the current record. In the next section, we will explore the DBGrid control, which is capable of displaying multiple records simultaneously.

> **NOTE**
>
> The RDC control that is visible on the Form is bound to the Authors table. As you navigate from row to row, the list box positions to the author's first name. The movement will appear to be random, but you are actually seeing the first name from the current author's record.

Using the DBGrid Control

The DBGrid control is a spreadsheetlike bound control that displays a series of rows and columns representing records and fields from a Recordset object. The Results pane in Visual Data Tools, discussed in Chapter 10, has the same look and feel as the DBGrid control. Also, if you have ever used Microsoft Access or Microsoft Query, you are familiar with the look and feel of the DBGrid control.

The DBGrid control provides a lot of "ready-made" functionality that allows you to browse and edit complete database tables or query results. When you set the DBGrid control's DataSource property to a data control or RDC, the DBGrid control is automatically filled, and its column headers are automatically set from the data control's recordset.

The DBControl provides in-cell editing and allows you to insert or delete entire database records. In addition, the DBGrid control provides a number of properties that can be set at design time or at run time to control the look and feel of the control.

The DBGrid control depends on two major objects:

- The Recordset object of the data control

- The Columns collection of the DBGrid itself

Figure 13.9 shows how the DBGrid is bound to an RDC.

FIGURE 13.9:

The DBGrid control bound to a RemoteData Control

The DBGrid control is a collection of Column objects corresponding to fields in a database and rows corresponding to records in the database.

You can specify the current cell in code, or the user can change it at run time by using the mouse or the arrow keys. When you change the current cell, the underlying data control's recordset is automatically repositioned to the record containing the selected cell.

You can edit cells interactively by typing in the cell or programmatically by changing the Value property of the currently selected Column object. Table 13.8 lists the properties used to fill and bind the DBGrid control or the RDC.

TABLE 13.8: The DBGrid Properties

Property	Description
DataMode	Sets a value specifying whether the DBGrid operates in bound or unbound mode. This property is not available at run time.
DataSource	The name of the data control or RDC that provides database access for the DBGrid.

The DBGrid control is not added to a new Visual Basic project by default. The next section shows you how to do this.

Adding the DBGrid Control to a Project

Follow these steps to add the DBGrid control to a project:

1. Start a new Visual Basic project.

2. Choose Project ➤ Components to display the Components dialog box.

3. Select Microsoft Data Bound Grid Control from the list of available controls.

The DBGrid control will be added to your Toolbox as shown in Figure 13.10.

FIGURE 13.10:

The Toolbox with the DBGrid control added

DBGrid control

In the next section, with the DBGrid control added to your Toolbox, we will create a sample project.

The DBGrid Project

The DBGrid project (shown in Figure 13.11) demonstrates a DBGrid control connected to the Publishers table through a connection to a RemoteData Control. This sample project includes one RDC and a DBGrid control.

> **NOTE**
>
> You'll find the DBGrid project in the Ch13/DBGrid folder on the CD that comes with this book.

FIGURE 13.11:

The DBGrid project

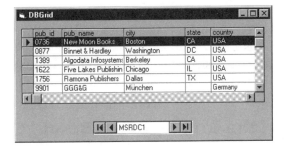

Creating the DBGrid project

Follow these steps to create the DBGrid project:

1. Add one RDC to Form1. This will be used to connect to the Publishers table in the Pubs database on your server.

2. Add one DBGrid control. This will display the records from the RDC.

3. Now, connect the RemoteData Control by setting the RDC properties according to Table 13.9.

TABLE 13.9: The MSRDC1 Property Settings

Property	Value	Description
Connect	DSN=KDHMAIN;UID=sa; PWD=;DATABASE=pubs;	Sets the server connect string
SQL	SELECT * FROM publishers	Provides the records for the DBGrid control

4. Set the DataSource property of the DBGrid control to MSRDC1 to connect the DBGrid control to the RemoteData Control.

Substitute your DSN in place of KDHMAIN or add a KDHMAIN DSN entry for the Pubs database, and supply a valid UID and PWD for your server. That's all there is to the setup. Now, let's test the project.

Testing the DBGrid Project

Press F5 to start the project. The Form will load, and the DBGrid will display the records from the Publishers table. Notice that the headings are created automatically. This is truly a drop-in database front end. In the next section, in order to round out our discussion on the bound controls commonly used in database front-end applications, we will look at using a standard Text Box control bound to an RDC.

Using the Text Box As a Bound Control

You can use a standard TextBox control as a bound control by setting the DataSource property to a data control or RDC and by setting the DataField property to a valid field in the data source. With these two properties set, the text box will take on the characteristics of a bound control and provide access to a database field. Figure 13.12 shows a text box bound to an RDC.

FIGURE 13.12:

A bound TextBox control

You can change the DataField or DataSource properties of the TextBox control at design time or at run time to change the source of the text box. All the standard properties apply to a bound text box.

NOTE   We'll look at bound TextBox controls in the FrontEnd project later in this chapter.

Bound controls provide an easy, powerful way to begin the process of building a front end. In the next section, we will look at how to use dialog boxes to enhance the functionality of front-end interfaces.

Incorporating Dialog Boxes into Front-End Interfaces

Visual Basic provides a standard suite of predefined dialog boxes in the CommonDialog control. This control provides dialog boxes for operations such as opening and saving files, setting print options, and selecting colors and fonts. It also has the ability to display Help by running the Windows Help engine.

The CommonDialog control provides an interface between Visual Basic and the routines in the Microsoft Windows dynamic-link library Commdlg.dll. To create a dialog box using this control, Commdlg.dll must be in your Microsoft Windows \System directory.

> **TIP**
>
> You cannot tell the dialog box where to display; however, with a little ingenuity, you can overcome this limitation. Create a separate Form with a CommonDialog control on it. Whenever you need to display a common dialog box, show this new Form at the desired location to position your dialog box where you want it.

You use the CommonDialog control in your application by adding it to a Form and setting its properties. The dialog box displayed by the control is determined by the methods of the control. At run time, a dialog box is displayed or the Help engine is executed when the appropriate method is invoked. Table 13.11 lists the dialog boxes provided as part of the CommonDialog control.

TABLE 13.11: Predefined Dialog Boxes in Visual Basic

Dialog Box	Description
Color	Allows the user to select a color from a palette or to create and select a custom color.
Font	Displays a dialog box in which the user can set the Font characteristics.
PrinterSetup	Displays a dialog box in which the user can select a printer and set printer options.
Help	Invokes Windows Help.
Open	Displays the standard File Open dialog box to allow the user to specify a drive, directory, file name extension, and a file name.
Save	Displays the standard File Save As dialog box to allow the user to specify a drive, directory, file name extension, and a file name.

If your application incorporates predefined dialog boxes where appropriate, it will take on the characteristics of a standard Windows application and, as such, be more likely to be accepted by your users. Another popular feature in front-end applications is the toolbar.

Accessing Menu Options with a Toolbar

Typically, a toolbar contains buttons that correspond to items in an application's menu, thus providing a graphical interface for the user to access an application's most frequently used functions and commands. Users of Windows applications have become accustomed to having toolbars available to them.

NOTE   We looked at toolbars in detail in Chapter 3.

With all the tools that Visual Basic provides, it is possible to design and build a commercial-quality Windows standard front end to your database applications. In the next section, we will look at putting the components from this chapter into practice as we create a sample Single Document Interface database front-end application.

The FrontEnd Project

The easiest and most common type of front-end interface to build is designed around a single Form, commonly referred to as an SDI application. An SDI application consists of one or more single Forms that allow the user to perform one task or to work with a single document. WordPad, Notepad, and Paint are SDI applications.

The sample FrontEnd project (shown in Figure 13.13) provides an interface to the Publishers and Titles tables in the Pubs database.

The FrontEnd Project consists of two Forms:

- The Main Form
- The About Form

FIGURE 13.13:

The FrontEnd project

The Main Form is a Master/Detail type Form that shows records from the Publishers table on the top and a DBGrid on the bottom with all the titles for the current publisher. The About Form is used to describe the application and show the current version.

A standard menu and a toolbar allow users to access the most common menu items. Also, whenever possible, we have incorporated Windows standard dialog boxes. In this application, the user will be able to do the following:

- Add records to the Authors table

- Display the predefined dialog boxes, including the Windows Help file

- Edit records for both the Publishers table and the Titles table

- Select the author's state from a DBCombo box

TIP

If you want to be able to delete records from the Publishers table, or Master table, you can write a cascading delete trigger to delete all the associated titles from the Titles table. See Chapter 12 for a discussion of triggers.

Connecting to the Pubs Database

The FrontEnd project connects to the database in three places:

- The datPrimaryRS
- The datSecondaryRS
- The datState RemoteData Controls

The datPrimaryRS is the recordsource connected to the Authors table in the Pubs database and is the main recordsource for the project. The datSecondaryRS is the recordsource for the associated records from the Titles table. The records are kept in sync in the Reposition event of the datPrimaryRS.

Code 13.1:   Repositioning the Detail DBGrid

```
Private Sub datPrimaryRS_Reposition()
  Screen.MousePointer = vbDefault
  On Error Resume Next
  'This will synch the grid
  'with the Master recordset
  datSecondaryRS.RecordSource = _
    "select [title_id],[title],[type],[pub_id]," _
    & "[price],[advance],[royalty],[ytd_sales]," _
    & "[notes],[pubdate] from [titles] " _
    & "where [pub_id]='" & _
      datPrimaryRS.Recordset![pub_id] & "'"
  datSecondaryRS.Refresh
  'This will display the current record
  'position for dynasets and snapshots
  datPrimaryRS.Caption = "Record: " & _
    (datPrimaryRS.Recordset.AbsolutePosition + 1)
End Sub
```

This code queries the Titles table in the Pubs database for all records where the pub_id field matches in the Publishers and Titles tables. The data source of the RDC for the DBGrid is set to the results.

The third connection is for the DBCombo box used to provide a list of states. The recordsource for this RDC is the state field in the Publishers table.

NOTE   See Chapter 11 for a complete discussion of how to connect to an ODBC data source.

After the RDCs are connected, it's time to add the fields to the Main Form.

Adding the Fields for the Main Form

The main Form in the FrontEnd project includes all the fields from the Publishers table in the Pubs database, with the exception of the state field, which is a DBCombo box.

Setting Up the State DBCombo Box Control

The state DBCombo box supplies a list of valid state abbreviations that can be used in our sample application. For this application, the user can select a state from the list, but cannot enter a state that is not already in use. This is accomplished by setting the Style property to 2- dbcDropDownList. Table 13.12 lists the styles available for the DBCombo box.

TABLE 13.12: Available Styles for the DBCombo Box Control

Style	Value	Meaning
vbComboDropDown	0	Default. Dropdown Combo. Includes a drop-down list and a text box. The user can select from the list or type in the text box.
vbComboSimple	1	Simple Combo. Includes a text box and a list, which doesn't drop down. The user can select from the list or type in the text box. By default, a Simple Combo box is sized so that none of the list is displayed. Increase the Height property to display more of the list.
vbComboDrop-DownList	2	Drop-Down List. Allows selection only from the drop-down list.

The DBCombo box list portion is bound to the datState RDC by setting the RowSource property to datState and by setting the ListField property to State. The state that is displayed from the Authors table is set by setting the DataSource

property to datPrimaryRS, the DataField property to state, and the
BoundColumn property to state.

By using two RDCs, it is possible to display a list of states from the Publishers
table and to display the current records state from the Publishers table.

TIP   You could add a new State table to the Pubs database that lists the abbreviations of all the states.

Using the Toolbar

The toolbar in our sample project provides easy access to the most frequently
used actions. The code for the toolbar calls the matching menu code. This process
is used so that you do not have code repeated in two places.

Code 13.2:   Responding to Toolbar Clicks

```
Private Sub Toolbar1_ButtonClick _
    (ByVal Button As ComctlLib.Button)
    On Error GoTo ErrorRoutineErr

    Select Case Button.Key
        Case "OpenFile"
            Call mnuOpenFile_Click
        Case "NewFile"
            Call mnuNewFile_Click
        Case "NewRecord"
            Call mnuNew_Click
        Case "SaveRecord"
            Call mnuSave_Click
    End Select
ErrorRoutineResume:
    Exit Sub
ErrorRoutineErr:
    MsgBox "Project1.frmauthors.Toolbar1_ButtonClick" _
    & Err & Error
    Resume Next
End Sub
```

Notice that error trapping is included. Since this code calls a second subroutine,
it will be helpful to know in which subroutine an error occurred. The error routine displays a message box with the subroutines name and the error message.

Accessing Common Dialog Boxes

Another feature of our FrontEnd application is the use of Windows standard common dialog boxes. Code 13.3, taken from the mnuOpenFile subroutine, accesses the dialog boxes.

Code 13.3: **Displaying the Common Dialog Boxes**

```
Private Sub mnuOpenFile_Click()
    On Error GoTo ErrorRoutineErr
    With CommonDialog1
        .DialogTitle = "Open File"
        .CancelError = True
        .ShowOpen
    End With
ErrorRoutineResume:
    Exit Sub
ErrorRoutineErr:
    If Err = 32755 Then
        'user chose cancel
        'put cancel code here
        Resume Next
    End If
    If glDebugMode = "True" Then
        MsgBox "Project1.frmauthors.mnuOpenFile_Click" _
            & Err & Error
    Else
        Call frmError.DisplayErrorForm _
        ("Project1.frmauthors.mnuOpenFile_Click", Err, Error)
    End If
End Sub
```

The only differences between calling an Open dialog box and a Save dialog box are the title and the ShowOpen command.

Notice the following line:

```
CancelError = False
```

If the user chooses the Cancel button on a dialog box, Visual Basic can raise error number 32755. If CancelError is set to True, the error will be raised, and you can write code to intercept and respond to the fact that Cancel was selected. If you do not need to know if the dialog option was canceled, set the CancelError property to False.

Now that we have looked at the major parts of the FrontEnd project, let's take it for a test drive.

Testing the FrontEnd Project

Follow these steps to test the FrontEnd project:

1. Press F5 to start the application. You should see the application as shown in Figure 13.13, earlier in this chapter

2. Click the OpenFile toolbar button to display the Open File dialog box.

> **NOTE** The New File, Open File, and Print Setup options display the appropriate common dialog boxes, but these dialog boxes are just for demonstration purposes. No action is taken in this sample program.

3. Click the arrow on the state DBCombo box to display a list of valid zip codes from the Authors table.

4. Select a new state to close the DBCombo box list portion and display the new state.

5. Click the Save icon or choose Edit ➢ Save to save the record with the new state.

6. Choose Help ➢ About to display the About screen. This is just a shell, but it gives you a start to building a complete About box.

7. To see the Windows Help file, choose Help ➢ Windows Help.

CHAPTER
FOURTEEN

14

Upsizing an Access Database to SQL Server 6.5

- Using the Microsoft Access Upsizing Wizard

- Preparing to upsize

- Evaluating cascading updates and deletes

- Upsizing the NWIND database to SQL Server 6.5

- Exploring the upsized NWINDSQL database

- Solving problems that arise during the upsizing process

As we discussed in Chapter 10, most applications being developed today provide some type of data access. More and more developers are adopting the client/server model as the basis for their applications—not because they want to, but because they have to.

Why is this happening? What drives developers to make the decision to move to this type of system? We believe it's for the following primary reasons:

- The need for enterprisewide access to corporate data

- The inadequacy of multiuser file-server applications

- The downsizing of mainframe and minicomputer database applications

- The flexibility, reusability, manageability, and ease of maintenance of the client/server model

In addition, more and more developers are using the Microsoft Access Database (MDB) to store data. It is important to understand that, even though the MDB supports multiuser access, it is not a true client/server implementation; it is a file server.

> **NOTE**   If you need to refresh your understanding of the differences between a file server and the client/server model, flip back to Chapter 9.

In this chapter, we will look at the steps to upsize the NWIND database from Microsoft Access to SQL Server 6.5. As you may recall from earlier chapters, NWIND is the sample database that is installed in the main Visual Basic installation directory. Upsizing from Microsoft Access to SQL Server means to make a copy of an Access database on SQL Server with the database structure and, if you choose, the data.

The Microsoft Access Upsizing Wizard

The Microsoft Access Upsizing Wizard is an add-in to Microsoft Access that can take an Access database and create an equivalent database on SQL Server with the same table structure, data, indexes, and many other attributes of the Access database.

NOTE　　You can download the Microsoft Access Upsizing Wizard free of charge from www.microsoft.com accessdev/a-free.htm.

The Wizard consists of two add-in applications:

Upsize to SQL Server is the actual Wizard that upsizes an Access database to SQL Server.

SQL Server Browser (shown in Figure 14.1) allows you to view, create, and edit SQL Server objects, including tables, views, stored procedures, and triggers. The browser has nearly the same functionality as the Microsoft SQL Server Enterprise Manager (discussed in Chapter 10), but has the look and feel of Access.

FIGURE 14.1:

The SQL Server Browser

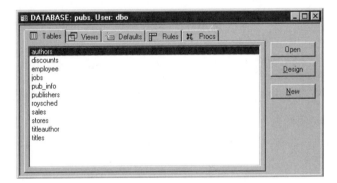

In the next section, we will take a look at some of the things you can do to get the most from the upsizing process.

Before You Upsize

Before you actually upsize, you can do several things to ensure that the process comes off without a hitch.

Backing Up

Backing up your data is always important, but it is essential when you make major changes to your database. The upsizing process does not alter the data in your Access database, but it is still a good idea to make a backup in case something unforeseen happens.

Using Windows Explorer or File Manager, make a backup copy of NWIND.mdb, the sample database, giving your file an extension of BAK.

Identifying the Changes SQL Server Makes to Your Access Data

In the upsizing process, SQL Server makes some changes, if needed, to your Access data to take advantage of all the advanced SQL Server features. Let's take a look at some of them.

The Need for a Key

Before you can update a SQL Server table through an ODBC data source, the table must have a unique index so that ODBC can identify the records. If you plan to use Visual Basic as the front end to your newly upsized database, you need to ensure that a unique key is defined for each table.

NOTE   See Chapter 10 for help on creating keys.

Identity Data Type

SQL Server has an automatically incrementing field called an *Identity field*, which is similar to the Microsoft Access AutoNumber field. When the Upsizing Wizard creates a table on the server with an Identity field, the functionality of the field is turned off with the IDENTITY_INSERT option. The data is copied with the current numbering, and then the IDENTITY_INSERT option is turned back on. This preserves the original AutoNumber values from your Microsoft Access table and begins future records with the highest number in your table, incrementing by one.

Testing for True and False

Microsoft Access stores either a zero (0) or a minus one (–1) in the Yes/No data type. Microsoft Access interprets zero as zero, No, or False. Microsoft Access interprets any nonzero value as –1, Yes, or True.

A bit field stored in SQL Server that is selected in ISQL/w appears as either a zero (0) or a plus one (1). Think of the result as True (1) or False (0). When you link to this table with Microsoft Access, you can accurately check for a value of zero but not 1. The correct method in Microsoft Access is to test for a value of True or False.

Data Type Conversions

When you move a Microsoft Access table to SQL Server either with the Upsizing Wizard or by exporting the table, the data types change to their corresponding SQL Server data types. SQL Server bases its data types on the C programming language, and Microsoft Access bases its data types on the Visual Basic programming language.

Here are the most common data type changes:

- Microsoft Access memo fields become SQL Server text fields.
- Microsoft Access OLE fields become SQL Server image fields.
- Microsoft Access text fields become SQL Server varchar fields (the default).

You can, however, modify the Upsizing Wizard to convert Microsoft Access text fields to char fields instead. Follow these steps:

1. Start Microsoft Access.
2. Choose File ➤ Open Database to open the Open dialog box, and select the database.

> **NOTE** The Upsizing Wizard library database for Microsoft Access 95 is Wzcs.mda, and Wzcs97.mda is the Upsizing Wizard library database for Microsoft Access 97.

3. When the database is open, select the Modules tab (as shown in Figure 14.2), and open the UT_modUserConstants module.
4. Search for the UT_USE_CHAR constant and change the default value from False to True.
5. Close the UT_ModUserConstants module window and answer yes to the message box.

Table 14.1 lists all the Microsoft Access to SQL Server data type conversions.

TABLE 14.1: Microsoft Access to SQL Server Data Type Conversions

Microsoft Access	SQL Server
Text	Varchar
Memo	Text
Byte	Smallint
Integer	Smallint
Long Integer	Int
Single	Real
Double	Float
Replication ID	Varbinary
Date/Time	Datetime
Currency	Money
Autonumber (Long Integer)	Int (Identity)
Yes/No	Bit
OLE Object	Image

NOTE   See Chapter 10 for a detailed discussion of SQL Server data types.

Evaluating Cascading Updates and Deletes

Cascading updates and deletes are features that cause a change in a record in a primary table to be automatically made in all related records in the related tables. For example, if you change a location code in an Inventory table from M1 to 1M, the location code will be automatically changed to 1M in all tables where referential integrity is linked with the Cascading Update option turned on. Also, if you delete a record in a primary table, all related records will be deleted in the related tables if referential integrity is linked and the Cascading Delete option is set.

Referential integrity maintains consistency among multiple tables of a database, and it is enforced by checking the validity of data to ensure that it exists within a range of values in another table.

In Microsoft SQL Server 6.5, referential integrity can be enforced in two ways:

- Programmatically by means of database triggers and stored procedures
- Declaratively by means of constraints defined with a table

A trigger, as you may recall from Chapter 10, is Transact-SQL code that runs when set off by an action such as INSERT, UPDATE, or DELETE. Triggers are flexible and can be written to do almost anything. Triggers are your only choice for cascading updates and deletes. The Upsizing Wizard writes them for you if you choose.

Declarative Referential Integrity (DRI) is similar to the referential integrity found in Microsoft Access and was first added in SQL Server 6. SQL Server's DRI will enforce referential integrity; however, DRI does not offer the cascading update feature. (For example, you cannot change the LocationCode to "Shelf 1" and expect all existing Parts Orders to be changed automatically.) Similarly, DRI does not support cascading deletes. In Microsoft Access, if you delete the Part 123, Access prompts you to delete all of 123's locations from the Locations table. With SQL Server DRI, you must do this in two steps:

1. Delete the part.
2. Delete the locations.

When there is inappropriate data, one drawback to using triggers is slower performance. If you use DRI, the primary key constraints are enforced before data is entered into the table, and any inappropriate data is rejected quickly. Triggers, on the other hand, permit the data to be entered into the table; then the trigger fires to validate the entry. If the relationship is not valid, the change to the table is rolled back.

Handling Required Data

The Upsizing Wizard uses triggers to prevent entry of data into fields that were marked as Required in Microsoft Access. SQL Server developers generally define a required field as NOT NULL when creating the table. You can configure the Upsizing Wizard to do that for you. Follow these steps:

1. Start Microsoft Access.

2. Choose File ➤ Open Database to open the Open dialog box, and select the database.

NOTE   The Upsizing Wizard library database for Microsoft Access 95 is Wzcs.mda, and Wzcs97.mda is the Upsizing Wizard library database for Microsoft Access 97.

---

3. When the database is open, select the Modules tab (as shown in Figure 14.2, earlier in this chapter), and open the UT_modUserConstants module.

4. Search for the UT_USE_NULL_CONSTRAINTS constant and change the default value from False to True.

5. Close the UT_ModUserConstants module window and answer yes to the message box.

Evaluating Object Names

SQL Server limits table names to 30 characters and allows no symbols other than #, $, and _. The first character of a table name cannot be a number, and you should not use the number sign (#) as the first character of an upsized table name because it indicates a temporary table.

Although the default installation is case-insensitive, you can install SQL Server with case sensitivity so that a table called MyTable is not the same as a table called mytable or MYTABLE. These three object names can coexist if you install SQL Server with a Case Sensitive sort order. To determine the sort order, run the stored procedure sp_helpsort. If you plan to change any table names, do it before the Upsizing Wizard starts copying your tables.

Object names in Microsoft Access can contain spaces. For example, you can name a table Inventory Locations. Microsoft SQL Server, however, does not permit spaces in table or column names. The Upsizing Wizard changes the spaces to underscores, transferring your table to SQL Server as Inventory_Locations.

Microsoft Access table names ending in "_local" cannot be upsized to SQL Server because the Upsizing Wizard renames all original Microsoft Access tables by adding "_local" to the original table name. This permits the new SQL Server table to be linked to the Microsoft Access database with the original name of *Inventory*, while leaving the original table untouched with the new name of *Inventory_local*.

A common way to avoid the underscores is to use capitalization to separate the portions of the names, such as InventoryLocations. If you have used this naming convention in your Microsoft Access tables, you needn't make any changes when moving your data to SQL Server.

In the next section, we will use the Upsizing Wizard to move the sample NWIND database, Nwind.mdb, to SQL Server 6.5.

Upsizing the NWIND Database to SQL Server 6.5

Now that all the preliminaries are out of the way, it's time to run the Upsizing Wizard. Load the Upsizing Wizard into Microsoft Access by double-clicking Aut97.exe. This places the Wzcs97.mda Wizard in your Microsoft Access directory and makes the necessary changes to your Windows Registry. Now, follow these steps:

1. Start Microsoft Access and load the NWIND.mdb file from the Ch14 folder on the CD that comes with this book.

NOTE   This sample database is the same as that included with Visual Basic 5.

2. Choose Tools ➤ Add-Ins ➤ Upsize to SQL_Server to start the Upsizing Wizard:

3. You can use an existing database or create a new one. For this example, choose Create New Database to have the Wizard create a new target database on SQL Server for you.

NOTE You must have rights on the server to create a database and database objects.

4. Choose Next to display the Select Data Source window:

5. Select a data source to use for your new database, and click OK to open the SQL Server Login dialog box:

6. Enter a valid login ID and password, and click OK to continue.

7. The Wizard will attempt to log you in to the server. If the login is successful, you will see this Upsizing Wizard window, in which you select a device to hold the new SQL Server database:

TIP
The Size field on this screen shows the size of the database device, not the size of your new database.

---

8. Accept the default device, and click Next to continue.

9. In this window, you set the name and the initial size of the new database. Accept the default name of NWINDSQL.

10. The NWIND database is approximately 1.5MB. The new database will be slightly smaller than this because it will not include the forms, reports, or queries. Set the initial size of the database to 10MB, and set the size for the log to 5MB. This will give the database room to grow. Choose Next to continue.

11. This window lists all the tables in the NWIND database in the Available Tables list box. Click the double-arrow button to add all the tables to the Export to SQL Server list box. Only those tables that you add to the Export to SQL Server list box will participate in the upsizing process. Choose Next to continue.

12. In this window, you set the attributes and options for your new database and instruct the Wizard on how to handle the upsizing:

You have the options described in the following section.

Selecting Options

You can use the Upsizing Wizard to export table attributes as well as data, and you can choose to link the upsized tables. You specify how you want this done by selecting from the following options.

Indexes   Indexes are easy to rebuild or drop and re-create; however, this can be time consuming if you have large tables. As a general rule, upsize the indexes of tables that are less than 10 or 20MB. If your tables exceed 100MB, skip the indexes until you are sure what you want. Selecting the Index checkbox will slow down the data transfer. You can also check the Index checkbox to accept the indexes you have been using in Microsoft Access. For our example, accept the default to create indexes.

Validation Rules   Validation rules are checked in almost all cases. If you have a validation rule (a rule in SQL Server) that says the OrderDate field must be greater than 01/01/1997 or the QuantityOrdered field must be greater than the ReorderPoint field, you should keep it. Since SQL Server rules do not allow you to display custom error messages, the Upsizing Wizard uses triggers to enforce field-level validation, and it codes an appropriate custom error message explaining why an invalid INSERT was rejected. Leave this box checked to create validation rule triggers.

Defaults   You should leave this option checked in almost all cases. A default value works the same in SQL Server as it does in Microsoft Access. The Upsizing Wizard provides the correct Transact-SQL syntax for common functions such as Date(). Leave this checked for our example.

Table Relationships   Selecting the Use DRI option creates the SQL Server tables with Declarative Referential Integrity, the designations that enforce foreign key to primary key relationships. SQL Server 6 and 6.5 do not enforce cascading updates and deletes, so if you have that selected in your relationships, you will get a dialog box reminding you that you are foregoing that feature.

If you select Use Triggers, the Upsizing Wizard writes triggers for your tables to enforce cascading updates and deletes. This may be a valid reason to make more than one pass through the Upsizing Wizard, selecting triggers to move the tables that have cascading updates or deletes and selecting DRI to move the tables that do not. All the tables involved in the relationships must be present or must have been created on the server with the DRI option; so move the triggered tables before you move the DRI tables.

If you uncheck the Table Relationships checkbox, DRI is ignored completely. This is a good choice for fast data transfer if you intend to evaluate the data and table structure after the data is loaded onto the server. For this example, accept the Use Triggers option.

Add Timestamp Fields to Tables?   You can add timestamp fields to tables and create a table structure without upsizing data. Selecting *Yes, let wizard decide* is recommended for now. Only select *No, never* or *Yes, always* if you understand the impact of data conversion and timestamps. A timestamp field is an easy way for Microsoft Access to tell if the data in a record has changed since its creation. This field is not visible to Microsoft Access users but can speed data entry and avoid the #Deleted error described later in the "Common Error Messages during the Upsizing Process" section of this chapter.

If you plan to use Microsoft Access to access your SQL Server tables, this is a good idea. If you plan to use Visual Basic 5 as your front end, it is not necessary to add a timestamp field. You will control, through your Visual Basic code, when and how to update tables.

For our example, change this option to *No, never* so that a timestamp field will not be added.

Only Create Table Structure, Don't Upsize Any Data   If you want to use the table structures but enter all new data, check this checkbox. This helps transfer tables that are large due to high quantities of data and insufficient database locks. Use this option to transfer the table structure, and then move the data in smaller chunks using APPEND queries. For our example, we want to move the data, so leave this option unchecked.

Link Newly Created SQL Server Tables   You can attach newly created SQL Server tables and save a password and user ID with linked tables. If you plan to use your Microsoft Access database as a front-end program to manipulate the SQL Server data, link to the tables. If you are abandoning your application because you plan to use ODBC from a Visual Basic–based application to connect to SQL Server, do not select this option. Uncheck this option for our example.

Save Password and User ID with Linked Tables   Do not select this option if you are using a trusted connection and integrated security. If you do not check this box, a user connecting with the Microsoft Access database is asked for a login ID and password when opening the table, a query, or a Form based on the linked table. This can be an important security feature. If you check this box, the login ID and password are cached with the connection, and users of the database have rights to the SQL Server database consistent with their login ID and password. If in doubt, avoid an inadvertent hole in your security by not checking this box. Since we are using Visual Basic as our front end and will most likely delete the Access database, do not check this box.

Now that we have set all the options, choose Next to continue.

Creating an Upsizing Report

The Upsizing Wizard now asks if you would like to create an upsizing report:

We strongly recommend that you select this option. The Upsizing Wizard intercepts many server error messages so that it can continue transferring tables without interruption and saves them for the report. Consequently, you will not see all the errors unless you see the report.

Well, that's it. Now it's time to run the upsizing process. Click Finish to run the Upsizing Wizard and create your new SQL Server database. A status dialog box will keep you apprised of the progress:

If all goes as expected, you will see a message box notifying you that the upsizing process has finished successfully.

In the next section, we will examine the new NWINDSQL database on the server and examine the Upsizing Wizard's handiwork.

WARNING   Do not close Microsoft Access. If you do, you will lose the upsizing report.

Exploring the Upsized NWINDSQL Database

Your new database should be available on the server. Open Microsoft SQL Server Enterprise Manager, and select the server that you used in the Upsizing Wizard. You'll see the new NWINDSQL database listed under the Database folder and all the tables listed under the Table folder as shown here.

See Chapter 10 for help on using the Microsoft SQL Enterprise Manager application.

Verifying the Data in the Customers Table

To see if the data was upsized properly, let's run a test query against the Customers table. Follow these steps:

1. Choose Tools ➤ SQL-Query Tool, and enter the following code in the Query window:

   ```
   SELECT * FROM Customers
   ```

2. Run the query to display the records in the Results tab:

In the next section we will use the upsizing report generated by the Access Upsizing Wizard to verify the upsizing process.

Viewing the Upsizing Report

Switch back to Microsoft Access, and the upsizing report will be open in the Access database. This report outlines most of the actions performed by the upsizing process and the results of those actions, as you can see in Figure 14.3. Table 14.2 lists and describes the major sections of this report.

FIGURE 14.3:

The Upsizing Report in the Upsizing Wizard

TABLE 14.2: Major Sections of the Upsizing Report

Section	Description
Database and Log	The database name and size.
Devices	The name of the database and log device.
Errors	Any error messages.
Upsizing Parameters	The options you selected during setup.
Table	A list of the tables and the fields, indexes, and triggers generated for each table.
Relationships	The fields, enforcing triggers, and attributes of the relationships.

WARNING You cannot save the upsizing report from Access. You can print the report from Access or from Microsoft Word. Once you close this screen, you cannot re-create the report.

In the next section, we'll look at how you can use the SQL Server Browser tool to view and maintain SQL Server databases.

Using the SQL-Server Browser Tool

The SQL-Server Browser is included as an add-in with the Upsizing Wizard. Follow these steps to start the SQL-Server Browser:

1. Start Microsoft Access if it is not already running.

2. Choose Tools ➤ Add-Ins ➤ SQL-Server Browser to open the Select Data Source dialog box.

3. Choose the data source, provide a valid login ID and password, and click the Options button.

4. Choose the NWINDSQL database from the list of available databases to open the Database dialog box. This interface will look familiar to Microsoft Access users.

NOTE   By default, you will be logged into the Master database if you do not make a selection.

In the Database dialog box, you can browse the data in tables, but you cannot edit the actual data. Click the Open button to open a table and view the data.

To alter a table, click the Design button to open the table definition window:

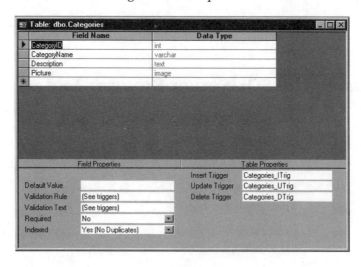

From this screen you can perform these actions:

- Alter the field names. Simply type a new field name. When you leave the current row, the changes are made.

- Set a default value. Enter a default value for the field in the Default Value text box.

- Create, view, edit, or delete triggers. Click a Trigger field, and an Ellipse button will appear next to the trigger. Click the Ellipse button to open the Trigger window. In this window you can create a new trigger or edit or delete an existing trigger.

To create a new table, click the New button to open the New Table dialog box. Here, you can enter the name of the new table and assign new fields and validation rules.

In the Database dialog box, select the Views tab and choose Ad-HocSQL to do the following:

- Administer users and groups
- Configure the server
- Perform backup and recovery tasks
- Set and maintain security options
- Define CHECK, FOREIGN KEYS, PRIMARY KEYS, and UNIQUE constraints and add Identity properties to a table

As you can see, you can use the SQL Server Browser to perform most of the SQL Server functions that you can do from SQL Enterprise Manager, and the interface is more Access-like.

In the next section, we will look at some of the most common errors that can occur during the upsizing process.

Common Error Messages during the Upsizing Process

Obviously, if you prepare for upsizing carefully, following the guidelines we gave you in the first part of this chapter, you can avoid many pitfalls. But inevitably you'll encounter some mishaps. Let's look at the most common and what you can do about them.

Table Name Skipped or Export Failed

The Upsizing Wizard provides this generic message whenever something goes wrong. For additional information, check the Error Message section on the upsizing report, or look in the SQL Server error log or the Windows NT Event Log.

If you can't find a more meaningful message, use the Upsizing Wizard to upsize the table structure without the data, link to the table, and then use an APPEND query to move the data from Microsoft Access to SQL Server.

ODBC Call Failed

This is an incomplete error message. After you click OK, it should be followed by the error that caused the ODBC call to fail:

```
ODBC Query Timeout
Server Error 0: Timeout expired
SQL that Caused Error(s)
UT_CopyData
```

The queries that move the data are internal to the Upsizing Wizard. Their time-out was lengthened programmatically to prevent the default 60-second timeout. If you have a table that is several megabytes or if your network has a lot of traffic, the timeout still may not be long enough. As a workaround, you can upsize the table structure without data, link to the new table, and then move the data into a Microsoft Access APPEND query. Either set the ODBC Timeout property to zero for your APPEND query, or use a criterion that selects and moves only a portion of the data at a time. Repeat this until the entire table has been moved.

If this problem is still creating a major stumbling block, try this workaround:

1. Close and reopen Microsoft Access.

2. Open the Wzcx.mda (Microsoft Access 95) or Wzcs97.mda (Microsoft Access 97) database.

3. Open the UT_modGlobals module and search for CLng(vODBCTimeout). You should find the following:

```
If Not IsMissing(vODBCTimeout) Then
qry.ODBCTimeout = CLng(vODBCTimeout)
End IF
```

4. Comment out this line:

```
'If Not IsMissing(vODBCTimeout) Then
```

5. Change the ODBC Timeout to zero.

   ```
   qry.ODBCTimeout = 0
   ```

6. Comment out this line:

   ```
   'End If
   ```

Now, the Upsizing Wizard should not time out.

SQL Server Error 1105: Can't Allocate Space

Here is the full error message:

```
Can't allocate space for object '<usually a table name>' in database
'<dbname>' because the '<name>' segment is full. If you ran out of
space in Syslogs, dump
the transaction log. Otherwise, use ALTER DATABASE or sp_extendsegment
to increase
the size of the segment.
```

This error message means that your database is full. This problem will occur in two situations. First, your database may be too small to hold the data. You must make the SQL Server database larger.

The second situation is more complicated. The Wizard moves the data in a table over in a transaction. Either it all transfers successfully, or none of it transfers. To compound this, the data is moved twice—once to the new database, and once to the log. You will, therefore, need twice the log space as normal. To work around this problem, consider upsizing the table structure only and then adding the data with an APPEND query.

Run Out of Locks

SQL Server is initially installed with the configuration setting of 5000 locks. If you run out of locks, you will receive this error message:

```
Server Error 1204: SQL Server has run out of LOCKS. Re-run your command
when there are fewer active users, or ask your System Administrator to
reconfigure SQL Server with more LOCKS.
```

Choose Server ➢ SQL Server ➢ Configure from SQL Enterprise Manager, and select the Configure tab to use the Server Configuration dialog box to increase the number of locks. You can increase the lock setting while you upsize your data and then reduce it for the smaller activity expected during normal use.

Alternatively, use the Edit Database dialog box to put your database in single-user mode so that SQL Server can maintain transaction integrity without using locking.

Table Is Read Only

Because the data in a SQL Server table is not in a native Microsoft Access format, Microsoft Access cannot manage it the same way it manages a native Microsoft Access table. It must have a unique index for identifying each row individually. For best performance, provide a unique index on each table.

Tables Do Not Show in SQL Enterprise Manager after Upsizing

Remember that SQL Enterprise Manager is not SQL Server; it is a client just like Microsoft Access. If you make a change to your server using SQL Enterprise Manager, it will reflect that change. If you make a change to the server from some other client (such as Microsoft Access), SQL Enterprise Manager will not reflect the changes until it has been refreshed. In the Server Manager window of SQL Enterprise Manager, right-click the appropriate place (Tables or Databases), and select Refresh from the shortcut menu.

Text Fields Are Incomplete

By default, a limit of 4Kb is transmitted for text fields. Increase this amount by using the SET statement. When upsizing tables, the Upsizing Wizard increases the text size to 2,147,483,647 bytes. You can do the same with the following command from the SQL Enterprise Manager Query Tool:

```
SET TEXTSIZE 2147483647
```

Remember, SET statements persist only for the current session and connection.

15

Three-Tiered Applications

- Understanding the three tiers

- Developing the Three-Tiered project

In Chapter 10, we discussed some aspects of three-tiered applications. In this chapter, we will build a sample three-tiered application based on the Pubs database and use SQL Server 6.5 as the database engine.

Three-tiered architecture partitions an application into three logical tiers, or services:

- User services (the front end)
- Business services (the middle)
- Data services (the back end)

By using three-tiered architecture, you can develop applications that separate user access, business rules, and data access into separate modules.

Understanding the Three Tiers

In our sample application, tier one, or user services, consists of one Form (shown in Figure 15.1) with the fields from the Authors table that will allow the user to do the following:

- Add new records to the Authors table
- Delete current records from the Authors table
- Find records based on an author's ID number that is actually a Social Security number
- Update records and change the current values

The user interface for tier one incorporates components that we discussed in many previous chapters, including:

- Menus
- Toolbars
- Status bars
- Advanced ActiveX controls

FIGURE 15.1:

The tier one Form

Tier two, business services, is a separate application compiled into a DLL. There is no interface for tier two because it receives requests from tier one and passes them on to the database through RDO 2 (Remote Data Objects 2).

> **NOTE**
>
> See Chapter 11 for a complete discussion of Remote Data Objects.

Tier three, data services, consists of the Pubs database, which we use throughout this book. It is the same sample database that comes with SQL Server 6.5 and is created when SQL Server is installed. In order to run the examples in this chapter, you must have access to the database. If the Pubs database is not installed on your server or if it has been altered, install it by running the Instpubs.sql script included on the CD that comes with this book.

The Three-Tiered Project

The Three-Tiered project is composed of two applications and the database. The front end, or tier one (as shown in Figure 15.1), provides the user interface for presenting information and gathering data. It gathers requirements from the user and presents data in response to a question or a query. The user can add, delete, update, and search records in the Pubs database.

NOTE

You will find the TierOne and TierTwo projects in the Ch15 folder on the CD that comes with this book.

Processing Toolbar Requests

Our application provides a toolbar (shown in Figure 15.2) with which users can interact with the program. The toolbar has four buttons that perform the following actions:

- Save Record sends a request to the tier-two application to save changes to the current record.

- Find sends a request to find the record that has the current AuthorID.

- New Record sends a request to add a new record to the database using the current field values.

- Delete Record sends a request to delete the current record.

FIGURE 15.2:

The tier-one toolbar

Code 15.1:   The Three-Tiered Application Toolbar

```
Private Sub Toolbar1_ButtonClick(ByVal Button _
    As ComctlLib.Button)
    On Error GoTo ErrorRoutineErr
    RichTextBox1.Visible = False
    Select Case Button.Key
        Case "Save"
            Call mnuSave_Click
        Case "Find"
            Call mnuFind_Click
        Case "New"
            Call mnuNew_Click
```

```
        Case "Delete"
                Call mnuDelete_Click
        End Select
    ErrorRoutineResume:
        Exit Sub
    ErrorRoutineErr:
        MsgBox "TierOne.Form1.Toolbar1_ButtonClick" _
        & Err & Error
    End Sub
```

As you can see, the toolbar simply calls the associated code in the menu to perform the request. This alleviates the need to duplicate the code.

Adding Records

To add a new author's record to the database, you simply click the Add button on the toolbar, as shown in Figure 15.2, or choose Edit ≻ New Record. This will call the mnuNew_click code as shown in Code 15.2.

NOTE   Remember: Tier one does not actually have any SQL statements or database code. It simply passes requests to tier two.

If all goes well, the record is added to the database, and the status bar is updated to display Record Added.

Code 15.2:   Sending a Request to Tier Two to Add a Record

```
Private Sub mnuNew_Click()
    On Error GoTo ErrorRoutineErr
    'Get the Authors ID
    clsAuthor.AuthorID = txtAuthorID

    'Assign the class values
    Call AssignValues

    'Add the new record
    clsAuthor.Add

ErrorRoutineResume:
    Exit Sub
ErrorRoutineErr:
    MsgBox "TierOne.Form1.mnuNew_Click" & Err & Error
    Resume Next
End Sub
```

NOTE

Notice the use of error-trapping code. Error-trapping code is always important, but here it is essential. You are calling a DLL, and if an error occurs, it is important for you to know where and why.

This code calls the Add subroutine in the TierTwo application, where all the work is performed. Tier one simply gathers requirements from the user and processes requests. It should not know or care how the data is processed.

When a request is processed, one of three things happens:

- The request is processed without any errors.
- A noncritical error occurs (for example, the record is not found).
- A database error occurs.

If the request is successful or if a noncritical error occurs, the TierTwo application raises the Action event in the TierOne application, and the status bar is updated.

Code 15.3:   Raising the Action Event in Tier One

```
Private Sub clsAuthor_Action(ByVal Status As Integer)
    'This event is raised by TierTwo.dll in the event
    'of a non-critical error

    'Define variables
    Dim Msg, Style, Title, Response

    'Clear the status
    StatusBar1.Panels(2).Text = ""

    Select Case Status
        Case 2
            'No record found
            Msg = "No Authors record was located" _
            & "with the AuthorID: " & txtAuthorID
            Title = "No Records Found"
            StatusBar1.Panels(2).Text _
            = "Record Not Found"
        Case 3
```

```
                  'Record not deleted
                  Msg = "No Authors record was located" _
                  & "with the AuthorID: " _
                  & txtAuthorID _
                  & Chr(10) _
                  & "No record was deleted"
                  Title = "Delete Error"
                  StatusBar1.Panels(2).Text _
                  = "Record Not Deleted"
            Case 4
                  'Record not updated
                  Msg = "No Authors record was located" _
                  & "with the AuthorID: " & txtAuthorID _
                  & Chr(10) _
                  & "No record was updated"
                  Title = "Update Error"
                  StatusBar1.Panels(2).Text _
                  = "Record Not Updated"
            Case 100
                  'Record Deleted
                  StatusBar1.Panels(2).Text _
                  = "Record Deleted"
                  Exit Sub
            Case 200
                  'Record Found
                  StatusBar1.Panels(2).Text _
                  = "Record Found"
                  Exit Sub
            Case 300
                  'record Added
                  StatusBar1.Panels(2).Text _
                  = "Record Added"
                  Exit Sub
            Case 400
                  'Record Updated
                  StatusBar1.Panels(2).Text _
                  = "Record Saved"
                  Exit Sub
      End Select

'Display the msgbox
DisplayMsgbox:
      Style = vbOKOnly + vbInformation
      Response = MsgBox(Msg, Style, Title)
End Sub
```

The code in the Action subroutine is passed an integer value from the TierTwo application in response to an action request. If no errors were found, a value of 100, 200, 300, or 400 is passed. The Action code interprets this value and constructs the proper status bar response.

If a record was not found, a value of 2, 3, or 4 is passed back. In this case, in addition to the status bar response, a message box is displayed, notifying the user of the error.

If a database error occurs while the record is being processed, the TierTwo application raises the Errors event in the TierOne application and calls the code in Code 15.4. This code displays a message box, notifying you that an error has occurred, and a RichTextBox control becomes visible between the author fields and the status bar, as shown in Figure 15.3. The rdoErrors, which contains details about remote data access errors, is written to the RichTextBox control, and the status bar displays Processing Error.

FIGURE 15.3:

The Three-Tiered application displaying error messages

Code 15.4:   Raising an Error

```
Private Sub clsAuthor_Errors(ErrMessages As Object)
    'This event is called from the TierTwo.dll
    'if errors are encountered.
    'Errors will be written to the RichTextBox control
```

```
        'Define variables
        Dim er As Object

        'Clear the status
        StatusBar1.Panels(2).Text = "Processing Error"

        'Clear the error text
        RichTextBox1.Text = ""

        RichTextBox1.Visible = True
        MsgBox "An error has occurred. Error messages" _
        & " will be displayed in the Errors box."

        'Write errors to the RichTextBox
        For Each er In ErrMessages
        RichTextBox1.Text = RichTextBox1.Text _
                & Chr(10) & er
        Next
    End Sub
```

This generic error-handling code module is raised, or called, from the TierTwo application in the event of a critical database error.

Deleting Records

Deleting records is easy in our application. With a valid AuthorID present, choose Edit ➤ Delete Record or simply click the Delete button, as shown in Figure 15.2, earlier in this chapter. A message box will ask you to confirm the delete request. If you select Yes, the record is deleted. Select No to cancel the request. When you delete the record, the status bar is updated to display Record Deleted to let you know that the delete was successful.

If an error occurs while the record is being processed, a message box notifies you that an error has occurred, and a RichTextBox control becomes visible between the author fields and the status bar. The rdoErrors is written to the RichTextBox control, and the status bar displays Processing Error.

The TierOne application uses the following code to request a delete from the TierTwo application.

Code 15.5:   **Sending a Delete Request**

```
Private Sub mnuDelete_Click()
    On Error GoTo ErrorRoutineErr
    'Declare variables
    Dim Msg, Style, Title, Response

    'Get the Authors ID
    clsAuthor.AuthorID = txtAuthorID

    'Confirm the delete request
    Msg = "Delete the current Author's record?"
    Style = vbYesNo + vbQuestion + vbDefaultButton1
    Title = "Confirm Delete"
    Response = MsgBox(Msg, Style, Title)
    If Response = vbYes Then
        'Delete the record
        clsAuthor.Delete
        Call PopulateTextBoxes
    Else
        'no action
        StatusBar1.Panels(2).Text = "Delete Aborted"
    End If

ErrorRoutineResume:
    Exit Sub
ErrorRoutineErr:
    MsgBox "TierOne.Form1.mnuDelete_Click" & Err & Error
    Resume Next
End Sub
```

This code gets the author's ID from the AuthorID field, which is used to actually locate the record for deletion. Next, a message box is constructed and displayed; it asks you to confirm the delete request. If you select Yes, the request is sent to the DLL; if you select No, the status bar is updated with `Delete Aborted`, and no action is taken.

Finding an Author's Record

Our application also makes easy work of searching for a particular author; you simply enter the author's ID number in the AuthorID field and click the Find icon, as shown in Figure 15.2 earlier in this chapter. The application gets the

AuthorID number from the TierTwo application and then sends a request to the application to create a recordset with the AuthorID number.

If the process is completed successfully and the record is found, the fields are filled in with the record, and the status bar is updated to display Record Found. As in the other cases, if an error occurs, the text box at the bottom of the screen displays the error messages. The following code sends the Find request to the DLL.

Code 15.6:   **Sending a Request to Find a Record**

```
Private Sub mnuFind_Click()
    On Error GoTo ErrorRoutineErr
    'AuthorID to find
    clsAuthor.AuthorID = txtAuthorID

    'Lookup
    clsAuthor.Search
    Call PopulateTextBoxes

ErrorRoutineResume:
    Exit Sub
ErrorRoutineErr:
    MsgBox "TierOne.Form1.mnuFind_Click" & Err & Error
    Resume ErrorRoutineResume
End Sub
```

This code is straightforward. First, the AuthorID number is retrieved from the AuthorID text box; then a request is sent to the TierTwo application to perform a search, and, finally, the new records populate the text boxes.

Updating a Current Record

From time to time, you will find it necessary to make changes to current records. Our application supports changes by sending an update request to the TierTwo application. To change a record, you simply locate a current record with the Find method, or add a new record and change one or more fields. Click the Save icon, as shown in Figure 15.2 earlier in this chapter, to send an Update request to the TierTwo application. If the record is successfully changed, the status bar displays Record Updated, notifying you that the change was successful. If an error occurs, the text box at the bottom of the screen displays the error message. The following code sends an update request to tier two.

Code 15.7:   Sending an Update Request to Tier Two

```
Private Sub mnuSave_Click()
    On Error GoTo ErrorRoutineErr
    'Get the Authors ID
    clsAuthor.AuthorID = txtAuthorID

    'Assign the class values
    Call AssignValues

    'Add the new record
    clsAuthor.Update

ErrorRoutineResume:
    Exit Sub
ErrorRoutineErr:
    MsgBox "TierOne.Form1.mnuSave_Click" & Err & Error
    Resume Next
End Sub
```

This code looks a lot like the code used to add or delete a record. First, the AuthorID number is retrieved from the AuthorID text box, and then the update request is sent. If the update is successful, the status bar displays `Record Updated`.

The user interface, or tier one, of a three-tiered application simply gathers requests and passes them to the business services, or second tier. No SQL statements or records are processed. In the next section, we will explore the tier-two application where the records are processed.

The TierTwo Application

In our sample application, the business services, or middle tier, is made up of a class module and is compiled into a dynamic-link library program, or DLL.

The TierTwo application does not have a user interface; in fact, the user really should not even know or care about this application. Its purpose is to receive requests from the front-end application, in our case the TierOne program, to process the requests and to notify the calling application of the status. In our case, this is accomplished with one class module.

Creating Properties, Methods, and Events

We created the class module in our TierTwo application with the help of the Class Builder add-in that comes with Visual Basic 5. The class module we will build consists of properties, methods, and events.

NOTE   For a complete discussion of Visual Basic classes, see Chapter 6.

Defining the Class Properties

The properties in our class are the fields from the Authors table in the Pubs database. Table 15.1 lists and describes them.

TABLE 15.1: The Class Properties

Property	Description
Address	The author's address
AuthorID	The author's Social Security number, which is the key to the table
City	The author's city
Contract	Signifies whether the author is under contract
FirstName	The author's first name
LastName	The author's last name
Phone	The author's phone number
State	The author's state
Zip	The author's zip code

Defining the Class Methods

The methods for our class module are the actions that can be performed from the front end, or the TierOne application. Table 15.2 lists and describes them.

TABLE 15.2: Methods Supported by the TierTwo Application

Method	Description
Add	Adds a new record to the authors table
Delete	Deletes the current record from the Authors table
Search	Locates a record matching the current AuthorID field
Update	Saves changes to the current author's record

Defining the Class Events

The events in our class module are raised and are available in the TierOne application. Table 15.3 lists and describes these events.

TABLE 15.3: Events Raised by the TierTwo Application

Event	Description
Action	Called in response to a method. If the method completes without a critical database error, the Action event is raised.
Errors	Raised if a critical database error occurs.

Accessing the Class Builder Utility

The Class Builder add-in is designed to help you build the class and collection hierarchy for your Visual Basic project. It keeps track of the hierarchy of your classes and collections and generates the framework code for implementing the classes and collections, including the properties, methods, and events.

Follow these steps to open the Class Builder add-in:

1. Choose Add-Ins ➤ Add-Ins Manager to display the Add-In Manager dialog box.

2. Select the VB Class Builder Utility from the list of Available Add-Ins and click OK to add the Class Builder Utility to the list of add-ins.

3. Choose Add-Ins ➤ VB Class Builder Utility to open the Class Builder dialog box:

Creating the Class Properties

Now, let's create the properties for our class module with the Class Builder Utility. Follow these steps:

1. Choose File ➤ New ➤ Class to open the Class Module Builder dialog box:

2. In the Name text box, enter **Authors** as the name for the new class.

3. In the Based On text box, accept the default (New Class), and in the Instancing section, select the Multi Use option to create the Class Module for multiuser use. Then click OK.

4. Choose File ➤ New ➤ Property to open the Property Builder dialog box:

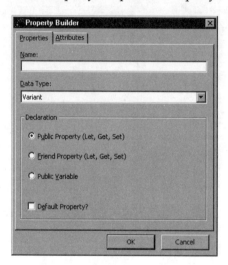

5. In this dialog box, you name the property as well as set the data type and declarations. Add the new properties by typing the name in the Name field according to Table 15.4, and then click OK.

TABLE 15.4: The Property Settings for the Authors Class

Property	Data Type	Declaration
Address	String	Public Property
AuthorID	String	Public Property
City	String	Public Property
Contract	String	Public Property
FirstName	String	Public Property
LastName	String	Public Property
Phone	String	Public Property

TABLE 15.4 (CONTINUED): The Property Settings for the Authors Class

Property	Data Type	Declaration
State	String	Public Property
Zip	String	Public Property

Creating the Methods

Follow these steps to create the methods for the Authors class:

1. Choose File ➤ New ➤ Method to open the Method Builder dialog box:

2. You use this dialog box to name the methods. These methods do not need a return value so leave the Return Data Type text box blank. Create the following methods by typing the name in the Name field and then clicking the OK button:

   Add

   Delete

   Search

   Update

Creating the Events

Follow these steps to create the events for the Authors class:

1. Choose File ➤ New ➤ Event to open the Event Builder dialog box:

2. Each event will have a name and an argument. Create two events according to Table 15.6. Enter the event's name in the Name text box, enter the argument's name in the Arguments text box, and then click the Plus button.

TABLE 15.6: Events for the Authors Class

Event Name	Argument Name	Data Type	By Val
Action	Status	Integer	Yes
Errors	ErrMessages	Object	No

Now that we have created all the properties, events, and methods, select the All tab to see a list of all these items. Choose File ➤Exit and answer Yes to the confirmation message box to close the Class Builder Utility and update the project.

In the next sections, we will discuss the TierTwo application flow and examine some of the code modules.

Writing the Code for TierTwo

As we discussed earlier in this chapter, the business services, or second tier, in a three-tiered application does not include a user interface. It is composed of class modules. In the previous sections, we used the Class Builder Utility to give us a headstart on writing the code. In this section, we will examine the major code sections created by the utility.

When we created the properties, events, and methods with the Class Builder Utility, Visual Basic 5 used our entries to generate code for those sections. A Get and Let property was created for each property. Code 15.8 shows the Property Get subroutine for the Address property.

Code 15.8:   The Address Property Get Subroutine

```
Public Property Get Address() As String
'Used when retrieving value of a property,
'on the right side of an assignment.
'Syntax: Debug.Print X.Address
    Address = mvarAddress
End Property
```

In addition to the property Get and Let code, the Class Builder Utility generated an empty procedure for the Add, Delete, Save, and Update methods. It is up to you to add code to these procedures. We added the following code for the Add method.

Code 15.9:   The Class Builder Utility Add Method Code

```
Public Sub Add(ByVal Status As Integer)

End Sub
```

As you can see, this is just the beginning of a procedure and has the name and event arguments that you defined.

The last code that the Class Builder Utility adds is for the Action and Errors events that you defined. The code in Code 15.10 has been added to the General Declarations section of the Authors class module.

Code 15.10:   Code Added for Events

```
'To fire this event, use RaiseEvent
'with the following syntax:
'RaiseEvent Action[(arg1, arg2, ... , argn)]
Public Event Action(ByVal Status As Integer)
'To fire this event, use RaiseEvent
'with the following syntax:
'RaiseEvent rdoe[(arg1, arg2, ... , argn)]
Public Event Errors(ErrMessages As Object)
```

This code defines the events that can be raised for the calling application, or, in our example, the TierOne application.

In the next section, we will add code to each of the methods to make them actually perform a function for us.

Coding the Methods

At this point, the methods that we have defined are just empty procedures. We need to add code to each one for it to actually perform a database function.

Adding Code to the Add Method

In our application, the Add method adds a new record to the Authors table in the Pubs database. The following subroutine clears the rdoError object to ensure that we do not get an error message left over from a previous action. Next, an INSERT SQL statement is constructed that inserts a new record in the Authors table based on the value from the text boxes on the TierOne application Form. The values are retrieved by the Property Get procedures in the TierTwo application. After the SQL Statement is constructed, it is executed with the EXECUTE statement.

If an error occurs, the Errors event is raised in the TierOne application. If no errors are encountered, the Action event is raised to notify the user that the record was added.

NOTE   See Code 15.3 earlier in this chapter for an explanation of the Action event, and see Code 15.4 for an explanation of the Errors event.

Code 15.11:   Adding a New Record

```
Public Sub Add()
    On Error Resume Next

    'Declare variables
    Dim ssql As String
    Dim er As Object

    'Clear rdo errors
    rdo.rdoEngine.rdoErrors.Clear

    'Construct SQL statement
    ssql = "INSERT INTO Authors(au_id,au_lname," _
        & "au_fname,phone,address,city,state,zip,contract)" _
    & "VALUES ('" _
    & AuthorID & "','" _
    & LastName & "','" _
    & FirstName & "','" _
    & Phone & "','" _
    & Address & "','" _
    & City & "','" _
    & State & "','" _
```

```
        & Zip & "'," _
        & Contract & ")"
        rdoConn.Execute ssql

        'Check for errors
        If rdo.rdoEngine.rdoErrors.Count > 0 Then
            'An error has occurred
            'Pass the rdoErrors to the calling application
          . RaiseEvent Errors(rdoErrors)
        Else
            'No error
            RaiseEvent Action(300)
        End If

    End Sub
```

Notice the On Error Resume Next statement. We included this because we want the errors to be raised in the Error event of the calling program.

Adding Code to the Delete Method

The Delete method deletes a record from the Authors table in the Pubs database. In the Delete subroutine, the rdoError object is cleared to ensure that we do not get an error message left over from a previous action. Next, a DELETE SQL statement is constructed and executed that attempts to delete the current record from the Authors table based on the value from the AuthorID text box on the TierOne applications Form. The value is retrieved with the Property Get AuthorID procedure in the TierTwo application.

If an error occurs during the delete attempt, the Errors event is raised in the TierOne application. In addition to checking for errors, the RowsAffected property of the rdoObject is checked to see if a row was actually deleted. If the RowsAffected value is greater that zero, you know the AuthorID was found and the record was deleted. If not, the Action event is raised with a value of 3. In the Action event in the TierOne application, the return value of 3 is interpreted, and a message notifies the user that the record was not found and was not deleted.

Code 15.12:   Deleting a Record

```
    Public Sub Delete()
        On Error Resume Next
         'Declare variables
        Dim ssql As String
```

```
'Clear rdo errors
rdo.rdoEngine.rdoErrors.Clear

'Build the SQL statement
ssql = "DELETE FROM Authors " _
& "WHERE au_id = '" & AuthorID & "' "

'Execute the Delete
rdoConn.Execute ssql

'Check for errors
If rdo.rdoEngine.rdoErrors.Count > 0 Then
    'An error has occurred
    'Pass the rdoErrors to the calling application
    RaiseEvent Errors(rdoErrors)
Else
    If rdoConn.RowsAffected > 0 Then
        'No error
        'Clear the values
        AuthorID = ""
        LastName = ""
        FirstName = ""
        Phone = ""
        Address = ""
        City = ""
        State = ""
        Zip = ""
        Contract = ""
        RaiseEvent Action(100)
    Else
        'There were no errors but,
        'no row was deleted
        'The record was not found
        RaiseEvent Action(3)
    End If
End If
End Sub
```

Adding Code to the Search Method

The Search method locates a record from the Authors table in the Pubs database by searching for the AuthorID. In the Search subroutine, the rdoError object is cleared to ensure that we do not get an error message left over from a previous action. Next, a SELECT SQL statement is constructed, and an rdoResultSet is created with the results of the search of the Authors table based on the value from the Author text boxes on the TierOne application Form. The value is retrieved with the Property Get AuthorID procedures in the TierTwo application.

If an error occurs during the creation of the rdoResultSet, the Errors event is raised in the TierOne application. In addition to checking for errors, the EOF, or End of File, property of the rdoObject is checked to see if a row was actually returned. If the EOF property is True, you know the AuthorID was not found because the recordset is at the end of file; the Action event is passed back with a value of 2, signifying that no record was found. If the rdoResultSet is not at EOF, the class properties are filled with the values from the current rdoResultSet record and the Action event is raised with a value of 200, signifying that the record was found.

Code 15.13:   Searching for a Record

```
Public Sub Search()
    On Error Resume Next
    'Declare variables
    Dim ssql As String
    Dim rdoRs As rdoResultset

    'Clear rdo errors
    rdo.rdoEngine.rdoErrors.Clear

    'Build SQL statement
    ssql = "SELECT * FROM Authors " _
    & "WHERE au_id = '" & AuthorID & "' "

    Set rdoRs = rdoConn.OpenResultset(ssql)

    'Check for errors
    If rdo.rdoEngine.rdoErrors.Count > 0 Then
        'An error has occurred
        'Pass the rdoErrors to the calling application
        RaiseEvent Errors(rdoErrors)
    ElseIf rdoRs.EOF = True Then
        'Record not found
        RaiseEvent Action(2)
```

```
       Else
           'No errors
           'Clear all except ID
           LastName = ""
           FirstName = ""
           Phone = ""
           Address = ""
           City = ""
           State = ""
           Zip = ""

           'Fill results
           LastName = rdoRs![au_lname]
           FirstName = rdoRs![au_fname]
           Phone = rdoRs![Phone].Value
           Address = rdoRs![Address]
           City = rdoRs![City]
           State = rdoRs![State]
           Zip = rdoRs![Zip]
           Contract = rdoRs![Contract]
           RaiseEvent Action(200)
       End If
  End Sub
```

Adding Code to the Update Method

The Update method changes a record in the Authors table. In the Update subroutine, the rdoError object is cleared to ensure that we do not get an error message left over from a previous action. Next, an UPDATE SQL statement is constructed and executed; it attempts to update the current record in the Authors table based on the values from the text boxes on the TierOne application Form.

If an error occurs during the update process, the Errors event is raised in the TierOne application. In addition to checking for errors, the RowsAffected property of the rdoObject is checked to see if a row was actually updated. If the RowsAffected value is greater that zero, you know the AuthorID was found and the record was updated. If not, the Action event is raised with a value of 4. In the Action event in the TierOne application, the return value of 4 is interpreted, and a message notifies the user that the record was not found and was not updated.

Code 15.14:   Updating a Record

```
Public Sub Update()
    On Error Resume Next
    'Declare variables
    Dim ssql As String

    'Clear rdo errors
    rdo.rdoEngine.rdoErrors.Clear

    'Build the SQL statement
    ssql = "UPDATE Authors SET " _
    & "au_lname = '" & LastName & " '," _
    & "au_fname = '" & FirstName & " '," _
    & "phone = '" & Phone & "'," _
    & "address = '" & Address & "'," _
    & "city = '" & City & "'," _
    & "state = '" & State & "'," _
    & "Zip = '" & Zip & "'," _
    & "contract = " & Contract & "" _
    & "WHERE au_id = '" & AuthorID & "' "

    rdoConn.Execute ssql

    'Check for errors
    If rdo.rdoEngine.rdoErrors.Count > 0 Then
        'An error has occurred
        'Pass the rdoErrors to the calling application
        RaiseEvent Errors(rdoErrors)
    Else
        If rdoConn.RowsAffected > 0 Then
            'No errors
            RaiseEvent Action(400)
        Else
            'Record was not found
            RaiseEvent Action(4)
        End If
    End If
End Sub
```

The Update code is similar to the Add and Delete code. Now that we have analyzed the program flow and discussed the major code, it's time to test the Three-Tiered application.

Testing the Applications

As we have already discussed, the TierTwo application is a DLL that must be referenced in the TierOne application.

Follow these steps to test the applications:

1. Start Visual Basic and open the TierTwo application.

2. Press F5 to run the TierTwo code.

3. Start another instance of Visual Basic, and open the TierOne application.

4. Choose Project ➤ References to open the References dialog box and check the TierTwo reference. This makes the TierTwo class available to the TierOne application.

5. Press F5 to run the TierOne application:

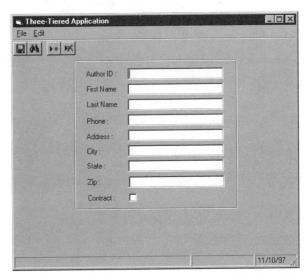

6. In the Author ID field, enter **172-32-1176,** and click the Find button to retrieve the first author's record.

7. Change the Last Name field to Johnston, and click the Save button. The record is saved, and the status bar shows Record Saved.

8. Change the Author ID field to **172-32-5555,** change the data in some of the other fields, and click the New Record button to add this as a new record.

9. With the record 172-32-5555 displayed from step 8, click the Delete Record button to delete this new record.

Now that we have tested the applications, let's look at how to compile the TierTwo application into a DLL.

Creating the TierTwo DLL

In the previous sections, we have been working with the TierTwo application in the Visual Basic design environment. To compile the application into a DLL, follow these steps:

1. Choose File ➤ Make TierTwo.dll to open the Make Project dialog box.

2. Click OK to compile the application and create the TierTwo.dll file.

PART IV

Programming for the Web

CHAPTER
SIXTEEN

Web Development Basics

- ■ Understanding the Web client/server model

- ■ Using Forms and controls

- ■ Embedding a script

- ■ Passing parameters to the server

- ■ Developing a Web page

ook discusses how to use Visual Basic on the Web. You can
edge to the Web in many ways. For example, you can create
eploy them on the Internet. You know how to design ActiveX
sily place them on a Web page. You can also turn your VB
documents and deploy them on the Web as well. Visual
ctiveX Document Migration Wizard that will do the conver-
ese technologies, however, are not yet mature, and they are not the
utter of Web developers and authors.

Only a small percentage of sites are using ActiveX controls, and ActiveX
Documents are simply not used on the Web. (Some intranets must make use of
ActiveX Documents, but they still can't be considered mainstream technology.)
One technology, however, has matured and is used on many Web sites: Active
Server Pages (ASP). Corporations are interested in flashy sites, but their primary
concern is to get their databases on the Web so that visitors can search their data-
bases and so that they can collect data (orders, whenever possible) from visitors.
Corporations aren't interested in putting together a game in Dynamic HTML;
they need applications that will allow visitors to interact with their sites. And this
is exactly what Active Server Pages are all about.

Using ASP, VB programmers can apply their knowledge in a profitable area of
the Web. ASP may not be the most interesting of all the technologies developed
by Microsoft to activate the Web, but it is surely the most practical. That's why
we'll focus on ASP and show you how to publish databases on the Web and how
to design pages that let visitors interact with a Web server.

Another reason for including Active Server Pages in this book is that the Web is
another implementation of the client/server architecture that you are so familiar
with by now. As far as database programming and client/server architectures are
concerned, you are ready to develop Web applications. The language you'll be
using is VBScript, a subset of Visual Basic. As you will see, Active Server Pages
use the ActiveX Data Objects to contact databases on the server, and they also rely
on objects.

We'll cover ASP in detail in the following chapter. In this chapter, we'll deal
with the prerequisites:

- How clients and servers interact

- The role of VBScript in building active Web pages

- The role of the server that makes this interaction possible

ASP is a component that runs on the server, and, in order to develop Active Server Pages, you must understand the role of the Web server, as well as how clients interact with the server. If you are familiar with this topic, you can jump to the next chapter. If you have only used the Web as a resource to retrieve information, you need the information in this chapter.

Clients and Servers on the Web

The computers that make up the World Wide Web can be classified in two categories:

- Clients
- Servers

The *clients* (the machines that run a browser such as Internet Explorer) request information. The *servers* (the machines that run a Web server such as the Internet Information Server) provide the requested information. The role of the Web server is to supply the documents requested by the client. This is an easy task, and setting up a Web server is straightforward. Today's Web servers, however, do a lot more than simply supply HTML documents. They process requests made by the clients, handle security, and more. To understand what the Web server does and to understand how to develop applications that interact with the server, let's start by examining what goes on between a client and a server on the Web.

When a client requests a document, it sends a URL (Universal Resource Locator) to the server. A URL is a unique address for every entity on the Web. Each server has a unique URL, and each document on the server has a unique URL. The Web server looks at the URL to determine the desired response for any given request. A Web server can process requests for:

- Ordinary Web pages (HTML documents)
- Common Gateway Interface (CGI) applications
- Active Server Pages (ASP)

Web pages are HTML documents that the browser renders on the screen as they arrive. These documents live on the server, and the server supplies them whenever a client requests them. CGI applications and scripts are applications that run on the server, and they produce HTML pages on the fly. CGI applications are used mostly on Unix machines (and most Web servers run on Unix machines), and they look a lot like C programs. Active Server Pages are simpler. They look a lot like HTML pages, and they contain VBScript code.

The URL is the string displayed in the browser's Address box every time you click a hyperlink (or the string you enter in the Address box to connect to a server). It looks like this:

```
http://www.servername.com/website/home.htm
```

A URL contains the following:

- Protocol (http://)

- Domain name (www.servername.com)

- Path (/website/home.htm) to the desired document

Within the path, rather than specifying a static HTML page as shown here, you can enter the file name of a script to run. In doing so, the server will commence the operation requested, if possible. If the server cannot fulfill the request properly, it will return an error message or the static contents of the file. In any case, the Web server returns the result of some local processing as an HTML document. Not all servers can process all types of requests mentioned here, but Microsoft's Web servers (Internet Information Server and the Personal Web Server) can do so.

A URL that requests an application on the Web server looks like this:

```
http://www.servername.com/website/register.asp?UserName=Evangelos&Email
=EP@Sybex.com
```

This URL contains the name of an application to run on the server (instead of an HTML document), followed by some parameters. The ASP file needs these parameters. The application on the server will process these values, and the results (for example, a confirmation message indicating that the user has been successfully registered or a report based on a database search) will be sent back to the client.

Sending information to the server is simple. The browser sends a string that looks like the URL of a document. For all the browser knows, it is requesting an HTML document. The server receives the request, sees that the client is contacting an application, and starts the application. At the same time, it passes the string with the parameters to the application. The application on the server processes the parameters, creates an output in HTML format, and submits it to the client. The client sees another HTML document and renders it on the screen.

How about HTML?

To develop Web sites, whether you're interested in working with the server or the client, you must learn HTML, which is a simple document formatting language. As a VB programmer, you can do so in less than a day with a good book.

NOTE   You might want to start with *Mastering HTML,* by Deborah S. Ray and Eric J. Ray, available from Sybex. Some excellent tutorials and reference material are available at the Microsoft Web site (www.microsoft.com). If you are going to do any work with HTML, you should also visit Microsoft's workshop site at www.microsoft.com/workshop/default.asp, a Web site dedicated to Web authors and developers and loaded with information and authoring tools.

We're including here the shortest introduction to HTML you'll probably ever find. This quick reference will give you the information you need to continue working through this chapter. It's not meant to explain HTML, but to convince you that not knowing HTML shouldn't keep you from getting involved with the Web and starting to develop Web pages immediately.

HTML is a lot like the RTF (Rich Text Format) language. An HTML document consists of text, which is displayed on the client as is, and formatting tags, which determine the appearance of the text in the browser's window. For example, to display a few words in bold, enclose them in a pair of <B> tags:

```
Some words in this sentence appear <B>in bold type</B>
```

The string "in bold type" will be displayed in bold. The <I> tags display text in italic, the <U> tags underline text, and so on. You can use the <FONT> tag to specify font attributes, as in the following example:

```
<FONT FACE = "Verdana" SIZE = 8>
```

Other, more complicated tags rearrange the text on the screen. You can use the table-related tags to create really elaborate tables. And you even insert images on a Web page with text tags. To insert an image at the current location on a page, use the <IMG> tag, whose syntax is:

```
<IMG SRC = "Bunny.bmp" ALT="Bunny Image">
```

When the browser sees the <IMG> tag, it contacts the server, requests the specified image file (the Bunny.bmp image happens to be in the same folder as the current document), and then displays it. While the image is being downloaded, the string "Bunny Image" is displayed in its place on the browser.

The tag that makes the Web tick is the <A> tag, which inserts hyperlinks. A hyperlink is a string, usually rendered in blue, that reacts to the mouse pointer. When the mouse pointer is over a hyperlink, it assumes the shape of a hand pointing up. If you click the mouse button on a hyperlink, the browser reads the destination of the hyperlink, contacts the server, and displays the new page. Here's how you would insert a hyperlink to Microsoft's home page in an HTML document:

```
For more information visit the <A
HREF="http://home.microsoft.com">Microsoft Web site</A>
```

The string "Microsoft Web site," which is enclosed in a pair of <A> tags, is displayed as a hyperlink when the document is rendered on the client computer. When the visitor clicks this hyperlink, the browser displays Microsoft's home page.

The most common use of hyperlinks is to take the visitor to another document on the same Web (our Web). The following hyperlinks create a table of contents when displayed:

```
<A HREF="HTMLDoc.htm">HyperText Markup Language</A>
<P>
<A HREF="VBSDoc.htm">Programming with VBScript</A>
<P>
<A HREF="JSDoc.htm">Programming with JavaScript</A>
<P>
```

To complete this speedy introduction to HTML, let's look at the structure of an HTML document. The <HEAD> section of an HTML document contains its title (which appears in the browser's title bar) and the scripts (if any). Next comes the <BODY> section, with the document's contents. If the page contains controls, where the visitor can enter information (such as registration data), they appear in a <FORM> section.

```
<HTML>
<HEAD>
<TITLE>The document's title</TITLE>
<SCRIPT LANGUAGE = VBScript>
Sub Window_OnLoad()
    MsgBox "You are about to enter our brave, active world!"
End Sub
</SCRIPT>
</HEAD>
<BODY>
<H1>The document's header</H1>
Here comes the document's body.
```

```
<P>
It consists of text, but we throw in a few pictures from time to time:
<IMG SRC = "Action1.gif">
<P>
No Web page would be complete without a hyperlink. So, click
<A HREF="http://www.nasa.org">here</A> to view some spectacular space
images.
Have fun with HTML!
</BODY>
</HTML>
```

This is a (not so) minimal HTML document, and with the exception of tables, you've seen all the tags you need in order to build Web pages. Indeed, the examples in the next chapter aren't much more complicated than that. If you can understand that the <TABLE> tag signifies the beginning of a table, that the <TR> tag signifies the beginning of a new row within a table, and that the <TD> tag signifies the beginning of a new cell in a row, you are ready to build tables too.

So don't let your ignorance of a simple language like HTML stop you from applying your hard-earned knowledge of Visual Basic on the Web. Of course, you can build complicated documents with HTML, and we don't want to downplay the importance of the language. But let's face it: HTML is not nearly as difficult as Visual Basic, and you can pick it as you go along.

Activating the Client with VBScript

The Web is by nature a client/server environment. The load is balanced between the server, where the information is stored, and the client, which does the processing. Until recently, processing consisted of rendering a Web page (including its graphics) on the client. With VBScript, you can add small programs to your pages, which are executed on the server. With the introduction of Dynamic HTML (DHTML), scripting languages such as VBScript and JavaScript, and ActiveX controls for the Web, an increasing amount of processing will move from the server to the client.

Web pages are by definition interactive: Each time visitors click a hyperlink, they are taken to another page. But this isn't the type of interaction with which Windows users are familiar. In addition, this type of interaction requires a trip to the server at each step. The Web page can't respond to events, such as the click of a button, because HTML isn't a programming language. It can't display the date or do a simple calculation. The latest trend in Web design is to make pages active.

An *active page* behaves like an application. It has its own user interface, composed of the common Windows elements (Command Buttons, text boxes, and all the new ActiveX controls released for the Web) and interacts with the visitor in a manner similar to a Windows application. An active page doesn't require a trip to the server to display the date or do some calculations.

The embedded application is called a *script*. Scripts are simple programs that are embedded into the HTML page as ASCII text. When the page is downloaded, the script is downloaded with it and is executed by the browser on the client computer. The idea behind active pages is to exploit the computing power of the client computer. With straight HTML, the client computer's task is to render the HTML documents on the screen. But most clients out there are powerful PCs, and they could do much more than simply display Web pages. Active pages can exploit the available computing power by passing much of the processing that would otherwise take place on the server to the client.

In the following sections, we are going to look at the differences between Visual Basic and VBScript, at the limitations of VBScript, and at a few features that are unique to VBScript 2. VBScript is a lightweight version of Visual Basic, but before you start developing scripts, you must understand the design philosophy of VBScript. The design environment is also quite different. VBScript doesn't come with an integrated editor. To insert a script on a page, you must edit the HTML file and insert the appropriate code. Once you learn the structure of a script and how it interacts with the rest of the document, you'll be ready to script your Web pages. You'll also be ready to design documents with Dynamic HTML, which relies on VBScript for the manipulation of its elements in real time.

VBScript and Windows 98

VBScript was designed to activate HTML pages, but it's not limited to the Web. Most of you probably remember the batch language that you could use to automate many tasks through BAT files. Windows 98 will be the first version of Windows to support a scripting language, and this language will be VBScript.

If you learn how to use VBScript on the Web, you will soon be ready to program the Windows 98 interface. After activating the Web, Microsoft is about to activate the Desktop, and the tool that does it is based on your favorite language.

VBScript Variables

To begin with, VBScript is a typeless language. All variables are treated as Variants, and VBScript converts them to the proper type before using them. You can declare variables before you use them, but not their type. For example, to declare the *UserName* variable, use the following statement:

```
Dim UserName
```

The language supports the usual data conversion functions, which you must use to call methods that expect their arguments to be of a specific type. You'll never have to convert argument types when calling VBScript procedures, which can only accept Variant arguments. However, if an ActiveX component provides a method that expects a double number as its argument, you must convert the value you pass to the method to a double value with the CDbl() function.

VBScript supports the VarType() function, which returns information about how your data is currently stored in a Variant data type. The VarType() function returns an integer that represents the type of its argument. The TypeName() function returns the actual name of a variable's type. You can also check for a specific data type by using the Is functions:

IsArray()

IsDate()

IsEmpty()

IsError()

IsNull()

IsNumeric()

IsObject()

VBScript variables declared in the procedures are local to these procedures. Variables declared outside procedures are global and are visible from within any procedure on the page. Since VBScript treats all variables as Variants, the only benefit of declaring variables is to write clean code and simplify debugging.

The variables declared in a procedure are local, and they have a limited scope. Only the function (or subroutine) in which they were declared can access them. They have a limited lifetime too. They exist only for as long as the procedure's code is executed. When the procedure exits, the local variables cease to exist. If the same procedure is called again, a new set of local variables is created and initialized. To make a local variable maintain its value between calls, declare it with the Static keyword. Static variables have a limited scope (they are local to the procedure), but the lifetime of a global variable. In other words, they maintain their values as long as the page with the script is active, but they can be accessed from within a specific procedure only. You can also make a variable global by declaring it with the Dim statement (and no type) outside any procedure.

VBScript Arrays and Dictionaries

VBScript supports arrays too, as well as a structure called *Dictionary*, which is equivalent to the Visual Basic collection. An array is declared with a Dim statement, without a type. The following statements declared two arrays:

```
Dim Days(7)
Dim Months(12)
```

VBScript arrays are zero based, and they may have multiple dimensions. For example, the array Temperatures, which holds the temperatures in various cities, can be declared as:

```
Dim Temperatures(1,99)
```

This array has enough elements to hold 100 city names and their temperatures. Since arrays are not typed, you can store any type of data in an array's elements.

Dictionaries are objects that can store index information, just like Visual Basic collections. The difference between an array and a Dictionary object is that in the array you use an index value to access the array's elements; in a Dictionary object, you use a key.

Back to our Temperature array. To read the temperature in a given city, you must know the city's index to the array and request the corresponding element. If New York's index in the array is 23, the temperature in New York city is Temperatures(23,1), and the name of the city is Temperatures(32,0).

If Temperatures were a Dictionary object, you would access the desired temperature by the name of the corresponding city, as in Temperatures("New York"). To use a Dictionary object in your code, you must first create an object variable with the CreateObject() function:

```
Dim Temperatures
Set Temperatures = CreateObject("Scripting.Dictionary")
```

In this case, *Temperatures* is an object variable, not an array. The *Temperatures* variable holds items, which can be any type (numeric or string). Each item is associated with a unique key that is used to retrieve an individual item and is usually an integer or a string, but can be anything.

To populate a *Dictionary* variable, use the Add method, which accepts two arguments: a value and a key. The following statements add cities and temperatures to the Temperatures Dictionary:

```
Temperatures.Add "New York", 82
Temperatures.Add "Atlanta", 79
Temperatures.Add "Houston", 73
```

If you attempt to add a pair with a key that exists already, an error will occur. You can either insert the appropriate error-trapping code or use the Exists method. The Exists method accepts as an argument a key and returns True if the key exists in the Dictionary; otherwise, it returns False. Call the Exists method every time you want to add a new pair to the Dictionary, to avoid multiple instances of the same value:

```
If Not Temperatures.Exists("Atlanta") Then
    Temperatures.Add "Atlanta", 79
End If
```

You can also remove items from the Dictionary with the Remove method, which accepts a key as an argument and removes the corresponding pair from the Dictionary. To remove the entry that corresponds to the temperature in Atlanta, use statements such as the following:

```
If Temperatures.Exists("Atlanta") Then
    Temperatures.Remove "Atlanta"
End If
```

You can also clear the entire Dictionary by removing all the pairs with the RemoveAll method, whose syntax is:

```
Temperatures.RemoveAll
```

These are the methods that let you set up Dictionaries and assign data to them. To retrieve a value stored in a Dictionary object, use the name of the *Dictionary* variable and pass to it the key as an argument. The temperature in Houston is:

```
Temperatures("Houston")
```

By default, keys are case-sensitive, and the keys "HOUSTON" or "houston" won't locate the desired item in the Dictionary. To change this behavior, use the

CompareMode property, which sets (or returns) the comparison mode for comparing string keys in a Dictionary object. Its syntax is:

```
Temperatures.CompareMode = 0
```

This property's value can be 0 (for binary, or case-sensitive, comparisons) or 1 (for text, or case-insensitive, comparisons).

To access the items and their keys in the Dictionary object, you must use the Items and Keys methods. The Items method returns an array containing all the items in a Dictionary object. Likewise, the Keys method returns an array containing all the keys in a Dictionary object. To access the elements of these two arrays, declare a new variable, and then assign the result of the corresponding method to the variable. The following lines demonstrate how to access the keys and their items:

```
Dim DItems, DKeys
{statements to assign values to the collection Temperatures}
DItems = Temperatures.Items
DKeys = Temperatures.Keys
For i = 0 To Temperatures.Count - 1
    Document.write DKeys(i) & " " &  DItems(i) & "<P>"
Next
```

This code segment displays the list of cities and their temperatures in the two columns of a table. The table is created on the fly with Document.write statements, which place strings directly on the current document.

In addition to the Items and Keys methods, which let you examine the items in a Dictionary object, you can use the Item and Key properties to manipulate the Dictionary's items. The Item property sets (or returns) an item for a specified key in a Dictionary object. To change the temperature of a city in the Dictionary object of the example, use a statement such as the following:

```
Dictionary.Item("Houston") = 84
```

You can also change the key of a given item with the Key property, although this isn't common practice. If users are looking up the temperature in Los Angeles using the key "LA," you can change the key of this item with a statement such as the following:

```
Dictionary.Key("Los Angeles") = "LA"
```

Finally, the Count property of the Dictionary object returns the number of items stored in it. To scan all the items in a Dictionary object, set up a For … Next loop that goes from zero to the value of the Count property minus 1.

VBScript Procedures

Like Visual Basic, VBScript supports two kinds of procedures:

- Subroutines
- Functions

Event handlers are implemented as subroutines, and their names are made up of the name of the control and the name of the event they handle, separated by an underscore character.

A subroutine is a block of VBScript statements, enclosed by the Sub and End Sub statements, that perform a specific action but don't return a value. To call a subroutine procedure from within another, type the name of the subroutine along with values for its arguments, separated by a comma. The Call statement is not required, but if you do use it, you must enclose any arguments in parentheses.

Functions are similar to subroutines, but they return a value. Functions consist of a block of VBScript statements enclosed by the Function and End Function statements. If a function doesn't require any argument, its Function statement must include an empty set of parentheses. The return type of a Function procedure is always a Variant data type.

Like Visual Basic, VBScript procedures accept arguments by value or by reference. The default is by reference, which means that the procedure accepts the actual argument (an address in memory where the argument is stored). Any changes to the arguments made by the procedure are permanent. If you want to pass an argument by value so that the procedure can't change its value, use the ByVal keyword.

And also like Visual Basic, event handlers in VBScript are implemented as subroutines. Any element on a Web page that has a name can recognize the usual mouse events. To implement a handler for an event, write a subroutine whose name consists of the element's name, the underscore character, and the name of the event.

VBScript Input/Output Functions

VBScript is limited when it comes to input and output functions. It supports the InputBox and MsgBox functions of Visual Basic, but your best bet is to avoid using them. This is not the way to build a user interface in the Windows environment. In

Visual Basic, we use controls on Forms to design elaborate user interfaces. HTML pages can also contain Forms with controls, only VBScript doesn't support as many controls.

NOTE   We are going to discuss VBScript's Forms and controls in the section "Forms and Controls."

VBScript doesn't provide any functions for writing output directly on the screen. You can use VBScript to update the display, but everything must be done within the framework of the current page. All you can do is create HTML code that can affect the current page, but there is no way to access a single pixel outside the client's window.

VBScript has no functions for opening and reading files. The reason is that VBScript is a "safe" language. Web pages that deploy scripts shouldn't be able to access the client system. Otherwise, every page you open with your browser would be a clear and present danger for your computer. To make VBScript safe, its designers had to eliminate many of the features of Visual Basic.

Updating the browser's window is usually done through the server. The visitor supplies information or simply clicks a hyperlink. The browser contacts the server, which supplies another Web page. It's quite simple, and it works very well. With the help of ActiveX controls, you can build elaborate user interfaces, but this requires that your visitors upload the ActiveX controls, which aren't safe.

By and large, visitors are reluctant to download and install new components on their computers from every Web site they visit. Eventually, the most commonly used and most useful ActiveX controls will be distributed with Internet Explorer, and Web developers will be able to use them. This, in turn, will make their pages dependent on Internet Explorer. The techniques we discuss in this book don't rely on specific ActiveX controls, and they apply to all browsers.

Web pages contain special sections called Forms on which you can place controls such as Command Buttons, CheckBoxes, and so on. These controls accept user input, and you can program them, just as you can program Visual Basic controls. But there is a major difference between scripts and Visual Basic applications. Visual Basic applications have Forms, and Forms can communicate via Public variables, but Web pages can't communicate.

You will find more information on passing information among the scripts of the various pages that make up a Web site in the next chapter in the section on cookies. In the following section, we are going to discuss how to create Web pages with Forms that can interact with the user.

Forms and Controls

As you know already, HTML pages contain controls that let the user enter information, similar to the usual Windows controls: text boxes, option buttons, and so on. The areas on the HTML page where these controls appear are called Forms, and the controls themselves are called *intrinsic controls*. HTML provides special tags for placing intrinsic controls on a Form.

NOTE   In addition to intrinsic controls, you can place ActiveX controls on your Forms. Because ActiveX controls must be downloaded to the client, and many visitors don't allow the installation of ActiveX controls on their systems, we are not going to discuss them.

Before placing a control on the page, you must create a Form, with the <FORM> tag. Its syntax is:

```
<FORM NAME=name ACTION=action METHOD=method>
</FORM>
```

All the controls must appear between these two tags. The NAME attribute (it's optional) is the name of the Form and is used when a page contains multiple Forms. The ACTION attribute is the name of an application on the server that will be called to process the information. The METHOD attribute specifies how the controls' values will be transmitted to the server. All the information needed by the browser to contact an application on the server is contained in the <FORM> tag. But more on this later, in the section "Passing Parameters to the Server."

HTML provides support for the following intrinsic controls. Figure 16.1 shows a Web page with a Form that contains most in HTML's intrinsic controls. You are going to see the HTML code that produced the page of Figure 16.1 in the section "The FORM.HTM Web Page," later in this chapter.

FIGURE 16.1:

This Form contains all the intrinsic HTML controls.

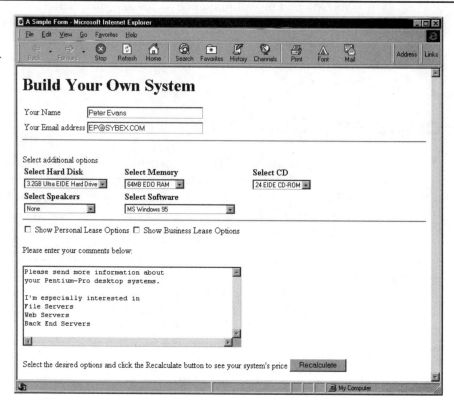

The Text Control

The Text control is a box in which visitors can enter a single line of text (such as name, address, and so on). To insert a Text control on a Form, use the following tag:

```
<INPUT TYPE = TEXT NAME = "Publisher" VALUE = "Sybex">
```

The VALUE attribute specifies the initial value. After the visitor changes this entry, VALUE holds the new string. To edit the contents of a Text control, the visitor can use the common editing keys (Home, Del, Insert, and so on), but the text can't be formatted.

To control the size and contents of the control, use the SIZE and MAXLENGTH attributes. The SIZE attribute specifies the size of the control on the Form, in number of characters, and the MAXLENGTH attribute specifies the maximum number of characters the user can type in the control. A variation of the Text control is the Password control, which is identical, but doesn't display the characters as they are typed. Instead, it displays asterisks, and it is used to enter passwords.

The TextArea Control

The TextArea control is similar to the Text control, but it allows the entry of multiple lines of text. All the usual navigation and editing keys work with the TextArea control. To place a TextArea control on a Form, use the <TEXTAREA> tag:

```
<TEXTAREA NAME = "Comments" ROWS = 10 COLS = 30>
The best editor I've ever used!
</TEXTAREA>
```

Because the TextArea control allows you to specify multiple lines of initial text, it's not inserted with the usual <INPUT> tag, but with a pair of <TEXTAREA> tags. The ROWS and COLS attributes specify the dimensions of the control on the page, in number of characters. Notice that the line breaks you insert between the two <TEXTAREA> tags are preserved when the text is displayed on the control. Even if you include HTML tags in the initial text, they will appear on the control.

The CheckBox Control

The CheckBox control is a little square with an optional checkmark, which acts as a toggle. Every time the visitor clicks it, it changes state. It is used to present a list of options, from which the visitor can select one or more. To insert a CheckBox control on a Form, use the <INPUT> tag:

```
<INPUT TYPE = CHECKBOX NAME = "Check1">
```

To initially check a CheckBox control, specify the CHECKED attribute in the corresponding <INPUT> tag. The control's value can be 0 or 1, indicating whether it's checked (1) or cleared (0).

The RadioButton Control

The RadioButton control is round and contains a dot in the center. RadioButton controls are used to present lists of options, similar to CheckBox controls, but only one of them can be selected at a time. Each time a new option is checked by the visitor, the previously selected one is cleared. To insert a RadioButton control on a Form use the following:

```
<INPUT TYPE = RADIO NAME = "Radio1">
```

Whereas each CheckBox control has a different name, a group of RadioButtons have the same name. This is how the browser knows that a number of RadioButton controls belong to the same group and that only one of them can be checked at a time. To specify the control that will be initially checked in the group, use the CHECKED attribute. The following lines insert a group of four RadioButton controls on a Form:

```
<INPUT TYPE = RADIO NAME = "Level">Beginner <BR>
<INPUT TYPE = RADIO NAME = "Level">Intermediate <BR>
<INPUT TYPE = RADIO NAME = "Level" CHECKED>Advanced<BR>
<INPUT TYPE = RADIO NAME = "Level">Expert <BR>
```

The Multiple Selection Control

The Multiple Selection control is basically a list that can contain a number of options. The visitor can select none, one, or multiple items in the list. The list is delimited with a pair of <SELECT> tags. Each item in the list is inserted with a separate <OPTION> tag. To place a Multiple Selection List on the Form, add the following lines:

```
<SELECT  NAME = "MemoryOptions" SIZE = 3 MULTIPLE = multiple>
<OPTION VALUE=16> 16 Mbytes</OPTION>
<OPTION VALUE=32> 32 Mbytes</OPTION>
<OPTION VALUE=64> 64 Mbytes</OPTION>
<OPTION VALUE=128> 128 Mbytes</OPTION>
<OPTION VALUE=256> 256 Mbytes</OPTION>
</SELECT>
```

The SIZE attribute specifies how many lines will be visible. If you omit it, the list will be reduced to a single line, and the visitor must use the up and down arrow keys to scroll through the available options. If the list contains more lines, a vertical scrollbar is automatically attached to help the visitor locate the desired item. The MULTIPLE attribute specifies that the visitor can select multiple items in the list by clicking on their names while holding down the Shift or Control key. If you omit the MULTIPLE attribute, each time an item is selected, the previously selected one is cleared.

The <OPTION> tag has a VALUE attribute that represents the value of the selected item. If the viewer selects the 64 Mbytes option in the earlier list, the value 64 is transmitted to the server. Finally, to initially select one or more options, specify the SELECTED attribute:

```
<OPTION  SELECTED VALUE=128> 128 Mbytes</OPTION>
```

The Command Button Control

Clicking a Command Button triggers certain actions. Without VBScript, Command Buttons can trigger only two actions:

- Submit the data entered on the controls to the server

- Reset all control values on the Form to their original values

With VBScript, Command Buttons can trigger any actions you can program in your pages.

You can place three types of buttons on a Form:

- Submit

- Reset

- Button

The most important is the Submit button: It transmits the contents of all the controls on the Form to the server. The Reset button resets the values of the other controls on the Form to their initial values. The Reset button doesn't submit any values to the server. Most Forms contain Submit and Reset buttons, which are inserted like this:

```
<INPUT TYPE = SUBMIT VALUE = "Send data">
<INPUT TYPE = RESET VALUE = "Reset Values">
```

The VALUE attribute specifies the string that will appear on the Command Button. The Submit button reads the name of the application that must be contacted on the server (the <FORM> tag's ACTION attribute), appends the values of the controls to this URL, and transmits it to the server.

The third, generic type of button has as its type simply Button and functions similar to the other buttons in the Windows interface. Clicking it triggers an event, which you can use to execute some VBScript code. To insert a generic Button control on your Form, use the <INPUT> tag:

```
<INPUT TYPE = BUTTON NAME = "ShowDate">
```

Every time this button is clicked, it triggers the ShowDate_Click event. Obviously, you must place the code that you want to execute every time this button is clicked in this event's handler:

```
Sub ShowDate_Click()
   MsgBox "The date is " & Date()
End Sub
```

If you're going to validate the data on the client's side, you shouldn't use the Submit button because that would transmit the data to the server as soon as the button is clicked. Instead, you must use the Button control to trigger your data validation routine. After you validate the data, you can submit it with the Submit method.

Here's a typical Command Button script that validates the data entered by the visitor and then submits the Form's contents to an ASP application on the server. The Command Button is a generic one and is placed on the Form with the following:

```
<INPUT TYPE = BUTTON NAME = SendData VALUE = "Register Now">
```

Code 16.1:   The Event Handler for the SendData Button's Click Event

```
<SCRIPT LANGUAGE = VBScript>
Sub SendData_Click()
    If Instr("@", EMail.Value) = 0 Then
        MsgBox "Invalid e-mail address." & chr(13) & _
                "Please enter a string like yourname@yourserver.com"
    Else If RealName.Value = "" Then
        MsgBox "You can't register without a name"
    Else
        RegistrationForm.Submit
End If
End Sub
</SCRIPT>
```

This script is invoked when the SendData button is clicked. First, it checks the contents of the EMail Text control. If the specified address isn't in the form name@server.com, it prompts the user to enter a valid e-mail address. It then checks the value of the RealName Text control. If the user hasn't specified a name, he or she is prompted accordingly. If both tests fail, the script submits the data on the Form (the Form may contain other controls too) with the Submit method. The Form's Submit method is equivalent to the Submit button. They both cause the browser to contact the application specified by the ACTION attribute of the <FORM> tag and pass to it the values of the controls as parameters. For the previous example, the browser will submit a string such as the following:

```
http://www.servername.com/Register.asp?EMail=EP@SYBEX.COM&Name=Evangelos+P
```

EMail and *Name* are the names of the parameters, as expected by the Register.asp application on the server. The values shown could be anything. Notice that strings are not enclosed in quotes, and spaces are replaced by plus signs.

Embedding a Script

The script is contained in the event handlers of the various controls, as well as procedures, just like regular Visual Basic applications.

You place scripts in the HTML file's SCRIPT section, which is delimited with a pair of <SCRIPT> tags. Because there is more than one scripting language, you must also specify the script's language in the <SCRIPT> tag. Here's a typical SCRIPT section:

```
<SCRIPT LANGUAGE = VBScript>
    {your scripting code}
</SCRIPT>
```

When the browser hits the <SCRIPT> tag, it calls the VBScript interpreter to compile and execute the following code. The code is usually placed in event handlers, but you can insert procedures that will be called from within event handlers. If some code appears outside any handler, as shown in the next listing, it is executed as soon as the page is downloaded and before the browser renders the document on the screen. The following script displays the current date as soon as the page that contains it is loaded:

```
<SCRIPT LANGUAGE="VBScript">
    MsgBox "The date is " & Date
</SCRIPT>
```

All intrinsic controls have a Name property (or attribute) that can be used to identify them in the script. Since the intrinsic controls are always placed on a Form, their complete name is the name of the Form, followed by a period and then the name of the control. The Button control, placed on a Form called RegisterForm with the following line:

```
<INPUT TYPE=BUTTON NAME="DateBttn" VALUE="Show Date">
```

can be accessed from within a script with this expression:

```
AppForm.DateBttn
```

For example, you can change the caption of the DateBttn with a statement such as the following:

```
AppForm.DateBttn.Value = "DATE"
```

All intrinsic controls, with the exception of the Select control, have a Value property too. A button's value is its caption, and a Text control's value is the text displayed on the control. The equivalent property of the Select control is the SelectedIndex property, which is the index of the item currently selected. You can manipulate the Value and SelectedIndex properties of the various controls from within your script.

Finally, the most common event in scripting Web pages is the Click event, which is generated when the visitor clicks a control. The Text, TextArea, and Select controls don't recognize this event. The most common event for these controls is the Change event, which takes place when the text in a Text or TextArea control is changed or when the visitor makes a new selection in the Select control.

This is all the information you need to start scripting your Web pages. VBScript is similar to Visual Basic, and we can look at an example next.

Passing Parameters to the Server

For the client to interact with the server, there must be a way for the browser to send information to the server, along with the name of the requested document. We mentioned already that, every time the viewer clicks a hyperlink, the browser sends a URL to the server. The hyperlink is the URL of another document.

To build truly interactive documents, browsers should be able to request not only documents, but invoke applications on the server and pass to the server data entered by the visitor. Indeed, this is how clients interact with the server. Instead of requesting another HTML document, they request an application, which is executed on the Web. Along with the name of the application, they pass visitor-supplied data. The application reads the data, processes them, and passes the results in the form of another HTML page, which is generated on the fly. Figure 16.2 shows a simple Web page (assuming that categories don't change daily) that displays the categories of the products stored in the NWIND database. When the visitor clicks a category name, the products in the selected category are displayed on a new page, shown in Figure 16.3.

FIGURE 16.2:

A Web page displaying product categories. Each category name is a hyperlink that leads to a page, like the one shown in Figure 16.3.

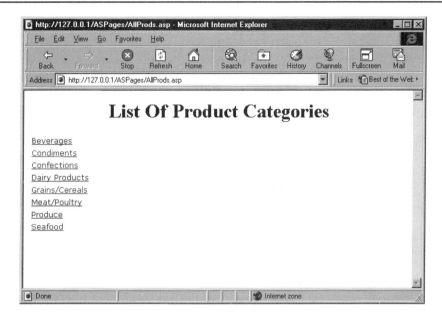

FIGURE 16.3:

The destinations of the hyperlinks on the page in Figure 16.2 display the products of the selected category.

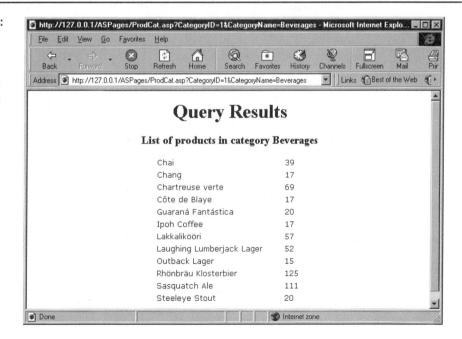

Each category could be a hyperlink, pointing to a different document, but you'd have to build a different HTML document for each category. This wouldn't be too time-consuming if products and prices didn't change frequently. In most cases, however, maintaining a separate document for each product category is more than a Webmaster can handle. If you wanted to display invoices, this approach simply wouldn't work.

Clearly, you should be able to write a program that runs on the server, accepts the category name (or category ID) as an argument, builds a new HTML page with the requested products (as shown in Figure 16.3), and submits it to the client. The HTML page generated by the application on the server exists only while it's being transmitted; it's not saved on the server. The client, on the other hand, has no idea what's happened; it sees another HTML page, which it renders on the screen.

The application that runs on the server is an Active Server Page. The HTML file shown in Figure 16.2 requests the document PRODUCTS.ASP. Along with the name, it passes to the server the value of the parameter CategoryID. The complete URL of the requested document is something like this:

```
http://www.myserver.com/products.asp?CateogryID=32
```

Everything preceding the question mark is the URL of a document. This document is not an HTML page, but the client doesn't care; it will receive an HTML document anyway. The question mark separates the URL of the requested document from the parameters. Parameters have a name and a value, and they are specified as:

```
parametername = parametervalue
```

The *parametername* parameter is the name, and *parametervalue* is the value of the parameter. If you are using a Form to collect information from the visitor, the parameter names are the names of the controls on the Form. Multiple parameters are separated by the ampersand (&) sign, as shown next:

```
http://www.myserver.com?LName=Evans&FName=Peter
```

If a value contains spaces, each space is replaced by the plus sign (+). With a different set of values, the previous URL would be:

```
http://www.myserver.com?LName=von+Kaiser&FName=Richter
```

Many characters have special meaning in HTML and the HTTP protocol, and they can't appear in the parameter string. For example, double quotation marks

(") can't appear in the parameter string following the application's URL. Other illegal characters are the forward slash (/) and the ampersand (&). All special characters (that is, every character that's not a letter or a numeric digit) are replaced with the hexadecimal representation of their ASCII value, prefixed with the percent (%) symbol. The ampersand (&) is encoded as %26, and the percent symbol itself is encoded as %25.

The parameters are encoded by the client, but you must be aware of this encoding scheme if you choose to create the URL from within a script. In some cases, you must also be able to decode the parameter string on the server, from within your application, by replacing the hexadecimal codes with the symbols they represent.

How does the client create the parameter string and append it to the URL of the application? When you include a Form in a Web page, you must supply the <FORM> tag. The <FORM> tag requires two parameters (it recognizes more optional parameters):

- ACTION
- METHOD

The ACTION parameter is the name of the application that will process the request. For the purposes of this book, this application is an Active Server Page (a file with the extension ASP). The METHOD parameter indicates the type of form-handling protocol that will be used to pass the parameters to the application, and it can have one of the values GET and POST. The application that receives the information usually dictates the method. Active Server Pages recognize both methods, but handle them differently. The simpler method is the GET method, and we are going to use it in our examples.

The browser, therefore, picks up the URL of the application from the <FORM> tag and appends the parameter/value pairs to it. Each pair corresponds to a control on the Form: The control's name is the parameter name, and the control's value is the parameter value. The whole thing is done automatically, and you don't have to provide any client scripts. And when does the browser submit the request to the server? When the Submit button is clicked. The Submit button's role on a Form is to submit the visitor-supplied values to the server.

The FORM.HTM Web Page

At this point, we can look at an example of a Web page with a Form that lets the visitor enter information, which is then submitted to the server. The FORM.HTM page is shown in Figure 16.4, and it contains many of the controls we discussed in the previous sections.

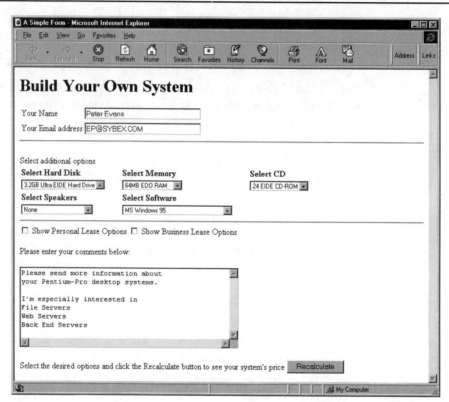

The HTML code of the page is straightforward, and you will be able to understand it even if you don't know HTML. The <TABLE> tag inserts a table at the current location in the HTML document and is used frequently to align controls (which explains why we used it in this document; the table isn't an essential feature of the page, but it wouldn't look nearly as good without it).

Code 16.2:   The FORM.HTM Page

```html
<HTML>
<TITLE>A Simple Form</TITLE>
<H1>Build Your Own System</H1>
<FORM name=ORDER method="POST"
action="http://127.0.0.1/aspages/param.asp">
<TABLE>
<TR><TD>Your Name</TD> <TD><INPUT TYPE=TEXT SIZE=30 MAXSIZE=30
NAME="Name"></TR>
<TR><TD>Your Email address</TD> <TD><INPUT TYPE=TEXT SIZE=30 MAXSIZE=30
NAME="EMail"></TR>
</TABLE>
<HR>
<P>
Select additional options
<TABLE>
<TR><TD><B>Select Hard Disk</B></TD>
<TD></TD>
<TD><B>Select Memory</B></TD>
<TD></TD>
<TD><B>Select CD</B></TD></TR>
<TR><TD><SELECT name="HardDisk" size="1">
<OPTION selected value="3.2G">3.2GB Ultra EIDE Hard Drive </OPTION>
<OPTION  value="4.3G">4.3GB Ultra EIDE Hard Drive </OPTION>
</SELECT>
</TD>
<TD>
      
</TD>
<TD>
<SELECT name="Memory" size="1">
<OPTION  value="32">32 MB EDO RAM</OPTION>
<OPTION selected value="64 MB">64MB EDO RAM</OPTION>
<OPTION  value="128">128 MB EDO RAM</OPTION>
<OPTION  value="256">256 MB EDO RAM</OPTION>
</SELECT>
</TD>
<TD>
      
</TD>
<TD>
<SELECT name="CD" size="1">
```

881

```
<option  value="">None</option>
<option selected value="CD12">12 EIDE CD-ROM</option>
<option selected value="CD24">24 EIDE CD-ROM</option>
</SELECT>
</TD>
</TR>
<TR>
<TD><B>Select Speakers</B></TD>
<TD></TD>
<TD><B>Select Software</B></TD>
<TD></TD>
</TR>
<TR>
<TD>
<SELECT name="Speaker" size="1">
<option selected value="">None</option>
<option value="S90">Altec ACS90 Speakers</option>
<option value="S290">Altec ACS290 Speakers</option>
</SELECT>
</TD>
<TD></TD>
<TD>
<SELECT name="Software" size="1">
<option selected value="WIN95">MS Windows 95</option>
<option value="WIN98">Microsoft Windows 98</option>
<option value="WINNT">Microsoft Windows NT Workstation 4.0 </option>
</SELECT>
</TD>
</TABLE>
<HR>
<INPUT TYPE=CHECKBOX VALUE=1> Show Personal Lease Options
<INPUT TYPE=CHECKBOX VALUE=2> Show Business Lease Options
<P>
Please enter your comments below:
<P>
<TEXTAREA NAME=Comments ROWS=8 COLS=50>
Please send more information about
your Pentium-Pro desktop systems.

I'm especially interested in
File Servers
Web Servers
Back End Servers
</TEXTAREA>
```

```
<P>
Select the desired options and click the Recalculate button to see your
system's price
<INPUT TYPE=SUBMIT VALUE="Recalculate">
</FORM>
</HTML>
```

Let's take a look at the parameters passed to the server by the FORM.HTM page. For the data shown in Figure 16.4, this is the URL prepared by the browser when the Command Button at the bottom of the Form is clicked:

```
http://127.0.0.1/aspages/param.asp?Name=Peter+Evans&EMail=EP@SYBEX.COM&
HardDisk=3.2G&Memory=64+MB&CD=CD24&Speaker=&Software=WIN95&Comments=
Please+send+more+information+about+your+Pentium-Pro+desktop+systems.
I'm+especially+interested+in+
File+Servers
Web+Servers
Back+End+Server
```

This is a lengthy string, but it isn't going to introduce any problems. The Web server will extract the values of the control, and you'll be able to access them through your Active Server Page as if they were variables. We'll discuss this topic in the next chapter.

The URL of the ASP application on the server (http://127.0.0.1/aspages/param.asp) is mentioned in the <FORM> tag's ACTION attribute. The names and values of the parameters are extracted from the controls on the Form and are encoded for transmission to the Web server. The PARAM.ASP application, which we'll present in the next chapter, displays the values submitted by the client in another HTML document.

You've seen how the client passes information to the sever. In the next chapter, you will see how an application running on the server processes this information. Between the client and the application that runs on the server is another program that coordinates them. As you probably know, this program is the Web server. The Web server communicates with the clients by receiving their requests, extracting the parameters they pass to the server, sending back HTML documents, and coordinating multiple clients. Without the Web server, your application would have to keep track of the connections and each client's requests, and, in short, it would be difficult to set up a Web site. The Web server is the most important part of the Web, and it's practically transparent to your applications.

Many Web Servers are out there, and most of them run on Unix machines. Microsoft has released two Web servers:

- Internet Information Server (IIS)
- Personal Web Server (PWS)

IIS is the professional Web server and can handle heavy traffic. The PWS is suitable for designing Web sites, as it runs on both Windows 95/98 and Windows NT. However, it supports Active Server Pages, and we are going to use it in the next chapter to demonstrate how to access ASP applications on the server.

The Personal Web Server

We'll end this chapter with a brief overview of the Personal Web Server. Microsoft's Personal Web Server (PWS) is the simplest way of sharing information with other users on an intranet or with the rest of the world on the Internet. PWS is a desktop Web server that simplifies Web site setup and maintenance and supports advanced features such as Active Server Pages (ASP). You can use it to develop and test Web sites and then move them to the Internet Information Server. The Personal Web Server 4 supports a maximum of 10 connections, so it isn't intended for running real Web sites.

To download the most recent version of PWS, go to the following site:

```
www.microsoft.com/msdownload/ntoptionpack/beta3
```

(You can also order PWS on CD. You'll find ordering information at the site.) We wrote this chapter using Beta 3 of Personal Web Server 4, which runs on both Windows 95/98 and Windows NT.

NOTE   Windows 98 may include the Personal Web Server.

Installing the software is practically automatic and takes place as you download nearly 40MB of data. A new icon is placed on the Desktop, which starts the Personal Web Manager application, as shown in Figure 16.5.

FIGURE 16.5:

Use the Personal Web Manager to manage your Web server.

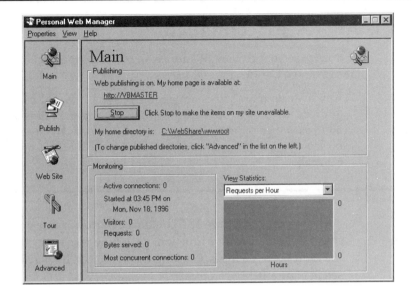

To test the PWS, start Internet Explorer and enter the following URL:

```
127.0.0.1
```

This is the IP address (Internet Protocol address) of the local computer, and it will connect you to the PWS on your own computer. You should see the home page that comes with the PWS. Any visitor who connects to your computer through the active Internet connection will also see this file. You should modify this document accordingly.

IP Addresses

Most computers on the Internet don't have a domain name. If you don't work for a corporation that has its own domain name (for example, www.sybex.com), you can run the WINIPCFG program to find out your current IP address (as well as some other information about your connection). Follow these steps:

1. Choose Start ➢ Run to open the Run dialog box.

2. In the Open text box, type **WINIPCFG** and click OK.

IP Addresses (continued)

You'll see your current IP address in the IP Configuration dialog box. It will be something like 192.210.54.102.

Any user with an active connection to the Internet can contact you at this address. If you disconnect from your ISP, the next time you connect, your IP address will be different. If you are on a network, any user can contact your site by specifying the IP address or the name of the machine on which the Web server is installed.

The window in Figure 16.5 contains a narrow frame on the left, where you can select an administrative function. Each time you select a function, the contents of the right frame changes. Clicking the Main icon displays the Main frame that you see in Figure 16.5.

In the following section, we are going to examine the Main and the Advanced functions of the Personal Web Manager. You can explore the other functions on your own:

- The Publish icon lets you create simple documents and publish them.

- The Web Site icon lets you structure your Web site (determine the documents you want to share with other users).

- The Tour icon is a guided tour of the product.

The Main Window

You start and stop the Web server in the Main window. To make the Web site available to other users, click the Start button. If the server is running and you want to stop sharing the Web site, click the Stop button. In the same frame, you can see the address of the machine on which the Web server is running and the site's home directory (this is where visitors are connected by default if they specify only the Web server's address). Both strings are hyperlinks, and you can click them to see the site's home page.

In the lower half of the Main window, you can monitor the activity of the Web server. You can see the number of visitors currently connected (Active connections), when the server was last started, the total number of visitors, how many requests they've made, and how many bytes have been sent out by the server. You can also view statistics on the usage of the Web site in the graph—by visitors or requests and on an hourly or daily basis.

The Advanced Window

This window, shown in Figure 16.6, contains the most important settings of the site, at least as far as Active Server Pages are concerned. In the upper zone of the window, you can edit the virtual directories. The home directory is your site's home. When users connect to the URL of the server, they are automatically connected to the home directory. If the home directory contains a home page, this page is displayed on the client.

FIGURE 16.6:

The Advanced window of the Personal Web Manager

Virtual Directories

To publish from any directory not contained within your home directory, you must create a virtual directory. A virtual directory is a directory that is not physically contained in the home directory, but that appears to the clients as though it were. You can chose to store your images in a folder that's not even on the same disk as the Web site. Instead of specifying long path names in your Web pages, you can create a virtual name for this folder—let's say you call it Images—and it will appear to be nested under the home directory. You can then reference any image in your Web page as `Images\Planets.bmp,` and the server looks for the `Planets.bmp` file in the physical folder that's mapped to the virtual name `Images.`

Virtual directories have aliases, which not only simplify coding, but add some security. Visitors don't know where your files are physically located on the server and cannot use that information to modify the actual files. Aliases make it easier for you to move directories in your site too. You can move an entire Web to another folder, map the home directory's virtual name to the new folder, and everything will work as before.

To add a new virtual folder, follow these steps:

1. Click the Add button to open the Add Directory dialog box:

2. In the Directory text box, enter the name of the physical folder or click Browse to locate it.

3. In the Alias box, enter a virtual name.

4. In the Access section, set the permissions for the new virtual directory and then click OK:

   - Check Read if you want clients to read documents stored in this folder. If a client requests a document in a virtual directory that doesn't have Read permission, the Web server returns an error message. Virtual directories that contain HTML documents should have their Read permission checked. Directories that contain scripts or executable files should not have Read permission.

   - Check Execute if the folder contains applications that can be executed on the server (ActiveX DLLs, for example).

   - Check Scripts if the folder contains scripts such as ASP applications.

NOTE   Scripts are text files, and you can easily check to see if they are doing anything to the system. Executable files that can be called from scripts aren't easy to control, so you should not trust other users to place executable files in a folder with Execute permission.

Home Directory and Default Documents

When visitors connect to your site by specifying a URL such as www.server.com or an IP address, the Web server connects them to the home directory. The home directory may contain a default document, which is displayed by default. For example, when you connect to the site www.sybex.com, the Web server at the specified location displays the default document in the home directory.

A default document is the document, usually in HTML format, that the server presents to site visitors when they have not specified a file name in the URL. Every home directory has a default document. Visitors can also specify the name of another document in the URL, in which case the Web server supplies the specified document instead of the default document.

Visitors can also specify a virtual directory, without a document name. If the specified directory has a default document, this document is sent to the client. By placing a default page in every virtual directory, you can assure that visitors find a home page on your site, regardless of how they got there. If no document is specified, they can either be allowed to browse the current directory or see an error message indicating that the requested document was not found.

NOTE   Of course, if visitors know the name of an HTML file, they can request it. This technique is used sometimes to allow trusted visitors to connect to a Web site. If the home directory contains the file Secret.htm, only visitors who know the name of the file can connect to the site by specifying the URL www.server.com/Secret.htm.

If you want to use default documents on your site, specify their names in the Default Document(s) text box. PWS supports the use of multiple default document names. When a request without a file name arrives, PWS searches for the first default document name in the directory specified in the URL. If it does not find a document with that name, it checks for the second default document name, and so on. In other words, you can have multiple default names and use a different one in each virtual directory. The simplest approach is to use the same file name for all virtual directories. The Personal Web Manager suggests the names `Default.htm` and `Default.asp` (depending on whether a directory contains HTML documents or ASP applications). The most common names are `Default.htm` and `Index.htm`.

Navigating by Using Directory Browsing

If you disable the Default Document(s) box and enable Allow Directory Browsing, visitors can view a list of all files in the directory specified in their URL. PWS automatically formats the file list in HTML format and transmits it to the client. When a visitor clicks the file name, the content of the document is displayed (assuming the visitor has a program compatible with the file format of the document).

When testing Web pages and ASP applications, consider disabling Default Document(s) and enable Allow Directory Browsing. Each time you create a new document and you want to test it, you won't have to specify its name or rename it to `Default.htm` or whatever the default document name is. With Allow Directory Browsing enabled, visitors can also navigate the subdirectories of the home directory.

Check the Save Web Site Activity Log if you want to log the activity of the Web server. Every new connection and every request for a document is logged by the server in a text file, which you can later open with a text editor.

CHAPTER
SEVENTEEN

Active Server Pages

- Understanding Active Server Pages

- Exploring the objects of Active Server Pages

- Creating an ASP page

- Using ActiveX Data Objects

- Understanding the File Access component

In the last chapter, you saw how a Web server sends information to the client in the form of HTML documents and how the client interacts with the server with hyperlinks. You also saw how to design Web pages that collect information from visitors on the client and submit it to the server along with the URL. When the server receives parameter values from a client, it must process them and return the results to the client in HTML format. In this chapter, we are going to discuss how parameters are processed on the server.

The parameters that a client submits can be anything—registration data, search arguments, customization data, anything. Businesses are interested in the information that is stored in databases and that must be retrieved as needed. To retrieve up-to-the-minute information through a Web server, the client must send back more information than simply the name of a hyperlink. For example, the user on the client might request the sales of a specific product in North Carolina or the most active customers in Texas. This information is encoded in a special format and transmitted to the server. As far as the client is concerned, it thinks it's requesting another URL.

Figure 17.1 shows a typical Web page that prompts the user to enter information, which will be used later to extract information from a database on the server. The site shown in Figure 17.1 is Infoseek, a widely used search engine on the Web. The search argument is "VB +books" (search for documents about VB that also contain the word *books*).

FIGURE 17.1:

The Infoseek site searches the Web for documents that contain user-supplied keywords.

When the Search button is clicked, the client sends the following URL to the server:

```
http://www.infoseek.com/Titles?qt=VB+%2Bbooks&rf=11&lk=noframes&st=10
```

Titles is the name of an application on the server that will search the database and supply the results. It's not an ASP application, but it doesn't make any difference. The same arguments would be supplied if it were an ASP application, and the same document would be returned to the client.

The parameters follow the question mark. The first parameter is qt, and its value is the string "VB+%2Bbooks". The space was replaced with a plus sign, and the plus sign in the original search argument was substituted with %2B (2B is the hexadecimal representation of the plus sign's ASCII value). The parameter lk=noframes tells the application on the server to generate an HTML document without frames, and the parameter st=10 specifies that it should display the second batch of ten matching titles. As you can see in Figure 17.1, the search recalled nearly 50,000 documents, but they can be displayed on the client 10 at a time. Each time you click the Next 10 hyperlink, the value of st is increased by 10 (and each time you click the Previous 10 hyperlink, the value of the parameter st is decreased by 10). This is all the information that the Titles application on the server needs to display the appropriate page with the results of the search.

The Web server can't decipher the requested URL, but it does have the intelligence to invoke the program whose name appears in the URL string and pass to it the parameters following the program's name. Traditionally, the programs that process client requests in real time on the server are called *scripts*, and most of them were written in Perl.

NOTE   Perl is an acronym formed from Practical Extraction and Report Language and is a scripting language for UNIX systems with which you can write powerful data and text manipulation routines. However, compared with Visual Basic and VBScript, Perl is a cryptic language, and it's not a language with which Windows programmers are familiar.

What Are Active Server Pages?

Microsoft introduced several methods for developing scripts on the server—some of them quite simple (such as the Internet Dababase Connector and the SQL Web Assistant), and others not as simple. There was a confusing time when companies did their best to simplify the development and deployment of server-side scripts, but none of these methods were particularly easy for Visual Basic developers or even for Web authors.

The situation changed drastically in 1996 with the introduction of Active Server Pages (ASP), an elegant solution to the problem of scripting. Active Server Pages are basically HTML pages that contain VBScript code which is executed on the server. The HTML code is transmitted to the client, as is. As a consequence, every HTML page you have authored can be turned into an Active Server Page. Not that you'll see any benefits in renaming your HTML documents, but you're ready to activate them with the inclusion of scripts.

The scripts included on an Active Server Page produce text and HTML tags that are also sent to the client, where they are rendered on the screen. An Active Server Page can produce any output, but only HTML documents can be rendered on the client. Since VBScript can contact the objects installed on the server, you are not limited to VBScript's native commands. You can contact ActiveX components to carry out complicated data processing, access databases, and so on. Which brings us once again to the ubiquitous objects. We didn't plan this book to revolve around objects, but there simply isn't a way around them! If you're planning to do some serious programming with Visual Basic, you can't go far without them.

Using the Server's Objects

In the last couple of years, we witnessed a dramatic shift from static Web pages to interactive applications that run in the browser's environment. Visual Basic's ActiveX documents are a perfect example. ActiveX documents, however, have not matured, and we have chosen not to discuss them in this book. They can't be considered mainstream technology yet, and many people still doubt their usefulness. (It doesn't take much longer to download a VB application that contacts your site to retrieve all types of information.) Instead, we decided to focus on more mature and far more popular methods of developing interactive Web pages, such as Active Server Pages.

HTML is a great language for displaying information on the client. HTML extensions made Web pages colorful, then interactive. But HTML is a simple language. It wasn't designed to be a programming language, and no matter how many extensions are introduced, HTML will never become a proper programming language.

To design interactive Web pages, we need a programming tool. VBScript could be the missing link, but VBScript (and any other scripting language) is also seriously limited because of security considerations. A scripting language that runs on the client must be safe, and, practically speaking, making a language safe for scripting is like crippling it. So, the answer is to do more on the server. The programming tool is still VBScript. But with the server's ability to create new objects, VBScript can now be extended with objects.

Among the objects you can access from within your Active Server Pages are the objects exposed by applications that support VBA, such as the Microsoft Office applications. Let's say you want to calculate complicated math expressions that the user entered on the client. Excel's Evaluate function is probably the simplest solution. Just pass the expression as entered by the visitor to the Evaluate function, wait for the result, and pass it to the client on a new HTML page.

To access databases, you can write custom objects similar to the ones we developed in Chapter 5. However, the simplest way to access databases through an ASP is via the Database component, which is based on the ActiveX Data Objects (ADO). ADO is a component that's installed along with ASP, and you can call it from within your ASP pages to access databases. The ADO component provides high-performance connectivity to any ODBC-compliant database or OLE DB data source. As such, it can be used from within a Web page's script to directly access remote databases. In other words, you can use the ADO component on the client script (provided that the component is already installed on the client computer) to build a Web front end for accessing corporate data, without developing additional scripts on the server. You will find more information on using the ActiveX Data Objects with Visual Basic in Chapter 11.

Why Use Active Server Pages?

Before we look at the structure of Active Server Pages and the objects they use, let's summarize the benefits of using Active Server Pages versus other, more traditional methods of server scripting. Active Server Pages enable HTML authors and Web developers to mix HTML with inline scripting using any authoring tool they are accustomed to (as long as they can comfortably open and edit the HTML documents). The scripts can reference components running on the server to perform complicated processing on the data submitted by the user.

Open Architecture

Active Server Pages are not limited to a particular scripting language. Currently, they support VBScript and Jscript, but third parties can provide support for other languages such as REXX (the OS/2 batch programming language), Perl, and so on. In addition, multiple scripting languages can be used interchangeably in the same ASP file.

You can create ActiveX components in virtually any language. This includes Visual Basic, which opens up a new field for VB programmers. You can easily apply your knowledge of Visual Basic components to Web development (several chapters on building ActiveX components are in the second part of this book). Even though most scripts in use today are still written in Perl (you see, Microsoft wasn't among the first to see the future of the Web and help it grow), the situation is changing rapidly with the introduction of Active Server Pages and the Internet Information Server. Any language that can produce ActiveX components can also be used in Web development.

Ease of Development

Active Server Pages make it easy for HTML authors to activate their Web pages on the server. You can develop customized pages immediately, without writing complicated CGI programs in unfamiliar languages. You can start developing Active Server Pages by writing an HTML document, using any tools you like, and then adding the script section, which provides the functionality that can't be achieved with HTML. You can also include server-side and client-side scripts on the same page, to balance the load between the two computers.

Processing on the Client or on the Server

In principle, any processing that can be carried out on the client shouldn't be moved to the server. Of course, a lot depends on the developer's abilities or other factors, such as the processing power of the client.

If an action takes a long time to complete on the client, consider bringing this part of the script to the server. This applies to intranets, however, because the time required to contact the Web server on the Internet and download a new page through a modem will more than offset any delays in processing the information.

Separation of Content and Logic

Web sites are designed by teams of professionals, including artists, HTML authors, programmers, and so on. One of the challenges in setting up a large Web site is to enable these professionals to work together efficiently. Developing large sites with straight HTML and traditional scripting tools leads frequently to one developer cutting into another developer's work.

The components provided by Active Server Pages allow teams to separate the programming from the design of visual elements. Each developer can focus on his or her part of the process (programming, back-end database management, renewing ads, visual design, and so on). This separation of the programming logic from the content allows more flexibility in Web site design, especially when it involves teams.

The last component of Active Server Pages is the scripting language, VBScript, which is the glue that holds these components together. Active Server Pages support multiple scripting languages, but in this book we'll focus on VBScript. Being a Visual Basic programmer, you will be able to apply your knowledge to the Web immediately—especially your knowledge of building and using ActiveX components.

Browser Independence

The output produced by an ASP is straight HTML code, which can be viewed with any browser. All application logic needed to generate dynamic content resides on the server. The server-side script can be as complicated as you can make it. Your visitors, however, don't see this complexity, and they aren't required to have a specific browser. Any browser that can handle the latest version of HTML will do. In the HTML documents you produce, you can include features that are unique to Internet Explorer, but this is up to you. Avoid browser-specific issues, and your ASP pages can be contacted by any browser.

The Objects of Active Server Pages

Active Server Pages follow the component-based development paradigm. All the standard functionality you need to build a Web site comes in the form of objects, which can be classified in two major categories:

- Intrinsic
- Basic

Intrinsic objects provide methods and properties that you need to access details of the incoming requests (such as the parameters of the request), handle cookies, and create the response to send back to the client. *Basic objects* provide functionality that is commonly used in Web development, such as the ADO component for accessing databases, the file system component for writing to and reading from local files on the server, and more. In the following two sections, we'll discuss these objects and give you some examples of how they are used in Web development. It goes without saying that you can build your own objects to address specific requirements.

Intrinsic Objects

ASP includes a number of built-in objects that free the developer from much of the grunt work of writing code to access details such as extracting the parameters submitted along with the URL, storing and retrieving cookies on the client computer, and directing the output to the client.

Request   This object gives you access to the parameters passed to the server by the client, along with the URL. These parameters are usually the values of the controls on the Form, but can be any string constructed on the client by a local script. Through the Request object, you can also recall the values of existing cookies on the client or create new ones.

Response   This object provides the methods you need to build the response, which is another HTML document. The Response object represents the output stream, which is directed by the Web server to the client, as if it were another HTML document.

Application   This object maintains information that's common to all users of an ASP-based application. The Application object provides events that let you set up variables that will be used by all users of the application.

Session   This object maintains information for individual users, while they are interacting with the application. A separate Session object is associated with each user, and its basic function is to maintain a state between sessions for that user. You can define variables in the Session object, and they will maintain their value even when the user jumps between pages in the application. The Session object's variables are released when the user terminates the session.

Server   This object allows your server-side script to create instances of ActiveX components that reside on the server. The Server object's CreateObject method is almost identical to the Visual Basic function by the same name, and it lets you incorporate the functionality of ActiveX components into your applications. Similarly, you can create object variables with the Server object and extend your Web pages with capabilities that are way beyond HTML.

Base Objects

To help you create Web applications, the Active Server Pages components of the Web server provide the following objects that provide the functionality that is not necessary (as is the functionality of the built-in objects), but that is commonly used in building applications for the Web.

Database   This object provides connectivity to any ODBC-compliant database or OLE DB data source. It is based on the ActiveX Data Objects and allows Web developers to easily link a database to an active Web page to access and manipulate data.

File Access   This is another useful object that lets you access text files stored on the server. As with client-side scripts, server-side scripts must be safe for the host system. The File Access object is fairly safe, because it allows developers to write and read only text files and only in specific folders on the server.

Content Linking   This object manages a list of URLs so that you can treat the pages in your Web site like the pages in a book. You author the pages, and the Content Linking object automatically generates and maintains tables of contents and navigation links to previous and following Web pages. With the methods and properties exposed by the Content Linking object, you can add, delete, and rearrange pages without editing the individual HTML files.

Browser Capabilities   With this object, ASP files can recognize the capabilities of the requesting browser and dynamically optimize the site's content for specific browser features. If you weren't able to write code that automatically recognizes the type of browser for a session, you'd have to create (and maintain) a series of duplicate pages for each browser, or you'd have to notify users that special features on your site can be viewed only with a specific browser.

Advertisement Rotator   As people realize the potential of the Web as a business medium and more and more sites become commercial, the need to manage ads on a Web increases. Web managers can't afford to manually place ads in their designs. Ads must not only be rotated, but selected according to user preferences. If your Web site has a search engine, it wouldn't make sense to advertise cars to a viewer who's looking for books or advertise magazines to people who are searching for programming tools. To simplify the handling of ads on a Web site, Active Server Pages comes with the Advertisement Rotator object. You can use this object to display ads based on preset criteria every time an ASP file is requested.

In this chapter, we'll cover only a few of the basic components of Active Server Pages. We'll discuss the built-in objects and a few of the basic objects, which will help you leverage your VB knowledge to the Web. We won't get into every ASP-related topic.

Creating an ASP Page

The simplest way to create an ASP page is to change the extension of an existing HTML document, from HTM (or HTML) to ASP. Then place the file in a new folder under your Web server's root folder. For the examples in this chapter, we will use the ASPages folder. All examples will reference ASP pages in the ASPages folder.

> **NOTE**
>
> You'll find all the Active Server Pages examples discussed in this chapter in the Ch17/ASPages folder on the CD that comes with this book.

ASP Files and Execute Rights

ASP files are text files by content, but they are also programs. When called, their scripts are compiled on demand, and the executable parts are loaded in the cache. Therefore, they must be placed in a folder with Scripts rights.

Through the Web server's administration utility, create a virtual directory, name it ASPages, and map it to the ASPages folder under the Web's root folder. (You can create the ASPages directory anywhere on your hard disk, but it's commonly placed under the root folder.) Then set the folder's Scripts permission. You need not set the Execution rights for the folder, because ASP files are not executable files.

Here's a simple HTML file that displays the time on the client.

Code 17.1:   The DATETIME.HTM File

```
<HTML>
<HEAD>
<TITLE>Simple ASP Demo</TITLE>
<SCRIPT LANGUAGE=VBScript>
Document.Write "<FONT SIZE=3 FACE='Verdana'>"
```

```
Document.Write "<H1>Welcome to the Active Server Pages</H1>"
Document.Write "The date is <B>" & Date() & "</B> and the time is <B>"
& Time() & "</B>"
Document.Write "<P>"
</SCRIPT>
</HEAD>
<BODY>
<B>Active Server Pages</B> contain text, HTML code and scripts that
are executed on the client, just like ordinary HTML documents. The
DateTime.asp  file contains a client-side script, which prints the
date and the time on the client and then displays the document's body.
<BR>
In addition, server-side scripts contain scripts that are executed on
the server and produce HTML output. The client never sees the server-
side script, just the output it produces.
</BODY>
</HTML>
```

The date and time are displayed from within a client-side script, which calls the functions Date() and Time(). This script is executed on the client, and as a consequence the date and time are read from the local computer's clock.

We'll revise this page to display the time on the server. To do so, we'll add statements that are executed on the server. Copy the DATETIME.HTM file to the SRVRTIME.ASP file and replace the <SCRIPT> tag with the following:

```
<SCRIPT LANGUAGE = VBScript RUNAT = Server>
Response.Write "<FONT SIZE=3 FACE='Verdana'>"
Response.Write "<H1>Welcome to the Active Server Pages</H1>"
Response.Write "The date is <B>" & Date() & "</B> and the time is <B>"
& Time() & "</B>"
Response.Write "<P>"
</SCRIPT>
```

The Response object is equivalent to the Document object, but the server can't access the Document object, which is available only on the client. Instead, it must use the Response object. The new page will produce the same output, but the date and time displayed will be the date and time on the server. The modifier RUNAT in the <SCRIPT> tag tells the Active Server Pages to execute this script on the server, not on the client.

Server-side scripts can also be enclosed in a pair of <% and %> tags. These tags enclose all the statements that must be executed on the server. Everything between these two tags is considered a server-side script, which is replaced by its output and never seen by the client.

Displaying the HTML Code

To open an ASP file (or ASP application, if you prefer), follow these steps:

1. Connect to your Web server. If you are developing on the machine where the Web server is installed, connect to the URL 127.0.0.1.

2. Open the ASPages folder.

3. Click the name of the ASP file you want to open.

If you double-click the name of an ASP file, you will see the HTML code, but none of the server-side statements will be executed. The browser skips the server-side script tags (<% and %>) because it doesn't know how to render them. These statements must be executed on the server, which happens only if a Web server furnishes the document.

Here's a more useful ASP page along the same lines. This page displays a different greeting depending on the time of the day.

Code 17.2:   An HTML Page with a Greeting

```
<HTML>
<BODY>
<%
If Time() >=#12:00:00 AM# And Time() < #12:00:00 PM#  Then
  greeting = "Good Morning!"
Else
  greeting = "Good Afternoon!"
End If
%>
<H1> <% =greeting %> </H1>
<BR>
<H2>and welcome to the Active Server Pages.</H2>
<BR>
More HTML lines follow
</BODY>
</HTML>
```

The statements between the first pair of server-side tags (<% and %>) do not produce any output for the client. They simply assign the proper value to the *greetings* variable. The value of this variable is then sent to the client by the line <% =greeting %>. The rest is straight HTML, which is rendered on the client as usual.

HTML and server-side statements can coexist on the same line too. The last example could have been implemented as follows:

```
<HTML>
<BODY>
<% If Time()  > = #12:00:00 AM# And Time() < #12:00:00 PM#  Then %>
<H1>Good Morning!</H1>
<% Else %>
<H1>Good Afternoon!</H1>
<% End If %>
<BR>
<H2>and welcome to the Active Server Pages.</H2>
<BR>
More HTML lines follow
</BODY>
</HTML>
```

Your server-side script can also call procedures you supply in addition to built-in procedures such as the Date() and Time() functions. You can write a function that returns the date formatted in a specific way with the FormatDate() function. To call this function from within your script, enclose its name in the server-side script tags:

```
<% =FormatDate %>
```

The actual definition of the function must appear somewhere in the same file. Since the entire procedure will be executed on the server and since it doesn't contain any HTML code to be sent to the client, you can place it in a pair of <SCRIPT> tags, similar to the client-side scripts, with an added qualifier:

```
<SCRIPT RUNAT=SERVER LANGUAGE=VBScript>
   function  FormatDate ()
   {
       function's statements
   }
</SCRIPT>
```

The procedure will be executed and will return the current date in a format determined by the code.

Included Files

Multiple scripts can use procedures such as the FormatDate() function. To avoid repeating code or to maintain identical code in multiple files, you can include a file with one or more procedure definitions in an ASP file. The included file can also contain HTML code; it doesn't really matter. It is inserted as is in the current ASP file and processed along with the rest of the file.

HTML provides the #INCLUDE directive, which inserts the contents of another text file into an ASP file before processing it. The #INCLUDE statement is called a directive, because it's not an executable statement; it simply instructs ASP to perform a simple insertion.

NOTE

C programmers will be quite familiar with the term *directive*. Normally, directives are processed by the preprocessor to prepare a file for the compiler.

The syntax of the #INCLUDE directive is:

```
<!- #INCLUDE VIRTUAL|FILE="filename" ->
```

The comment tags ensure that this line will not be sent to the client by mistake. If the file resides in a virtual folder (or a subfolder under a virtual folder), use the VIRTUAL keyword. If you'd rather specify an absolute path name, use the FILE keyword. Either keyword must be followed by the path name to the file to be included. Included files do not require a special extension, but the extension INC is commonly used.

To include the DateFunctions.inc file in the Support folder under ASPages, use the following line:

```
<!-#INCLUDE VIRTUAL="/ASPages/Support/DateFunctions.inc"->
```

If the DateFunctions.inc file resides in the same folder as the ASP file in which it will be included, you can use the #INCLUDE directive with the FILE keyword:

```
<!-#INCLUDE FILE="DateFunctions.inc"->
```

If the included file resides in the Support subfolder under the folder of the ASP file, the following line will insert it in the current ASP file:

```
<!-#INCLUDE FILE="Support/DateFunctions.inc"->
```

Relative paths use the ASP file's folder as the starting point. You can also use the ../ qualifier to specify parent folders:

```
<!-#INCLUDE FILE="../Support/DateFunctions.inc"->
```

Included Files: Dos and Don'ts

Included files can, in turn, include other files. You must ensure that the #INCLUDE directives don't form a loop. For example, `Document1.asp` includes `file1.inc`, which in turn may include `file2.inc`. `File2.inc`, however, can't include `file1.inc` (and neither can an included file include itself). ASP detects circular references and aborts the processing with an error message, which will appear in the browser.

Advanced programmers might even attempt to use the script to generate the included file's name. This is an interesting technique with VB applications, but it won't work with Active Server Pages. The #INCLUDE directives are processed before the script is executed, and the name of the included file won't be available the moment it must be inserted.

Finally, an included file must contain scripts in their entirety. In other words, you can't start a script in one included file and end it in another; neither can you include a file in the middle of script. The following script won't work:

```
<%
    {server-side script statements}
    <!-#INCLUDE FILE="DateFunctions.inc"->
    {more statements}
%>
```

You must break the script into two segments, as follows:

```
<%
    {server-side script statements}
%>
    <!-#INCLUDE FILE="DateFunctions.inc"->
<%
    {more statements}
%>
```

Mixing Server-Side and Client-Side Scripts

An ASP file can contain both server-side and client-side scripts. If you want to include a script section in your Web page, simply insert the scripting commands between the <SCRIPT> tags in the file. Figure 17.2 shows the output of another ASP file that is a variation of the script that displays the server's date on the client. The TIMESRVR.ASP page displays the time on the client through a client-side script, and it displays the time on the server through a server-side script. If the client and server computers are in different time zones, the difference in the time is an integer number of hours, plus a few seconds that it may take for the HTML code to arrive at the client.

FIGURE 17.2:

The TIMESRVR.ASP pages combines client-side and server-side scripts to display the time on the client and the server.

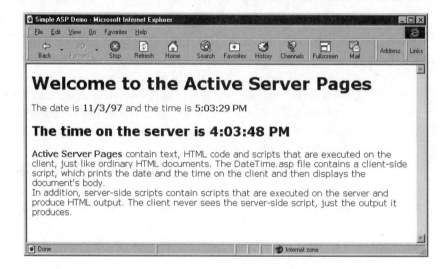

Here is the listing of the TIMESRVR.ASP file. Notice that the client-side script is inserted with the <SCRIPT> tag, as if it were included on a regular HTML page. The server-side script isn't really a script, just a call to the Time() function. You could have inserted as many statements as necessary, as long as they were included in a pair of <%> tags.

Code 17.3:   The TIMESRVR.ASP Page

```
<HTML>
<HEAD>
<TITLE>Simple ASP Demo</TITLE>
<SCRIPT LANGUAGE=VBScript>
Document.Write "<FONT SIZE=3 FACE='Verdana'>"
Document.Write "<H1>Welcome to the Active Server Pages</H1>"
Document.Write "The date is <B>" & Date() & "</B> and the time is <B>"
& Time() & "</B>"
Document.Write "<P>"
</SCRIPT>
</HEAD>
<BODY>
```

```
<H2>The time on the server is <% =Time() %></H2>
<P>
<B>Active Server Pages</B> contain text, HTML code and scripts that are
executed on the client, just like ordinary HTML documents. The
DateTime.asp file contains a client-side script, which prints the date
and the time on the client and then displays the document's body.
<BR>
In addition, server-side scripts contain scripts that are executed on
the server and produce HTML output. The client never sees the server-
side script, just the output it produces.
</BODY>
</HTML>
```

After this introduction to the basic structure of ASP files, we can turn our attention to the objects of the Active Server Pages and see how they can help you develop interactive Web pages. In developing ASP applications, we are primarily interested in interacting with the client, rather than writing elaborate HTML code or even client-side scripts.

The emphasis is in writing server-side code that reads data submitted by the client, processes them on the server (in most cases with ActiveX components that reside on the server), and produces Web pages on the fly, which are transmitted back to the client. With any other server, this process requires CGI scripts and, in general, programming in C-like languages. With Active Server Pages and the built-in objects, the tasks that would normally require Perl or C++ programming can be taken care of with VBScript.

In the rest of the chapter, we are going to examine these objects and see how they simplify scripting on the server. At the end of the chapter, we'll look at some of the basic components, especially the Database component, which lets your script access databases on the server.

The Response Object

Use the Response object to send information to the client. ASP files may contain straight HTML code that's sent directly to the client. However, if you want to control the output programmatically from within the script, you must write it to the Response object. The Response object supports the following methods and properties.

Write Method

Everything you write to the Response object with the Write method is sent to the client. Normally, the information written with the Write method must be an HTML document. Here's a simple, but working example of the Response object's Write method:

```
<HTML>
<SCRIPT LANGUAGE=VBScript RUNAT=Server>
   Response.Write "<HTML>"
   Response.Write "<HEAD>"
   Response.Write "<TITLE>Response.Write Demo</TITLE>"
   Response.Write "</HEAD>"
   Response.Write "<H1>"
   Response.Write "Response Object:Write Method"
   Response.Write "</H1>"
   Response.Write "This document was created on the fly by an ASP file
on the server"
   Response.Write "</HTML>"
</SCRIPT>
</HTML>
```

The outer pair of HTML tags delimits the ASP file (they are not really required), and the pair of HTML tags written to the Response object delimit the HTML file seen by the client. If there's one method used in nearly every ASP file, it is the Response.Write method, and you will see many more examples of it in this chapter.

NOTE   The Write method of the Response object is the primary way to send data to the client. ASP also uses this method behind the scenes. Let's say you want to output the value of a variable, and you mistype the expression, as shown here: Welcome back < % =UserName %>. (The mistake is an extra space between the characters < and %.) When the script that contains this line is processed, the error message that is displayed on the client indicates that the error occurred in the method Response.Write, even though this method is not directly called by the script!

Here's a more practical example of the Response object's Write method. Let's say you are constructing a page with various levels of headings that are determined by the variable *iHead*. This variable is incremented and decremented by an algorithm you provide. If *iHead* is 2, a level 2 heading is inserted, with a statement such as the following:

```
Response.Write "<H" & iHead & ">"
```

When this statement is executed with iHead = 2, the tag <H2> is sent to the client.

Later in this chapter, you will see how to use the File Access object to read from text files on the server. If you want to read the text and send it to the client, you use the Write method to write the incoming text stream to the Response object.

Redirect Method

This method redirects the client to another URL. If you move your site to another URL, write a short ASP application such as the following to redirect the visitor automatically to the new URL.

```
<HTML>
<%
Response.Write "Our site was moved at a new URL."
Response.Write "Your browser will be redirected to the new URL
automatically."
Response.Redirect newURL
%>
</HTML>
```

The *newURL* variable is the Web's new URL.

Clear Method

This method clears the data written to the Response object and is used only when the Buffer property is set to True (when the output is buffered until the entire page has been processed, before it's sent to the client).

NOTE   See the discussion of the Buffer property, later in this section, for more details on using the Clear method.

ContentType Property

This property determines the type of document you will send to the client. The ContentType property applies to the entire page and must be set before you write any information to the output stream with the Write method.

You'll find the various content types in the File Types tab of the Windows Explorer's Options dialog box. (In any Explorer window, choose View ➤ Options and select the File Types tab.)

For example, if you want to send source code of an ASP page, set ContentType to "text/plain", rather than to "text/html", which is the default content type:

```
<% Response.ContentType = "text/plain" %>
```

The browser displays the page as text, instead of rendering it as an HTML page.

Cookies Property

Use this property to send cookies to the client. Cookies are special strings that are stored on the local computer, and your ASP application can read them back with the Request method.

In effect, cookies are a way to pass values between the pages of your Web. The HTTP protocol used on the Web is stateless. Each document is requested by the client and transmitted by the server, and the transaction completes at this point. If the same client requests another document from the same server, neither the client nor the server has any recollection of the previous transaction.

Maintaining variables between different pages is a problem with a stateless protocol, which is solved with the help of cookies. If your Web pages use a consistent, but user-defined background color, you can store this value to a cookie, let's call it BColor, and then read it before constructing and transmitting a new page. *BColor* is the name of a variable that is stored on the client computer with the Cookies method of the Response object. To read its value, you access the Cookies property of the Request object.

For more information on using cookies, see the section "Storing and Recalling Cookies," later in this chapter.

Buffer Property

By default, the Response object sends its output to the client as soon as it can, and it doesn't wait for the entire page to complete. If you want to process the entire page before sending any output to the client, set the Buffer property of the Response object to True. Let's say that as you process the page (with an ActiveX component or by reading data from a database), you discover that you need not send the previous data to the client or that you must redirect the client to another URL. If the Buffer property was set to True, you can cancel the processing and clear the output stream with the Clear method of the Response object. Here's a typical scenario:

```
<%
Reponse.Buffer = True
{script statements}
If SupplierName = UserName Then
    Response.Clear
    Response.Redirect "/Suppliers/AllSuppliers.html"
    Response.End
End If
%>
```

This script builds a page by reading data from a database, until it discovers that the visitor is actually one of the suppliers and then it clears the output created so far, ends the Response object, and redirects the visitor to another page. If your script takes too long to process, however, nothing will appear on the client's monitor, and visitors may think they are not getting a response. Normal HTML pages are not buffered, so you should not buffer your ASP pages by default.

The Request Object

To interact with the visitor, your script should be able to request information that the visitor enters on a Form and read the values of cookies. Reading data back from the client has been a sore point in server scripting. ASP has simplified the process of reading the data submitted by the client by encapsulating all the complexity of the operation into a few properties of the Request object. This single feature of ASP would be adequate to make it a major server-scripting tool.

The Request object has five properties, all of which are collections:

> **QueryString** contains the values passed to the server with the GET method.

> **Form** contains all the Forms on the page.

> **Cookies** contains all cookies that have been written to the client by the Web site.

> **ServerVariables** contains all the HTTP variables, which are determined by the server.

> **ClientCertificate** contains all the client certificates installed on the client.

The QueryString Collection

The collection you'll be using most often in developing ASP applications is the QueryString collection. This property gives you access to all the parameters passed along with the URL by the client. If the names of the parameters are known at the time you develop the ASP file, you can request their values by name, with expressions such as the following:

```
reqProdName = Request.QueryString("ProductName")
```

If the names of the parameters are not known when you develop the ASP file or if you want to process them all serially, you can use a loop such as the following:

```
Set Params = Request.QueryString
    For Each param in Params
    {process parameter param}
Next
```

Figure 17.3 shows a simple HTML page with a Form; the visitor can enter information by selecting options in list boxes.

NOTE   The HTML page is called SRVRFORM.HTM, and you will find it in this chapter's folder on the CD.

FIGURE 17.3:

A typical Form on an HTML page

The names of the List Box controls on the SRVRFRM page are: HardDisk, Memory, CD, Speaker and Software. The possible values for each setting are listed in the <OPTION> tags of each <SELECT> tag. The options of the Select Memory list box have the values 32, 64, 128, and 256. The Memory query parameter will have one of these values, depending on which option was selected on the Form.

Code 17.4: The SRVRFRM.HTM File

```
<H1>Build Your Own System</H1>
<FORM name=ORDER method="GET"
action="http://127.0.0.1/aspages/param.asp">
<TABLE>
<TR>
<TD><B>Select Hard Disk</B></TD>
<TD></TD>
<TD><B>Select Memory</B></TD>
<TD></TD>
<TD><B>Select CD</B></TD>
</TR>
<TR>
<TD><SELECT name="HardDisk" size="1">
<OPTION selected value="3.2G">3.2GB Ultra EIDE Hard Drive </OPTION>
<OPTION  value="4.3G">4.3GB Ultra EIDE Hard Drive </OPTION>
</SELECT>
</TD>
<TD>
      
</TD>
<TD>
<SELECT name="Memory" size="1">
<OPTION  value="32">32 MB EDO RAM</OPTION>
<OPTION selected value="64 MB">64MB EDO RAM</OPTION>
<OPTION  value="128">128 MB EDO RAM</OPTION>
<OPTION  value="256">256 MB EDO RAM</OPTION>
</SELECT>
</TD>
<TD>
      
</TD>
<TD>
<select name="CD" size="1">
<option  value="">None</option>
```

```
<option selected value="CD12">12 EIDE CD-ROM</option>
<option selected value="CD24">24 EIDE CD-ROM</option>
</select>
</TD>
</TR>
<TR>
<TD><B>Select Speakers</B></TD>
<TD></TD>
<TD><B>Select Software</B></TD>
<TD></TD>
</TR>
<TR>
<TD>
<select name="Speaker" size="1">
<option selected value="">None</option>
<option value="S90">Altec ACS90 Speakers</option>
<option value="S290">Altec ACS290 Speakers</option>
</select>
</TD>
<TD></TD>
<TD>
<select name="Software" size="1">
<option selected value="WIN95">MS Windows 95</option>
<option value="WIN98">Microsoft Windows 98</option>
<option value="WINNT">Microsoft Windows NT Workstation 4.0 </option>
</select>
</TD>
</TABLE>
<BR><BR>
Select the desired options and click the Recalculate button to see your
system's price
<INPUT TYPE=SUBMIT VALUE="Recalculate">
</FORM>
</HTML>
```

The ASP page that processes this Form doesn't do much (it doesn't actually recalculate the price of the configuration, but once you know the options specified by the visitor, it's relatively easy to calculate the price of the selected configuration). It generates another HTML page on the fly with the names and values of the parameters and sends it back to the client. The server's response is shown in Figure 17.4.

The names and values of the query parameters submitted to the server by the Form in Figure 17.3.

The PARAM.ASP page that processed the data on the Form on the server uses a For Each loop to scan all the items of the QueryString collection and display their names and values in a new table. Each parameter is stored in the variable *PValue*. The default property of this variable is the name of the parameter. To access the value of the parameters, use Params(PValue).

Code 17.5:   The PARAM.ASP File

```
<HTML>
<%
  Response.Write "<HTML>"
  Response.Write "<BODY>"
  Response.Write "<TABLE BORDER RULES=ALL>"
  Response.Write "<TR><TD><B>Parameter Name</B></TD><TD><B>Parameter
Value</B></TD></TR>"
  Set Params = Request.QueryString
  For Each PValue in Params
  Response.Write "<TR><TD>" & PValue & "</TD><TD>" & Params(PValue) &
"</TD></TR>"
  Next
  Response.Write "</TABLE>"
  Response.Write "</HTML>"
%>
</HTML>
```

To access individual parameters, you can use the collection Request.QueryString followed by the name of the parameter whose value you want. The following lines will return the specifications of the memory and the hard disk, as entered by the visitor on the Form in the page SRVRFRM.HTM:

```
MemorySpec = Request.QueryString("Memory")
HDiskSpec = Request.QueryString("HardDisk")
```

TIP

It is possible for multiple controls on a Form to have identical names. In this case, the QueryString collection contains an array of values. For example, if the Form contains three TextBoxes named "Name," you can access them as Request.QueryString("Name")(1),Request.QueryString ("Name")(2), and Request.QueryString("Name")(3).

The Form Collection

This collection is similar to the QueryString collection in that it contains data that the visitor entered on a Form. Whereas the QueryString collection contains all the parameters submitted to the server, regardless of whether they belong to a Form, the Form collection contains the values of the parameters that come from controls. It is possible to build a URL followed by a number of parameters on the fly, from within a client script. These parameters will be reported by the QueryString collection, but not by the Form collection.

NOTE

You will see examples of URLs with parameters constructed by the client in the section "Using the ActiveX Data Objects," later in this chapter.

To access the value of a specific parameter in the Form collection, use a statement such as the following:

```
FullName = Request.Form("LastName") & ", " % Request.Form("FirstName")
```

The ServerVariables Collection

This collection contains a number of standard environment variables, which you can access from within your script. Basically, the ServerVariables collection contains all the information available about the client and the server. Here are some of the most commonly used server variables:

SERVER_NAME: The server's DNS or IP address.

SERVER_PROTOCOL: The name and revision number of the protocol used for the request. It's usually HTTP/1.0.

SERVER_PORT: The TCP/IP port number on which the server accepts requests. It's usually 80.

SERVER_SOFTWARE: The name and version of the HTTP server software on the server machine.

SCRIPT_NAME: The path to the script being executed.

QUERY_STRING: The information that follows the question mark (?) in a URL. The GET method uses this variable, and you can retrieve it with the QueryString collection. This string is encoded according to the following two rules:

- Spaces are converted to plus signs.

- Any character may be represented as a hexadecimal number (representing the character's ASCII value) prefixed with the percent sign. The plus sign is encoded as %2B.

REQUEST_METHOD: The HTTP method being used to send client data to the server. The possible values are GET and POST.

CONTENT_TYPE: The type of data sent to the server. This variable is always `application/x-www-form-urlencoded`.

CONTENT_LENGTH: The length of the string holding the data. This variable is used with the POST method.

REMOTE_HOST: The full domain name of the client that made the request.

REMOTE_ADDR: The IP (Internet Protocol) address of the requesting client.

The file SRVRPARAM.ASP contains a short script that displays all the server variables, as shown in Figure 17.5.

NOTE
You'll find the SRVRPARAM.ASP file in the Ch17 folder on the CD that comes with this book.

Code 17.6:   The SRVRPARAM.ASP File

```
<HTML>
<%
  Response.Write "<HTML>"
  Response.Write "<BODY>"
  Response.Write "<TABLE BORDER RULES=ALL>"
  Response.Write "<TR><TD><B>Parameter Name</B></TD><TD><B>Parameter
Value</B></TD></TR>"
  Set Params = Request.ServerVariables
  For Each Pvalue in Params
  Response.Write "<TR><TD>" & Pvalue & "</TD><TD>" & Params(pValue) &
"</TD></TR>"
  Next
  Response.Write "</TABLE>"
  Response.Write "</HTML>"
%>
</HTML>
```

FIGURE 17.5:

The SRVRPARAM.ASP file displays the names of all server variables and their values on a Web page.

The Cookies Collection

This collection is discussed in detail in the "Storing and Recalling Cookies" section, later in this chapter. Cookies are basically variables stored by the server on the client computer and can be accessed by name, similar to parameters.

The ClientCertificates Collection

This collection contains all the certificates installed on the client computer and is needed only when your ASP applications install ActiveX components on the client. This property is supported only by Internet Explorer clients.

The Server Object

The Server object controls the environment in which the server-side scripts are executed. The single most important member of the Server object is its CreateObject method, which can create a new instance of an object from a registered class.

The CreateObject Method

The Server object's CreateObject method is identical to the Visual Basic CreateObject function. It accepts as an argument the programmatic ID of the object and returns an instance of the object. The syntax of the CreateObject method is:

```
Server.CreateObject("progID")
```

To access a database through the ADO component, for instance, you first create a Connection object and a Recordset object with the following statements (see the section "Using ActiveX Data Objects," later in this chapter, for more details on accessing databases through ASP):

```
Set ADOConnection = Server.CreateObject("ADODB.Connection")
Set ADORS = Server.CreateObject("ADODB.Recordset")
```

Similarly, you must create object variables to access the other basic components of ASP, such as the File Access component and the Advertisement Rotator component. You can also use the Server's CreateObject method to create object variables for accessing your own custom ActiveX components. For example, you can use the DBClass ActiveX server we created in Chapter 6 to access Microsoft Access databases. Or you can build an ActiveX component that contacts Excel to evaluate math expressions with the Evaluate method. In short, the CreateObject method lets you extend Active Server Pages by plugging into it almost any component you need.

The MapPath Method

Another commonly used method of the Server object is the MapPath method, which maps virtual folders to actual path names. This method is useful in developing server-side scripts for a very simple reason: All the files you access are stored in virtual folders. You can rearrange the entire folder structure of a Web site and then rename a few virtual folders, and your scripts will never know. In some situations, however, you need to know the actual path to a file, and the MapPath method will return this value.

> **NOTE**
>
> In the last section of this chapter, "The File Access Component," you will find an example of using the MapFolder method.

The Session and Application Objects

The Session object maintains variables that apply to a specific session. Before we examine the members of this object and how it's used in developing an ASP application, let's look at how the ASP component maintains sessions with a stateless protocol.

As we mentioned, HTTP is a stateless protocol. Each time the client requests a new document, a new transaction is initiated. Then how does the ASP know that a new request from a client belongs to an existing session? The answer is that ASP uses cookies.

When the client connects for the first time, the server sends the ASPSESSIONID cookie, which is stored on the client computer. Then, every time the client contacts the server, the ASPSESSIONID cookie is transmitted along with the request's header.

> **NOTE**
>
> The header contains information that both computers use to communicate, but you don't have to know what type of information is transmitted or change the default headers.

ASP processes this cookie and uses it to restore the variable values saved previously in the Session object. The ASPSESSIONID cookie doesn't have an expiration value and expires automatically when the client disconnects. The next time the same client connects, a new cookie is sent, and a new session is created. To maintain information between sessions, you must store a cookie with an expiration date on the client, read it as soon as the client connects to the Web server, and use it as a key to a database with relevant data (such as user preferences, access rights, and so on).

Some browsers don't support cookies (a rather rare situation today). These browsers don't support sessions either. Basically the only limitation that ASP imposes on the client (if it can be considered a limitation) is that it support cookies.

The Application object plays a similar role. It maintains a set of variables, not for each session, but for the application. Simple examples are a welcome message that's displayed on each client's window and a visitor counter. To implement a visitor counter with ASP, all you have to do is create an application-wide variable and increment it every time a client hits your home page (which must be an ASP document).

To create a new Session or Application variable, you need only reference it in your code (this is VBScript; you are not required to declare variables). The statement:

```
<% Session("UName") = Request.QueryString("UserName") %>
```

assigns the value of the cookie UserName (which presumably has been set by the client) to the Session variable *UName*. You can also assign function values to the Session variables, as the following statement does:

```
<% Session("Connected") = Now() %>
```

The name of the variable is on the left side of the above expressions. You can use Session variables to build all types of expressions and statements with VBScript. The following statement terminates a client connection if it's been active for more than 12 hours:

```
<% If Hour(Now() - Session("Connected")) > 12 Then
    Session.Abandon
End If
%>
```

The Abandon method terminates the current session.

Application variables are declared and used in the same manner, but since multiple scripts can access Application variables, there is always a chance that more than one script will attempt to change the value of an Application variable. The Application object provides the Lock and Unlock methods, which must be called before and after setting the variable:

```
Application.Lock
Application("VisitorCounter") = Application("VisitorCounter") + 1
Application.Unlock
```

The Session and Application objects support object variables too, created with the CreateObject method of the Server object. The difference is that object variables stored in the Session object can't be accessed by other sessions. If you have many clients accessing the same object (the same component on the server), you will be creating many instances of the same component, which may affect performance. This isn't as simple as it sounds. An object can be accessed by multiple sessions only if it has been designed to support multiple threads of execution.

The Start and End Events

Both the Session and the Application objects support a Start and an End event, which signal when a Session or Application starts and when it ends. The Start events are:

- Session_OnStart
- Application_OnStart

The End events are:

- Session_OnEnd
- Application_OnEnd

These procedures include code you want to run whenever an application or a session starts or ends. If an application and a session start at the same time, the Application_OnStart event is executed first. These events are important in developing ASP applications, but they are not available from within the script. You must enter them in the GLOBAL.ASA file, which lives in the root folder of the application (the folder where the first ASP file to be requested by the client is stored). Typically, the GLOBAL.ASA file contains the Start and End events of the Session and Application objects, as well as variable definitions.

For example, if you want to implement a variable that stores the number of visitors hitting the site, initialize it in the Application_OnStart event. Enter the following code in the GLOBAL.ASA file:

```
<SCRIPT LANGUAGE=VBScript RUNAT=Server>
Sub Application_OnStart
    Application("Visitors") = 0
End Sub
</SCRIPT>
```

This event takes place every time the Web server software starts. Since you don't want to reset this counter every time you stop and restart the server, you can save the value of the variable *Visitors* to a text file on the server's disk, as explained in the sections "The FileSystemObject Object" and "The TextStream Object," later in this chapter. In the Application_OnStart event you read the value of the variable from the text file, and in the Session_OnStart event you increase it by one:

```
<SCRIPT LANGUAGE=VBScript RUNAT=Server>
Sub Session_OnStart
    Application("Visitors") = Application("Visitors") + 1
End Sub
</SCRIPT>
```

You must also enter this procedure in the GLOBAL.ASA event. This technique works well. The number will not increase each time a visitor hits the home page during the same session, because the Session_OnStart event is only triggered the first time.

Displaying a fancy counter on your pages is a different story. You can simply display this number in a large font on your home page, or you can generate a GIF file on the fly and display it on the home page. The Structured Graphics control that comes with Internet Explorer 4 lets you create elaborate graphics with simple text commands. This control is probably the simplest way to display a graphic that shows the number of visitors.

If your pages call a specific component frequently during a session, you can declare an object variable in the session's Start event. This variable will be available from within any page during the current session. Here's a simple example that creates an object variable referencing the MyObject component:

```
<SCRIPT LANGUAGE=VBScript RUNAT=Server>
Sub Session_OnStart
    Set Session("MyObj")=Server.CreateObject("MyObject")
End Sub
</SCRIPT>
```

Any page in the current session can use the *MyObj* object variable, and each session's *MyObj* variable is independent of the other sessions' *MyObj* variable.

Storing and Recalling Cookies

You have certainly noticed that some of the sites you've visited (Microsoft's home page is one of them) can be customized according to the visitor's preferences. How is it done? How does the server know each visitor's preferences between sessions? If each user had a fixed IP address, it would be possible (although not practical) for the server to maintain a database with IP addresses and the preferences for each visitor. The IP address of the client computer is given by the ServerVariables collection of the Server object. But most clients have different IP addresses each time they connect, so this approach is out of the question.

If you think about it, you will see that the only way for the server to maintain information about specific clients is to store this information on the client computer itself and recall it each time the client connects to the server. The information is stored on the client computer by the browser, in a special folder, in the form of variables and values. But instead of variables, they are called *cookies*.

NOTE *Cookies* is another Unix term if you were wondering what cookies have to do with your computer. And, no, cookies can't be used as Trojan horses.

Cookies are also used to pass information between pages on the same site. Let's say you're building a Web site for online orders. The site is made up of many pages, and visitors can order items on many pages. How do you keep track of the visitors' orders? Each page can have its own script, and each page can have its own global variables, but their scope is limited to the page on which they were declared. There is no way for two or more pages to share common variables. This is a direct consequence of HTTP being a stateless protocol. Each time a new page arrives at the client, the browser forgets everything about the current page (except for its URL, so that it can jump back to it). Orders made on one page can be stored on the client computer in the form of cookies and can be read by any other page on the same site.

Since cookies are managed by the browser, Web pages can't access your computer's hard disk directly (that's why cookies are safe). Moreover, when a page requests the values of the cookies, the browser supplies only those cookies that were stored by pages on the same site. In other words, cookies left on your computer by Microsoft's Web site can't be read by pages of other sites. The browser supplies to each page only the cookies left by other pages on the same site.

Cookies have expiration dates too. If a cookie is stored without an expiration date, it ceases to exist after the current session. A cookie with an expiration date remains on the client computer until it expires.

To store a cookie to the client computer, use the Cookies property of the Response object. The Cookies property is a collection, and you can create and access individual cookies by name. To create a new cookie, use a statement such as the following:

```
<% Response.Cookies("FavoriteSport")="Hockey" %>
```

If the cookie FavoriteSport exists on the client computer, its value is overwritten. If not, a new cookie is created. This cookie is released as soon as the current session ends.

You can specify the expiration date and time with the Expires property of the cookie, as follows:

```
<% Response.Cookies("FavoriteSport").Expires = "December 31, 1998
12:00:00 GTM" %>
```

Cookies have other properties too:

Domain: If specified, the cookie value is sent only to requests from this domain. This property is used along with the Path property.

Path: If specified, the cookie is sent only to requests made from this path on the server, and not to every page on the same site.

HasKeys: Specifies whether the cookie contains multiple keys (in which case, it's a dictionary). This property is read-only.

To create cookies with keys, use the same cookie name with multiple attributes, as in the following statements:

```
<%
Response.Cookies("Preferences")("Books") = "Mystery"
Response.Cookies("Preferences")("News") = "Sports"
%>
```

To request the value of a specific cookie from the client, use the Cookies collection of the Request object. The number of cookies in the Cookies collection is given by the Request.Cookies.Count property.

You can write a For ... Next loop that scans the collection, or you can write a For Each ... Next loop such as the following:

```
<%
For Each cookie In Request.Cookies
    {process current cookie, which is Request.Cookies(cookie)}
Next cookie
%>
```

Normally, the script on the server knows the names of the cookies and can request them by their names:

```
BookType = Request.Cookies("FavoriteSport")
```

If you need to find out the names of the cookies, use the For Each ... Next structure. At each iteration, the value of the *cookie* variable is the name of the cookie, and *Request.Cookies(cookie)* is its value.

If a cookie has keys, you must access them as elements of a collection. Let's assume you've sent a cookie with keys to the client with the following statements:

```
<%
Response.Cookies("Background") = "Planets.bmp"
Response.Cookies("Preferences")("Books") = "Mystery"
Response.Cookies("Preferences")("News") = "Sports"
%>
```

The first cookie determines the visitor's favorite background patterns. The next two values can be used to create a custom home page. The following loop reads all the cookie values, including the key values:

```
<%
For Each cookie In Request.Cookies
    If Request.Cookies(cookie).HasKeys Then
        For Each cookie In Request.Cookies(cookie)
            { Process current cookie. Its value is
              Request.Cookies(cookie)(scookie) }
        Next
    Else
        { Process current cookie. Its value is Request.Cookies(cookie)
    End If
Next
%>
```

Cookies are used for many purposes other than to exchange information among different pages on the same site. Every site that provides customized start pages uses cookies to store user information. Some Web sites may store information about the topics you search most often and adjust the ads they present to you.

Using ActiveX Data Objects

The most important component of ASP is the Database component, which is nothing else than the ADO. We left this topic for last so that we can use the objects discussed earlier in this chapter to build more elaborate and practical examples. Although you can use other components to access databases on the server, most Web developers use the ADO component.

As you recall from our discussion in Chapter 11, the ADO is the simplest object for accessing databases. It's object model is much simpler than that of DAO (Data Access Objects) or even the RDO (Remote Data Objects). Yet, the ADO is the most powerful component and is used on most sites that deploy Active Server Pages. You can also use the DAO component and even develop your own ActiveX components to access databases on the server. This approach will work, but if you are setting up a new Web site, you should seriously consider ADO. It's faster, consumes fewer resources on the server (an important consideration for servers with a heavy load), and will eventually replace the DAO.

Setting Up an ODBC Data Source

To access a database on the server through the Database component, you must first define a System ODBC data source for the database, using the ODBC Data Source Administrator. Follow these steps:

1. Choose Start ➤ Settings ➤ Control Panel.

2. Double-click 32bit ODBC (the ODBC Administrator) to open the ODBC Data Source Administrator dialog box:

3. Select the System DSN tab to see the installed data sources. For the examples of this chapter, we are going to use the NWIND sample database; so let's create a data source for the NWIND database.

4. Click the Add button to open the Create New Data Source Wizard. In this window, you will see the names of all ODBC drivers. Select the Microsoft Access driver and click Finish.

5. In the ODBC Microsoft Access 97 Setup dialog box, enter **NWINDDB** in the Data Source Name text box (you'll use this name to access the database). Enter a description in the Description text box, and then click Select to select the NWIND.MDB database in your VB folder.

6. Click OK to return to the ODBC Data Source Administrator dialog box. The new data source will now appear in this window.

Opening the Database

To access the NWIND database from within an Active Server Page, you must create a Connection object with the Server.CreateObject method, as shown here:

```
Set DBConnection = Server.CreateObject("ADODB.Connection")
```

This variable establishes a connection to the database when you call its Open method, whose syntax is:

```
DBConnection.Open "NWINDDB"
```

The first argument following the Open method's name must be the name of the data source that corresponds to the database you want to access. After you access the database to build the HTML page, you must release the Connection object by closing the connection with the Close method:

```
DBConnection.Close
```

TIP

This is the preferred method for accessing Microsoft Access databases. If you use the SQL Server instead, you can set up the *DBConnection* variable in the Application_OnStart event. This way it will be available to all clients that need to access the NWIND database. SQL Server supports multiple threads, and this technique will work. The Microsoft Access ODBC driver does not. Instead, there's a pool of connections, and the first available one is used. That's why you must release each connection object when you no longer need it.

Building a Recordset

After you establish a connection to the database, you can access it with SQL statements. To issue an SQL statement, use the Execute method of the Connection object, and pass the SQL statement as an argument. The syntax of the Execute method is:

```
DBConnection.Execute SQLStatement
```

The *SQLStatement* argument can be a string with the SQL statement or the name of a stored procedure. If the SQL statement returns records (as does the SELECT statement), the Execute method returns a recordset and should be called as follows:

```
Set SelRecords = DBConnection.Execute(SQLStatement)
```

The Execute method accepts two optional arguments:

- The number of records affected by the operation (this parameter is set by the driver)
- Whether the SQL statement is SQL text or the name of a stored procedure

The method's complete syntax is:

```
DBConnection.Execute SQLStatement, numRecords, SQLText
```

The *SQLText* argument can have the value adCmdText or adCmdStoredProc.

A second way to execute a SQL statement against the database is to create a Command object with the statement:

```
Set SQLCommand = Server.CreateObject("ADODB.Command")
```

You can then execute SQL statements with the SQLCommand object's Execute method. The Command object exposes several properties that let you specify the statement and how it will be executed.

For example, you can specify the Connection object to which the Command object applies (should you have multiple connections open), specify parameter values for stored procedures, and so on.

NOTE   For a complete discussion of the ADO object, see Chapter 11.

Here's how the Command object is typically used:

```
Set DBConnection = Server.CreateObject("ADODB.Connection")
Set SQLCommand = Server.CreateObject("ADODB.Command")
Set ParamItem = Server.CreateObject("ADODB.Parameter")

SQLCommand.ActiveConnection = DBConnection
SQLCommand.CommandText = "ProductsByCategory"
SQLCommand.CommandType = adCmdStoredProc
SQLCommand.ParamItem
SQLCommand.ParamItem.Name = "@ProductCategory"
SQLCommand.ParamItem.Value = 31
SQLCommand.Parameters.Append ParamItem
SQLCommand.Execute
```

These statements set up the SQLCommand Command object to execute a stored procedure with parameters. The same code can be simplified using a With structure:

```
Set DBConnection = Server.CreateObject("ADODB.Connection")
Set SQLCommand = Server.CreateObject("ADODB.Command")
Set ParamItem = Server.CreateObject("ADODB.Parameter")

With SQLCommand
    .ActiveConnection = DBConnection
    .CommandText = "ProductsByCategory"
    .CommandType = adCmdStoredProc
    With ParamItem
        .Name = "@ProductCategory"
        .ParamItem.Value = 31
        .Parameters.Append ParamItem
    EndWith
    .Execute
End With
```

Using the Recordset

Most ASP applications that access databases use recordsets to retrieve and display records, rather than edit them remotely. Recordsets have two important properties:

CursorType indicates the type of cursor used with the Recordset object.

LockType indicates the type of lock to be placed on a record during editing.

Cursors are similar to DAO's Recordset types: They determine the degree of navigation and the freshness of the recordset. There are four Cursor types:

ForwardOnly: This cursor is the most efficient and the fastest, but the least flexible. Its contents do not reflect the changes made by other users. It contains an image of the records at the moment they were retrieved from the database. ForwardOnly recordsets can only be scanned forward; they support only the MoveNext method.

KeySet: This cursor is more flexible than the ForwardOnly cursor. It lets you scan forward and backward and use bookmarks, but it doesn't automatically reflect changes made by other users. However, you can synchronize the recordset with the database with the ReSync method. Except for an initial overhead, the KeySet cursor is more efficient than a Dynamic cursor (discussed next), but if you don't want the recordset to be continuously synchronized, you should prefer the KeySet cursor over the Dynamic cursor type.

Dynamic: This is the most flexible, but the most expensive cursor type. It can be scanned forward and backward and reflect changes made to the records by other users. To make sure that the cursor's records are always up-to-date, the driver is constantly checking the records in the database to see if any have changed. Don't use this type of recordset on the Web because records can change while their previous values are being transmitted.

Static: KeySet and Dynamic cursors do not contain the actual fields of the records. Instead, they contain keys to the records and retrieve them from the database as needed. Static cursors contain the actual records (avoid them with very large recordsets) and provide forward and backward navigation. They do not reflect changes made by other users.

The LockType property determines when pages are locked and can have one of the following values:

- ReadOnly (default)
- Optimistic
- Pessimistic
- Batch Optimistic

NOTE   We discuss the various locking methods in Chapter 11.

To navigate through the recordset, use the MoveNext, MovePrevious, MoveFirst, and MoveLast methods. You can also bookmark certain records so that you can return to them instantly. To display all the records in the recordset, set up a loop like the following:

```
<%
Do While Not SelRecords.EOF
    {process fields}
    SelRecords.MoveNext
Loop
%>
```

To access the fields of the recordset, use the name of the recordset and the name of the field or its order in the recordset. For example, to access the field ProductName in the current record of the SelRecords recordset, use the expression:

```
SelRecords("ProductName")
```

Or, if the ProductName field is the first one (this is determined by the SQL SELECT statement), use the expression:

```
SelRecords(1)
```

NOTE We discuss the ActiveX Data Object in detail in Chapter 11.

The overview we presented in this chapter should be adequate for building interactive ASP Web applications that access databases on the server and display selected records. In the examples that follow, you will see how these objects are used in building Active Server Pages. The following examples are all based on the NWIND sample application, and we are assuming that you have set up a data source for this database.

The ALLPRODS.ASP Page

The ALLPRODS.ASP page displays a list of all the product categories in the NWIND database, as shown in Figure 17.6.

NOTE You'll find the ALLPRODS.ASP file in this chapter's folder on the CD that comes with this book.

The ASP page retrieves the category names and formats them as hyperlinks. When the visitor clicks a category name, the hyperlink takes him or her to another ASP page, the PRODCAT.ASP page, which displays all the products in the selected category, along with their prices and the number of units in stock. The output of the PRODCAT.ASP page is shown in Figure 17.7.

NOTE You'll find the PRODCAT.ASP file in this chapter's folder on the CD that comes with this book.

FIGURE 17.6

The ALLPRODS.ASP page displays the product categories in the NWIND database as hyperlinks.

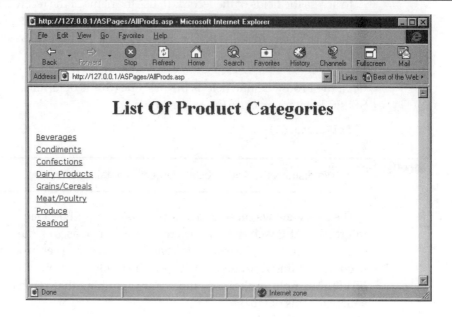

FIGURE 17.7:

The PRODCAT.ASP file displays the products in the category selected in Figure 17.6.

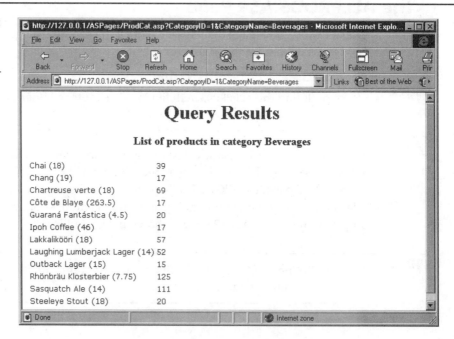

Let's examine the code of the ALLPRODS.ASP page. There's very little HTML code on this page; it's a server-side script that opens the NWINDDB database, creates a recordset with all the category names, and displays them as hyperlinks.

The line that inserts the hyperlinks is the most interesting code in this listing. If you ignore the expression surrounded by the server-side script tags, it's a simple HTML tag for inserting a hyperlink. Because the hyperlink's name and destination are not known at the time of this file's design, we insert them as expressions, which are substituted by the Active Server Pages when the file is processed.

Notice that all hyperlinks call the same URL on the server (the file PRODCAT.ASP), but each hyperlink passes a different parameter to it. The parameter is the ID of the category since this is the field stored in the Products table of the NWIND database, along with each product. The PRODCAT.ASP page uses this parameter to retrieve the products that correspond to the selected category. In addition, it passes the name of the category as the second parameter. This value is not needed in extracting the requested products from the database, but the script uses it to display the name of the selected category. Had we omitted this parameter, the PRODCAT.ASP page would have to open the Categories table to find out the name of the selected category, display it in the page's header, and then open the Products table to retrieve the product names. By passing the name of the category as a parameter, we save the script from establishing a new connection to the database to read a value that's already known.

Code 17.7:   The ALLPRODS.ASP File

```
<HTML>
<%
Set DBObj = Server.CreateObject("ADODB.Connection")
DBObj.Open "NWindDB"

SQLQuery = "SELECT CategoryID, CategoryName FROM Categories"
Set RSCategories = DBObj.Execute(SQLQuery)
%>

<CENTER>
<H1>List Of Product Categories</H1>
</CENTER>

<TABLE>
<% Do While Not RSCategories.EOF %>
```

```
    <TR>
    <TD> <FONT FACE="Verdana" SIZE=2>
       <% CategoryName = RSCategories("CategoryName") %>
       <A HREF="/ASPages/ProdCat.asp?CategoryID=<%
=RSCategories("CategoryID") %>&CategoryName=<% =CategoryName  %> "> <%
= CategoryName %> </A>
       </FONT>
    </TD>
    </TR>
<%
RSCategories.MoveNext
Loop
DBObj.Close
%>

</HTML>
```

The PRODCAT.ASP file, which processes requests made by the ALLPRODS.ASP
page, is a bit more complicated. First, it must extract the values of the parameters
passed by the client. The following statements:

```
ReqCategory=Request.QueryString("CategoryID")
ReqName=Request.QueryString("CategoryName")
```

store these values to the variables *ReqCategory* and *ReqName*. The QueryString collection contains these values for you, and you don't have to do anything special to
read them. Simply access them by name. The value of *ReqCategory* is then used to
build the SQL statement that will retrieve the records from the Products table:

```
SQLQuery = "SELECT ProductName, UnitPrice, UnitsInStock FROM Products
WHERE CategoryID = " & ReqCategory & " ORDER BY ProductName"
```

This SQL statement returns a recordset with the products in the selected category. The script scans the records, one at a time, and displays each record on a
new row of a table. The code that builds the table looks quite complicated
because it combines HTML code and script statements. Replace every expression that appears between the <%> tags with a likely value (a product name for
the expression <% = RSProducts("ProductName") %> and so on) to see how
these lines gradually build the table in Figure 17.8, later in this chapter.

Code 17.8:   The PRODCAT.ASP File

```
<HTML>
<%
ReqCategory=Request.QueryString("CategoryID")
ReqName=Request.QueryString("CategoryName")
Set DBObj = Server.CreateObject("ADODB.Connection")
DBObj.Open "NWindDB"
SQLQuery = "SELECT ProductName, UnitPrice, UnitsInStock FROM Products
WHERE CategoryID = " & ReqCategory & " ORDER BY ProductName"
Set RSProducts = DBObj.Execute(SQLQuery)
%>

<CENTER>
<H1>Query Results</H1>
<H3>List of products in category <% = ReqName %></H3>
</CENTER>

<TABLE>
<% Do While Not RSProducts.EOF %>
  <TR>
  <TD> <FONT FACE="Verdana" SIZE=2>
      <% = RSProducts("ProductName") & " (" & RSProducts("UnitPrice") &
")" %>
    </FONT></TD>
  <TD><FONT FACE="Verdana" SIZE=2>
      <% = RSProducts("UnitsInStock") %>
    </FONT></TD>
  </TR>

<%
RSProducts.MoveNext
Loop
%>
</TABLE>
</HTML>
```

This example was fairly simple. Some of the code may look complicated, but try to separate the expressions that will be evaluated on the server from the pure HTML code. You can use symbolic names—ProdName and UnitPrice in your code—and after you make sure it works, replace these symbolic expressions with the actual server-side script variables.

The PRDSALES.ASP Page

Our next example is along the same lines, but the script is a bit more complicated. This time we'll start with the list of product categories. When the user selects a category, its products are displayed in the table shown in Figure 17.8. Each category hyperlink calls the PRODINV.ASP page, which responds by generating the page shown in Figure 17.8. The code of the PRODINV.ASP page is similar to the code of the PRODCAT.ASP page we examined in the previous section, only the lines that build the output are a bit more complicated.

FIGURE 17.8:

The PRODINV.ASP page displays a table with details about the products of a specific category.

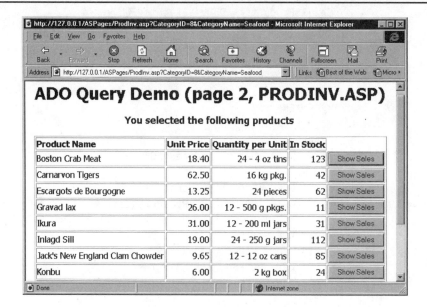

Not only can you see more details about each product, but you can click the Show Sales button to see the total sales for the specific product. From within the Click event of each button, the page requests another URL, which is the INVOICES.ASP page, and passes the product's name and ID as a parameter. The INVOICES.ASP page displays the total sales for the product, as shown in Figure 17.9. You can add more controls to the page in Figure 17.9 to let the user specify a time interval in which the totals will be calculated.

FIGURE 17.9:

The INVOICES.ASP
page retrieves and
displays the total
sales for a product.

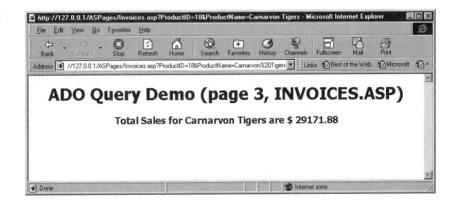

The code behind the ASP pages of this example is quite similar to the code of the ALLPRODS application, and we are not going to repeat it here. You will find all the files on the CD, and you can examine them. We will only discuss briefly the code that generated the table with the Command Buttons.

Code 17.9:   Constructing the Table

```
<% Do While Not RSProducts.EOF %>
  <TR>
  <TD>
      <% =RSProducts("ProductName") %>
  </TD>
  <TD ALIGN=right>
      <% =RSProducts("Price") %>
  </TD>
  <TD ALIGN=right>
      <% =RSProducts("QuantityPerUnit") %>
  </TD>
  <TD ALIGN=right>
    <% =RSProducts("UnitsInStock") %>
    </FONT></TD>
  <TD ALIGN=center>
    <INPUT TYPE=SUBMIT VALUE="Show Sales" _
        OnClick="Window.Navigate('/ASPages/Invoices.asp?ProductID=<%_
        =RSProducts("ProductID") %>&ProductName=<% _
        =RSProducts("ProductName") %>')">
  </TR>
```

```
<%
RSProducts.MoveNext
Loop
%>
```

The syntax of the tag for inserting a command button on an HTML page is:

```
<INPUT TYPE=SUBMIT VALUE="caption" ONCLICK="action">
```

The ONCLICK option lets you specify the action to take place when a button is clicked. Usually, we call a procedure on the same page (a client-side script) to carry out some action. In this example, we call the Navigate method of the Window object. The line is fairly lengthy, but looking at the code it produces when processed might help you understand it. If you open the PRDSALES.ASP file with Internet Explorer and look at the source code (choose View ➢ Source), you will see the actual HTML code generated by the ASP application. Here are the lines that correspond to the first product:

```
<TR>
  <TD>
      Boston Crab Meat
  </TD>
  <TD ALIGN=right>
      18.40
  </TD>
  <TD ALIGN=right>
      24 - 4 oz tins
  </TD>
  <TD ALIGN=right>
    123
    </FONT></TD>
  <TD ALIGN=center>
    <INPUT TYPE=SUBMIT VALUE="Show Sales" _

OnClick="Window.Navigate('/ASPages/Invoices.asp?ProductID=32&ProductName
=Boston Crab Meat')"
  </TR>
```

With these two examples, we end our discussion of using the Database component with Web pages. The Database component is based on the ActiveX Data Objects, and you should read Chapter 11 for information on this very flexible and powerful data component.

The File Access Component

The second basic component of the Active Server Pages we are going to discuss is the File Access component, which gives your server-side scripts access to text files on the server. The File Access component consists of two objects:

- FileSystemObject
- TextStream

The FileSystemObject object gives your script access to the server computer's file system, and the TextStream object lets your script open, read from, and write to text files.

The FileSystemObject Object

The FileSystemObject object gives your script access to the server computer's file system. To gain access to the server's file system, you create a FileSystemObject object with the CreateObject method of the Server object, as usual:

```
Set fs = Server.CreateObject("Scripting.FileSystemObject")
```

The *fs* entry is an object variable that represents the file system on the server. With the FileSystemObject variable's methods, you can open existing files and create new ones. The methods that open a file return a TextStream object, which provides the methods for reading and writing data. Let's look at the methods of the FileSystemObject object first.

The CreateTextFile Method

This method creates a text file and returns a TextStream object that can be used to read from or write to the file. The syntax of the CreateTextFile method is:

```
fs.CreateTextFile(filename, overwrite, unicode)
```

The *filename* variable is the path of the file to be created and is the only required argument; *overwrite* is a Boolean value that indicates whether you can overwrite an existing file (if True) or not (if False). If the *overwrite* argument is omitted, existing files are not overwritten. The last argument, *unicode*, indicates whether the file is created as a Unicode or as an ASCII file. If omitted, an ASCII file is assumed.

To create a new text file, you first create a FileSystemObject object variable and then call its CreateTextFile method as follows:

```
Set fs = CreateObject("Scripting.FileSystemObject")
Set TStream = fs.CreateTextFile("c:\testfile.txt", True)
```

The *TStream* variable represents a TextStream object, whose methods allow you to write to or read from the specified file.

The OpenTextFile Method

In addition to creating a new text file, you can open an existing file with the OpenTextFile method, whose syntax is:

```
Set Tstream = fs.OpenTextFile(filename, iomode, create, format)
```

The OpenTextFile method opens the specified file and returns a TextStream object that can be used to read from or write to the file. The *filename* argument is the only required one. The value of the *iomode* argument is one of the following constants:

> **ForReading**: The file is opened for reading.

> **ForAppending**: The file is opened for appending data.

The *create* optional argument is a Boolean value that indicates whether a new file can be created if the specified file name doesn't exist. The last argument, *format*, is also optional, and if it's True, the file is opened in Unicode mode. If it's False or omitted, the file is opened in ASCII mode.

To open a TextStream object for reading from a text file, use the following statements:

```
Set fs = CreateObject("Scripting.FileSystemObject")
Set TStream = fs.OpenTextFile("c:\testfile.txt", ForReading)
```

The TextStream Object

After you create a TextStream object with one of the FileSystemObject object's methods, you can use it to read from and write to the file.

The Methods of the TextStream Object

The methods of the TextStream object are equivalent to Visual Basic's file I/O functions. They allow you to read lines from and write lines to text files. The following methods apply to a *TextStream* object variable, which represents a file that has already been opened for input and/or output.

Read   This method reads a specified number of characters from a TextStream object. Its syntax is:

```
TSream.Read(characters)
```

The *characters* variable is the number of character to be read from.

ReadAll   This method reads an entire TextStream (text file) and returns the resulting string. Its syntax is simply:

```
TStream.ReadAll
```

ReadLine   This method reads one line of text at a time (up to, but not including, the newline character) from a TextStream file and returns the resulting string. Its syntax is:

```
TStream.ReadLine
```

Skip   This method skips a specified number of characters when reading a TextStream file. Its syntax is:

```
TStream.Skip(characters)
```

The *characters* variable is the number of character to be skipped.

SkipLine   This method skips the next line when reading from a TextStream. Its syntax is:

```
TStream.SkipLine
```

The characters of the skipped lines are discarded, up to and including the next newline character.

Write   This method writes a specified string to a TextStream file. Its syntax is:

```
TStream.Write(string)
```

The *string* variable is the string (literal or variable) to be written to the file. Strings are written to the file with no intervening spaces or characters between them. Use the WriteLine method to write a newline character or a string that ends with a newline character.

WriteLine   This method writes the specified string, followed by a newline character to the file. Its syntax is:

```
TStream.WriteLine(string)
```

The *string* variable is the text you want to write to the file. If you call the WriteLine method without an argument, a newline character is written to the file.

WriteBlankLines   This method writes a specified number of blank lines (newline characters) to the file. Its syntax is:

```
TStream.WriteBlankLines(lines)
```

The *lines* variable is the number of blank lines to be inserted in the file.

The Properties of the TextStream Object

The TextStream object provides a number of properties, which allow your code to know where the pointer is in the current TextStream.

AtEndOfLine   This is a read-only property that returns True if the file pointer is at the end of a line in the TextStream object and False otherwise. The AtEndOfLine property applies to files that are open for reading. You can use this property to read a line of characters, one at a time, with a loop similar to the following:

```
Do While TSream.AtEndOfLine =False
    newChar = TStream.Read(1)
    {process character}
Loop
```

AtEndOfStream   This is another read-only property that returns True if the file pointer is at the end of the TextStream object. The AtEndOfStream property applies only to TextStream files that are open for reading. You can use this property to read an entire file, one line at a time, with a loop such as the following:

```
Do While TStream.AtEndOfStream = False
    newChar = TStream.ReadLine
    {process line}
Loop
```

Column   This read-only property returns the column number of the current character in a TextStream line. The first character in a line is in column 1. Use this property to read data arranged in columns, without tabs or other delimiters between them.

Line Property   This read-only property returns the current line number in the TextStream. The Line property of the first line in a TextStream object is 1.

Using the TextStream Object

Here's a simple ASP page that demonstrates several of the TextStream object's methods. When this file is requested by the client, it creates a text file on the server computer and writes a few lines in it. Then, it opens the file, reads its lines, and displays them on an HTML page, which is returned to the client computer. As you will see, it uses the Write method of the Response object to send its output to the client.

Code 17.10:   Writing to and Reading from Text Files

```
<HTML>
<HEAD>
<TITLE>Working with Text Files</TITLE>
</HEAD>
<CENTER>
<H1>Working with Text Files</H1>
</CENTER>
<%
  Set FileObj = Server.CreateObject("Scripting.FileSystemObject")
  TestFile = Server.MapPath ("/AXPages\textfile.txt")
  Set OutStream= FileObj.CreateTextFile (TestFile, True, False)
  str1 = "This file was created on " & Now()
  OutStream.WriteLine Str1
  OutStream.WriteLine "This is Tip # 1"
  OutStream.WriteBlankLines(1)
  OutStream.WriteLine "This is Tip # 2"
  Set OutStream = Nothing

  Response.Write "The contents of the textfile.txt '" & TestFile &
"':<BR>"
  Response.Write "<HR>"
  Set InStream= FileObj.OpenTextFile (TestFile, 1, False, False)
%>
</BODY>
</HTML>
```

The Server object's CreateObject method creates a FileSystemObject through which the script can access the server's hard disk. It then calls the MapPath method to map a virtual folder to the actual folder name and specify a full path name. The path name of the text file is then passed to the CreateTextFile method to create the *OutStream* object variable. The second argument of the CreateTextFile method specifies that the text file should be overwritten if it already exists. After the desired lines have been written to the file, we set the *TextStream* object variable to Nothing to release it.

In the second half of the script, we create another TextStream object to read the lines of the same file. The file's lines are read with a While...Wend loop, which examines the value of the TextStream object's AtEndOfStream property to find out how many lines to read from the file:

```
While InStream.AtEndOfStream = False
    Line = Instream.ReadLine
    {process Tline text line}
Wend
```

Server-side scripts don't use text files frequently. Information is usually stored in databases, but it's not uncommon to store common variables in text files. We already discussed how you can implement a visitor counter with an Application variable. To make sure that this variable isn't reset every time you restart the Web server, you can store it to a text file. You can also use text files from within your scripts to store debugging information or to log information that's not available through the server's administration logging utilities (such as the duration of each session). In general, short pieces of information that don't justify the use of a database are usually stored in text files on the server.

PART V

Programming Office 97

CHAPTER

EIGHTEEN

18

An Introduction to VBA

- Programming with objects

- Using the VBA Editor to create macros

- Automating Microsoft Office applications

- Designing and using VBA Forms with Visual Basic

For several years, VBA (Visual Basic for Applications) was the programming language to use with Microsoft Office applications. VBA is a simple programming language that allows programmers (and power users as well) to do the following:

- Extend and automate Office applications,

- Integrate Office applications and their data with other applications

The basic idea is really simple: Create a common language and programming environment for a number of applications so that people can customize applications and add capabilities to suit their own environment. As such, VBA had to be simple. You can't use VBA to develop just any type of application you may need or think of. VBA provides only the basic control structures, math and string functions, and variable manipulation capabilities. The real power of VBA comes from the objects of the applications that support it.

With the introduction of VBA 5, Microsoft started licensing the language to manufacturers who want to add programmable features to their products, for example, Autodesk's AutoCAD. AutoCAD has been a programmable environment for many years, but its programming language was unique to AutoCAD and couldn't be shared with other applications. Many other manufacturers included scripting languages or other means of automating their software. But the need for a global language that would act as the glue in putting together pieces of many applications was clear. Finally, Microsoft came up with a version of VBA that meets the needs of other manufacturers, and VBA is on its way to becoming a universal language for automating applications under Windows.

Most companies today use off-the-shelf software and need to customize it. More than half the corporations in the United States use Microsoft Office products, and many of them use VBA to customize these applications to suit their business needs. This trend will continue and become stronger in the future. There is already a need not to simply customize applications, but to tie them together so that they can communicate. VBA does that too, and as a result, the need for VBA programmers will increase in the next few years.

Today's applications are so powerful and so feature-rich that it no longer makes sense to develop custom applications. Instead, it makes sense to customize existing applications and make them work together. Even the Office 97 applications are adequate for addressing most of the day-to-day computer operations of a typical corporation. With a host of third-party applications supporting VBA, you can easily guess its importance in corporate environments.

In this chapter, we'll introduce you to the parts and pieces of VBA and show you in general how you can use it with Visual Basic. In the following three chapters, we'll get into the specifics, discuss the objects of the major Office applications, and give you some concrete examples of how you can use them from within your own applications.

The examples in this and the following three chapters assume that you have Word and Excel installed on your system. You can automate other applications with VBA, but we are going to focus on the primary Office applications, since most of the VBA code written today applies to them. Because VBA depends on the functionality and the objects exposed by each individual application, you can apply the information in this chapter to other applications.

Programming with Objects

The theme running throughout this book is object programming. We have looked at all types of objects you will run into as a VB programmer, and VBA is no exception. The goal of VBA is to access the functionality of applications and either automate them (with macros—procedures made up of VBA commands) or control them from within other applications. And, as you no doubt know so well by now, applications make their functionality available to other applications via objects. Applications expose objects, which represent their programmable entities:

The Visual Basic IDE exposes the CommandBars collection, which represents the toolbars of the Visual Basic IDE. The DAO (Data Access Object) exposes the Database object, which represents an entire database. Likewise, Word exposes the ActiveDocument object, which represents the current document, the Selection object, which represents the current selection, and so on. Excel exposes a different set of objects, better suited for the type of data it can handle. Instead of the ActiveDocument object, it exposes the ActiveSheet object, which represents the active worksheet.

All these objects have properties, which are also objects or collections of objects. For instance, the Documents collection contains an item for each open document. Each Document object, in turn, contains a Paragraphs collection, which represents all the paragraphs in the document. You already know that you can access each paragraph of a DOC document, and as you will see, you can access individual words and characters.

For example, to access the first paragraph of the document DevHandbook.doc, you use an expression such as the following:

```
Documents("DevHandbook.doc").Paragraphs(1)
```

To set the Bold attribute of this paragraph, you must use an even longer expression:

```
Documents("DevHandbook.doc").Paragraphs(1).Font.Bold
```

NOTE   Bold is a property of the Font object, as you may recall from Chapter 5.

Expressions involving objects exposed by Office applications can get quite lengthy, but they are usually simple to build and understand. The object model of each application forms a hierarchy, which represents the structure of the documents each application can handle.

When an application is manipulated from within another, we say that the application is *automated*. You can't really program Word to do something it doesn't know how or can't do. You must call functions already built into Word to access the objects exposed by Word itself. In essence, you are automating Word. You are telling Word to carry out an action that isn't implemented as a menu command, to carry out an action repeatedly on each paragraph, and so on. VBA is not a complete language. Instead, it relies on the functionality of the applications that support VBA and expose it via an object model.

The same object can also be used from within other applications. You can write Word macros that rely on Excel to retrieve data and then format them as DOC files. You can also borrow the functionality of Office applications from within your Visual Basic applications. You will see later in this chapter how to use Word's spell-checking capabilities to verify the spelling of a document from within a Visual Basic application and how to use Excel capabilities to evaluate a math expression from within your Visual Basic application.

The New VBA Editor

VBA is not a new language; it's been around for several years, although limited to Office applications. And, as you probably know, the simplest way to program in VBA is to record a macro. Every operation you can perform with the keyboard and menu commands in Word or Excel can be recorded as a macro. Macros can be executed (or played back) to perform the same operation on different data.

The most common use of macros is to assign formatting commands to keystrokes. Let's say you are using Word to prepare elaborate documents, with many formatting options. If your documents contain code segments, you probably want to format these segments in Courier New 10 or 11 point and indent their left edge more than the text. Instead of selecting every code segment in the document and then applying the formatting manually, you can record a macro that contains all the commands you must issue to apply the desired formatting. You can also assign these commands to a keystroke, such as Alt+C. Then, each time you want to format a section as a code segment, all you have to do is select the text and press Alt+C.

In older versions of VBA, macros were the only means of programming, or automating, Office applications. You could edit macros, but there were no debugging tools and no special editor (an editor with an Auto List Members features, for example). With VBA 5, a new editor was introduced, which is nearly identical to the IDE editor of Visual Basic 5. As you type the name of an object variable, the editor displays the names of its members in a drop-down list, where you can select the desired member. The new VBA editor is a programmer's editor, and it simplifies the manual coding of macros as much as an editor can. VBA 5 comes with an integrated development and debugging environment, which was sorely missing from previous versions of VBA.

Using the Auto List Members Feature

If you're a seasoned programmer, you may find the Auto List Members feature a real annoyance. But you will find it extremely useful with VBA because Office applications expose their own objects and most VB programmers just aren't familiar with these objects. A reminder won't hurt.

If you want, you can turn off the Quick Tip feature and type the names of the members in lowercase. If the member is supported by the object, the VBA editor will adjust the spelling of the member's name the moment your pointer leaves the line.

For example, you can type the following:

Application.activeprinter

If the Application object supports the property ActivePrinter, the editor automatically changes the name of the property to Application.ActivePrinter when you press Enter (or move the pointer to another line).

Another limitation of previous versions of VBA was the lack of Forms. VBA macros were limited to the user interface of the application. You could add a few dialog boxes, but not elaborate Forms, such as the ones you can design with Visual Basic. VBA 5 has a Form Designer that lets you design Forms just as you do with Visual Basic and incorporate them in a macro. As you can see, with a proper editor, debugging tools, and a Form Designer window, VBA is no longer a macro language. It's a fully developed language with which you can write real applications in the environment of Office 97, not just customize applications.

Recording Macros

The example of a paragraph formatting macro is a trivial one, but you will see shortly how to develop more elaborate macros that behave like applications. But let's start with the simplest operation of all—recording a macro.

No matter how elaborate your VBA programs are, macros are indispensable. The Macro Recorder will generate most of the trivial code of your macro. As you will see, VBA is a verbose language, and the more code you can generate automatically, the better—less typing, fewer chances for mistakes, and less testing.

Let's start by looking at the VBA code of a common operation, searching for a string:

1. Start Word and open an existing file, or create a new one and enter some text.

2. Choose Tools ➢ Macro ➢ Record New Macro to open the Record Macro dialog box:

3. In the Macro Name box, enter the name of the new macro. You can click the Toolbars or the Keyboard button to assign the new macro to a keystroke or to the toolbar. (This is a simple test, and you don't need to make the macro permanent. We'll delete it shortly anyway.)

4. The default macro name is Macro1, and if a macro by the same name exists, Word will ask you whether it should overwrite it.

5. Click OK, and you will see a small window on your screen, with two VCR-style buttons: Stop Recording and Pause Recording. Every action you perform on the current document with the keyboard or the mouse from now on will be recorded. To pause the recording of the commands (say you want to look up the Help files), click the Pause Recording button. To end the recording of the macro, click the Stop Recording button.

Now perform the following actions:

1. Press Ctrl+Home to move to the top of the document.

2. Choose Edit ➤ Find to open the Find and Replace dialog box.

3. In the Find What box, enter the string you want to look for (in this example, our text included the word *macro,* and we searched on that string), and click the Find Next button. Word locates and highlights the first instance of the word *macro* in the document. Because we did not check the Match Case box or the Find Whole Words Only box, it locates any instance of the word, regardless of case or whether the word is part of another word.

4. The macro is now recorded. Click the Stop Recording button.

Now let's open the macro to see its code. Follow these steps:

1. Choose Tools ➤ Macro ➤ Macros to open the window where all available macros are displayed.

2. Select the Macro1 entry (or whatever the macro's name is) and then click the Edit button to open the VB Editor window. You will see the listing of the Macro1 macro, as shown in Figure 18.1.

FIGURE 18.1:

In the Visual Basic Editor window, you can edit any macro recorded in a Word session.

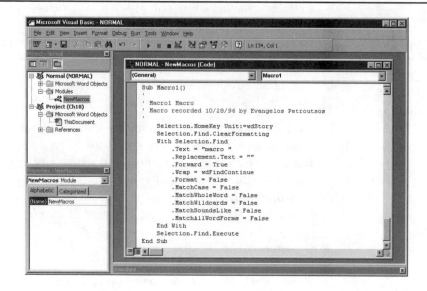

Code 18.1:   The Macro1 Macro

```
Sub Macro1()
'

' Macro01 Macro
' Macro recorded 10/26/96 by Evangelos Petroutsos
'

    Selection.HomeKey Unit:=wdStory
    Selection.Find.ClearFormatting
    With Selection.Find
        .Text = "macro"
        .Replacement.Text = ""
        .Forward = True
        .Wrap = wdFindContinue
        .Format = False
        .MatchCase = False
        .MatchWholeWord = False
        .MatchWildcards = False
        .MatchSoundsLike = False
        .MatchAllWordForms = False
    End With
    Selection.Find.Execute
End Sub
```

The first line of code represents the Ctrl+Home keystroke, which took us to the beginning of the document. All the following lines represent the Find operation. Since we are not replacing the word we found, you can omit the following line:

```
.Replacement.Text = ""
```

To find another word, simply replace the string "macro" with any other string. If you want to perform a more elaborate search, use the macro recorder to capture the appropriate commands. Figure 18.2 shows the Find and Replace dialog box with the arguments of another, more complicated search operation. By specifying the word *replace* and checking the Find All Word Forms box, you're telling Word to find not only the instances of the word *replace*, but the words *replaced* and *replacing* as well. The new macro is identical to the previous one, except for the last option:

```
.MatchAllWordForms = True
```

FIGURE 18.2:

The Find and Replace dialog box for a more complicated search

The With Structure

You are probably familiar with the With structure. It's a shorthand notation for referencing objects' properties and methods. Objects can have really long names. The expression Selection.Find represents the Find dialog box, and each option in this dialog box is another property of this object. The expression Selection.Find.Text represents the text to search for.

Instead of repeating the object's name over and over (thus making the code harder to type and read), you can type the names of the properties within a With structure. The object name following the With keyword determines the object to which these properties apply.

Developing a "Real World" Word Macro

Let's look at a more meaningful example of automating Word. When preparing long documents with many figures, such as this chapter, we avoid inserting figures in the text. This would slow down many normal editing operations, not to mention that, in general, the figures are not available at the time of the writing or they must be revised later.

To make sure that we have all the figures we need for a chapter, we like to collect all the figure captions at the end of the chapter or in a separate file and use this file to capture the appropriate figures. When all figure captions, along with their numbers, are listed in the same order as they appear in the text, we can easily check whether we've skipped a figure number. This simple operation is done with the CollectCaptions macro we'll develop in this section.

> **NOTE** You'll find the CollectCaptions macro in the Ch18\WMacro folder on the CD that comes with this book.

The CollectCaptions macro is based on the one you recorded earlier, only it repeats the search as many times as necessary to extract all the captions from the text. Clearly, we must place the lines generated earlier by the Macro Recorder into a loop structure, which will repeat them as many times as there are captions in the document. The captions copied by the macro will be appended to a string variable, and, when done, we'll paste this variable at the end of the document.

To implement the new macro in the Visual Basic Editor of Word, follow these steps:

1. Start Word, and choose Tools ➢ Macro ➢ Visual Basic Editor to open the VB Editor window for Word, which looks a lot like the Visual Basic window.

> **NOTE** In the next chapter, we'll explore the components of the Visual Basic Editor interface in detail.

Standard toolbar   Procedure drop-down list   Object drop-down list

Project Explorer

Code Window

Properties Window

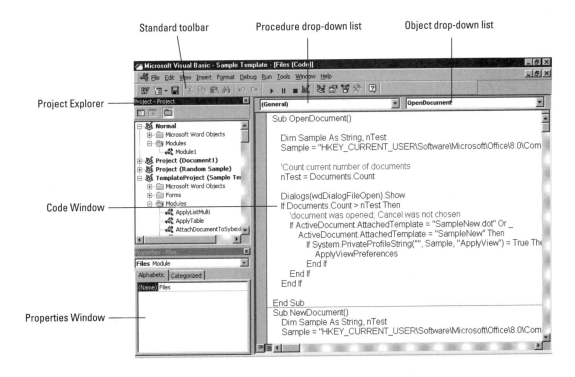

2. Open the Code window and create a new subroutine and name it CollectCaptions. In other words, enter the following lines in the Code window:

```
Sub CollectCaptions()
End Sub
```

3. Copy the contents of the Macro1 macro and paste them in the new procedure's body.

The specification .Wrap = wdFindContinue tells Word to ask the user whether to continue searching the document from the beginning, once it reaches the end. Since we are going to start the Find operation at the first character of the document, we don't need to display this prompt; so remove this line from the code or comment it out as we've done in the listing.

Next, we must decide how many times to loop. Since we don't know in advance how many captions the document contains, we must set up a While... Wend loop that will keep finding the next caption until a search operation ends unsuccessfully. When a Find operation ends unsuccessfully, the Found property of the Find object is False. Our code will examine the value of this property and end the loop by setting the value of the FindMore variable.

Code 18.2:   **The CollectCaptions Macro**

```
Sub CollectCaptions()
'

' CollectCaptions Macro
' Macro recorded 10/25/96 by Evangelos Petroutsos
' This macro collects all figure captions in the text
' and appends them to the document.
' Captions are formatted with the Caption style, which is
' used to locate them in the text

Dim CaptionsText As String

' Move to beginning of document
Selection.HomeKey Unit:=wdStory
' Set up the Find & Replace dialog box's parameters
Selection.Find.ClearFormatting
Selection.Find.Style = ActiveDocument.Styles("Caption")
With Selection.Find
    .Text = ""
    .Replacement.Text = ""
    .Forward = True
'    .Wrap = wdFindAsk
    .Format = True
    .MatchCase = False
    .MatchWholeWord = False
    .MatchWildcards = False
    .MatchSoundsLike = False
    .MatchAllWordForms = False
End With
' Now execute the Find operation
Selection.Find.Execute
CaptionsText = CaptionsText & Selection.Text
If (Not Selection.Find.Found) Or Selection.End Then
    FindMore = False
End If
FindMore = True
' Repeat the Find operation as long as there are more instances
' of the text being searched
While FindMore
    Selection.Find.ClearFormatting
    Selection.Find.Execute
' Stop searching if last find operation was not successful
    CaptionsText = CaptionsText & Selection.Text
```

```
        If (Not Selection.Find.Found) Then
            FindMore = False
        End If
    Wend
    ' Insert spaces before the list of captions
    CaptionsText = vbCrLf & vbCrLf & vbCrLf & "L I S T   O F   C A P T I O N S"
    & vbCrLf & CaptionsText
    ' Append list of captions to text
    Selection.EndKey Unit:=wdStory
    Selection.Text = CaptionsText
    ' Set Normal style, or else it may be formatted in the
    ' document's last paragraph's style
    Selection.Style = "Normal"
    End Sub
```

Figure 18.3 shows the CollectCaptions macro being edited in Word's Visual Basic Editor. Notice that the Find object's properties need not be defined at each iteration. We can simply call the Execute method of the Find object. Each time a new caption is located in the text, we copy it and append it to the local variable *CaptionsText*. When the loop ends, we paste the variable *CaptionsText* at the end of the document. We move to the end of the document and paste the string as a Selection object. This highlights the new text so that we can apply the Normal format to it. If you don't reformat the pasted text, it will be formatted according to the format of the last paragraph in the document (which could be another caption, for all we know).

FIGURE 18.3:

The CollectCaptions macro being edited in the VBA Editor

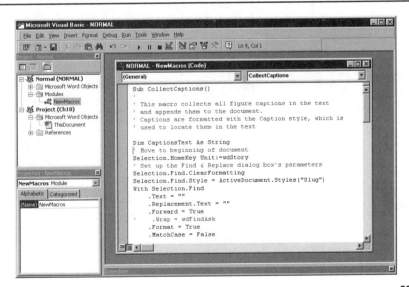

Automating Office Applications

In this section, we'll explore how you can automate Office applications from within your Visual Basic applications. The idea is to exploit the functionality of the various applications without having to rewrite the code. One of the things you can do so well with Word is spell-check your documents, but this feature is useful in the context of other applications. If you want to add spell-checking capabilities to a VB application, you can "borrow" the spell-checking capabilities of Word and incorporate them in your application. You can even hide Word, and users need not know you are contacting Word to do all the work. However, the Word application must be installed on the host system.

Rich Services and the Operating System

Shouldn't basic services, such as document editing, spell-checking, charting, and so on, be part of the operating system? Right now, they are part of Office applications, and you can't assume that Office applications will be available on every system.

It would work much better if these basic features were part of the operating system, but these features are costly. Someone has to pay for their development, and Microsoft decided that including them with Office applications is the best way to recover the cost.

Eventually, all these services may end up in the operating system, and you will be able to expect that your applications will run on every host system. You can also purchase a spell-checker and install it along with your application. However, Office applications are popular, and you can expect to find them installed on many host systems. Moreover, by developing custom applications based on the Office applications, you may be able to justify the cost of installing Office on a standalone system or on a corporate network.

To access an Office application from within a VB application, you must first create an object variable that references the desired application, just as you did for the ActiveX components you developed in Chapter 6. You declare this variable as Object, with the following statement (change the name of the variable according to the application you want to access):

```
Dim AppExcel As Object
```

To actually instantiate the AppExcel, you use the CreateObject or the GetObject function. The CreateObject function creates a new instance of an object. To create a new instance of Excel from within your VB application, use this statement:

```
Set AppExcel = CreateObject("Excel.Application")
```

The string "Excel.Application" is the programmatic ID of the application that supplies the object. This variable references the application itself. The CreateObject method starts a new instance of the application (or ActiveX component), even if an instance of it is already running.

If one or more instances of the application is already running, you can contact this instance of the application instead of creating a new one. The obvious advantage of this technique is that no additional resources are required. To do so, use the GetObject method, whose syntax is:

```
Set objectvariable = GetObject([pathname] [, progID])
```

The pathname argument can be the path to an existing file or to an empty string, or it can be omitted entirely. If you omit it, the *progID* argument is required. If you specify the path to an existing file, the GetObject method will create an object using the information stored in the file (it will start the application associated with this file). If it's a DOC file, for example, it opens the specified file in an existing instance of Word. If Word isn't running at the moment, it will be started, and the specified file will be opened in its main window. Using an empty string for the first argument causes GetObject to act like CreateObject—it creates a new object of the class whose programmatic identifier is *progID*.

To open the file SALES97.XLS with Excel, you can use the statements:

```
Dim XLObj As Object
Set XLObj = GetObject("C:\SALES\SALES97.XLS")
```

When the second line executes, the file SALES97.XLS either opens in a running instance of Excel or starts a new instance of Excel and opens the XLS file in it. When you supply the *pathname* argument (the file name of a document), you need not specify the *progID* argument.

If you omit the name of the file in the GetObject() function, the function returns a handle to the running instance of Excel or an error message if Excel isn't running. If you want to use the running instance of Excel to evaluate a math expression (an operation that doesn't entail any changes in the currently open document), you can contact a running instance of Excel, call its Evaluate method, and then release the object variable, as shown here:

```
Dim XLObj As Object
Set XLObj = GetObject(, "Excel.Application")
If Err.Number <> 0 Then
    ' Excel isn't running, you must start a new instance
    Set XLObj = CreateObject("Excel.Application")
End If
X = XLObj.Evaluate("3*sin(2/log(45.5))"
```

Object Variables and Early Binding

The object variables we created in the previous section are not of a specific type. As we mentioned time and again in the second part of this book, Visual Basic doesn't have enough information about them at design or compile time to check the validity of their members. This means that the variables will be late bound; not only will the application be slower at run time, but any reference to nonexistent members will cause a run-time error. Whenever possible, declare object variables with specific types.

If you enter the following line in the Visual Basic Editor (not the VBA Editor), you would expect to see a variable type that matches the object you want to reference.

```
Dim AppWord As
```

Such a type doesn't appear in the drop-down list. Does this mean you can't use early binding with object variables that reference Office applications and/or their objects? Not at all. You see the Auto List Members drop-down box because Visual Basic doesn't know that you want to reference another application from within your program. When the line that sets the object variable is reached during execution, Visual Basic locates the application you are referencing in the Registry and starts it in the background.

To be able to declare the *AppWord* and *AppExcel* variables with an explicit type (and not as Object type), you must first add a reference to the type library of the application you want to reference. To do so, follow these steps:

1. Choose Project ➤ References to open the References dialog box.

2. Check the boxes Microsoft Excel 8.0 Object Library and Microsoft Word 8.0 Object Library, as shown in Figure 18.4.

FIGURE 18.4:

Use the References dialog box to add the object libraries of other applications to your Visual Basic application.

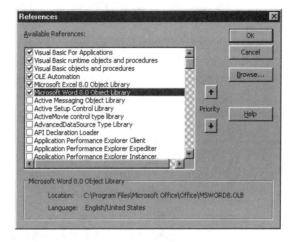

NOTE   See Chapter 19 for much more information on the References dialog box.

3. Now enter the same line in the Form's declaration section and scan the list of available variable types in the Auto List Members drop-down list box (shown in Figure 18.5).

FIGURE 18.5:

Add the object libraries of the applications you want to reference, and their types will appear in the Auto List Members box as you enter VB code.

The declarations of the object variables *AppExcel* and *AppWord* should be:

```
Dim AppWord As Word.Application
Dim AppExcel As Excel.Application
```

These declarations are all the information Visual Basic needs to early bind the variables and check the validity of their members at design time.

The VBAObjects Application

Now that we have seen how to create object variables that represent the Office applications, let's build an application that demonstrates these techniques. The VBAObjects application lets you start a new instance of Excel or Word, create a new Word document or a new Excel worksheet, and manipulate it from within a Visual Basic application. The application's main Form is shown in Figure 18.6.

NOTE   You'll find the VBAObjects application in the Ch18\VBAObjs folder on the CD that comes with this book.

FIGURE 18.6:

The main Form of the VBAObjects application

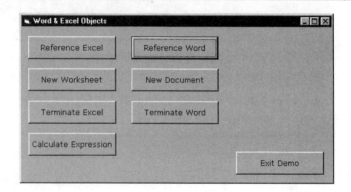

When you run VBAObjects, all buttons are disabled except for the two buttons that reference Excel and Word. When these buttons are clicked, the program creates a new instance of Excel or Word and enables the remaining buttons on the Form. (We'll discuss the operation of these buttons later in this chapter.)

The object variables that represent the two applications are declared outside any procedure:

```
Dim AppWord As Object
Dim AppExcel As Object
```

Both buttons create a new instance of the application, and they assign it to an object variable, which is used later by the other procedures in the program.

Code 18.3:   The Click Event Handler of the Reference Excel Button

```
Private Sub Command1_Click()

    Screen.MousePointer = vbHourglass
    Set AppExcel = CreateObject("Excel.Application")
    Screen.MousePointer = vbDefault
    Command3.Enabled = True
    Command5.Enabled = True
    Command8.Enabled = True

End Sub
```

The code for the Reference Word button is similar, except that it passes the Class Word.Application to the CreateObject method.

We will examine the code behind the other buttons on the VBAObjects Form later, but you can run the application now. Instantiate the *AppExcel* and *AppWord* object variables, and then break the application and check out the members of the two object variables in the Immediate window. (In the examples below, the results displayed in the Immediate window are underlined.) You can find the names of the applications that these two variables reference.

```
Print AppExcel.Name
    Microsoft Excel
Print AppWord.Name
    Microsoft Word
```

Or you can ask Excel to evaluate math expressions:

```
Print AppExcel.Evaluate ("log(999.333)")
    2.99971022893117
```

You can use the AppWord object to find out whether a word is spelled correctly:

```
Print AppWord.CheckSpelling("Antroid")
    False
```

Or you can display the names of the fonts installed:

```
For i=1 To AppWord.FontNames.Count: Print AppWord.FontNames(i):Next
    Times New Roman
    Arial
    Courier New
    {more font names}
```

Simply type the name of the object variable followed by a period and then select a member (property or method) from the drop-down list that appears automatically, as shown in Figure 18.7.

FIGURE 18.7:

Use the Visual Basic Immediate window to check out the members of the *AppWord* and *AppExcel* object variables.

You might want to change the declarations of the *AppWord* and *AppExcel* object variables to generic object variables to see how they are going to affect the application at design time and at run time. The Auto List Members feature will be practically useless, and all references to the wrong members will cause run-time errors.

The Application Object

When an application is executed in the background, you can access it via the Application object, which represents the running application and is common to all Office applications. You can think of the Application object as a container for the application's objects. Besides being your back door to the running application, the Application object has a few members of its own. Here are the most important:

ActivePrinter: Returns or sets the name of the active printer.

ActiveWindow: Returns the handle to the application window that has the focus.

Caption: Returns or sets the string that appears on the application window's title bar. You can use this property to find out whether a window contains a specific document.

DisplayAlerts: Normally, Office applications display dialog boxes to confirm certain actions (such as deleting a large amount of data) or irreversible actions (such as closing a document without saving it). If you are running the application in the background and you don't want users to see any dialog boxes other than the ones displayed by your application, set this property to False. When your procedure ends, the DisplayAlerts property is reset to True automatically.

ScreenUpdating: Normally, when a macro is executed, the application's window is updated after the completion of each command. This is usually unnecessary, as these actions take place too quickly and the user can't follow them anyway. In general, it's a good idea to turn off the updating of the screen from within your macros. To do so, set the ScreenUpdating property to False. When you are done, remember to turn it on again; this property isn't reset automatically.

Top, Left: These two properties return or set the position of the application's window.

Width, Height: These two properties return or set the dimensions of the application's window.

UsableWidth, UsableHeight: These properties return the dimensions of the document window within the application's window. Normally, they are the window's total width (or height), minus the space taken by scrollbars, menu bars, and toolbars.

Visible: Hides (if False) or displays (if True) the application's window.

Windows: This property is a collection of Window objects, which represent the application's windows.

WindowState: This property returns or sets the state of the application's main window. The window's state can be:

    Maximized: xlMaximized or wWindowStateMaximize

    Minimized: xlMininized or wWindowStateMinimize

    Normal: xlNormal or wWindowStateNormal

The Application object supports a few methods as well, which are different depending on the application. You can use these methods to tap into the functionality unique to the application. Both Excel's and Word's Application objects provide the OnTime method, which executes a procedure at a specified time. Its syntax is:

```
Application.OnTime when, name, tolerance
```

The argument *when* is a date and time expression indicating when the procedure will be invoked; *name* is the name of the procedure that will be executed, and the *tolerance* argument is the delay (in seconds) you are willing to tolerate, with respect to the argument *when*.

Another common method is the Move method, which repositions the window on the screen and is equivalent to changing the Top and Left properties. The methods that apply to all applications are more or less generic. However, a few methods expose unique functionality that you can access from within your applications. One of them is the CheckSpelling method, which can spell-check a word or an entire document. The CheckSpelling method is a member of the Application object and of the Selection object, which represents the current selection. When used as a method of the Application object, its syntax is:

```
Application.SpellCheck(word, CustomDictionary, IgnoreUpperCase)
```

The *word* argument is the word to be spelled, *CustomDictionary* is the file name of a custom dictionary, and *IgnoreUpperCase* specifies whether words in uppercase will be ignored. The SpellCheck method returns a True/False result, indicating whether the word is spelled correctly. The same method is also available with Excel's Application object.

In the following sections, we are going to look at the basic objects of Word and Excel, and we'll present a few examples. In the following chapters, we are going to look at each application's objects in depth and show you how to automate Office applications with macros or from within your VB applications.

Working with Word VBA Objects

Word provides numerous objects with which you can program any action that can be carried out with menu commands. Under the Application object is the Documents collection, which contains a Document object for each open document. Using an object variable of Document type, you can access any open document (or open and create new documents). The most important object that each document exposes is the Range object, which represents a contiguous section of text. This section can be words, part of a word, characters, or even the entire document. Using the Range object's methods, you can insert new text, format existing text (or delete it), and so on.

To address specific units of text, use the following collections:

- Paragraphs, which are made up of Paragraph objects

- Words, which are made up of Word objects

- Characters, which are made up of Character objects

These objects represent a paragraph, word, or character in the object to which they apply. For example, if you access the Paragraphs collection of a specific document, you retrieve all the paragraphs of the document. If you apply the same method to the current selection (represented by the Selection object), you retrieve all the paragraphs in the selected text.

The Documents Collection and the Document Object

The first object under the Word Application object hierarchy is the Document object, which is any document that can be opened with Word or any document that can be displayed in Word's window. All open documents are represented by a Documents collection that is made up of Document objects. Like all other collections, it supports the Count property (the number of open documents), the Add method, which adds a new document, and the Remove method, which closes an existing one. To access an open document, you can use the Item method of the Documents collection, specifying the document's index:

```
Application.Documents.Item(1)
```

or the document's name:

```
Application.Documents.Item("VBHandbook.doc")
```

Since Item is the collection default property, you can omit its name altogether:

```
Application.Documents(1)
```

To open an existing document, use the Documents collection's Open method, whose syntax is:

```
Documents.Open(fileName)
```

The *fileName* argument is the document file's path name.

To create a new document, use the Documents collection's Add method, which accepts two optional arguments:

```
Documents.Add (template, newTemplate)
```

The argument *template* specifies the name of a template file to be used as the basis for the new document. The *newTemplate* argument is a Boolean value. If it's set to True, Word creates a new template file.

Most of the operations you will perform on text apply to the active document, which is represented by the ActiveDocument object. This is the document in the active Word window. You can also make any document active by calling the Activate method of the Document object. To make the document MyNotes.doc active, use the following statement:

```
Documents("MyNotes.doc").Activate
```

After the execution of this statement, the MyNotes.doc document is active, and your code can refer to it through the object ActiveDocument.

Objects That Represent Text

The basic object for accessing text in a Word document is the Range object, which represents a contiguous segment of text. To extract some text from a document, you can use the Document object's Range method, which accepts as arguments the positions of the starting and ending characters in the text. The syntax of the Range method is:

```
Document.Range(start, end)
```

The *start* and *end* arguments are two numeric values. Oddly enough, the first character's position in the document is zero. The statement:

```
Range1 = Document.Range (0, 99)
```

extracts the first 100 character of the document represented by the *Document* object variable. These characters are assigned to the *Range1* object variable, which represents a Range object.

In the previous expressions, the *Document* variable must first be set to reference an existing object, with a statement such as the following:

```
Set Document = Documents(1)
```

You can also replace the variable *Document* with the built-in object AppWord.ActiveDocument, which represents the active document (the one you've set with the Activate method).

Words, sentences, and paragraphs are more meaningful units of text than characters. We mentioned these collections earlier in this chapter, and you'll find more information on them in the following chapters. The Word, Sentence, and Paragraph objects are better suited for text manipulation, and you commonly use these objects to access documents. These objects, however, don't support all the properties of the Range object. Therefore, in addition to the Range method, there is a Range property, which returns a Word, Sentence, or Paragraph object as a Range.

For example, the following statement:

```
Document.Paragraphs(3).Range
```

returns the third paragraph in the document as a Range object. You can then access the Range object's properties to manipulate the third paragraph. The Paragraph object doesn't have a Font property or a Select method. To change the appearance of the third paragraph in the document, you can use a statement such as the following:

```
Document.Paragraphs(3).Font.Bold = True
```

Document is a properly declared Document variable, or you can use the AppWord.ActiveDocument object.

The following statement selects (highlights) the same paragraph:

```
Document.Paragraphs(3).Select
```

Once a paragraph (or any other piece of text) is selected, you can apply all types of processing to it (edit it, move it to another location, format it, and so on).

The two methods of the Range object that you will use most often are:

- InsertAfter, which inserts a string of text after the specified Range
- InsertBefore, which inserts a string of text in front of the specified Range

The following statements insert a title at the beginning of the document and a closing paragraph at the end:

```
AppWord.ActiveDocument.Select
AppWord.ActiveDocument.Range.InsertBefore "This is the document's title"
AppWord.ActiveDocument.Range.InsertAfter "This is the closing paragraph"
```

The Select method of the ActiveDocument object selects the entire text. The selected text is assigned to the Range object. The InsertBefore and InsertAfter methods place some text before and after the Range object.

VBAObjects: Creating a New Document

Now we can examine the code behind the New Document button of the VBAObjects application, which we looked at earlier in this chapter. When this button is clicked, the program does the following:

- Connects to a new instance of Word

- Creates a new document

- Inserts some text and formats it

- Counts the paragraphs, words, and characters in the new document and displays them in a message box

These actions take place from within the Visual Basic application, and Word is running in the background. The user doesn't see Word's window, not even as an icon on the taskbar. Clicking the OK button in the message box opens the Word window and displays the newly created document, as shown in Figure 18.8. At this point you can edit the document or shut down Word.

The code behind the New Document button is straightforward. It uses the object AppWord.Documents(1).Range to manipulate the text (insert new paragraphs and format them). Notice how it changes the alignment of the first text paragraph with the Alignment property of the Paragraph object.

FIGURE 18.8:

This document is created by a Visual Basic application, which manipulates the objects exposed by Word.

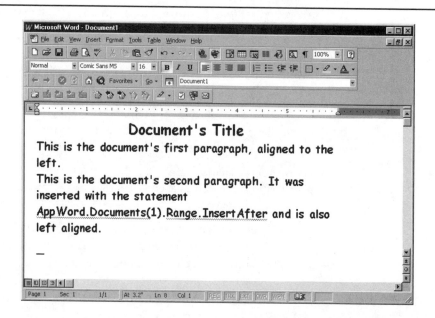

Code 18.4: The New Document Button

```
Private Sub Command4_Click()
Dim wDoc As Document
Dim tmpText As String
Dim parCount As Long, wordCount As Long, charCount As Long
Dim msg As String

    If AppWord.Documents.Count = 0 Then
        AppWord.Documents.Add
    End If
    AppWord.Documents(1).Range.InsertAfter "Document's Title" & vbCr
    AppWord.Documents(1).Range.Font.Bold = True
    AppWord.Documents(1).Range.Font.Size = 16
    AppWord.Documents(1).Range.Font.Name = "Comic Sans MS"
    AppWord.Documents(1).Range.InsertAfter "This the document's first _
            paragraph, aligned to the left." & vbCr
    AppWord.Documents(1).Range.InsertAfter "This the document's second _
            paragraph. "
    AppWord.Documents(1).Range.InsertAfter "It was inserted with the _
            statement "
    AppWord.Documents(1).Range.InsertAfter _
            "AppWord.Documents(1).Range.InsertAfter "
    AppWord.Documents(1).Range.InsertAfter "and is also left aligned." _
& vbCrLf

    parCount = AppWord.Documents(1).Paragraphs.Count
    wordCount = AppWord.Documents(1).Words.Count
    charCount = AppWord.Documents(1).Characters.Count
    msg = "The new document contains " & vbCrLf
    msg = msg & parCount & " paragraphs" & vbCrLf
    msg = msg & wordCount & " words" & vbCrLf
    msg = msg & charCount & " characters"
    MsgBox msg

    AppWord.Documents(1).Paragraphs(1).Alignment = _
wdAlignParagraphCenter
    AppWord.Visible = True

End Sub
```

The code behind the Terminate Word button is more interesting. To shut down Word, all you really need is the Quit method of the Application object. It would be quite simple if Word were running in the background only. But since we display Word's window, the user can close it before switching back to the VBAObjs application. If we attempt to close an application that has been closed already, we'll end up with a run-time error. To avoid a run-time error, the procedure that terminates Word uses an error handler.

The program closes Word with the Quit method and resumes with the next statement, if an error occurs. The next executable statement attempts to read the name of the application. If the error occurs because this particular instance of Word was already closed, an error will occur again, and the program will simply disable the New Document and Terminate Word buttons. If no error occurs, the two buttons are not disabled and the procedure ends.

Code 18.5:   The Terminate Word Button

```
Private Sub Command6_Click()

    On Error Resume Next
    AppWord.DisplayAlerts = False
    AppWord.Quit
Dim wRunning As String
    wRunning = AppWord.Application.Name
    If Error Then
        Command4.Enabled = False
        Command6.Enabled = False
    End If
End Sub
```

Spell-Checking Documents

One of the most useful features of Word (and of every Office application) is the ability to spell-check a document. This functionality is also exposed by Word's VBA objects, and you can borrow it for use within your VB applications. This is not only possible, it's quite simple. To call upon Word's spell-checking routines, you need to know about two objects:

- The ProofreadingErrors collection
- The SpellingSuggestions collection

The ProofreadingErrors collection is a property of the Range object, and it contains the misspelled words in the specified Range. If you want Word to spell-check a range of text and populate the ProofreadingErrors collection, call the Range object's SpellingError method. This method returns a result that must be stored in an object variable of type ProofreadingErrors:

```
SpellCollection As ProofreadingErrors
Set SpellCollection = DRange.SpellingErrors
```

The second line populates the *SpellCollection* variable with the misspelled words. You can then set up a loop to read the words from the collection.

Besides locating spelling errors, Word can also suggest a list of alternate spellings or words that sound like the misspelled one. To retrieve the list of alternate words, you call the GetSpellingSuggestions methods of the Application object, passing the misspelled word as an argument. Notice that this is a method of the Application object, not the Range object you are spell-checking. The results returned by the GetSpellingSuggestions method must be stored in a similar object variable, declared as SpellingSuggestions type:

```
Public CorrectionsCollection As SpellingSuggestions
Set CorrectionsCollection = AppWord.GetSpellingSuggestions("antroid")
```

The second line retrieves the suggested alternatives for the word *antroid*. To scan the list of suggested words, you set up a loop that retrieves all the elements of the CorrectionsCollection collection. The example in the next section demonstrates the use of both methods from within a Visual Basic application.

The SpellDoc Application

In this section we are going to look at the SpellDoc application (see Figure 18.9), a VB application that uses Word's methods to spell-check a document.

NOTE   You'll find the SpellDoc application in the Ch18\SpellDoc folder on the CD that comes with this book.

FIGURE 18.9:

The SpellDoc application's main Form

The user can enter text in the multiline TextBox control (or paste it from another application) and then spell-check it by clicking the Check Document button.

The results, which are the misspelled words, are displayed on a different Form, shown in Figure 18.10. The ListBox control on the left shows all the misspelled words returned by Word. Word can not only locate misspelled words, but suggest alternatives as well. To view the correct words suggested by Word for each misspelled word, click the corresponding entry in the list of misspelled words. The SpellDoc application doesn't replace the misspelled word in the document with the selected alternative, but this is straightforward code that manipulates strings. Once you have the list of misspelled words and the alternatives, you can design any number of interfaces that allow the user to correct the original document with point-and-click operations.

FIGURE 18.10:

This Form of the SpellDoc application displays the misspelled words and possible alternatives.

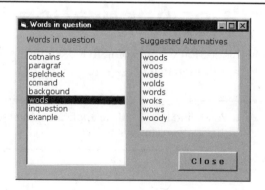

The program uses three public variables, which are declared as follows:

```
Public AppWord As Application
Public CorrectionsCollection As SpellingSuggestions
Public SpellCollection As ProofreadingErrors
```

The *SpellCollection* variable is a collection that contains all the misspelled words, and the *CorrectionsCollection* variable is another collection that contains the suggested alternatives. The *CorrectionsCollection* variable's contents are assigned every time the user clicks another misspelled word.

When the Check Document button is clicked, the program contacts the Word application. First, it attempts to connect to an existing instance of Word, with the GetObject function. If no instance of Word is currently running, it starts a new instance of Word.

Code 18.6:   The Check Document Button

```
Set AppWord = GetObject("Word.Application")
    If AppWord Is Nothing Then
        Set AppWord = CreateObject("Word.Application")
        If AppWord Is Nothing Then
            MsgBox "Could not start Word. Application will end"
            End
        End If
    End If
```

After contact with Word is established, the program creates a new document and copies the text there, using the InsertAfter method of the Range object:

```
AppWord.Dcouments.Add
DRange.InsertAfter Text1.Text
```

Now comes the interesting part. The VB code calls the Range object's SpellingErrors method, which returns a collection of Word objects. The result of the SpellingErrors method is assigned to the object variable *SpellCollection*:

```
Set SpellCollection = DRange.SpellingErrors
```

The following lines add the words contained in the *SpellCollection* variable to the left list of the second Form, and then they display the Form.

Code 18.7:   The Check Document Button

```
Private Sub Command1_Click()
Dim DRange As Range

    Me.Caption = "starting word ..."
On Error Resume Next
    Set AppWord = GetObject("Word.Application")
    If AppWord Is Nothing Then
        Set AppWord = CreateObject("Word.Application")
        If AppWord Is Nothing Then
            MsgBox "Could not start Word. Application will end"
            End
        End If
    End If
On Error GoTo ErrorHandler
    AppWord.Documents.Add
    Me.Caption = "checking words..."
    Set DRange = AppWord.ActiveDocument.Range
    DRange.InsertAfter Text1.Text
    Set SpellCollection = DRange.SpellingErrors
    If SpellCollection.Count > 0 Then
        SuggestionsForm.List1.Clear
        SuggestionsForm.List2.Clear
        For iWord = 1 To SpellCollection.Count
            SuggestionsForm!List1.AddItem SpellCollection.Item(iWord)
        Next
    End If
    Me.Caption = "Word VBA Example"
    SuggestionsForm.Show
    Exit Sub

ErrorHandler:
    MsgBox "The following error occurred during the document's
spelling" & vbCrLf & Err.Description
End Sub
```

On the second Form of the application, all the code is concentrated in the "Words in Question" list's Click event. Every time an entry in this List is clicked, the code calls the AppWord object's GetSpellingSuggestions method, passing the selected word as an argument. Notice that we add 1 to the List's ListIndex property to offset the fact that the indexing of the elements of a collection starts at 1, while the indexing of the elements of a ListBox control starts at zero. The GetSpellingSuggestions method returns another collection, with the suggested words, which are placed in the list on the right.

Code 18.8:   The List's Click Event

```
Private Sub List1_Click()

    Screen.MousePointer = vbHourglass
    Set CorrectionsCollection = _
        AppWord.GetSpellingSuggestions(SpellCollection.Item _
        (List1.ListIndex + 1))
    List2.Clear
    For iSuggWord = 1 To CorrectionsCollection.Count
        List2.AddItem CorrectionsCollection.Item(iSuggWord)
    Next
    Screen.MousePointer = vbDefault

End Sub
```

The SpellDoc application can become the starting point for many VB applications that require spell-checking, but that don't need powerful editing features. This situation isn't common, but in some cases you might want to customize spelling. In a mail-aware application, for example, you can spell-check the text and exclude URLs and e-mail addresses. You first scan the words returned by the SpellingErrors method to check which ones contain special characters and omit them.

As you can see, tapping into the power of the Office applications isn't really complicated. Once you familiarize yourself with the objects of these applications, you can access the Office applications by manipulating a few properties and calling the methods of these objects.

Working with Excel VBA Objects

The objects that Excel exposes have different names, but they form an equally sensible and structured hierarchy for accessing data stored in a tabular arrangement. Just as Word's basic unit of information is the text segment (not characters or words), Excel's basic unit of information is a Range. A Range object can contain a single cell or an entire worksheet (and everything in between).

The Application object represents an instance of Excel, and it supports most of the basic properties and methods of Word's Application object. In addition, it supports a few more methods that are unique to Excel. The most important methods of Excel's Application object are:

- Calculate
- OnKey
- Evaluate

The Calculate method recalculates all open worksheets. The OnKey method allows the programmer to specify a procedure to be executed each time the user presses a specific keystroke. The syntax of this method is:

```
Application.OnKey(key, procedure)
```

The *key* argument represents the keystrokes that will initiate a procedure, and the *procedure* argument is the procedure that will be executed each time the specified key combination is pressed. Table 18.1 shows the strings you can use for the *key* argument.

TABLE 18.1: The Settings of the OnKey Method's *key* Argument

Key	Expression
Arrow Dn	"{DOWN}"
Arrow Left	"{LEFT}"
Arrow Rt	"{RIGHT}"
Arrow Up	"{UP}"
Backspace	"{BACKSPACE}"
Break	"{BREAK}"
Caps Lock	"{CAPSLOCK}"
Delete	"{DELETE}", "{DEL}"
End	"{END}"
Enter	"{ENTER}", "{~}"
Esc	"{ESCAPE}", "{ESC}"
Home	"{HOME}"

TABLE 18.1 (CONTINUED): The Settings of the OnKey Method's *key* Argument

Key	Expression
Help	"{HELP}"
Insert	"{INSERT}"
NumLock	"{NUMLOCK}"
Page Dn	"{PGDN}"
Page Up	"{PGUP}"
Scroll Lock	"{SCROLLLOCK}"
Tab	"{TAB}"
F1 – F12	"{F1}" – "{F12}"

The Evaluate method evaluates math expressions and returns the result. The following statement:

```
Application.Evaluate "cos(3/1.091)*log(3.499)"
```

returns a numeric value that is the value of the math expression passed to the Evaluate method as an argument. You can also use variables in your expressions, as long as you store their values in specific cells and use the addresses of these cells in the expression. The following statement:

```
Application.Evaluate "log(" & Application.Range("A1") & ")"
```

returns the logarithm of the numeric value stored in cell A1. The Range object represents one or more cells, depending on the address you supply. In this example, we addressed a single cell (A1). You will see how you can address and access specific cells in an Excel worksheet in the following two sections.

The Sheets Collection and the Sheet Object

Each workbook in Excel contains one or more worksheets. The Worksheets collection, which is similar to Word's Documents collection, contains a Worksheet object for each worksheet in the current workbook. To add a new worksheet, use the Add method, whose syntax is:

```
Application.Worksheets.Add(before, after, count, type)
```

The *before* and *after* arguments let you specify the order of the new worksheet in the workbook. You can specify one of the two arguments, and if you omit both, the new worksheet is inserted before the active worksheet. The *type* argument specifies the type of the new worksheet and can have one of the following values:

xlWorksheet (the default value)

xlExcel4MacroSheet (a worksheet with Excel 4 macros)

xlExcel4IntlMacroSheet (a worksheet with Excel 4 international macros)

To access a worksheet, use the collection's Item method, passing the index or the worksheet's name as an argument. The following expressions are equivalent (if the second worksheet is named `SalesData.xls`):

```
Application.WorkSheets.Item(2)
Application.Worksheets.Item("SalesData.xls")
```

Since Item is the collection default property, you can omit its name altogether:

```
Application.Worksheets(2)
```

Objects That Represent Cells

Excel is an application for manipulating units of information stored in cells, but the basic object for accessing the contents of a worksheet is the Range object, which is a property of the Worksheet object. There are several ways to identify a Range (and we discuss them in detail in Chapter 20), but here's the basic syntax of the Range method:

```
Worksheet.Range(cell1:cell2)
```

Here, `cell1` and `cell2` are the addresses of the two cells that delimit a rectangular area on the worksheet. They are the addresses of the upper-left and lower-right corners of the selection (which is always rectangular; you can't select disjoint cells on a worksheet). Of course, you can address cells in several ways, but we will not discuss them here. In this section, we are going to use the standard Excel notation, which is a number for the row and a letter for the column, for example, C3 or A103.

You can also retrieve a single cell as a Range object, with the Cells method, whose syntax is:

```
Worksheet.Cells(row, col)
```

The *row* and *col* arguments are the coordinates of the cell as numbers. Finally, the Rows and Columns methods return an entire row or column by number. The following two expressions:

```
Worksheet.Rows(3)
Worksheet.Columns("D")
```

return the third row and the fourth column as Range objects.

The Range object is not a collection, but you can access individual cells in a Range object with the Cells method. The Cells method accepts a single argument, which is the index of the cells in the range. The index 1 corresponds to the upper left cell in the range, the index 2 corresponds to the second cell of the first row, and so on up to the last cell in the first row. The next index corresponds to the first cell of the second row and so on up to the last row. The Text property returns the cell's contents as a string, and the Value property returns the cell's contents as a string (if it's text) or as a numeric value (if it's numeric).

Another way to work with cells is to make a selection and access the properties and methods of the Selection object. To create a Selection object (which represents the cells that are highlighted if you select them with the mouse), use the Range object's Select method:

```
Range("A2:D2").Select
```

This statement creates a new Selection object, which you can access by name. Because a worksheet has only one selection, you don't have to specify any arguments. To change the appearance of the selection, for instance, use the Font property:

```
Selection.Font.Bold = True
Selection.Font.Size = 13
```

Now that we've looked at the basic objects of Excel VBA, we can examine the code behind the New Worksheet button of the VBAObjs application.

VBAObjects: Creating a New Worksheet

The VBAObjs application's New Worksheet button demonstrates how to access a worksheet, populate it with data, and then format the data. The program starts by examining the number of open workbooks. If no workbook is open, the program creates a new one. If a workbook exists, the program assigns it to the *wBook* object variable:

```
Dim wSheet As Worksheet
Dim wBook As Workbook

    If AppExcel.Workbooks.Count = 0 Then
        Debug.Print "Adding a new Workbook"
        Set wBook = AppExcel.Workbooks.Add
    End If
    Set wSheet = AppExcel.Sheets(1)
```

TIP

Before you run the VBAObjs application, be sure that you don't have an instance of Excel with useful data running. Or, add a new worksheet to the workbook, and give it a unique name (unless you don't mind overwriting the data of the open worksheet, of course).

The code then populates the first four cells on the first and second rows. Figure 18.11 shows the worksheet after it has been populated and formatted by the VBAObjs application. To populate the worksheet, the program uses the Cells object, as shown in the following lines:

```
wSheet.Cells(2, 1).Value = "1st QUARTER"
wSheet.Cells(3, 1).Value = 123.45
```

FIGURE 18.11:

The VBAObjs application populated and formatted this worksheet.

To format a range of cells, the code uses the Select method of the Range object to create a selection and then manipulate the appropriate properties of the Selection object. The following lines format the headings of the worksheet shown in Figure 18.11:

```
Range("A2:D2").Select
With Selection.Font
    .Name = "Verdana"
    .FontStyle = "Bold"
    .Size = 12
End With
```

While the worksheet is being populated and formatted, Excel is running in the background. Users can't see Excel, although they will notice activity (the disk is spinning, and the pointer assumes an hourglass shape for several seconds). After all operations complete, the program displays Excel by setting its Visible property to True.

Code 18.9:   The New Worksheet Button

```
Private Sub Command3_Click()
Dim wSheet As Worksheet
Dim wBook As Workbook

    If AppExcel.Workbooks.Count = 0 Then
        Debug.Print "Adding a new Workbook"
        Set wBook = AppExcel.Workbooks.Add
    End If
    Set wSheet = AppExcel.Sheets(1)
    wSheet.Cells(2, 1).Value = "1st QUARTER"
    wSheet.Cells(2, 2).Value = "2nd QUARTER"
    wSheet.Cells(2, 3).Value = "3rd QUARTER"
    wSheet.Cells(2, 4).Value = "4th QUARTER"
    wSheet.Cells(3, 1).Value = 123.45
    wSheet.Cells(3, 2).Value = 435.56
    wSheet.Cells(3, 3).Value = 376.25
    wSheet.Cells(3, 4).Value = 425.75

    Range("A2:D2").Select
    With Selection.Font
        .Name = "Verdana"
        .FontStyle = "Bold"
        .Size = 12
    End With
```

```
Range("A3:D3").Select
With Selection.Font
    .Name = "Verdana"
    .FontStyle = "Regular"
    .Size = 11
End With

Range("A2:D2").Select
Selection.Columns.AutoFit
Selection.ColumnWidth = Selection.ColumnWidth * 1.25
Range("A2:E2").Select
Selection.HorizontalAlignment = xlCenter

AppExcel.Visible = True

End Sub
```

VBAObjects: Using Excel As a Math Parser

In the section "Spell-Checking Documents," you saw how you can steal the spell-checking capabilities of Word. Now, we'll do something similar with Excel. Excel is a great tool for doing math. At the same time, Visual Basic doesn't provide a function or a method for evaluating math expressions. With the little information on VBA programming we have presented so far, you can exploit this capability of Excel and use it as a server in the background to calculate math expressions.

To calculate a math expression such as the following with Excel:

```
1/cos(0.335)*cos(12.45)
```

all you have to do is enter the expression in a cell and let Excel calculate the cell. For Excel to recognize that the text you've entered is a formula and treat it accordingly, you must prefix the expression with the equals sign.

That's exactly what the Calculate Expression button does. It contacts Excel, builds a new worksheet (if needed), and then copies a user-assigned math formula to a cell. The formula is prefixed with the equals sign so that Excel will calculate the value of the expression and place it in the same cell. The value of this cell is then read back and displayed from within the VBObjs application (see Figure 18.12).

Code 18.10: **The Calculate Expression Button**

```
Private Sub Command8_Click()
Dim wSheet As Worksheet
Dim wBook As Workbook
Dim expression

    expression = InputBox("Enter math expression to evaluate (i.e.,
1/cos(3.45)*log(19.004)")
    If Trim(expression) <> "" Then
        If AppExcel.Workbooks.Count = 0 Then
            Debug.Print "Adding a new Workbook"
            Set wBook = AppExcel.Workbooks.Add
        End If
        Set wSheet = AppExcel.Sheets(1)
        On Error GoTo CalcError
        wSheet.Cells(1, 1).Value = "=" & expression
        wSheet.Calculate
        MsgBox "The value of the expression " & expression & vbCrLf & "
is " & wSheet.Cells(1, 1).Value
    End If
    Exit Sub

CalcError:
    MsgBox "Error in evaluating expression"
End Sub
```

FIGURE 18.12:

Using Excel's Evaluate
method to evaluate
math expressions

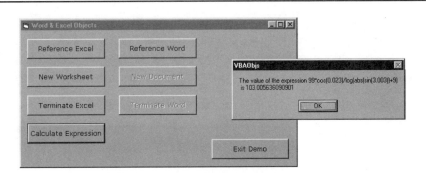

VBA and Form Design

Besides the VB Editor, Office applications come with a Form Designer that is similar to the Form Designer in the Visual Basic IDE. With VBA 5, you can create Forms and display them from within your VBA applications. In the past, VBA programs were limited to the user interface of the Office application. A Word macro that called some of Excel's methods to streamline the transfer of data from Excel to Word and format them in Word could use the user interface of Word or Excel and display a few simple dialog boxes on its own, but not a real Form such as the ones you can build with Visual Basic. Custom Forms were not an option.

The situation has changed, and now you can design Forms similar to Visual Basic Forms, program their events, and display them from within your macros. This significant development was the next step in the evolution of Word and Excel applications to fully programmable environments. In the following sections, we'll describe how to design and use Forms with Excel's Visual Basic Editor and how to import these Forms into Visual Basic applications.

VBA Forms

We'll demonstrate the VBA Form Designer with a simple, but typical, example, the VBAExcel application. The Form shown in Figure 18.13 is displayed from within Excel. It summarizes the data shown on the Excel spreadsheet. You could just as easily process the data in Excel, but in some situations it is best to not extract the information from a spreadsheet, process it, and display the results on a different Form.

FIGURE 18.13:

The Order Details Extended query returns the details of all invoices in the NWIND sample database.

NOTE   You'll find the VBAExcel application in the Ch18\VBAExcel folder on the CD that comes with this book.

The data come from the NWIND database (we've used it many times in the previous chapters of the book), but you won't find the spreadsheet on the CD. To import the data into Excel, follow these steps:

1. Start Access, and open the NWIND database (you will find it in the VB folder).

2. In the Queries tab of the Database window, double-click the Order Details Extended box to display all the invoice details.

3. Select the data on the data grid (shown in Figure 18.13) and copy them.

4. Start Excel.

5. Paste the data from the clipboard in the first cell.

6. Select the following columns (by clicking their headings) and remove them from the grid by choosing Edit ➤ Delete:

   - Product

   - Unit Price

   - Quantity

   - Discount

What you have now on the spreadsheet are the details of all invoices recorded in the NWIND database. Your Excel window should look like the one shown in Figure 18.14. However, there are no totals for each invoice. The specific query returns the detail lines. Notice that the same invoice number is repeated on the spreadsheet as many times as there are lines in the invoice.

The invoice details of the grid shown in Figure 18.13 in an Excel spreadsheet

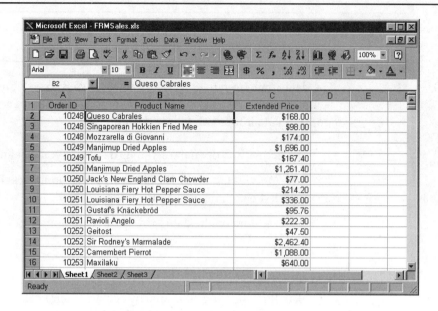

Assuming we are not interested in taxes or other charges, we can calculate the total for each invoice by running down the details and summing the Extended Prices for all lines with the same OrderID field. All it takes is macro that loops through the spreadsheet's rows, compares the OrderID cell with the previous one, and adds the Extended Price to the running total. But how about displaying the totals? One approach is to insert a new row after each invoice's lines. Another is to place the total in the cell next to each invoice's last Extended Price cell.

To demonstrate the design of Forms, we are going to display the totals for each in a separate Form, as shown in Figure 18.15. This Form looks like an ordinary VB Form, but it was designed with Excel's Visual Basic Editor and displayed in Excel's environment. You don't even need to have Visual Basic installed to design and display this Form. In the next section, we are going to export this Form and use it with a VB application.

FIGURE 18.15:

The totals for the invoices shown in Figure 18.14 displayed in a ListBox control on a VBA Form

You may be wondering, Why deploy a new Form instead of using Excel's subtotaling features? Keep in mind that this is a simple example. The processing of the data may be more complicated, and it may not always be convenient to display the results on the same spreadsheet. This example does not demonstrate the need to deploy custom Forms, but everyone who's programmed Excel in the past will admit that they wished they could pop up a similar Form at one time or another.

Forms are the next step in Excel's evolution toward a fully programmable environment. Once you understand the structure of a spreadsheet and the objects that expose this structure to other applications, programming Excel will be no different from programming with Visual Basic, including Form design. You can even "dress your application up" with Forms so that users will see very little Excel, and they may even think that the spreadsheet is another data-entry window in your application.

Designing a Form

To design a new VBA Form with Excel, open a new worksheet and choose Tools ➤ Macro ➤ Visual Basic Editor. You will see the window shown in Figure 18.16. To get the Form shown in Figure 18.16, open the VBA Editor and choose Insert ➤ UserForm. This window contains the usual Project, Properties, and Form panes, just like the Visual Basic Editor. The Project pane contains all the components of the Excel project, including the spreadsheets and the modules (recorded macros are stored in the project's main module). If you select the Form, you will see a Toolbox, similar to the one in the Visual Basic editor, except that it doesn't contain as many controls. If you don't see the Toolbox, click the Form to display it. When you are not designing a Form's interface, the Toolbox remains hidden.

FIGURE 18.16:

The Visual Basic Editor's window for a typical Excel project

To design the Form shown in Figure 18.15, earlier in this chapter, place the ListBox control on it, add a Command Button to the right side of the control, and place two Label controls on top of the List control. The exact placement of the two labels depends on the size of the tab character between the two columns on the ListBox control, and the first time you can only position the labels approximately.

The data should be loaded when the Form is initialized, which is signaled by the Initialize event. In this event's handler, we must set up a loop to scan all the rows of the spreadsheet and sum the prices while the OrderID field is the same. As each invoice is processed, the new total is added to the list. The OrderID fields are accessed by the following expression:

```
Range("A" & curRow)
```

in which *curRow* is the row's number, and it's increased by 1 with every iteration. Many of the lines deal with formatting the numbers, and you can ignore them initially.

Code 18.11:   The Initialize Event

```
Private Sub UserForm_Initialize()
Dim InvoiceValue As String

curRow = 2
Range("A" & curRow).Select
curInvoice = ActiveCell.Value
curRow = curRow + 1
While curInvoice <> ""
    Range("A" & curRow).Select
    InvoiceNumber = ActiveCell.Value
    If InvoiceNumber = curInvoice Then
        invoicetotal = invoicetotal + Range("C" & curRow).Value
    Else
        InvoiceValue$ = Format$(invoicetotal, "#.00")
        InvoiceValue$ = Space(12 - Len(InvoiceValue$)) & InvoiceValue
        ListBox1.AddItem InvoiceNumber & Chr(9) & Chr(9) &
InvoiceValue$
        invoicetotal = Range("C" & curRow).Value
        curInvoice = InvoiceNumber
    End If
    curRow = curRow + 1
Wend
DoEvents
End Sub
```

The List's Font property is set to a monospaced font to simplify alignment. There are better ways to align multiple columns in a ListBox control, but for this example we wanted to keep the code's complexity to a minimum.

To display the Form, press F5, or choose Run ➢ Run Sub/User Form. The Form will be loaded, and a couple of seconds later the invoice totals will appear, as shown in Figure 18.15. The Close button simply hides the Form with the following statement:

```
Me.Hide
```

Using VBA Forms with Visual Basic

You can use the Forms and applications that you design with VBA with Visual Basic by making a few adjustments in the code. This means that you can start with VBA and move your designs to Visual Basic, or vice versa. Both the user interface and the code can be reused and shared by people in different environments.

To reuse a VBA Form in a Visual Basic application, first export it by choosing File ➢ Export.

NOTE   VBA Forms are saved automatically with the current project, and you don't have to save them separately. Every time you save the workbook, the Forms (and macros) you designed in the current session are also saved as part of the project.

Choosing File ➢ Export saves the current Form in an FRM file. You can then import this file into a Visual Basic project by choosing Project ➢ Add Form. Save the Form you designed in the last section (you can also find it in the VBAExcel folder on the CD) and then start a new Visual Basic project.

Choose Project ➢ Add Form to add the VBA Form. Visual Basic creates a new folder in the Project window, the Designers folder, and places the VBA Form there. This folder contains Forms designed outside Visual Basic. The UserForm1 Designer is quite similar to a Visual Basic Form, but you can't add to it all the controls you can use with regular Visual Basic Forms. If you click UserForm1, you will see the same Toolbox as you see in the VBA Editor (see Figure 18.17). The Designer should be usable in the environment in which it was created, even after it's been edited with Visual Basic.

FIGURE 18.17:

To adjust the interface of a Designer, you must use the same Toolbox as the application in which the Designer was created.

If you open the UserForm1 Form's Code window, you will see that it doesn't support all the events recognized by regular Forms. Most of the events are still present, and the code you entered in the VBA Editor is still there.

To complete the application VBExcel, add a new module (the InvModule) and enter the following lines:

```
Public appExcel As Object

Sub Main()
    On Error Resume Next
    Set appExcel = GetObject(App.Path & "\FRMSales.xls",
"Excel.Application")
    If appExcel Is Nothing Then
        Set appExcel = CreateObject("Excel.Application")
        appExcel.Workbooks.Open App.Path & "\FRMSales.xls"
    End If
    VBEXCEL.Show
End Sub
```

As you can guess, the code of the UserForm1 Form's code isn't going to work as is. When executed from within Excel's VB Editor, it can safely assume it's connected to an instance of Excel. This is no longer the case. The VB application must first establish a connection to an instance of Excel and then show the Form.

The code of the Main subroutine does exactly that. It instantiates the *appExcel* object variable, assigns the FRMSales spreadsheet to it, and then displays the VBEXCEL Form, shown in Figure 18.18. This Form simply waits for the user to click the Show Invoice Totals button or terminate the application. The project's Startup Object is the subroutine Main (open the Project Properties window and select Sub Main in the Startup Object list).

FIGURE 18.18:

The VBExcel application's starting Form. As the program reads the invoice lines, it displays its progress on the Form.

The code of the Show Invoice Totals button's Click event doesn't do much. It simply loads and displays the UserForm1 Form with the statement:

```
UserForm1.Show
```

When UserForm1 is loaded, it's Initialize event is triggered, and the data are read from Excel. We must adjust the code of the Initialize event. The necessary corrections are quite simple. When this code is executed in Excel's environment, we don't have to tell it which spreadsheet to access. We can call the Range method to access the cells of the active spreadsheet. Now, however, the Range method isn't adequate. We must tell Visual Basic that it must now contact a server application (appExcel) and request data from the first worksheet ("Sheet1" or any other name you may have used in Excel). All instances of the methods called in the Initialize event handler must now be prefixed with the following string:

```
appExcel.Sheets("Sheet1")
```

To read the value of the active cell, for example, we use the expression:

```
appExcel.ActiveCell.Value
```

The revised code of the UserForm1 object's Initialize event handler is shown next.

Code 18.12:   The UserForm1_Initialize Event Handler

```
Private Sub UserForm_Initialize()
Dim InvoiceValue As String

curRow = 2
appExcel.Sheets("Sheet1").Range("A" & curRow).Select
curInvoice = appExcel.ActiveCell.Value
curRow = curRow + 1
While curInvoice <> ""
    appExcel.Sheets("Sheet1").Range("A" & curRow).Select
    InvoiceNumber = appExcel.ActiveCell.Value
    If InvoiceNumber = curInvoice Then
        invoicetotal = invoicetotal +
appExcel.Sheets("Sheet1").Range("C" & curRow).Value
    Else
        InvoiceValue$ = Format$(invoicetotal, "#.00")
        InvoiceValue$ = Space(12 - Len(InvoiceValue$)) & InvoiceValue
        ListBox1.AddItem InvoiceNumber & Chr(9) & Chr(9) &
InvoiceValue$
        invoicetotal = appExcel.Range("C" & curRow).Value
        curInvoice = InvoiceNumber
        InvCounter = InvCounter + 1
    End If
    VBEXCEL.Label1.Caption = "Processing invoice line # " & curRow
    VBEXCEL.Label2.Caption = "Number of Invoices " & InvCounter
    curRow = curRow + 1
    VBEXCEL.Refresh
Wend
End Sub
```

If you load the VBExcel application from the CD, be sure that the FRMSales.xls file (the worksheet with the invoice details) has been prepared and resides in the same folder as the application. Moreover, you may have to change the addresses of the cells. In the project's code, we assume that the OrderID values are stored in the first column (A) and the prices in the third column (C). If you paste the data in a different location on the worksheet, adjust the references in the code accordingly. Figure 18.19 shows the Form being used within a VB application.

The NWIND database contains more than 2,000 invoice lines, and processing them won't be instant, even on a fast machine.

FIGURE 18.19:

A VBA Form being used from within a Visual Basic application

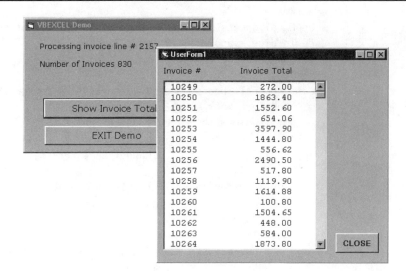

This example concludes our introduction to the basic objects exposed by Excel and Word. You have now seen how you can build applications to control these applications by manipulating their objects. In the following chapters, you will find a complete discussion of all the objects exposed by Word and Excel and lots of examples.

CHAPTER

NINETEEN

Using the Visual Basic Editor with Word and Excel

19

- Using the Visual Basic Editor

- Choosing options for the Visual Basic Editor

- Recording and creating macros

- Creating Forms

- Finding the VBA objects you need

In this chapter, we'll discuss how to use the Visual Basic Editor to create and edit code and Forms for Word and Excel. If you're familiar with the Visual Basic Integrated Development Environment (IDE), you'll find that many of the features in the Visual Basic Editor are familiar, though some work in somewhat different ways in the Visual Basic Editor than in the Visual Basic IDE.

> **NOTE** You'll find that the Word documentation and help files use the term *user-form* instead of *Form*, which is the term we use throughout this book. The terms are synonymous, and you'll find that Excel (which we discuss in the next chapter) uses both of them.

Word and Excel use the same Visual Basic Editor, but always in separate sessions launched from the host application: You run a Visual Basic Editor session for Word from Word, and you run a Visual Basic Editor session for Excel from Excel. If you have the Visual Basic Editor open for Word and choose to display the Visual Basic Editor for Excel, Excel opens its own session of the Visual Basic Editor.

We'll start by discussing the components of the Visual Basic Editor, what does what, and how to use the Visual Basic Editor. We'll then run through how to use the Visual Basic Editor to create code and Forms for Word and Excel. Finally, we'll look at how to find the objects you need in VBA.

> **NOTE** Most of the information in this chapter also applies to using the Visual Basic Editor with PowerPoint, but we won't discuss PowerPoint in this chapter.

Opening the Visual Basic Editor

You can open the Visual Basic Editor for Word and Excel in any of several ways:

- Choose Tools ➤ Macro ➤ Visual Basic Editor.

> **NOTE** If the Visual Basic Editor for the current application is already displayed, Word or Excel switches to it. If a session of the Visual Basic Editor is open for another application, Word or Excel starts its own session of the Visual Basic Editor.

- Press Alt+F11 from within Word or Excel.

- Choose Tools ➣ Macros ➣ Macros (or press Alt+F8) in Word or Excel to display the Macros dialog box. Select the macro you want to edit, and click the Edit button. (Alternatively, you can create a macro by typing a name for it in the Macro Name text box in the Macros dialog box and then clicking the Create button. Word or Excel displays the Visual Basic Editor and creates the macro in it ready for editing.)

To switch back to Word or Excel from the Visual Basic Editor, click the View Microsoft Word button or the View Microsoft Excel button on the Standard toolbar. Alternatively, press Alt+F11.

The Visual Basic Editor Interface

Parts of the Visual Basic Editor will be immediately familiar from the Visual Basic IDE. As you can see in Figure 19.1, the Visual Basic Editor typically displays three windows—the Project Explorer, the Properties window, and the Code window—and a Standard toolbar.

FIGURE 19.1:

The Visual Basic Editor

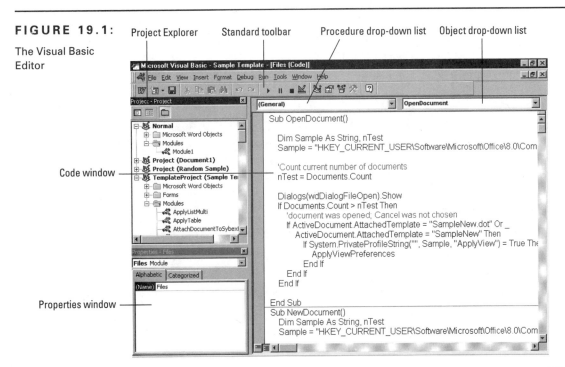

In the previous chapter, we took a quick look at the components of the Visual Basic Editor. Now, we'll look at them in detail and discuss how to use them.

Similarities between the Visual Basic Editor and the Visual Basic IDE

The first time you display the Visual Basic Editor for Word and Excel, you'll be struck by its similarities to the Visual Basic IDE. Not only does the interface of the Visual Basic Editor have a similar layout to that of the Visual Basic IDE, but many (if not most) of the features in the Visual Basic Editor are the same as or similar to those in the Visual Basic IDE.

For example, most of the code-completion and visual help features from the Visual Basic IDE—such as the Complete Word feature, the List Properties/Methods and List Constants features, and the Quick Info and Parameter Info features—are present in the Visual Basic Editor as well. Likewise, most of the keyboard commands in the Visual Basic Editor are the same as those in the Visual Basic IDE.

For example, you can press the F7 key to view the code for an object, and you can press Shift+F7 to return from viewing the code to viewing the object to which the code belongs. Further, as you'll see later in this chapter, the commands for arranging controls on Forms in the Visual Basic Editor are mostly the same as those in the Visual Basic IDE.

However, you'll also notice a number of differences, such as the following:

- The Visual Basic Editor has no Form Layout window to give you a quick view of the Form you're creating.

- The Visual Basic Editor has no Property Pages.

- The Visual Basic Editor does not have explanatory help text at the bottom of the Properties window as does the Visual Basic IDE.

- The Visual Basic Editor has fewer controls available than the Visual Basic IDE.

- When you drag an object on a Form, the Visual Basic Editor does not display the coordinates at which the outline of the object is currently located as does the Visual Basic IDE.

If you've spent any time working with macros in earlier versions of Word or Excel, you'll find a number of differences in the Visual Basic Editor that take some getting used to. Whereas Word versions through Word 95 and Excel versions through Excel 95 used a macro-editing window within the host application window, the Visual Basic Editor runs as a separate application window. It has its own Taskbar button so that you can switch to it easily and close it from the Taskbar. (Be warned, though, that the Visual Basic Editor shares the same memory space as the host application. If you crash the Visual Basic Editor, it's wise to close and restart the application as well, even if the crash doesn't take the application down by itself—or, if you're using Windows 95, shut down and restart the operating system. If you crash Word or Excel, it will almost invariably take down its session of the Visual Basic Editor as well.)

The Project Explorer

As in the Visual Basic IDE, you use the Project Explorer to navigate among projects and components of projects in the Visual Basic Editor for Word and Excel. The Project Explorer lists all open projects for the current session of the host application, representing each project as an item in the Explorer-style hierarchical list. You can click the boxed plus sign (+) to the left of a project or project component to expand the view to display the contents of the project component, and you can click the resulting boxed minus sign (–) to the left of a project or project component to collapse the view again. You can double-click an item to display it or its code in the Code window.

Because the Project Explorer provides fast and efficient navigation among the various elements of your VBA projects, it's usually easiest to keep it displayed unless you're desperately short of screen space. Given that you'll usually be working with multiple projects in Word and Excel, the Visual Basic Editor can quickly become more cluttered than the Visual Basic IDE normally does. So it makes sense to keep the Project Explorer displayed to make it easy to navigate from one project element to another.

To display the Project Explorer, choose View ➤ Project Explorer, press Ctrl+R, or press the F4 key. To close the Project Explorer, click its Close button.

Projects in the Project Explorer for Word

In this section, we'll discuss the projects that you'll see in the Project Explorer in Word. Figure 19.2 shows the Project Explorer window in the Visual Basic Editor for Word with several projects open.

FIGURE 19.2:

The Project Explorer with several Word projects open

The Visual Basic Editor for Word displays the following projects in the Project Explorer:

- The template project for the NORMAL.DOT template (the global template). This project is identified as Normal and appears at the top level of the Project Explorer. This project is always displayed, even when no document is open.

- One template project for each open global template. Each project is identified by the keyword TemplateProject, followed by the name of the global template in parentheses. For example, the project for a global template named NADIR CO. GLOBAL TEMPLATE would appear as TemplateProject (Nadir Co. Global Template) in the Project Explorer. As you can see in Figure 19.2, the Project Explorer does not present a global template differently from a regular template, but you can identify a global template because the project for any global template loaded is always displayed, even when no document is open. You'll also notice that the project for each global template is locked: You cannot edit a global template when it is loaded. (The locking isn't peculiar to global templates, because any template can be locked, but it can be a hint that a template is a global template.)

- One document project for each open document. Each document project is identified by the keyword Project, followed by the name of the document in parentheses. For example, the project for a document named ESTONIAN PEASANT REBELLIONS.DOC would appear as Project (Estonian Peasant Rebellions) in the Project Explorer.

- One template project for each open document template. This project is identified by the keyword TemplateProject, followed by the name of the template in parentheses. For example, the project for a global template named INDUSTRIAL DESIGN.DOT would appear as TemplateProject (Industrial Design) in the Project Explorer.

The order in which the document projects and template projects are listed varies from session to session and will change as you open and close documents. The project for the Normal template is always listed first in the Project Explorer.

Running Multiple Word and Visual Basic Editor Sessions

If you run multiple sessions of Word, you can open a session of the Visual Basic Editor for each Word session. Each session of the Visual Basic Editor will show the projects open in the corresponding session of Word. As long as you do not have the same document or template open in two or more sessions, you can make and save changes to the document projects and template projects. However, the Normal template will be controlled by the first Word session and its corresponding Visual Basic Editor session.

If you try to save changes to the Normal template from a second or subsequent Word session or from its corresponding Visual Basic Editor session while the first Word session is running, Word will alert you to the problem and prompt you to save the template under a different name.

If you try to save changes to the Normal template from a second or subsequent Word session or its corresponding Visual Basic Editor session after closing the first Word session, Word will warn you that NORMAL.DOT was being edited by another Word session and that saving these changes as NORMAL.DOT will overwrite any changes made in the other session. You can then choose to overwrite the previous copy of NORMAL.DOT or to save the other session of the template under a different name.

Components of Word Projects

As in the Visual Basic IDE, you can expand the projects in the Project Explorer to view their contents by clicking the plus (+) sign to the left of the project name. Figure 19.3 shows the expanded view of a typical project.

FIGURE 19.3:

The expanded view of a typical project, showing its component objects

Each Word project can contain the following elements:

Microsoft Word objects: Typically, each document project or template project contains an object named ThisDocument that contains the properties for the document or template. For example, the project for the Normal template contains an object named ThisDocument that contains the properties for the Normal template.

Userforms (for dialog boxes or Forms): You can save a Form to a separate FRM file.

Modules (which typically contain macros, procedures, and functions): You can save a module to a separate BAS file.

Class modules: You can save a class module to a separate CLS file.

References: To object type libraries, ActiveX controls, or other projects. For example, when you need to use a Form or procedure stored in a different document or template, you can add a reference to that document or template to make it available to the current project. Each document project contains a reference to the template to which it is currently attached.

Projects in the Project Explorer for Excel

In this section, we'll discuss the projects that you'll see in the Project Explorer in Excel. Figure 19.4 shows the Project Explorer for the Visual Basic Editor for Excel with several projects open.

FIGURE 19.4:

The Project Explorer with several Excel projects open

The Visual Basic Editor for Excel displays the following projects in the Project Explorer:

- One project for each add-in file (XLA) you have loaded. This project is identified by the name of the add-in, followed by its file name in parentheses. For example, if you load the Web Form Wizard add-in (`webform`), its project will appear in the Project Explorer as webform (`WEBFORM.XLA`). Projects for add-ins are always displayed while the add-ins are loaded, even when no workbook is open.

- The project for the Personal macro workbook, if one exists for this copy of Excel and (for systems with multiple users defined) for this user. This project is identified as VBAProject (`PERSONAL.XLS`) and is displayed whether the Personal macro workbook is hidden or displayed. This project is always displayed in the Project Explorer, even when no workbook is open.

- One project for each open workbook. Each workbook project is identified by the keyword VBAProject, followed by the name of the document in parentheses. For example, the project for a workbook named `NEW MODEL WORKBOOK` `.XLS` would appear as VBAProject (New Model Workbook.xls) in the Project Explorer.

Running Multiple Excel and Visual Basic Editor Sessions

As with Word, you can run multiple sessions of Excel, with a separate session of the Visual Basic Editor for each Excel session. However, Excel is more protective of the PERSONAL.XLS Personal macro workbook than Word is of the NORMAL.DOT Normal template. If you start a new Excel session when an Excel session is already running, Excel displays the File Reservation dialog box shown here to warn you that the Personal macro workbook is being modified. (If you don't have a Personal macro workbook, Excel will not display this message box.)

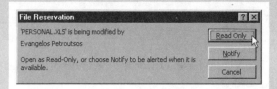

You then have three choices:

- Click the Read Only button to open PERSONAL.XLS as a read-only file (so that you will not be able to modify it).

- Click the Notify button to open a second (or subsequent) Excel session without PERSONAL.XLS. After you close the first Excel session, the second Excel session will display the File Reservation dialog box shown here to notify you that PERSONAL.XLS is available for editing. Click the Read-Write button to open PERSONAL.XLS for editing.

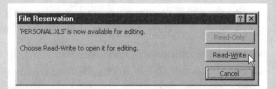

- Click the Cancel button to open a second (or subsequent) Excel session without PERSONAL.XLS.

Because you can therefore make changes to PERSONAL.XLS from only one Excel session at a time, there's no possibility of two sessions trying to write changes to PERSONAL.XLS. You can safely make changes to any Excel workbook project or template project open in any Visual Basic Editor session.

Components of Excel Projects

Each Excel project can have the following components:

> **Microsoft Excel Objects**: Each workbook project or template project contains an object named ThisWorkbook that contains the properties for the workbook or template. For example, the project for the PERSONAL.XLS macro workbook contains an object named ThisWorkbook that contains the properties for PERSONAL.XLS. Each worksheet appears as an object identified by a default name based on its position in the workbook (Sheet1, Sheet2, and so on) and any name assigned to its tab. For example, in Figure 19.4, earlier in this chapter, Sheet1 is named 1997, and Sheet2 is named 1998.

> **Forms** (for dialog boxes or Forms): You can save a Form to a separate FRM file.

> **Modules** (for macros, procedures, and functions): You can save a module to a separate BAS file.

> **Class modules**: You can save a class module to a separate CLS file.

The Code Window

As in the Visual Basic IDE, the Code window in the Visual Basic Editor is where you'll do most of the actual work of creating and editing your macros. The Visual Basic Editor provides a Code window for each open project, for each document section within the project that can contain code, and for each code module and Form in the project. Each Code window is identified by the project name, the name of the module within the project, and the word *Code* in parentheses.

The Visual Basic Editor Code window provides a half-dozen features for helping you create code efficiently and accurately. You'll recognize most of these features if you're familiar with the Visual Basic IDE.

> **Complete Word** completes the word you're typing once you've typed enough letters to distinguish that word from any other. To activate Complete Word, press Ctrl+spacebar or click the Complete Word button on the Edit toolbar.

> **Quick Info,** which is on the Edit toolbar, displays syntax information on the current variable, function, method, statement, or procedure.

List Properties/Methods displays a pop-up list box containing properties and methods for the object you've just typed so that you can quickly complete the expression. List Properties/Methods is switched on by default and will automatically pop up the list box when you type a period within an expression. You can select a property or a method by clicking it with the mouse, by using ↑ and ↓, or by typing the name of the property or method until the Visual Basic Editor can identify it. To enter the property or method into the code, you can double-click it or do one of the following:

- Press Tab or the spacebar and continue working on the same line.
- Press Enter and start a new line.
- Press the comma key (,) followed by a comma.
- Press the period key (.) followed by a period.

List Constants displays a pop-up list box containing constants for a property that you've typed so that you can quickly select the constant needed to complete the expression. Again, you can use either the mouse or the keyboard to select the constant, and you can enter the constant by double-clicking it or by pressing Tab (to continue working on the same line) or Enter (to start a new line).

Data Tips displays a screentip containing the value of a variable that the mouse pointer moves over when the Visual Basic Editor is in Break mode.

Margin Indicators lets you quickly set a breakpoint, the next statement, or a bookmark by clicking in the left margin of the Code window.

Apart from these features, the Visual Basic Editor includes standard Office editing features such as copy and move; cut and paste; and drag-and-drop. Drag-and-drop is particularly useful because you can drag code from one macro or module to another.

The Properties Window

The Visual Basic Editor provides a Properties window that you can use to view the properties of an object such as a project, a Form, or a control. Use the drop-down list at the top of the Properties window to select the item whose properties you want to view. The Alphabetic tab presents an alphabetic list of the properties in the item, and the Categorized tab presents a list of the properties broken down into categories. Figure 19.5 shows the properties for a relatively straightforward Word document.

FIGURE 19.5:

Use the Properties window to view the properties of a project, a Form, or a control.

These properties map to document or template information (in Word) or workbook or template information (in Excel) that you're probably familiar with. For example, the Saved property stores information on whether the document or workbook contains unsaved changes. If the document or workbook does not contain unsaved changes, this property will be set to True (because all the information in the document or workbook is saved); if the document or workbook does contain unsaved changes, this property will be set to False.

To display the Properties window, press F4, click the Properties Windows button on the Standard toolbar, or choose View ➤ Properties Window. To change a property, click in the right column and change the value. You'll be able to choose different values depending on the type of property. For a True/False property, you'll be limited to those two choices in the drop-down list; for a text property such as Name, you can enter any valid Visual Basic name.

Other Windows in the Visual Basic Editor

In this section, we'll discuss the other windows that the Visual Basic Editor provides for working with code:

- Object Browser
- Locals

- Watch

- Immediate

Unlike the Project Explorer, the Code window, and the Properties window, these windows are not displayed by default in the Visual Basic Editor; you can display them whenever you find them helpful. Like the Project Explorer, the Code window, and the Properties window, these windows work in a similar way to their equivalents in the Visual Basic IDE.

The Object Browser

The Object Browser in the Visual Basic Editor provides information classes, properties, methods, events, and constants for both built-in objects and custom objects you create. Figure 19.6 shows the components of the Object Browser.

FIGURE 19.6:

The Object Browser provides information on built-in objects and custom objects.

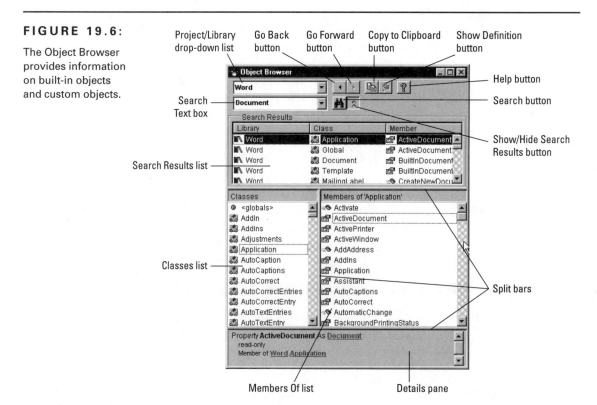

Here's what the elements of the Object Browser do:

- The **Project/Library drop-down list** provides a list of object libraries available to the current project. Use the drop-down list to choose the object libraries you want to view.

- In the **Search Text box**, enter the string you want to search for: Either type it in, or choose a previous string in the current project session from the drop-down list. Then either press Enter or click the Search button to find members containing the search string.

TIP

To make your searches more specific, you can use wildcards such as ? (representing any one character) and * (representing any group of characters). You can also choose to search for a whole word only (rather than matching your search string with part of another word) by right-clicking anywhere in the Object Browser (except in the Project/Library drop-down list or in the Search Text box) and choosing Find Whole Word Only from the shortcut menu. The Find Whole Word Only choice will have a checkmark next to it in the shortcut menu when it is active; to deactivate it, choose Find Whole Word Only again on the shortcut menu.

- Click the **Go Back button** to go back one by one through your previous selections in the Classes list and the Members Of list. Click the **Go Forward button** to go forward through your previous selections one by one. The Go Back button will become available when you go to a class or a member in the Object Browser; the Go Forward button will become available only when you use the Go Back button to go back to a previous selection.

- Click the **Copy to Clipboard button** to copy the selected item from the Search Results box, the Classes list, the Members Of list, or the Details pane to the clipboard so that you can paste it into your code.

- Click the **Show Definition button** to display a Code window containing the code for the object selected in the Classes list or the Members Of list. The Show Definition button will be available (undimmed) only for objects that contain code, such as macros and Forms that you've created.

- Click the **Help button** to display any available Help for the currently selected item.

- Click the **Search button** to search for the term entered in the Search Text box. If the Search Results pane is not open, the Object Browser will open it at this point.

- Click the **Show/Hide Search Results button** to toggle the display of the Search Results pane on and off.

- The **Search Results list** in the Search Results pane contains the results of the latest search you've conducted for a term entered in the Search Text box. If you've performed a search, the Object Browser will update the Search Results list when you switch to a different library by using the Project/Library drop-down list.

- The **Classes list** shows the available classes in the library or project specified in the Project/Library drop-down list.

- The **Members Of list** displays the available elements of the class selected in the Classes list. A method, constant, event, property, or procedure that has code written for it appears in boldface. The Members Of list can display the members either grouped into their categories (methods, properties, events, and so on) or ungrouped as an alphabetic list of all the members available. To toggle between grouped and ungrouped, right-click in the Members Of list and choose Group Members from the shortcut menu. When members are grouped, the Visual Basic Editor displays a checkmark next to the menu item.

- The **Details pane** displays the definition of the member selected in the Classes list or in the Members Of list. For example, if you select a macro in the Members Of list, the Details pane displays its name, the name of the module and template, document, or workbook in which it is stored, and any comment lines you inserted at the beginning of the macro. The module name and template name will contain hyperlinks so that you can quickly move to them.

- Drag the three **split bars** to resize the panes of the Object Browser to suit you.

Adding and Removing Object Libraries

You can add and remove object libraries by using the References dialog box (we looked at this dialog box briefly in the previous chapter). By adding object libraries, you can make available additional objects to work with; by removing object libraries that you do not need to view or use, you can reduce the number of object references that VBA needs to resolve when it compiles the code in a project, thus allowing it to run faster.

You can also adjust the priority of references by adjusting the order in which the references appear in the References dialog box. The priority of references matters when you use in your code an object whose name appears in more than one reference: VBA checks the order in the References list of the references that contain that object name and uses the first of them.

Adding and Removing Object Libraries (continued)

To add or remove object libraries, follow these steps:

1. Right-click anywhere in the Object Browser window other than in the Search Text box, and choose References from the shortcut menu, or choose Tools ➣ References in the Visual Basic Editor, to display the References dialog box (shown here).

2. In the Available References list box, select the checkboxes for the references you want to have available, and clear the checkboxes for the references you want to remove.

3. Adjust the priority of the references if necessary by selecting a reference and using the up- and down-arrow Priority buttons to move it up or down the list. Usually, you'll want to keep Visual Basic for Applications and the Microsoft Excel 8.0 Object Library at the top of your list when you're working with Excel, and the Microsoft Word 8.0 Object Library if you're working with Word. You can add further reference libraries by clicking the Browse button to display the Add Reference dialog box, selecting the library file, and clicking the Open button.

4. Choose the OK button to close the References dialog box and return to the Object Browser.

The Locals Window

The Locals window provides a quick readout of the value and type of all expressions in the active procedure via a collapsible tree view. The Expression column displays the name of each expression, listed under the name of the procedure in which it appears; the Value column displays the current value of the expression (including Empty if the expression is empty, or Null or Nothing as appropriate); and the Type column displays the data type of the expression, with variants listed as "Variant" along with their assigned data type (for example, "Variant/String" for a variant assigned the string data type).

To display the Locals window, click the Locals Window button on the Debug toolbar or choose View ➤ Locals Window; to remove the Locals window, click its Close button. From the Locals window, you can also click the button marked with an ellipsis (...) to display the Call Stack dialog box.

The Watch Window

In the Watch window you can track the values of variables and expressions as your code executes. To display the Watch window, click the Watch Window button on the Debug toolbar or choose View ➤ Watch Window in the Visual Basic Editor. To hide the Watch window, click its Close button.

The Watch window displays watch expressions you set ahead of time to give you a running display of the value of a variable or an expression. This allows you to pinpoint the location of an unexpected value for a variable or an expression as your code executes. The Watch window lists the names of the watched expressions or variables in the Expression column, their values in the Value column, their type (Integer, Byte, String, Long, and so on) in the Type column, and their context (the module and macro in which they are operating) in the Context column.

NOTE   If a variable or an expression in the Watch window has not been initialized, the Watch window will display "<Out of Context>" in the Value column and "Empty" (for a variable other than a Variant) or "Variant/Empty" (for a Variant) in the Type column.

The Visual Basic Editor updates all watch expressions in the Watch window whenever you enter Break mode and whenever you execute a statement in the Immediate window (more on this window in the next section). So if you step through a macro in the Code window, you can watch the value of a variable or an expression as each statement executes. This is a great way to pinpoint the location of an error or an unexpected value and is much easier than moving the mouse over each variable or expression in question to check its value by using the Auto Data Tips feature.

Before you can display a variable in the Watch window, you need to declare it (otherwise the Visual Basic Editor will respond with a "Variable not created in this context" error).

Because watch expressions slow execution of your code, the Visual Basic Editor does not save them with the code—you need to place them separately for each editing session. The Visual Basic Editor stores watch expressions during the current editing session, so you can move from procedure to procedure without losing your watch expressions.

To set a watch expression, add it to the list in the Watch window:

1. Select the variable or expression in your code, or position the insertion point in it. (This step is optional, but recommended.)

2. Right-click in the Code window or in the Watch window and choose Add Watch from the shortcut menu, or choose Debug ➢ Add Watch to display the Add Watch dialog box. If you selected a variable or an expression in step 1, it will appear in the Expression text box.

3. If necessary, change the variable or expression in the Expression text box, or enter a variable or an expression if you didn't select one in step 1.

4. If necessary, adjust the settings in the Context group box. The Procedure drop-down list will be set to the current macro, and the Module drop-down list will be set to the current module.

5. In the Watch Type group box, adjust the option button setting if necessary:

   - The default setting, Watch Expression, adds the variable or expression in the Expression text box to the list in the Watch window.

   - *Break when value is true* causes VBA to enter Break mode whenever the value of the variable or expression changes to True.

   - *Break when value changes* causes VBA to enter Break mode whenever the value of the watch expression changes. Use this setting either when dealing with a watch expression whose value you do not expect to change but which appears to be changing or when dealing with a watch expression whose every change you need to observe.

1025

TIP

The *Break when value is true* option button allows you to run your code without stepping through each statement that does not change the value of the watch expression to True. The *Break when value changes* option button allows you to run your code and stop with each change of the value.

6. Click the OK button to add the watch expression to the Watch window.

TIP

You can also drag a variable or an expression from the Code window to the Watch window. This sets a default watch expression in the current context; to set *Break when value is true* or *Break when value changes*, edit the watch expression after dragging it to the Watch window.

To edit a watch expression, right-click the watch expression in the Watch window and choose Edit Watch from the shortcut menu, or select the expression in the Watch window and choose Debug ➢ Edit Watch. Either action displays the Edit Watch dialog box with the watch expression selected in the Expression box. Change the context or watch type for the watch expression by using the settings in the Context group box and the Watch Type group box, and then click the OK button to apply your changes.

To delete a watch expression, right-click it in the Watch window and choose Delete Watch from the shortcut menu. You can also delete the current watch expression by clicking the Delete button in the Edit Watch dialog box.

Using the Quick Watch Feature

For times when you don't want to create a watch expression for an expression or a variable, you can use the Quick Watch feature, which displays the Quick Watch dialog box showing the context and value of the selected expression.

To use Quick Watch, select the expression or variable in the Code window and then click the Quick Watch button on the Debug toolbar, choose Debug ➢ Quick Watch, or press Shift+F9. (If you're already working in the Quick Watch dialog box, you can click the Add button to add the expression to the Watch window.)

The Immediate Window

The Visual Basic Editor provides an Immediate window that you can use as a virtual scratchpad to enter lines of code that you want to test without entering them in the macro itself or to display information to help you check the values of variables while a macro is executing. In the first case, you enter code in the Immediate window; in the second, you use statements entered in the Code window to display information in the Immediate window, where you can easily view it. You can execute code in the Immediate window *only* when your code is running—for example, when you have a project in Break mode and are stepping through it.

To display the Immediate window, click the Immediate Window button on the Debug toolbar, choose View ➤ Immediate Window, or press Ctrl+G. To hide the Immediate window again, click its Close button.

A number of restrictions apply to the code you can use in the Immediate window:

- You cannot use declarative statements (such as Dim, Private, Public, Option Explicit, Static, or Type) or control-flow statements (such as GoTo, Sub, or Function). These will cause VBA to throw an "Invalid in Immediate Pane" error.

- You cannot use multiline statements (such as block If statements or block For…Next statements) because there is no logical connection between statements on different lines in the Immediate window; each line is treated in isolation. You can get around this limitation by entering block If statements on a single line, separating the statements with colons, and using the underscore line-continuation character to break the resulting long lines into two physical lines while keeping them as one logical line.

- You cannot place breakpoints in the Immediate window.

The Immediate window supports most standard Windows key combinations and most of the Visual Basic Editor keystrokes and key combinations (such as F5 to start a procedure or Form running). There are, however, two exceptions:

- Pressing Enter runs the current line of code.

- Pressing Ctrl+Enter inserts a carriage return.

As well as entering statements in the Immediate window for quick testing, you can include in your macros statements to print information to the Immediate window by using the Print method on the Debug object. This provides you with a way of viewing information as a macro runs without having to be in Break mode or having to display a message box or dialog box that stops execution of the macro.

The syntax for the Print method is:

```
Debug.Print [outputlist]
```

The `outputlist` argument, which is optional, specifies the expression or expressions to print. For example, you could print the names and paths of all open documents to the Immediate window by using the following statements in a macro for Word:

```
For Each doc in Documents
     Debug.Print doc.FullName
Next
```

The Visual Basic Editor Toolbars

The Visual Basic Editor for Word and Excel provides four toolbars:

- Standard
- Edit
- Debug
- UserForm

You can display and hide these toolbars by using conventional Office methods: Right-click anywhere in the menu bar or in any displayed toolbar and choose the name of the toolbar from the shortcut menu of toolbars; or choose View ➢ Toolbars and make your selection from the Toolbars submenu.

The following sections discuss each of the toolbars in detail.

Standard Toolbar

The Standard toolbar (see Figure 19.7) provides commands for working with and running macros.

FIGURE 19.7:

Use the buttons on the Standard toolbar for working with macros.

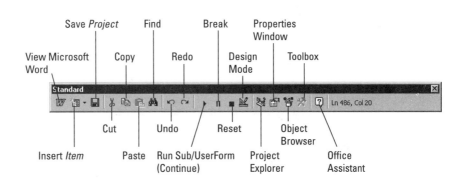

Here's what the buttons on the Standard toolbar do:

View Microsoft Word displays Word.

Insert *Item* inserts the currently selected item—UserForm, Module, Class Module, or Procedure. You can click the drop-down button and select a different item from the drop-down list.

Save *Project* (*Project* is the name of the current project) saves the current project and all code in it.

Cut, **Copy**, and **Paste** work as usual.

Find displays the Find dialog box for finding and replacing text.

Undo and **Redo** work as usual.

Run Sub/UserForm (Continue) starts the current procedure or Form running. If the current procedure or Form is already running and is stopped in Break mode, clicking the Run Sub/UserForm (Continue) button starts the procedure or Form running again. (If no procedure is current, clicking this button displays the Macros dialog box for you to choose the macro to run.)

Break places the Visual Basic Editor in Break mode, interrupting the execution of any code that is running. (When the Break button is not visible, you can enter Break mode by pressing Ctrl+Break.)

Reset stops the current procedure and clears all its variables.

Design Mode toggles Design mode on and off.

Project Explorer displays the Project Explorer window (if it is not displayed) and activates it.

Properties Window displays the Properties window (if it is not displayed) and activates it.

Object Browser displays the Object Browser (if it is not displayed) and activates it.

Toolbox displays or hides the Toolbox when it is available.

Office Assistant starts the Office Assistant.

Edit Toolbar

The Edit toolbar (see Figure 19.8) provides more commands for running and editing macros.

FIGURE 19.8:

Use the buttons on the Edit toolbar for running and editing macros.

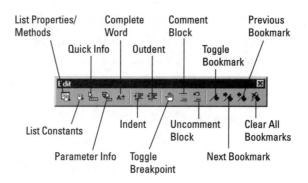

Here's what the buttons on the Edit toolbar do:

List Properties/Methods displays the pop-up List Properties/Methods list box when it is available.

List Constants displays the pop-up List Constants list box when it is available.

Quick Info displays information about the code at which the insertion point is currently located.

Parameter Info displays pop-up information about the parameter at which the insertion point is currently located.

Complete Word completes the word in which the insertion point is currently located.

Indent and **Outdent** indent and un-indent the current line of code or the currently selected lines.

Toggle Breakpoint toggles on and off a breakpoint at the current line.

Comment Block comments out the current line or selected lines by putting an apostrophe at the beginning of the line. The Visual Basic Editor displays comment lines in a different color (by default, green) so that you can readily identify them.

> **NOTE**
> When you comment a block, any lines already commented receive a second apostrophe. When you uncomment a block, the Visual Basic Editor removes only the first apostrophe from each line so that any lines commented before the block was commented remain commented when you uncomment the block. You can remove such commenting by clicking the Uncomment Block button again.

Uncomment Block removes commenting from the current line or selected lines.

Toggle Bookmark adds a bookmark to the current line (if it doesn't already have one) or removes a bookmark if the line already has one.

Next Bookmark moves the insertion point to the next bookmark.

Previous Bookmark moves the insertion point to the previous bookmark.

Clear All Bookmarks removes all bookmarks from the current project.

Debug Toolbar

The Debug toolbar (see Figure 19.9) contains commands for running and debugging your macros. The Debug toolbar shares three buttons—Run Sub/UserForm (Continue), Break, and Reset—with the Standard toolbar; the others are specific to running and debugging macros.

FIGURE 19.9:

The Debug toolbar provides 13 commands for debugging your macros.

Here's what the buttons on the Debug toolbar do:

Design Mode/Exit Design Mode toggles in and out of Design mode, which you use for creating Forms.

Run Sub/UserForm (Continue), **Break**, and **Reset** work as described in the "Standard Toolbar" section earlier in this chapter.

Toggle Breakpoint toggles on and off a breakpoint at the current line.

Step Into steps into the current procedure in Break mode.

Step Over executes the whole of a procedure or function called from the current procedure (instead of stepping through the called procedure statement by statement). This button becomes available when you enter Break mode.

Step Out runs the rest of the current procedure. This button becomes available when you enter Break mode.

Locals Window displays the Locals window.

Immediate Window displays the Immediate window.

Watch Window displays the Watch window.

Quick Watch displays the Quick Watch dialog box containing the context and value of the selected expression.

Call Stack displays the Call Stack dialog box.

UserForm Toolbar

The UserForm toolbar (see Figure 19.10) contains buttons for working with Forms. This toolbar contains some of the same buttons as the Form Editor toolbar in the Visual Basic IDE.

FIGURE 19.10:

The UserForm toolbar

Here's what the buttons on the UserForm toolbar do:

Bring to Front places the selected object, objects, or group of objects in front of the other objects on a form.

Send to Back places the selected object, objects, or group of objects behind the other objects on a form.

Group groups the selected objects.

Ungroup ungroups the selected objects.

Align aligns the selected objects using the alignment last chosen (for example, Align Middles). The Align drop-down list offers the horizontal alignments Lefts, Centers, and Rights; the vertical alignments Tops, Middles, and Bottoms; and To Grid.

Center centers the selected object, objects, or group of objects using the centering last chosen (for example, Center Vertically). The Center drop-down list offers the choices Horizontally and Vertically.

Make Same Size makes the selected objects the same size in the dimension or dimensions last used (for example, Make Width Same Size). The Make Same Size drop-down list offers the choices Width, Height, and Both.

Zoom zooms the controls on the Form.

Choosing Options for the Visual Basic Editor

The Visual Basic Editor provides a number of options to let you customize its look and its actions. You'll find many of these options similar to those in the Visual Basic IDE.

To choose options for the Visual Basic Editor, select Tools ➤ Options to open the Options dialog box and make choices on the four tabs. The following sections describe the options.

Editor Tab Options

The Editor tab of the Options dialog box (see Figure 19.11) includes the following settings:

Auto Syntax Check controls whether the Visual Basic Editor automatically checks your syntax as you type expressions. This is usually helpful because the Visual Basic Editor can instantly point out errors that otherwise would have remained unseen until you tried to run or debug your code. But if your style is to flit from one unfinished line of code to another (and ultimately finish lines at your convenience), you may want to turn off this feature.

Require Variable Declaration governs whether you declare variables explicitly or implicitly. Select this checkbox to have the Visual Basic Editor require you to declare variables explicitly. The Visual Basic Editor will place an Option Explicit statement at the beginning of each module you create when this option is selected.

Auto List Members controls whether the List Properties/Methods and List Constants features automatically suggest properties, methods, and constants as you work in the Code window.

Auto Quick Info controls whether the Quick Info feature automatically displays information as you work in the Code window.

Auto Data Tips controls whether the Visual Basic Editor displays ScreenTips when you move the mouse pointer over a variable.

Auto Indent controls whether the Visual Basic Editor automatically indents subsequent lines of code after you've indented a line.

Tab Width sets the number of spaces in a tab. You can adjust this from 1 to 32 spaces.

Drag-and-Drop Text Editing controls whether the Visual Basic Editor supports drag-and-drop. (This is usually a good idea.)

Default to Full Module View controls whether the Visual Basic Editor displays all the macros in one module together in one list or displays them one at a time. If you're working with short macros, you may find the list view useful; for most other purposes, the individual view provides a less cluttered and more workable effect. To switch to individual view, clear this checkbox, close the Options dialog box, and then open the module you want to work with by choosing it from the Procedure drop-down list at the top of the Code window. (If you already have the macro displayed in the list view, you'll need to close this window to switch to the individual view.)

Procedure Separator controls whether the Visual Basic Editor displays horizontal lines to separate the macros within a module shown in list view in the Code window. Usually these lines are helpful, providing a quick reference to where one macro ends and the next begins. (If you're using the individual view, this checkbox is not relevant.)

FIGURE 19.11:

The Editor tab of the
Options dialog box

Editor Format Tab Options

The Editor Format tab of the Options dialog box (see Figure 19.12) controls how
text in the Visual Basic Editor appears. You can change the default colors for various types of text used in macros by choosing any of them (one at a time) in the
Code Colors list box and selecting colors from the Foreground, Background, and
Indicator drop-down lists.

FIGURE 19.12:

The Editor Format tab of
the Options dialog box

You can change the font and size of all the text in the Code window by using the Font and Size drop-down lists. To increase the size of the Code window a fraction, you can also prevent the display of the margin indicator bar (in which items such as the Next Statement and Breakpoint icons appear) by clearing the Margin Indicator Bar checkbox.

General Tab Options

The General tab of the Options dialog box (see Figure 19.13) contains categories of settings. The Form Grid settings control how the Visual Basic Editor handles Forms for items such as dialog boxes. Note that unlike the Visual Basic IDE, the Visual Basic Editor uses twips as its measurement unit for the grid.

- Select the Show Grid checkbox if you want the Visual Basic Editor to display the grid pattern of dots on Forms.

- Specify the distance between the lines in the grid pattern by setting the Width and Height text boxes.

- Select the Align Controls to Grid checkbox if you want the Visual Basic Editor to automatically snap the controls to the grid as you place them.

FIGURE 19.13:

The General tab of the Options dialog box

The Notify before State Loss checkbox controls whether the Visual Basic Editor warns you when you're running a module and you try to take an action that will require VBA to reset the values of all variables in the module.

The Error Trapping group box controls how VBA handles errors that occur when you're running code:

Break on All Errors sets VBA to enter Break mode when it encounters any error, no matter whether an error handler is active or whether the code is in a class module. This option is useful for pinpointing where errors occur; if you have an error-handling mechanism in place, you probably won't want to use this option.

Break in Class Module is the default setting for the Error Trapping group box, and it's the most useful option for general use. When VBA encounters an unhandled error in a class module, it enters Break mode at the offending line of code in the module.

Break on Unhandled Errors is useful when you have constructed an error handler to handle predictable errors in the current module. If there is an error handler, VBA allows the handler to trap the error and does not enter Break mode; but if there is no error handler for the error generated, VBA enters Break mode on the offending line of code. An unhandled error in a class module, however, causes the project to enter Break mode on the line of code that invoked the offending procedure of the class, thus enabling you to identify (and alter) the line that caused the problem.

The Compile group box controls when the Visual Basic Editor compiles the code for a project. Select the Compile on Demand checkbox if you want the code to be compiled only as needed; if you do so, you can also select the Background Compile checkbox to have the Visual Basic Editor use idle CPU time to compile the code while the project is not running.

The Show ToolTips checkbox controls whether the Visual Basic Editor displays ToolTips (a.k.a. ScreenTips) for its toolbar buttons.

The Collapse Proj. Hides Windows checkbox controls whether the Visual Basic Editor hides the Code window and other project windows that you collapse in the Project Explorer.

Docking Tab Options

The Docking tab of the Options dialog box (see Figure 19.14) controls whether the various windows in the Visual Basic Editor are dockable or not—that is, whether they attach automatically to a side of the window when you move them there. As in the Visual Basic IDE, keeping windows dockable usually makes for a more organized interface, but you may find it useful to make the windows undockable so that you can drag them off the edge of the screen as necessary and generally arrange them however makes most sense to you.

The Docking tab of the Options dialog box

Working with the Visual Basic Editor and the Visual Basic IDE

Both the Visual Basic IDE and the Visual Basic Editor provide an enormous amount of help when you're working in them. In most cases, the best way of creating code that uses VBA and the Office applications is to use all the help that you can get. This means working in the environment most suited to helping you create the code you need.

As discussed earlier in this chapter, the Visual Basic Editor interface provides help and prompting for creating VBA code to work with the host application for the Visual Basic Editor session through features such as Auto Complete and List Properties/Constants. Because these and other features of the Visual Basic Editor are not available when you are working in the Visual Basic IDE and referencing Word or Excel VBA objects, it's usually a good idea to create the prototype for the code in the Visual Basic Editor and then transfer it to the Visual Basic IDE when you're sure it works: When creating a Visual Basic project that manipulates Word, create the Word statements in the Visual Basic Editor in a session started from a Word session. (The Visual Basic Editor provides help on the host application only. If you reference another application—for example, if you use VBA in Word to create an Excel object—the Word VBA session cannot provide help on Excel VBA.)

When you move code from the Visual Basic Editor to the Visual Basic IDE, you will have to adjust the references in the code from the Visual Basic Editor to correspond with the command structure you've used in the Visual Basic IDE, but doing so is usually much faster than debugging code statement by statement in the Visual Basic IDE because you've missed (or mistyped) an argument that the Visual Basic Editor could have supplied (or highlighted) instantly had you been working in it.

Recording a Macro

If you're not intimately familiar with the object model of Excel or Word (which we'll be examining in Chapters 21 and 22), recording a macro is by far the easiest way of creating VBA code that you can then move to the Visual Basic IDE: You simply switch on the macro recorder and record the actions you want the macro to take. When you finish recording, you can switch to the Visual Basic Editor and work with the code representing the actions.

Even if you *are* familiar with the object models of the Office applications, a macro can still be a handy way of quickly assembling the details of the code you need. Either way, you will usually want to adjust the code recorded in a macro before moving it to the Visual Basic IDE.

In Chapter 18, we gave you the short version of how to record a macro. Here's a more detailed look:

1. First, start the macro recorder by choosing Tools ➤ Macro ➤ Record New Macro. (In Word, you can also double-click the REC indicator on the status bar instead.) Excel or Word displays the Record Macro dialog box. Figure 19.15 shows the Record Macro dialog box for Word; Figure 19.16 shows the Record Macro dialog box for Excel.

FIGURE 19.15:

In the Record Macro dialog box, enter a name for the macro you're about to record, and enter a description in the Description box if necessary. This is the Record Macro dialog box for Word.

FIGURE 19.16:

The Record Macro dialog box for Excel

2. Enter a name for the new macro in the Macro Name text box. The macro name can be a maximum of 80 characters and can contain both letters and numbers, but it must start with a letter. It cannot contain spaces, punctuation, or special characters (such as ! or *), though underscores are allowed.

NOTE   Neither Excel nor Word will prevent you from typing a space or a forbidden character in the Record Macro Name text box. But when you click the OK button, Excel will display a message box telling you the name is not valid and will return you to the Record Macro dialog box to allow you to fix the name. Word will display a message box telling you that the procedure name is invalid and will close the Record Macro dialog box.

3. If you care, you can enter a description for the macro in the Description box. This description is to help you (and anyone you share the macro with) identify the macro. If you're creating the macro with the intention of cannibalizing it immediately for a Visual Basic project, don't waste time adding a description to it.

4. In Word, if you want to restrict the macro to just the current template, choose that template from the Store Macro In drop-down list. If you want the macro to be available no matter which template you're working in, make sure the default setting, All Documents (NORMAL.DOT), appears in the Store Macro In drop-down list box.

    In Excel, if you want the macro to be available only to the current workbook, choose This Workbook in the Store Macro In drop-down list. If you want the macro to be available to all workbooks, choose the Personal Macro Workbook option. If you want to store the macro in a new workbook, choose the New Workbook option.

5. Next, you can assign a way to run the macro. Again, if you're creating a scratch macro for immediate reuse, this isn't worth the effort. Otherwise, see the sidebar for how to assign a toolbar button, menu item, or shortcut key.

Assigning a Way to Run a Macro

You can assign a macro to a toolbar button, to a menu item, or to a shortcut key. The process is a little different, depending on whether you're working in Excel or in Word.

In Excel, click in the Shortcut Key text box and press the key that you want to use with Ctrl as a shortcut key. Press the Shift key if you want to add Shift to the key combination. (For example, you can use Ctrl+k and Ctrl+Shift+K to run different macros stored in the same workbook if you so choose.)

In Word, click the Toolbars button or the Keyboard button in the Assign Macro To group box. If you choose Toolbars, Word displays the Customize dialog box with the Commands tab displayed and Macros selected in the Categories list box. Now, follow these steps:

1. Click the macro's name in the Commands list box and drag it to any convenient toolbar or to the menu bar. Word will add a button or menu item for the macro, giving it the macro's full name and context, such as NORMAL.NEW-MACROS.MyNewMacro.

2. You can now rename the button or menu item by right-clicking it and entering a suitable (and probably shorter) name in the Name text box on the shortcut menu that appears.

3. To assign an access key to an item, put an ampersand (&) before the character that you want to use as the access key.

4. Click the Close button to close the Customize dialog box.

If you choose Keyboard, Word displays the Customize Keyboard dialog box. Place the insertion point in the Press New Shortcut Key box and then press the key combination you want. A key combination can be any one of the following:

- Alt plus either a regular key not used as a menu access key or a function key

- Ctrl plus a regular key or a function key

- Shift plus a function key

- Ctrl+Alt, Ctrl+Shift, Alt+Shift, or Ctrl+Alt+Shift plus a regular key or function key

Check the Current Keys list box to make sure the key combination you chose isn't already in use (if it is, press Backspace and press another combination), and then click the Assign button. Click the Close button to close the Customize Keyboard dialog box. Excel or Word will now be ready to start recording the macro.

6. Excel or Word will now be ready to start recording the macro. You'll see the application display the Stop Recording toolbar and add a cassette-tape icon to the mouse pointer to remind you that you're recording. In Word, the REC indicator in the status bar will be darkened (activated) as well.

7. Now record the sequence of actions for the macro:

    • In Word, you can use the mouse to select items from menus and toolbars and to make choices in dialog boxes, but not to select items within a document window—to select items in a document window, you must use the keyboard.

    • To perform any actions that you don't want recorded, you can pause the macro recorder at any time by clicking the Pause Recording button on the Stop Recording toolbar. Click the Pause Recording button again to resume recording.

NOTE When you make choices in a dialog box—for example, the Paragraph dialog box in Word—the macro recorder records the current settings for *all* the options on that tab of the dialog box when you click OK. So when you make a change to, say, the left indention of a paragraph, Word records all the other settings on the Indents and Spacing tab as well (Alignment, Before and After spacing, and so forth). You'll need to edit the unnecessary commands out of the resulting macro.

8. To stop recording, click the Stop Recording button on the Stop Recording toolbar. The macro recorder will have recorded the VBA commands for the actions you performed. If you chose to assign the macro to a control or a keystroke, the application will have assigned it.

You'll probably need to edit the macro you've recorded, either to adapt it or to tighten it. We'll look at editing macros in the Visual Basic Editor in just a moment, in "Editing a Macro in the Visual Basic Editor."

Creating a Macro from Scratch in the Visual Basic Editor

Instead of recording a macro from Excel or Word, you can create the macro from scratch in the Visual Basic Editor. There are a couple of main advantages to doing so:

- First, you can write code that you will not need to tighten or edit down. If you want to use only one setting in, say, the Paragraph dialog box in Word, you will not need to record every other setting on that tab of the dialog box as well.

- Second, you can create code that you would not be able to record using the macro recorder. For example, while working interactively with Excel or Word, you can work only with the active workbook or document: Any workbook or document that you need to work with, you must first make active. By writing VBA code, on the other hand, you can work with workbooks or documents other than the active one. This can greatly help you write efficient macros.

The disadvantage to writing a macro from scratch is that you need to know which objects you want to manipulate—or be prepared to do some research. This is why the macro recorder makes a great tool for getting a macro started.

You can start creating a macro from scratch in any of several ways:

- From Excel or Word, choose Tools ➤ Macro ➤ Macros to open the Macros dialog box. Enter the name for the new macro in the Macro Name text box, add a description in the Description text box if necessary, select the template, document, or workbook to store the macro in, and then click the Create button. Excel or Word opens the Visual Basic Editor and displays the macro in a Code window.

    Excel will store the macro in a new module named Module*n*—Module1, Module2, and so on, where *n* is the number higher than any consecutive number used so far for such a module name. Excel will continue to use this module for further macros you create in the same Excel session. For macros you create in a subsequent Excel session, Excel will create a new module with the next higher consecutive number.

Word will store the macro in a module named NewMacros, creating the module if it does not already exist.

- From the Visual Basic Editor for the appropriate host application, open the module in which to store the macro. Choose Insert ➤ Procedure to open the Add Procedure dialog box (see Figure 19.17). Enter the name for the new procedure in the Name text box. In the Type group box, choose the type of procedure to create: Sub, Function, or Property. (For a macro, choose Sub.) In the Scope group box, select the Public option button or the Private option button to specify public or private scope for the procedure. Click the OK button to close the Add Procedure dialog box. The Visual Basic Editor places the appropriate statements for the macro—for example, Public Sub *MacroName*(), a blank line, and an End Sub statement—in the module.

FIGURE 19.17:

Name the macro and specify its scope in the Add Procedure dialog box.

- In the Code window, type **Sub** (or **Private Sub** or **Public Sub**, as appropriate for the scope of the macro you want to create), followed by the name you want the macro to have, and press Enter. The Visual Basic Editor will automatically add parentheses (unless you typed them), a blank paragraph, and an End Sub statement.

You can now create the macro by entering code in the Code window, using the help features that the Visual Basic Editor provides.

Debugging a Macro in the Visual Basic Editor

In this section, we'll touch on the types of errors to expect in VBA and the main ways of debugging a macro in the Visual Basic Editor. Both these topics should be familiar to you from Visual Basic and the Visual Basic IDE, so we won't linger on them. We'll simply point out the few differences between debugging in the Visual Basic Editor and debugging in the Visual Basic IDE.

Types of Errors to Expect

You can confidently expect to see language errors, compile errors, and run-time errors when working with VBA. Whether you see program logic errors as well is up to you.

The Visual Basic Editor's help features help eliminate language errors (also known as *syntax errors*) and some compile errors when entering code. For example, the Visual Basic Editor will alert you to an error such as omitting the Then from an If… Then construction by checking the statement when you move the insertion point to another line in the Code window. Language errors that the Visual Basic Editor doesn't catch as you create them usually show up as compile errors when the Visual Basic Editor compiles the code for a procedure.

Compile errors occur when VBA cannot compile a statement correctly—when it cannot turn a statement that you've entered into viable code. For example, if you tell VBA to use a property for an object that doesn't have that property, you'll cause a compile error. Likewise, if you mistype an argument in a statement, as in the example below (FileMame instead of FileName), it will usually show up as a compile error.

```
ActiveDocument.SaveAs FileMame:="My File.doc"
```

As well as the errors that the Visual Basic Editor actively helps you avoid, as in the examples above, you can avoid other errors by watching the Visual Basic Editor's behavior closely as you're creating your code. Say you're trying to enter a Documents.Close statement and mistype Documents as Docments—easy enough to do. In this case, the Visual Basic Editor will not display the Properties/Methods list because you haven't entered a valid object. Not seeing the list should alert you that something is wrong, unless you've turned off the Auto List Members option. If you continue anyway and enter the Docments.Close statement (again, easy enough to do if you're not watching the screen), the Visual Basic Editor will not spot the mistake, and it will show up as a "Run-time error 424: Object required" when you try to run the macro.

In a similar vein, if you specify a property or a method for an object to which that property or method does not apply, VBA will generate a compile error. For example, say you forget the Add method and enter Documents.Create instead. VBA will highlight the offending word and will generate a compile error "Method or data member not found," which tells you there's no Create method for the Documents collection.

Run-time errors occur while code is executing, caused by a statement that makes VBA try to perform an impossible operation. For example, your code might require opening a document that doesn't exist, closing a workbook when no workbook is open, or performing something mathematically impossible such as dividing by zero.

Program logic errors—errors that produce incorrect results, though the code compiles and runs correctly—are entirely up to you. They also tend to be the hardest errors to catch, because you'll have less of an indication as to where things start going wrong—or how many things are going wrong.

Troubleshooting Problems in Procedures

This section contains some suggestions for troubleshooting problems in procedures in the Visual Basic Editor.

First, make the most of Break mode for pinpointing where things go wrong in your code:

- When a macro stops and the Visual Basic Editor displays the Microsoft Visual Basic *Code execution has been interrupted* dialog box, click the Debug button to access and view the problem line in your code straightaway. If your code gets stuck in a loop, press Ctrl+Break to enter Break mode and display this dialog box.

- Alternatively, set breakpoints at lines of code that may be problematic.

- Use Stop statements if you need to keep a breakpoint in your code from one editing session to another. Like the Visual Basic IDE, the Visual Basic Editor doesn't save breakpoints with your code: You have to place them for each editing session. This serves as a handy way to avoid leaving breakpoints in your code unintentionally, but at times you'll want to use a Stop statement instead to halt execution.

- Use the Step Through and Step Out commands to avoid stepping command-by-command through code that you know to be working fine.

- After you fix an error in the code in Break mode, use the Set Next Statement command to continue execution from wherever is most advantageous. Click in the line from which to start and choose Debug ➤ Set Next Statement, or right-click in the line and choose Set Next Statement from the shortcut menu.

Don't let your error handlers hide errors from you:

- Make your error handlers as specific as possible. When you're creating an error handler, use a Debug.Print statement to place the error number in the Immediate window and then copy the number into your handler. Check to make sure that this error number solves the problem: Often, you'll get various errors from the same line of code, depending on the condition of the host application. For example, if the user tries to specify a drive that is not available, VBA responds with an error that is different from the one it displays when a user tries to access a folder that does not exist. Trap each error by number, and take action accordingly, rather than using a blanket error handler that will quash any other error that you encounter.

- If you're using one or more error handlers that prevent you from seeing certain errors in your code, use the Break on All Errors setting in the Options dialog box to cause VBA to enter Break mode from any error without your having to disable your error handler or handlers.

Comment out lines that may be problematic, and rerun the code to see if that makes a difference.

Keep a close eye on the value of variables and expressions:

- When you hit an error, check as many of the variables and expressions as possible, looking for unexpected values.

- Use the Immediate window to test data or expressions or to print information at strategic points in the macro.

- Use the Locals window to track the values of all the declared variables in the current procedure.

- Use the Watch window (and the Quick Watch dialog box when necessary) to watch the value of selected expressions.

- Use the Call Stack dialog box to track which procedures are called.

To watch what is happening as a macro executes, arrange the Visual Basic Editor and the host application windows so that you can see them both. Then step through the questionable part of the macro command by command. Watching the effect of each command as it is executed is a powerful tool in helping to establish what's going wrong. Is a macro failing because the required object is not available (for example, because the relevant document or workbook is not open when the macro expects it to be) or because the wrong object is being manipulated (for example, if you have selected a different range than you intended)?

NOTE　　Beyond the necessary differences in the menus to deal with the different capabilities of the Visual Basic IDE and the Visual Basic Editor, you'll find small inconsistencies that take a little getting used to. For example, the Run menu in the Visual Basic IDE contains a Restart command with the access key R, whereas the Run menu in the Visual Basic Editor contains the Reset command instead, also with the access key R. This Reset command performs the equivalent of the Visual Basic IDE's Run ≻ End command. If you're used to using Alt+R, R to restart a project from Break mode, you'll get a little surprise when you use that key combination in the Visual Basic Editor.

Creating Forms in the Visual Basic Editor

Creating Forms in the Visual Basic Editor is similar to creating Forms in the Visual Basic IDE. In this section, we'll briefly discuss the process of creating Forms in the Visual Basic Editor, touching on some of the differences from the Visual Basic IDE. We'll look at how the controls in the Visual Basic Editor compare with those in the Visual Basic IDE and at how you can customize the Toolbox in the Visual Basic Editor.

To create a new Form in a project, follow these steps:

1. Right-click the project in the Project Explorer and choose Insert ≻ UserForm from the shortcut menu. The Visual Basic Editor creates and displays a new Form of the default size and names it UserForm*n*, where *n* is the next highest unused consecutive number. Figure 19.18 shows a new Form in the Visual Basic Editor. The Visual Basic Editor places this Form in the Forms collection for the project. If the project does not have a Forms collection yet, the Visual Basic Editor creates one and places the Form in it. The Visual Basic Editor also displays the Toolbox.

NOTE

If you don't have the Project Explorer displayed, choose Insert ➢ UserForm, or click the Insert button on the Standard toolbar and choose UserForm from the drop-down list. The Insert button has four manifestations: Insert UserForm, Insert Module, Insert Class Module, and Insert Procedure, depending on the last item created from this button. If the current button is Insert UserForm, you can click the button to create a Form rather than using the drop-down list.

FIGURE 19.18:

Creating a Form in the Visual Basic Editor

2. Add controls to the Form. Click the Toolbox button for the control you want to create. The mouse pointer changes to a crosshair with the button symbol for the item that you will create. Click once in the Form to place a default-size control; the upper-left corner of the control will be placed where you click. Click and drag in the Form to place and size a custom control. You can drag in any direction after clicking—the point at which you click does not have to be the upper-left corner of the control.

3. Adjust the controls as necessary:

   • Drag them about with the mouse.

   • Use the Properties window to adjust their properties.

   • Use the commands on the UserForm toolbar and on the Format menu to adjust the placement, grouping, and layering of the controls.

NOTE
The Visual Basic Editor provides several commands that the Visual Basic IDE does not. The Group and Ungroup commands let you work swiftly with groups of controls; the Bottom and Right commands on the Arrange Buttons submenu let you quickly arrange the command buttons in a Form; and the Size to Fit command automatically resizes an object to an appropriate size. On the other hand, the Visual Basic Editor does not provide a Lock Controls command as the Visual Basic IDE does.

4. Add code to the code sheet for the Form:

   - Display the code sheet for the Form. You can do so in several ways: Press F7; right-click the Form itself or the Form's name or icon in the Project Explorer and choose View Code from the shortcut menu; select the Form's name in the Project Explorer and click the View Code button on the Project Explorer's toolbar; or choose View ➤ Code. To create a procedure associated with a particular control, double-click that control. The Visual Basic Editor will display the code sheet for the Form and will create a private procedure for the default event of that control. For example, if you double-click an option button named optAutomatic, the Visual Basic Editor will create a procedure associated with the Click event for the option button and name it Private Sub optAutomatic_Click. (If a procedure with that name exists already, the Visual Basic Editor will display the procedure.)

   - Enter the code for the procedures as usual.

   - Create an initialization macro if you need to initialize any of the controls in the Form. This macro does not take the name of the Form. It needs to be named UserForm_Initialize:

     ```
     Private Sub UserForm_Initialize()
     'Commands for initializing the Form
     End Sub
     ```

5. Adjust the tab order of the controls on the Form as necessary. Choose View ➤ Tab Order to display the Tab Order dialog box. Select one or more controls in the Tab Order list box (Shift+click or Ctrl+click to select multiple controls) and click Move Up and Move Down to get the controls into the appropriate order. Click the OK button to close the Tab Order dialog box.

6. If necessary, create a macro to display the Form:

- To load a Form, use the Load statement. To unload a Form, use the Unload statement. The Load statement loads the Form into memory so it is available to the program, but does not display the Form. The Unload statement unloads the Form from memory and reclaims any memory associated with that object. If the Form is displayed when you run the Unload statement on it, VBA removes the Form from the screen. The following statement loads the Form named frmOptions:

```
Load frmOptions
```

- To display a Form, use the Show method. You can display a Form by using the Show method without explicitly loading the Form with a Load command first; VBA takes care of the implied Load command for you. To hide a Form, you use the Hide method. The following statement displays the Form named frmOptions:

```
frmOptions.Show
```

NOTE   If you run a Hide method without having loaded the dialog box into memory by using the Load statement or the Show method, VBA will load the dialog box but not display it on-screen.

Controls in the Visual Basic Editor

Although the Visual Basic Editor provides fewer controls for Forms overall than the Visual Basic IDE, it has a number of controls that the Visual Basic IDE does not. Table 19.1 shows how the controls stack up in the Visual Basic IDE and the Visual Basic Editor.

TABLE 19.1: The Visual Basic IDE Controls and the Visual Basic Editor Controls

Visual Basic IDE Control	Visual Basic Editor Control
CheckBox	CheckBox
ComboBox	ComboBox
CommandButton	CommandButton
Data	—
DirListBox	—

TABLE 19.1 (CONTINUED): The Visual Basic IDE Controls and the Visual Basic Editor Controls

Visual Basic IDE Control	Visual Basic Editor Control
DriveListBox	—
FileListBox	—
Frame	Frame
HscrollBar	—
Image	Image
Label	Label
Line	—
ListBox	ListBox
—	MultiPage
OLE	—
OptionButton	OptionButton
PictureBox	—
Shape	—
—	SpinButton
—	TabStrip
TextBox	TextBox
Timer	—
—	ToggleButton
VScrollBar	ScrollBar

As you can see, the Visual Basic Editor does not provide the DriveListBox, DirListBox, and FileListBox controls for working with drives, directories (folders), and files. Instead, you can use list boxes or combo boxes to display arrays of files. But you'll often find it easier to use built-in dialog boxes in the Visual Basic Editor than list boxes or combo boxes with arrays. For example, you can display a built-in dialog box such as the Open dialog box to allow the user to choose a file—either to open it or simply to select it. Alternatively, you might want to select or open a file by using a Form in the Visual Basic IDE before manipulating it in the Visual Basic Editor.

Neither does the Visual Basic Editor provide a Timer control. You can use the OnTime method of the Application object to run a procedure at a specified time.

The Visual Basic Editor provides only a vertical scrollbar control, named ScrollBar, whereas the Visual Basic IDE provides the VScrollBar vertical scroll bar control and HScrollBar horizontal scroll bar control.

The Visual Basic Editor provides the following controls that are not present in the basic set of controls in the Visual Basic IDE:

ToggleButton toggles between an On state and an Off state.

SpinButton increments and decrements numbers. Typically, you use a SpinButton control to adjust the value of another control, in many cases in preset increments or decrements (for example, adjusting the cost of a service in five-cent steps).

TabStrip presents sets of controls. For example, you might use a TabStrip control to move from one record to another, where each record used the same set of controls.

MultiPage presents different sets of controls on pages of a Form, as in dialog boxes such as the Options dialog box in the Visual Basic IDE and the Visual Basic Editor. The pages in MultiPage controls are often described as "tabs." The MultiPage control is similar to the Microsoft Tabbed Dialog control that you can add to the controls in the Visual Basic IDE Toolbox.

There are some minor differences between the Visual Basic Editor and the Visual Basic IDE when it comes to working with controls:

- To denote the access key for a control, in the Visual Basic Editor you set the Accelerator property for the control to the appropriate letter. In the Visual Basic IDE, you place an ampersand before the appropriate letter.

- To copy an object in the Visual Basic Editor, you can hold down Ctrl and drag the object (instead of using a Copy command).

- You can also use Copy and Paste to copy an object. Unlike Visual Basic, the Visual Basic Editor will not ask if you want to create an array, but will create a copy of the object, resetting its name to the next generic name for that type of object but leaving all relevant properties set as they were. For example, if you create a CommandButton object named cmdOK, set its properties as you want them, and then copy it, the Visual Basic Editor will name the copy CommandButton1 (or CommandButton2 or CommandButton3, as appropriate) but will leave the other properties as they were.

Customizing the Toolbox

In the Visual Basic Editor, as in the Visual Basic IDE, you can customize the Toolbox. You can change the controls on its default page if you wish, or you can add extra pages to it and place on them both existing controls and custom controls of your own creation.

By customizing the Toolbox, you can avoid having to create custom controls from scratch each time you need them. For example, in most dialog boxes, you'll want to have an OK button and a Cancel button. You can create these easily by using CommandButton objects and setting the relevant properties (Name, Height, Width, Accelerator, Default, and so on). Once you've created one CommandButton object with the right properties, you can simply put a copy of it in your Toolbox and reuse it when you need it.

You can also add to the Toolbox complex controls that extend the things you can do with dialog boxes and Forms.

Working with Toolbox Pages

Here's how to work with Toolbox pages. You can add pages, rename them, move them to different positions in the Toolbox or even save them to separate files.

To Add a Page to the Toolbox   Right-click the tab at the top of a page (or the label on the tab) and choose New Page from the shortcut menu. The Visual Basic Editor adds a new page named New Page, to which it will add the Select Objects control. This control appears on every tab in the Toolbox (so that it's always at hand), and you cannot remove it.

To Change the Name of a Page   You'll usually want to change the name of a page after adding it to the Toolbox. Right-click its tab or label, and choose Rename from the shortcut menu to display the Rename dialog box. Enter the name for the page in the Caption text box; enter any control tip text you want to appear in the Control Tip Text text box; and click the OK button to close the dialog box.

To Remove a Page from the Toolbox   Right-click its tab or label, and choose Delete Page from the shortcut menu. The Visual Basic Editor removes the page from the Toolbox without any confirmation, whether the page contains controls or not.

To Save Toolbox Pages As Separate Files   You might want to do this when creating a backup or for distribution purposes. Toolbox pages have a PAG extension. To import a Toolbox page, right-click the tab or label on an existing page in the Toolbox and choose Import Page from the shortcut menu to display the Import Page dialog box. Select the page you want to import and choose the Open button. The Visual Basic Editor adds the new page after the last page currently in the Toolbox and names it New Page. To export a Toolbox page, right-click its tab or label and choose Export Page from the shortcut menu to display the Export Page dialog box. Enter a name for the page (change folders if necessary) and click the Save button to save it.

To Move a Page in the Toolbox   Right-click its tab or label and choose Move from the shortcut menu to display the Page Order dialog box. In the Page Order list box, select the page or pages that you want to move (Shift+click to select multiple contiguous pages, Ctrl+click to select multiple pages individually) and use the Move Up and Move Down buttons to rearrange the pages as desired. Click the OK button to close the Page Order dialog box when you've finished.

Working with Toolbox Controls

To customize the pages of the Toolbox, you can add and remove controls, rename controls, and assign pictures to their Toolbox icons.

To Add Controls to the Toolbox   You can add to the Toolbox either custom controls from a displayed Form or additional controls installed on your computer:

- To copy a control from a displayed Form to the Toolbox, drag the control from the Form and drop it where you want it in the Toolbox.

- To add controls to the Toolbox, right-click in the tab to which you want to add controls, and choose Additional Controls from the shortcut menu to display the Additional Controls dialog box (see Figure 19.19). In the Available Controls list box, select the check boxes for the controls you want to add to the Toolbox, and then click the OK button. (To collapse the list to only the items currently selected, select the Selected Items Only checkbox in the Show group box.)

You can move a control from one page of the Toolbox to another by dragging it from the page it is on, moving the mouse pointer (still dragging) over the tab of the destination page to display that page, then moving the mouse pointer down (again, still dragging) into the body of that page, and dropping the control on it. To copy a control from one page to another, hold down the Ctrl key as you drag the control.

FIGURE 19.19:

In the Additional Controls dialog box, select the checkboxes for the controls you want to add, and then click the OK button.

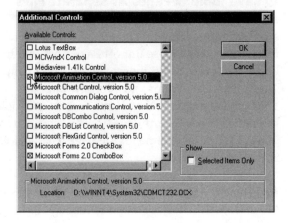

To Rename a Toolbox Control Right-click it in the Toolbox and choose the Customize item from the shortcut menu to display the Customize Control dialog box, shown in Figure 19.20. (The menu item will be identified by the name of the control—for example, if the control is identified as New Label, the menu item will be Customize New Label.)

FIGURE 19.20:

In the Customize Control dialog box, enter the name for the control in the Tool Tip Text text box, and then click the Edit Picture button or the Load Picture button to assign a button to it.

Enter the name for the control in the Tool Tip Text text box; this name will appear as a screentip when the user moves the mouse pointer over the control in the Toolbox. Then, if you wish, assign a different picture to the control's Toolbox icon as described in the next section, or click the OK button to close the Customize Control dialog box.

To Assign a Picture to a Control's Toolbox Icon To edit the picture assigned to the control, right-click the control, choose Customize from the short-cut menu to display the Customize Control dialog box, and click the Edit Picture button to display the Edit Image dialog box. Here, you can adjust the picture in the Picture edit box, pixel by pixel, by choosing the appropriate color or choosing the Erase tool in the Colors group box and clicking in the square you want to change. Click the Move buttons to move the entire image around the edit box (each direction button is available only if the image does not touch that edge of the edit box); click the Clear button to erase the entire image so that you can start from scratch. Use the Preview group box to see how the picture looks at the resolution at which it will be displayed in the Toolbox. When you finish adjusting the image, click the OK button to return to the Customize Control dialog box, and click the OK button to close that dialog box.

To load an existing picture for a control, right-click the control, choose Customize from the shortcut menu to display the Customize Control dialog box, and click the Load Picture button in the Customize Control dialog box to display the Load Picture dialog box. Select the picture and click the Open button to load it.

To Remove a Control from the Toolbox   Right-click it, and choose Delete from the shortcut menu. The item will be identified by the name of the control—for example, if you right-click a control named Company Name Combo Box, the menu item will be named Delete Company Name Combo Box. If the item is a custom control, this action gets rid of the control, and you will not be able to restore it (unless you have a copy elsewhere). If the item is a Microsoft-supplied control, you can restore it from the Additional Controls dialog box by selecting the checkbox for the appropriate object (for example, Microsoft Forms 2.0 CommandButton).

You can also remove controls from the Toolbox by deleting the entire page they are on, as we discussed earlier in this chapter.

Finding the VBA Objects You Need

In this section, we'll discuss how to find the VBA objects, methods, and properties you need. You find objects, methods, and properties in the same way in both Excel and Word, though the specifics naturally vary.

In addition to the List Properties/Methods feature and to recording a macro to identify the objects you need to manipulate, you can find objects in two main ways:

- By using the Object Browser
- By using the Help system

Navigating with the Object Browser

The Object Browser in the Visual Basic Editor works in a similar way to the Object Browser in the Visual Basic IDE, which we looked at in Chapter 5. Here's how to find the objects you need by using the Object Browser.

1. Display the Object Browser (see Figure 19.6, earlier in this chapter) by choosing View ➢ Object Browser, by pressing the F2 button, or by clicking the Object Browser button on the Standard toolbar. If the Object Browser is already displayed, make it active by clicking in it or by selecting it from the list at the bottom of the Window menu.

2. In the Project/Library drop-down list, select the name of the project or the library that you want to view. The Object Browser displays the available classes in the Classes list.

3. In the Classes list, select the class you want. For example, if you chose a template in step 2, select the module you want to work with in the Classes list.

4. If you want to work with a particular member of the class or project, select it in the Members Of list. For example, if you're working with a template project, you might want to choose a specific macro or Form to work with.

5. Once you select the class, member, or project, you can take the following actions:

   - View information about it in the Details pane at the bottom of the Object Browser window.

   - View the definition of an object by clicking the Show Definition button. Alternatively, right-click the object in the Members Of list and choose View Definition from the shortcut menu. (The definition of a macro is the code that it contains; the definition of a module is all the code in all the macros that it contains; the definition of a Form is the code in all the macros attached to it.) The Show Definition button will be available (undimmed) only for objects that contain code, such as macros and Forms that you've created.

   - Copy the text for the selected class, project, or member to the clipboard by clicking the Copy to Clipboard button or by issuing a standard Copy command (for example, Ctrl+C or Ctrl+Insert).

Using Help to Find the Object You Need

VBA's Help system provides another easy way to access the details of the objects you want. The Help files provide you with a hyperlinked reference to all the objects, methods, and properties in VBA, including graphics that show how the objects are related.

The quickest way to access VBA Help is to activate the Visual Basic Editor and then press the F1 key. (If you've disabled the Office Assistant, you can also choose Help ➤ Microsoft Visual Basic Help.) VBA will respond by displaying the Visual Basic Reference window.

TIP

> To get help on a specific object, keyword, and so on referenced in your code, place the insertion point in the appropriate word before pressing the F1 key. VBA will display the Help for that topic.

Click the Help Topics button at the top-left corner of the Visual Basic Reference window to display the Help Topics dialog box. Click the Index tab to display it if it isn't already displayed. In the top text box, start typing the name of the object about which you want to get information, and then select the appropriate entry in the list box and click the Display button to display the entry.

For example, if you display help on the Word Document object, you'll see a Help window like the one shown in Figure 19.21.

FIGURE 19.21:

Here's what you'll get if you search for help on the Document object.

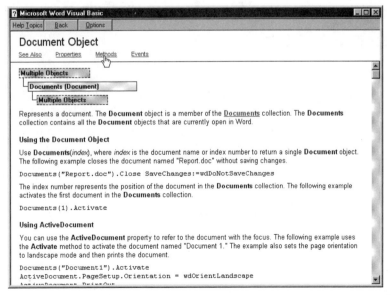

Apart from the regular Help information you'll find in the Help window, you can use the following features to get some additional information:

- Use the graphic at the top of the Help listing to understand the relationship of the current object to the object (or objects) that contain it and to the objects it contains. Click either of these objects to display a list of the relevant objects.

- Click any See Also hyperlink at the top of the window to display a Topics Found dialog box showing associated topics.

- Click the Properties hyperlink at the top of the window to display a Topics Found dialog box listing the help available on the properties of the object. You can then display one of the topics by selecting it in the list box and clicking the Display button or by double-clicking it in the list box.

- Click the Methods hyperlink at the top of the window to display a Topics Found dialog box listing the help available on the methods available for use on the object. Again, you can display one of these topics by selecting it in the list box and clicking the Display button or by double-clicking it in the list box.

- Some objects also have one or more events associated with them. If the object has any events associated with it, you can access them by clicking the Events hyperlink at the top of the window to display a Topics Found dialog box.

Saving Your Work and Closing the Visual Basic Editor

To save your work in the Visual Basic Editor, choose File ➤ Save *projectname* to save the document, template, or workbook and the changes you've made to it. Then choose File ➤ Close and Return to Microsoft Word or File ➤ Close and Return to Microsoft Excel to close the Visual Basic Editor and return to Word or Excel.

NOTE   You can also press Alt+Q to quit the Visual Basic Editor and return to its host application.

CHAPTER
TWENTY

20

Excel 97 Objects

- The Excel object model

- Working with the Excel application

- Working with workbooks and worksheets

- Working with ranges

- Using Find and Replace

- Using Excel's built-in dialog boxes

In this chapter, we'll discuss the objects in Excel 97, the Excel object model that describes how they are arranged, and how to work with them to get things done in VBA.

To manipulate Excel with VBA, you use the VBA objects that Excel exposes. These objects range from the Application object that represents the Excel application to Range objects that can be used to represent ranges of cells. By controlling these objects, you can take actions in Excel.

Because Excel is such a complex application, it exposes many more VBA objects than we can deal with in this chapter. So here we'll discuss the most important Excel objects—those you are most likely to work with first when automating procedures involving Excel. In discussing these objects, we will highlight the most useful properties and methods for each. We will not list or discuss every single property and method for each object. Likewise, for each method we mention, we will present the most useful arguments, not an exhaustive list of every argument that can be used with the method. The goal of this chapter is to give you the information you need to start working effectively with Excel through Visual Basic, not to bore you beyond tears.

The Excel Object Model

The Excel object model describes the theoretical architecture underlying Excel. By understanding the Excel object model, you can manipulate the objects in Excel and work effectively with VBA.

The Application object, at the top level of the Excel object model, represents the Excel application. Figure 20.1 shows the objects and collections contained in the Application object. From the Application object, you can access almost any Excel object by manipulating the appropriate object or collection. The plural names with singular names in parentheses indicate collections and the individual objects they contain. For example, the Addins collection comprises all Addin objects in the Application object, and the Workbooks collection contains all the open Workbook objects in the Application object.

FIGURE 20.1:

The Excel Application object. The shaded boxes denote objects and collections; the unshaded boxes denote objects only.

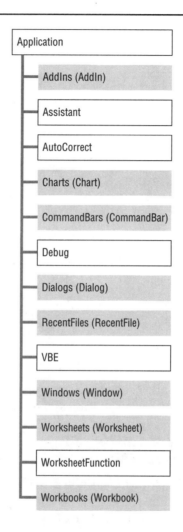

Application
AddIns (AddIn)
Assistant
AutoCorrect
Charts (Chart)
CommandBars (CommandBar)
Debug
Dialogs (Dialog)
RecentFiles (RecentFile)
VBE
Windows (Window)
Worksheets (Worksheet)
WorksheetFunction
Workbooks (Workbook)

The most-used objects in the Application object are the Workbooks collection, the Worksheets collection, and the Windows collection. By using these, you can manipulate the workbooks, the worksheets, and the windows that are open. Figure 20.2 shows the collections and objects contained in the Workbooks collection.

FIGURE 20.2:

The collections and objects contained in the Workbooks collection

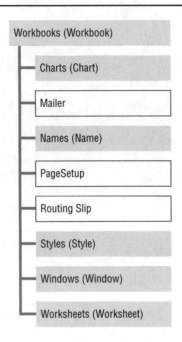

FIGURE 20.2:

The collections and objects contained in the Workbooks collection

The Worksheets collection gives you access to the worksheets in the active workbook (when you access the Worksheets collection from the Application object) or in the specified workbook (when you access the Worksheets collection from a Workbook object). Figure 20.3 shows the collections and objects contained in the Worksheets collection.

The Windows collection provides access to the windows in the active workbook (when you access the Windows collection from the Application object) or in the specified workbook (when you access the Windows collection from a Workbook object).

FIGURE 20.3:

The collections and objects contained in the Worksheets collection

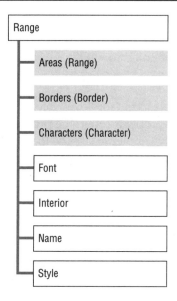

Working with the Excel Application

The Application object represents the Excel application. It contains properties that control application-wide settings, such as options in the Options dialog boxes. For example, the following statement turns off the EditDirectlyInCell property, the equivalent of clearing the Edit Directly in Cell checkbox on the Edit tab of the Options dialog box:

```
Application.EditDirectlyInCell = False
```

The following statement displays a message box containing the Path property of the Excel application:

```
Msgbox Application.Path
```

Accessing the Application Object

You can access the Excel Application object from within the Excel VBA environment. You can also access it either from VBA from another Office application (for example, from Word) or from Visual Basic.

The Application property returns the Application object. You can apply properties to the Application object to access objects and collections within it. The following statement accesses the Caption property of the first Window object in the Windows collection in the Application object:

```
Application.Windows(1).Caption
```

You can access top-level objects such as ActiveCell, ActiveSheet, and ActiveWindow through the properties available in the Application object, but it is usually simpler to use the top-level objects without the Application object qualifier. The following statements both return the Address property of the active cell. The first statement uses the ActiveCell property of the Application object, whereas the second statement is more concise and easier to use:

```
Application.ActiveCell.Address
ActiveCell.Address
```

To access the Application object from within another VBA environment or from Visual Basic, use the GetObject function or the CreateObject function. The GetObject function returns a reference to an existing object, and the CreateObject function creates a new object and returns a reference to it.

The following statements create a new Excel Application object and return a reference to it:

```
Dim vbExcel As Object
Set vbExcel = CreateObject("Excel.Application")
With vbExcel
    'Statements here
End With
```

The following statements return a reference to an existing Excel object:

```
Dim MySpreadsheet As Object
Set MySpreadsheet = GetObject("c:\Corporate\Sales Forecast.xls")
With MySpreadsheet
    'Take actions here
End With
Set MySpreadsheet = Nothing
```

To display an Excel object that you have created or accessed, set its Visible property to True:

```
vbExcel.Visible = True
```

To close the Excel application, use the Quit command:

```
With vbExcel
     'Take actions here
     .Quit
End With
```

Once you've closed the Excel application or the Excel object, use a Set statement with the Nothing keyword to release the memory:

```
Set vbExcel = Nothing
```

Working with Workbooks

The Workbooks collection represents all open workbooks. You can work either with Workbook objects that you access through the Workbooks collection or with the ActiveWorkbook object, which represents the currently active workbook.

Depending on the type of procedure you are creating, it's usually easy to decide whether to work with one or more Workbook objects in the Workbooks collection or to work with the ActiveWorkbook object. Use the Workbooks collection when you need to specify a workbook by name or when you need to work with a workbook that is not (or may not be) the active workbook. When performing complex procedures for the user, it is sometimes beneficial to work with a workbook other than the active workbook so that the user cannot see what Excel is doing. Use the ActiveWorkbook object when you do not know (or need to know) the name of the workbook you're working with (for example, in a simple macro the user runs on a workbook of their choosing), to find out which workbook is active, or when you want to display a procedure on screen so that the user can see it.

Activating a Workbook

To activate a workbook, use the Activate method. The Activate method makes the specified workbook the active workbook, so you can work with it as the ActiveWorkbook object.

The following statement makes the open workbook named CANDIDATES.XLS the active workbook:

```
Workbooks("Candidates.xls").Activate
```

NOTE Running the Activate method on a workbook that is already the active workbook does no harm.

Opening a Workbook

To open a workbook, use the Open method with the appropriate Workbook object. The following statement opens the file named CONTRIBUTION ANALYSIS.XLS in the U:\VPS\FINANCE\ folder:

```
Workbooks.Open "u:\vps\finance\Contribution Analysis.xls"
```

NOTE If the workbook you want to open is in the current folder, you do not need to specify the path. For example, the previous statement could be simply `Workbooks.Open "Contribution Analysis.xls"`. However, unless you can be sure that the current folder contains the workbook you want to open, it's wise to include the full path in the statement.

The only argument required when opening a workbook in Excel is the FileName string argument, which can be supplied implicitly, as in the previous example.

Important optional arguments for opening workbooks include the following:

- Use the UpdateLinks argument to specify how to update any links in the workbook. Use the value 0 to specify that no links be updated, 1 to specify that external references be updated but remote references not be updated, 2 to specify that remote references be updated but external references not be updated, or 3 to specify that both external references and remote references be updated. If you omit the UpdateLinks argument and the workbook being opened contains one or more links, the user will be prompted to choose how to update the links. The following statement opens the workbook C:\TEMP\MY_LINKS.XLS and updates all references in it:

  ```
  Workbooks.Open FileName:="c:\temp\My_Links.xls", UpdateLinks:=3
  ```

- To open a workbook in read-only mode, use the optional ReadOnly argument set to True:

  ```
  Workbooks.Open FileName:="c:\temp\My_Links.xls", _
  UpdateLinks:=3, ReadOnly:=True
  ```

- To add the workbook you're opening to the most recently used file list for Excel, use the AddToMRU argument set to True, as shown in the following statement. (The default value of the AddToMRU argument is False; so if you omit this argument, the workbooks you open from VBA will not be added to the most recently used file list.) The following statement opens the workbook C:\TEMP\MY_LINKS.XLS and adds it to the most recently used file list:

```
Workbooks.Open FileName:="c:\temp\MyWork.xls", AddToMRU:=True
```

NOTE
When you open a workbook using VBA, Excel does not run any Auto_Open macro associated with the workbook—so you don't need to worry about automatic macros when opening a workbook programmatically.

Opening a Recently Used File

As well as opening any file by name, you can open a recently used file. Excel stores the list of recently used files as RecentFile objects in the RecentFiles collection, which can contain 0 to 9 files, depending on the Recently Used File List setting chosen on the General tab of the Options dialog box.

To open one of the recently used files, access its RecentFile object by its index number in the RecentFiles collection. For example, to access the most recently used file, use the following statement:

```
Application.RecentFiles(1).Open
```

To open all the recently used files, you could use the following statements:

```
With Application
    For i = 1 to .RecentFiles.Count
            .RecentFiles(i).Open
    Next i
End With
```

Closing a Workbook

To close a workbook, use the Close method with the appropriate Workbook object. The following statement closes the active workbook:

```
ActiveWorkbook.Close
```

You can use the Close method without any arguments, but usually in automated procedures you'll want to allow for the workbook containing unsaved changes. To do so, use the optional SaveChanges argument to specify whether to save changes to the workbook: A value of True saves the changes to the workbook; a value of False closes the workbook without saving changes. If you omit the SaveChanges argument and the workbook contains unsaved changes, Excel prompts the user with a message box asking whether to save changes. The following statement closes the workbook named COMPETITIVE REPORT.XLS and saves any unsaved changes:

```
Workbooks("Competitive Report.xls").Close SaveChanges:=True
```

You can also use a FileName argument to specify the file name under which the workbook should be saved as it is closed. The following statement closes the workbook named COMPETITIVE REPORT.XLS and saves any unsaved changes under the name UPDATED COMPETITIVE REPORT.XLS:

```
Workbooks("Competitive Report.xls").Close SaveChanges:=True, _
FileName:="Updated Competitive Report.xls"
```

Note that if a file with the name specified by the FileName argument already exists, Excel will prompt the user whether to replace it. If the user selects the No button or the Cancel button in the dialog box, the Close method will fail, causing an error.

> **NOTE** When you close a workbook using VBA, Excel does not run any Auto_Close macro associated with the workbook.

Creating a Workbook

To create a new workbook, use the Add method with the Workbooks collection.

- To create a new workbook based on a template, specify the template by using the Template argument. The following statement creates a new workbook based on the INVOICE.XLT template in the C:\PROGRAM FILES\ MICROSOFT OFFICE\TEMPLATES\SPREADSHEET SOLUTIONS\ folder.

  ```
  Workbooks.Add Template:="c:\Program Files\Microsoft
  Office\Templates\Spreadsheet Solutions\invoice.xlt"
  ```

- To create a new workbook based on the default template, omit the Template argument:

  ```
  Workbooks.Add
  ```

- To create a new template, start a new workbook using one of the above techniques, and then save it as a template, as discussed in the next section.

Saving a Workbook

To save an existing workbook under its current name and path, use the Save method, which takes no arguments. (If the workbook has never been saved, Excel will save it under its default name, such as BOOK2.XLS.) The following statement saves the active workbook:

```
ActiveWorkbook.Save
```

To save a new workbook for the first time or to save a workbook under a different name, use the SaveAs method with the appropriate Workbook object. Use the FileName argument to specify the file name under which to save the file. Include the path in FileName unless you want to save the workbook in the current folder. If you do not specify FileName, Excel will save the workbook under the current name (for example, BOOK1.XLS for a new, unsaved workbook).

The following statement saves the active workbook as C:\TEMP\OUTPUT.XLS:

```
ActiveWorkbook.SaveAs "c:\temp\Output.xls"
```

Important optional arguments for saving a workbook include the following:

- Use the FileFormat argument to specify the file format in which to save the file. The following list shows the most commonly used file formats:

xlAddIn	Excel add-in
xlCSV	Comma-separated value
xlExcel4	Excel 4 format
xlExcel5	Excel 5 format
xlWorkbookNormal	Excel 97 format
xlTemplate	Excel template

- Use the CreateBackup argument with a value of True to create a backup file of the workbook. Note that the backup of a workbook is created only the second and subsequent times the workbook is saved, not the first time.

- To add the workbook you're saving to the most recently used file list for Excel, use the AddToMRU argument set to True. (The default value of the AddToMRU argument is False; so if you omit this argument, the workbooks you save from VBA will not be added to the most recently used file list.)

The following statement saves the workbook named TORQUE FRAGILITY.XLS under the name TORQUE FRAGILITY TESTS.XLS in Excel 5 format in the current folder:

```
Workbooks("Torque Fragility.xls").SaveAs _
FileName:="Torque Fragility Tests.xls", FileFormat:=xlExcel5
```

Printing a Workbook

To print a workbook, use the PrintOut method. The following statement prints the current print area of the active workbook:

```
ActiveWorkbook.PrintOut
```

> **NOTE** You can also use the PrintOut method with other objects, such as a worksheet or a window.

Important optional arguments for the PrintOut method include the following:

- Use the From variant argument to specify the number of the page at which to start printing.

- Use the To variant argument to specify the number of the page at which to stop printing.

- Use the Preview variant argument set to True to display Print Preview of the workbook before printing.

- Use the Copies variant to specify the number of copies of the item to print. If you omit the Copies argument, VBA prints one copy.

The following statement prints three copies of pages 2 through 4 of the active workbook:

```
ActiveWorkbook.PrintOut From:=2, To:=4, Copies:=3
```

Code 20.1: **Creating, Saving, and Closing a Workbook**

```
Dim vbExcel As Object
Set vbExcel = CreateObject("Excel.Application")

With vbExcel
    .Workbooks.Add
    With .ActiveWorkbook
        .SaveAs "z:\common\Manufacturing Capacity.xls"
        'Manipulate the contents of the workbook
        .Close SaveChanges:=True
    End With
    .Quit
End With
```

Working with Worksheets

The Sheets collection represents the worksheets within a workbook. You can use the Sheets collection to access worksheets, activate worksheets, add worksheets, delete worksheets, or rename worksheets. You can use the ActiveSheet object to work with the active worksheet, and you can use the SelectedSheets collection in the active window to work with all selected sheets.

To work with worksheets within a workbook, you use the Sheets collection. You can return the Sheets collection by using the Worksheets property:

- Use the Worksheets property with the Application object, with the ActiveWorkbook object, or without an object to return the Sheets collection for the active workbook. All three of the following statements return the Sheets collection for the active workbook:

```
Set mySheets = Application.Worksheets
Set mySheets = ActiveWorkbook.Worksheets
Set mySheets = Worksheets
```

- Use the Worksheets property with the Workbook object to return the Sheets collection for that workbook. For example, to print a list of the worksheets in the open workbook named EXPANSION PLANS.XLS to the Immediate window, you could use the following statements:

```
For Each wks In Workbooks("Expansion Plans.xls").Worksheets
    Debug.Print wks.Name
Next
```

To select a worksheet, use the Select method. The following statement selects the worksheet named Frame Relay Charges in the active workbook:

```
ActiveWorkbook.Sheets("Frame Relay Charges").Select
```

To add a worksheet to a workbook, use the Add method with the Sheets collection. The following statement adds a worksheet to the workbook named GIGABIT.XLS:

```
Workbooks("Gigabit.xls").Sheets.Add
```

To delete a worksheet from a workbook, use the Delete method. The following statement activates the workbook named 1999 SALARY PROJECTIONS.XLS and deletes the worksheet named Vice-Presidents from it:

```
Workbooks("1999 Salary Projections.xls").Activate
Sheets("Vice-Presidents").Delete
```

You cannot delete all the worksheets in a workbook, because each workbook needs to contain at least one visible sheet at all times. The following statements check to make sure that not all worksheets in the active workbook are selected before deleting the selected sheets. If all the worksheets in the workbook are selected, a message box warns the user of the problem:

```
With ActiveWindow
    If .SelectedSheets.Count < ActiveWorkbook.Sheets.Count Then
        .SelectedSheets.Delete
    Else
        MsgBox "You cannot delete all the sheets in the workbook.", _
        vbOKOnly + vbCritical, "Deletion Failed"
    End If
End With
```

To rename a worksheet, change its Name property. The following statement changes the name of the active sheet in the active workbook to Spot Prices:

```
ActiveSheet.Name = "Spot Prices"
```

To move a worksheet within a workbook, use the Move method. The Move method takes either a Before argument or an After argument, specifying the worksheet before which or after which to place the worksheet being moved. The following statement moves the worksheet named Results in the workbook named REMOTE OFFICES.XLS to the position after the worksheet named Projections:

```
Workbooks("Remote Offices.xls").Sheets("Results").Move
After:=Sheets("Projections")
```

NOTE Without a Before argument or an After argument, Excel will create a new default workbook and move the specified sheet to it.

To move a worksheet from one workbook to another, specify the destination workbook in the Before or After argument, as appropriate. The following statement moves the worksheet named Results in the workbook named REMOTE OFFICES.XLS to the position before the worksheet named Vice-Presidents in the workbook named 1999 SALARY PROJECTIONS. Note that the destination workbook will be the active workbook after the worksheet is moved.

```
Workbooks("Remote Offices.xls").Sheets("Results").Move _
    Before:=Workbooks("1999 Salary Projections.xls").Sheets("Vice-Presidents")
```

To copy a worksheet from one workbook to another, use the Copy method with either a Before argument or an After argument, as appropriate.

The following statements provide an example of how you might copy a worksheet from a workbook located on a local drive to a workbook located on a network drive using Visual Basic.

Code 20.2:   Copying a Workbook from One Drive to Another

```
Set vbExcel = CreateObject("Excel.Application")
With vbExcel
    'Open source workbook and destination workbook
    .Workbooks.Open "d:\Finance\Office Current.xls"
    .Workbooks.Open "\\Mercury\Mercury_D\Finance\Company Current.xls"
    'Copy worksheet from one to the other
    .Workbooks("Office Current.xls").Sheets("October Sales").Copy _
        Before:=.Workbooks("Company Current.xls").Sheets(1)
    'Save destination workbook
    .Workbooks("Company Current.xls").Save
    'Close both workbooks
    .Workbooks("Company Current.xls").Close
    .Workbooks("Office Current.xls").Close
    'Close Excel application object
    .Quit
End With
'Release object variable to free memory
Set vbExcel = Nothing
```

Working with Ranges

The Range object can represent any range of cells, from a single cell to a 3-D range of cells. The Range object does not have an associated Ranges collection object—you might say it acts as its own collection when it represents more than one cell.

Specifying a Range

To work with a range, you first specify it. You can specify a range in several ways:

- To specify a simple range (consisting of one contiguous block of cells), use an A1-style reference. The first of the following statements sets the Formula property of cell Z28 on the second worksheet in the active workbook to =SUM(C28:Y28). The second statement sets the Value property of the cells in the range A1:L1 to 1999:

```
ActiveWorkbook.Sheets(2).Range("Z28").Formula = "=SUM(C28:Y28)"
ActiveWorkbook.Sheets(2).Range("A1:L1").Value = 1999
```

- Alternatively, use the Range property with Cell1 and Cell2 arguments to specify the extent of a range. The following statements create a range named newRange that refers to cells A2:E2 on the third worksheet and then apply bold font formatting to the range:

```
Set newRange = Worksheets(3).Range(Worksheets(3).Cells(2, 1), _
Worksheets(3).Cells(2, 5))
newRange.Font.Bold = True
```

- You can also create a range by specifying its row index and column index. The following statement sets the font of cell E4 (the fourth row, the fifth column) on the specified worksheet to Times New Roman:

```
Workbooks("Sales Forecast.xls").Sheets("Western Region") _
.Cells(4, 5).Font.Name = "Times New Roman"
```

Looping on Row Numbers of Column Numbers

Specifying the row index and column index of a cell is less intuitive than using an A1-style reference, but it enables you to create For... Next loops on row numbers or column numbers. The following statements check the values of the cells in the range named Totals and apply red font color to any cell whose value is 1000 or greater:

```
With Range("Totals")
    For i = 1 to .Columns.Count
        If .Cells(1, i).Value >= 1000 Then _
        .Cells(1, i).Font.ColorIndex = 3
    Next i
End With
```

- To specify a range by its position offset from another range, use the Offset property with Row and Column arguments. The following statements select the range named Conclusions in the active sheet; create a range named Cost offset from the selection by three rows (down) and no columns, and spanning the columns A through F of the row in questions; and enter **Cost** in each cell in the range:

```
Conclusions.Select
Set Cost = Selection.Offset(3, 0).Range("A1:F1")
Cost.Value = "Cost"
```

- To specify a multiple-range area consisting of two or more contiguous blocks of cells, use the Union method with as many Range*n* arguments as necessary. The following statements create a range named EmphasisRange that consists of the ranges Headings, Totals, and Conclusions and apply font formatting to it if it is not already applied:

```
Dim EmphasisRange, Headings, Totals, Conclusions As Range
Set Headings = Range("A1:F1")
Set Totals = Range("A7:f7")
Set Conclusions = Range("A11:F11")
Set EmphasisRange = Union(Headings, Totals, Conclusions)
With EmphasisRange.Font
    If .Name <> "Gill Sans Ultra Bold" Then _
    .Name = "Gill Sans Ultra Bold"
    If .Size <> 24 Then .Size = 24
End With
```

TIP   Use the Areas property to find out how many areas are in a given selection before trying to take an action that works only with simple selections.

Identifying the Current Range

If you allow users to specify a range in your code, you may need to identify the range they select in order to work with it effectively. Two useful tools for doing so are the CurrentRegion property and the UsedRange property.

Using the CurrentRegion Property

The CurrentRegion property returns the current region of the specified sheet. The current region is the range of contiguous cells around the insertion point, bordered by either empty rows or columns, or the boundaries of the spreadsheet. For example, if a worksheet contains entries in every cell in the range C3:Z28, an entry in cell A1, and an entry in cell Z80, the current region will be C3:Z28 if the active cell is within the C3:Z28 block. If the active cell is cell A1, the current region will be cell A1. If the active cell is cell Z80, the current region will be Z80.

The following statements check that the current region is large enough for a procedure to have enough data to operate. If the current region does not contain at least 10 columns and 5 rows, a message is displayed asking the user to place the active cell in a suitable range.

```
With ActiveCell.CurrentRegion
    If .Rows.Count < 5 Or .Columns.Count < 10 Then
        MsgBox "Please place the active cell in a range of data at
least 10 columns wide by 5 rows deep.", vbOKOnly, "Select Range for
Procedure"
        End
    End If
End With
```

Using the UsedRange Property

The UsedRange property defines the range of cells used on the specified worksheet. The used range is understood to be the range marked by the first (upper-left) and last (lower-right) cells used in the worksheet. For example, if a worksheet contains entries in every cell in the range C3:Z28, an entry in cell A1, and an entry in cell Z80, the used range will be A1:Z80. The following statement returns the used range for the active worksheet:

```
MsgBox ActiveSheet.UsedRange
```

Manipulating a Range

Once you've specified a range, you can manipulate its properties and methods and those of the objects contained within it:

- To select a range, use the Select method. The following statement selects the range named EmphasisRange:

  ```
  EmphasisRange.Select
  ```

- To access a cell within the range, specify it by reference within the range: The top-left cell in a range is Cells(1, 1) for the range, the cell to its right is Cells(1, 2), and so on. The following statement selects the second cell in the second row of the range qRange:

```
qRange.Cells(2,2).Select
```

- To apply formatting to the range, manipulate the properties of the appropriate object for the range: Use the Style object to return or change the style of the range, use the Font object to return or change the font of the range, and so on. The following statements create a range named TR referring to cell K11 (of the active sheet) and truncate the contents of the cell to five characters if the contents are more than five characters long:

```
Set TR = Cells(11, 11)
If TR.Characters.Count > 5 Then
    TR.Value = TR.Characters(1, 5).Text
End If
```

- To copy the contents of a range to the clipboard, use the Copy method. To copy the contents of a range to another range, set the value of the second range to the value of the first. The following statements copy the content of the range named TempRange into the range named PermRange:

```
Range("PermRange").Value = Range("TempRange").Value
```

- To clear the contents of a range, use the ClearContents method. The following statement clears the contents of the range named TempRange:

```
Range("TempRange").ClearContents
```

Working with Name Objects

You can use the Names collection and the Name objects it contains to work with named objects in a workbook. Because named objects let you easily access predefined areas of a workbook without specifying the location by worksheet or by cell, they are useful for automated procedures.

To return the Names collection for a workbook, use the Names property of the workbook. The following statement returns the Names property of the first named object in the workbook:

```
n1 = Names(1).Name
```

To return the range a named object refers to, use the RefersTo property. The following statements display a message box containing a list of the named objects in the active workbook together with their ranges. If the active workbook contains no named objects, the message box displays a message to that effect.

```
Dim Msg, msgTitle As String
msgTitle = "Named Objects in " & ActiveWorkbook.Name
If Names.Count = 0 Then
    Msg = "The workbook contains no named objects."
Else
    Msg = "The workbook contains the following named objects:" & vbCr &
vbCr
End If
For j = 1 To Names.Count
    Msg = Msg & Names(j).Name & ": " & Names(j).RefersTo & vbCr
Next j
MsgBox Msg, vbOKOnly + vbInformation, msgTitle
```

To add a named object to the Names collection, use the Add method with a Name argument specifying the name and a RefersTo argument specifying the address. Specify the RefersTo argument using A1-style notation, including dollar signs when the reference should be absolute rather than relative to the active cell. The following statement creates a named object called InterestRates that refers to the range Q33:Q36 on the sheet named 1999 in the active workbook:

```
Names.Add Name:="InterestRates", RefersTo:="1999!$Q$33:$Q$36"
```

To delete a named object, use the Delete method with the appropriate item in the Names collection. The following statement deletes the named object InterestRates in the active workbook:

```
Names("InterestRates").Delete
```

Working with Windows

VBA provides two Windows collections: one containing Window objects that represent the windows available in the Application object, and another containing Window objects in a Workbook object. Usually, you'll want to work with the Windows collection for the Application object, though at times it's useful to work with the Windows collection for a Workbook object. Each Window object contains a Panes collection of Pane objects that represent the panes for the window.

These are the actions you're most likely to need to perform with Window objects and the Windows collection:

- Use the window name or index number with the Windows collection to return a Window object. Windows(1) is always the active window. The following statement displays a message box containing the name of each Window object in turn:

```
For i = 1 To Windows.Count
    MsgBox Windows(i).Caption
Next i
```

- Use the WindowState property to return or adjust the window state of the active window. Use the arguments xlMaximized to maximize the window, xlMinimized to minimize the window, or xlNormal to "restore" the window. The following statements maximize the active window if it is not already maximized:

```
With ActiveWindow
    If .WindowState <> xlMaximized Then .WindowState = xlMaximized
End With
```

- Use the Zoom property to adjust the zoom level in the window. The following statement sets the zoom percentage to 90%.

```
ActiveWindow.Zoom = 90
```

- Use the DisplayVerticalScrollBar property and the DisplayHorizontalScrollBar property to return or set the display of the scrollbars in the window. The following statements make sure both scrollbars are displayed:

```
With ActiveWindow
    If .DisplayHorizontalScrollBar = False Then _
    .DisplayHorizontalScrollBar = True
    If .DisplayVerticalScrollBar = False Then _
    .DisplayVerticalScrollBar = True
End With
```

- Use the Arrange method with the ArrangeStyle argument to arrange the open document windows in the application window. Use xlArrangeStyleTiled (or omit the argument) to tile the windows. Use xlArrangeStyleCascade to cascade the windows (overlapping, with the title bar of each visible). Use xlArrangeStyleHorizontal to arrange the windows horizontally. Use xlArrangeStyleVertical to arrange the windows vertically. The following statement cascades the windows:

```
Windows.Arrange ArrangeStyle:=xlArrangeStyleCascade
```

- Use the Count property of the Windows collection for a Workbook object to make sure the appropriate number of windows (usually only one) are displayed for a workbook you want to work with.

- Use the Split property to split or unsplit a window, and use the FreezePanes property to freeze or unfreeze the panes of a window. Both Split and FreezePanes are Boolean properties. The following statements work with the active window to unfreeze the panes if they are frozen and unsplit the window if it is split:

```
With ActiveWindow
    If .FreezePanes = True Then .FreezePanes = False
    If .Split = True Then .Split = False
End With
```

Working with the Active Cell

The ActiveCell property returns the ActiveCell object, which represents the active cell. The ActiveCell object has the same properties and methods as a Range object.

If you do not specify a Window object, Excel returns the active cell in the active window. The following statements both return the active cell in the active window:

```
ActiveCell
ActiveWindow.ActiveCell
```

You can specify a Window object to return the active cell from that window. The following statement displays a message box containing the contents of the active cell in the window 2000 SALARY PROJECTION.XLS:

```
MsgBox Windows("2000 Salary Projections.xls").ActiveCell
```

NOTE   If no worksheet is displayed, the ActiveCell property fails. If a range of cells is selected, the ActiveCell property returns the active cell within the range—not the whole range.

To manipulate the active cell, work with its properties and methods and those of the objects it contains. For example, to return the address of the active cell, use its Address property:

```
ActiveCell.Address
```

The following statements enter in the active cell the text from a text box named txtMyText in a Visual Basic Form:

```
Dim vbExcel As Object
Set vbExcel = CreateObject("Excel.Application")
vbExcel.Workbooks.Add
vbExcel.ActiveCell.Value = txtMyText.Text
```

You can set the active cell by using the Activate method on a cell. For example, to make cell Z80 on the worksheet named Captains of Industry the active cell, enter the value "Moderator" into it, and apply the style named Emphasis, you could use the following statements:

```
With Worksheets("Captains of Industry")
    .Activate
    .Range("Z80").Activate
    With ActiveCell
        .Value = "Moderator"
        .Style = "Emphasis"
    End With
End With
```

To move the active cell, you can use the Activate method with the Offset property of the ActiveCell object. The Offset property uses two optional variant arguments, RowOffset and ColumnOffset, for specifying the number of rows and columns by which to move the active cell. The following statement moves the active cell down one row:

```
ActiveCell.Offset(1,0).Activate
```

Working with Find and Replace

You can use the Find and Replace methods in your macros and procedures to find or replace specific information in a given range.

Using the Find Method

The Find method in VBA corresponds to the Edit „ Find command in the Excel user interface. The Find method has the following syntax:

```
Expression.Find(What, After, LookIn, LookAt, SearchOrder,
SearchDirection, MatchCase)
```

The Expression argument and the What argument are required:

- *Expression* is an expression that specifies the Range object for the Find operation. The Find operation starts in the upper-left cell in the range unless you specify a different starting location by using the After argument. Find wraps to the beginning of the range after reaching the end, so if you use an After argument, you will sometimes need to stop Find from wrapping by comparing the location of the currently found cell with the location of the first found cell. If Find does not find a match for the specified information, it returns Nothing.

- *What* is a variant argument specifying the data you want to search for.

The following statements use a Set statement to perform a Find operation for the string "Paris". If the string is found, VBA displays a message box showing the address. If it is not found, VBA displays a message box informing the user.

```
Set Found = Cells.Find(What:="Paris")
If Found Is Nothing Then
    MsgBox "The item was not found.", vbOKOnly, "Find Unsuccessful"
Else
    Found.Cells.Font.Bold = True
    MsgBox Found.Cells.Address, vbOKOnly + vbInformation, "Location"
End If
```

Find operations such as this do not move the selection or the active cell. Use the Activate statement to perform a Find operation and move the active cell to the information found, as happens in searches performed through the user interface. The following statement searches for the string "Paris" on the active worksheet and moves the active cell to the first instance of it (if there is one):

```
Cells.Find(What:="Paris").Activate
```

These are the most useful optional arguments for the Find method:

- Use the After variant argument to specify the cell after which to begin the search. This argument must be a single cell rather than multiple cells and must be in the range being searched. The following statement specifies that the search begin after the active cell:

```
Set Found = Cells.Find(What:="Paris", After:=ActiveCell)
```

- Use the LookIn variant argument to specify whether to look in formulas (xlFormulas), values (xlValues), or notes (xlNotes). This corresponds to the Look In drop-down list in the Find dialog box in the Excel user interface.

- Use the LookAt variant argument to specify whether to search for a whole cell (xlWhole) or a part of a cell (xlPart) containing the specified item. This corresponds to the Find Entire Cells Only checkbox in the Find dialog box.

- Use the SearchOrder variant argument to specify whether to search by rows (xlByRows) or by columns (xlByColumns). This corresponds to the Search drop-down list in the Find dialog box.

- Use the SearchDirection variant argument to specify whether to search down (xlNext) or up (xlPrevious). The default setting is xlNext.

- Use the MatchCase variant argument set to True to perform a case-sensitive search. The default setting is False.

NOTE Like the settings in the Find dialog box, which they affect and which affect them, the settings for LookIn, LookAt, SearchOrder, and MatchCase are sticky. So if you set SearchDirection to xlPrevious in one procedure, it will remain set to xlPrevious until you change it. It's a good idea to set each argument explicitly when you use the Find method, to make sure you get the effect you intended.

Finding the Next or Previous Instance

To find the next instance of the item you last searched for, use the FindNext method. Use an After argument if you need to specify the cell after which to start the search. The following statement searches for the next instance of the last item searched for:

```
Set nFound = Cells.FindNext(After:=ActiveCell)
```

To find the previous instance of the item you last searched for, use the FindPrevious method. Use an After argument if you need to specify the cell *before* which to start the search.

Using the Replace Method

The Replace method corresponds to the Edit ➤ Replace command in the Excel user interface. Replace works in a similar way to the Find method and has the following syntax:

```
Expression.Replace(What, Replacement, LookAt, SearchOrder, MatchCase)
```

Here, Expression, What, LookAt, SearchOrder, and MatchCase work in the same way as their counterpart arguments for the Find method; Expression and What are required, and LookAt, SearchOrder, and MatchCase are optional. Replacement is a required string expression specifying the replacement string for the Replace operation; Replacement corresponds to the Replace With text box in the Replace dialog box. As with the Find method, the arguments for Replace operations stick and affect (and are affected by) the settings in the Replace dialog box, so it's best to specify them in each Replace operation.

The Replace method returns True if the specified item is found one or more times in the specified range.

The following statement replaces all instances of the word *prognosis* in the sheet named March in the workbook SALES RESULTS.XLS with the word *forecast*:

```
Workbooks("Sales Results.xls").Sheets("March").Cells.Replace _
    What:="prognosis", Replacement:="forecast", LookAt:=xlWhole
```

Looping through an Excel Collection

By looping through a collection, you can check or take action on each item in the collection without having to establish how many items there are. Earlier in the chapter, we looked at how to open all the recently used files by looping through the RecentFiles collection using a For... Next loop. You can also loop through a collection by using a For Each... Next loop.

The For Each... Next loop performs one iteration of the loop for each object in the collection. The following statements use a For Each... Next loop to close any workbook that has never been saved to disk. The statements check the Path property of each of the workbooks in the Workbooks collection. If the Path property of a workbook is an empty string—that is, if it has never been saved to disk—the workbook is closed without saving changes.

```
For Each wBook In Workbooks
    If wBook.Path = "" Then wBook.Close SaveChanges:=False
Next
```

Using Excel's Built-In Dialog Boxes

In this section, we'll discuss how to use Excel's built-in dialog boxes in procedures you create. You can use Excel's built-in dialog boxes to get past the limitations of the standard selection of controls that the Visual Basic Editor provides for Forms. Moreover, you can save time and trouble by using a built-in dialog box, and you can be confident that users of your applications or procedures will recognize the dialog box and know how to use it, particularly if it is a common dialog box (for example, an Open dialog box, a Save dialog box, or a Print dialog box).

Displaying a Built-In Dialog Box

Built-in dialog boxes in Excel are identified by constants starting with *xlDialog*, followed by the name of the dialog box. For instance, the constant for the Open dialog box is xlDialogOpen; the constant for the Print dialog box is xlDialogPrint; and the constant for the Save As dialog box is xlDialogSaveAs. The naming conventions are not entirely consistent. For example, the constant for the Delete dialog box is xlDialogFileDelete rather than xlDialogDelete, because there is also an xlDialogEditDelete dialog box that identifies itself only as Delete.

To identify a dialog box, use its constant with the Dialogs property of the Application object, which returns the Dialogs collection. The following statement refers to the Delete dialog box:

```
Application.Dialogs(xlDialogFileDelete)
```

To display a dialog box, use the Show method. The Show method displays the specified Dialog object and executes the actions the user takes in the dialog box. For example, if you use the Show method to display the xlDialogOpen dialog box and the user chooses a file to open and clicks the Open button, VBA will open the file.

In VBA, Excel treats its multipage dialog boxes as individual dialog boxes, except for the Page Setup dialog box, which has its regular four tabs. For example, you cannot display the same Format Cells dialog box through VBA that you can display when working live in Excel, but you can display the six pages (tabs) of the Format Cells dialog box—Number, Alignment, Font, Border, Patterns, and Protection—individually by using the constants xlDialogFormatNumber, xlDialogAlignment, xlDialogActiveCellFont, xlDialogBorder, xlDialogPatterns, and xlDialogCellProtection. Similarly, the Excel Options dialog box is divided into its eight component pages.

If you look through the list of built-in dialog boxes for Excel, you'll notice a number of other peculiarities, including multiple copies of a number of dialog boxes. For example, there are four Paste Special dialog boxes, each of which has arguments suitable for a different situation.

WARNING   Don't try to display the xlDialogMacroOptions dialog box. It generates enough of an error to crash Excel.

Setting Options in a Built-In Dialog Box

Most of the built-in Excel dialog boxes have a number of arguments that you can use for retrieving or setting values in the dialog box. To set an option in a built-in dialog box, you use the appropriate argument. For example, the xlDialogSaveAs dialog box has the arguments shown in Table 20.1.

TABLE 20.1: The Arguments for the xlDialogSaveAs Dialog Box

Argument	Type	Explanation
document_text	Text	The name in the File Name text box
type_num	Numeric	The entry in the Save As Type drop-down list
prot_pwd	Text	The password for opening the file
backup	True/False	Whether the Always Create Backup checkbox in the Save Options dialog box is selected
write_res_pwd	Text	The password for modifying the file
read_only_rec	True/False	Whether the Read-Only Recommended checkbox in the Save Options dialog box is selected

TIP The names of arguments tend to be cryptic and are almost impossible to guess from the names of the corresponding options in the dialog boxes. To access a list of Excel dialog boxes and the names of the arguments they take, look up the topic "Built-In Dialog Box Argument Lists" in the Index of the VBA Help file for Excel.

You can specify the arguments either explicitly or implicitly. The following statement uses explicit arguments to display the Save As dialog box with the suggested file name of MY TEST FILE.XLS, a file-opening password of **mytest**, a file-modifying password of **testme**, and the backup option selected:

```
Application.Dialogs(xlDialogSaveAs).Show arg1:="My Test File.xls",
arg3:="mytest", arg4:=True, arg5:="testme"
```

The following statement uses the arguments implicitly. Note the extra comma to indicate that the second argument is skipped:

```
Application.Dialogs(xlDialogSaveAs).Show "My Test File.xls",, "mytest",
True, "testme"
```

Returning the Button the User Chose in a Dialog Box

To find out which button the user clicked in a dialog box, check the return value of the Show method. The OK button or equivalent (the Open button, the Save button, and so on, depending on the dialog box) returns True, whereas the Cancel button or equivalent (the Close button, say) returns False.

For example, you could display the Open dialog box so that the user could open a workbook. By checking the return value of the Open dialog box, you could display a warning (or terminate the procedure) if the user clicked the Cancel button instead of opening a workbook. The following statements prompt the user to terminate the procedure:

```
TryAgain:
Clicked = Application.Dialogs(xlDialogOpen).Show
If Clicked = False Then
    If MsgBox("Do you want to terminate this procedure?", _
    vbYesNo + vbExclamation, "Terminate Procedure?") = vbYes Then
        End
    Else
        GoTo TryAgain
    End If
End If
```

The following procedure, run from Visual Basic, accesses a Word document, brings information from it into Excel, and prompts the user to save the resulting workbook under a different name.

NOTE To display a built-in Excel dialog box from Visual Basic, add to the Visual Basic project a reference to the Microsoft Excel 8.0 Object Library.

Code 20.3:   Working with Excel from Visual Basic

```
'Declare object variables for Excel and Word
Dim vbExcel, vbWord As Object

'Return Excel and Word application objects
Set vbExcel = CreateObject("Excel.Application")
Set vbWord = CreateObject("Word.Application")

'Open Word document, select bookmark, copy it
'Close Word document without saving changes; quit Word
With vbWord
    .Documents.Open "d:\temp\newinfo.doc"
    .Documents("newinfo.doc").Bookmarks("info").Select
    .Selection.Copy
    .Documents("newinfo.doc").Close SaveChanges:=wdDoNotSaveChanges
    .Quit
End With

'Release Word object variable
Set vbWord = Nothing

'Display Excel, open workbook, add and name sheet
'Display Save As dialog box for user to save workbook under a new name
'Close workbook and quit Excel
With vbExcel
    .Visible = True
    .Workbooks.Open "u:\testing\fiscal\FY99 Master.xls", ReadOnly:=True
    .Sheets.Add Before:=Sheets(1)
    .Sheets(1).Name = "Antwerpen"
    With .Sheets("Antwerpen")
        .Cells(2, 2).Select
        .Paste
    End With
```

```
    .Dialogs(xlDialogSaveAs).Show arg1:="u:\testing\fiscal\FY99 Master
(adapted).xls"
    .ActiveWorkbook.Close SaveChanges:=False
    .Quit
End With

'Release Excel object variable
Set vbExcel = Nothing
```

CHAPTER TWENTY-ONE

Word 97 Objects

- The Word object model

- Working with documents

- Working with windows and panes

- Working with ranges and the Selection object

- Looping through a collection

- Using Word's built-in dialog boxes

In this chapter, we'll discuss the objects in Word 97, the Word object model that describes how they are arranged, and how to work with them to get things done in VBA.

To manipulate Word with VBA, you use the VBA objects that Word exposes. These objects range from the Application object that represents the Word application, to Document objects that represent individual documents, to collections such as Words and Paragraphs that represent components of documents. By controlling these objects and adjusting their properties, you can take actions in Word.

Like Excel, Word is highly complex and exposes many more VBA objects than we can deal with in this chapter. To get you started manipulating Word with VBA, we'll discuss the most important Word objects—the objects likely to be most useful to you when you are accessing Word from Visual Basic. As in the previous chapter, we'll highlight the most useful properties and methods for each object but will not list or discuss every single property and method for each object. We'll present the most useful arguments for each method discussed here, not a complete list of the arguments for the method.

We'll start by looking at the Word object model and examining the logical structure of the application as VBA sees it.

VBA Takes Over from WordBasic

VBA is new to Word 97, replacing the WordBasic language used in previous versions of Word up to Word 95. In many ways, VBA is the most important new feature in Word 97, because it provides far greater capabilities overall than any other new feature.

If you've used WordBasic in previous versions of Word, there's good news and bad news. The bad news is that VBA works very differently from WordBasic, and you'll have to adjust your thinking to VBA's object-dominated structure. The good news is in two parts: First, if you know Visual Basic, you'll find VBA straightforward; and second, VBA in Word includes full support for WordBasic through the WordBasic property.

In a pinch, you can leverage your knowledge of WordBasic through VBA to get things done. For a few disparate maneuvers, you will find that WordBasic offers functionality that VBA does not or that by using a WordBasic statement through the WordBasic property, you can achieve the same effect more concisely than you can with VBA. In most cases, though, VBA offers equivalent functionality to or greater functionality than WordBasic.

VBA Takes Over from WordBasic (continued)

If you have Word 6 or Word 95 templates containing macros that you need to use with Word 97, you can open the templates and have Word convert the macros to VBA procedures, with some statements using the WordBasic property. VBA's conversion is impressive and mostly successful, though some WordBasic structures are beyond its conversion capabilities; you'll have to fix such structures manually when the converted macros fail. You'll also find less-than-concise renderings that you can improve manually if you have the inclination.

The Word Object Model

In this section, we'll look at the Word object model, which describes the theoretical architecture underlying Word. By understanding the Word object model, you can manipulate the objects from which Word is built and work quickly and effectively with VBA.

Because the Word object model is extremely complex, we will look only at the most important objects in this chapter. But by understanding the structure of Word, and by using the techniques described in Chapter 19, you should be able easily to find the objects you need.

The Application object, at the top level of the Word object model, represents the Word application. Figure 21.1 shows the Application object and the objects it contains. The plural names with singular names in parentheses indicate collections and the individual objects they contain. For example, the Addins collection comprises all Addin objects in the Application object, and the Documents collection contains all the open Document objects in the Application object. The arrows to the right of the AutoCorrect, Documents, Selection, Templates, and Windows objects indicate that these objects and collections contain further objects.

FIGURE 21.1:

The Application object and the objects it contains. The unshaded boxes denote objects and collections; the shaded boxes denote objects only.

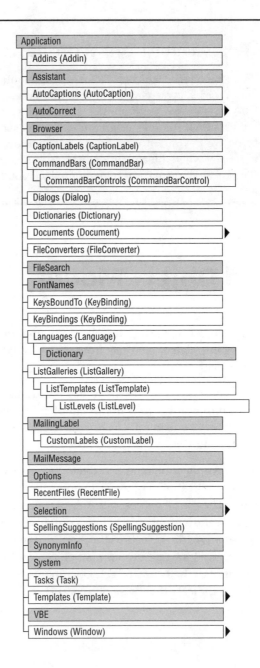

The three most-used objects in the Application object are the Documents collection, the Windows collection, and the Selection object. By using these, you can manipulate the documents that are open, the windows that are open, and the current selection in the active document. Figure 21.2 shows the collections and objects contained in the Documents collection and the Document object.

FIGURE 21.2:

The collections and objects contained in the Documents collection and the Document object

The Selection object enables you to work with the current selection. Figure 21.3 shows the collections and objects contained in the Selection object.

FIGURE 21.3:

The collections and objects contained in the Selection object

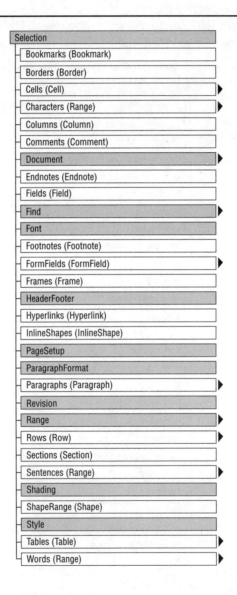

The Windows collection object gives you access to the Window objects for all the available windows in the application. Figure 21.4 shows the collections and objects contained in the Windows collection object.

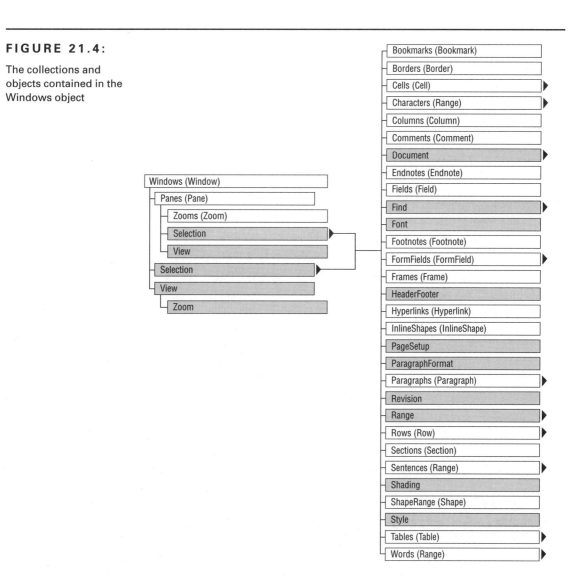

The collections and objects contained in the Windows object

Working with the Word Application

As we just mentioned, the Application object represents the Word application. You can use the Application object to control many aspects of Word's behavior, from the size of the application window to global preferences such as whether AutoCorrect features are switched on.

The Application object contains properties and methods that return top-level objects, including:

- An ActiveDocument property to return the active document
- A Documents property to return the Documents collection
- A CommandBars property to return the CommandBars collection

You can access the most-used interface objects without using the Application object qualifier. For example, both the following statements display the name of the active document; the second statement is more concise:

```
MsgBox Application.ActiveDocument.Name
MsgBox ActiveDocument.Name
```

To set application-wide preferences, set the appropriate property of the Application object. For example, to make Word visible or to hide it, set the Visible property to True or False:

```
Application.Visible = False
```

To run Word from another application, use the CreateObject function or the GetObject function, as discussed for Excel in Chapter 20:

```
Set vbWord = CreateObject("Word.Application")
With vbWord
    'Statements here
    .Quit
End With
Set vbWord = Nothing
```

Working with Documents

To work with documents in Word, you can use either the Documents collection or the ActiveDocument object. The Documents collection represents all open documents; the ActiveDocument object represents the currently active document.

Depending on the type of procedure you are creating, it's usually easy to decide whether to work with one or more Document objects in the Documents collection or to work with the ActiveDocument object. Use the Documents collection when you need to specify a document by name or when you need to work with a document that is not (or may not be) the active document. For example, in some procedures you might prefer to work with a document other than the active document so that the user cannot see what is happening. Use the ActiveDocument object when you do not know (or need to know) the name of the document you're working with (for example, in a simple macro that users run on a document of their choosing), to find out which document is active, or when you want to display a procedure on screen so that the user can see it.

TIP To prevent the user from seeing what is happening, you can also turn off screen updating by setting the ScreenUpdating property of the Application object to False, as discussed in Chapter 18.

Activating a Document

To activate a document, use the Activate method on its Document object. The Activate method makes the specified document the active document, and you can then work with it using the ActiveDocument object. The following statement makes the open document URUGUAY VISIT.DOC the active document:

```
Documents("Uruguay Visit.doc").Activate
```

NOTE Running the Activate method on a document that is already the active document does no harm.

Opening a Document

To open a document, use the Open method with the appropriate Document object. The following statement opens the document named VP MEMO.DOC in the folder F:\USERS\JSMITH\:

```
Documents.Open "f:\users\jsmith\VP Memo.doc"
```

TIP Before trying to open a document, be sure that it exists. Alternatively, trap the run-time error 5174 that results when a document does not exist, or trap the run-time error 5273 that results when the path does not exist.

The only argument required when opening a document is the FileName string argument, which can be supplied implicitly, as in the above example. Important optional arguments for opening documents include the following:

- Use the ConfirmConversions variant argument set to True if you want Word to display the Convert File dialog box if the file is in a format other than Word 97.

- Use the ReadOnly variant argument set to True to open the document as read-only.

- Use the AddToRecentFiles variant argument set to True if you want Word to add the file name to the list of recently used files at the foot of the File menu. (The default is not to add the file to the recently used files list.)

- The Revert argument is a variant that specifies what Word should do if the FileName argument matches a file already open. By default, Revert is set to False, so Word activates the open instance of the document (if it is not the active document) and does not open the saved instance. Set Revert to True if you want Word to open the saved instance of the document and discard any changes to the open instance.

- Use the Format variant argument with the appropriate wdOpenFormat constant (see the list below) to specify the file converter with which to open the document:

Constant	Effect
wdOpenFormatAuto	Word chooses a converter automatically. This is the default setting.
wdOpenFormatDocument	Word opens the document as a Word document.
wdOpenFormatRTF	Word opens the document as a Rich Text Format file.
wdOpenFormatTemplate	Word opens the document as a template.
wdOpenFormatText	Word opens the document as a text file.
wdOpenFormatUnicodeText	Word opens the document as a Unicode text file.

- Use the Format variant argument with the appropriate FileConverter object and the OpenFormat property to specify an external file format (one not included in the above list). The following statement opens the Write file TEST.WRI in the current folder:

```
Documents.Open FileName:="Test.wri", _
    Format:=FileConverters("MSWinWrite").OpenFormat
```

Finding FileConverter Objects

Here's how to find out the names of the FileConverter objects you need:

1. In Word, choose Help ≻ About Microsoft Word to display the About Microsoft Word dialog box; or, in the Visual Basic Editor, choose Help ≻ About Microsoft Visual Basic to display the About Microsoft Visual Basic dialog box.

2. Click the System Info button to run the Microsoft System Information application in its own window.

3. In the tree in the left panel, expand the Text Converters object (if it's collapsed) by clicking the boxed plus sign to its left.

4. Select the Registry Settings item under Text Converters. Microsoft System Information will display a list of installed text converters in the panel on the right. The Key column shows the name you need to specify. For example, the import filter for Word 6 is named MSWord6, and the import filter for WordPerfect 6.x is WordPerfect6x. Specify this name for the FileConverter object.

To close Microsoft System Information, click its close button or choose File ≻ Exit.

Closing a Document

To close a file, use the Close method with the appropriate Document object. The following statement closes the active document:

```
ActiveDocument.Close
```

Important optional arguments for the Close method include the following:

- SaveChanges is an optional variant you can use to specify how to handle unsaved changes. Use wdDoNotSaveChanges to discard changes, wdPromptToSaveChanges if you want Word to prompt the user to save changes, or wdSaveChanges to save changes without prompting.

- OriginalFormat is an optional variant you can use to specify the save format for the document. Use wdOriginalDocumentFormat if you want Word to use the original document format, wdPromptUser if you want Word to prompt the user to choose a format, or wdWordDocument to use the Word 97 document format.

The following statement closes the document ESTONIAN PEASANT REBELLIONS .DOC and saves any unsaved changes to it:

```
Documents("Estonian Peasant Rebellions.doc").Close _
SaveChanges:=wdSaveChanges
```

The following statement closes all open documents, prompting the user whether to save any document that contains unsaved changes:

```
Documents.Close SaveChanges:=wdPromptToSaveChanges
```

Creating a Document

To create a new document, use the Add method with the Documents collection. The following statement creates a new document based on the Normal template:

```
Documents.Add
```

To create a new document based on a template other than the Normal template, use the optional Template argument. Specify the path unless the template is in the default template folder or global template folder. (If you omit Template, Word uses the Normal template.) The following statement creates a new document based on the template INDUSTRIAL DESIGN.DOT stored in the folder U:\COMMON\PROGRAM FILES\MICROSOFT OFFICE\TEMPLATES\:

```
Documents.Add Template:="u:\common\Program Files\Microsoft Office\
Templates\Industrial Design.dot"
```

To create a template rather than a document, use the NewTemplate variant argument set to True. The following statement creates a new template based on the Normal template:

```
Documents.Add NewTemplate:=True
```

You can also create a new document by using the SaveAs method (discussed later in this chapter) on an existing document.

Saving a Document

To save a document or a template, use the Save method or the SaveAs method, depending on whether you're saving a previously saved file, saving a file for the first time, or saving a previously saved file under a new name.

Saving a Previously Saved File

To save a previously saved file, use the Save method. The following statement saves the active document:

```
ActiveDocument.Save
```

The following statement saves the open document named STRIFE IN GEORGIA .DOC:

```
Documents("Strife in Georgia.doc").Save
```

The following statement saves all open documents:

```
Documents.Save
```

If you use the Save method the first time you save a file, Word displays the Save As dialog box for the user to enter a name and choose a drive and folder for the document.

Saving a File for the First Time

To save a file for the first time, use the SaveAs method. Use the FileName optional variant argument to specify the name and path for the document. (FileName is optional in that if you omit the argument, VBA will use the current folder and the default file name of DOCN.DOC for a document and DOTN.DOT for a template, where n is the next higher unused consecutive number.) If a document with the name and location specified in FileName already exists, VBA will overwrite it without warning.

The following statement saves the active document under the name TEST DOCUMENT.DOC in the folder C:\TEMP\:

```
ActiveDocument.Save FileName:="c:\temp\Test Document.doc"
```

Use the FileFormat optional variant argument to specify the format in which to save the document. Word provides eight wdSaveFormat constants for quick reference, as shown in Table 21.1.

TABLE 21.1: The Word wdSaveFormat Constants

Constant	Saves Document As
wdFormatDocument	A Word 97 document
wdFormatDOSText	A DOS text file
wdFormatDOSTextLineBreaks	A DOS text file with layout
wdFormatRTF	A Rich Text Format file
wdFormatTemplate	A Word template
wdFormatText	A text file (plain ASCII)
wdFormatTextLineBreaks	A text file with line breaks
wdFormatUnicodeText	A text file with Unicode characters

The following statement saves the active document as a text file under the name INVESTIGATION.TXT in the current folder:

```
ActiveDocument.SaveAs FileName:="Investigation.txt",
FileFormat:=wdFormatText
```

Use FileFormat with the appropriate value for the SaveFormat property of the FileConverter object to save a document in a different format. The following statement saves the active document in Word 5.1 for the Macintosh format:

```
ActiveDocument.SaveAs
FileFormat:=FileConverters("MSWordMac51").SaveFormat
```

To add the document to the list of recently used files, use the AddToRecentFiles variant argument set to True:

```
Documents(11).Save FileName:="c:\temp\Test Document.doc",
AddToRecentFiles=True
```

Saving a Document under a Different Name

To save a previously saved document under a different name, use the SaveAs method and specify the FileName argument implicitly or explicitly. The following statement saves the open document named OCTOBER REPORT.DOC under the name NOVEMBER REPORT.DOC in the current folder:

```
Documents("October Report.doc").SaveAs "November Report.doc"
```

Printing a Document

To print a document, use the PrintOut method on the appropriate document object. The following statement prints the open document named GENERATING LEADS.DOC:

```
Documents("Generating Leads.doc").PrintOut
```

The PrintOut method has a number of optional arguments that correspond to options in the Print dialog box and the Print tab of the Options dialog box. Use the Range variant argument to specify the range to print:

- Use wdPrintAllDocument to print the whole document.

- Use wdPrintCurrentPage to print the current page.

- Use wdPrintFromTo with From and To arguments to print a simple range of pages (from one numbered page to another numbered page):

  ```
  Documents("Generating Leads.doc").PrintOut Range:=wdPrintFromTo,
  From:=11, To:=22
  ```

- Use wdPrintRangeOfPages with a Pages argument to print a simple range of pages or a complex range of pages:

  ```
  Documents("Generating Leads.doc").PrintOut
  Range:=wdPrintRangeOfPages, Pages:="1, 3, 5, 11-21"
  ```

- Use wdPrintSelection to print the current selection.

Checking Whether a Document Contains Unsaved Changes

To find out whether a document contains unsaved changes (if it is dirty) or not (if it is clean), check the Saved property of its Document object. This Boolean property reads True if the document contains no unsaved changes and False if the document contains unsaved changes. The following statement checks the active document for unsaved changes and saves it if it contains any:

```
If ActiveDocument.Saved = False Then ActiveDocument.Save
```

NOTE A newly created document is considered clean until you make changes to it, even if it contains a vast amount of text from the template on which it is based. So a document that has never been saved to disk can be clean or dirty, and you won't necessarily be able to tell from its contents (or lack of them). As soon as the user enters even a space in the document or deletes existing content, it becomes dirty.

Checking Whether a Document Exists

To check whether a document exists, use the Dir function with the file name. The following procedure prompts for a file name to test and displays a message box saying whether the file exists:

```
Sub UsingDir()
    Dim TestName As String, Msg As String
    TestName = InputBox("Enter the name and path of the document:", _
        "Demonstration of Dir Function")
    If Dir(TestName) <> "" Then
        Msg = TestName & " exists."
    Else
        Msg = TestName & " does not exist."
    End If
    MsgBox Msg, vbOKOnly + vbInformation, _
        "Demonstration of Dir Function"
End Sub
```

Deleting a Document

To delete a document (or other file) from VBA, use the Kill statement with the path and file name. The following statement deletes the document C:\TEMP\SCRATCH1.DOC:

```
Kill "c:\temp\Scratch1.doc"
```

WARNING Two quick caveats: First, *Kill deletes files irrevocably*—it does not send them to the Recycle Bin. Second, Kill will not work if the file in question is open—instead, you'll get a run-time error 75 in Windows 95 ("Path/File access error") and a run-time error 70 in NT ("Permission Denied"). If you need to kill an open file, close it first.

The following statements provide an example of how you can close and delete the active document. If the document has never been saved, there is no need to use the Kill statement—closing it gets rid of it:

```
Dim DocToKill As String, TestDoc
DocToKill = ActiveDocument.FullName
ActiveDocument.Close
TestDoc = Dir(DocToKill)
ActiveDocument.Close SaveChanges:=wdDoNotSaveChanges
If Len(TestDoc) <> 0 Then Kill DocToKill
```

To delete multiple files at the same time, use the wildcards * (for multiple characters) and ? (for single characters). The following statement deletes all the DOC files in the C:\WINDOWS\TEMP\ folder:

```
Kill "c:\windows\temp\*.doc"
```

Getting Document Information

Word keeps a full set of information on each document. Here's how to return the most useful information:

- Use the Path property to return a document's path:

  ```
  MsgBox ActiveDocument.Path
  ```

- Use the Name property to return the file name without the path:

  ```
  MsgBox ActiveDocument.Name
  ```

- Use the FullName property to return a document's full path and name:

  ```
  MsgBox ActiveDocument.FullName
  ```

- Use the Application.PathSeparator property to add to the path the backslash used to separate folders and drive letters:

  ```
  MsgBox ActiveDocument.Path + Application.PathSeparator
  ```

- Use the Count property of the Characters, Words, Sentences, or Paragraphs collection to get a count of the characters, words, sentences, or paragraphs in the document.

You can also retrieve built-in document properties by using the BuiltIn-DocumentProperties property for a document. Word provides the built-in document properties shown in Table 21.2.

TABLE 21.2: The Built-In Document Properties of Word

Property	Meaning
wdPropertyBytes	The number of bytes the file occupies.
wdPropertyCharacters	The number of characters in the document, not including spaces, paragraph marks, and other "noncharacter" characters.
wdPropertyComments	The contents of the Comments field in the Properties dialog box.
wdPropertyKeywords	The contents of the Keywords field in the Properties dialog box.
wdPropertyLastAuthor	The name of the last user to work on the document.
wdPropertyLines	The number of lines in the document.
wdPropertyPages	The number of pages in the document.
wdPropertyParas	The number of paragraphs with contents in the document; does not include blank paragraphs.
wdPropertyRevision	The number of times the document has been saved.
wdPropertySubject	The subject of the document (as set in the Properties dialog box).
wdPropertyTemplate	The template to which the document is attached.
wdPropertyTimeCreated	The date and time at which the document was first created.
wdPropertyTimeLastPrinted	The date and time at which the document was last printed. This property returns an error if the document has never been printed.
wdPropertyTimeLastSaved	The date and time at which the document was last saved. Returns an error if the document has never been saved.
wdPropertyTitle	The Title of the document (as set in the Properties dialog box).
wdPropertyVBATotalEdit	The time spent editing the document.
wdPropertyWords	The number of words in the document

To use one of these built-in document properties, specify it like this:

```
ActiveDocument.BuiltInDocumentProperties(wdPropertyWords)
```

Changing the Default File Paths

Word maintains a number of default file paths, from the program path to the tutorial path (where tutorial files are located). You'll often want to retrieve these paths to establish where particular types of files should be located on a computer; occasionally, you may want to change the paths in your macros.

Table 21.3 displays the most useful of Word's default file paths. Some of these are accessible on the File Locations tab of the Options dialog box; others are accessible only through the Registry.

TABLE 21.3: Default File Paths in Word

Constant	Specifies the Path To
wdAutoRecoverPath	AutoRecover files
wdCurrentFolderPath	The current folder
wdDocumentsPath	The default location for documents
wdGraphicsFiltersPath	The location of graphics filters (usually the COMMON FILES\MICROSOFT SHARED\GRPHFLT\ folder)
wdProgramPath	The location of the Word EXE files (usually the MICROSOFT OFFICE\OFFICE\ folder)
wdStartupPath	The Startup folder
wdTempFilePath	The folder where Word stores temporary files
wdTextConvertersPath	The folder containing the text converters (usually COMMON FILES\MICROSOFT SHARED\TEXTCONV\)
wdToolsPath	The folder containing Word tools (usually the MICROSOFT OFFICE\OFFICE\ folder)
wdUserOptionsPath	The folder in which user options are stored
wdUserTemplatesPath	The folder containing user (local) templates (usually the PROGRAM FILES\TEMPLATES\ folder)
wdWorkgroupTemplatesPath	The folder containing workgroup (shared) templates

To return a default file path, use the DefaultFilePath property of the Options object with the appropriate argument. The following statement displays a message box containing the program path:

```
MsgBox Options.DefaultFilePath(wdProgramPath)
```

The following statement sets the workgroup templates path:

```
Options.DefaultFilePath(wdWorkgroupTemplatesPath)=
"f:\common\Templates"
```

Working with Folders

VBA provides the following commands for working with folders:

- Use the Dir function with \nul to check whether a folder exists. The following statements save a document if the specified folder exists and display a warning message box if the folder does not exist:

```
If Dir("d:\temp\nul") <> "" Then
    ActiveDocument.SaveAs "d:\temp\Sample Document.doc"
Else
    MsgBox "The folder d:\temp does not exist.", vbOKOnly + _
vbCritical
End If
```

- Use the ChDir statement to change the current directory or folder on the specified drive. The following statement changes the current folder on drive D to D:\TEMP:

```
ChDir "d:\temp"
```

- Use the ChDrive statement to change the current drive. ChDrive uses only the leftmost character of the string you give it. The following statements both change the current drive to D:

```
ChDrive "d"
ChDrive "d:\temp\testing"
```

- Use the CurDir function to return the current folder:

```
MsgBox "The current folder is " & CurDir & ".",, "Current Folder"
```

- Use the MkDir statement to create a folder. MkDir takes a path argument specifying the path of the folder to create. The following statement creates the folder C:\WINDOWS\TEMP\TESTING\:

```
MkDir "c:\Windows\Temp\Testing"
```

- Use the RmDir function to delete a folder. RmDir takes a path argument specifying the path of the folder to delete. Before using RmDir, you need to remove all the contents of the target folder (for example, by using a Kill statement) and make sure the target folder is not the current folder.

- To delete a folder and its contents, use a Shell statement and the DELTREE command. Shell uses a DOS box.

Working with Windows and Panes

VBA provides two Windows collections: one containing Window objects that represent the windows available in the Application object, and one containing Window objects in a Document object. Usually, you'll want to work with the Windows collection for the Application object, though at times it's useful to work with the Windows collection for a Document object.

Each Window object contains a Panes collection of Pane objects that represent the panes for the window. Each window and pane can have a different Selection object, though only one Selection object can be active at a time.

These are the actions you're most likely to need to perform with Window and Pane objects and their collections:

- Use the window name or index number with the Windows collection to return a Window object. The following statement displays a message box containing the name of each Window object in turn:

```
For i = 1 To Windows.Count
    MsgBox Windows(i).Caption
Next i
```

- Use the WindowState property to return or adjust the window state of the active window. Use the arguments wdWindowStateMaximize to maximize the window, wdWindowStateMinimize to minimize the window, or wdWindowStateNormal to "restore" the window. The following statement maximizes the active window if it is not already maximized:

```
If ActiveWindow.WindowState <> wdWindowStateMaximize Then _
ActiveWindow.WindowState = wdWindowStateMaximize
```

- Use the View object to adjust the view in the window. For example, for many procedures you will want a document to be in Normal view rather than Outline view, Print Preview, or another unsuitable view. The following statements store the current view, change to Normal view if necessary, and then restore the previous view if necessary:

```
With ActiveWindow
    If .View <> wdNormalView Then
        CurView = .View
        .View = wdNormalView
    End If
    'Take other actions here
    If CurView <> "" Then .View = CurView
End With
```

- Use the Zoom property of the View object to adjust the zoom level in the window. The following statement sets the zoom percentage to 125%.

```
ActiveWindow.View.Zoom = 125
```

- Use the Arrange method with the ArrangeStyle argument to arrange the open document windows in the application window. Use wdTiled to tile maximized or "restored" windows, or use wdIcons to arrange minimized window icons:

```
Windows.Arrange ArrangeStyle:=wdTiled
```

- Use the Count property of the Windows collection for a Document object to make sure that only one window is displayed for a document you want to work with. Note that Print Preview uses a second window.

- For many procedures, you'll want to make sure that the insertion point is in the main document before taking action. This enables you to, say, avoid creating a whole document in a header, footnote, or comment pane. To find out which pane the insertion point is in, try using the SplitSpecial property of the View object for the appropriate pane. (We say "try using" because for us, SplitSpecial consistently causes GPFs under both Windows 95 and NT.) Failing that, you can close every pane beyond the first to make sure the main document is active:

```
With ActiveWindow
    Do While .Panes.Count > 1
        .Panes(.Panes.Count).Close
    Loop
End With
```

Inserting Text in a Document

You can insert text in either the active document or a specified Document object.

When working with the active document, you can use the Selection object for working with text:

- To insert text at the position of the insertion point, use the TypeText method of the Selection object:

```
Selection.TypeText "Report for April 1, 1998"
```

> **NOTE**
>
> Before inserting text, make sure the current selection is suitable, as discussed in the next section. Usually, you'll want to make sure the selection is wdSelectionIP.

- To insert text before or after the current selection, use the InsertBefore and InsertAfter methods on the Selection object. VBA will extend the selection to include the inserted text. The following statements insert Professor and a space before the current selection and the content of the string expression Course after it:

```
Selection.InsertBefore "Professor "
Selection.InsertAfter Course
```

To insert text in a document other than the active document, identify the document and the position in which to insert the text. The following statement inserts the string Title at the beginning of the document named Weekly Report.doc:

```
Documents("Weekly Report.doc").Characters(1).InsertBefore Title
```

You can insert a paragraph in any of several ways:

- Use the InsertParagraph method to insert a paragraph at the current position of the insertion point:

```
Selection.InsertParagraph
```

- Use the InsertParagraphAfter or InsertParagraphBefore method to insert a paragraph either after or before the selection or range:

```
Selection.InsertParagraphBefore
```

- Use the TypeText method to enter the vbCr constant or the carriage-return character, Chr(13):

```
Selection.TypeText vbCr
Selection.TypeText Chr(13)
```

Working with the Selection Object

The Selection object represents the selection in the Application object, a Window object, or a Pane object. Use the Selection object with the Application object to return the active selection in the active document; use the Selection object with a Window object or a Pane object to return the selection in that pane. Each window in each open document can have a Selection object, but only one Selection object can be active at any time in any Word session: the selection in the active document. The Selection object is analogous to the insertion point or current selection when you are working interactively with Word.

The Selection object can be collapsed to an insertion point, or it can contain one or more characters or document items, up to the entire content of any document story. (Word recognizes eleven *stories*—parts of a document—including the main text, the comments section, text in frames, and the header and footer sections. See "Using Range Properties" later in this chapter for a list of Word stories and their associated constants and values.)

Checking the Type of Selection

To find out what type of selection you currently have, return the Type property of the Selection object:

```
If Selection.Type = wdSelectionIP Then MsgBox "Insertion point"
```

Word differentiates the types of selections shown in Table 21.4.

TABLE 21.4: The Types of Selections in Word

wdSelectionType constant	Value	Meaning
wdNoSelection	0	There is no selection
wdSelectionIP	1	The selection is a plain insertion point—nothing is selected.

TABLE 21.4 (CONTINUED): The Types of Selections in Word

wdSelectionType constant	Value	Meaning
wdSelectionNormal	2	A "normal" selection, such as a selected word or sentence.
wdSelectionFrame	3	A frame is selected.
wdSelectionColumn	4	A column or part of a column (two or more cells in a column, or one cell in each of two or more columns) is selected.
wdSelectionRow	5	A full row in a table is selected.
wdSelectionBlock	6	A block is selected (a vertical part of one or more paragraphs).
wdSelectionInlineShape	7	An inline shape or graphic is selected.
wdSelectionShape	8	A shape object is selected.

Manipulating the Current Selection

To manipulate the current selection, use the properties and methods of the Selection object and the objects and collections it contains. The Text property contains the text of the Selection object:

```
MsgBox Selection.Text
```

You can perform operations such as cut, copy, and paste. The following statement copies the current selection from the active document:

```
Selection.Copy
```

To work with part of the current selection, specify it by using the appropriate object. The following statement sets the font size of the second word in the selection to 48 points:

```
Selection.Words(2).Font.Size = 48
```

To work with the current paragraph (the paragraph in which the insertion point resides, or the paragraph that is selected or partly selected), use the Paragraphs object to specify it:

```
Selection.Paragraphs(1)
```

Extending a Selection

To extend a selection, use the EndOf method for a Range or Selection object. EndOf takes an optional Unit argument (see Table 21.5) and an optional Extend variant argument: wdMove moves the selection or range and is the default setting; wdExtend extends the selection or range.

TABLE 21.5: Unit Arguments

Unit	Meaning
wdCharacter	A character
wdWord	A word (the default setting if you omit Unit)
wdSentence	A sentence
wdLine	A line (can be used only with Selection objects, not with ranges)
wdParagraph	A paragraph
wdSection	A section of a document
wdStory	The current story
wdCell	A cell in a table
wdColumn	A column in a table
wdRow	A row in a table
wdTable	A whole table

The following statement extends the current selection to the end of the paragraph:

```
Selection.EndOf Unit:=wdParagraph, Extend:=wdExtend
```

The following statement moves the selection (that is, the insertion point) to the end of the paragraph:

```
Selection.EndOf Unit:=wdParagraph, Extend:=wdMove
```

The following statement selects from the current insertion point or selection to the end of the current Word story:

```
Selection.EndOf Unit:=wdStory, Extend:=wdExtend
```

Canceling a Selection

You can cancel (deselect) a selection in any of several ways:

- Collapse the selection to the start of the selection by using the Collapse method:

    ```
    Selection.Collapse wdCollapseStart
    ```

- Reduce the selection to just one point by setting the end of the selection to be equal to the start of the selection:

    ```
    Selection.End = Selection.Start
    ```

- Reduce the selection to one point by setting the start of the selection to be equal to the end of the selection:

    ```
    Selection.Start = Selection.End
    ```

- Collapse the selection and move the insertion point to the end of the selection:

    ```
    Selection.Collapse wdEnd
    ```

Getting Other Information about the Current Selection

VBA can provide full information about the current selection, from its font and size to its borders. To access this information, check the property of the relevant object.

For further information, use the Information property to return information about a selection or range and about what's happening in the Word environment. Table 21.6 lists the available information.

TABLE 21.6: Information Available in the Information Property

wdInformation Constant	Returns this Information
Environment Information	
wdCapsLock	True if Caps Lock is on.
wdNumLock	True if Num Lock is on.
wdOverType	True if Overtype mode is on.
wdRevisionMarking	True if change tracking is on.

TABLE 21.6 (CONTINUED): Information Available in the Information Property

wdInformation Constant	Returns this Information
Environment Information	
wdSelectionMode	The current selection mode: 0 indicates a normal selection; 1 indicates an extended selection (Extend mode is on); and 2 indicates a column selection.
wdZoomPercentage	The current zoom percentage.
Selection and Insertion Point Information	
wdActiveEndAdjustedPage-Number	The number of the page containing the active end of the selection or range. This number reflects any change you make to the starting page number; wdActiveEndPageNumber does not.
wdActiveEndPageNumber	The number of the page containing the active end of the selection or range.
wdActiveEndSectionNumber	The number of the section containing the active end of the selection or range.
wdFirstCharacterColumnNumber	The character position of the first character in the selection or range. If the selection or range is collapsed to an insertion point, this returns the character number immediately to the right of the insertion point. (This "column" is relative to the currently active left margin and does not have to be inside a table. This is the number that appears in the Col readout in the status bar.)
wdFirstCharacterLineNumber	Page Layout view and Print Preview, returns the line number of the first character in the selection. In non-layout views (for example, Normal view), this returns –1.
wdFrameIsSelected	True if the selection or range is a whole frame or text box.
wdHeaderFooterType	A value that specifies the type of header or footer containing the selection or range: –1 indicates that the selection or range is not in a header or footer; 0 indicates an even page header; 1 indicates an odd page header in a document that has odd and even headers, and the only header in a document that does not have odd and even headers; 2 indicates an even page footer; 3 indicates an odd page footer in a document that has odd and even footers, and the only footer in a document that does not have odd and even headers; 4 indicates a first-page header; and 5 indicates a first-page footer.

TABLE 21.6 (CONTINUED): Information Available in the Information Property

wdInformation Constant	Returns this Information

Selection and Insertion Point Information

wdHorizontalPositionRelative-ToPage	The horizontal position of the selection or range—the distance from the left edge of the selection or range to the left edge of the page, measured in twips (20 twips = 1 point; 72 points = 1 inch).
wdHorizontalPositionRelative-ToTextBoundary	The horizontal position of the selection or range—the distance from the left edge of the selection or range to the text boundary enclosing it, measured in twips.
wdInCommentPane	True if the selection or range is in a comment pane.
wdInEndnote	True if the selection or range is an endnote (this is defined as appearing in the endnote pane in Normal view or in the endnote area in Page Layout view).
wdInFootnote	True if the selection or range is in a footnote (this is defined as appearing in the footnote pane in Normal view or in the footnote area in Page Layout view).
wdInFootnoteEndnotePane	True if the selection or range is in a footnote or endnote.
wdInHeaderFooter	True if the selection or range is in a header or footer (defined as appearing in the header or footer pane in Normal view or in the header or footer area in Page Layout view).
wdInMasterDocument	True if the selection or range is in a master document (a document containing at least one subdocument).
wdInWordMail	A value that specifies the WordMail location of the selection or range: 0 indicates that the selection or range is not in a WordMail message; 1 indicates that it is in a WordMail send note; and 2 indicates that it is in a WordMail read note.
wdNumberOfPagesInDocument	The number of pages in the document in which the selection or range appears.
wdReferenceOfType	A value that specifies where the selection is in relation to a footnote, endnote, or comment reference.
wdVerticalPositionRelative-ToPage	The vertical position of the selection or range—the distance from the top edge of the selection to the top edge of the page, measured in twips.
wdVerticalPositionRelative-ToTextBoundary	The vertical position of the selection or range—the distance from the top edge of the selection to the text boundary enclosing it, measured in twips.

1123

TABLE 21.6 (CONTINUED): Information Available in the Information Property

wdInformation Constant	Returns this Information
Table Information	
wdWithInTable	True if the selection is in a table.
wdStartOfRangeColumnNumber	The number of the table column containing the beginning of the selection or range.
wdEndOfRangeColumnNumber	The number of the table column containing the end of the selection or range.
wdStartOfRangeRowNumber	The number of the table row containing the beginning of the selection or range.
wdEndOfRangeRowNumber	The number of the table row number containing the end of the selection or range.
wdAtEndOfRowMarker	True if the selection or range is at the end-of-row marker in a table (not the end-of-cell marker).
wdMaximumNumberOfColumns	The largest number of table columns in any row in the selection or range.
wdMaximumNumberOfRows	The largest number of table rows in the table in the selection or range.

Creating and Using Ranges

In Word, a *range* is a contiguous area of a document with a defined starting point and ending point. For example, you can define a range that consists of the first paragraph in a specified document. The starting point of the range will be the beginning of the paragraph, and the ending point of the range will be the end of the paragraph. Likewise, you can define a range that consists of the 100th to 200th characters in a document or a range that consists of a specified number of words in a certain paragraph.

You can use ranges with VBA for the same reason you use bookmarks when working interactively with Word: to mark a location in a document that you want to be able to access quickly or manipulate easily. Like a bookmark, a range can contain any amount of text in a document, from a single character to all the contents of the document; a range can even have the same starting point and ending point, which gives it no contents and makes it in effect an invisible mark in the document that you can use to insert text. Once you've created a range, you can refer to it, access its contents or insert new contents in it, or format it, all by using the properties of the range and the methods that apply to it.

In practical terms, the main difference between a range and a bookmark is that the lifetime of a range is limited to the VBA procedure that defines it, whereas a bookmark is saved with the document or template that contains it and can be accessed at any point (whether or not a procedure is running).

Using range objects gives you far more flexibility than working with the current selection. Whereas there can be only one active selection in a given Word session, you can define multiple ranges in each of the documents you have open. Moreover, you can define and manipulate ranges in documents other than the active document, and you can work with ranges without affecting the current selection.

Defining a Named Range

You can create a Range object by using a Set statement in either of two ways:

- Use the Range method on a Document object.
- Use the Range property for an object that supports it.

To use the Range method, use the following syntax, where RangeName is the name you are assigning to the range, and Start and End are optional arguments specifying the starting and ending points of the range.

```
Set RangeName = Document.Range(Start, End)
```

To use the Range property, use the following syntax:

```
Set RangeName = Object.Range
```

The following statement uses the Range property of the Paragraphs collection to define a range named FirstPara that consists of the first paragraph of the active document:

```
Set FirstPara = ActiveDocument.Paragraphs(1).Range
```

The following statements uppercase the first three words of the active document:

```
With ActiveDocument
    Set FirstThree =.Range(Start:=.Words(1).Start, End:=.Words(3).End)
    FirstThree.Case = wdUpperCase
End With
```

The first statement defines the range FirstThree as a range in the active document, from the beginning of the first word to the end of the third word. The second statement changes the case of the FirstThree Range object to uppercase. Because FirstThree is now defined as a Range object for the duration of the procedure that declares it, you can return to FirstThree and manipulate it later in the procedure if you want to.

Working with Unnamed Ranges

You don't have to assign a name to a range to work with it—you can also use the Range object without assigning a name. For example, if you didn't want to revisit the FirstThree range that we defined in the previous example, you could skip the step of naming the range and instead apply the Case method to the Range object, as in the following statement:

```
With ActiveDocument
    .Range(Start:=.Words(1).Start, End:=.Words(3).End).Case = _
wdUpperCase
End With
```

Redefining a Range

To redefine a range, use the SetRange method with the optional Start and End arguments. The following statement redefines the range FirstThree (which was defined as the first three words of the active document) to refer to the first character of the document:

```
FirstThree.SetRange Start:=0, End:=1
```

> **NOTE** You can also redefine a range by using the Set method again, in essence re-creating the range from scratch.

Using Range Properties

The Range object has a large number of other properties associated with it, from contents properties such as a Words property and a Characters property (as well as a Cells property, a Columns property, and a Rows property for ranges that contain tables) to formatting properties such as a Font property, a Bold property, and an Italic property. For manipulating a range, the most important properties are the Start property, the End property, and the StoryType property:

- Use the Start property to set or return the starting character position of the range.

- Use the End property to set or return the ending character position of the range.

- Use the StoryType property to set or return the type of story (document area) associated with the Range:

wdStoryType Constant	Value	Meaning
wdMainTextStory	1	Main text of the document
wdCommentsStory	4	Comments section
wdEndnotesStory	3	Endnotes section
wdFootnotesStory	2	Footnotes section
wdTextFrameStory	5	Text in frames
wdPrimaryFooterStory	9	Main footer
wdEvenPagesFooterStory	8	Even-page footer
wdFirstPageFooterStory	11	First-page footer
wdPrimaryHeaderStory	7	Main header
wdEvenPagesHeaderStory	6	Even-page header
wdFirstPageHeaderStory	10	First-page header

The following statement compares the story type of the range MyRange to the main text of the document and terminates the macro if it is not the main text of the document:

```
If MyRange.StoryType <> wdMainTextStory Then End
```

Working with a Range

Once you've defined a range, you can specify it by name to quickly work with its contents. The following statements define a range named WorkRange that references the first sentence in the document and then works with it:

```
Set WorkRange = ActiveDocument.Sentences(1)
With WorkRange
    .Font.Name = "Arial"
    .Font.Size = "48"
    .Font.Underline = wdUnderlineSingle
End With
```

Working with Formatting and Styles

By using VBA, you can apply the same three types of formatting to your documents as you can manually: paragraph styles, character styles, and direct formatting.

Applying Paragraph Styles

To apply a paragraph style, use the Style property of either the Paragraphs collection, a Range object, or the Selection object. The following statement applies the Heading 1 style to the current selection:

```
Selection.Style = "Heading 1"
```

You can apply a style to all the paragraphs in a document by specifying the Paragraphs collection. The following statement applies the Body Text style to all the paragraphs in the document A QUESTION OF STYLE.DOC:

```
Documents("A Question of Style.doc").Paragraphs.Style = "Body Text"
```

Applying Character Styles

To apply a character style, identify the target text and use the Style property of a suitable object, such as the Characters collection or the Words collection. The following statement applies the character style Bold Italic to the first word of the second paragraph of the active document:

```
ActiveDocument.Paragraphs(2).Range.Words(1).Style = "Bold Italic"
```

To apply a character style to selected text, use the Style property of the Selection object. The following statement applies the character style Dialog Text to the current selection:

```
Selection.Style = "Dialog Text"
```

NOTE   You cannot apply a character style to a Paragraph object directly—you need to specify a range, some characters, or some words.

Applying Direct Formatting

You can apply direct formatting as well as (or instead of) paragraph styles and character styles. Although direct formatting has a number of disadvantages (such as that carelessly applying other styles to text that has direct formatting can remove formatting attributes from it), you may want to use direct formatting from time to time in your macros. Here are two examples.

To apply font formatting, manipulate the Font property of the object in question. The following statement italicizes the first paragraph in the document named ARIZONA SALES.DOC:

```
Documents("Arizona Sales.doc").Paragraphs(1).Range.Font.Italic = True
```

To apply paragraph formatting to a paragraph, use the ParagraphFormat object. The following statement applies Left alignment to the current selection:

```
Selection.ParagraphFormat.Alignment = wdAlignParagraphLeft
```

Working with Find and Replace

Word's Find and Replace features are as powerful tools in procedures as they are for working interactively with Word. You can use Find and Replace operations on either the ActiveDocument object or a Document object.

The Find Object

The Find object, which applies to the Range and Selection objects, has properties and methods that match the options in the Find and Replace dialog box. The easiest way to use the Find object is with the Execute property and specify the parameters for the Find operation as arguments in the Execute statement. You can also set the parameters beforehand using properties.

Table 21.7 describes the most useful properties for common search operations. You'll see a lot of overlap between these and the arguments for the Execute statement, which we'll look at in a moment; essentially, they cover the same ground, but with different syntax.

TABLE 21.7: Properties for Common Search Operations

Find Property	Meaning
Font	Font formatting you're searching for (on either specified text or an empty string).
Forward	A Boolean argument specifying whether to search forward (True) or backward (False) through the document.

TABLE 21.7 (CONTINUED): Properties for Common Search Operations

Find Property	Meaning
Found	A Boolean property that is True if the search finds a match and False if it does not.
Highlight	A Long argument controlling whether highlighting is included in the formatting for the replacement text (True) or not (False).
MatchAllWordForms	A Boolean property—True or False—corresponding to the Find All Word Forms checkbox.
MatchCase	A Boolean property corresponding to the Match Case checkbox.
MatchSoundsLike	A Boolean property corresponding to the Sounds Like checkbox.
MatchWholeWord	A Boolean property corresponding to the Find Whole Words Only checkbox.
MatchWildcards	A Boolean property corresponding to the Use Wildcards checkbox.
ParagraphFormat	Paragraph formatting you're searching for
Replacement	Returns a Replacement object containing the criteria for a replace operation.
Style	The style for the search text. Usually, you'll want to use the name of a style in the current template, but you can also use one of the built-in Word constant style names, such as wdStyleHeading1.
Text	The text you're searching for—what you would enter in the Find What box in the Find and Replace dialog box. To search only for formatting, use an empty string ("").
Wrap	A Long property that governs whether a search that starts anywhere other than the beginning of a document (for a forward search) or the end of a document (for a backward search), or a search that takes place in a range, wraps when it reaches the end or beginning of the document or the end or beginning of the selection.

The Replacement Object

The Replacement object specifies the replace criteria in a replacement operation. The Replacement object has the following properties, which correspond to the properties of the Find object (but pertain to the replacement operation instead):

- Font
- Highlight

- ParagraphFormat
- Style
- Text

Using the Execute Method

The easiest way to execute a Find operation is to use the Execute method with the Find object. The syntax for the Execute method is:

```
Find.Execute(FindText, MatchCase, MatchWholeWord, _
MatchWildcards, MatchSoundsLike, MatchAllWordForms, _
Forward, Wrap, Format, ReplaceWith, Replace)
```

The parts of this statement are as follows:

- FindText is an optional variant specifying the text for which to search. Though this argument is optional, you'll almost always want to specify it, even if you specify only an empty string ("") to allow you to search for formatting. (If you do not specify FindText, you run the risk of searching inadvertently for the previous item searched for.) You can search for special characters (such as ^p for a paragraph mark or ^a for an annotation) and for wildcards by using codes. For wildcards to work, set MatchWildcards to True. To search for a symbol, enter a caret and a zero followed by its character code. For example, to search for a smart double closing quote, specify ^0148, because its character code is 148.

- MatchCase is an optional variant that you can set to True to make the search case-sensitive.

- MatchWholeWord is an optional variant that you can set to True to restrict the search to finding whole words rather than words contained in other words.

- MatchWildcards is an optional variant that you can set to True to use wildcards in the search.

- MatchSoundsLike is an optional variant that you can set to True to have Word find words that sound similar to the Find item specified.

- MatchAllWordForms is an optional variant that you can set to True to have Word find all forms of the Find item specified.

- Forward is an optional variant that you can set to True to have Word search forward (from the beginning of the document toward the end) or False to have Word search backward.

- Wrap is an optional variant that governs whether a search that begins anywhere other than the beginning of a document (for a forward search) or at the end of a document (for a backward search), or a search that takes place in a range, wraps (continues) when it reaches the end or beginning of the document. Word offers the following options for Wrap:

WdFindWrap Constant	Value	Meaning
wdFindAsk	2	Word searches the selection or range or from the insertion point to the end or beginning of the document and then displays a message box prompting the user to decide whether to search the rest of the document.
wdFindContinue	1	Word continues to search after reaching the end or beginning of the search range or the end or beginning of the document.
wdFindStop	0	Word stops the Find operation upon reaching the end or beginning of the search range or the end or beginning of the document.

- Format is an optional variant that you can set to True to have the search operation find formatting as well as (or instead of) any Find text you've specified.

- ReplaceWith is an optional variant specifying the replacement text. You can use an empty string for ReplaceWith to simply remove the FindText text; you can also use special characters for ReplaceWith as you can for the FindText argument. To use a graphic object, copy it to the clipboard and then specify ^c (the contents of the clipboard).

- Replace is an optional variant that controls how many replacements the Find operation makes: one (wdReplaceOne), all (wdReplaceAll), or none (wdReplaceNone).

To clear formatting currently set for the Find object or the Replace object, use the ClearFormatting method. The following statements clear formatting on both the Find and Replacement objects:

```
With ActiveDocument.Content.Find
    .ClearFormatting
    .Replacement.ClearFormatting
End With
```

Find and Replace in Action

The simplest way to use Find and Replace is to specify as many parameters as you need in an Execute statement, leaving out any optional parameters that you don't need to specify. For example, to replace all extra paragraph marks in the active document, you could search for **^p^p** and replace it with **^p** with the following statement:

```
ActiveDocument.Content.Find.Execute FindText:="^p^p" _
ReplaceWith:="^p",Replace:=wdReplaceAll
```

Alternatively, use a With statement to specify the properties for a Find and Replace operation:

```
With ActiveDocument.Content.Find
    .Text = "^p^p"
    .Replacement.Text = "^p"
    .Forward = True
    .Wrap = wdFindContinue
    .Execute Replace:=wdReplaceAll
End With
```

Working with Bookmarks

Word's bookmarks provide a quick and easy way of identifying and referring to parts of documents quickly and easily. Bookmarks are particularly useful for automating the flow and transfer of information from document to document or from Word to another application. To access bookmarks, use the Bookmarks collection.

VBA's ranges provide another way of working with a specified part of a document. The advantage of a bookmark over a range is that you can save a bookmark in a document, whereas a range lasts only while the procedure that defines it is running.

Not only can you create bookmarks of your own, but Word includes a number of hidden, built-in bookmarks that you can use to access information about a document.

Working with User-Defined Bookmarks

In this section, we'll discuss how VBA handles user-defined bookmarks—the ones that you add to a document either manually or by using macros.

Inserting a Bookmark

To insert a bookmark, use the Add method. The Add method takes a required Name string argument that specifies the name of the bookmark. Bookmark names can contain underscores but not spaces, can contain alphanumerics but not symbols, and can be a maximum of 40 characters. You can also use an optional variant Range argument to specify the range for the bookmark to mark. The range can contain text or graphical elements or can be collapsed to a single point.

The following statement adds a bookmark named Meeting_Location to the active document at the current position of the insertion point or the current selection:

```
ActiveDocument.Bookmarks.Add Name:="Meeting_Location"
```

The following statement uses a Range argument to add a bookmark named Request_Number to the first word of the open document named PERSONNEL REQUEST.DOC:

```
Documents("Personnel Request.doc").Bookmarks.Add _
    Name:="Request_Number", _
    Range:=Documents("Personnel Request.doc").Words(1)
```

Finding Out Whether a Bookmark Exists

To find out whether a bookmark exists, use the Exists property for the Bookmark object in the Bookmarks collection. The following statements display a message

box stating whether the bookmark Request_Number exists in the document
PERSONNEL REQUEST.DOC:

```
With Documents("Personnel Request.doc")
    If .Bookmarks.Exists("Request_Number") = True Then
        MsgBox "The bookmark exists."
    Else
        MsgBox "The bookmark does not exist."
    End If
End With
```

Going to a Bookmark

To move the insertion point to a bookmark, use the Select method for the
Bookmark object. The following statement moves the insertion point to the bookmark named MyTemp in the active document:

```
ActiveDocument.Bookmarks("MyTemp").Select
```

Finding Out Where a Bookmark Is Located

To find out where a bookmark is located, use the Start and End properties of its
Range object, which return the character position of the start and end of the bookmark's range. The statements below display a message box listing the start and
end positions of the bookmark named CEO_Salary:

```
Set CurDoc = Documents("Industry Survey.doc")
BookStart = CurDoc.Bookmarks("CEO_Salary").Range.Start
BookEnd = CurDoc.Bookmarks("CEO_Salary").Range.End
MsgBox "Start position:" + Str(BookStart) & vbCr & "End position:" _
 & Str(BookEnd), vbOKOnly + vbInformation, "Bookmark Information"
```

NOTE   If the start and end of the bookmark's range are in the same place—that is, if
the bookmark marks a collapsed selection—the start and end positions will
be the same.

Returning the Contents of a Bookmark

To return the contents of a bookmark, use the Text property of the Range object of
the Bookmark object. The following statement returns the contents of the bookmark CEO_Salary in the active document:

```
MsgBox ActiveDocument.Bookmarks("CEO_Salary").Text
```

To find out whether a bookmark is empty, check to see if its Empty property is True.

Deleting a Bookmark

To delete a bookmark, use the Delete method with the Bookmark object. The following statement deletes the bookmark named Employee_Idea in the document NEW IDEAS.DOC:

```
Documents("New Ideas.doc").Bookmarks("Employee_Idea").Delete
```

To delete all the bookmarks in a document, you could use a For Each...Next statement with the Bookmarks collection. The following macro deletes all bookmarks in the active document.

```
Sub Delete_All_Bookmarks()
    With ActiveDocument
        For Each Mark In .Bookmarks
            .Bookmarks(Mark).Delete
        Next Mark
    End With
End Sub
```

Using Word's Built-In Bookmarks

Word provides a number of built-in bookmarks (see Table 21.8) that it uses in the background to perform standard operations. You can use these bookmarks for your own purposes.

TABLE 21.8: Word's Built-In Bookmarks

Bookmark	Returns
\Sel	The current selection.
\PrevSel1	The location of the most recent edit (Shift+F5 manually).
\PrevSel2	The location of the second most recent edit (Shift+F5 twice manually).
\StartOfSel	The start of the current selection if there is one; otherwise, the location of the insertion point.
\EndOfSel	The end of the current selection if there is one; otherwise, the location of the insertion point.

TABLE 21.8 (CONTINUED): Word's Built-In Bookmarks

Bookmark	Returns
\Line	The first line of the current selection if there is one; otherwise, the line on which the insertion point resides. If the insertion point is positioned at the end of any line other than the last line in the paragraph, this bookmark includes the whole of the next line. If there's a space after the insertion point at the end of the line, you'll get the current line instead of the next line.
\Char	The first character of the current selection if there is one; otherwise, the character to the right of the insertion point.
\Para	The current paragraph, or the first paragraph if part or all of two or more paragraphs are selected. This bookmark includes the paragraph mark unless the paragraph in question is the last paragraph in the document.
\Section	The current section, or the first section if there is a selection that contains part or all of two or more sections.
\Doc	All the contents of the active document except for the last paragraph mark.
\Page	The current page, or the first page if there is a selection that spans two or more pages. If the page in question is the last page in the document, this bookmark does not include the last paragraph mark.
\StartOfDoc	The beginning of the document.
\EndOfDoc	The end of the document.
\Cell	The current cell in a table, or the first cell if there is a selection that spans two or more cells.
\Table	The current table, or the first table if there is a selection that spans part or all of two or more tables.
\HeadingLevel	The current heading and any subordinate headings or text. If the current selection is not a heading, VBA selects the heading that precedes the selection, together with any subordinate headings or text.

NOTE Before using the PrevSel1 or PrevSel2 bookmark, check that it exists by using a statement such as `If ActiveDocument.Bookmarks.Exists ("\PrevSel2") = True Then ActiveDocument.Bookmarks ("\PrevSel2").Select`.

The following statements delete the current paragraph in the active document:

```
ActiveDocument.Bookmarks("\Para").Select
Selection.Delete
```

Looping through a Collection

By looping through a collection, you can quickly perform an action on all the objects in it without testing to see how many objects there are. To loop through a collection, use a For Each...Next statement. The following statements set the ShowAll property (which displays paragraph marks, spaces, tabs, and so on) for each window to False and the WrapToWindow property to True:

```
For Each Win In Windows
    Win.View.ShowAll = False
    Win.View.WrapToWindow = True
Next Win
```

The following procedure shows how you might search the contents of each document for a particular word or phrase and close each document that did not contain it:

```
Sub Close_Documents_without_Specified_Text()
    Dim SearchText As String
    SearchText = InputBox("Enter the text to search for:", _
        "Close Documents without Specified Text")
    For Each Doc In Documents
        With Selection.Find
            .Text = SearchText
            .Execute
            If .Found = False Then Documents(Doc).Close
        End With
    Next Doc
End Sub
```

Using Word's Built-In Dialog Boxes

In this section, we'll discuss how to use Word's built-in dialog boxes in procedures you create. Using the built-in dialog boxes is an easy way to present the user with choices that Word already offers. Furthermore, you can use built-in dialog boxes to get past the limitations of the standard selection of controls that the Visual Basic Editor provides for Forms. (For example, as we saw in Chapter 20, the Visual Basic Editor does not offer the FileListBox, DirListBox, and DriveListBox controls that the Visual Basic IDE offers.) Moreover, you can save time and trouble by using a built-in dialog box, and you can be confident that users of your applications or procedures will recognize the dialog box and know how to use it, particularly if it is a common dialog box (such as an Open dialog box, a Save dialog box, or a Print dialog box).

The main disadvantage to using a built-in dialog box is that it may not be 100 percent suitable for what you want it to do: It may not offer all the actions you want, or it may offer the user actions that you do not want them to take. For example, you might require the user to open a file only from a given folder, in which case the Open dialog box would not be suitable, as it lets the user access any folder to which they have file-viewing rights.

You can choose whether to display a built-in dialog box and let the user use it in the normal fashion or to display a built-in dialog box, check the choices the user makes in it, and execute only appropriate choices. Doing the latter enables you to prevent the user from taking inappropriate actions in the dialog box.

Displaying a Built-In Dialog Box

Built-in Word dialog boxes are identified by constants starting with *wdDialog*, followed by the name of the dialog box. The name is derived from the menu commands required to display the dialog box. For example, the constant for the Open dialog box is wdDialogFileOpen (File ➤ Open); the constant for the Print dialog box is wdDialogFilePrint (File ➤ Print); and the constant for the Font dialog box is wdDialogFormatFont (Format ➤ Font).

NOTE   To display a Word dialog box from Visual Basic, you need to add a reference to the Microsoft Word 8.0 Object Library.

To display a dialog box, you use its constant with the Dialogs collection. There are two methods for displaying a built-in dialog box:

- The Show method displays the specified Dialog object and executes the actions the user takes in the dialog box. For example, if you use the Show method to display the wdDialogFileSaveAs dialog box, and the user enters a name for the file in the File Name box and clicks the Save button, VBA will save the file with the given name in the specified folder (and with any options the user chose). The following statement displays the Save As dialog box:

```
Dialogs(wdDialogFileSaveAs).Show
```

- The Display method displays the dialog box on-screen but does not execute the actions the user takes in the dialog box. Instead, it allows you to return the settings from the dialog box once the user dismisses it and use them for your own purposes. For example, you could display the Open dialog box to allow the user to select a file. Instead of opening the file, you could then manipulate it in a different way. The statements below use the Display method to display the Open dialog box and then display a message box containing the name of the file selected.

```
Set MyFileOpen = Dialogs(wdDialogFileOpen)
MyFileOpen.Display
MsgBox "You chose " & MyFileOpen.Name & "."
```

If the dialog box has tabs, the tabs have names built from the name of the dialog box, the word *Tab*, and the name of the tab. So the constant for the Bullets and Numbering dialog box is wdDialogFormatBulletsAndNumbering, and the constant for its Outline Numbered tab is wdDialogFormatBulletsAndNumberingTab-OutlineNumbered. Likewise, the Character Spacing tab of the Font dialog box is wdDialogFormatFontTabCharacterSpacing. To specify the tab to display, you use the DefaultTab property. The following statements display the Font dialog box with the Character Spacing tab foremost:

```
With Dialogs(wdDialogFormatFont)
    .DefaultTab = wdDialogFormatFontTabCharacterSpacing
    .Show
End With
```

To execute the settings in a built-in dialog box displayed with the Display method, use the Execute method. The statements below display the Open dialog box and then execute the user's choices in it. The comment line indicates where you could take actions to ensure the user had chosen a suitable file.

```
Set MyFileOpen = Dialogs(wdDialogFileOpen)
With MyFileOpen
    .Display
    'Check the file chosen by the user; set options as appropriate
    .Execute
End With
```

You can also use the Execute method on a built-in dialog box you've displayed using the Show method, but typically you won't need to, because the user's actions will make the dialog box execute appropriately.

Setting Options in a Built-In Dialog Box

To set an option in a built-in dialog box, use a Set statement to return a dialog object that refers to the object in the Dialogs collection. For example, to set the contents of the File Name text box in the Save As dialog box, you could use the statements shown below:

```
Set SaveMe = Dialogs(wdDialogFileSaveAs)
SaveMe.Name = "Baroque Castles in Bavaria, Introduction.doc"
```

Alternatively, you can use a With statement to work with the dialog box:

```
With Dialogs(wdDialogFileSaveAs)
    .Name = "My Visit to Neuschwanstein"
    .Display
End With
```

Most of the built-in Word dialog boxes have a number of arguments that you can use for retrieving or setting values in the dialog box. For example, the Open dialog box has arguments for Name, ConfirmConversions, ReadOnly, LinkToSource, AddToMRU (adding the document to the Most Recently Used document list at the foot of the File menu), PasswordDoc, and more. Some of these are options that you'll see in the Open dialog box itself; others are associated options that you'll find on the various tabs of the Options dialog box.

You can deduce the names of many of the arguments for a built-in dialog box from the names of the options in the dialog box. For example, in the Font dialog box (wdDialogFormatFont), the Font drop-down list is identified by the Font argument, and the Color drop-down list is identified by the Color argument. Other options, however, have different names. For instance, the Size drop-down list in the Font dialog box is identified by the Points argument.

Look up the topic "Built-in Word dialog boxes, argument list" in the Index of the VBA Help file for Word to get a list of all the built-in Word dialog boxes and the names of the arguments they take.

For example, you could display the Open dialog box showing all the TXT files in the \PUBLIC\COMMON\folder on the networked drive \\ERASER_D\ by setting the Name argument for the dialog box to *.txt and using the ChangeFileOpenDirectory statement to change the folder displayed in the Open dialog box:

```
ChangeFileOpenDirectory "\\Eraser_D\public\common"
With Dialogs(wdDialogFileOpen)
    .Name = "*.txt"
    .Show
End With
```

TIP

To change the folder in the Open dialog box, use the ChangeFileOpenDirectory method before displaying the dialog box. ChDrive and ChDir will not affect the folder displayed in the Open dialog box. The File-Open-Directory setting is set to a default folder when Word is launched, and it changes when the user manually changes folders in the Open dialog box.

Retrieving Values from a Built-In Dialog Box

When you use the Display method to display a dialog box, you'll need to return information from the dialog box so that you can take action with it. You may also need to return information from a dialog box displayed using the Show method.

To return a value from a built-in dialog box, use a Set statement to identify the dialog box:

```
Set mySaveAs = Dialogs(wdDialogSaveAs)
```

Then display the dialog box to let the user choose settings. If you want to be able to approve the settings before implementing them, use the Display method instead of the Show method so that VBA does not execute the settings when the user dismisses the dialog box. Then check the settings, change any that need changing, and use the Execute method to apply the settings.

For example, you could display the User Info tab of the Options dialog box from Visual Basic and make sure the user had entered text in each of the three text boxes by using the following code. Note that the dialog box uses the Execute method to execute any changes the user made to the information in the dialog box even when the user has not supplied complete information. Without this Execute method, the Display method will not bring in updated information on each loop back to the Redisplay label.

```
Set MyWord = CreateObject("Word.Application")
With MyWord
    .Visible = True
Redisplay:
    With Dialogs(wdDialogToolsOptionsUserInfo)
        .Display
        'Substitute a more effective check for the next line
        If .Name = "" Or .Initials = "" Or .Address = "" Then
            .Execute
            MsgBox "Please complete your information.", vbOKOnly _
            + vbCritical, "Information Inquisition 1.1"
            GoTo Redisplay
        Else
            .Execute
        End If
    End With
    .Quit
End With
Set MyWord = Nothing
```

Getting the Current Values for a Dialog Box

To get the current values for a dialog box, use the Update method. For example, the following statements show how you might display the Find and Replace dialog box, take other actions (indicated by the comment line), and then use the Update method to get the current values for the Find and Replace dialog box:

```
Set MyFind = Dialogs(wdDialogEditReplace)
MyFind.Display
'Take other actions here
MyFind.Update
```

NOTE   In most cases, it makes more sense to delay calling the dialog box until it is needed. By doing so, you will get the current values for the dialog box and will not need to use the Update method.

Returning the Button the User Chose in a Dialog Box

To find out which button the user clicked in a dialog box, check the return value of the Show method or the Display method. Table 21.9 shows the return values.

TABLE 21.9: The Return Values of the Show and Display Methods

Return Value	Button Clicked
−2	Close
−1	OK
0	Cancel
1	The first Command Button
2	The second Command Button
>2	Subsequent Command Buttons

For example, you could display the Paragraph dialog box and check which button the user clicked by using the following statements:

```
With Dialogs(wdDialogFormatParagraph)
    ButtonClicked = .Display
    Select Case ButtonClicked
    Case -1                        'User clicked the OK button
        MsgBox "You clicked the OK button.", vbOKOnly
    Case 0                         'User clicked the Cancel button
        MsgBox "You clicked the Cancel button.", vbOKOnly
    End Select
End With
```

Specifying a Timeout for a Dialog Box

You can a specify a timeout for a built-in dialog box, instead of having it displayed until the user dismisses it, by using the TimeOut variant argument with the Show method or the Display method. You specify TimeOut as a number of units, each of which is approximately a thousandth of a second (if the system is busy with many other tasks, the units may be longer). So you could display the User Information tab of the Options dialog box for about 15 seconds by using the following statements:

```
With Dialogs(wdDialogToolsOptions)
    .DefaultTab = wdDialogToolsOptionsTabUserInfo
    .Show (15000)
End With
```

NOTE The TimeOut argument works only for built-in Word dialog boxes; it does not work for custom dialog boxes.

Index to Code Listings

INDEX

Note to the Reader: Throughout this index **boldfaced** page numbers indicate primary discussions of a topic. *Italicized* page numbers indicate illustrations.

for collections, **302**
in CommandBarControl control, 518, 520, 522
in ContainedVBControl class, 452, 509–510
in Document objects, 1106
in Documents collection, 975–976
for names, 1082
in rdoConnections collection, 680
in Sheets collection, 1076
in TabStrip project, **150–151**
in TierTwo application, 836, **843–844**
in Toolbar buttons, 114
for TreeView control nodes, **164–165**
in VBComponents collection, 491
in VBProjects collection, 459
in VBScript, 865
for workbooks, 1072–1073
in Worksheets collection, 987–988
Add MOVE Command button, 488, 519–520
Add Printer Tab button, 147
Add Procedure dialog box, 1044, *1044*
Add Properties window, 410, *410*
Add Property Page dialog box, 407–408
Add Watch dialog box, 1025
AddFile method, 491
AddFromFile method, 459
AddFromString method, 515
AddIn module, **475–477**
Addin object, **458**
adding
code to forms, **515–516**
collection elements, **302**
controls to forms, **509–510**
fields to forms, **791–792**
IDE menu commands, **519–522**, *521*
ImageList control images, **112–113**, *112*
methods to class modules, **311–313**
names to Name collection, 1082
object libraries, **1022–1023**
properties to class modules, **313–316**
rdoConnection objects, 680

records
with parameter queries, **700–701**
in three-tiered applications, **827–831**
in TierTwo applications, **843–844**
status bar panels, **138–142**, *138*
tabs, **149–151**
Toolbar images and buttons, **115–117**, *116*, **121**
Toolbox pages and controls, **1054–1055**, *1056*
TreeView controls nodes, **164–166**
VBScript Dictionary entries, 865
watch expressions, 1025
worksheets, 1076
AddIns collection, **458**
addition, 725
Additional Controls dialog box, 1055, *1056*, 1057
Additional Network Support option, **617–618**
Address property, 841–842
addresses, IP, **885–886**
AddToAddInCommandBar function, 482
AddToIni function, 475–477, 485
AddToMRU argument
for Open method, 1071
for Save method, 1074
AddToRecentFiles argument
for Open method, 1103
for SaveAs method, 1108
administrative improvements in SQL Server
backup and recovery, **603–604**
Database Maintenance Plan Wizard, **601**
external tools support, **601–603**, *602*
fallback support, **604**
print support, **603**
remote server management, **605**
SNMP enhancements, **604–605**
SQL Mail, **604**
ADO and SQL Server Developer's Guide, 714
ADO Online Help file, 714
ADOs. *See* ActiveX Data Objects (ADOs)
Advanced Optimization option, 194–195, 199
Advanced Optimizations dialog box, 194, *195*, **333–334**

B

(

D

E

F

H

J

M

N

0

Q

R

S

T

U

W

X

Y

Z

Your Way to | Internet.Netcom.

Fast, Reliable Internet Access

Sign up today with Netcom*

If you want flexible, easy to use access to the Internet, then Netcom has a solution for you. We provide fast, reliable worldwide access to the Net, complete Internet software and advanced communication tools. Choose from a choice of scalable service plans.

- *Fast, reliable access* from over 330 local access points worldwide from 33.6 Kbps to 128 Kbps ISDN
- *Netcom's Internet Access Kit* includes Netcomplete 4.0, with Microsoft Internet Explorer™ 4.0, Claris HomePage™ Lite, Adobe Acrobat Reader® and more! Software included is a $50 value that you receive for FREE!
- *Choose the Netcomplete plan* and price tailored to your needs
- *Additional mailboxes* and mail forwarding services**
- *Free web page* with FTP support
- *Free customizable enhanced news* and financial information
- *World class* customer support

When You Need More, We're Ready!

Netcom also offers ISDN connectivity, web hosting solutions to create a distinctive presence on the Net, and connectivity solutions that provide high speed access. For more information call 1-888-280-6911.

Find Netcom's Internet Access Kit inside Sybex's CD-ROM

Sign-up with Netcom now and save $25 on your set-up!

US Robotics
X2 56Kbps modem
TECHNOLOGY

*If you are a Canadian customer, please call 1-800-NETCOM-1 for more information.
If asked, please use registration code #91959.

**Available with select service plans.

Netcom™

Visual Basic 5 Developer's Handbook Companion CD-ROM

*F*or Windows 95 and NT4 users, this *autoplay* CD-ROM automatically displays the Sybex interface for access to the different products on the CD. Just pop it in the CD-ROM drive and let the autoplay CD boot the Sybex interface. At this interface you'll find the following software products:

- **Complete Code from Book.** All the code from the book's chapters in one .exe file for a simple transfer to your hard drive.

- **Visual Quantify 4 by Rational Software.** A powerful Visual Basic profiling tool for optimizing VB5 code.

- **Visual Applet Designer by TVObjects.** Generate 100% Pure Java source and byte code from Visual Basic projects (modules, classes and forms). Converts ActiveX controls written within Visual Basic to Pure Java object code.

- **LeadTools 8 by LeadTools.** The leading image development toolkit, with controls for almost 300 functions, methods and properties, with imaging technology in 12 general categories including: scanning, color conversion, display, annotation, image processing (more than 50 different filters with region of interest), animation, compression.

- **Sp_assist and WinAPI Oblets by Sheridan Software.** Sp_assist is an enhanced development environment for SQL Server. WinAPI Oblets is a collection of 24 programmable application objects that encapsulate the functionality of the most commonly used Microsoft Windows API functions.

- **RoboHTML by Blue Sky Software.** An HTML Help Authoring tool that provides rich WYSIWYG editing capabilities with full drag and drop support, automated project management, and complete testing features.

- **NETCOMplete Online Signup.** In case you don't have access to the Net yet, Sybex and Netcom have included the latest version of NETCOMplete with Netscape Navigator 3. Check out the ad on the preceding page for details.

- **VSDocx Controls.** Videosoft's suite of ActiveX controls, including VSdata, VSsdirect, VSflex, VSOCX, VSspell, VSview3.

In addition, four appendices are included in pdf format. You can view these appendices with the included Adobe Acrobat Reader.

- **Appendix A:** *Chapter 1 API Functions.* Includes the declarations, parameters, and return values for all the Win32API functions used in Chapter 1. A Remarks section is included in some functions to provide additional information.

- **Appendix B:** *Chapter 2 API Functions.* Lists and explains the API functions used in the Registry projects in Chapter 2.

- **Appendix C:** *New and Enhanced Features in SQL Server 6.5.* Describes the functions, statements, and procedures new to SQL Server 6.5. Use this appendix while reading Chapter 9.

- **Appendix D:** *Visual Basic 5 Service Pack 2 Changes and Additions.* Describes changes and fixes included in service pack 2. Describes apartment threading model and when to use it as opposed to single threads.